Changing Families

RELATIONSHIPS IN CONTEXT

Second Canadian Edition

Anne-Marie Ambert
York University

Pearson Canada
Toronto

Library and Archives Canada Cataloguing in Publication

Ambert, Anne-Marie
    Changing families : relationships in context / Anne-Marie Ambert. — 2nd Canadian ed.

Includes bibliographical references and index.

ISBN 978-0-205-83202-6

1. Family—Textbooks. I. Title.

HQ560.A34 2011   306.85   C2010-906304-X

ISBN 978-0-205-83202-6

Vice-President, Editorial Director: Gary Bennett
Editor-in-Chief: Ky Pruesse
Editor, Humanities and Social Sciences: Joel Gladstone
Marketing Manager: Lisa Gillis
Developmental Editor: Rema Celio
Project Manager: Marissa Lok
Production Editor: Heather Sangster, Strong Finish
Copy Editor: Aspasia Bissas, Strong Finish
Proofreader: Kathy White, Strong Finish
Compositor: MPS Limited, a Macmillan Company
Photo Researcher: Anne-Marie Ambert
Permissions Researcher: Anne-Marie Ambert
Art Director: Julia Hall
Cover Designer: Rod Bravo
Interior Designer: Miguel Acevedo
Cover Image: Getty Images

1 2 3 4 5   15 14 13 12 11

Printed and bound in the United States of America.

Brief Contents

Contents

2   History and Cultural Diversity of Canadian Families   34

3   Contemporary Issues in Family Life   65

5 Impacts of Neighbourhoods and Housing Conditions on Family Life   122

PART 4   COUPLE AND FAMILY RELATIONSHIPS   252

10 The Parent-Child Relationship and Child Socialization   283

13   Family Violence, Abuse, and Neglect   379

14   Family Futures and Social Policies   413

Preface

The field of family studies has recently benefited from an injection of innovative research from other areas of sociology as well as from other disciplines, particularly demography and psychology. *Changing Families: Relationships in Context* is the first family textbook, whether Canadian or American, to integrate this new body of knowledge—which also includes additional theoretical perspectives—in such a comprehensive manner. It follows that this book is different from others in terms of some of its contents. As well, some aspects of its format and organization are distinct. This second Canadian edition includes *many new sections* that reflect more recent developments in the contexts within which Canadian families live.

CONTENTS

This second Canadian edition of *Changing Families: Relationships in Context* contains several chapters and many new sections that are entirely innovative and even "outside the box" in usual family textbooks. This is particularly evident in Part 2, where we look at how various aspects of the changing economy, neighbourhoods, and educational institutions affect families and human development within these families. The contents of these chapters reflect the fact that the best scholarly journals in sociology, family studies, and child development now regularly publish articles in these domains as do Statistics Canada researchers. This is probably the only family sociology textbook on the market that focuses on these areas combined, including the role that religiosity plays in marriage and child socialization. As well, the media as a sociocultural context for family life is also discussed more extensively than is done elsewhere and contains new material on video games, for instance (in Chapter 3).

Further, an entire chapter is devoted to siblings: their relationship, how they grow up to be different, and how they relate to their parents. The second Canadian edition also includes new sections on polygamy, online dating and infidelities, adolescent sexuality, condo living, military families, and antisocial behaviours in and around schools, among others. It has also retained its substantial sections on adoption, foster families, reproductive technologies, the impact of children's peers on the family, same-sex-parent families, and ex-spouses' relationships after divorce. It includes new perspectives on cohabitation as well as more pages on families' elders. Thus, this text contains a more complete overview of families and a greater diversity of domains relevant to family dynamics.

In the same vein, I have introduced a wide range of theoretical frameworks. In addition to the better-known theories, such as structural functionalism and symbolic interactionism, others, including social constructionism, are much in evidence. For instance, interactional-transactional theories are used in the chapters in which the parent-child relationship is discussed. Not only do we look at the socialization of children by parents but we also examine how children affect their parents' ability to raise them within specific environments—in other words, how parents, children, and their environment interact. Furthermore, I have borrowed from the field of behaviour genetics in order to acquaint students with new concepts, ideas, and explanations that are now regularly encountered in the area of family research and even in the popular media: the interaction between nature and nurture or genes and environment. Students can examine behaviour genetics within a critical sociological framework alongside interactional-transactional theories and even symbolic interactionism.

FORMAT AND RESEARCH

The text of this book includes a great deal of qualitative sociology in the form of quotes, case studies, and summaries from my fieldwork. Unlike other textbooks, where qualitative material tends to be presented separately in boxed inserts as anecdotes, here it is an integral part of the contents. Moreover, I present a great deal of information, both quantitative and qualitative. How this information is obtained and research is carried out are important issues to me as an instructor. As a result, I have included one Family Research insert in most chapters: These Family Research features say, "Here is how various researchers do it, and how they get their information on family life." In other words, these inserts illustrate various research methods that will allow students to get a better idea of the range of methods that are used in family studies, both qualitative and quantitative.

Canadian research on various aspects and contexts of family life has flourished since the first Canadian edition of this book was published in 2006. This development is reflected in an increasing recourse to works published in Canada—by researchers from Canadian universities, various research centres, and Statistics Canada—as well as Canadian research published internationally, particularly in American scholarly journals. While this textbook focuses on Canadian families, it also contains material from other societies, particularly the U.S., because this is the society that is the most relevant to the daily lives of Canadians—via its economic supremacy, media colonization, and general cultural and historical interchanges.

ORGANIZATION OF THE TEXT

This second Canadian edition of *Changing Families: Relationships in Context* remains divided into five parts. Part 1, Foundations of Family Studies, introduces definitions, perspectives, and issues pertaining to families. This includes theoretical perspectives; a historical and cross-cultural overview; a discussion of current concerns about family functions; and contemporary developments, especially pertaining to the audiovisual media. Part 2, Social and Cultural Family Contexts, focuses on the macrosociological settings and conditions that affect family life and structure. These include the changing dynamics of the global and technological market economy;

neighbourhoods and housing conditions; schools; and religious participation. The contents of Part 3 reflect its title, Patterns of Partnering and Family Formation, but also focus on sexual relations.

Part 4, entitled Couple and Family Relationships, introduces successive chapters on the spousal, parent-child, and sibling relationships. Part 5, Family Challenges and Solutions, begins with a chapter on divorce, widowhood, and repartnering, particularly remarriage. The next chapter examines violence, abuse, and neglect within the family. The last chapter re-examines the themes that have linked the contents and then focuses on future family trends. It then addresses social policies and suggestions designed to prevent or ameliorate problems faced by families. A special emphasis is placed on policies that could alleviate family poverty, improve child care, support conjugal units and the parental role, as well as provide a better environment for families' care of their elders.

PEDAGOGY

Each chapter begins with a detailed outline. Throughout the text, many concepts and themes are bolded or italicized in order to help students memorize key concepts and ideas and to note emphases. Concepts that might need additional explanation are further defined in the Glossary at the end of the book. This Glossary contains fewer but lengthier definitions to serve as a reference for students who have never taken a sociology course before. Each chapter has a clearly identified but brief conclusion that serves an integrative function. As is the convention, chapters end with a Summary, Analytical Questions, Suggested Readings, as well as Suggested Weblinks.

SUPPLEMENTS

The first Canadian edition had an Instructor's Manual, which has been updated. To this has been added a Student's Study Guide. The following instructor and student supplements are available for downloading from a password-protected section of Pearson Education Canada's online catalogue (**vig.pearsoned.ca**). Navigate to your book's catalogue page to view a list of available supplements.

Instructor's Manual: This manual contains a variety of additional instructor resources, including:

- **Additional Class Material** expands upon topics introduced in the text or adds new topics relevant to a chapter.
- **Chapter Linkages and Modules** help point out to students how various sections and themes in one chapter relate to their counterparts in other chapters.
- **Help with Analytical Questions** offers suggestions for those questions placed at the end of each chapter.
- **Suggestions for Discussion, Projects, Papers**
- **Short Essay Questions.**
- **Suggested Media Options** are occasionally found.

Test Item File: Available in Microsoft Word / Adobe Acrobat format, this test bank includes almost 1,000 multiple-choice, true/false, and essay questions.

Student's Study Guide: New to the second Canadian edition is a text enrichment site featuring an online Student's Study Guide. You can access the text enrichment site at **www.pearsoned.ca/text/ambert**.

The Student's Study Guide contains the following *for each chapter:*

- **Learning Objectives** that help students focus on the main educational goals of each chapter. By the same token, these objectives will allow students to evaluate how successful they have been in terms of having acquired the knowledge and critical thinking required by each chapter. These objectives are useful both to orient students before they begin a chapter and as a self-evaluation of their own learning process after the chapter is concluded.

- **Questions Students Ask.** Often, students see certain results and statistics that may appear to be negative and want to know how these might apply to them or, yet, why they are not following the "averages." Or they want to know why they have or have not been affected by given situations. A few of these questions are answered in this feature.

- **Relevance to Students' Lives.** This feature complements the section on Questions Students Ask. Students wishing to utilize this section will be encouraged to ask themselves how some of the contents of each chapter are applicable to their own lives and how they can situate themselves within the contexts presented by each chapter. This section may help students analyze their own family and partner situations, as is the case, or goals, and discover other alternatives, where relevant.

- **Work-Related Relevance.** This section will help students see where some of the contents of each chapter can be utilized in various types of work, such as clinical work with families and children, social work, teaching, health-related work, as well as research work.

- **Key Concepts and Themes** complement the Learning Objectives.

COURSESMART FOR INSTRUCTORS

CourseSmart goes beyond traditional expectations—providing instant online access to the textbooks and course materials you need at a lower cost for students. And even as students save money, you can save time and hassle with a digital eTextbook that allows you to search for the most relevant content at the very moment you need it. Whether it's evaluating textbooks or creating lecture notes to help students with difficult concepts, CourseSmart can make life a little easier. See how when you visit **www.coursesmart.com/instructors**.

COURSESMART FOR STUDENTS

CourseSmart goes beyond traditional expectations—providing instant online access to the textbooks and course materials you need at an average savings of 50%. With instant access from any computer and the ability to search your text, you'll find the content you need quickly, no matter where you are. And with online tools like highlighting and note-taking, you can save time and study efficiently. See all the benefits at **www.coursesmart.com/students**.

mysearchlab

MySearchLab offers extensive help to students with their writing and research project and provides round-the-clock access to credible and reliable source material.

- **Research.** Content on MySearchLab includes immediate access to thousands of full-text articles from leading Canadian and international academic journals, and daily news feeds from The Associated Press. Articles contain the full downloadable text—including abstract and citation information—and can be cut, pasted, emailed, or saved for later use.
- **Writing.** MySearchLab also includes a step-by-step tutorial on writing a research paper. Included are sections on planning a research assignment, finding a topic, creating effective notes, and finding source material. Our exclusive online handbook provides grammar and usage support. Pearson SourceCheck™ offers an easy way to detect accidental plagiarism issues, and our exclusive tutorials teach how to avoid them in the future. And MySearchLab also contains AutoCite, which helps to correctly cite sources using MLA, APA, CMS, and CBE documentation styles for both endnotes and bibliographies.

To order this book with MySearchLab access at no extra charge, use ISBN 978-0-13-259621-3.

Take a tour at **www.mysearchlab.com**.

ACKNOWLEDGEMENTS

The following reviewers have provided extensive comments and suggestions that were greatly useful in guiding the structural and substantive improvements brought to the second Canadian edition: Terry Murphy, College of the North Atlantic; Penny Poole, Fanshawe College; Denis Wall, University of Toronto; Adenike Yesufu, Grant MacEwan University. Their very detailed suggestions resulted in the elimination of two chapters and the addition of several sections as well as an improvement in the Supplements for both instructors and students. In addition, the following reviewers are acknowledged for their help and suggestions regarding the first Canadian edition: Paula Chegwidden, Acadia University; Debra M. Clarke, Trent University; Patience Elabor-Idemudia, University of Saskatchewan; Scott Kline, St. Jerome's University, University of Waterloo; Stephen Riggins, Memorial University; Noreen Stuckless, York University; Franc Sturino, York University; Alison M. Thomas, University of Victoria; Vappu Tyyskä, Ryerson University; and Mike Wahn, University of Winnipeg. These reviewers together have made me rethink and rework many sections and I am most grateful to them. I hope that I have done justice to their thoughtful input.

I have appreciated a neighbour's assistance in locating relevant information regarding Home Children. Irene Relph is gratefully acknowledged. Last but not least, I am indebted to my daughter, Stèphanie, who, despite her own heavy professional commitments (also related to family life) has continued her tradition of entering the Bibliography section—something she has been doing since age 12.

I also acknowledge the advice and help provided by Joel Gladstone, Acquisitions Editor at Pearson Canada, and that of Rema Celio, who was my Developmental Editor. It was a pleasure working with both of them. Heather Sangster, Aspasia Bissas, and Kathy White of Strong Finish have provided invaluable assistance in copy editing, formatting, and proofreading.

I am especially indebted to the hundreds of couples, ex-couples, as well as parents and children who have given so generously of their time and their hospitality for my various research projects over the past decades. Quotes and case studies from these families have greatly enriched this text, as has the material gathered from the over 1,500 students who wrote semi-structured autobiographies in my classes for more than 30 years. I am also indebted to the 232 adoptees, adoptive parents, and birth parents who, more recently, sent me unsolicited email information on their personal history and experience following an article I had published on a related website. As acknowledged at the beginning of Chapter 1, most of my research ideas and theoretical revisions throughout my career have been influenced by this spousal, parental, child, and student contribution to my knowledge of real life as lived by others in their diverse family situations.

Anne-Marie Ambert

CHAPTER 1

Introduction to Family Studies

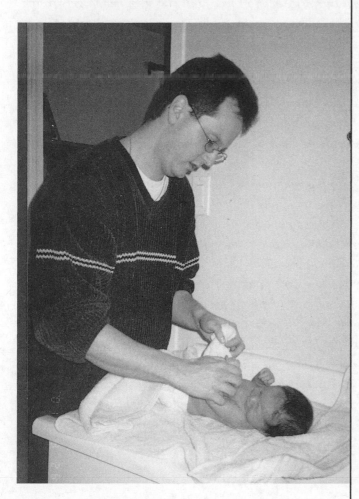

My publisher suggested that I begin this chapter by answering a personal question: What in my own family life has led to my becoming interested in family studies? Simply put: I do not think that my early family life had much to do with this interest, although it certainly influenced my personal choices later on. Rather—and this may at first appear to be a strange answer coming from a sociologist—I am convinced that my interest was intrinsic to who I was (am) and stemmed largely from my genes, because I clearly recall being fascinated by family matters as young as age six. Further, when I was small, there was no environmental reason for this interest because my family life was then uneventful for me. As well, the sociocultural climate of the time and place in which I lived was certainly not conducive to fostering the intellectual curiosity I was developing—at any rate, girls were not supposed to be "intellectual"! Finally, it bears mentioning that my own family life course, either as a child or as an adult, does not have much to do with the topics I ended up studying.

Overall—and I will return to this point in the last chapter—what has most influenced my scholarly perspectives on family life, apart from readings, has been the fieldwork I have done for my research: learning about the lives of the hundreds of children, adolescents, parents, and couples I have interviewed, observed, and exchanged emails with. Furthermore, as the reader will see at the end of this chapter, many of my students have written about their families in autobiographies and a large number of persons involved in adoptions provided me with a rich gamut of unsolicited (online) but welcome perspectives. These lives, put together, have shown me that the questions asked in family research, especially about the parent-child relationship, were often not the right ones. The theories were too limited and did not always fit the facts I was discovering. This led me early on to search for and consider a wider range of theoretical perspectives, including feminist theories in the late 1960s, interactional approaches in the 1970s and 1980s, as well as social constructionism and behaviour genetics in the 1990s until now.

Notice that the title of this book contains the word *families* rather than *the family*; indeed, several types of families exist under one rubric. Despite this diversity, families can be analyzed as an institution. In fact, families are the most basic institution of any society: It is within their folds that citizens are born, sheltered, and begin their socialization. **Socialization*** is the process whereby children learn how to think and

* Words are bolded to accentuate key concepts and themes or to serve as additional subtitles within a section. Therefore, these words do *not* necessarily appear in the Glossary.

behave according to the ways of the society and the group in which they are born and raised. Children are not, however, passive recipients in this process: They respond according to their personalities, needs, and accumulated experiences. They accept, reject, or transform the cultural messages that they receive from parents and others. It is thus through this process that a society transmits its culture, with some or many modifications, to the next generation. It is also through socialization that a society perpetuates and reconstructs its gender, racial, and economic structure as well as the roles that flow from it.

Why are families called an institution? An **institution** is a recognized area of social life that is organized along a system of widely accepted norms that regulate behaviours. The elements of organization and norms contribute to the predictability of life: People know what to expect—it is a shared culture. Over time, each society evolves a set of norms or rules that guides the behaviours of family members toward one another and toward other institutions. Other key institutions in a society are the religious, educational, economic, as well as political contexts. We will study these institutions as they intersect with families in subsequent chapters, particularly in Part 2 and in the last chapter.

Canadian society is constituted by people from many different backgrounds; thus, there is less consensus about family norms and behaviours as well as less stability than would be the case in a smaller and more homogeneous society. Change has become a part of the institution of the family, as it is in nearly all large societies of the world. As we see in Chapter 3, this situation leaves many people uncomfortable about the future of the family and raises concerns in their minds about its fragility. But, as we will also see, although family forms may change, *the institution itself remains* while its functions evolve and even multiply.

HOW CAN FAMILIES BE DEFINED?

The task of defining what families are is a difficult one these days because our society is experiencing many changes and, consequently, experts do not all agree in this respect. Some want to eliminate the institutional aspect from the definition and replace it with a focus on close and sexually intimate relationships, however temporary. Others include networks of friends as a kind of family. For them, the emphasis is on the voluntariness ("chosen") and the relational aspects of the relationships. For the purpose of the census, Statistics Canada broadened its definition in 2002 in order to reflect some of the current processes. For instance, Statistics Canada's definition (2002a) includes a couple, of any sexual combination, with or without children, married or cohabiting, as well as "a lone parent of any marital status, with at least one child living in the same dwelling," or a grandparent raising a grandchild.

In this book, the definition adopted reflects current changes but also retains the institutional aspect and focuses on the intergenerational dimension of families. A family is a social group, an institution, and an **intergenerational** group of individuals related to one another by blood, adoption, or marriage/cohabitation. It is a group that endures over several generations (White and Klein, 2002). The minimum requirement to meet this definition at the nuclear level (see Table 1.1) is the combination of

TABLE 1.1 | **Typology of Families and Unions**

Type	Description
Families	
Nuclear family	At least one parent and one child living together
Conjugal	Husband, wife, and child(ren)
	Cohabitants with child
	Same-sex parents with child
Single parent	One parent and his or her child living together
Grandparent/grandchild	One grandparent or two grandparents and grandchild living together
Reconstituted	Remarried spouses or cohabiting spouses when at least one had a child from a former union
Horizontal	Sisters or brothers or cousins living together without the parent generation
Extended family	All the members of a family, including child, parents, grandparents, and other ascendants, plus uncles, aunts, and cousins (by blood, adoption, or marriage)
In one household	Generally involves three generations: at least one parent and his or her child living with another relative, usually the child's grandparent or aunt or uncle
In multiple households	Members of a family, including child, parents, grandparents, and other ascendants, plus uncles, aunts, and cousins (by blood, marriage, or adoption) living in separate dwellings and interacting on a regular basis
Unions	
Legal marriage	Socially/legally/religiously sanctioned union, which is generally heterosexual but could also be of same-sex partners, depending on the jurisdiction involved
Cohabitation	Consensual union that is not legally (common-law) sanctioned but is legally protected in Canada: It can involve same-sex or opposite-sex partners
Living apart together (LAT)	Union in which the two partners maintain separate residences
Monogamy	A legal marriage or cohabitation involving only two partners
Serial monogamy (serial polygamy)	Sequence of spouses or partners over time as in the sequence of marriage, divorce, and remarriage; spouses or cohabitants succeed each other
Polygamy	Multiple partners or spouses at the same time
Polygyny	One man married to more than one woman at the same time
Polyandry	One woman married to more than one man at the same time

two generations in one household, or the nuclear family. Or it can refer to persons living together who are related to one another through another generation, such as siblings or cousins. Finally, it should be added that families as a system existed among pre-humans and still exist among primates and other animals. It is an evolutionary and necessary system for the care of the young and helpless, and for the survival of the species (Sprey, 2009). In this respect, families should not be equated with marriage, which is a late cultural invention in the history of humanity—even though many animal species are monogamous for life.

Therefore, the typology of families presented here does *not* include unrelated single people living together, even though they constitute a **household** unit or share an address. Such persons are members of their families of origin or of procreation but do not themselves constitute a family. Although this definition is restrictive in terms of what constitutes a family (not a couple, not roommates sharing a house, not friends), it is quite inclusive as to the number and sex of parents present and takes recent social changes into consideration. In contrast, past definitions of the nuclear family did not include unmarried mothers or same-sex-parent families, for instance. This definitional distinction is important, not only in terms of accuracy but also because it carries family policy implications. For example, one often reads that children are born more and more "outside of the family." Such a statement is accurate when older definitions are applied, but is inaccurate as soon as one accepts a mother and her child as a type of nuclear family.

As mentioned, some critics opt for a much broader definition of the family. This definition includes any person one wishes to recognize as such or feels close to or shares a household with. Thus, best friends can become a family, and so can neighbours who help each other a great deal, as well as former partners, ex-spouses, and friends' relatives. The emphasis is on "intimate relations," which, it is claimed, are more egalitarian and inclusive than families. This broad inclusiveness as to what constitutes a family is quite problematic for analytical and social policy purposes.

To begin with, such an inclusive family group overlaps with the concepts of social networks and support networks. Second, social policies designed to facilitate family life do need a modicum of definitional precision. Third, if we so broaden the definition of the family, it runs the risk of becoming useless. Basically, if we choose to include anyone we are close to at the moment as a family member, the concept of family will become so elastic that it will be meaningless and will have no continuity over time. As O'Brien and Goldberg (2000:136) put it, membership in a family is an **ascribed status** while friendship networks are acquired. "Status ascription is one of the reasons that family relations tend to be enduring, whereas friendships change over time, especially when significant changes take place in a person's life." As well, a *family is enduring*. For instance, when a couple has children and separates, each ex-spouse remains part of their children's families as parents. The children then have a binuclear family and remain in both nuclear family systems. By using an intergenerational perspective, this text repositions procreation and related linkages as central to the definition of families—no matter the gender or number of parents.

Nuclear Families

A parent and his or her children as well as two parents with their children form the most elementary type of family—referred to as the nuclear family. When a person or a couple has a child, whether by birth, adoption, or surrogacy, a nuclear family of **procreation** is formed. What is important is not whether the offspring are biological or adopted but that *a new generation is added*. Under this definition, a grandmother who raises her grandson also constitutes a nuclear family and so does a single man who has an adopted son. However, a husband and wife, a cohabiting couple, and a same-sex couple fall under the category of *couples* (see the lower panel of Table 1.1). They constitute a nuclear family only upon the arrival of their first child. These couples are, however, members of their own families of **origin** or **orientation**. That is, they "belong to" or originate from their parents and their parents' families.

This said, who constitutes a nuclear family and under what circumstances calls for some flexibility. For instance, when young adults move out of their parents' house and set up a new *household*, are they still part of the parents' nuclear family or do the parents become their extended family? One has to consider the fact that parents and their adult children who live separately may still consider themselves a nuclear family. Similarly, in a situation of divorce, children may experience what is termed a **binuclear** family; that is, half of their nuclear family is constituted by themselves and their mother and the other half by themselves and their father. When brothers and sisters share a household together without their parents, this is often referred to as a **horizontal** nuclear family because there is only one generation involved—but this generation originates from that of the parents.

Extended Families

Other relatives constitute the *extended* family or *kinship* group: grandparents, aunts, uncles, cousins, and in-laws. There is fluidity between nuclear and extended families. It is not an either-or category (see upper part of Table 1.1). Most people belong to an extended family as well as to a nuclear family. Contrary to what is often believed, extended families living together under one roof (**multi-generational households**) have never been the norm in Canada, except among certain Aboriginal groups. English and French people arrived here with a tradition of nuclearity (Thornton, 2005). Even rural Quebec was an exception rather than a rule when, in the 19th and early 20th centuries, most elderly parents lived with one of their many children when widowed or ill.

Three-generational households have increased in Canada in the past two decades, largely as a consequence of immigration from Asia and the return home of adult children with their own children. The majority of these extended families live in cities, and in 48 percent of the cases such families contain one or two grandparents with a single parent and his or her children. Yet, despite this increase, in 2001, only 4 percent of Canadians lived in multi-generational households and only 1.6 percent of Québécois did (Milan and Hamm, 2003). It is estimated that only about 7 to 10 percent of adult children in Canada live with an *elderly* parent (Mitchell, 2003).

The level of exchange taking place between the nuclear family and the extended family varies by coresidence, proximity of neighbourhood, and even for emotional reasons. In North America, most relationships between members of an extended kin system are optional—perhaps with the exception of communities in Newfoundland and Labrador because of the historical isolation of these fishing communities, the harsh environment, and dangerous subsistence activities. All these led to a greater reliance on kin and near kin. But, overall, in North America, for example, if two brothers and their wives or children do not get along, they are not forced to see each other, particularly if they live at a distance. In contrast, the kinship group is still a key organizational unit in many African and Asian societies today. As we see in Chapter 2, most newly arrived families are more kinship oriented than are average Canadian-born families. Among the former, the extended family is more institutionalized: They often entertain higher values of reciprocity and have more exact rules of behaviour concerning their extended kin (Barrow, 1996).

In some ethnic groups—of Latin American descent, for instance—friends may be assimilated into the family as they become godparents to children. This is the system of *compradazgo*. When a father's friend is a frequent visitor to the house, he may be called an uncle (*tio*) and a mother's friend becomes an aunt (*tia*), thus creating what some researchers call **fictive kinship** bonds. Many Inuit groups similarly extend their kin system to the kin of kin (Miller, 2005:177). For many individuals who belong to a large extended family group living in close proximity, there is often less of a necessity to make friends outside the family, as all interactional needs are met within this system. This situation is further explained by a student belonging to a "white ethnic" family:

> *"We've always lived near my grandparents and several uncles and aunts on both sides of the family so I grew up with a very secure feeling of belongingness. There was always someone to play with or talk to and we never had to kill ourselves making friends at school because we had so many cousins."*

Types of Union and Marriage

As indicated in Table 1.1, there are several types of union and marriage in the world. In Canada, the only two types of marriage and common-law union that are legally accepted are between one man and *one* woman or between *two* persons of the same sex. Polygamy in the form of **polygyny** (a man married to two or more women) became illegal in 1878 both in Canada and the U.S. **Polyandry** (a woman married to two or more men) is less frequently encountered across the world and tends to be localized in smaller societies.

Polygamy as a Conjugal and Family Type

Polygamy, in the form of a man married to two or more wives (polygyny), has resurfaced as an issue both in Canada and the U.S. in the past few years. It has received wide media attention in 2008 and 2009, in Canada particularly with respect to Bountiful, British Columbia, and even Toronto (Javed, 2008). Indeed, an unknown number of polygamous Mormon families still exist in the U.S. and Canada, although they are not recognized by the mainstream Utah-based Church of Jesus Christ of Latter Day Saints. In 2009, 81 percent of Canadian adults disapproved of polygamy: 90 percent of women and 70 percent of men (MacQueen, 2009).

Polygyny was far more widespread throughout the world in the past and is mentioned in the Old Testament. It could be found in Asia, Europe, in non-Muslim parts of Africa, and some of the First Nations of the Americas. It is recognized in the Qur'an and accepted as a practice but *not* as a requirement. Today, polygamy is a minority phenomenon, even in countries that recognize it legally. It is said to be practised mainly by well-to-do men, as the Qur'an specifies that a husband has to have the means to support all his wives. But some men in poverty resort to it. Generally women are more likely to enter a polygamous marriage when they are rural, have little education, and come from a disadvantaged family (Al-Krenawi et al., 2006). Historically, polygamy was rooted in agrarian societies where men who owned a great deal of land, for instance, benefited from the help of several wives and an extensive progeny. Wives and children were signs of wealth and producers of wealth. Plural marriages were also useful for the purpose of integrating widows and their children into another household in countries where women had no independent standing.

At the demographic level, and disregarding the issue of equity, there is a question of **sex ratio imbalance** that arises where polygamy is practised by a segment of the population, even if it is a minority one. That is, as a proportion of men acquire more than one wife, there are not enough potential wives left. As a result, other men, generally the less fortunate ones, cannot marry, or have to wait until they are much older to do so. Or, yet, they may have to take a very young bride, or one who would not otherwise be "marriageable." Consequently, age at marriage is generally low, often as low as the 9- to 14-year range, as occurs in Afghanistan and Yemen, for instance. As a result of this scarcity of women, their parents may focus on the girls' role in the marriage market to the detriment of their education. In offshoot Mormon communities in the west of Canada and the U.S., many teenage boys have been expulsed from their familial enclaves and rejected from their group so that they would not compete for wives with the more senior males. This demographic structure is similar to what happens in countries such as China and parts of India where female infanticide and abortion of female fetuses was and is still practised: The male-to-female ratio increases, leaving many men unmarried and childless (Attané, 2006; Das Gupta et al., 2009; Guilmoto, 2009).

Polygamy tends to be practised more in rural areas where agricultural activities can benefit from the birth of many sons and where **co-wives** have more space in which to establish quasi-separate residences with their children within the patrilocal compound. It is not coincidental that, both in Canada and the U.S., polygamy exists mainly in rural enclaves isolated from mainstream culture. One can, therefore, ask how polygamy can be functional in societies that are highly urbanized and technological; need an educated workforce, including women's labour outside the home; and have a high population density. Within this analysis, polygamy can be seen as an outdated institution that no longer provides any economic benefit. In fact, more and more Asian and African societies are limiting its scope; some are introducing a gradual reduction in the number of wives permitted, while others are outlawing it outright (Coontz, 2006).

At the interpersonal level, the results of polygamy differ. There may be competition between co-wives for a husband's attention and, especially, for material necessities. Which of their children will the husband favour is also a great and divisive concern. Indeed, the mother of a favourite son can expect a more comfortable old age. Many co-wives learn to enjoy the benefits that additional hands bring to household labour, child care, chores related to small-business ownership, and help in horticultural activities. They may together obtain concessions from their shared husband and exercise a certain degree of power in the household and status in the community. In some countries, the senior wife, especially when she has had sons, benefits from having a co-wife: This raises her status and she may even help her husband in selecting subsequent wives. When co-wives are sisters or kin, their relatedness may help them adapt to each other and offers a certain level of protection (Yanca and Low, 2003). Even in American polygamous communities, many women report benefiting from the help and companionship they provide to one another (Forbes, 2003).

What about the children? It is very difficult to assess the research literature on how children are affected because the effects of polygamy certainly depend on the cultural and socio-economic context in which it is embedded. Therefore, the studies that exist in Africa and Asia cannot be applied to the cases found in Canada, the U.S., or Great Britain, where polygamy is not institutionally supported (Campbell, 2005).

When polygamous families immigrate to western cities, as has been the case for a long period in France, they cannot afford a separate residence for each wife and her children. As a result, family members live in crowded conditions fostering stress and conflict between co-wives and their children. "There have been reports of women treated in Paris hospitals for physical injuries resulting from confrontations among family members, often co-wives" (Campbell, 2005:2). It is impossible to estimate how many polygamous families are in Canada as a result of recent **immigration** from African and Asian countries. Two women students mentioned it in their autobiographies in 2005; in one case, one of the two wives had arrived here as the "sister" of her husband in order to be accepted by Canadian Immigration. In the other case, the older wife, who was the student's mother, had been left behind ten years earlier with few resources.

> *"I am working very hard to get a good job to sponsor my mother* [who was only 38 years old] *and we will live together . . . I'll find a job for her, not too hard because she always slaved for my father and his side of the family and I want her to have some happiness. I won't tell my father because he might claim her to use her. . . . When I get married I'll take her with me because she couldn't survive alone, she's too inexperienced with life . . . I'll have to be very careful because my father may want to marry me off as soon as I graduate here and I should count myself lucky that this hasn't already happened but I don't think that he'll ship me off back home for this but just in case, I've made contacts with a group of women and I'm planning on moving to* [deleted] *as soon as I save money but the other problem will be to hide my pay check from my father . . ."*

When the law of a society such as Canada does not allow for multiple wives, one of the wives who is not the "legal" one may be unprotected—even though some provincial laws, such as the *Ontario Family Law Act*, provide spousal support and welfare benefits. But these women may not be aware of these benefits and it is more than likely that their husband would not want them to know. This is one of the key questions that some Canadian legal experts are debating (Bala et al., 2005): Such wives may have no recourse in terms of support for themselves and their children after a religious divorce; they may even lose their children, especially when they are left behind in the home country. Hence, polygamous immigrant families face multiple challenges: Not only do they have to adapt to a new country but they also have to adapt to a different legal family situation law and the criminalization of wife abuse.

Basically, throughout the world, the success of polygamy (that is, how happy and well functioning the spouses and their children are) depends on the sociocultural context within which a polygamous family lives, including the fair treatment received by women within this type of family—a difficult balance to achieve (Hassouneh-Phillips, 2001; Madhavan, 2002). Al-Krenawi et al. (2006:184) concludes that "problematic family functioning is more characteristic of polygynous families than monogamous families"—perhaps a result of the greater complexity of this type of family structure (Al-Krenawi et al., 2002). A sophisticated analysis of the evolution of social inequalities shows that polygamy is a key indicator of inequality in societies throughout the world (Nielsen, 2004).

WHAT THEORETICAL PERSPECTIVES INFORM FAMILY STUDIES?

The study of families requires a multidisciplinary approach, from demography and economics to psychology and social work. In the same vein, several theoretical perspectives are necessary to guide and explain family research (White, 2005). A **theory** is a set of interrelated propositions that explains a particular phenomenon and guides research. In this section, some of the main theoretical perspectives that are encountered in the sociological study of families in western countries are examined. Two others are added that, although psychological in origin, are sociologically oriented and inform several discussions in this text. Each theory that follows explains certain aspects of family life, but no theory alone explains it in its entirety and all its contexts. Often, two or three theories combined provide a more thorough explanation of reality. The study of families is the ideal meeting point of theoretical perspectives because families are a nexus of interactions informed by cultures and contexts (Tudge, 2008). In turn, families create culture via their interactions and socialization of generations. This being said, how these theories apply to non-western countries, especially less developed rural ones, remains to be tested (Arnett, 2008).

Structural Functionalism

Structural functionalism analyzes a society's organization, its structure, and the linkages between its various systems (Merton, 1968). Within this perspective, the family is an important unit that fulfills key **functions** for society, such as child socialization. In turn, a society's social structure provides the overall cultural and organizational contexts that influence family life. The analogy is organic: An organism (the society) is a system with many subsystems that collaborate or function together to optimize its success. The various systems fulfill functions or do things for one another.

The sociologist responsible for the propagation of structural functionalism was Talcott Parsons (1951). Structural functionalism was, to some extent, a theory with *assumptions of consensus or equilibrium*. It left little room to address and redress inequalities in the social structure, because these inequalities were perceived to be fulfilling necessary functions for the entire social system. Thus, this framework was not sufficiently flexible to analyze family developments. The changing role of women, for instance, could not be adequately examined because, under this perspective, even maternal employment threatened families' equilibrium.

As well, the differentiation along gender lines between the **instrumental role** (father as the breadwinner responsible for linking the family to the society at large) and the **expressive role** (mother who cares for children, maintains relationships, and does the housework) was not sustainable with the return to paid employment of a majority of women and the changes in gender ideologies. Further, subsuming all the instrumental tasks carried out by mothers under the rubric of the "expressive" realm did not do justice to reality (Luxton, 2009). Nevertheless, if one rereads Parsons and Bales's *Family, Socialization and Interaction Process* (1955), much of their analysis of the family as a system is still relevant. Particularly important is the view that, as agents of socialization, parents must "interpenetrate" other systems in order to be successful in their role (p. 35), a perspective that is linked to the discussion of family functions in Chapter 3 and of the linkages between families and schools in Chapter 6.

Structural perspectives have since emerged to explain social inequalities based on the organization of society. This **social structural** orientation is evident in this text when inequalities between families are discussed, particularly in Part 2. In this respect, it is similar to a political economy approach to the family (Baker, 2001). Families' living conditions are analyzed through political, economic, and even cultural arrangements of society rather than through individuals' deficits or merits. This interpretation does not defend the status quo; rather, it suggests the necessity for change at the global level.

Functionalist terminology has been utilized in family research without its original, consensual focus. Such is the case of the concept of **dysfunction**. At the individual level, a dysfunctional characteristic, such as hyperactivity, is one that prevents a child from doing well at school or from integrating himself or herself within the peer group. A dysfunctional family is one that is so disorganized or debilitated by conflict, incompetence, and various deficiencies that it is unable to care for its members and socialize its children. This perspective also allows us to see in other chapters that a majority of "dysfunctional" families have so become or are so labelled because they have been socially marginalized by poverty or discrimination.

Social Exchange and Rational Theories

Both social exchange and rational theories are the products of the sociocultural environment of the 20th century and their development was influenced by the discipline of economics. For its part, exchange theory owes a great deal to the influence of the philosophical perspective of utilitarianism, which is based on the assumption of individual self-interests (White and Klein, 2002:33). Resources occupy a key role in both these perspectives.

Social Exchange Theory

The early proponents of exchange theory were psychologists John Thibaut and Harold Kelly (1959) along with sociologists George Homans (1961) and Peter Blau (1964). Homans and Blau agreed that all the parties involved in an exchange should receive something that they perceive to be equivalent; otherwise imbalance will occur: One person will have power in the relationship while the other will be at a disadvantage. In this context, Homans used the term "distributive justice" while Blau referred to "fair exchange." However, Blau saw exchange as a more subjective and interpretive phenomenon than did Homans.

The basic assumption behind social exchange theory is that people interact and make choices so as to *maximize* their own *benefits* or rewards and to *minimize* their *costs*. In the market metaphor of exchange theory, **resources** and **power** occupy a central position—a perspective anticipated in Blood and Wolfe's (1960) research design in the mid-1950s. As explained by Sabatelli and Shehan (1993:386), "Each spouse's resources and each spouse's dependence on the relationship must be taken into account, for example, when attempting to study marital power." The spouse who has alternatives outside a marriage weighs the advantages of these alternatives against those secured in the current marriage. This theory has also given rise to the equity model or the perception of equity (see Sprechner, 2001). Thus, social exchange theory focuses on rational choices. Its emphasis on resources, which is called capital in rational theory below, brings an element of commonality between the two theories.

Exchange theory has been particularly useful in explaining gender relations, the household division of labour, and why people enter into, remain in, or leave relationships (Sassler, 2010). See Chapters 7 and 9, for instance. As well, decisions concerning separation or divorce are affected by the relative resources of the spouses and the perceived alternatives. The spouse with the most alternatives may be the least committed (Blau, 1964). However, one can argue that this principle does not always apply in the decision to divorce because more women than men now decide to divorce despite the fact that they have fewer alternatives after. Yet, if women make this step, it is often because of a perceived inequity within their marriage.

This market or economic orientation to human relations presents some difficulties for researchers whose values may be more **altruistic** and collectivist. In other words, it is difficult to believe that western parents make so many sacrifices for their children on the basis of the expectation of rewards. In fact, there is often an imbalance of power in favour of children when parents raise adolescents who are particularly difficult (Ambert, 2007). This, in itself, flies in the face of another tenet of exchange theory: that social groups such as the family exist and endure because they allow individuals to maximize their rewards. In contrast, Becker's (1974) concept of altruistic motives was tied to a sense of duty or moral obligation (Rajulton and Ravanera, 2006b). As Carroll et al. (2005) point out, morality and altruism are key motivators, especially in family life, and social exchange cannot account for these. In fact, in some areas, particularly isolated coastal communities in Newfoundland and Labrador and among the Inuit, survival depended, and still does to some extent, on others' help and altruistic exchanges. Another critique of this orientation resides in the fact that people's choices are not always made purposively or objectively (Parsons, 2005:14).

Rational Theory

Resources are also a key element of rational theory, which is currently used in the study of certain domains of family life. James Coleman (1990a) has been at the origin of this theoretical interest in family research in North America, albeit preceded by the French sociologists Durkheim (1951) and Bourdieu (1977). What I have exercised from this theory for the purpose of this book is the concept of capital—social, human, and cultural (Coleman, 1988, 1990b). These concepts, particularly evident in Chapter 6, are used extensively to explain the socialization outcomes of children of various social classes, for instance (Bourdieu, 1977). In this sense, rational theory is more one of capital and community than one of choice by individuals, as is the case for exchange theory.

Human capital refers to abilities, skills, education, and positive human characteristics inherited or acquired by a person. This concept is of paramount importance in knowledge-based economies that require skills largely shaped by early childhood education (Bogenschneider and Corbett, 2010). **Cultural capital** refers to parents' general knowledge and aspects of their lifestyle that can promote their children's achievement. **Social capital** refers to resources that individual families are able to secure on the basis of membership in social networks (Portes, 1998; Statistics Canada, 2004l). But social networks and communities themselves are not equal in terms of the resources they can transfer to families (Furstenberg, 2005). In this text, social resources enhance families' sense of belonging, child socialization, and the acquisition of human and cultural capital (Coleman, 1990a). One type of social capital is evident when parents cooperate, agree, and share authority, which allows their children to learn norms more effectively. The same result occurs when the parental role is supported by a community. In both cases, **social closure** exists (White, 2005:71); that is, social networks are closed so that children are less subjected to conflicting norms. Another type of social capital refers to friendships, contacts with neighbours, and participation in volunteer work within communities, a key to well-being among older Canadians (Theurer and Wister, 2010).

Further, Coleman and Hoffer (1987) have been the proponents of the **effective community**, which I have adopted as one of the themes of this book. An effective community exists when neighbours are willing to take responsibility for all the children in their community (Sampson et al., 1999). This situation, whereby groups of parents share a particular prosocial set of values, enhances individual parents' social capital and contributes to the monitoring of all children (Aird, 2001). It allows for social closure and constitutes an element of *collective socialization*. In simple terms, parents are not alone and this refers us to the often-heard catch phrase that "it takes a village to raise a child."

This three-year-old girl has five grandmothers: a grandmother and a great-grandmother on her father's side; a grandmother, great-grandmother, and great-great-grandmother on her mother's side. She knows each by name, "Gran Jeanne," "Gran Maria," and so on, and is well aware of their individual characteristics. She benefits from a rich web of intergenerational social capital.

Symbolic Interactionism

Symbolic interactionism is a popular theory in family research (White and Klein, 2002). It is favoured by qualitative family researchers and, as such, constitutes both a theoretical perspective and a methodological orientation. It is a sociopsychological theory in which the **self**, social self, and **role** occupy a singular position, as do societal contexts whose meanings and structures are perceived by individuals while interacting with one another. People develop their self-concepts and the definition of the roles they occupy through other people's views of them. The concepts of "reflected appraisals" and the "looking glass self" were originally used by Cooley in 1902 and Mead in 1934. Basically, individuals acquire their self-definition through interaction with **significant others**—that is, people who play an important role in that individual's life, such as parents. Parents, teachers, peers, and even sports figures, singers, and movie stars may become **reference groups** for children as they grow up and learn the roles they are playing and will play as adults. This means that children look up to these individuals and groups and use them as role models or as points of reference to guide their own behaviours, develop their sense of self, and interpret social contexts.

Symbolic interactionism is most suitable for the study of personal and familial phenomena that have not been sufficiently researched. As Daly (2003:775) points out, "Emotions are rarely foregrounded in our theories about families, and yet much of the everyday rhetoric of living in families is about love, jealousy, anger, disappointment, hurt, tolerance, and care." Families construct an environment based on the reflections of self and on the perceptions of significant others, all key themes of this theory. Families constitute their own symbolic world through myth and rituals (Gillis, 1996).

The best-known symbolic interactionists are George Herbert Mead (1934), Herbert Blumer (1969), and Erving Goffman (1959). Symbolic interactionism encompasses two orientations (White and Klein, 2002). The first focuses more on family processes. The second focuses more on roles, is more structural, and has been heavily influenced by Goffman. He became the most popular symbolic interactionist upon the publication of his *The Presentation of Self in Everyday Life* (1959), perhaps in great part because he focused on dramaturgy (using theatre or drama terms such as *roles, actors, frontstage,* and *setting*). This orientation indicates that role strain is reduced when individuals perceive greater consensus in the expectations surrounding their role. One can think of the role of parents here. If parents perceive that their role is well defined, they are less likely to feel insecure about it and role strain will be reduced. This will become important in Chapter 10 on the parent-child relationship.

Interactional-Transactional Perspectives

The interactional-transactional framework goes beyond symbolic interactionism: It posits that an individual creates his or her own environment, at the interpersonal level, at the same time that he or she is being shaped by this environment (Maccoby and Jacklin, 1983). It views socialization as a process whereby children participate in the formation of their identities. The more recent perspective on the **child as a social actor** belongs to this theoretical perspective (Corsaro, 1997).This theory is particularly useful in the study of the parent-child relationship: It corrects the biases or flaws inherent to earlier socialization and child development framework whereby children were seen as the passive recipients of their parents' actions. Instead, the child is studied as an active social actor with individual characteristics, as are parents (Ambert, 2001). *Interactions* between parents and children *feed back* on each other. Similarly, the socialization process involves the interaction between children's personalities and parental teachings (Ambert, 1997). The child actively participates in the socialization process, albeit often unconsciously so. The child becomes **coproducer** of his or her own development. Although this dynamic was recognized as early as 1968 by Bell, it has been largely ignored in the design of research projects.

The interactional causality model is multidimensional and **bidirectional**. It flows *both* from parents and children interacting with and reacting to each other and responding to the environment that affects them (Magnusson, 1995). Thus, the interactional perspective is also *transactional* in the sense that it involves a multiplicity of causality; in other words, it involves transactions between a child, his or her parent, and their environment within a **feedback model**. Interactional-transactional perspectives are very sensitive to the diversity of a family's environment, including culture and ethnicity (Sameroff, 2010). This theory applies equally well to other interactions within the family, such as between spouses or between siblings. Several chapters are informed by the interactional-transactional perspective, particularly Chapters 9 through 13.

Interactional theories are often developed within a larger framework whereby the various levels of a child's or a family's environment influence development and interactions (Sameroff, 2010). In other words, whereas children are coproducers in their development, both parents' and children's actions are enhanced, limited, and constrained by the larger **environment** in which they are situated (Bronfenbrenner, 1989), which is a tenet of transactional theories and is a guiding principle in this textbook. When the term "interactionist perspective" is used, it refers to the interaction between several variables whereas contributions from a social variable, such as poverty, to negative child outcomes is then combined with other parental or child variables to create further negative (or positive) child outcomes (Conger et al., 2010).

Developmental (Life Course) Perspectives

As White and Klein (2002) point out, family development theory is the only socio-logical theory created specifically for the study of families. Paul Glick (1947) and Evelyn Duvall (1957) were the first to propose a sequencing to family life. Indeed, family **life stages** help structure Chapter 10 on the parent-child relationship. In this text, we see that families have a *life course* or trajectory that it is now more fluid than it was in the past; as well, not all families follow the same sequencing of events (Laszloffy, 2002). Developmental theories are both micro- and macrosociological. At a more micro level, families are viewed as long-lived groups with a history of internal interactions as well as transactions with the rest of society. This theory has been particularly useful in the study of intergenerational phenomena and relations in the context of different historical periods. Indeed, at the macro level of analysis, families are considered within the **historical context** of their society. Not only do families change and adapt but they do so under the influence of more global social develop-ments (McDaniel, 2002). The effect of technology on family life is a case in point (Chapters 3 and 8) as is the economy in general (Chapter 4).

One key contribution of the developmental perspective has been to present a more **longitudinal** or long-term framework for research on families (Aldous, 1996). Longitudinal studies follow individuals or families over time as opposed to inter-viewing them just once. Furthermore, the developmental perspective examines the careers of families within their particular socioeconomic context, and takes into con-sideration the dynamics between the various trajectories and life stages of its mem-bers (Elder, 1998).The concept of role recurs in this perspective as each individual's role evolves when additional members arrive, as children age and enter the economic system or depart, and as grandchildren are born.

Dynamic concepts include transition or passage from one stage to the next as well as individual transitions within a particular family stage, such as when an older child moves out while the other child remains at home (Macmillan and Copher, 2005). **Timing** is a key concept (Ravanera et al., 2004). For instance, today, norma-tive timing includes a 25-year-old woman who marries and has her first child two years later. Less normative is the 17-year-old who has a baby. The first woman is "on time," whereas the second is "off time" (that is, too young according to the norms of society). Similarly, a 45-year-old woman who gives birth to her first child is considered to be off time, although such delayed transitions are becoming more com-mon (Beaujot, 2004). Transitions may also include changes in family structure, such as the occurrence of divorce, with the recognition that parents' timing may not always mesh with the stage of life in which their children are (Chapter 12).

Developmental perspectives allow us to see how family stages relate to parents' own life course. For instance, a couple who has their first child at age 28 compared

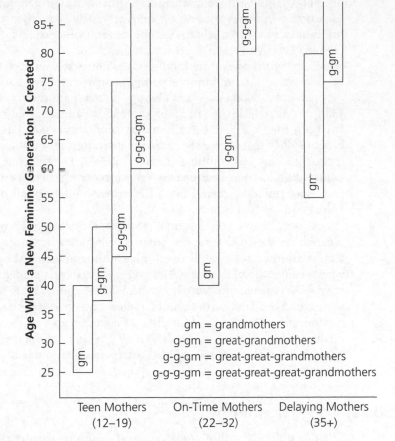

FIGURE 1.1

Generation Successions: How a Woman Creates Generations Depending on Her Age at the Birth of Her First Child

with another one who is 40 to 50 when this event occurs are at the same stage in terms of **family development** but belong to two stages in terms of **individual development**. This difference has consequences on how they live this experience, on family dynamics, and even child development. It also means that the life course of the older couple's family may be less complex and contain fewer generations, as seen in Figure 1.1. Thus, mid-life is a particularly diverse life stage in individual development because it cuts across several different family life cycles (McDaniel, 2003).

Whether one looks at delayed or youthful generation creation, the life course perspective shows the extent to which the "circumstances experienced by one member of the family impact on the lives of other family members and create change for them" (Martin-Matthews, 2000:335). When a 16-year-old has a baby, she initiates a generational chain of events in her family. If she is her mother's first child to have a baby, she creates a young grandmother, as described in Figure 1.1, and may be creating a young great-grandmother and so on up the generational line. This family is "**age condensed**": It has multiple generations closely succeeding each other. In the case of an on-time or yet older mother, the opposite occurs and the family has an "**age gap**" as the generations are less close in age (Milan and Hamm, 2003).

Early births accelerate family stages and stack up several generations of *young* people within a same family—young people who have had little time to devote to their own developmental tasks before creating another generation (Burton, 1996). They have had little time to accumulate social and material resources that could benefit both the youngest and the oldest generations (see East and Jacobson, 2000). **Early fertility** that is repeated across generations contributes to an increase in social inequalities between families (Beaujot, 2004). The opposite is more likely to occur when adults become grandparents at an older age. The two older generations have had more time for education and asset accumulation, all of which can benefit the young and the frail elderly.

As well, with a young mother, the generational gap between mother and child is blurred: As the child ages, the young mother may act more like a peer or a sibling. Unless another adult takes over, this child can lack the benefit of having a parent who assumes moral authority and who can serve as a guide. A 12-year-old child may have a 27-year-old mother who goes to clubs, dates, and is obviously sexually active with men who are not the child's father. The child may become a peer who is not monitored nor guided, and the risks of delinquency and the transmission of off-time births are high (Levine et al., 2001:369). Such a child has a very different life compared with a child whose single mother is older, more mature, and authoritative (Chapter 8).

Social Constructionism

There is diversity within constructionist positions (Crotty, 1998; Potter, 1996), and some are more psychological than sociological. Social constructionism has its roots in the classical sociology of knowledge, from Karl Mannheim's *Ideology and Utopia* (1936) through the better known Berger and Luckmann's *The Social Construction of Reality* (1966). The theory argues that various phenomena that are taken for granted and seem natural are actually culturally defined or socially constructed: A **social construct** is a social and cultural creation or interpretation. A case in point is childhood, which has been redefined throughout the centuries according to prevailing socioeconomic changes (Ariès, 1962; Parr, 2003). William Kessen explained in 1979 how children are socially constructed by psychologists. He described the American child and psychology as two cultural "inventions," or social constructs. Indeed, childhood is lived very differently in smaller, less stratified societies (Hewlett and Lamb, 2005). Gergen et al. (1996) even analyzed the discipline of psychology as a western product.

Family life is socially redefined according to the socioeconomic needs of a society at any point in time (Ferree et al., 1999). This social construction of family life generally comes from those who are in **power** as well as from **experts** who produce the knowledge that is valued by a society at a particular time in its history (McCarthy, 1996). Such valued knowledge can be religious, medical, psychological, economic, or even legal expertise—all of which have evolved from a masculine power base. It is not surprising, then, that social constructionism is related to feminism (D. E. Smith, 1993). Both emphasize culture as an explanation for the definition of gender roles as well as masculinity and femininity. Both approaches present a critique of certain aspects of society (Calixte et al., 2010). Furthermore, this critique can be used to alleviate certain social conditions created by the constructs, whether it be motherhood, adoption, or adolescence, as examples.

The Gendered Social Construction of Parenthood

One of the most important influences on individuals' lives arises from the gendered social construction of parenthood. The overall social stratification by gender dictates that women and men fulfill different functions in their respective parenting roles. The consequent household division of labour is largely unequal and gives far more flexibility to males, who can choose the activities they engage in at home (Fox, 2001). However, as we see in Chapter 4, changes in the economy and at the cultural level are altering the framework within which fathers and mothers interpret their roles. As well, a few fathers share equally in parenting while others are their children's only visible parents (Doucet, 2006).

Motherhood

Probably the most salient metamorphosis that occurs in the formation of a new nuclear family is the transformation of a girl or a woman into a mother. Motherhood is, above all, a social and cultural phenomenon (Arendell, 2000): *It is socially constructed to serve the culture of the time and the economic system of a society.* It is also defined according to the prevailing definition of childhood and of children's needs and roles within a particular economic system (Wall, 2004). The "nature" of childhood is socially constructed and thus differs from culture to culture and from century to century. Thus, mothering is defined along with the nature of childhood, as the "needs" of children differ culturally (Ambert, 1994b). For instance, in North America, it is believed that small children need to be talked to, given affection, allowed some autonomy, and prepared for school. As well, their self-esteem has to be nurtured, despite the fact that an overly high self-esteem may be detrimental (Menon et al., 2007). More and more, the emphasis is placed on the development of intellectual abilities and achievement from a young age, particularly among middle-class parents (Lareau, 2003). Such beliefs about children's needs place specific demands on how women mother (Hays, 1996). In other societies, such as the Efe foragers and the Lese farmers of Zaire, small children are defined as needing assistance from older children, having to learn how to help in and around the house and how to get along with others (Hewlett and Lamb, 2005). Such needs place fewer demands on mothers and bring vastly different socialization practices.

Once there is agreement in a society or in a social class on what is "in the best interest of the child," that is, within a particular economy, what mothers should do and should be is implicitly and explicitly constructed (Miller, 2005). For instance, the Gusii in East Africa, an agrarian people, focus on the health and survival of their infants because of high mortality. The role of caregivers is accordingly scripted around child safety and feeding. Notions pertaining to the development of self-esteem, attachment, and intellectual abilities simply do not exist (in Hewlett and

Lamb, 2005). Thus, the role description of Efe, Lese, and Gusii mothers does not include activities and concerns about these aspects of development. Whiting and Edwards (1988:94) have found that, in some societies, mothers initiate very few nurturing acts, such as cuddling; they leave these aspects of child care to older children. This observation led Whiting and Edwards to suggest that current stereotypes regarding the nature of the maternal role should be revised.

Further, in western societies, it is believed that mothers are absolutely essential to children's well-being, and that women have a natural or "instinctual," rather than learned, aptitude for mothering (Eyer, 1992). Although it may be that mothers are indeed the most important persons and parents in a majority of children's lives in modern societies, this should not be taken to mean that *one* mother is a necessity of human nature. Indeed, the western focus on individual mothers at the core of children's development is not universal. Many anthropologists question it as an *ethnocentric phenomenon* (LeVine, 1990). That is, motherhood is defined according to western criteria.

The reality is that multiple mothering and even **multiple parenting** are in the majority in many agrarian and gathering societies where several women in a community share in the care and supervision of children (Rogoff et al., 1991; Scarr, 1998). Members of the village are responsible for all children; older siblings or other youngsters are often small children's caregivers as well as their main source of psychological comfort and discomfort (Harkness and Super, 1992). To some extent, one encounters multiple parenting among North American blacks and even more so in some Caribbean as well as in some Aboriginal communities (Barrow, 1996; Collins, 1992). The care of small children by older ones was widely practised in black families during slavery (Illick, 2002).

In contrast, many western societies require **intensive mothering**—mothering that is expert-guided, is labour intensive at the middle-class level, and emphasizes the child's psychological development, particularly the promotion of self-esteem and individualism (Harkness and Super, 2002; Lareau, 2003). The child is seen as a project that has to be perfected (Wall, 2001). Hays (1996) discusses the cultural contradictions of what is involved in this type of motherhood. She points out that this social construct requires mothers to expend a tremendous amount of time, energy, and money in raising their children. Yet, in consumerist western economies, two salaries are often necessary, so neither parent can afford to stay home and care for their children 24 hours a day. Thus, at the same time that the ever-demanding economy propels men and women into the workplace, it also requires of these parents that children be raised intensively. The end result is that the requirements of the current social constructions of motherhood and childhood compete (Hays, 1998). This may be reflected in the fact that, in a Canadian longitudinal survey, having children at home was related to elevated risk of distress among women but a substantially reduced risk of such among men (Orpana et al., 2009).

Another example of the social construction of motherhood rests on the changes that have taken place regarding what is the **"proper" feeding of infants**. Before the 1970s, to breast-feed or bottle-feed was a choice on the part of mothers (Blum, 1999). Since then, various "moral entrepreneurs" have transformed this choice into a directive highlighting the superiority, even the necessity, of breast-feeding—both for mothers and infants (Knaak, 2005). As a result, mothers who do not breast-feed are often led to feel guilty and inadequate, even "bad" mothers. Maternal needs are no longer considered. As Knaak (p. 23) puts it: "It is an ideological blanket . . . that undermines mothers' abilities to feel confident about" their decision and themselves.

Another anomaly inherent to the social construction of intensive motherhood in a society where women are employed resides in the division of labour between fathers and mothers (Luxton and Corman, 2001). As we see in Chapter 4, even a mother who has a career as demanding as that of her husband spends more time in child care and housework than he does (Nelson and Robinson, 2002). This division of labour includes 24-hour-a-day maternal availability if the child is ill or needs special atten-tion. Even the task of hiring nannies or locating daycare facilities is usually a woman's responsibility. Mothers also worry more about their children (Hays, 1996:104) and are blamed when a child "goes wrong" or develops problems (Ambert, 2001).

Mother blaming is an old phenomenon. It is also a very useful political tool to use when social structures and safety nets fail individual families (Robson, 2005). Mothers often become children's only safety net. For instance, children with disabil-ities are more likely to live with a lone mother (Cohen and Petrescu-Prahova, 2006). Children themselves internalize the cultural definition of motherhood and behave accordingly: They demand more of their mothers than of anyone else in society, including their fathers. Therefore, the transition to parenthood affects a **woman's role** in terms of daily activities and preoccupations far more than a man's role. A new father retains his primary identity as a worker, whereas a new mother acquires another identity that may supersede identities that she has devoted years to acquire by going to professional school, for instance.

Fatherhood

The social construction of fatherhood has evolved substantially, particularly in the way researchers view it, and is affected by the ethnic and educational status of fami-lies (Coley, 2001). Although fathers are still defined as the chief breadwinners in two-parent families, the reality that mothers contribute heavily to the family's econ-omy contradicts this social construction and brings considerable unease to a segment of men (Gazso, 2010). Thus, there has been a shift in the social construction of fa-therhood, in great part as a result of women's increased participation in the labour force. The ideal father is now often described as the one who is involved with his children and shares household responsibilities with the mother (Doucet, 2006; Dubeau, 2002). But reality clashes with this cultural shift, as paternal involvement in children's daily lives remains comparatively low.

Further, a **dual practice of fatherhood** exists: one for intact families and one for what are called absent fathers (Eggebeen and Knoester, 2001). The more remote the *legal* paternity linkage to mothers, the less involved fathers are. Most are less involved after divorce, even though they may share legal custody, and are even less involved when the custody is not shared (Seltzer, 1998). When fathers remarry and have other biological children, their first set of children is often dis-placed or, as Cooksey and Craig (1998) put it, "crowded out." After separation, common-law fathers are far less likely to support their children than are divorced

Both symbolic interactionist and interactional perspectives view the child as a social actor who coproduces his or her development. A mother can teach her child to read, for instance, only with the child's cooperation and active participation. In turn, the child's inherited abilities also enter in the equation and set limits or enhance the learning process.

fathers. Finally, men who father children non-maritally, especially when they have not lived with the mother, are the least involved of all parents.

In contrast, mothers generally maintain a high level of emotional investment with children, even during marital conflict and divorce. The role of fathers is less "scripted" and is consequently more influenced by situational variables (Doherty et al., 2000). Thus, fathers' investment in children decreases as fathers' relations with mothers deteriorate: Mothers constitute a key context for fathering (Doucet, 2006; Madden-Derdich and Leonard, 2000). A husband who perceives that his wife has confidence in his parenting ability is far more involved in the care of their children. These results clearly show another set of differences between motherhood and fatherhood. The latter depends to a large extent on the relationship with the children's mother (Pasley et al., 2002). In contrast, motherhood exists on its own: A good relationship with the father helps, but does not determine the presence or absence of mothering. Fathering is "a more contextually sensitive process than mothering" (Doherty et al., 1998).

Behaviour Genetics

The framework of behaviour genetics, which was casually introduced in my autobiographical opener, is not well known to sociologists. It should not be confused with sociobiology, which explains human behaviours and social institutions on the basis of evolution. Nor should it be equated with approaches that foster the notion of inequalities based on presumed genetic inferiority versus superiority between racial groups, for instance. Rather, the field of behaviour genetics studies *within*-family phenomena to explain how **nature and nurture** (or genetics and environment) *combine* and *interact* to produce personalities, parent-child interactions, the home environment, how parents raise their children, and why children grow up to be who they become (Beaver et al., 2009; Plomin et al., 2008).

Parents influence their children, both through their behaviours and attitudes, and also the genes they transmit to them and the indirect effect of their own genes on the family environment (Schnittker, 2008). Parents' genes are expressed through their personalities, their socialization practices, and the lifestyle choices they make for their families, all of which are even more influenced by their environment (Rutter, 2002). A parent's environment includes his or her economic and cultural situation and relationship with the other parent; it also includes his or her children, their personalities, and their behaviours, which in turn affect the parent and his or her socialization practices. In other words, in a family, *each person is part of the other's environment*. Behaviour genetics, then, is closely related to the multicausality model of interactional and transactional theories.

Because of their different personalities, siblings in a family do not experience their **shared environment** in exactly the same way (see Chapter 11). The shared environment consists of family events and circumstances in which everyone partakes, such as family outings, meals together, parental teachings, and even divorce (Booth et al., 2000). Therefore, depending on their own temperament, birth order, and spacing, siblings experience the shared environment differently. (There is a link with symbolic interactionism here in terms of the development of different meanings attached to experiences.) If one adds other experiences that children in the same family do not necessarily share—such as illnesses, classrooms, and peers (the **nonshared environment**)—it is not surprising that siblings grow up to be different to some extent (Lemelin et al., 2007).

The closer the genetic link between two persons, the more similar their personalities and personality-driven behaviours. Identical twins raised together resemble each other more than fraternal twins, as detailed in Chapter 11. Further, the closer the cultural link between two persons, the more similar their behaviours become. Therefore, identical twins raised together resemble each other behaviourally more than identical twins raised separately. Genes and the environment constitute the two engines that guide human development—*not* the environment alone and *not* genes alone (Meaney, 2010). For instance, high parental involvement (environment) can compensate for a child's genetic liabilities (Shanahan et al., 2008). Thus, behaviour genetics represents an important perspective for sociologists because nearly all the research on families has ignored the fact that human beings are biochemical entities that affect and are affected by their environment (D'Onofrio and Lahey, 2010). Behaviour genetics *complements* sociological perspectives (Sercombe, 2009).

WHY IS FEMINISM A PARTICULARLY IMPORTANT PERSPECTIVE?

There is a great deal of philosophical diversity within feminism ranging from liberalism to radicalism (Calixte et al., 2010; Hamilton, 2005). Feminist scholars, therefore, vary in the extent to which they emphasize certain elements over others (Luxton, 2009): Socialist feminists are more likely to seek to redress inequities in gender and class through changes in the state and in its policies; liberal feminists seek equality of opportunity for women in "all areas of social, economic, legal, and political life" (Calixte et al., 2010:3). Radical feminists, for their part, focus on patriarchy and how women's daily lives are affected, whether through violence or pornography, as basic examples. This said, these theoretical distinctions are more ideal than real: Very few feminist scholars do not utilize more than one of these orientations, or, yet, have not emphasized one of these at some point in their lives while drifting into another later.

In summary, feminism is an interdisciplinary set of perspectives and theories united by a common analysis of the patriarchal organization of society. This social structure privileges male attributes and male morality and leads to unequal gender roles in all social settings, beginning with the family (Thorne, 1992). These trends combined have provided most of the critique that has served as a basis for a reformulation of research on family life, often by researchers in general. Yet, it is still the case that only a minority of research on families utilizes feminist perspectives, even broadly defined (Wills and Risman, 2006).

There have been several waves of feminism in North America since the 19th century (Chunn, 2000), but ultimately feminist theories are woman-centred and aim at documenting and explaining the feminine experience (D. Smith, 1999). Feminist scholars have highlighted the fact that women's and men's experiences of life are largely different and unequal. This theme has a multitude of ramifications for family life even if feminists by and large, as Hilda Nelson (1997:3) points out, have neglected family issues other than the division of labour. Canadian theorists are, however, notable exceptions in this respect.

The Analysis of Gender Stratification and Gender Roles

Gender roles return us to social constructionism: They represent the social definition of what, in a society, is constructed as appropriately masculine or feminine in terms of behaviour. **Gender roles** are norms or rules that define how males and females should think and behave. They have the result of making men and women accept their proper place in society according to the dictates of the overarching structural arrangement by gender. The transmission of gender roles occurs at the interface of macro- and microsociological levels (see Glossary).

At the macro level, gender roles are supported by the masculine organization or **stratification** system of the society, which provides more resources, authority, and opportunities to men than to women (Ferree, 2010). In other words, men in general have more *power* and, at the micro level, this affects the way they think and behave—differentiated gender roles. Girls and boys are socialized to occupy different roles in society, to think and feel differently, beginning with a preference for separate toys and activities. This process of socialization is so subtle that it is taken for granted as normal or as a result of nature, thus unavoidable. Consequently, on average, boys and girls grow up along divergent developmental paths and experience relationships as well as family life differently, even as adults. This fact is particularly relevant in the study of families. Feminist theories have influenced researchers who study men as well as the development of boys (Messner, 1997). For instance, there is a great deal of concern over the problems created and encountered by boys as a result of their masculine socialization emphasizing toughness, emotional distance, and even bravado (Garbarino, 1999).

Feminist theories also contribute to the examination of social inequalities and diversities in general as well as in societies that have been subjected to colonization (e.g., Mohammed, 2002). As such, they are useful in the domains of state and social policies (Eichler, 1997; Luxton, 1997), particularly with regard to racism (Baca Zinn, 2007; Dua, 1999; Rezai-Rashti, 2004) and, more recently, gender and sexual differences (Baber, 2010). In this respect, feminist theories have made it possible to examine the patriarchal structure of society from the perspective of anti-racism so as to study the impact of this double stratification on the lives of non-white women and on their families (Das Gupta, 2000). This analysis has been extended to wars (masculine) and violence against women in zones of conflict (Giles and Hyndman, 2004; MacKinnon, 2006). The phenomenon of immigration has been examined, including that of foreign domestic workers in Canada as well as the role played by gender in the cultural adaptation of immigrant families (Bakan and Stasiulis, 1997; Dion and Dion, 2001).

Feminist Analyses of the Family

Families cannot be understood outside of the forces in society that are dominated—at the political and economic levels—by a gendered as well as a racial structure (Ferree, 2010). The resulting division of labour by gender, both within society at large and within households, is a fundamental focus of feminist analyses (Bradbury, 1996). Thus, feminism emphasizes the fallacy of the family as an entirely private world that is untouched by society's inequities. In this respect, there is a kinship to structuralism as used in this text. Feminists see the division of individuals' lives between the **public** and the **private spheres** as analytically flawed (MacKinnon, 2005). Not only is the private domain affected by the public (culture, economy, polity), but the private becomes a political issue. For instance, the notion that family relations, including wife battery, are purely a personal matter has been challenged by feminists and successfully placed on the social policy and legislative agendas. As well, private decisions—such as a woman's choice to have fewer children as a personal adaptation to having the major responsibility for those children—carry important social consequences (Beaujot, 2000).

Feminism also analyzes motherhood as a social construct rather than as a purely natural product. Therefore, many aspects of feminist theories are related to social constructionism and have informed as well as expanded this perspective. Marriage is seen as an institution that generally contributes to feminine inequality and perpetuates it in private life. The gendered nature of marriage is particularly evident in the division of labour concerning household work and child care, one of the topics in Chapters 4 and 10. Other analyses examine the gap in parenting, what Jensen (1995) has called the "feminization of childhood," which leads to a discussion of how in our type of society the interests of women and children may be at odds (Presser, 1995).

However, feminist theories have been underutilized when studying older persons and their families (Chappell and Penning, 2001) and, especially, caretaking (Keating et al., 2003; McDaniel, 2009; Martin-Matthews, 2007). Further, feminist analyses have not sufficiently included women (and men) who might choose to be full-time parents to the exclusion of paid employment or those who have too little education to be competitive on the labour market and instead remain as homemakers (Evans, 1996; Marks, 2004). In a sense, feminist analyses have been developed by career-oriented women within an economic system of paid employment controlled by men and within a technology designed by men to serve the capitalist economy. These existential conditions have affected theory and research and have unwittingly devalued "feminine" qualities and overvalued "masculine" ones as well as the male structure of work.

WHAT ARE THE MAIN THEMES IN THE TEXT?

Within the theoretical perspectives just described, this book emphasizes several themes that provide the distinct conceptual framework and flavour or "voice" of this text. Social class or socioeconomic status (SES), gender, and race or ethnicity, which are key demographic variables in sociological analyses in general, are woven into this multiple thematic framework.

The first theme of **social inequalities** is the dominant perspective of Part 2 and other chapters. This theme is informed by structural, political economy, and ecological theories as well as by social capital or rational theory. Based on their economic situation and their ethnicity, families have unequal access to the key resources of their society. This is complemented by a feminist analysis as well as social constructionism, which inform us that **gendered inequalities** and consequent **gender roles** cut across economic and ethnic stratification: Men and women have a differential access to societal resources and opportunities. Gender roles form the cornerstone of several specific discussions throughout the text, particularly the domestic division of labour, relationship maintenance, and kin keeping.

A second theme is related but not limited to the first one: **family diversity**—that is, diversity in structure, culture, and inequalities. Therefore, inequalities and diversity are the two overarching themes guiding Parts 1 and 2. My concerns about *social policies* pertaining to families flow from these two themes as well as from family functions. Social policies are intended to prevent and remedy familial difficulties created by social inequality (i.e., poverty) as well as diversity (i.e., one- versus two-parent families). Diversity also includes class, ethnicity, and religion as well as ideologies leading to distinct lifestyles (Biles and Ibrahim, 2005).

The third theme, which will be initially examined in Chapter 3, focuses on **family functions**; it is related to structural functional theories. The text will document that, not only has the family not lost its functions, as is commonly believed, but it has actually acquired new ones. Above all, the book will document how individual families are too often ill-equipped to fulfill their functions, in part because of a lack of social investment in families—an important social policy critique that recurs and is expanded upon in the final chapter.

A fourth theme running through the text is that of the **effective community**, particularly the role it plays or can play in child socialization and the successful integration of families in society. This theme, which is inspired by rational theories, emphasizes how effective communities constitute social capital that supports families. In turn, this social capital allows children to develop their own human capital: positive qualities, socially acceptable behaviour, and school completion and achievement, among others. An effective social community should also help in the care of frail elderly family members and of those with special challenges so that women are not unavoidably the chief occupiers of this role—particularly women who are already caring for their nuclear family (Beaujot, 2000).

A fifth theme revolves around the **cultural context** and includes a recourse to *social constructionism.* An example is the social construction of adoption and how it can affect children's development (see Chapter 8). Another example involves adolescence and the salience of age-segregated peer groups—all western phenomena that are not universal (Kağitçibaşi, 2007; Kitayama and Cohen, 2006; see Chapter 10). The cultural context also involves the audiovisual media and its impact on family interaction and child socialization. The issue of *media influence* first appears in Chapter 3. Not only have the media restructured family time but they have also offered social constructs of reality that affect adults' and children's mentality. The cultural context also joins the theme of diversity inasmuch as families belong to a wide range of religious, ethnic, and ideological spectra.

The sixth theme in this book is especially important for Parts 4 and 5 and has a double theoretical focus. First, it emphasizes the **interactional** aspect of family relations as opposed to previous models that, for instance, tend to explain children's problems strictly through their parents' negative socialization approach. This aspect implicates feedback between environment, parents' characteristics and behaviours, and children's characteristics. Second, this theme points to the complementary importance of paying attention to family members' embodiment and **genetic inheritance** as well as the interaction of genetic inheritance with the environment in creating personalities and family relationships.

WHAT METHODS ARE USED IN FAMILY RESEARCH?

Let's briefly return to the matter of **theory.** As defined earlier, a theory is a set of interrelated propositions that explains a particular phenomenon and guides research. A good theory can be tested against facts with a set of hypotheses. A **hypothesis** is a testable proposition or sentence. For instance, exchange theory can give rise to the following hypothesis: Employed wives are less happy with their marriage when they perceive inequity in the household division of labour (Lavee and Katz, 2002). In methodological language, marital happiness is the *dependent variable*—it depends on the wives' perceptions of inequity. Inequity then becomes the independent variable, the one that will make marital happiness change. The independent variable (perceived inequity) is one of the presumed sources of the dependent variable (marital happiness).

Theories inform the questions that researchers ask about families and provide explanatory models. **Methods** are the means or tools utilized to answer researchers' questions or obtain information. The methods utilized in family research are those of sociology, psychology, and demography in general. They are summarized in five categories in Table 1.2. This table will be useful throughout the following chapters where these methods are mentioned or are described in conjunction with various results found by researchers on a wide variety of topics. Further, one special Family Research box on methods of particular interest appears in most subsequent chapters.

The matter of methods is a serious one with great consequences: The utilization of inappropriate methods simply creates useless and even misleading or false results. In turn, false or misleading results could lead legislators to enact family policies that might have negative consequences. One such example is the belief,

TABLE 1.2	**Methods in Family Research**	
Surveys	Questionnaires given in groups (such as a classroom)
	Questionnaires distributed to homes (includes Canadian census) and via the Internet
	Face-to-face interviews in homes or elsewhere
	Phone interviews
Observations	Observation in natural settings (at homes, public places, village centres, streets)
	Participant observation where the researcher plays a role in the life of the respondents
	Laboratory observations (particularly of mother/child interactions) and one-way mirror; events are recorded as they occur
Experiments	"Natural" experiments: the study of families before and after a social event or a natural phenomenon occurs (for instance, introduction of the Internet in the home; earthquakes)
	Laboratory experiments (observations, questionnaires, interviews) before and after a variable is introduced or while the dynamics of an interaction are ongoing
Evaluative research	May involve any of the above methods in order to study the impact of social policy initiatives and clinical interventions
Content and secondary analyses	Content analysis of public documents, media programs, newspapers, books, songs, videos
	Content analysis of archives and personal documents such as diaries for historical research
	Content analysis of diaries and autobiographies
	Secondary analyses of surveys, the census, and other statistical sources (*secondary* refers to the fact that the researchers who do the analyses were not the ones who had designed the original study or data gathering)

particularly in the U.S., that welfare availability has been a main cause in the past of rising rates of single motherhood. This belief, based on inherently flawed research, has recently led to a severe curtailment of help to poor families in the U.S. and in most Canadian provinces, with potentially damaging consequences for children in the future.

Qualitative and Quantitative Methods

Methods are generally separated into two large categories: quantitative and qualitative. *Quantitative methods* are based on numbers, percentages, and averages; they are shown in tables and charts and are expressed in statistical tests of significance such as time-series analyses or, at a more basic level, correlations. In contrast, *qualitative research* reports what family members say, write, and do in the form of extracts, quotes, case studies, and summaries, in order to describe and explain various family phenomena in depth and to arrive at conclusions. The reader will find many examples of such reports throughout the text, particularly in quotes from students' autobiographies, excerpts from conversations with parents during interviews, unsolicited email responses regarding adoption, and various case studies from my fieldwork. Qualitative researchers may also want to know about the impact of their study on their respondents (Campbell et al., 2010). Above all, the methodological basis of qualitative methods focuses on a more holistic perspective, on letting respondents express their realities, and on informing theory. Many qualitative researchers use **grounded theory** (Corbin and Strauss, 2008). This is a *methodological* approach guiding the study of the family via qualitative methods (LaRossa, 2005). Grounded theory emphasizes individual experience from which to build research results and even theory (Gilgun, 2005).

Statistical designs generally begin with a set of hypotheses and usually consist of multiple-choice or "close-ended" questions. Nevertheless, qualitative researchers may also use the information they have gathered and summarize it numerically. For instance, they may present averages and percentages to provide an overall view of the themes and situations that have emerged in their narrative material. This is particularly useful when large samples are involved. Qualitatively-gathered material can lead to more sophisticated statistical analyses. Therefore, the two methods do not need to be so entirely separate.

A distinction has to be made between qualitative data and "anecdotal" material. Qualitative research follows rigorous methods of information gathering. In contrast, anecdotes are gathered casually. Every individual has stories to tell about his or her life that may hold great emotional and personal meanings for that person. But these have limited *research* value because they reveal no information about general trends and do not explain where each anecdote is situated along a continuum of life experiences on a given topic. In other words, although one life incident can be the source of inspiration for future research, it does not form a sociological perspective.

In this text, the quotes presented throughout are part of rigorously designed studies seeking to obtain a wide range of family experiences so as to offer larger perspectives that lead to conclusions. An example of anecdotes, in contrast, can be found on p. 290 of Chapter 10, where I report conversations overheard accidentally. But, because they are guided by a researcher's theoretical framework—in this case, the interactional perspective—these anecdotes can constitute *exploratory data*. These are insights gathered informally that can then be used to design state-of-the-art qualitative or quantitative studies later on, particularly with the goal of testing hypotheses.

Qualitative and quantitative research methods are *equally scientific* and complement each other (Ambert et al., 1995); they are found within all five categories summarized in Table 1.2. In other words, both sets of methods can be used in surveys, observations, experiments, evaluative research, and content analysis. The latter includes historical documents. Both groups of methods can also be utilized to test hypotheses based on most theories described earlier.

Family sociologists should be concerned with choosing a research approach that can best describe the human reality they wish to study *within its social context*, whether it is a qualitative or quantitative approach or a combination of both. Methods should be selected depending on what is being investigated and on their ability to minimize the influence of social desirability (Whisman and Snyder, 2007). For instance, sensitive issues lend themselves well to audio-computer assisted self-interviews (Nooner et al., 2010). As well, if one wants to study the well-being of children in a country, then clearly a large sample is required and statistical analysis is needed. The Canadian **National Longitudinal Survey of Children and Youth** is a good example (Willms, 2002a, b). Statistics Canada's various **General Social Surveys** (GSS) are another. At the same time, however, one might want to inject more human texture and depth into the statistics by including qualitative information. This can be achieved by intensive interviewing of a small subsample of the larger one to allow the interviewees to talk at some length about the issues raised, their experiences, and feelings. One salient problem in much of the research is that only one family member, or one parent, or one spouse, is generally interviewed. In some instances, there are discrepancies in reports of facts and perceptions. Unfortunately, these can be addressed only when more than one person is interviewed (e.g., Lin, 2008b).

An Example of Qualitative Methods: Students' Autobiographies

As pointed out in the Preface, one key source of qualitative material for this book is the research I have done from my students' autobiographies. This type of research falls under the rubrics of surveys and content analysis in Table 1.2. Throughout the years, students in some of my classes have written autobiographies that were semi-structured (i.e., in response to a set of **open-ended questions**). Such questions allow respondents to say anything they want; they are the opposite of multiple-choice questions. This project was first initiated when a format was tested on several hundred students. Two years later, students' responses had confirmed that the questionnaire was nonsuggestive (I was not putting words into their mouths), easily understood, and yielded answers that could be analyzed into themes. Questions have been added and some deleted throughout the years. More than 1,500 autobiographies have been collected.

The core of the autobiographies resides in the following questions: "When you look back on your early childhood (0–5 years), what is it that you like best to remember about it? (What made you the most happy?)" and "What is it that you remember being most painful to you? (What above all else made you unhappy?)" These two questions are repeated for the 6–10, 11–14, 15–18, and current age brackets. Initially, I worried that students might resent an intrusion into their recent personal lives, so I did not go beyond the 11–14 age bracket. This ethical concern was superfluous, however, as students were actually quite happy about the entire exercise. Consequently, in future years, I added questions to cover later ages and let students choose where they wanted to stop their personal narrative.

A great proportion of the autobiographical pages are devoted to these core questions as students utilize them to narrate the main themes of the story of their lives. There are other questions whose answers are used in this textbook. These result in descriptions of students' neighbourhoods and their relationships with parents, siblings, and peers within each age bracket. No question was asked about age, race, ethnicity, religion, or marital status, as these could help identify individual students. Nevertheless, most students provided this information somewhere in their narratives.

The autobiographies (as well as all other papers and tests) were submitted *anonymously,* via their university identification number on the cover page only. After the autobiographies were read, the cover sheets were torn off, brought to class where the grades were entered on the class list in front of students. The autobiographies were an *option*; however, each year, only one or two students chose to do a conventional research paper instead. Many students elected to write well beyond the required minimum of 12 single-spaced pages. A formal 1990 evaluation of this assignment indicated that students not only trusted the anonymity of the procedure but also felt that they generally had benefited from the experience (Ambert, 1994a). Students' answers indicated that they had tried very hard to project themselves back into the particular age brackets. A frequent remark is, "Of course, when I think about this now, I laugh, but it was really a terrible problem for me at that age." Other analyses I performed showed the trustworthiness of their efforts (Gilgun, 2005).

CONCLUSIONS: UNITY IN DIVERSITY

Families are tremendously diverse but they are united under the rubric of the family as an *intergenerational institution*. The theories used to study and explain the family are numerous but they form a totality that allows one to see the family in its entirety—to study families in the plural and yet to find important similarities among them. Furthermore, the various theories discussed in this chapter illustrate the fact that the family is an ideal phenomenon for a linkage, rather than a polarization, between the macro and micro levels of sociological analysis. That is, some of the chapters that follow have a societal framework, specifically Chapters 2 through 6 on ethnicity, the economy, neighbourhoods, and educational institutions, as well as religion. Yet, family interactions and dynamics (micro level) are discussed within the larger contexts presented by these same chapters.

On the other side of the coin, some chapters have a microsociological framework. Cases in point are the "relationship" chapters in Part 4 and much of the two "challenges" chapters in Part 5. Yet, these relationships and challenges are situated within and are explained by their larger context. Similarly, the themes that form the basis of this text, although diverse, are unified because, when placed together, they present a holistic view on family life. This view can then be translated into social policies pertaining to supporting the family as an institution and consequently supporting individual families, however diverse they are in terms of structure, social class, and culture.

Summary

1. The family is defined as an institution and an intergenerational group of individuals related by blood or adoption. The nuclear family is generally enclosed in an extended network of kinship. Polygamy is examined as a conjugal and family type in its social contexts.

2. The main theoretical perspectives informing family research are as follows: (a) Structural functionalism emphasizes global forces in society that affect family life, with a focus on the functions fulfilled by social systems and their subsystems. (b) Resources occupy a central position in social exchange and rational theories. Social exchange theories see people interacting so as to maximize their own benefits and minimize their costs. Rational theory also focuses on resources in the guise of social and human capitals in the area of child socialization. The concept of the effective community is also important. (c) Symbolic interactionism focuses on shared meanings, self-concept, reference groups, and roles. (d) The interactional- transactional perspective explains how family members create their environment at the interpersonal level while also being shaped by this environment. It considers bidirectional feedback between parents and children; the latter are coproducers of their development. (e) Developmental or life course perspectives emphasize the longitudinal approach, transitions, timing, as well as the personal and historical contexts in which family stages evolve. Generational successions are examined, including age-condensed versus age-gapped generations. (f) Social constructionism argues that social phenomena that are taken for granted and seem natural are actually culturally defined or socially constructed. The gendered social construction of motherhood and fatherhood is a prime topic of analysis by both social constructionists and feminists. (g) Behaviour genetics studies within-family phenomena to explain how genes and environment combine and interact to produce personalities and the home environment, and how they affect parent/child relations as well as child socialization.

3. Feminism is a particularly important theoretical perspective in family studies because the intimate world of the family is guided by gender roles that are supported by the patriarchal organization of society at large. Important aspects of feminism include the transmission of gender roles, the social construction of motherhood, and the study of the family from a female perspective.

4. This text emphasizes six themes that recur throughout the chapters: social inequalities, including gender inequalities and roles; family diversity; family functions; the effective community; the cultural context and social constructionism; interactional and behaviour genetics perspectives.

5. Qualitative and quantitative research methods in family research are equally scientific and complement each other. Qualitative methods, often based in grounded theory, are distinguished from mere anecdotes. Qualitative researchers do in-depth interviewing or observation. Quantitative methods use statistics. The description of students' autobiographies used in this text is presented as an example of a qualitative study.

6. The chapter concludes by emphasizing the unity in the family as an institution that exists amidst the diversity of levels of analysis and theoretical as well as thematic approaches to the study of the family.

Analytical Questions

1. Some instructors prefer to teach "Intimate Relations" rather than Families classes; some say that teaching about "families" is obsolete. How can you respond to this position?
2. Which of the theories described in this chapter interests you the most? Be prepared to make a reasoned case for your response.
3. Link each of the main themes of this book to a theoretical perspective and analyze how

these themes unite some of the theories herein presented.
4. How do qualitative and quantitative methods differ and complement each other? What are their respective limitations for the study of families?

Suggested Readings

Hamilton, R. 2005. *Gendering the vertical mosaic: Feminist perspectives on Canadian society*, 2nd Ed. Toronto: Pearson. Overview of feminist viewpoints concerning Canadian society. This book ranges from a discussion of the development of the women's movement, to the gendered division of labour, to the constructs of sexual desirability, to globalization.

Mandell, N. (Ed.). 2010. *Feminist issues: Race, class, and sexuality*, 5th Ed. Toronto: Pearson Education. The articles in this book contain discussions exemplifying how feminism relates to race, class, and sexuality.

Nelson, A., and Robinson, B. W. 2002. *Gender in Canada*, 2nd Ed. Toronto: Pearson Education. The authors present a feminist analysis of several aspects of family life.

White, J. M., and Klein, D. M. 2008. *Family theories*, 3rd Ed. Thousand Oaks, CA: Sage. The authors focus on five theoretical perspectives in family research: exchange, symbolic interactionism, family development, systems theories, and the ecological perspective.

Suggested Weblinks

The **National Council on Family Relations** in the U.S. is host to the *Journal of Marriage and Family* as well as *Family Relations*. It is the focal point of information dissemination for researchers, theoreticians, as well as educators regarding families, not only in the U.S. but throughout the world.

www.ncfr.com

Two American websites that present different ideological perspectives on family are **Council on Contemporary Families**

www.contemporaryfamilies.org

and the **Institute for American Values**

www.Americanvalues.org

Feminist Majority Foundation is an American website that presents news from the entire world on women's issues and includes a list of feminist journals.

www.feminist.org

Canadian Families Project provides some information about the historical approach to the study of families.

http://web.uvic.ca/hrd/cfp

CHAPTER 2

History and Cultural Diversity of Canadian Families

I am grateful to Catherine Krull, Queen's University, for her contribution to several sections of this chapter in the previous edition.

"I find it difficult here at the university because there are not many Native persons like me and I don't even look like the stereotypical Native that people have in mind because my mother is part Native and my father's family was from Scotland and no one in my family looks alike but we speak English different, sort of slow and quiet and we live at the edge of town many of us together but we travel back and forth to visit our relatives north of here. . . . I am the first person in my family to go to university and my mother is very proud of this but at the same time this makes me different than my people . . . and I know for a fact that many Natives that got an education in the past have assimilated themselves into the rest of Canadians, so it's all very difficult to fit in anywhere completely." [A female Aboriginal student, one of only three who were ever enrolled in my classes while teaching at York University for more than 30 years; see also Mayer, 2008.]

"At that age [10–14] it was total rebellion at home: My parents were first-generation immigrants but I was born here and I wanted nothing to do with being different, poor, them having an accent, not being allowed out at night with the others. . . . Now looking back I realize that it must have been a horrible time for my parents: They only wanted the best for me."

"I am very happy to be in Canada because the country where I come from does not value girls. In Canada I can be anything I want. I just have to study hard. Even my father respects his daughters now."

"Things are different for my younger brother and sister than for me because they mix much more than I do with kids from backgrounds other than Chinese whereas in my time we had to work harder and we lived in Chinatown so it was difficult to meet other children and it's still difficult for me now. But I can see how different things have become in just 10 years even in my own family, especially now that we have moved out and up."

These students' comments exemplify the number of ways in which ethnic, including Aboriginal, and immigrant origins can profoundly affect people's lives and that of their families. Scrolling down through the past of Canadian families to present day allows us to examine how diverse family systems have always been and how the various waves of immigration have transformed our familial landscape into one of cultural diversity. We also see how some tragedies in our history, particularly concerning Aboriginals, have had negative effects on families that are felt to this day.

CANADIAN FAMILIES OF THE PAST

This chapter begins with a description of the structure and functions of families in the three founding nations of Canada: the First Nations, the French, and the British. It also discusses the family life of a small but important black community early on in Canada and the large-scale immigration after to western Canada of Chinese and Europeans with more diverse origins after 1867.

Early First Nations Families

When Europeans *officially* "discovered" the Americas in the 1490s, Aboriginal people in what is now Canada numbered well over 200,000. The most densely populated areas were in the woodlands along the St. Lawrence River and the Great Lakes and in the forests and coastal regions of future British Columbia. The nations in these regions were both hunter-gatherers and horticulturalists. They lived in settled villages and engaged in some trade. In the other regions, especially in the Prairies, the north, and the Maritimes, Aboriginal nations were almost exclusively hunter-gatherers and followed a nomadic existence because of the need to pursue migratory game. There were more than 300 First Nations in North America by the 1490s, with unique histories, cultures, laws, various levels of economic complexity, and diverse languages. Some lived peacefully with neighbouring nations while others were more warfare oriented.

Before the European arrival, the First Nations were political, social, and cultural entities built around families and kinship. Some nations, such as the Pacheenaht on Vancouver Island were **patrilineal**—that is, they recognized descent and inheritance through the father's line. Others, such as the Iroquois in the St. Lawrence Valley, were **matrilineal**, whereby descent and inheritance were through the mother's line. Nonetheless, the basic social unit of all First Nations was the extended family within bands, clans, tribes, and nations. These families were communal, and they shared responsibilities and resources—everything from childrearing to food. Two contrasting examples of First Nations are provided, but we always have to keep in mind that we know next to nothing about these nations' histories before the conquest.

Plains Cree and Iroquois Families

The Plains Cree were a nomadic people, and their society tended to be patriarchal and patrilineal. Families united to form a band in order to better protect themselves against attack and to facilitate communal hunting (Mandelbaum, 1979). Varying in size from 80 to 250 persons, bands normally comprised a male chief, his parents, brothers and their families, plus other families that may or may not have been related (Binnema, 1996). Informal councils composed of male members advised a chief, and band unity was provided by the chief's prestige and power (Christensen, 2000). Yet, while band leadership rested on consensus-building among families, membership was not fixed (Binnema, 2001). For instance, if individual disputes occurred, young men could join another band, perhaps even marrying within it. If a band as a whole encountered difficulties, say the death of the chief, entire families could leave and unite with some relatives in other bands (McLeod, 2000).

The type of economy structured gender roles. Men hunted, cared for horses (after they were re-introduced), and served as warriors in defending the band and its territory (Friesen, 1999). Women reared children, prepared food, and made clothing and domestic implements. The band provided for needy members, especially the elderly and widows who could not hunt, and older people were at times adopted by younger families. Orphans and boys whose families were in difficult situations could live with the families of the chief or other men of high rank. They were then considered members of these families, and in return for work, were given food and clothing. Like the other male children, they received instruction in hunting and warfare; female children were taught the domestic skills needed for band survival.

In contrast to the Cree, the Iroquois were a group of settled people that included the Nadouek, with territories extending across the future Canada–U.S. border. By the beginning of the 14th century, they had embarked on intensive agriculture. Their tribes were matrilocal and matrilineal: Women owned all property and determined kinship (Danvers, 2001). Therefore, when marrying, a man moved in with his wife's family and, when children were born, they became members of their mother's clan. All clan members were responsible for childrearing. Iroquois settlements were defensive fortifications and contained a series of longhouses, one for each clan, which were often more than 100 feet long; these settlements served as the political and economic centres of each tribe. The Iroquois had to abandon their settlements periodically, either because their farmland ceased to be productive or in order to improve their defensive position.

It was these two elements of social survival—producing food and defence—that saw gendered divisions of labour among the Iroquois. In terms of food production, since women possessed clan land, they worked the fields that produced crops such as corn. Men hunted and fished, and warfare was their principal vocation (Recht, 1997). But warring societies require political organization. Given the matrilineal nature of Iroquois society, women chose the male leaders from amongst warriors in the settlements. Women of high status were often consulted even on matters of war (Magee, 2008). Family life in Iroquois society, therefore, was based on the implicit concept of gender equality, with men and women each having a range of specific responsibilities and rights (Brandáo, 2003; Engelbrecht, 2003). When the individual Iroquois nations coalesced into the Iroquois League, influential clan mothers continued this tradition by determining their nation's representatives within the governing council of the league (Fenton, 1998).

Families of New France

European and Native Precursors

It is difficult to evaluate the changes that might have taken place among eastern Native nations before the official "discovery" date of 1534 for, indeed, Scandinavians already had seasonal settlements in what is now Newfoundland, at Anse aux Meadows, for instance. Breton fishers had been exploiting cod stocks along the coast all the way to Cape Breton in Nova Scotia, where they had carried out exchanges with the Mi'kmaq, including down the coast of Maine in 1524 (Trudel, 1973). Although the Mi'kmaq still exist in several Maritime provinces

(Critchley et al., 2007), these sporadic contacts with northern Europeans could already have resulted in some degree of *métissage* and in epidemics of influenza and chicken pox, for instance, for which the Native peoples had no immunity. As a result, their **demographic profile** might already have deteriorated via imported diseases and, later, loss of territories and food sources (Northcott and Wilson, 2008:25), as happened to the Beothuk of Newfoundland, who were extinct as a nation by the mid-1850s.

It was not until Jacques Cartier came to Gaspé in 1534 that the first regular trading took place with the Mi'kmaqs and Iroquois; in fact, it is these same Iroquois who helped Cartier push his discoveries to Quebec. After Roberval and Cartier's failure in 1541–43, only Basques, Breton, and Norman fishers continued yearly trips to the eastern regions and initiated the fur trade: One can only speculate about the changes that might have been brought to some of the Native peoples' ways of life. For instance, iron objects received in trade seemed to have been bartered all the way to Huron territories in what is now Ontario. When Champlain arrived in 1603, most of the villages that Cartier had encountered were gone; Algonquins and Montagnais nations seemed to have replaced the Iroquois along the St. Lawrence—in itself an indication of profound demographic changes. By the 1620s, some tribes had already noticed an increase in mortality as their contact with the French intensified. They were being decimated by disease.

While the Aboriginal tribes in these areas and even beyond were adopting some European habits and objects including tools, clothing, food (such as bread), alcohol, and armaments, a great deal of their ways of living also penetrated the early colonial culture and allowed it to survive. This includes indigenous food, tobacco, forced germination of seeds, clothing better suited to the harsh winter climate, as well as means of transportation such as toboggans and canoes.

What kind of family structure did the French bring? As Thornton (2005) has well documented, northern Europeans had, well before the 1600s, already developed an emphasis on individualism and the **nuclear family** within one household. By the 1800s, many other countries had adopted a neolocal system of residence (Ruggles and Heggeness, 2008). In northern Europe, including northern France, couples married in their twenties because of the necessity of establishing a separate household—a very modern situation already. As well, most young people were fairly autonomous in terms of choosing a mate—even though parents among the nobility still arranged marriages, as exemplified in biographies such as Amanda Foreman's *Georgina, Duchess of Devonshire*. But for the remainder of the population, affection and companionship were already important elements of courtship and marriage, perhaps since the 1300s. In summary, the northern European family was already adapted to the future requirements of industrialization and may have contributed to its rapid ascent in northern Europe, particularly in England.

Settlement and Colonial Families

The territory rediscovered by Jacques Cartier in 1535 and then by Champlain in 1603 did not become part of France's overseas empire until 1608, when an expedition of 28 men established the colony of New France at what is now Quebec City. Only eight survived the harsh living conditions (Cartier, 2008). After many failed attempts, it is only in 1618 that the settlement at Quebec started holding, with vegetables and other crops growing. And it is only in 1642, more than a century after Jacques Cartier, that a settlement in Montreal was undertaken. These very slow beginnings were due both to France's lack of interest in settling Canada and the difficulties that the harsh climate imposed on the few French would-be colonizers. Parallel to these developments was the establishment of British and French communities in Newfoundland and Labrador in the 17th century.

The first French-Canadian colonists were **fur traders**, or *coureurs de bois*, who constructed a frontier society while confronting many difficulties: extreme weather, conflict with the Iroquois, and later on intermittent warfare against the English colonies for the control of the fur trade. Until the mid-1600s, there were very few European women in New France. The 1665–66 census indicated that there were 2,034 males and only 1,181 females, including children (Statistics Canada, n.d.). French male colonists were involved in the fur trade, military service, and administration. A significant number took First Nations women as wives—called *les femmes du pays*—in unions outside of the Church (Dickason, 2002). As marriage partners, these women played an important role in the early development of New France. Not only were their domestic skills key to survival but their knowledge about skinning animals and preserving fur pelts, their ability in using First Nations languages, and their peoples' traditions as traders all contributed to the growth of the fur trade (Jamieson, 1986).

However, the nature of French Canada's economy and society changed over time and this affected these families: The fur trade began to weaken, and perhaps more importantly, intermarriage between French colonists and First Nations women declined. Rather, the Roman Catholic Church encouraged colonists to marry Métis women—those of mixed French and First Nations ancestry—and, later, white women. Between 1667 and 1673, at the request of the first intendant, Jean Talon, France sent almost 1,000 young women, 800 of whom were called *les filles du roi* (the King's daughters), to the colony to marry bachelor settlers (Cartier, 2008). Although most women were married, they adopted a wide range of roles. Some became merchants and administrators while others founded religious institutions and even became missionaries (Clio Collective, 1987:49).

By 1700, however, four major events had combined to relegate women to more specialized female roles and promote family life even more prominently than it was in France itself. The first event was economic and pertained to the demise of the fur trade and the coinciding **rise of agriculture**. Although women had some freedom, large families became essential for the settlement of communities because farm life required numerous workers (Noël, 2001). And, as French women had been scarce for many decades, a trend toward early age at marriage was established, in contrast to later ages in France at the time. Under French law, a seigneur—akin to France's minor nobility—owned the land, and tenant farmers worked it. The number of land concessions from the Crown worked by a tenant family depended on the number of sons a couple had.

The second event was a strategic consideration: Government policy promoted **large families** to strengthen the colony against British advances (Krull, 2003). Rather than encouraging massive immigration from France, the French Crown promoted high fertility to increase its colonial population. Women's options for economic security were quickly reduced to either marrying or entering the convent. In 1666, there were only 3,215 Europeans but by 1763, when the English regime began in Canada, 70,000 French-speaking people lived in North America (Beaujot and McQuillan, 1982). They descended from only about 10,000 French immigrants, who travelled to North America over a 150-year period. This growth constituted an extraordinary rate of natural population increase.

The third event influencing women's role and family life concerned the expanding authority of the **Catholic Church**. As farming communities and parishes increased, the Church gained more power and influence over the colonial population. By controlling education, for instance, the Church developed a gender-specific curriculum: Girls were taught to be good wives, mothers, and servants of the Church. Although also instructed to serve the Church, boys were tutored in the ways of the world. The Church played a major role in implementing the Crown's pronatal agenda (Krull and Trovato, 2003a).

The fourth event, a peace settlement with the Iroquois in 1701, produced a more secure agrarian society. With the family as the base of this society, continued population growth remained the order of the day. Couples in New France kept marrying at a much younger age than elsewhere (Beaujot and McQuillan, 1982). This tendency was reinforced by government policies that gave monetary rewards to females who married before the age of 16 and males before 20. Other policies to strengthen people's desire to have large families included monetary rewards to couples with at least 10 legitimate children. Marriage was viewed as a natural state that all colonists would eventually enter and in which they would remain until their death. Consequently, divorce was almost unheard of.

Early colonial families shared several characteristics such as sex-segregated roles, pronatalist attitudes, a neolocal nuclear household, self-selection in mating (but with parental approval), and kin interaction (Nett, 1993:102). These values, the agrarian framework of the new society, and the structure of the Québécois family, which continued well into the 20th century, may have contributed to slow down industrialization and economic development in what is now Quebec compared with the emerging American states south of the border.

Families during British Colonial Rule

Before Britain's conquest of Quebec in 1759–1760, the British colonial presence in what is now the United States had surpassed the French in terms of both wealth and population. Although the original purpose for Britain's presence mirrored that of France—commercial pursuits centring largely on the fur trade—its demographic superiority lay with London's policy of populating its Empire by massive emigration from the British Isles (Games, 1999). Entire families were a large part of this migration. After the American Revolution of 1776–1782, the British presence in North America remained through control of Quebec and Newfoundland/Labrador, the loyalist colonies in the other Maritime provinces, and Upper Canada or modern southern Ontario (Reid, 1990).

Families in Upper Canada and the Maritimes

Families in Upper Canada and the Maritimes during the period of British colonial rule, which lasted until 1867, were different from their counterparts in Quebec. Given their greater population, these British colonies experienced relatively faster urbanization and more rapid industrialization than in Quebec. Major towns emerged: Halifax, York (now Toronto), Kingston, Fredericton, among others. The emphasis on private property also facilitated another economic transition, this time from a preindustrial agricultural economy to a capitalist and industrial one.

Social stratification solidified along classes of merchants, professionals, artisans, farmers, and labourers. Moreover, also reflecting British society, an aristocratic element was introduced when British noblemen and their families came to Canada to govern, lead the army and navy, and establish estates. A distinction arose between nuclear families and households: Households included domestic workers, servants, and labourers and their families who worked for and were supported by the patriarch's family (Hoffman and Taylor, 1996). In all classes in the colonies, therefore, there was an intimate connection between family life and production: "The household was the centre around which resources, labour, and consumption were balanced"(Tilly and Scott, 2001:78).

British families in Upper Canada and the Maritimes were nuclear ones built around English Christian principles (MacDonald, 1990; Potter-MacKinnon, 1993). There was no central religious power equivalent to the Roman Catholic Church in Quebec: The several Protestant religious authorities included Anglicans, Methodists, Quakers, Puritans, and Presbyterians. Christian notions that fathers and husbands owned property and were responsible for subservient children and wives underpinned this colonial society. Having custody of their families' moral character as well as their economic well-being, men often worked outside the home. More importantly, British common law gave legal rights to men as the heads of their families. Women were restricted to the home as cooks, cleaners, and caregivers for their children and, sometimes, for elderly parents. But they could take a leading role within households (Smith and Sullivan, 1995). On a husband's death, for example, widows could inherit land and manage their families' interests on their own. Divorce in Upper Canada was only possible after 1839, but when it occurred, men received better treatment from the law, including custody of their children (Johnson, 1994).

Within the working class, children were crucial for the economic survival of families. After receiving rudimentary education, they worked to help support the family (McClare, 1997). Most working-class boys learned farming, logging, and, in the Maritime colonies, fishing, while others apprenticed in trades such as carpentry and blacksmithing. Within the upper classes, male children had access to good schooling, including university, to prepare for the professions and government. With some exceptions (den Boggende, 1997), upper-class females received a general education that prepared them to take their place in society (Errington, 1995). At lower levels, girls entered domestic service as young as 10 years old, and remained there until they either became financially independent or married. Overall, children only married when their contribution to the family was no longer essential; this translated into the age of marriage being higher in Upper Canada and the Maritimes than in Quebec

(Krull and Trovato, 2003b). For very poor families, who had no home and no income, begging was not uncommon (Hoffman and Taylor, 1996). Charity from well-to-do families rather than from the government helped less fortunate ones.

Quebec Families under British Rule

In the period between the British conquest of Quebec (1763) and Confederation (1867), when Upper Canada, Quebec, and the Maritime colonies (except Newfoundland and Labrador) joined to form an independent Canada, the Québécois continued to develop a distinct society with the family at its core (Berthet, 1992). The British could not afford the troops that would have been necessary for a cultural conquest. Therefore, to keep their new French-speaking colony stable, the British let the Québécois use their language; put no strictures on the Roman Catholic Church, and allowed French civil law to remain. The result was that, beneath the English political and economic domination of Quebec, a Catholic, agrarian, and French-speaking society continued to exist as before, and became very homogeneous in its rural world.

Marriage in French Canada not only remained as the natural state for every colonist, it was seen as essential for the survival of Quebec's distinct culture and society (Krull and Trovato, 2003b). Of course, some women and men chose not to or failed to marry. They generally stayed with their families and, in the case of older daughters, often remained to care for elderly parents. Others entered religious orders and, until the 1960s, most large Québécois families were proud to have a priest or a nun among their children. French-speaking government officials and the Church promoted family growth and more sons were needed to open new territories farther north. Divorce remained extremely rare, as family solidarity was more important than marital happiness. In this way, the nature of Quebec families did not change despite the British conquest. The established pattern of marrying at an early age continued along with large families.

Montreal became one of Canada's major industrial cities, with a growing immigrant population from Europe seeking employment. But the majority of Québécois in the 19th century lived outside of Montreal; and because Quebec's population was expanding, its best farmland was occupied, and the British had commercial monopoly, some Québécois saw the possibility of a better life for their families outside of the Canadian colonies: Québécois families began moving south to find jobs in industries. Indeed, 900,000 Québécois settled in the U.S., from Maine to Michigan, between 1840 and 1940 (Lavoie, 1981).

First Nations Families under French and British Rule

Contact with both British and French societies continued to bring great changes to First Nations and their families, which became more fragile in the face of increasing European supremacy. At first, the contacts had saved the French colonists, who learned to adapt to the harsh climate from the Native peoples. There was a level of equity for some decades and this frequently occurred as well when hard-working *coureurs de bois* cohabited with Aboriginal women who, along with their villages, proved to be very helpful to the French. Later, it was largely the progeny of such *métissage* (hence the nation of Métis) that contributed to the expansion of trade in the north and Manitoba (Van Kirk, 1992). But this mutually advantageous state of affairs did not last. Eventually, throughout the decades, close to 3,000 Aboriginals were enslaved. Fur traders often exchanged alcohol and arms, along with new foods, and these created an economic dependency amongst Aboriginal people on the French and later the British colonizers—in addition to implanting alcoholism. As well, Aboriginal tribes were often pushed one against the others. To these problems were then added the calculated plans by both the French and British colonial governments and Christian missionaries to eradicate First Nations' culture by assimilating them (Fiske and Johnny, 2003:182).

The European educational system played a key role in colonizing Aboriginal culture. The Jesuits in Quebec opened schools to educate Aboriginal children about religion and French culture. The British did the same and, by the end of the colonial period and the early years of Confederation, every region in Canada had **residential schools** for Aboriginal children (Harrison and Friesen, 2004), with the Métis situation being somewhat less clear-cut (Chartrand et al., 2006). Children, now wearing uniforms, were alienated from their families and stripped of all identifiers of Aboriginal culture. They were forced to take Christian names and forbidden to speak their mother tongue. One Aboriginal woman recalls that:

> *"When I got into school, everything changed for me all at once. My parents didn't have a say any more in the way my life went. When I came in off the land, the people with any type of authority were Qallunaat [non-Aboriginal]. . . . They treated us like we belonged to them, not to our parents. . . . They taught us a new culture, a different culture from our own, they taught us that we have to live like the white people. We had to become like the white people."* (Emberley, 2001:61)

First Nations families were extended and often shared a common dwelling in which all the generations lived in close and constant proximity. This communal life meant that all family members were responsible for the rearing of children. They formed an effective community.

Many children were assaulted. Thus, the residential schools have had lasting negative consequences both for the individuals who attended them and their families (Barman, 2003). "Generations of depression, alcoholism, suicide, and family breakdown are the legacy of such traumatic experiences and are described as the 'residential school syndrome' by native people themselves" (Chartrand and McKay, 2006).

Some academics have argued that British colonial relations with Aboriginal peoples were based on a patriarchal domestic model that also ultimately "structured the proper meaning of 'the family' for aboriginal cultures" (Emberley, 2001:60). In this context, the First Nations people were treated as unruly children and the government as the benevolent father (Chartrand et al., 2006). Beginning in 1870, a series of *Indian Act*s reinforced the concept of the

British nuclear family model by forcing First Nations to change their traditional family structures. These changes ranged from "marriage practices, adoptions, and residence rights to an inability to bequeath property according to established custom" (Fiske and Johnny, 2003:183). With the help of the Church, the Europeans adopted a strategy of biological and cultural assimilation of Native peoples (Das Gupta, 2000:150). As well, their means of production—their economy—was replaced.

Early Black-Canadian Families

First Nations families were not the only ones whose family structures and social institutions were affected by the cultural imperatives of the Europeans. Even before the conquest of Quebec by the British, a black community lived in what is now Canada. Slavery, which until then had been practised only toward some Aboriginal tribes, was not widespread in France but was in its colonies. Black Africans were brought to New France in the century after 1650 to serve as house servants and general labourers for the French religious, military, aristocratic, and commercial elite (Trudel, 1973; Walker, 1980). Taken from their homes and families in West Africa, only a rudimentary family life was possible for them because their owners determined almost all facets of their lives, as was the case for slave families in the southern U.S. (Gaspar and Hine, 1999). Slavery was curtailed in Quebec in 1793 by legislation making it illegal to bring people into the colony to become slaves. The British Parliament passed the *Slavery Abolition Act* in 1833.

Then, a second wave of black immigration occurred: It was a mixture of free blacks and the more than 2,000 slaves who came north after the American Revolution (Simms, 1993). The free blacks were Loyalists and the slaves belonged to white Loyalists who fled the new United States. The third wave consisted of American slaves who escaped their bondage before the 1860s and made their way to Canada (Sharon, 1995).

As occurred in New France, the institution of slavery severely weakened the structure of the family among slaves in Upper Canada and the Maritimes as, legally, blacks had no marital or parental rights (Nicholson, 1994). For their part, Loyalist blacks and former American slaves who reached Canada encountered racial discrimination and social prejudice (Winks, 2000). In one example, Loyalist blacks, compared with Loyalist whites in Nova Scotia, received few land grants after coming north, and whatever land was granted was marginal at best (Calliste, 2003). In another example, in Ontario, although official policy after 1833 was to treat blacks as free citizens equal with whites before the law, they encountered general hostility from white officialdom, even though there was a strong abolitionist movement in Ontario before the American Civil War (Martin, 1974: Stouffer, 1992).

Given their lesser economic status, black husbands and wives commonly worked outside the home, as labourers and domestic servants. Consequently, there was a reliance on the extended family to help in childrearing through a tradition of taking relatives and others who were destitute into family homes; they could help with domestic chores or could earn money. There was a reverence for elder blacks who could also join households to help themselves and the family with which they lived (Dunaway, 2003). In this context, older blacks would have adoptive titles such as

"Aunt" or "Uncle" to show that they were part of these extended families. Black Loyalist households could include neighbours, orphans, members of the local church, the widows or widowers of friends, and so on (Walker, 1976). Importantly, given that black men could not always find employment, when black wives and mothers worked in domestic service and other areas at the lower end of the economy, their unemployed husbands stayed home, minded the children, and did what they could to keep their families together (Calliste, 2003).

A more communal way of life emerged for black Canadians in which bonds of kinship became extremely important for their physical and spiritual survival as an identifiable minority. In some places, both in Upper Canada and, later, when western Canada was being settled, entire black communities were founded. Amber Valley in Alberta was such a community, established in 1911 by 90 black families from Oklahoma. The problem was that the white majority was prejudiced against black rural settlers, so that not every effort by blacks to build a family life in Canada was successful (Shephard, 1997). In other places such as the Africville area of Halifax, black urban communities evolved as a result of both segregation and black leaders' efforts to organize themselves for mutual assistance, property ownership, and education (Clairmont and Magill, 1999). Black women also played a significant role in these efforts to reinforce their communities by strengthening the family (Fingard, 1992; Yee, 1994). A distinctive black family structure and culture had emerged in Canada by the early part of the 20th century.

Families during Industrialization and the Settling of the West

The 19th century was a period of industrialization for parts of Canada, chiefly Upper Canada and the Maritimes. In this context, urbanization was also a new element of social and economic development; it affected the family and related social constructs. As this was occurring during the high point of the Victorian period, middle-class notions of women as being naturally endowed to provide the moral education of their children and to nurture their sensitivities became widespread (Hoffman and Taylor, 1996:41–91). In the realm of men, no matter their class, the demands of employment took them increasingly from home. There was a heavy emphasis on masculinity (Moss, 1998). The result was that the division of labour within marriage became even more differentiated, especially within the middle classes, and gender roles overlapped less.

Childhood: A New Social Construct in Context

By the 1840s, the concept of *childhood* began to emerge; urban social reformers became concerned about childhood employment in dangerous and unsanitary conditions, such as in mines (McIntosh, 2003). Reflecting new ideas that children were actually innocent beings who needed to be protected and educated, laws were passed to restrict child labour and allow for better educational opportunities. But as this new perspective on childhood developed—and no doubt led slowly to the improvement of the life conditions of many children—treatment of certain categories of children did not follow this new trend. Apart from the mistreatment of Aboriginal children, one childhood topic that is rarely mentioned in sociology chapters on the history of families is that of the **"Home Children"** (2009; Parr, 2003).

In poor households, children contributed to their families' economic survival well into the 20th century. Many Home Children laboured heavily, especially in rural areas. Thus, the social reconstruction of children's roles did not reach all social classes or groups of children simultaneously.

Well over 100,000 children, from a few months old to 18 years of age, were sent to Canada from the British Isles between 1869 and the late 1930s (Ontario Heritage Foundation, 1997); approximately 10 percent of the Canadian population descends from them. Who were these children? They were the poor. Some were taken off the streets while the majority came from workhouses that could no longer afford to keep them. Others had been in reformatories, generally for minor thefts while still others came from various "homes" of philanthropic institutions (BIFHSGO, 2010). They were not generally orphans but poverty had prevented their parents from caring for them. Both the Canadian and British governments supported this immigration program. It reduced British welfare costs and provided apprentices in Canada as well as adoptions by interested families for the children younger than 10 (Neff, 1996). After 1925, only children who had completed their education in Britain and had reached the age of 14 could be brought to Canada (BIFHSGO, 2010).

Many of these children found a better life in Canada but probably many more were maltreated, abused, and exploited. Many were placed on farms (Parr, 1994). Often, they were no better than slaves and had to sleep in cold barns with the animals, had no shoes, and were isolated (Thompson, 2010). They had been taken away from their own families and cut from their roots and identities. Although many served with the Canadian and British Forces during both World Wars, many of their descendants are still trying to find their parents', grandparents', and even great-grandparents' roots and are discovering distant relatives in the process. The Home Children and their immediate descendants constitute an example of resilience in adversity and family reconstruction within one generation.

The Beginning of Family Ethnic Diversity

By the middle of the 19th century, what is now western Canada was a vast area where a small number of white persons, principally British and French, engaged in fur and other trading with First Nations. After Confederation in 1867, the new federal government decided that the western regions of Canada should be populated as quickly as possible to counteract U.S. expansion westwards and to ensure Canada's sovereignty over its territory. A transcontinental railway was begun in the 1870s to link the west with the eastern regions. A police force, the North West Mounted Police, was created and dispatched to the Prairies to ensure law and order. There was a conscious effort by Ottawa to encourage immigration from Europe to populate the west.

Thus, unlike the Maritimes and Upper Canada, which were populated almost exclusively by British immigrants, and Quebec, which contained a relatively homogeneous francophone population, the Canadian west came to be settled by increasing numbers of new Canadians arriving from more diverse parts of Europe along with a significant Chinese population brought to work on the railway. As the railway pushed westwards linking the emerging provinces with central and maritime Canada, groups of Swedes, Germans, Ukrainians, Italians, and other nationalities settled in the west, including a good number of Home Children and Québécois in search of opportunities (Farnam, 1998; Gagnon, 1994; Stambrook and Hryniuk, 2000).

Initially, these new Canadians created an agrarian society (Darlington, 1997). Men tended the land and herds; women were responsible for domestic chores and childrearing (McManus, 1999). In the early period of settlement, access to education was limited. Hence, male children helped their fathers as soon as they were physically able; female children acquired domestic skills from their mothers. Once schooling was available, children had a few years of learning before working on the family farm or ranch. Communities evolved rather quickly, as groups of immigrants with the same ethnic background or even from the same region of Europe settled close together (Bennett and Seena, 1995; Voisey, 1987).

Within a generation of the railway being built, urbanization and industrialization emerged in a few cities like Winnipeg and Edmonton, and in a host of smaller towns like Brandon, Prince Albert, and Red Deer. As a result, social stratification in urban areas began to spread again: Western urban families began to experience different levels of education, labour, and social status. As time passed, groups of immigrants from the same places in Europe—for instance, Italian immigrants in Calgary and Polish ones in Edmonton—began to live in particular parts of these urban areas (Aliaga, 1994; Lukasiewicz, 2002). Although British political and social custom dominated, large-scale immigration in western Canada (and that of Canada as a whole) began transforming it into a multicultural society with a variety of ethnicities. During this process, Aboriginal societies were further marginalized.

Among Asian immigrants who in the late 19th century settled chiefly in British Columbia and the Prairies were Chinese men and women referred to as "sojourners" because they did not intend to remain permanently in this country. Their purpose was to supplement their incomes in the home countries where their families still lived. Married sojourners were prohibited from bringing their spouses and children to Canada. They worked in railway- and road-building, in the lumber industry, and in mining, to name a few of their generally dangerous and low-paying jobs. Asian female sojourners worked as domestics (Das Gupta, 2000). The Chinese faced discrimination from the moment they arrived. In 1885, to limit their immigration, the government imposed a head tax of $50 on each Chinese entering the country. The head tax was raised to $100 in 1902 and to $500 in 1903. In 1923, the federal government passed the *Chinese Immigration Act*, also known as the "*Chinese Exclusion Act*": Until its annulment in 1947, it barred new Chinese immigrants. Further, all Chinese in Canada, including those born here, had to register with the authorities and a great deal of discrimination occurred at all levels (e.g., Stanley, 2003).

By 1947, the injustice of these policies began to be called into question, especially since Chinese Canadians had served in the Canadian armed forces during the Second World War. By the early 1950s, Asian Canadians in general were given the right to vote in federal and provincial elections and were allowed to work in professional fields heretofore closed to them. With the passage of the 1967 *Immigration Act*, the Chinese and the Japanese received the same rights as other groups of immigrants and began to reunify their families in Canada.

CURRENT DIVERSITY OF CANADIAN FAMILIES

Of the 1.1 million immigrants to Canada between 2001 and 2006, approximately 58 percent came from Asian countries and the Middle East, while only 16 percent came from Europe. The foreign-born numbered 6,186,950 in 2006 and constituted 20 percent of the total 31.2 million Canadians—the highest proportion since 1931 (Statistics Canada, 2009b). In addition, fully 75 percent of immigrants who recently arrived belong to a non-white minority. The highest proportions of immigrants came from China and India, then Pakistan, the Philippines, and Iran as well as Sri Lanka and others from South Asia (Statistics Canada, 2008a). In this section, we complete the overview of the development of families' structure, culture, and conditions of life in Canada by examining current trends and outcomes in family diversity. We return to Aboriginal and Québécois families—the original two groups of founding families. We then return to black families before examining more recent families, including Chinese and Indian.

Aboriginal Families

In the 2006 census, close to 1.2 million Canadians, or about 3.8 percent, identified themselves as an Aboriginal person. Of these, 698,025 were First Nations (or 60 percent of all Aboriginals), 389,785 were Métis (or 33 percent), and more than 50,000 were Inuit (Statistics Canada, 2009a). As we see later in Family Research 2.1, adding multiple identities gives us a total of over 1.6 million Aboriginals, or 5 percent of the Canadian population. This is a huge change over just 10 years ago, perhaps due to an increased tendency to identify as Aboriginal as a result of a renewed pride in their unique heritage and the fact that more reserves have participated in this census (see also Lawrence, 2004; Naumann, 2008). As well, children born to an Aboriginal parent and a non-Aboriginal one now tend to identify as Aboriginal (Robitaille et al.,

2010). **High fertility rates** also contribute; although these rates have declined over the past four decades, they still remain much higher than the Canadian average of 1.6 children per woman (Statistics Canada, 2009q). The Inuit have the highest fertility rate, with an average of 3.4 children per woman, followed by status Indians with 2.8 children, the Métis with 2.4 children, and non-status Indians with 2.0 children (Beaujot and Kerr, 2004).

Some provinces have a higher proportion of Aboriginals in their population. For instance, while they represent less than 2 percent in Ontario, they constitute over 10 percent of Saskatchewan (Gionet, 2009). Approximately 58 percent of Aboriginals who are registered as status Indians live on one of the 2,284 **reserves** throughout the country. Reserves are lands that have been set aside by the Canadian government explicitly for Aboriginal peoples (Harrison and Friesen, 2004:228). The primary unit of First Nations social structure is the **band**, which originally described small cultural and linguistic groups who either lived together or came together at various times of the year (Harrison and Friesen, 2004). In more recent times, a band refers to an administrative unit that operates under the *Indian Act* of 1876. There are currently 621 bands in Canada (Frideres, 2000).

We have discussed residential schools earlier: The end result has been a legacy of trauma with which the First Nations people are still trying to cope (Grant, 2004; Kirmayer et al., 2007). For example, because they were isolated from their own families, students of residential schools were deprived of nurturing and of First Nations familial role models (Das Gupta, 2000). Poor parenting skills subsequently prompted **Children's Aid Services** to remove many children from their families. A 1979 Canadian report on adoption and welfare found that 20 percent of children in state care were Aboriginal, which is a number disproportionate to their share of the Canadian population (Das Gupta, 2000). Today, over 27,000 Aboriginal children are in foster care (Monsebraaten, 2009). In addition, rates of domestic violence and abuse are extremely high, with women, children, the elderly, and persons with disabilities the most affected (Chartrand and McKay, 2006).

Large numbers of Aboriginal children were also taken from their homes and adopted by non-Aboriginal families. "In many cases, children

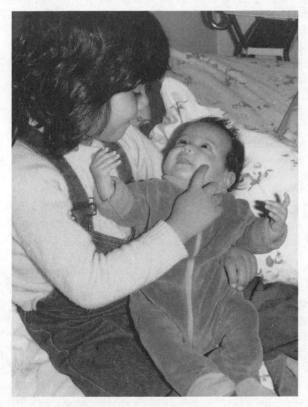

First Nations families are, on average, larger and younger than other families in Canada. In Aboriginal communities, many of the childrearing functions fulfilled by parents in Canadian society at large are shared with relatives, including older children. Sibling influence may be even more important on Aboriginal reserves compared with its importance in society at large—a hypothesis that remains to be tested.

were taken from parents whose only crime was **poverty**—and being aboriginal" (Fournier and Crey, 1997:85). As a result, several Aboriginal communities lost nearly an entire generation (Johnston, 1983). As one woman recalls: "Our family life was shattered after seven of my eight siblings and I were split apart into separate foster homes. We were never again to reunite as a family" (Fournier and Crey, 1997:85). There were so many Aboriginal children adopted out during the 1960s that Patrick Johnston, a researcher for the Canadian Council on Social Development, referred to this mass exodus of children as the "Sixties Scoop." By the late 1970s, one in four status Indian children could expect to be separated from his or her parents for all or part of childhood. Nearly half of all legal wards in British Columbia are First Nations children (Kershaw et al., 2005).

It was not until the 1980s before the last residential school was closed. At that time, the administration of most reserve schools was handed over to Aboriginal school boards (Harrison and Friesen, 2004). Nonetheless, although many traditional First Nations family structures have ceased to exist, either because of government policies or because of a mass movement from reserves to cities where non-Aboriginals form the majority, the notion "of the caring, effective, extended family, co-extensive with community, continues to be a powerful ideal etched deep in the psyche of Aboriginal people" (Castellano, 2002:16). The importance of the **extended family** in terms of social identity, economic support, and psychological nurturing cannot be overstated. Urban Aboriginals generally remain connected to their kin (UAPS, 2010). Fiske and Johnny (2003:182) argue that the "importance of family and kin relations takes precedence over all other emotional and social ties in most, if not all, First Nations communities." Their **kin networks** are twice as extensive as those of other Canadians, and they are able to identify more than 50 different familial relationships to people living with them (Buchignani and Armstrong, 1999). The importance of kin may be one of the reasons why Aboriginal victims of family violence vastly under-report their situation (ANAC and RCMP, 2001). (This topic is addressed at greater length in Chapter 13.)

Within an extended family structure, **elders** tend to be respected and identified as key sources of tradition and wisdom (Buchignani and Armstrong, 1999). Most live with their children or another family member. Elder care is primarily informal, an arrangement which is consistent with traditional values that emphasize familial obligation. Both elder care and visits to elderly family members are generally carried out by women, especially daughters. However, Aboriginal elders face more hardships than other Canadian elders and they suffer a great deal of abuse (Chartrand and McKay, 2006). As well, their income is typically below the poverty line and many support their unemployed children, which means that an extended family lives on less than required for bare subsistence (McPherson, 1998). Disability rates for Aboriginal seniors are twice the national average, and nursing care facilities on reserves are rare, which forces many to live in nursing homes away from their families and friends. Buchignani and Armstrong (1999) have found that First Nations elders were three times more likely to report their health as "fair" or "less than fair" than other Canadians of comparable age. Similarly, Aboriginals in general, including those living off-reserve, have a poorer health status than other Canadians (Statistics Canada, 2010c).

Statistics Canada and Ethnic Groups

Census statistics regarding ethnicities are at times difficult to interpret because the definition of what is a person's ethnicity is a matter of self-definition. As well, the Canadian census allows persons to self-identify with only one group or, if they wish, more than one. Partly as a result of this, the various tables and articles published by Statistics Canada often give different numbers depending on the basis of calculation. For instance, we have seen earlier that there are two estimates for the Aboriginal population, ranging from a low of 1.17 million to a high of 1.67 million, depending on the number of self-identities chosen.

For Indians, the total is 962,670 and includes 780,175 with only this identification and another 182,495 with more than one self-identity. For Chinese, the total number is 1,346,510, which includes 1,135,370 with one identification and 211,145 with more than one (Statistics Canada, 2009e). The larger number is generally given but this is not always the case for Aboriginals—perhaps reflecting the greater complexity in the ancestry of Aboriginals due to higher rates of racial mixing historically and currently.

Over the past few decades, Aboriginals have developed strategies to achieve **self-determination** and self-government. Some have used traditional games, such as gambling, as a means of expanding their economy (Belanger, 2008). The federal government is currently negotiating various forms of self-government with approximately 90 different indigenous groups. There have been strong collective efforts to renew traditional knowledge, values, cultural activities, and customs and a determination to take charge of social services and child welfare (Kumar and Janz, 2010). Various healing groups have been formed; some encompass research (e.g., Bopp et al., 2003; Lane, 2002), including some that are specific to the Métis experience (Chartrand et al., 2006). Some reserves in British Columbia have acquired the right to own their homes.

As well, First Nations families have demanded the right to teach their young people and to develop a curriculum that embraces Aboriginal practices and ways of knowing. Given the importance of language in "the transmission and survival of Aboriginal knowledge and culture," the revival of First Nations language is viewed as pivotal to this process (Harrison and Friesen, 2004). Of the 50 distinct Aboriginal languages known to have once been spoken in Canada, only three are now considered secure: Cree, Inuktitut, and Ojibway. The remaining languages have either disappeared or are spoken by only a few people (Beaujot and Kerr, 2004). Families and schools are cornerstones to these efforts to revive these cultures.

Québécois Families

Since the early 1960s, Quebec society has seen fundamental changes to family life. In 1960, a reformist Liberal government took power and undertook wide-ranging reforms. The economy shifted to one based more on finance and industrialization.

Québécois began to replace anglophones in leadership roles. The French language was used increasingly in the workplace. The power of the Catholic Church was curtailed: Its domination of education was replaced by secular government control and its influence over moral issues, such as the prohibition on divorce, was diminished (Laplante et al., 2006). As well, the Church's political alliance with the conservative political elite was broken. Women's rights were expanded and entrenched: Until then, women had had few property rights, limited access to education beyond primary school (even then concentrating in the domestic sciences), and few legal rights.

Nationalism, pronatalism, and feminism are powerful elements in understanding contemporary Quebec families. Québécois feminists, a relatively small group in 1960, supported the reforms. But by the end of the decade, as Quebec feminists became more organized, the province experienced a second wave of feminism: By 1985, there were more than 300 women's groups involved in political action (Dumont, 1995). Women's roles changed; therefore, so did family life. **Marriage rates** have plummeted since the early 1970s, from 8.2 per 1,000 population in 1971 to only 2.7 in 2001, well below the national average of 5.0 (Girard, 2008). Divorce is now much higher in Quebec than in the rest of Canada. The percentage of never-married individuals at age 50 is almost twice as high in Quebec, and the average age at marriage is one year later (Krull, 2003). Moreover, by 1991, Quebec already had the lowest proportion of married-couple families in all of Canada: 69 percent compared with 80 percent in the other provinces.

The rapid decline of Quebec's **birth rate** since 1960 clearly changed family structures in the province, as large nuclear families were replaced by smaller ones and many were led by single or cohabiting parents. Québécois society went from exceptionally high and sustained reproductive levels—spanning more than 300 years—to fertility rates that have now reached historic lows. This situation has proven problematic in the relations between women's groups and Quebec nationalists. On the one hand, many feminist groups support Quebec nationalism. But nationalists are concerned about the decline of Quebec's francophone population. In their estimation, for Quebec nationalism and the French language to survive—even if sovereignty is impossible—francophone women must produce more babies. However, Québécois women increasingly control their own lives—cohabiting or marrying as they like; pursuing education and careers; gaining financial independence; and limiting their fertility. As one francophone student from Quebec points out:

> *"I find that girls here* [Ontario] *are less independent than at home especially when it comes to becoming mothers. Here they all say they want children but it was not like that at UQAM, many of us didn't want any or* [wanted] *only one. I have two older sisters and they both put their babies in child care and don't have any problem with this. Here I noticed that women are more hung up about this. . . . They still feel guilty about it. . . . Women also breast-feed longer in Montreal than in Toronto. . . . Anyways . . . I met this guy but I am worried that his family will find me too liberal for them. So that's my problem right now, figuring out where to go."*

To push their agendas in the 1980s and 1990s, both Liberal and Parti Québécois provincial governments supported pronatal policies (Ansen, 2000). Financial rewards for women who had children were $500 for a first birth, $1,000 for the second, and $8,000 for the third and for each subsequent birth. Incentives also included a family allowance for all children under 18 years and an additional allowance for children under age six (Baril et al., 2000). Québécois feminists argued that, by advancing pronatal policies, the Quebec government was supporting a "traditional" family structure in which women are valued primarily for their domestic role. Accordingly, the birth rate did not increase and Quebec abandoned its pronatal policies in favour of **pro-family policies** to recognize that people who have children are helping their society.

In 2000, for instance, Quebec introduced a progressive, government-subsidized daycare program for working families, at a cost of only $5 per day per child. With the cost now at $7 per day, the program has a waiting list of up to three years. Yet, because every subsidized daycare in Quebec follows a formal, age-appropriate curriculum that emphasizes school readiness and basic skills such as language and socialization, the Canadian Policy Research Network points out that "Quebec is the only province in Canada that has made a commitment to early-childhood education, and not just daycare" (Anderssen and McIlroy, 2004). In addition, the provincial government is proposing to expand its provision for parental leave and, in 2006, 56 percent of Quebec fathers compared with only 11 percent in the rest of Canada availed themselves of this program (Statistics Canada, 2008b).

Black-Canadian Families

There are important cultural differences among blacks: Those not born in Canada are coming from the Caribbean, the Americas, or Africa. They differ in their history, language, geography, social experiences, family structures, and in their reasons for emigrating (Galloway, 2004). They also differ by religion; yet, religiosity is a key element in black family culture (Taylor et al., 2004). There are other common experiences shared by black families. For instance, most black-Canadian parents believe that the community is important and tend to "share the African proverbial saying that it takes the whole community to educate a child. While parents believe that individual rights are important, they also think they should be matched with a strong sense of social responsibility" (Dei, 1993:47). Unfortunately, few studies exist on Canadian black families and given their longstanding presence in this country, this lack of research illustrates their marginality (Calliste, 2003; Christensen and Weinfeld, 1993).

The number of black families in Canada dramatically increased after racial barriers were removed from immigration laws in the 1960s. During the 1970s and 1980s, the majority of black immigrants came from the Caribbean, South America, and Central America; since 1990, the proportion of black immigrants arriving from Africa has increased. Forty-eight percent of black persons are Canada born; of the foreign born (Statistics Canada, 2009c),

- 26 percent come from Jamaica
- 15 percent from Haiti
- 12 percent from other Caribbean nations
- 20 percent from several African countries

Black-Canadian families have a varied cultural and social heritage. They also include a wide range of family structures and patterns, which have constituted adaptive strategies that have allowed them to survive in rather difficult environments.

Blacks, who represent 2.5 percent of the Canadian population, constitute the third largest non-white minority group with close to 800,000 persons (Statistics Canada, 2008a). Cultural factors retained by black immigrants when they come to this country, as well as racism and structural inequalities, have played some part in the evolution of black family patterns and coping strategies. For instance, despite their growing numbers, black families continue to be disadvantaged. Blacks—particularly black women—experience unemployment and income inequality more than any other minority group (Calliste, 2003; Galloway, 2004). Statistics Canada (2004h) recently pointed out that Canadian-born blacks between the ages of 24 and 54 earned on average $7,500 less per year than other Canadians with the same education. A black student indirectly recalls how her economic problems tainted her relationship with her parents when she was 10 to 14 years of age:

> *"We all had a hard time together mainly because our parents couldn't cope with us three children. We weren't bad or anything of the sort but we lived in a cramped apartment near a subsidized project and there were kids, kids, kids everywhere. We had a lot of fun some days but my parents didn't. They were trying to raise us well but the other kids we were always hanging around with would have none of it and their parents weren't always the best either, they'd let them stay out late at night, go wherever, invade and control the hallways, parking lots, you name it. They were up to no good but my sister, brother and myself couldn't appreciate that our parents were trying to protect us from this mayhem. I resented my parents but at the same time I loved them and we had the only father on the block and that made us special also."*

Black families have tighter connections to their extended kin (Gosa and Alexander, 2007). A related issue that middle-class black students often mentioned in their autobiographies was that of having poor relatives and even siblings who were unemployed, out of money, and even criminal—elements less often mentioned by others (Heflin and Pattillo, 2006). These relatives, who as one woman put it, "have a sense of entitlement," were often draining their own families' resources.

Low socioeconomic status and few employment opportunities have contributed to family breakdown. Black spouses, especially in working-class families, are more likely to be separated or divorced and less likely to be formally married, a situation also found in the U.S. and throughout the Caribbean region (Christensen and Weinfeld, 1993). Conflicts pertaining to money frequently arise as an issue explaining this racial disparity (Bryant et al., 2008). As a result of disadvantaged economic circumstances, blacks place less importance on marriage as a context for childbearing (see Chapter 8). However, upper-income blacks are more likely to marry before having children, and this class difference also holds in the Caribbean (Barrow, 1996). The high divorce rate and the higher tendency for black women to have nonmarital births have resulted in many black families being headed by a woman: Black children are approximately three times more likely than other Canadian children to be living in a low-income, single-parent family. Also contributing to low marriage rates is an **imbalance in the gender ratio** of potential mates available. There are more black women of marriageable age in Canada than black men, primarily the result of earlier policies that admitted massive numbers of black women as domestics and the greater tendency among black men than among women to enter into interracial marriages (Calliste, 2003; Harknett, 2008).

Moreover, black female domestics were also denied reproductive freedom in that they were not allowed to marry or have children without facing deportation, a restriction that did not apply to white immigrant women. However, a sizeable proportion of these domestic workers from Caribbean countries already had had one or more children who were left behind, generally in the care of grandmothers. These grandmothers raised and loved these small children. Many were sponsored by their mothers and arrived in large Canadian cities, particularly Toronto and Montreal, at times in winter, to live with a mother they had barely known. This mother may have had a live-in boyfriend or another child. This situation is well expressed by a student:

> *"The most painful part of my life was when I had to leave my grandmother in Jamaica and come here to my mother I had seen only a few times in ten years. I didn't know her and I hated her and I refused to do anything she asked. . . . Even to this day we aren't close but at least I can feel for her terrible situation."* [This student's brother is now in a penitentiary.]

These immigrant children have great difficulties adjusting to life in a high-density, low-income neighbourhood where gangs at times rule. Despite all these problems caused by systemic forces, the fact that most of these families find ways of thriving is testament to their resilience and adaptive ability.

Chinese-Canadian Families

Marriage and Fertility in China

For almost 2,000 years, China's family life was shaped by Confucianism. Marriage partners were chosen based on family needs and values rather than on attraction and love (Engels, 1995). It was common practice for parents to negotiate a marriage contract when their children were young; some children were betrothed before they were born. The groom's family was expected to pay a **bride price** and the bride's family was to provide a **dowry**. The Chinese family was patrilineal, patrilocal, and patriarchal, and overwhelmingly favoured sons. Prior to the founding of the People's Republic of China in 1949, women were barred from participating in public life, had few employment opportunities, and 90 percent were mostly illiterate (SCIO, 2000). Few resources were spent on daughters. Custom dictated that a son reside with his parents after he married but that a daughter depart to live in her husband's home. It was not uncommon for poor families to sell daughters into servitude to pay the bride price for a son's wedding.

Families underwent tremendous changes in 1949. The communist government passed a marriage law meant to replace traditional family structures with a democratic marriage system. Arranged and coerced marriages were abolished, monogamy became the norm, and the rights and interests of women and children were protected through law (SCIO, 2000). Child betrothal was abolished; men had to be 22 years old and women 20 years before a marriage could be contracted. Moreover, the law discouraged patrilocal residence. However, China was still plagued by its considerable and rapidly growing population. Even though contraceptive technology was officially approved in 1954, fertility rates remained high. In 1970, each woman was having an average of six children, a rate well above that of western countries. To promote modernization, the Chinese government needed a strategy to reduce the number of people who would be competing for resources (Fong, 2002). The solution came in the form of a one-child-per-family policy in 1979 and a new marriage law in 1980.

The implementation of the **one-child policy** has varied by region and over time. For example, great resistance to the policy emerged in the countryside because rural parents depended on their children, especially sons, to work on farms and support them in old age. In the 1980s, the government revised the policy so rural couples could have two children but urban couples were still restricted to one child. These various policies were enforced at the provincial level with rewards and punishments. Pregnant women having an approved birth received free obstetric care and could obtain better housing, extra food rations, and cash subsidies as an incentive to have no further children. However, couples who had an unapproved birth not only paid for their prenatal care, they also faced substantial fines, usually ranging from 20 to 50 percent of a family's annual income. Women were subjected to a number of intrusive enforcement tactics, including coercive sterilization programs and mandatory IUD insertions and abortions (Short and Fengying, 1998).

These policies had unexpected negative effects. For example, Doherty et al. (2001) found that women who had an unapproved birth, and thus were not eligible for free obstetric care, were more at risk of prenatal complications and even maternal death than women who had approved births. As well, the policies did not diminish the traditional preference for sons over daughters, and unusually low numbers of female babies were born in comparison to male babies (Guilmoto, 2009). A normal **sex ratio** at birth is 105 boys for every 100 girls. But, currently, in China, there are 120.5 males for every 100 females—112 in Hong Kong and 109.6 in Taiwan. This imbalance is the result of female infanticide, parents' refusal to register daughters, parents' abandonment or neglect of daughters, and selective abortion of female fetuses following ultrasound tests (Zhu et al., 2009).

On the positive side, two years after implementing the one-child policy, fertility decreased dramatically to two children per woman. A Chinese woman now has on average 1.5 children, which is below replacement level (Morgan et al., 2009). Chinese families today, especially in urban areas, tend toward greater gender equality and have become neolocal and bilineal. In eastern cities, such as Beijing and Shanghai, son preference is diminishing and daughters help their elderly parents (Fong, 2002). Nevertheless, the preference for male children has not entirely disappeared, especially in rural areas, and numerous orphanages exist to shelter abandoned baby girls: Thousands of western couples and single women adopt these infant girls. However, with continuing economic and social development, China's sex ratio imbalance may slowly disappear, as has been the case in South Korea (Das Gupta et al., 2009).

Chinese Families in Canada

Chinese Canadians currently represent Canada's largest non-white group: Over 1.3 million Canadians, or 4 percent of the population, come from or trace their descent to China (Statistics Canada, 2008a, 2009d). But despite a long history in Canada, family formation by Chinese immigrants has only taken place over the past four decades—after the passage of the *Immigration Act* of 1967. Although Chinese-Canadian communities existed in every province and region of the country, the majority of Chinese immigrants settled in British Columbia and tended to reside with other Chinese Canadians in the same areas. This produced a series of Chinatowns with shops, restaurants, and other cultural and social elements of life. Today, approximately 72 percent of the Chinese people in Canada live in Vancouver or Toronto.

As the Chinese-Canadian population grew, it transplanted a number of traditions from China, Taiwan, and Singapore into its Canadian communities, including the dominance of patriarchy, extended families, and social stratification based on wealth (Burney, 1995). However, although it is not unusual for three generations to reside together, this is no longer the dominant Chinese-Canadian family structure, and couples tend to live near extended family members rather than with them. There is still a strong family support network, particularly in child care and assistance in housework (Man, 2001). Two Chinese-Canadian students describe how these social networks maintain cultural identity and help parents reinforce traditional values in their children:

> *"I live in a big house in Toronto with my parents, and my grandparents live in a nearby condo and I have all in all six uncles and aunts who live around and in Markham. So it's easy for us to remain Chinese and my grandparents never have to speak English. They might as well be in Hong Kong for all I know. . . . Sometimes though it's hard because I'd like to be more Canadian but there is so much pressure to be and marry within our group, I feel like I am being choked and I'd like to move to Vancouver later but then who would babysit for me?"*

"My peers' values have always been similar to those of my family's because I have always hung around with other Asians. Living in Chinatown has made my life easier. . . . We are different but I do not think that we ever cared much because there always were so many of us."

As pointed out by the first student, without their extended families, women may encounter problems with child care and household maintenance, which are considered the wives' responsibility. Man (2001:434) reports from her study on Hong Kong female immigrants to Canada that "the physical spread of Canadian cities, and the lack of transportation systems in suburbia—where most of the Hong Kong immigrants reside—heighten children's dependency on their mothers, intensifying women's workloads. Consequently, some of them experience an intensification of traditional roles, unequal distribution of household labour, and gender and sexual oppression in the home." Moreover, she found that most Chinese women linked power to the ability to manage and control every aspect of family life, and thus, to relinquish control is to relinquish power or to lose face. Chinese women are reluctant to ask their husbands for help, even though they are less traditional than men with respect to gender roles and family hierarchy (Tang and Dion, 1999).

Chinese-Canadian family relationships are, for the most part, based on the notion of filial piety: respect, obedience to one's parents, reverence for and assistance to the elders in the communities. This helping behaviour is reciprocal, as parents often assist their adult children with financial matters and child care. When one or both parents are not proficient in English, young Chinese immigrants are often faced with having to link the two cultures by taking on the role of **cultural brokers**. This role entails serving as translators for their parents, which often requires accompanying them as they take care of their daily needs, such as shopping and paying bills.

Chinese-Canadian parents tend to be indulgent until their children reach school age, although many remain authoritative (Cheah et al., 2009)—not to be confused with authoritarian. Then, children may fall under stricter control, although the level of parental supervision varies greatly. Chinese-Canadian adolescents state that their parents want to choose careers for them more often than is the case for other Canadian adolescents. Moreover, a large majority of Chinese parents expect their children to go to university, whereas fewer other Canadian parents have such expectations. Overall, Chinese-Canadian parents have so far been quite successful at helping their children retain their values (Su and Costigan, 2009). For instance, Chinese youths are generally more conservative sexually. Adolescents of Chinese origin are slow to shift their expectations toward the North American model of early autonomy because of the effectiveness of the family in transmitting its values (Liu et al., 2005).

Indo-Canadian Families

Once the racial barriers in Canada's immigration policies were lifted in the 1960s, many Asians immigrated, especially Indians, who now number more than 900,000, or about 2.9 percent of the Canadian population (Statistics Canada, 2009d). The roles and status of family members are well defined and understood within the ideal model of the Indian family structure, which is extended and patrilocal (Fuller and Narasimhan, 2008). Roles and status are challenged when members of extended

First- and second-generation Indian families have assimilated into the Canadian economy while at the same time retaining many elements of their culture. This is particularly evident at weddings where couples begin life within the rituals of their culture.

families move to Canada and must live as nuclear families—although many still live in three-generational households. For many Indian and other Asian immigrant families, including families from the Middle East, economic survival depends on the wife taking on paid employment. This process not only challenges established gender roles, it accounts for increased conflict between many husbands and wives. However, many Indian wives are happy and feel free because they no longer fall under the control of their **husband's mothers** who are very powerful—even though about half of families are already nuclear in India (Niranjan et al., 2005). When asked about her current happiness, an Indo-Canadian student conveyed anguish over her mother's situation:

"At this stage of my life I am not the happiest. I would like to leave my parents' home because it is really not their home, it's my grandparents' and it is too painful for me to see how badly my grandmother treats my mother as [if] *she is her slave and my father lets her do it. . . . She even treats my father badly* [she prefers the student's uncle who still lives in India]. *I don't understand that my father accepts this because he owns his home and he paid for his parents to come here and my mother worked hard helping him do this. It hurts me so much that I want to run away and take my mother with me."*

Let's look at the cultural heritage that Indian families bring with them. "Love-marriages" have been legal since 1872, but they continue to be rare; yet, many couples in the younger generations are engaging in such marriages, albeit with some parental consent (Derne, 2008). This occurs even in villages (Ahearn, 2001). But, overall, **arranged marriages** still predominate in India (Mody, 2002). There are strict criteria used to determine an appropriate partner for one's child. For example, the future bride and groom need to be matched in terms of caste position, socioeconomic status, age, education, and of course, religion. Emphasis is placed on social compatibility and duty to parents and ancestors rather than on individual compatibility and personal desires for love and intimacy. Indeed, Muslims, Hindus, and Sikhs view the obligation to marry within the group as essential (Mody, 2002).

When Indian families migrate to Canada, they are exposed to a social construction of marriage that emphasizes romantic love and companionship. Two results can follow. First, many established couples experience marital strain, at least as perceived by their children. As one woman explains in her autobiography:

"I would rate my parents' marital satisfaction differently, with my father's being high because he has what he needs which is a traditional Indian marriage while my mother is so lonely for just a bit of attention from him . . . and also because she sees that her cousins who came here before get along better and have a good relationship. It's very hard on my mother and it will be terrible when my father's mother eventually moves here from India to be with us."

Second, most Indo-Canadian female university students still undergo some form of arranged marriage—and some even expect to be sent to the U.S. for this purpose; others are still married against their will during trips to India. In England, the Foreign Office's **Forced Marriage Unit** received 1,600 such reports in 2008 and intervened in 420 cases (Aulakh, 2009). In fact, in the Punjab city of Ludhiana, each year several hundred cases of brides abandoned by husbands abroad are registered. "Canada-based families are said to be among the worst offenders," with many husbands living in the Toronto area (Westhead and Aulakh, 2009). But, overall, most will have a greater say than would have been the case a decade ago (Zaidi and Shuraydi, 2002). One married woman student was introduced to her future husband,

" . . . But my mother made it clear to me, him, and my father that I had to like him. So he visited me at my home several times and I really liked him; he was so nice and brought me and my mother little gifts. I asked him all kinds of questions. Then, after several weeks, we went out with my brother who left us alone most of the time, we held hands at the movies and he even asked my brother if he could kiss me and my brother said 'go for it' and here I am, married, and pretty happy. . . . I think that when arranged marriages work out, they're great because your parents do all the preliminary work for you. It's a great tradition to this extent."

The parent-child relationship is considered the most intimate and fulfilling familial relationship. **Motherhood** is a key source of *power* for Indian women. According to Kohler Riessman (2000), a child solidifies a wife's often fragile bond with a spouse in an arranged marriage and improves her status in the joint family and larger community; and with a child, she can eventually become a mother-in-law. Moreover, women rely on their children, particularly on their sons, to support them in old age. Indeed, preference for male children exists in many parts of India, especially the Punjab and Rajasthan, where **sex ratios** in the population are 123.8 and 120.7, respectively (Guilmoto, 2009). In the well-to-do classes, selective abortion takes place. Among the poorer, female malnutrition, non-vaccination, and non-treated illnesses before age five produce an excess of female mortality (Oster, 2009). Two problems exacerbate the situation: first, a dowry, which, although legally abolished, is still paid to the future husband's family; and second, the huge costs of wedding ceremonies—which can last for several days—and which families have to bear to enhance their status. When the bride price is unpaid or too low, many brides are abused and even maimed by their in-laws' families; others are pushed into suicide so that the husband can find another bride with better means.

The parent-child role among Indo Canadians has also undergone major changes (Nayar, 2004). Although first-generation immigrants have strong expectations that their children will uphold the tradition of arranged marriages, these wishes are often challenged by children who are raised in a culture that devalues such marriages. Yet, many other young adults feel comfortable within this cultural perspective (Porter, 2003). Although marriage may not play the role that it does in western societies, it would be wrong to assume that the relationship between husbands and wives in India is unavoidably weak or deficient or lacks in companionable values, at least at the ideal level (Orsini, 2007; Zysk, 2002). Zaidi and Shuraydi (2002:512) found a definite "cultural" generation gap between the family values of second-generation Muslim Pakistani immigrant women and their parents, who typically favour arranged marriages. "This non-conformity to arranged marriages creates a mood of uncertainty for many females as they feel confused, uncertain, and torn between their own thoughts and their parents' belief system."

Although other Asian women have made advances such as being able to pursue post-secondary education and seek a career, it is not always easy. For instance, Talbani and Hasanali (2000:625–626) found that second-generation Asians tend to adapt to Canadian material culture but "find it difficult to negotiate between cultural control and individual freedom." Among Muslim immigrants, however, there may also be issues of others' reaction to "Islamism" that confronts them (Moghissi et al., 2009). But just as Chinese-Canadian families continued to adapt to Canadian society, so too do other Asian ones. And the result will probably be the same—finding a balance whereby the family as the core of various Asian ethnic identities will change but not be destroyed.

CONCLUSIONS: EVOLVING CANADIAN FAMILIES IN DIVERSITY

Territorial conquests, cultural contacts, and economic development all have a major impact on the structure of families as well as on gender roles and general family functions. Prior to contact with the French and the British, Aboriginal families were complex social and economic institutions that allowed for survival in a difficult land. Contact with the colonizers destroyed many of these cultures and family systems. For their part, the British and French brought their own forms of neolocal family structure and adapted them to Canada as conquest, modernization, and industrialization brought economic and social transformations requiring change. The settlement of the Prairies and the West diversified families as other people from Europe and Asia arrived to populate this vast region of the country. But even these families had to evolve to respond to urbanization and industrialization.

Thus, the family, a crucial institution of Canadian cultural heritage, includes many structures and systems of roles related to the various ethnic and immigrant groups comprising this society. Therefore, being a member of a First Nations family, or a Québécois family, or a black or a Jewish family has a different meaning, connotations, and identities for its members than those of being a member of an Indo-Canadian or Chinese-Canadian family. However, it is key to recall that all these families show a great deal of variation *within their own groups*. No group is totally homogeneous and this makes for even greater diversity of family life in Canada.

Summary

1. Whether patrilineal or matrilineal, Aboriginal families have historically been distinguished by communal living and the practice of sharing responsibilities and resources. The Plains Cree and Iroquois families are described.

2. There had been contacts between northern European fishers/explorers and Aboriginal peoples before 1534. These contacts altered the demographic profile of Aboriginals. For their part, northern European families had long been nuclear.

3. The first settlers from France were immensely helped by Aboriginals in the fur trade and in terms of sheer survival. Intermarriages were common. Later, European nuclear families had increasing importance in the development of colonial New France. For economic (agriculture), religious, cultural, and social reasons, marriage became the norm and large families were encouraged and predominated.

4. Colonial British Canada—Upper Canada and the Maritimes—quickly evolved from a preindustrial agricultural economy to a capitalist industrial one and social stratification solidified. Legal and religious traditions imported from the British Isles reinforced the nuclear family structure that made patriarchy dominant. Children's work was important. Under British rule, Quebec continued as a culturally and demographically separate society.

5. Both French and British colonial governments—and the government of Canada after 1867—worked to assimilate First Nations into the dominant European society. Assimilation resulted in a loss of language and culture, and a weakening of Aboriginal family structures built around communal living and shared responsibilities.

6. Black Canadians developed a more communal and extended family life by the early 20th century—an amalgamation of their West African traditions that survived slavery, and newer ones that derived from living in French and then British Canada.

7. The 19th century witnessed industrialization and modernization for parts of Canada, chiefly Upper Canada and the Maritimes. Along with urbanization, these economic changes affected the family, especially in terms of the social constructs of childhood, the role of mothers, and the repositioning of men's employment away from the home. Divisions of labour within marriage became more pronounced, especially in the middle classes.

8. The development of western Canada brought new European immigrants: Germans, Ukrainians, Italians, and others. The vast majority of new Canadians brought with them family cultures derived from their various homelands. However, Chinese immigrants were long prohibited from bringing their families. The case of "Home Children" is discussed.

9. Since Confederation, immigrants increasingly came from Asia, Africa, Latin America, and the Caribbean. More recently, immigrants have come mainly from Asia and Africa.

10. Aboriginal families are still based on kinship, communal sharing, and defined familial responsibilities for all members. Despite a range of social, economic, and other problems affecting their society, First Nations are the fastest growing group in Canada. The extended family remains an important emotional and social foundation for them even though it has been severely affected by residential schools, the loss of their territories, and life on reserves. Elders still have a special role but many burdens as well.

11. In the 1960s, Quebec's family structure was transformed and women's rights were

expanded. Smaller families have replaced large ones and many are led by single or cohabiting parents. Worried about preserving French culture, the Québécois government has encouraged larger families and has worked to strengthen family life by introducing innovative policies such as universal daycare.

12. Blacks now represent the third-largest visible minority group in Canada. Migration policy and women's domestic labour have created difficulties for black families, with an unbalanced gender ratio, resulting in lowered marriage rates and high rates of single motherhood.

13. In terms of cross-cultural perspectives on family, the People's Republic of China provides an important case study showing how demographic policy can influence family structure. China has introduced tough laws to ensure one-child families and abolish arranged marriage as well as bride price.

Preference for sons is diminishing in some areas. Canadian-Chinese families have retained their filial values related to family life as well as expectations for their children's economic success.

14. In India, arranged marriages continue to be the norm for both Hindus and Muslims. Motherhood is a sacred duty. Indo-Canadian families have made some compromises in terms of gender roles and arranged marriages are perhaps more open, although the value of marriage itself and of sons has remained. Immigrant families in Canada are also marked by generational differences, and they reflect the different cultures of Canada's older and recent immigrant arrivals.

15. Families have evolved since the advent of the colony and have continued to adapt and to diversify according to their origins. Diversity also exists within cultural groups.

Analytical Questions

1. What accounts for the differences in family structures found between early Iroquois and Plains Cree people?
2. What can explain the development of communal and extended family life among black Canadians by the early 20th century?
3. How is childhood affected by and linked to the concept of industrialization and modernization? And how does this relate to theories of social constructionism discussed in the previous chapter?
4. How has racism influenced government policies historically in Canada? Include all affected cultural groups.
5. How can you analyze the implications of such cultural heritage as arranged marriages, forced marriages, and imbalanced sex ratios?

Suggested Readings

Clio Collective (M. Dumont et al.). 1987. *Quebec women: A history.* Toronto: Women's Press. This book offers an in-depth history of the women who have lived in Quebec during the past four centuries. Its six sections each reflect an important era in Quebec's history.

Fournier, S., and Crey, E. 1997. *Stolen from our embrace: The abduction of First Nations children and the restoration of Aboriginal communities.* Vancouver/Toronto: Douglas and McIntyre. A compelling account of how Aboriginal family life was decimated by government policies. The book concludes with a discussion of how Aboriginal people have begun to empower themselves and help their families.

Gaspar, D. R., and Hine, D. C. (Eds.). 1999. *More than chattel: Black women and slavery in the Americas.* Bloomington: Indiana University Press. A collection of articles that provide a wide-ranging coverage of the conditions of feminine slavery throughout the Americas. Childbearing, cycles of work, social construction of these women, family life, resistance—only a sample of the topics covered.

Harrison, T., and Friesen, J. 2004. *Canadian society in the twenty-first century: A historical sociological approach*. Toronto: Pearson/Prentice Hall. Through a variety of perspectives, this book explores three major relationships responsible for shaping Canada's development.

Lavell-Harvard, D. M., and Corbiere Lavell, J. (Eds.). 2006. *"Until our hearts are on the ground": Aboriginal mothering, oppression, resistance and rebirth*. Toronto: Demeter Press. A collection of essays on Aboriginal women's diverse roles as mothers and activists, reclaiming their cultural identities. The diversity of the motherhood experience is highlighted. The effects of social policies are discussed.

Lynn, M. (Ed.). 2003. *Voices: Essays on Canadian families*, 2nd Ed. Scarborough: Thomson Nelson. This book offers a rich and diverse collection of cross-cultural perspectives on family life in Canada.

Moghissi, H., Rahnema, S., and Goodman, M. J. 2009. *Diaspora by design. Muslim immigrants in Canada and beyond*. Toronto: University of Toronto Press. This book presents the results of a fairly large study on four groups of recent immigrants to Canada: Pakistanis, Afghans, Palestinians, and Iranians, and compares their adaptation in Canada to the adaptation of similar groups in other countries. A substantial part of this research pertains to family life.

Whyte, M. K. (Ed.). 2010. *One country, two societies. Rural-urban inequality in contemporary China*. Cambridge, MA: Harvard University Press. This collection of articles by economists, sociologists, and historians offers critical analyses with supporting data on the widening gap between rural and urban communities in China. Rural migration to cities, schooling, and health care, as well as past and present policies are discussed. This book provides a socioeconomic context from which to understand the condition of families and gender roles in China.

Suggested Weblinks

The **Aboriginal Canada Portal** offers a variety of Canadian online resources, information, and research.

www.aboriginalcanada.gc.ca

Assembly of First Nations

www.afn.ca

Health Canada dedicates a section of its site to immigrant and refugee health. Lists of research publications are given on various topics including family violence, immigrant women, and isolation of older immigrants.

www.hc-sc.gc.ca/hl-vs/jfy/spv/immigrants-eng.php

Canadian Heritage is responsible for national policies and programs that promote Canadian content, foster cultural participation, and strengthen connections among Canadians. Their website includes a variety of

links on diversity and multiculturalism, including recent articles that have appeared in the media.

www.pch.gc.ca/index_e.cfm

and **www.culture-canada.ca**

Citizenship and Immigration Canada's website offers practical information and advice as well as news, research, and policy papers.

www.cic.gc.ca

Aboriginal Healing Foundation includes news, policy suggestions, and research.

www.ahf.ca

Aboriginal Nurses Association of Canada is a practical website with information as well as research.

www.anac.on.ca

CHAPTER 3

Contemporary Issues in Family Life

"Right now I am not so sure that I want to have children because I am afraid that I couldn't handle everything that we have to do for children nowadays, I can't imagine having to do what my mother has done and is still doing with me and my brothers, taking us here and there, parents' nights at school, us always sneaking behind their [parents'] back and actually doing things that could be considered dangerous or could ruin our reputation or could get us into a lot of trouble for a very long time."

"What made me the happiest at that age [11 to 14] was all the sports and activities I was in. My parents were running like crazy trying to meet all of our sports and arts schedules but I had the greatest time. It was exciting, I was never home. (But now my parents admit that they were burdened and were glad when it was over.)"

"The hardest month of my life happened during the winter when I was 13 when I got ganged on by the guys in my hockey team after a game in the locker room because I had scored in our net. They hit me with sticks and one stomped on me with his skate.... I was cut, bruised and had some cracked bones and spent a painful month at home and that was the end of my hockey career. This episode was also painful for my entire family not excluding that my mother had to stay home from her work to put me back together!"

"I don't know how my parents can stand us because we are never home and when we are we are always in our rooms on the computer or watching television or doing video games and when they talk to us we grunt and just keep doing what we're doing. My parents really don't have a life as parents that they can brag to their friends about and I admit that I should feel guilty and I do at times but the whole bunch of us we're addicted to television and video games and it's so much more fun than parents.... [In 10 years] I guess I won't have much to show for myself... and my relationship with my parents will be gone and I will regret it but it will be too late because I will have grown into some kind of media freak." [This was written before the advent of Facebook and smartphones.]

As indicated in the previous chapter, the structure and dynamics of family life have evolved considerably over the centuries. But certain trends, which appear to be recent, were already in evidence in the 19th century and early in the 20th century. Before the anomalous years from 1945 to 1960 that followed the Second World War, fertility had long begun a slow decline in most societies of the western world.

Further, single-parent families had always existed because life expectancy was low: Children were often orphaned. Remarriage and stepparenting were common. Female labour had been widespread in previous centuries, although it generally took place within the household economy. Some of these trends, such as lower fertility and later age at marriage, were briefly reversed following the Second World War—and these few years are the "golden" yardstick by which we tend to compare current families to those of the past. Yet, this "good old past" was an anomaly in the long history of families.

As well, the years following the 1950s witnessed important changes in families. For instance, as the economy and technology evolved, so did the nature of people's employment—including that of women. Further, certain aspects of family structure have exhibited a dramatic transformation. Divorce, cohabitation, births to single mothers, and same-sex-parent families have all increased substantially and have transformed the profile of families. Even children's roles have changed and the cultural context within which families live has been altered by information technology.

Concepts such as "traditional," and "new" or "alternative" forms of families are labels that reflect our value system (Thornton, 2005). They are relatively meaningless because the traditional families of the 1950s were actually an alternative to what had just preceded that decade. Labelling prevents us from focusing on the multiple functions that all families fulfill. For instance, cohabiting-parent families are "alternatives"; yet, they fulfill "traditional" family functions. Similarly, same-sex-parent families are "new" forms; yet, they also fulfill traditional family functions. For example, they all raise their children, love them, and integrate them to the best of their ability within the society in which they live.

Thus, in this chapter, I begin by examining the misleading and much heralded loss of family functions. Then, we will examine three circumstances that shape how a growing minority of families function: transnational, military families, and couples living apart. This discussion will be followed by an examination of what European sociologists refer to as the defamilialization of children. I will then turn to the impact of certain aspects of the media on family life and child socialization.

HAS THE FAMILY LOST ITS FUNCTIONS?

There is no doubt that the family has lost some of its functions if we compare today's situation with that of the preindustrial period. As Hareven (1994a) puts it, in those days "the family not only reared children but also served as workshop, a school, a church, and a welfare agency. Preindustrial families meshed closely with the community and carried a variety of public responsibilities within the larger society." But many of the functions that the family has lost in western societies, such as training apprentices, were tied to a specific type of economic and technological tradition that vanished long ago. Thus, these familial functions are no longer necessary for the survival of society and for the integration of family members into society.

However, what is often overlooked—and is the focus of this section—is that the family as an institution has acquired other functions. It is also recapturing some "traditional" ones because the social safety net and social policies fail society's most vulnerable members, particularly children, the elderly, and the mentally, emotionally, as well as physically challenged (Luxton, 1997). Above all, the family as an institution has become more specialized in certain domains, a phenomenon already noted in 1926 by E. W. Burgess (Bengtson, 2001). These situations are well illustrated in the quotes opening this chapter.

Functions That Have Remained with the Family

1. It is often said that the family has lost its **reproductive function** because, until recently, births generally took place within wedlock. However, wedlock is a marital status rather than a family. As we have seen in Chapter 1, a married couple is not a family until the two spouses have their first child. Similarly, a woman's nonmarital sexual reproduction serves as the foundation to a family form: the mother-headed nuclear family. Understandably, the single-mother form of nuclear family is at times more fragile and at a greater risk of being unable to fulfill its functions as adequately as those headed by two married parents (Chapter 8). Therefore, while it is true that a large proportion of children are born to single parents and to cohabiting couples, this does not change anything in terms of families' reproductive function.

   The family will lose its reproductive function only when children are conceived, then cut away from their parents, and raised separately in special institutions. Actually, were such a point to be reached, the family as we understand it would disappear because it would lose its intergenerational dimension and all the other functions that flow from it.

2. The **socialization** or sociocultural reproduction of children still begins within the family. While other institutions soon complement parents or even take over their role, particularly child care centres and schools, parents are still children's most important agents of socialization until mid-adolescence. Even with adolescents, parents often are able to counterbalance negative peer and media influences when they exist. As is the case in all societies, our families prepare children for the economic system in which they are embedded, albeit, as we see in Chapters 4 and 6, with different levels of success.

3. The **economic** function of the family is still salient. True, the family no longer is the prime unit of production that it used to be. But all the unpaid *work* that takes place at home, mainly by women (housework, child care, elder care), constitutes economic activities—but just not the ones that a male world values. As well, families contribute to the formation of future workers and taxpayers. Thus, families affect a society's level of productivity (Bogenschneider and Corbett, 2010). Feminists have consistently pointed this out (Gazso, 2010). In addition, many persons now do paid work from home. Therefore, it is false to think that the family, as a unit at home, no longer fulfills an economic function: It fulfills many. The family has also remained the key unit of consumption.

4. The family continues to meet its members' needs for physical security as it did in the past. Families still provide **shelter**, attend to basic nutritional needs, and

ensure physical **health** according to their means. With the drastic cuts in the health care system, families are called upon to expand their functions in these domains (FSAT, 2004).

5. The family confers to its members their place within the social stratification system, at least until children are on their own. This is referred to as the **status function**. That is, young members of a family belong to their parents' socioeconomic group—or to their grandparents'. Thus, the reproduction of the class system begins within the family, although Canada experiences a great deal of downward and upward social mobility of adult children compared with their own parents (Corak, 1998). Further, the family contributes to the reproduction of the **religious and ethnic status** of a group, through socialization practices and the structure of opportunities available to its members in a racialized society.

6. The family still serves as an agency of psychological stabilization and provides a sense of identity and **belongingness**, particularly for its children. For instance, a French study found that 86 percent of adults mention their family when asked what defines them (Housseaux, 2003). It follows that the family fulfills many **affective functions**. It is within its boundaries that the young child learns to love and be loved, where attachment first develops, where trust is built. The family is one of the prime movers in **personality development** for children and adults alike. However, the family shares this function with a person's genetic background and with other social systems such as schools, work, as well as the peer group. When adults become parents, their personality development continues as they extend themselves into this new role.

New Functions Imposed upon Families

Not only has the family retained some of the functions it has fulfilled throughout centuries past, but it also has acquired many new ones, most of which are actually performed in great part by *mothers*.

1. Parents have become the coordinators of the education and the services that their children receive from various institutions (Coontz, 2000). Thus, the family has acquired the function of **coordination** or **management**: Parents must make the extra-familial environment (whether schools, child care, or the media) accessible to and safe for their children. They must also interpret these contexts to their children within the perspective of their values. Further, the various institutions and services available to children, especially schools, make great demands on parents' time, and even more so on mothers. The latter, for instance, have to monitor and help in their children's intellectual development, and this includes homework (Mandell and Sweet, 2004). In turn, because of a longer life span, when elderly parents become frail, children must manage the care they receive.

2. The family has now been charged with the responsibility of policing what its children and youth access on television, the Internet, their cellphone, and what they want to buy (Moscovitch, 2007). Thus, parents have to filter out noxious influences, whether in terms of consumerism, individualism, violence, or

exploitative sexual content, which the media unleash upon everyone (Ybarra et al., 2009). This in itself is a very onerous function for which most adults are ill prepared and receive little social support. While in the past parents had to be vigilant concerning the potentially negative influence of the printed media, contemporary parents have to be vigilant on all fronts of a vastly expanding web of audiovisual media, in addition to the remaining printed media. Thus, the role of **agency of social control** that the family has always fulfilled has vastly expanded in terms of the cultural territory covered.

3. By the same token, the family prevents the fragmentation of its young members' lives that would unavoidably occur in view of the numerous and often conflicting sources of socialization to which children are subjected. As Hays (1996:175) puts it, "the more the larger world becomes impersonal, competitive, and individualistic and the more the logic of that world invades the world of intimate relationships, the more intensive child rearing becomes." The family serves as an **agency of integration** at the personal and social levels. This family function is particularly important in view of the *surfeit of choices* and alternatives that the consumer market economy and an urbanized society present (Bumpass, 2001). The family serves as a *lone* anchor because, in the past, this function was generally fulfilled with the help of the parish, village, or neighbours.

Additional Responsibilities Taken on by Some Families

1. A significant number of families provide the entire special care needed by their intellectually, emotionally, or physically challenged children and, in some cases, frail elderly parents. The family is again becoming a **welfare agency**, as was the case in the "old" days. However, currently, the family is rather isolated in this role while, in the past, it might have received more help from the community. Further, in the past, the frail elderly had a more restricted life span, and most physically challenged children did not survive because medicine was too rudimentary to support them. Contemporary advances in nutrition, sanitary conditions, and medicine have increased the longevity and survival rates of the weakest. As a result, families have been forced to be the main caretakers or supervisors of the help that these relatives in precarious health receive—and women do a great proportion of this work (Mitchell, 2004).

2. Many families fulfill additional functions for their members, depending on their means, social class, racial/ethnic membership, religion, as well as citizenship status. For instance, some families remain a centre of worship and religious education while others provide at-home schooling. Still others continue to serve as a centre of leisure activities, both for their children and adult members. Amish families are a good example in this respect (Hostetler, 1993); until very recently, extended families also fulfilled this function in Newfoundland and in Inuit rural communities. Furthermore, many of the functions performed at the nuclear level (father and/or mother) are being transferred to the extended family, especially to grandparents. One can think here of the increase in the number of

grandparents who are completely in charge of raising grandchildren. This situation occurs as a result of problems at the nuclear family level, as well as when both parents are in the military and have to participate in war or peacekeeping duties abroad.

3. Many families, particularly those on farms and owners of small enterprises, still form a unit of production: They train, employ, and pay their members.

4. Finally, immigrant families serve important functions for their members, as many subsidize the immigration of their kin and support their resettlement to Canada. Others send remittances to their relatives in their home country and contribute not only to the sustenance but also to the economic survival of entire societies. Cases in point are the Philippines, Vietnam, Cuba, and Romania.

An Overabundance of Family Functions

In short, while Canadian families in general are not always a haven and many are far from perfect, the functions that they fulfill cover an amazing range of personal, social, cultural, and economic needs. And families do so, particularly mothers, with far fewer moral and social resources than was the case in the past, when communities were more cohesive and there was greater value consensus. As imperfect and, at times, limping as it is, *the family still does more and better than any other social institution for its members,* particularly its children and youth (Bogenschneider and Corbett, 2010). Thus, the fact is not that families have become obsolete or irrelevant. The contrary has actually happened: Families have become burdened with new functions foisted upon them by technology, consumerism, and urbanization (Castaneda, 2002). Hence, one can only be concerned about families' burden rather than obsolescence when discussing functions.

As we have seen, the concern over the "decline" in family functions stems from an inappropriate comparison of today's families with those of centuries past. It also stems from an idealization of the late 1940s and the 1950s when several unusual circumstances coalesced: early age at marriage; higher fertility; low divorce rates; relatively few births to single women, particularly single teens; fathers in the role of breadwinner; and stay-at-home mothers. As well, there is the ethnocentric factor in all these musings about the demise of family functions: Across the world, people emphasize familial obligations and mutual support far more than is the case here (Kağıtçıbaşi, 2007; Shweder et al., 2006). *Is it not possible that this dismissal of family functions simply provides a rationale for not better supporting individual families?* As Ravanera and McQuillan (2006:10) aptly put it, "All of society benefits when families work well. Thus, it is in our collective interest to find ways to support families in achieving their goals."

Society's Failures Become Families' Burdens

Another source of concern over this alleged decline in family functions is probably the result of an analytical and social policy misunderstanding: It results from equating *individual* families' inability or failure to fulfill certain functions with a loss of functions by the family as an **institution**. People correctly observe that more children are problematic, unhappy, and in foster care than was the case 50 years ago. But the error begins when this is seen as a failure of *the* family as an institution rather than of individual families—or of society as a whole.

The new social structure based on the market economy, information technology, and the retrenchment of social policies has bestowed upon the family a new set of responsibilities or functions (Wall, 2004). It is therefore not surprising if more individual families fail at these than in the past: Families are more unstable structurally, are more isolated socially, and are less well supported by other institutions at the cultural, economic, and political levels. Thus, too great a proportion of our families are ill equipped to fulfill their functions, particularly in terms of supervising, guiding, and educating their youth and caring for their elders. Economic deprivation, segregation, social stigmatization and isolation, singlehood, and members' personal deficiencies are among the elements that prevent individual families from fulfilling their functions adequately. Most of these are socially driven problems, not family-produced ones (Connidis, 2010).

For instance, at the macrosociological level of analysis, there is a **lack of social and political support** that would provide more resources to families and their special-needs members. A second source, also systemic, sees countless families forgotten by society and relegated to segregated enclaves where they are visible only when their members commit crimes. A third cause resides in the absence of an effective community surrounding families. The structural conclusion one arrives at is that the family as an institution certainly requires far more assistance from other institutions to fulfill its numerous functions adequately. Were this assistance forthcoming at the institutional family level, most individual families would benefit and fewer would fail in this respect.

By the last decades of the 20th century, and the first decade of the 21st century, **unplanned change** may well be occurring too rapidly for the good of families as an institution. As a result, families have suddenly inherited a pileup of new functions and responsibilities. Unfortunately, this pileup took place at the same time as drastic changes were occurring in family structure. These changes have actually reduced the number of adults or parents available to children, thus diminishing many families' ability to fulfill their functions adequately, particularly in terms of child socialization.

A concurrent problem resides in governments having failed to plan or even keep up with change. Political institutions have failed to create social policies favourable to families of all types, as well as policies protecting families and their members, particularly children, against the potentially harmful impacts of technology. We could think here in terms of the structure of the workweek and the workplace, the relative lack of child care centres, and the noxious contents of the media. But we can also think in terms of failure to more adequately assist near-poor and poor families and, soon, we will be mentioning policy failures to protect the natural environment in which families live (Gore, 2006; Suzuki and Taylor, 2009).

Are Family Values Necessarily under Attack?

As sociologists, we have to consider two other cultural as well as political realities concerning family change. First, in an individualistic, democratic society, everyone is entitled to his or her religious and moral beliefs about family life. Except for abusing one's children or one's partner, an individualistic democracy such as Canada ensures individuals' right to live their lives and their relationships according to their personal beliefs. But this democratic right also presumes an obligation: the tolerance of the different ways and values of other families.

This leads us to the second reality: the diversity of family life in the postmodern era. Not only are there more divorces than in 1950 (but fewer than in the mid-1980s), and more children living in one-parent families, but same-sex couples are now raising and reproducing children. A new wave of immigration has also contributed to further diversify the familial landscape. Nevertheless, these culturally and structurally diverse families not only fulfill similar functions but share some common concerns, such as the desire to see their children do well, and for many, the hope that they will have a better life than their parents—all cherished Canadian values. While family structures are fluid, family functions remain.

Therefore, if family values are under attack, it is from the roadblocks created by the materialistic forces of society that prevent families from fulfilling their functions. What is certainly a concern is that, under individualistic pressures and attacks from various professional interests, many parents themselves have lost their moral authority. Hence, family diversity in itself should not be analyzed within a concern over the loss of traditional family values or the "decline of the family." Rather, perhaps we should be concerned over the loss of traditional forms of **support** for the family—whether structural, cultural, or environmental—and over the modern burdens placed upon families.

Family life viability and family values are far more endangered by other cultural and economic forces than they are by changes in the structure of the family. As we see in a subsequent section and in Chapter 4 on economic context, one can think here of certain television content promoting infidelity and "sex as leisure"; or of the distorting effect that widely accessible pornography may have on real-life couple relationships (Paul, 2004); and of consumerism, which often controls family time and individual family members' values. Another set of forces that is affecting families negatively and may bring more burdens are environmental ones such as disappearing farmlands, threatened water sources, pollution, and climate change.

CHILDREN ARE DEFAMILIALIZED AND SEGREGATED

Another two-fold contemporary development in family life pertains to children: Children's lives have become more defamilialized and segregated. The concept of **defamilialization** was introduced by European sociologists and refers to children being increasingly taken care of by non-family members who earn their living doing so. Children spend less and less time at home interacting with their parents and enter care or educational institutions at an earlier age than was the case before the 1980s. This change began with industrialization, when the family lost its key economic function of the production of goods (clothes, shoes, metalwork), which was one of its foundations of solidarity and of child integration (Martin, 1997). Compared with the 19th century, for instance, when children helped in family productivity, today, urban youth, especially from educated families, now rarely work with their families or other families—unless they belong to a farming household or their parents own a

Children's "free time" is now more structured and age-segregated than was the case 50 years ago. This results from a combination of circumstances, including both parents' employment outside the home, concerns for children's safety, and a construction of children as "projects" to be perfected for the future.

small store (Bradbury, 2000; Bullen, 2000; Tudge, 2008).

By the same token, children are an important source of economic activities in postindustrial societies because they create work; that is, service work carried out by adults as they care for and educate children as well as organize and control their activities. These workers include teachers, child-care personnel, social workers, clinicians, and various other child specialists. Thus, childhood as a structural category creates employment opportunities for adulthood outside the familial realm. As British sociologist David Oldman (1994) puts it, it is one of the paradoxes of the current economic situation "that parents need non-familial supervision of their own children so they can be paid for providing that non-familial supervision for other children." For instance, parents hire babysitters so that they can become teachers to other adults' children.

Danish sociologist Jens Qvortrup (1995) defines children as useful members of the economy, not only because they create work but because children themselves do work: Their labour consists of **schoolwork**. Children participate in the societal division of labour by obtaining an education. In preindustrial societies, children were useful because, like most adults, they engaged in manual labour. But today they are useful by attending school, preparing themselves for their future as voting citizens, adult workers, parents, and taxpayers. As well, by remaining in school longer, children prevent the large-scale unemployment that would inevitably occur were they to enter the labour market prematurely and compete with adults (Côté and Allahar, 1994).

In contrast, children living in the small villages and rural areas of Africa and many Asian countries are fully integrated in the life of the community and in their parents' world, including work that is basically familial. Children learn their adult roles by imitating their parents as they help them. They are totally familialized, even though they may attend the village school. Moreover, these children play in mixed-age groups, the 6-year-olds or 10-year-olds watching over the babies collectively (Hewlett and Lamb, 2005).

This leads us to the second sociological development regarding children's place in society: They are more **age segregated** and, at the middle-class level, their lives have become more structured. That is, children's lives are more **organized**, regimented, less spontaneous and free ranging than in the past (Perry and Doherty, 2005). Institutions such as daycare centres, kindergartens, schools, organized extracurricular activities, day and overnight camps, and so on contribute to child socialization, leisure, and experience (Lareau, 2003). Children are segregated in supervisory settings (Coakley and Donnelly, 2004). Therefore, children's time is rationalized and institutionalized in order to increase their safety and prepare them for the growing rationalization of postmodern life (Boekhoven, 2009). Not only do these institutions regiment children's lives into organized time segments, but as children spend less time within the folds of the family and are increasingly "serviced" by other adults and institutions, they are further defamilialized and families become underconnected, especially across the generations (Uhlenberg, 2009). Within this analytical framework, educational institutions are **institutions of exclusion**, even exclusion of children from their parents' world, largely to suit the needs of the economy (Côté and Allahar, 2006; Schlegel, 2003).

Thus, in western societies, not only are children segregated into age groups, they are also especially segregated from many of the activities carried out by their parents. As Coontz (2000:290) points out, while youth today are more excluded from productive roles, they are paradoxically much more fully involved in **consumer roles**. This age segregation is promoted by consumerism and is often self-chosen and reinforced by the peer culture that has evolved along age lines. As illustrated in an opening quote, even when they are at home, children may watch different television programs or surf the web and send text messages in their rooms and may be served dinner separately by their mothers. Hence, children themselves contribute to their defamilialization, which, in North America, is often referred to as the process of **individuation**. This psychological term refers to children's gaining a sense of identity separately from their connection to their parents. Individuation is largely absent as a notion in many more-collectivist societies of the world and even in many Aboriginal groups in Canada that are more oriented toward their families (Arnett, 2008).

FAMILIES AND COUPLES LIVING APART

Another very contemporary situation returns us to a topic initially raised in Chapter 1 when presenting various family types. Thus, in this section, we will focus on transnational families, military families, and couples living apart.

Transnational Families

Globalization has had a tremendous impact on migration and family structures. With more international trade and exchange, international boundaries have become blurred. Many men and women now cross nation-state boundaries to live and work as easily as they once travelled to different cities in the same country. As a result, transnational families have become more commonplace in recent times. These are "families that live some or most of the time separated from each other, yet hold together and create something that can be seen as a feeling of collective welfare and unity, namely 'familyhood,' even across national borders" (Bryceson and Vuorela, 2002:3).

But as Beaujot and Kerr (2004:98) point out, "There are winners and losers in globalization, and the glaring disparities in standards of living around the world are themselves a leading cause of migration." Consequently, the experiences of transnational families vary by ethnicity, gender, country of origin, and occupational class. For instance, "guest workers" on a two-year visa to work for an industry or a farm, who may number over 200,000 in Canada currently, certainly experience a transnational family life that does not compare with that of an educated executive on leave to Dubai or Hong Kong. These low-skilled and low-paid workers often become "illegals" after losing their job. Then, as illegal workers, they are further exploited (Contenta and Monsebraaten, 2009).

As part of a project on immigrant families, Waters (2002) was particularly interested in the experiences of Taiwanese and Hong Kong "astronaut" wives, immigrant women whose husbands, within a few months after their arrival, had returned to their country of origin to work. For the most part, Chinese and Taiwanese astronaut families in Vancouver—and also in Toronto—are of higher social class. According to Waters (2002:118), such families exemplify "the ways in which social relationships can operate over significant distance, spanning national borders, and reducing the importance of face-to-face context in personal interaction." Thus, current trends in transnational families find children increasingly separated from one of their parents. Traditionally, the father is away and the mother raises the children alone.

However, a global market economy has also resulted in an increase in female-headed transnational families where the mother works in a country different from where some or all of her children reside. Indeed, developed countries continue to demand low-wage female domestics and caretakers from less fortunate countries. This trend in transnational mothering has disrupted the notion of family in one place. But often overlooked are the detrimental effects of mothering one's children from a distance, a situation often forced on migrant **domestic workers** with children. In the absence of their mothers, children of transnational women are generally raised by their grandmothers. When these children are reunited with their mothers, they often resent her authority, not wanting to obey a mother they have never met or have rarely seen. A student who was reunited with her transnational mother explains:

> *"What was the hardest at that age* [10–14] *was leaving my grandmother behind in Jamaica. I had been so excited about living with my mother. . . . I had seen her only three times since she left when I was 4. . . . She really was like a stranger and she was so busy. . . . I thought she had money but we had to live in a poor place, real tough kids that I can see now were bad but for me they were exciting because life with my mother and her boyfriend was no fun. I paid no heed to her and him and I skipped school. . . . I missed my grandmother and I wanted her here but she had to help with my other cousins over there."*

Military Families

Military nuclear families often become transnational, albeit temporarily. All army personnel are members of families, whether their parents' families with whom they may still have been living when they were recruited or their spouses and children. The Canadian Forces (CF) are involved in many peacekeeping operations throughout the world and some of these missions take place within war zones. It is when army personnel are mobilized abroad, especially in war zones, such as Afghanistan at the time that this text was written in 2010, that the impact on their families is the greatest. Currently, being a soldier posted in Afghanistan is a high-risk occupation, mainly because of improvised explosive devices that maim and kill so many soldiers and civilians. Therefore, the soldiers are affected in a dire way. In addition, many return home suffering from post-traumatic stress disorder, serious injuries, and amputations.

For their part, families are affected because they are separated from their loved one, are worried, and their daily routines are changed. Even very young children develop fears of what could happen to the parent who is deployed abroad and this type of parental absence is related to anxiety and even behavioural problems (Booth et al., 2007; Dekel and Goldblatt, 2008). Adolescents report signs of depression, stress, and "short fuse" in their at-home parent while the other is deployed. When the parent returns, adjustment difficulties include reintegrating the parent into the daily routine and helping with his or her difficulties in recognizing the changes that have occurred in the children during the parent's absence (Huebner and Mancini, 2005). It is assumed that repeated separations are more disruptive of family life (Orthner and Rose, 2009).

How do these families function? What coping mechanisms do they use? What are their main sources of support? In Canada, research is only beginning with a new project headed by Deborah Harrison, which is being carried out at several universities. For their part, American academics have begun publishing research reports. The armed forces themselves, whether Canadian or American, are also conducting some basic research. Both forces recognize the importance of their personnel's families and their websites offer Support Resources for them. The Canadian Forces (2008) have found that "spouses play a vital role in promoting the well-being, readiness and performance of military members and their ability to carry out missions." Given this, "it is crucial to understand how families maintain or enhance resiliency during and after military deployments and separation." However, rates of divorce, particularly among women soldiers, have recently increased in the U.S. military (Teachman and Tedrow, 2008).

The CF are trying to keep track of stressors involved and factors that could mitigate or exacerbate these outcomes. For its part, the U.S. military has found that remarried parents with children from a previous union encounter more family problems in part because the children may have a wider range of adaptations to make than other children. Yet, these same families were the most likely to be satisfied with military resources and support and willing to re-enlist (Adler-Baeder et al., 2005). They were also happier in the military than couples in their first marriages: A more mature outlook to couple life is discussed as the main reason for this finding. Through these internal studies, military officials have concluded that more resources in mental health and better access to medical care were key areas that needed attention.

The military profession carries another negative economic impact on families: Salaries are low for recruits and often the spouse left behind has difficulty finding employment, so that army families are often disadvantaged economically compared with others. The average recruit is generally a young person, often out of high school, and consequently with no savings or resources, and may have a young spouse and small children. Because of their young age, these families are doubly disadvantaged at the economic level (Uecker and Stokes, 2008). Army couples often have children at a younger age than persons in other occupational categories (Lundquist and Smith, 2005). Younger persons may have more difficulties adapting than older persons with more life experience (Adler-Baeder et al., 2005). This is why accessibility to quality child care is so important (MacDermid et al., 2004).

A topic that is salient on the CF website is family violence, particularly spousal abuse, because it is an issue against which the army has taken a strong official stand with its Family Violence Action Plan (Herrington, 2009). It is pointed out, in these analyses, that certain aspects of military life make it more difficult to cope with spousal violence than is the case in the population at large. These difficulties include "victims' economic dependency on their CF spouses, frequent postings, an unfamiliar and closed environment [on army bases], peculiarities of Married Quarters neighbourhoods, and, in some cases, language disadvantages" (Herrington, 2009). But the best predictor of spousal abuse in the army is a history of such before entering the military. However, rates of spousal abuse have diminished in the military as has been the case in the remainder of the population. For its part, child abuse in the military is more likely to occur with younger than older parents (Booth et al., 2007). It may also be more frequent during periods of transition in times of deployment (Huebner et al., 2009).

Couples Living Apart

Couples who live apart together (LAT) maintain separate households, may or may not be married (Borrell and Karlsson, 2002), and some may be simply "dating." In 2001, 8 percent of Canadian adults lived in LAT unions (Milan and Peters, 2003). Although most (56 percent) occurred among the 20- to 29-year-old age group, another 11 percent were found among those older than 50. For the older and widowed, this arrangement protects their children's inheritance. Others are professionals whose careers cannot be accommodated within the same geographical area. LATs are also becoming more common in some Asian countries, particularly Japan where 70 percent of women involved in these unions are still living with their parents (Jones, 2007).

According to Villeneuve-Gokalp (1997), nearly two-thirds of LAT couples lead this lifestyle because of family duties or work requirements, while the other third mention the need to retain their independence. Levin and Trost (1999) found that nearly half of these persons expected eventually to live with their partner, but only a minority of those older than 50 held such expectations (Bawin-Legrow and Gauthier, 2001). The latter may prefer to retain their own residence and ways of living.

Persons who choose this lifestyle hold less traditional ideas concerning the importance of having long-term relationships than either married or cohabiting persons (Milan and Peters, 2003). Unfortunately, the studies do not tell us what proportion, even though small, of such couples are actually married to each other, and even living in separate cities, countries, or continents—closely resembling what has often been referred to as "commuter marriages." When young couples have to be separated for work reasons, they may choose to cohabit rather than marry, at least for the duration of the separation period (Binstock and Thornton, 2003).

This phenomenon of extra-residential unions is widely found in the Caribbean region as an adaptive response to the socioeconomic conditions that require women to head households with very little or no economic support from their co-progenitors (Barrow, 1996). In Canada, LATs are found across all income levels but especially more so among those who earn less than average.

THE AUDIOVISUAL MEDIA AND FAMILY LIFE

Perhaps one of the most salient historical developments for society, its families, and their children has occurred relatively recently. It resides in the introduction of the audiovisual media, particularly television, video games, the Internet, and now smart cellular phones to the cultural landscape. Major events are now experienced and socially constructed through the prism of these media, whether it is the news, sports, talk shows, "reality" shows, sitcoms, social networking, or "tweets."

The Restructuring of Family Life

In 1951, there were 90,000 television sets in Canadian homes, all receiving American programming. Three months after the advent of the CBC in 1952, this number grew to 224,000 sets (Gorman, 1997). Television represented a mode of "family entertainment" that was to prove radically different from anything in the past. It had no historical precedent in terms of its ability to inform, influence, and structure daily life. Between 1951 and 1955, nearly two-thirds of the nation's homes acquired a television set. By 1960, almost 90 percent had at least one set and, at that point, the average person watched television about five hours a day. By the 1960s, television had replaced the piano in family rooms and "TV dinners" (the precursor to prepared food) appeared in grocery stores.

Television changed family leisure patterns: As people watched it, less time became available for reading and the development of skills, such as musical abilities, creative play, and for family entertainment that might involve all the members (whether dancing, singing, playing card games, or just visiting). Television changed family leisure patterns. Early studies summarized by Andreasen (1994) indicate that, by 1952 in large cities, a great proportion of families reported regularly eating with the television on, which meant less interpersonal exchange during dinner. Families with a television set went to bed later, talked less, and often ate separately while watching different programs at different times—trends that are even more pronounced now (Moscovitch, 2007).

Today, children and particularly middle-class adolescents have their own personal entertainment centres in their **bedrooms,** where they choose what they want to watch or which video game to play (Livingstone and Bovill, 2001). In the U.S., low-income children are even more likely than others to have this equipment in their bedrooms, except for the Internet, and they also read less. Overall, only a proportion of children report having **rules** set by parents about their use of what they see or do and time spent with media. For instance, Rideout et al. (2010) found that 64 percent of 8- to 10-year-olds had rules set by parents, but in only 38 percent of these cases did parents enforce them. Parents with a high level of education tend to restrict television

The black American politician, Jesse Jackson, has called television "the third parent." It would be interesting to know whether children build more connections among themselves within a family via videos and television programs they share or via social games and activities they engage in together.

more during mealtimes and to have more rules concerning viewing, especially for small children; their children also read more.

Family members who view television together find the experience more pleasant than when they watch it alone. Unfortunately, in a good proportion of families, television is on most of the time, even when no one is watching, and especially during **meals**. This limits familial conversations (Kirkorian et al., 2009). Further, many parents use videos specifically made and advertised to enhance infants' intellectual and verbal development when, in fact, they may actually retard it. There are suggestions that television and videos contribute to hyperactivity (Christakis, 2009).

Nearly all students today have grown up with television, video games, the Internet, and cellphones. Few know what family life is without these media. For most, the low level of time currently spent talking and sitting in the den or in the backyard just enjoying one another's company seems normal. As well, more and more youth access the media through their cellphones and laptop computers. When parents control media access, children spend less time with these media than their peers. This is important because children and youth who are heavy media users do less well in school, get along less well with their parents, "get into trouble" more, and are often sad and unhappy (Rideout et al., 2010).

The Family on Television: A Historical Overview of Contents

The first television show geared to children, *Howdy Doody*, ran from 1947 to 1960, and with it, the debate about the effect of television on children began and has continued to this day. The debate has not, however, been accompanied to the same extent by discussions over the impact of television on adults and on family life, although the research done for advertising and marketing firms indicates strong media effects on adults' beliefs, lifestyles, approach to medication, as well as on family life. *Howdy Doody* also marked the beginning of the impact of audiovisual **advertising** on children.

Sesame Street, which began in 1969, presented a revolutionary format, and is still widely watched by the nation's small children. This program emphasizes the acceptance of ethnic differences, as well as values of cooperation and environmentalism. It is devoid of commercialism, violence, and sex. Its goal is to provide skills to help prepare children for school, and research has shown that children from varied backgrounds do learn by watching it (Christakis, 2009). *Sesame Street* complements parents' role as educators and does not conflict with family values.

Situation comedies, or **sitcoms**, began with *I Love Lucy* in 1951. This was the first show with a woman as its superstar. Except for sports and newscasts, women are the prime TV audience, and the orientation of Lucille Ball's show around themes that concerned couples, and particularly wives, contributed to women's devotion to this medium. *Ozzie and Harriett* and, a little later, *Leave It to Beaver* became **family shows** par excellence. The latter ran from 1957 through 1963 and represented the ideal American family at the time: white, middle-class, with a working father, a stay-at-home mother, and two sons. The program was child-centred; that is, it offered a perspective on family life from a child's point of view. Not only did *Leave It to Beaver* become a cultural icon in later decades when American and Canadian families had changed from the idealized type of the 1950s, but it also set the stage for the nostalgia of what Stephanie Coontz called *The Way We Never Were* (1992).

Another family-related show that has remained popular, mainly through reruns, is *The Brady Bunch* (1969–1974). Its cast consisted of a widow with three girls who marries a widower with three boys. Like *Leave It to Beaver*, the young actors provided a child's view of the world and child-sized problems. Any child between 6 and 12 years of age could identify with a same-age character, as there were offspring of various ages in this television family. This reconstituted family anticipated the coming wave of real-life stepparenting situations created by rising divorce rates, which may explain why reruns of *The Brady Bunch* have remained popular.

Soap operas had long been a staple of radio programming in Quebec. Therefore, it is not surprising that television adopted this genre early on in the 1950s in Quebec, with programs focusing on family relationships in small communities, as in the very popular turn-of-the-century *Les Belles Histoires des Pays d'En Haut*. In the U.S. in the 1960s, programs such as *As the World Turns* and *Peyton Place* centred more on couples. These melodramas generally ran during the afternoons, which meant that they largely targeted a feminine audience. They included a mixture of largely segregated gender roles and family life on the one hand, with powerful examples of sexually liberated women on the other hand. Other soap operas soon followed: *All My Children, The Young and the Restless, The Bold and the Beautiful, Dallas, General Hospital,* and, more recently, *Desperate Housewives*, to mention only a few.

The plots of the soap or melodrama genre generally revolve around couples or families. The children who are born soon disappear to resurface only when they are old enough to be wrapped up in romantic dramas or scandals of their own. These shows contain many weddings, love triangles, breakups, and more adopted as well as lost or kidnapped children than exist in reality. Soaps focus on feelings, melodrama, and talk. Overall, they present a sharp contrast with the daily routine of real-life families and, as such, provide women with an escape from domestic reality.

In the 1970s, *The Mary Tyler Moore Show* represented a turning point in sitcoms—it focused on single adults, particularly in the workplace. The main character was a woman. The U.S. Commission on Civil Rights (1977) found that, in the period between 1969 and 1972, almost one-half of the female characters portrayed on television were married, yet fewer than one-third of the males were. At about the same time, McNeil (1975) revealed that 74 percent of the female interactions on television took place within the context of problems associated with romance and family, compared with only 18 percent of male interactions. Thus, *The Mary Tyler Moore Show* was overcoming many **gender stereotypes**. For the first time, employment was depicted as a salient aspect in the life of a woman—albeit a single woman, not a married one with children—just as more and more women were entering the labour force. This show paved the way for *Murphy Brown* (and nonmarital parenthood on TV) and *Ally McBeal*, both profiling single, professional women.

The Cosby Show, running from 1984 to 1992, represented yet another milestone, as it introduced a black family headed by two professional parents. The family came closer to approximating a two-paycheque family than any other show had done. In the mid-1980s, it was still quite unusual to think of a black family as well-to-do. It was probably the first sitcom with which black families could identify, at least in terms of race if not necessarily lifestyle. Then, the *Fresh Prince of Bel Air* followed a similar format, but within an even more affluent and yet more "hip" context.

The last sitcom to be mentioned here is *Roseanne*, which began in 1988: The show introduced a blue-collar family with a hard-working mother, three kids, and loud-mouthed parents, and dealt with issues such as teen sex, among others. Parents and children alike could be unpleasant creatures! Roseanne also departed from the usual tendency of representing the feminine body in terms of slimness. All these factors combined to reflect changes in the depiction of family life. In the 1990s and early 2000s, many shows simply dispensed with family life or focused on emotional"families" or sets of couples. One can think of *Friends, South Park,* or *Party of Five* (Kanner, 2001). Other more recent sitcoms, such as *Grey's Anatomy* and *Little Mosque on the Prairie*, have become more inclusive in terms of ethnic and cultural diversity, and even environments in the latter case.

Then, problematic aspects of family life started to be reflected in the many **talk shows** that began appearing in the mid- to late-1980s, such as *Donahue, The Oprah Winfrey Show, Jenny Jones, Geraldo,* and so on—not to omit more recent arrivals such as the *Maury Show* and later *Dr. Phil*. Many of these programs place the spotlight on the self-disclosure of problems and even deviances, from weight problems to sexual infidelity, attempted suicide, drug addiction, and incest.

The Continued Effects of the Audiovisual Media: The Internet and Cellular Phone

A contemporary and much debated issue is the role that the media play in the development of children's attitudes and behaviours (Garbarino, 2006). Some contend that the media have no effect. However, it is illogical to deny that violent or sex-suffused media have no effect, while at the same time accepting the fact that the tobacco industry's ads foster smoking among adolescents. Further, why would companies invest so many billions in advertising if it had no effect? Observing how children and even some adults dress in imitation of their favourite stars provides a clear indication that the media **create needs** and a reality, while reinforcing stereotypes of ideal feminine body types and of a tough masculinity (Abu-Laban and McDaniel, 2004; Malszecki and Cavar, 2004). As well, there are fears in some quarters that accepting research results pointing to the media in the causality chain of children's problematic behaviours might lead to censorship. Lawyers for the media industry are particularly active in promoting this fear. This is a **political issue:** The media constitute a very powerful and increasingly interconnected industry and lobby. For instance, many news magazines and newspapers are owned by mega corporations that include television stations, cable networks, film and music companies. Thus, the media can easily prevent the wide dissemination of research results that could be damaging to their image—and to their bottom line.

It can also be argued that the media **distort reality** itself. For instance, over 50 percent of the crimes shown on television are murders, while murders represent only 0.2 percent of the crimes reported by the FBI (Bushman and Huesmann, 2001). As well, between 1950 and 1995, families with children headed by two parents have been underrepresented in television stories in every decade, while those with a single father have been overrepresented (Robinson and Skill, 2001).

In the following sections, we focus on the role that the audiovisual media may play in various aspects of family life and in child development. However, one question that we cannot address is: What growing-up experiences do children *not* get when they spend so much time watching TV, playing video games, surfing the net, and texting on their cellphone? We can also be concerned about the consequences for young adults and particularly adolescents of presenting themselves and their lives to a larger than normal circle of family and friends via Facebook. Many parents now even create Facebook pages for their school-age children or, yet, the children do it themselves. In terms of symbolic interactionism, children and adolescents now put their own lives on a **stage** and manipulate their self-presentations to fit a circle of what are consumers of their own lives. Every adolescent can now be on a stage. What does this do to children's development to have their fabricated selves on stage and how, at such a young age, can they differentiate between their real selves, as they evolve, and these reflections of themselves? Research has yet to catch up on the effects of such cultural developments.

The Issue of Sociability in Family Life

Apart from the fact that the media such as television, the Internet, and video games cut down the time that a young person spends on *face-to-face* sociability, both in and out of the family, there is surprisingly little research devoted to how these media can foster sociability and human relations within the family. For instance, the new "reality" shows, whether *Dancing with the Stars* or *Canadian Idol*, are all competitive and little cooperation is required of contestants. Many, including *Survivor*, are based on voting people out, exclusion, and **competition**. Values of altruism are out of the question and a great deal of **bullying** takes place at a time when this problem in schools is exacerbated by the public aspects of Facebook and cellphones.

What does the Internet do in terms of family life? Since the 2000s, many families take advantage of email and Facebook and now Skype and texting to keep in touch with their children in college and other relatives, and teenagers exchange messages with their classmates after school. As well, some parents use the Internet in order to find information about various aspects of family life, including parenting (Keown, 2009). These media can also break senior citizens' social isolation when they are place-bound (Clark, 2001).

However, large-scale Canadian data analyzed by Williams (2001a) clearly indicate that a good minority of people cut down on visiting or talking with family (14 percent) and friends (13 percent) because of the time they spend on the Internet. Heavy Internet users are even more likely to reduce time interacting with family—and, perhaps, so do heavy cellphone users? After comparing the results of the 1998 and the 2000 General Social Surveys, Williams concluded that Internet users spend about 48 fewer minutes per day in social contact with others in their households, but spend about 72 minutes more in contact with people outside their households. This would probably be even more so now since the advent of Facebook, which can be very time consuming.

Internet use is even more **individualistically oriented** than television viewing. It follows that extensive Internet exposure by family members, often in their own separate bedrooms/studies, may contribute to lack of interaction and a loss of communication skills. In fact, parents and children's cyber worlds diverge widely (Taylor, 2002). For instance, while a majority of parents say that they talk to their children about the children's Internet activities, only 24 percent of children report the same. Furthermore, 83 percent are alone when they go online (Taylor, 2002).

The next few years will indicate the direction that the Internet and cellphones are taking culturally and the type of use family members will make of these. But, as Williams (2001b) points out, when we include all the modes of electronic communication in the possession of all family members and the incessant recourse to them many make (particularly cellphones), we may well be "too connected" in general—but, one might fear, less so with our family in terms of *face-to-face interaction*. How often do we observe mothers or fathers pushing a baby in a stroller or walking with a small child while being entirely absorbed in a cellphone conversation? These parents miss out on the possibility of a quiet moment of interaction with their child. As well, how often can we observe entire peer groups of youths in subway cars or on the street, fresh out of school, all interacting with their cellphones, texting friends who are elsewhere while ignoring friends who are with them? Does this enhance or decrease the ability to verbally and emotionally connect with peers?

The Issue of Violence vs. Prosocial Behaviour

The average child has witnessed well over 8,000 murders on television by the end of elementary school. In the U.S., the National Television Violence Study (1998) found that over 40 percent of violent acts are perpetrated by "good" characters—thus glamorizing violence—and over 55 percent of victims of violence show little pain or suffering, thus desensitizing people to its true effects (Donnerstein and Linz, 1995). The rate of violent crimes in the U.S. and other western countries rose dramatically after 1965, coinciding with the coming of age of the first generation of children raised with television (Bushman and Huesmann, 2001).

FAMILY RESEARCH 3.1

Experimenting with Real-Life Situations to Determine Causality

In the fall of 1973, a study on the effect of television on children was initiated by creatively exploiting a naturally occurring social situation: At that time, a Canadian town, renamed Notel, was to receive television transmission for the first time. Notel was not isolated but was located in a valley, which prevented transmission. A nearby town, called Unitel, had already been receiving one Canadian channel for seven years, and a third town, called Multitel, had been receiving several U.S. channels in addition to a Canadian one for about 15 years. Notel (no television) became the experimental town; Unitel (one channel) and Multitel (several channels) became the two control towns.

In Phase 1, in 1973, students in Grades 4 and 7 from the three towns were tested on a wide range of behaviours and skills. In a longitudinal design, they were retested two years later (Phase 2), in Grades 6 and 9, to measure the effects of television. In order to rule out maturation or growing-up influences, additional students in Grades 4 and 7 were also included in Phase 2. The children in the town that had received television two years earlier showed a substantial increase in aggressiveness that was not observed among the youngsters in the other town (Joy et al., 1986). They also exhibited a sharp increase in sex-role stereotyping (Kimball, 1986).

In the 1980s, researchers began harvesting the results of **longitudinal studies** (see Family Research 3.1). They found that young adults tended to act more aggressively when they had watched more violence as eight-year-olds or as adolescents (Johnson et al., 2002). The link between adult aggressiveness and childhood viewing of violence on TV was even stronger than it had been at age eight. Boys who had not been aggressive at age eight but had watched more violence had become more aggressive young adults than a similar group of non-aggressive boys who had watched fewer episodes of violence (Bushman and Huesmann, 2006). Studies of more recent cohorts have shown that television violence now affects American girls' level of aggressiveness as well (Huesmann et al., 2003). Other studies continue to show that exposure to TV is an independent contributing risk for aggressive behaviours in children as young as three years old (Manganello and Taylor, 2009).

Even when it is a predilection for aggressiveness that leads children to select television violence, this violence then leads to aggressiveness (Manganello and Taylor, 2009). Although exposure to violent television and videos is not the main factor in the etiology of aggressiveness, it is part of the **enabling environment** for problematic behaviours (Garbarino, 1999). Viewing violence may teach children that conflict can be resolved only with verbal or physical aggressiveness. It may also be related to the development of a lower threshold for frustration, so that children tolerate irritants less easily and react to them more explosively. As well, exposure to violence may desensitize viewers to the severity of its consequences, so that even killing can appear routine (Cantor and Nathanson, 2001).

In fact, killing is often the goal in **video games:** Children learn aggressive techniques such as how to punch, kick, and kill. Indeed, a link has also been found between this interactive media and aggressive thoughts and behaviours (Anderson et al., 2004). However, the research on the effect of video games still has to include longitudinal studies, although one short-term longitudinal study did find that children who played violent video games became more aggressive later in the school year (Anderson et al., 2007). Further, research would need to separate the effect of violence on television from that on videos, not exactly a small task today (Wartella et al., 2004). As Funk et al. (2000) point out, at the very least, playing violent video games will not improve children's overall behaviour, although it may improve their visual-manual coordination.

Several studies have also shown that positive thoughts and behaviours can follow when contents are prosocial. First, listening to prosocial lyrics increases empathy and positive behaviour (Greitemeyer, 2009). Second, prosocial video games increase willingness to cooperate, to intervene when someone is harassed, and to be more willing to devote time to help (Gentile et al., 2009; Greitemeyer and Osswald, 2010). These studies even conclude that the effects of video games, whether aggression or positive behaviour, may be more powerful than those of television: "Video games teach whatever concepts are repeatedly rehearsed within them" (Buckley and Anderson, 2006:366).

Another related issue that society faces, often within the context of families, occurs both on the sports fields and especially on television: **violence in sports** (Coakley and Donnelly, 2004). This issue is salient because about 54 percent of children aged 5 to 14 regularly participate in organized sport activities, including 25 percent who play hockey (Kremarik, 2000b). In Canada, the problem centres on hockey violence—among professional players, among children on competitive teams, often by parents against coaches or other parents, and even in situations where parents encourage their sons to "beat up" opposing team members. At any rate, the constructs of masculinity as related to violence are evident in the culture of sports (Burstyn, 1999; Malszecki and Cavar, 2004).

In addition, in the U.S., the off-field behaviour of professional football and basketball celebrities is a concern: Many players have been arrested for criminal behaviours, including rape and murder. Too many have been implicated in fatal traffic and boating accidents, while others father children in an assembly line fashion! A July 18, 2003, *Toronto Star* article proclaims, "Bad boys of the NBA." Violence in sports is a problem that plagues the entire society. It is promoted by the mass media because it "sells." Overall, a climate of violence, when it exists, is certainly not an ideal one within which to form relationships and raise children (Garbarino, 2006).

The Issue of Consumerism and Lifestyle

The advertising industry spends over $12 billion a year marketing directly to children, who see over 40,000 ads a year on television alone (Moscovitch, 2007). Further, pop stars promote lifestyles (clothing, for instance) that preteens and adolescents try to emulate (Chaplin and John, 2005). Thus, mass culture creates **false needs**, which then contribute to less prosocial attitudes and even behaviours, both among parents and children. The American Psychological Association's Task Force on Advertising and Children points out that "advertising might trigger materialistic attitudes by teaching children to measure personal worth by the products they own" (Dittman, 2002).

Children learn how to dress and to behave according to this clothes-related self-presentation from the media (Quart, 2003). When ads, pop stars, and words in song lyrics promote premature sexiness in children, for instance, one should study how this inappropriate socialization might affect their sexual behaviour a few years later. One might also want to know if clothing styles promoted by certain popular entertainers relate to difficult behaviours down the road. In other words, there is no research on how children's consumer behaviours may be linked to the development of problematic or positive behaviours (Côté and Allahar, 1994). As Seiter (1993:193) points out concerning the mass-media targeting of children, "A distinctive, peer-oriented consumer culture now intervenes in the relationship of parents and children, and that intervention begins for many children as early as two years of age."

Whenever experts give conferences on issues of media effect, they unavoidably remind parents that they have to exercise control over what children view, and that they should discuss potentially detrimental programs with children. The entertainment industry follows suit and shamelessly places the entire responsibility on parents' shoulders—*one additional family function.* How this responsibility affects parents and their relationship with their children is not addressed. At least one observational study has shown that, in a supermarket, 65 percent of all parents' refusals to buy food items advertised on TV resulted instantly in parent-child conflict or arguments (Atkin, 1978). I have often observed children having screaming fits in these contexts. One can only wonder about the level of conflict that takes place in the privacy of the home when parents attempt to curtail TV viewing (Alexander, 1994:52).

The Issue of Sexuality

One also has to consider the impact of the media's sexual contents (Mitchell et al., 2001). For instance, Lowry and Towles (1989) compared the sexual content in soap operas in 1979 and 1987: There were more episodes depicting sexual behaviours per hour in 1987 than in 1979. The U.S. Kaiser Family Foundation (2003) also found that 64 percent of 1,123 randomly selected programs contained sexual material in 2002: 14 percent included sexual intercourse, up from 7 percent only four years earlier. Nearly all soap operas and movies had sexual content, as did a majority of comedies, dramas, and talk shows. Greenberg and Busselle (1996) found that the average number of sexual incidents in soap operas increased from 3.7 per hour in 1983 to 5.0 in 1994. There was also an increase in sexual behaviours between unmarried characters. Lowry and Towles (1989) concluded that the 1987 contents gave the following messages:

> *Nonmarital sex is the most exciting; spontaneous sex is very romantic, especially between unmarried persons; it carries no consequences such as unplanned pregnancy and sexually transmitted infections (STIs), which are rampant among some teen groups (Tu et al., 2009); all unmarried people engage in sex, often with several partners.*

Sapolsky and Tabarlet (1991) also found that the majority of sexual action and language depicted on television involved unmarried characters. Chandra et al. (2008) have reported that young teens who watch many programs that include sexual content have a greater risk of pregnancy later. Others have found that sexual content relates to earlier sexual activities in some groups of young teens (Brown et al., 2006).

In Brazil, the country's famed soap operas or novellas broadcast nationally "have pushed the limits of permissiveness" in the 1990s. Reboucas (2002) links this observation to the fact that, by the late 1990s, the age of first sexual intercourse had declined: Of adolescents who had ever had sex, 40 percent had had intercourse before reaching the age of 14. Of these, 64 percent originated from single-parent families.

The new genre of "reality" shows that began in 2003, such as *Temptation Island, The Bachelor, The Bachelorette,* and *EX-treme Dating,* promotes sexuality, infidelity, lack of commitment, and superficiality in the selection of partners. Not only do these shows promote values that have been found to relate to low marital quality and high divorce rates, they do not represent reality. One can only wonder how adolescents are affected by such portrayals, whether in terms of expectations, attitudes, and behaviours in their own dating relationships. As may be the case for the effect of violence, the effect of sexuality on television may already have reached its saturation point, at least among adolescents, because American high-school students initiated sexual intercourse in 2001 at a later age than in 1991 (U.S. Department of Health and Human Services, 2002).

Second, it is estimated that there are tens of thousands of websites throughout the world with pedophiliac and pornographic content. The exploitation of children becomes more widespread because the Internet is not easily policed. In a survey, a quarter of children aged 9 to 17 reported that they intentionally entered porn sites, while 53 percent have ended up on such a site by accident (Taylor, 2002). This is hardly surprising if one considers that pornography constituted at least 7 percent of the 3.3 billion web pages indexed by Google in 2003 (Paul, 2004). Furthermore, chat rooms that are preyed upon by pedophiles are a danger to children that parents have to monitor (Wolak et al., 2008). As well, adult pornographic, racist, and hate websites are so easily accessible by children and adolescents that some schools have had to monitor closely their students' use of the Internet during class time.

The Issue of Education

Children and adults use media presentations as a source of information. TV and the Internet have become what the critical sociologist Habermas (1987:16) called an insulating expertise that splits children and adults from "the context of everyday practice" and leads to cultural impoverishment. On the one hand, children are active social actors and participate in the reconstruction of the messages they receive from the media. However, they can make a realistic reconstruction only to the extent that the real world around them, particularly their families, their peers, and schools, offers them this possibility. Yet, not all children benefit from such healthy environments (Garbarino, 2006). In fact, perhaps 25 percent of children do not have a home/peer/school environment that can counterbalance the negative effects of the media on their attitudes and behaviours.

Parents are also subjected to media contents of dubious value and many use talk shows as educational sources. Yet, the contents of these shows often focus on the sensational: conjugal infidelities, incest, child prostitution, pregnancies of unknown paternity following intercourse with several sexual partners, and so on. Parents, especially the less educated, show great interest in these shows. What, then, can they teach their children (Austin, 2001)? As well, while parents watch television and videos, they often include their babies: This begins when the infants are three months of age in about 40 percent of babies and this premature exposure has been related to delays in speech development (Tanimura et al., 2007).

While the Internet and cellphones now displace television to a great extent, they also take away from time spent on homework and studying. Canadian data clearly indicate that students aged 15 to 24 spend over an hour less studying and over one hour more in leisure activities than in 1986 (Fast et al., 2001). An American survey of first-year university students revealed that, during their last high-school year, they had spent less time on homework and studies and more on surfing the net (HERI, 2003). In 2008, 70 percent of boys and 58 percent of girls exceeded the two-hour-a-day limit of time spent on television, video games, and the Internet that is considered healthy (CIW, 2010). In 2009, 32 percent of male high-school students in Ontario played video games daily (Paglia-Boak et al., 2010).

Children aged 9 to 17 report spending 38 percent of their online time on homework—while their parents' perception is that 68 percent of their children's time is so spent (Taylor, 2002)! Children's favourite online activities include downloading music and emailing, as well as visiting chat rooms. Facebook use is widespread and a great proportion of adolescents openly display their own risky behaviours, whether violence or sexuality (Moreno et al., 2009). These facts lead us to pause when we consider that, already a decade ago, 25 percent of elementary school children and 50 percent of high-school students reported that they had email accounts of which their parents were unaware (Taylor, 2002).

Therefore, as is the case with television, the Internet also contains dangers. For instance, it is far from an unmitigated blessing in terms of providing reliable information, because information is generally mixed with advertising. It is often difficult to assess the origin and accuracy of the material presented on websites. Erroneous and misleading information is too frequently accepted by a population that has faith in the power of technology to inform accurately. As well, the constant use of the Internet is changing the way youth process information, evaluate it, and use this technology to replace traditional skills while, at the same time, new skills are not compensating for this loss (Levey, 2009). One can also be concerned that the time itself spent with the new media may place at risk the continuation of the artistic cultural heritage that is so obvious in provinces such as Quebec and Newfoundland/Labrador.

CONCLUSIONS: FAMILIES HAVE TO BE REEMPOWERED

The research presented in this chapter does not support the pessimistic view of a general family decline and loss of functions. Rather, the research supports pessimism concerning *individual* families' ability to fulfill their ever-increasing functions adequately, particularly that of the socialization of children. On the one hand, the family as an institution is highly valued and demands are placed on it in terms of its responsibilities in ever-expanding domains. But, on the other hand, this exacting sociocultural context generally fails to provide individual families with equivalent moral support and practical as well as financial help that could allow them to fulfill their functions.

For instance, society is choosing to embrace information technology and market forces as values and as a way of life. Unavoidably, there are high costs to such a choice and families bear a disproportionate burden in this respect, especially those that are marginalized by poverty, segregation, and lack of access to the new types of jobs. As Blank (1997:198) phrases it, given that our society "has chosen a market-oriented economy, it has a responsibility to those who cannot survive in the market on their own." This responsibility should not be displaced onto families. Unfortunately, this is exactly what is happening.

As Hewlett and West (1998:34) point out, too many **conservatives** fail to recognize the ways in which *market values are destroying families and family values.* For their part, too many on the **liberal** side, with their emphasis on rights and freedoms, "fail to understand that we need to rein in untrammelled individualism if we are to recreate the values that nurture family life." The family is the cornerstone of society because it reproduces, nurtures, and socializes society's future workers, citizens, taxpayers, and leaders. Thus, *a private institution subsidizes an entire society.* When families "fail," largely due to income and cultural causes within the same society, such families produce society's future unemployed poor, welfare recipients, and even criminals. In other words, what happens within the family affects the entire society just as the economic and cultural agenda of society has an impact on its families. There is an incessant feedback dynamic between the private and the public spheres of life—between the family and society at large.

In most western societies, the family is a small and relatively isolated unit in terms of the mediocre support it receives while being much affected by its environment. In recent decades, this cultural and socioeconomic environment has broadened considerably because of globalization and a more pervasive as well as **intrusive technology**. At the dawn of the new millennium, families experience change at a rapid pace, are contextualized in a larger world, but receive relatively fewer resources in terms of instrumental and effective moral support. Empowering families, no matter their structure, is one of the key social challenges of the 21st century.

Summary

1. Although the family has lost a few historical functions, it has gained a number of new ones. Its main functions are reproducing, socializing children, coordinating and managing the external services children receive, stabilizing personalities, meeting affective needs, and providing a sense of belongingness, health care, a place to live, and care of family members who have special needs. There is an overabundance of family functions created by a lack of social support for the frail. Thus, too many individual families are unable to fulfill their functions, which should not be taken to mean a loss of functions by the family as an institution. Family-oriented values are threatened, not by changes in the structure of families, but by the lack of social support they face.

2. Children spend more time outside of their families and have become defamilialized. Childhood has become more structured in terms of activities than in the past. Children produce work that adults do to educate them and organize their activities. Thus, children are useful to society via their schoolwork and the work they produce for the employment of adults. But children in industrialized nations are separated from adults, whereas in non-industrialized societies, they are fully integrated into village life and their parents' work and are totally familialized. This is in contrast to a high level of defamilialization in many western countries.

3. Globalization has made transnational families more numerous and diverse than in the past, both ethnically and economically. Military families face particular challenges that deserve more research in Canada. Couples choosing to live apart together (LAT) are a fairly new phenomenon in Canada and also exist in some Caribbean nations.

4. An important historical development took place at the cultural level between 1951 and 1955, as nearly two-thirds of the nation's homes acquired a TV set. As people watched television, less time was left for the development of certain skills and family sociability. A historical overview of the trends in television programming pertaining to family life and norms highlights the changes in the content of programs as the decades went by.

5. Family life and time continued to evolve with the introduction of the Internet and cellphones. Various issues pertaining to family life and child development are reviewed as families are affected by the contents of the media and the time devoted to these media. These are issues of sociability, violence, prosocial behaviour, consumerism, sexuality, and education.

6. Sociologists are generally concerned that certain types of family structure are not sufficiently supported by the economy and the polity. Another concern is the potentially negative impact of the rapid pace of technological change.

Analytical Questions

1. Now that you have completed this chapter, revisit Analytical Question 1 in Chapter 1: What more can you say?
2. Can you think of additional functions that families fulfill in Canada, and especially in other countries?
3. Are military families a new development historically and cross-culturally?
4. Does television reflect reality or does it create a reality? What is the role of advertising in this respect?
5. Write down a hypothetical time diary that would illustrate your family life on a daily basis this coming week, were you without television, Internet, and cellphones.
6. Write down how you would describe your family life to a researcher. Then, write how you would present it on Facebook. Which theoretical perspective would explain discrepancies, if any?

Suggested Readings

Côté, J. E., and Allahar, A. L. 2006. *Critical youth studies. A Canadian focus.* Toronto: Pearson. This book provides the economic and sociocultural context that affect the current life conditions of young people: The focus is on market forces as the main catalyst in youth living conditions.

Suggested Weblinks

Media Awareness Network provides reports on the use of the Internet by youth, on media portrayal of minorities, and on violence.

www.mediaawareness.ca

SafeSurf: This site provides information on how to make the Internet safer for children and to improve the quality of programming in the media.

www.safesurf.com

CHAPTER 4

Effects of Economic Changes and Inequalities on Families

"In 10 years from now I will be either a lawyer or a doctor. I want to make money, lots of it. That's my primary goal."

"In 10 years I hope to be out of this noisy apartment building and live in a modest house in the countryside. I hope to have travelled a bit and especially help my mother and sister out of here. I would want my mother to stay home and not to have to worry about money for the first time in her life."

"Right now my big problem is lack of money, nothing new here but now that I am getting close to becoming a teacher and having a bit for myself for the first time in my life, I can't stand it any longer!"

"This autobiography is going to be rather boring. I have lived the typical 'American dream' or should I say 'Canadian'? Born to poverty, hard working parents, moves to better neighbourhoods and now our dream come true: a big house on a street with other big houses."

"My father is a lawyer and when I turned 10 my mother became a stock broker. . . . We've always lived in the same lovely neighbourhood in a fairly large home with lots of trees and flowers, in two homes actually because my parents at some point decided to have a house with a two-level foyer with French doors and matching staircase."

"At that age [10 to 14] all I can remember is being hungry most of the time but especially by the end of each month and never having something special or nice that belonged to me. I don't have one pleasant memory."

In the preceding quotes, we hear from students who want to become doctors or lawyers because their dreams include a lot of money, students who simply want to have just enough for a decent life, students who suffered from the deprivations and fears of poverty, and others who lived in affluence. As these quotes begin to illustrate, economic circumstances and the economic system in which people live affect all facets of their lives and of their families' lives. The decades of the 1970s through the 2010s are characterized by an economy that has been radically transformed by information technology, which in turn has contributed to globalization. These sweeping changes have contributed to the contemporary profile of families and to what some see as upheavals in the social fabric. Without some understanding of the economy, we cannot fully grasp the sources of the recent family transformations that are discussed in this book.

There is a historical parallel between the Industrial Revolution, which came to Canada in the 19th century, as discussed in Chapter 2, and the ongoing technological revolution: Both have had an impact on families' lives and roles.

OVERVIEW OF ECONOMIC CHANGES

We now live in what is called the postindustrial economy. It is characterized by **information technology**; high finances, including "paper" speculation (the stock market); and the predominance of the service sector. The economy is no longer organized along regional or even national lines; rather, it is international or global. This phenomenon is referred to as the **globalization of the economy** and is driven by multinational corporations operating throughout the world. In order to increase their profits, corporations move production plants and call centres around the globe, depending on the availability of cheap labour. It is a world of mergers and acquisitions, speculation, and of restructuring and downsizing (Moen and Roehling, 2005). Hence, national economies are at the mercy of **worldwide financial fluctuations** more than ever before and this was very apparent in the recent 2008–09 recession largely generated by a lack of controls over the paper economy and risky borrowing that originated in the U.S.

It is now difficult for governments to control their country's labour markets and, especially, financial sectors: Multinational corporations, hungry for profit for their **shareholders,** dictate trade and commercial laws as well as who will work, where, at what wage, and under what conditions. Therefore, globalization and various free trade agreements have important consequences for families: Governments now have more difficulties stepping in to improve the economic opportunities of a disadvantaged neighbourhood or of an area that is threatened by plant closure, for instance. As well, powerful financial companies such as Goldman Sachs are too connected with the American government. This prevents decisions from being taken in the best interest of the general public rather than speculators. For instance, two of Goldman Sachs' past four leaders have served as head of the U.S. Treasury. Even worldwide, a majority of countries' finance officials attending G-8 meetings have recently been former Goldman Sachs men.

Until the 1970s, some of the largest Canadian employers were industries producing materials and goods such as steel and cars. In 1951, 27 percent of jobs were in **manufacturing**, but this number had plummeted to 15 percent by 1995 (Glenday, 1997). Manufacturers provided well-paying entry-level jobs, employment security, and, later on, benefit packages to young workers fresh out of high school. These industries hired large numbers of youths, often immigrants. With such jobs, youths, especially males, could marry and support a family. After the 1970s, as technology progressed, fewer low-skilled workers were needed. Plant closures, downsizing, relocation, and imports from abroad, particularly Asia, followed and the proportion of males working in manufacturing declined. All of these and other factors began to restrict working-class individuals' ability to earn decent wages and secure a job during certain periods, such as the early 1990s, the early 2000s, and then 2008–10. In the 1990s, even traditionally feminine domains of employment were affected by job losses, whether clerical or in the clothing industry (Phillips and Phillips, 2000). However, in the 2008–09 recession, some of the feminine domains such as health, education, and service sectors sustained fewer losses than the more masculine manufacturing, mining, farming, and even oil sectors.

Also, by the late 1970s, another phenomenon was occurring that changed the entire employment profile: The **service sector** expanded, a large segment of which offered only low-paying and part-time jobs—for example in the restaurant, hotel, and retail industries. These jobs constituted only 18 percent of the labour market in 1951 but employed 37 percent by 1995 (Glenday, 1997). Furthermore, in the face of a more competitive and high-tech economy and the requirements of corporations' shareholders, many jobs have been downsized into **part-time positions** and contracts; these are less secure, less well paid, and do not provide any health or pension benefits—and ultimately contribute to poverty. In 2004, 19 percent of all Canadian workers were employed part-time: 27 percent of employed women and 11 percent of employed men. Women constitute 70 percent of all part-time employees (Lindsay, 2006). Although women turn to part-time work in order to combine employment with maternal duties, 30 percent would prefer full-time jobs.

Thus, the traditional gender division of labour and of income, with women earning less, remains in the new economy (Statistics Canada, 2009h). Feminine activities continue to be devalued (England, 2010). This **detrimental feminine wage** and labour situation contributes to poverty in single-mother families and in low-income families in which two salaries are necessary. However, at the two-parent family level, the losses incurred by males on the labour market were accompanied by feminine gains. The former affected couple formation while the latter affected fertility. Despite this increase in two-earner couples, families are not much better off financially than they were in the 1960s (FSAT, 2004).

Another consequence of the emergence of the postindustrial economy has been an **inflation in educational requirements**. About two-thirds of all new positions created—even some low-paying ones—require at least 12 years of formal education and 45 percent require more than 16 years. In turn, the need for a longer education forces youths to seek part-time and summer jobs to defray the increasing costs of their scholarization (Beaujot, 2004). In this type of economy, school dropouts and youths with only high-school diplomas face a life of part-time or low-wage jobs (Côté and Allahar, 2006). Indeed, Canadians with only a high school diploma are more likely to earn low wages and to be unemployed than their better educated peers (Chung, 2006). This leads to a new and more intractable type of poverty. However, compulsory education also has had the effect of increasing income and preventing more widespread poverty (Oreopoulos, 2006). Yet, at the same time, heavy student loans also delay young people's ability to accumulate assets (Luong, 2010).

The **gap between the rich and the poor** in terms of **wealth** (assets such as real estate, stocks, and savings accounts) has also increased—and this gap favours the more educated (Frenette et al., 2007). For instance, between 1999 and 2005, the net worth of the 20 percent of the top earning families increased by 19 percent (Morissette and Zhang, 2006). Not only are the rich getting richer, but the middle class may be losing ground (Sauvé, 2009b). This gap is in part related to marital status, as married couples have more assets (Ozawa and Lee, 2006). It is also related to the fact that marriages increasingly consist of two high-earning or two low-earning spouses (Schwartz, 2010). As well, the **debt** load of Canadians has increased substantially so that, by 2008, the ratio of debt to disposable income had reached 127 percent (Sauvé, 2009a). One result is that a higher number of bankruptcies take place and less well-off families have more difficulties repaying their debts and securing home equity.

EFFECTS OF ECONOMIC CHANGES ON FAMILIES

Overall, the new economy presents a less secure employment and financial environment for families than was the case in the 1950s and 1960s when goods were manufactured. It is a more demanding environment, which has many consequences for family structure, lifestyle, and dynamics. Among these consequences are the increase in maternal employment and two-income families, as well as the "time crunch," the rise of a consumerist culture, and the lengthening of youths' dependence on parents—the latter discussed in Chapter 10. Other consequences such as delayed couple formation and fertility are discussed in subsequent chapters.

The Rise of Feminine Employment and the Dual-Income Family

The first effect of the new economic situation on families has resided in an **increase in feminine employment** and consequently in **two-income families**. In 2000, 79 percent of Canadian families headed by a non-retired couple had two or more earners (Sauvé, 2002). Without the earning of the second worker, the number of families living in poverty would double. Indeed, in two-parent families, mothers' wages have become increasingly important and now account for 41 percent of total family earnings (Statistics Canada, 2009f). This percentage is, however, much lower when there are children below the age of six. In 2000, among married couples with children, when both husbands and wives were employed, the average income was over $61,000 (after transfers and income taxes) compared with $43,000 when the wife was not employed.

By 2003, about 29 percent of wives earned more than their husbands, up from only 11 percent in 1987: They are the "primary earners" in their families, and most earned twice as much as their husbands. Although more educated than other wives and even than husbands who are primary earners in the other families, their wages and family incomes were, on average, lower than those of families whose main breadwinner is the husband (Sussman, 2006). Why? Because of the lower wages that women in general receive and the "glass ceiling" preventing some of them from reaching the top of their career. As well, hourly wages of women with children is 12 percent lower than wages of childless women and this gap widens so that by the time mothers are 40 years old, they earn 21 percent less than childless women (Statistics Canada, 2009g).

Recourse to women's labour for family survival is a recurrent theme in history (Bradbury, 2000; Parr, 2000). Not only did women (and children) fully participate in the family economy in past centuries, but in the 19th century, many low-income families already had (needed) two or more incomes (Bradbury, 1996; Parr, 1980). What is now unprecedented is that the majority of women of all classes work for wages while children no longer do; also unprecedented is the combination of economic and cultural forces driving feminine employment (Moen and Roehling, 2005). In many two-parent families, two wages have become a necessity because of a rise in economic instability and consumer expectations (Edwards, 2001). As husbands' salaries plunge or as they lose their jobs, wives increase their own labour market participation (Morissette and Hou, 2008). Further, higher divorce and single parenting rates make it necessary for divorced and unmarried mothers to be employed.

But feminine employment would have nevertheless grown despite these economic necessities, although perhaps to a lesser extent. Indeed, the 1970s wave of the Women's Movement has led to the liberalization of attitudes concerning women's roles in society. This cultural change has allowed women to enter the labour force in greater numbers and to penetrate occupational fields that had been traditionally masculine, such as law, medicine, and the physical sciences.

Below, we note the sharp increase in the percentages of married women in the labour force from decade to decade (Statistics Canada, 2003a):

1931	3.5%
1951	11
1961	22
1971	37
1981	52
1991	63
1998	78
2003	80

In Table 4.1, we compare the overall employment rates for 1995 with those in 2007 by age of youngest child still at home: Mothers' labour participation has increased at each child age level.

There were, however, differences by province, with Quebec and the Maritime provinces having the highest rates of maternal employment and the Prairie provinces the lowest. These differences may arise because of the types of jobs created and the higher number of immigrant women in the east (Roy, 2006), as immigrant women tend to seek employment more because of economic necessity.

TABLE 4.1	**Percentages of Mothers Who Are Employed by Age of Youngest Child at Home in 1995 and 2007**		
	Youngest child is 0–2	Youngest child is 3–5	Youngest child is 6–16
1995	61	68	76
2007	69	77	84

Source: Beach et al., 2009, from Table 2. Adapted with permission.

Recent studies have found that women who **delay childbirth** by at least one year past the average age at first birth for their cohorts earn higher salaries—up to 17 percent higher. Postponing a first birth is even more important among younger cohorts of women, in part because of the types of careers now open to them. As Drolet (2003:21) points out, "wage growth and promotion opportunities are substantial early in one's career." Women who delay childbirth are more flexible for career moves, additional training, and may also be inherently more career oriented than women who begin childbearing earlier. As well, career interruptions of more than three years have a great impact on mothers' wages; by age 40, they earn close to 30 percent less than other mothers and childless women (Statistics Canada, 2009g).

These observations are important in view of the fact that **women's wages** still lag behind men's, even among younger cohorts: This is a fairly universal phenomenon, even among the very educated (Brouillet, 2004). This gap in part stems from women occupying positions that are less well remunerated in the service sector (such as retail salespersons, cashiers, and babysitters) and also because a larger proportion work part-time. Thus, women experience only 78.7 percent of the time men actually spend employed (Drolet, 2001). In 2007, women earned only 65.7 percent of what men earned (Statistics Canada, 2009h).

As women try to link their paid work life with their home life (production and reproduction), they often have to choose economic sectors that have more flexible hours but pay much less; or they have recourse to part-time employment; others interrupt their work cycle for a substantial period of time, thus delaying promotions and salary increases. One should, however, consider that a proportion of women still choose and enjoy being homemakers and full-time parents and have minimal aspirations as far as paid employment is concerned. There is a lack of attention in feminist theories to this aspect of many women's condition, as we have tended to focus on paid employment (Marks, 2004). One could as easily see that many men might also want to become full-time fathers were they socialized within this perspective.

At another level, 30 percent of men and 28 percent of women engage in **shift work**; they report higher levels of work-related stress and work overload. This is even more so for women than men (Williams, 2008). As well, both men and women on evening shifts report more relationship problems with their spouses and lower well-being than those with daytime employment (Davis et al., 2008; Shields, 2003). Another study has found that children whose parents have nonstandard work schedules have more social and emotional difficulties, in part as a result of lower parental well-being and less effective parenting (Strazdins et al., 2006).

Domestic Division of Labour along Gender Lines

As we have just seen, a majority of mothers, even those with very young children, are gainfully employed. Paradoxically, this shift toward maternal employment has occurred at a time when the requirements of care of small children have become more labour intensive and the pressure on women as mothers has mounted (Hays, 1996). The net result is what sociologist Arlie Hochschild has, in 1989, called *The Second Shift*. That is, although society has become more accepting of women's status and role in the workplace, this development has not been accompanied by a similarly

TABLE 4.2	Housework by Men and Women for 1986 Compared with 2005	
	1986	**2005**
% of men who do housework daily	54%	69%
% of women who do housework daily	90%	90%
# of hours of housework (for men who do any)	2.1 hours	2.5 hours
# of hours of housework (for women who do any)	4.8 hours	4.3 hours

Source: Marshall, 2006, Statistics Canada; Table adapted by Ambert with permission from Statistics Canada.

liberating one on the domestic front. In the "second shift," women come home from work to work even more. After picking up children at the daycare centre or at the sitter's, they cook and serve dinner, prepare lunches for the next day, perhaps do laundry, and help the children with their homework and bedtime (Hochschild, 1997).

In Table 4.2, we see that women do more housework than men, although masculine participation has increased. Not shown is the fact that there is a similar pattern for child care. Further, wives who are not in the labour force do more housework than other wives, and wives employed part-time do more than wives employed full-time. The scenario that comes closest to equality in terms of housework is when the husband is not in the labour force but his wife is employed full-time. When both spouses are employed full-time, wives still do more child care and housework than husbands (Moen and Roehling, 2005). Overall, married fathers have more leisure time per day than married and single mothers also employed full-time. One consequence of this overload is that women take more time off work for family reasons other than maternity. In fact, in 2000, married women with children took 12 days off versus one day for married men with children and four for single-parent women, because employed mothers are more time stressed than fathers (Marshall, 2006).

An important gap in the literature is the lack of widespread research on **children's contributions** to household tasks and child care—including self-care. Not only do we need to know how much work children do and what they do, but how easy or difficult it is for parents to obtain their cooperation in this respect. For instance, only 4 out of 10 teens do some housework daily, for about one hour—although they average 9.2 hours of work per day at school and part-time jobs (Statistics Canada, 2008g). Further, 10 percent of husband-wife households employ some domestic help (Statistics Canada, 2003d). In fact, 43 percent of households with income of $160,000 and over hire **domestic help** (Marshall, 2006). They are more likely to be hired when wives' incomes constitute a greater share of the joint income and house size is larger (Palameta, 2003). Among couples and professional singles, domestics, who are usually immigrant women, contribute to alleviating better-off women's own domestic burdens and time squeeze, thus participating in the gendered division of household labour.

Employed mothers, whether married or single, have little time for themselves, are overworked and stressed, frequently worry about their children, and often feel guilty, even more so when child care arrangements are not optimal or when their children are alone at home after school or in the company of problematic peers. Overall, there are both negative and positive work/family spillovers, but these differ depending on each family's context (Grzywacz et al., 2002). A national survey reveals that fathers and mothers in two-parent families are happier at home than at work, but divorce often reverses this trend (Kiecolt, 2003). However, for women who shoulder most of the burden at home, paid work outside is often less stressful than housework and childrearing (Larson and Richards, 1994). It is, nevertheless, quite possible that the ideological devaluation of housework in recent decades has contributed to the fact that it is now generally viewed as stressful and as something that everyone prefers to avoid (Zimmerman, 2003).

The Discussion Concerning the Effect of Maternal Employment on Children

The research literature, public policy debates, talk shows, and magazines still focus on the effects of maternal rather than paternal employment. Why is so much attention devoted to maternal employment and its presumed negative consequences on children? Why not consider fathers' employment in these respects? The answer to this question resides in the overall gender stratification and social constructions of motherhood and fatherhood, as discussed in Chapter 1. Under the existing gender-based division of responsibilities, mothers are still viewed as children's primary care-givers. But the notion that mothers are children's best caregivers is unscientific. If mothers were "by nature" the best caregivers, why would an army of social workers be needed to watch over the thousands of children abused or neglected by their biological mothers and fathers? Being a competent child-care giver is more a matter of training, personality, and social encouragement than femininity versus masculinity.

This concern about the effect of maternal employment arose at a time when mothers were encouraged to leave work after their Second World War effort in order to give back jobs that "naturally" belonged to returning male veterans. Not only were women "sent home" but child care centres built during the war were dismantled, thus making it difficult for mothers to continue their employment activities. However, very little in the way of negative impact of maternal employment was ever found in the research. Possible exceptions may exist for very small children (Han et al., 2001), especially when their mothers work more than 30 hours a week (Brooks-Gunn et al., 2002), or children of mothers whose employment is substandard (Raver, 2003). Thus, in more recent studies, when the impact of maternal employment on children is examined, mothers' work circumstances, stressors, earnings, and the quality of care children received are considered, especially within the first year of a child's life (Waldfogel et al., 2002).

So what can we conclude? All things being equal, children whose mothers are employed do not have more negative outcomes than children of stay-at-home mothers. Maternal employment may even be advantageous to some children, particularly girls, in terms of school achievement and self-esteem. This is especially so when mothers' occupations are highly skilled (Cooksey et al., 1997). Even for disadvantaged children, a mother's salary may raise the family's standard of living and thus provide compensation against risks for children.

Parental Employment in General and Its Effects on Children

It is important to reframe the question of maternal employment within the context of parental employment. For instance, the proportion of families with two parents working *full time* has more than doubled between 1980 and 2005, from 15 to 32 percent (LaRochelle-Côté and Dionne, 2009). Low-income single mothers also saw their work status shift to full time, from 8 to 20 percent. Analyzed within an interactional and transactional perspective, the effect of the employment of one parent cannot be separated from the effect of the employment of the other parent. To begin with, no matter what their social class, when both parents work long hours and there are no adult substitutes at home, children and adolescents may not have sufficient interaction with caring authority figures (Moen and Roehling, 2005).

A study looking at the effect of both parents' employment found that, when mothers' hours at work increased, fathers became more aware of their 8- to 10-year-old children's activities, as a compensating mechanism (Crouter et al., 1999). But researchers also found that children were less well monitored when both parents had demanding jobs (Bumpus et al., 1999). Other studies show that, when parents work long hours, they report more stress (LaRochelle-Côté and Dionne, 2009). This is certainly why at least one of two parents works fewer hours when children are younger than six to avoid role overload. Indeed, the combination of long hours at work with more work at home takes a toll on women's well-being and, therefore, on children (Burton and Phipps, 2007; MacDonald et al., 2005).

According to Coleman's (1990a) rational theory, in situations where parents are overworked, children are deprived of social resources or social capital. Children go unsupervised, which is a risky matter in this society where opportunities for problematic and even delinquent behaviours abound. Actually, there is a direct correspondence between physical and sexual assaults on children and lack of supervision by adults in general, including parents (AuCoin, 2005:68). In other words, the better supervised adolescents are, the less likely they are to commit delinquent acts. When no adults are in charge, children may fail to learn certain coping skills, others may not do their homework, and still others may not learn how to communicate effectively. In other words, even when their parents are relatively affluent, many of these children may not develop sufficient human capital and may be undersocialized. That is, they may not learn what they are required to know at a given age in order to function effectively and ethically in this society.

Another potential problem related to parental employment resides in the combination of materialistic values with a preoccupation for upward mobility, or "moving up socially." These parents (who also have a high divorce rate—see Clydesdale, 1997) spend many hours at the office or on business trips and, when at home, often pursue their career-related activities rather than engage in family interactions. Cell phones and laptop computers certainly contribute to parents remaining connected to work. Such parents do not have the time to relate to their children authoritatively or to teach them appropriate values. Also, the lives of working parents' children are sometimes hectically packed with activities and their days are lived at a frenetic pace. Let's look at the example of a young, affluent family from my 1998 home interviews of two-career couples.

This suburban family consists of two parents, aged 35 (husband) and 33 (wife), both professionals in large brokerage firms, and two boys of three and six years of age. The family rises at 6:00 a.m. The parents alternate taking the boys to the day care centre where they arrive at 7:00 a.m. From there, Glenn, the oldest, is picked up by minivan at 8:45 and brought to a nearby school, where he is in grade 1. The parents take turns fetching the children at 6:00 p.m. at the daycare, where Glenn has been since 3:15, after another ride in the minivan. Once a week, a taxi drives him to music classes after school and returns him to the centre. One parent takes the hungry children home and promptly serves them supper; the other parent arrives at 7:00 p.m., equally hungry and tired. The children are in bed at 8:00, quite exhausted by then.

Saturday morning, the father takes the boys for swimming lessons; the mother takes them for skating lessons in the afternoon. Sunday is spent going to church, shopping, and visiting with friends and relatives. Both parents are intelligent, attractive, and sociable. The boys get along well and play together in the few hours of unstructured time they have. They are apparently intelligent. However, Glenn's report card indicates that his verbal skills are below his grade level. His visiting grandmother explains that this is due to the fact that the children are always in the company of other children and are rarely alone with adults who, at any rate, are obviously of no interest to the child-oriented boys. The boys basically spend only two hours daily with their parents who are all the while busily catching up with housework activities. Little conversation takes place. Life is fast paced.

Economic Realities and Changing Family Time

When both parents, and especially mothers, have demanding hours, less time is available for personal needs, as well as family and couple interaction (Clark, 2002). However, when adults feel that their work environment provides flexibility, they benefit from a more favourable work-family balance (Hill et al., 2001). As well, when children's activities outside school are regimented into a variety of lessons and sports, they have less time for spontaneous play—even though these structured activities may be favourably related to cognitive development (Hofferth and Sandberg, 2001). Further, information technology has spawned "gadgets" such as cellphones, to which adults and children are tethered, and which occupy a great deal of their time in interaction with other persons, often to the detriment of face-to-face interactions with family members.

Thus, another effect of economic changes on families consists of what is called the **time crunch**: Too many activities are crammed into too few hours, as seen in the example above (CIW, 2010). Spouses have less time for each other, especially if they work different shifts, and parents can devote far fewer hours to their children. The use of the Statistics Canada Time Crunch Instrument has revealed that 23 percent of parents of children under the age of six are "highly time-stressed"; 68 percent feel that they do not spend enough quality time with their children (Invest in Kids, 2002). The U.S. Bureau of the Census has estimated that, between 1960 and 1986, parental time available to children has diminished by 10 hours per week for whites and 12 for blacks (Fuchs, 1990). The phenomenon of "latchkey" children comes to mind here, as well as of older siblings taking care of a younger one after school (Riley and Steinberg, 2004). Not only do parents work more hours, but the average Canadian now spends nearly 12 full days commuting to and from work a year—14 days in Toronto (Turcotte, 2006).

In 2005, the average worker was spending 45 minutes less with his or her family during weekdays compared with 20 years earlier. In part, this is due to the fact that Canadians work longer hours than two decades ago. These data are very solid because they are based, not on retrospective information, but on time journals provided in the General Social Survey on Time Use (Statistics Canada, 2007c).Other researchers have found that adolescents now spend an average of three hours a day alone at home (Schneider et al., 2000). In 2005, only 35 percent of 15- to 17-year-olds ate a meal with their parents on a typical day (CIW, 2010). As well, another study found that, "In low and high income households, parents report spending under 5 minutes a day reading or talking with their children and less than 20 minutes a day playing with them" (Williams, 2002:10).

However, while total parental time has diminished in two-parent families, time per child may have increased—because there are fewer children (Wolff, 2001). Other research indicates that parents of small children (five and younger) spend more time with them than was the case in 1960 (Gauthier et al., 2004). Therefore, when considering studies of parental time with children, one has to look at the age of the child. Still, overall, mothers have been able to balance their hours with children by doing less housework, having less leisure, and having fewer children (Schor, 2001). Both mothers and fathers would prefer to have more family time, and half of them wish that their partner would spend more time with the children (Bond et al., 1998). It is difficult, however, to know if the children themselves feel deprived of "family time." High-income families may be even more affected than low-income families in patterns of time consumption. Parents with a higher income work at least six hours more per week than those on a low income (Williams, 2002). As an illustration of this time squeeze, let's hear what another young professional couple, with both spouses employed full-time, said when interviewed:

> The spouses in their early thirties both complained during their separate interviews that they had "no time for each other; it's even difficult to put some sex in our lives because we are always on the run" [wife]. For his part, the husband felt that his wife "could work fewer hours; that way, it would be easier to arrange our schedules so that we can take some time out for our relationship." He did not mention that he could also work fewer hours, a realistic possibility, given that he stayed at the office daily until 8 p.m. This was an affluent couple with extremely high material expectations—costly expectations. In contrast to the other couples interviewed, this couple was not concerned about having practically no time for their four-year-old son. Fortunately, the little boy appeared to be good-natured and easily contented. He made no demands during the two hours I spent at his home and he occupied himself peacefully.

The Rise of Consumerism in Family Life

One reason families now need larger incomes resides in the rise of consumerism fuelled by advertising and television programming, which all contribute to a sense of relative deprivation (Easterbrook, 2003). For instance, when families watch certain shows focusing on the well-to-do, they may feel deprived in comparison. New "needs" are created by advertisers, whether for clothes, cellphones, computers, entertainment units (DVD players, large flat-screen TVs), or more cars per family. Children are particularly rewarding "targets" of such advertising and play a very active role as consumers, often as a result of peer pressure (Cook, 2004). As well, the size of houses has increased substantially as has their cost, and these large spaces have to be furnished.

Family members dream of objects, shop for them, buy them or fail to do so, agree or disagree on their necessity, their costs, their appropriateness, and develop a sense of identity in part related to their possessions (Côté, 2000). Further, consumerism—looking at catalogues and online displays, going to malls, searching for items in mega stores—takes time. This time could be used for other family activities; thus, consumerist activities may compound the time crunch felt by parents. More positively, Little (2006) has shown that, between 1998 and 2003, Canadian households have spent 41 percent more on movies, performing arts, and spectator sports as well as museums. It is not known, however, if such activities take place at the family level.

Long ago, the sociologist Thorsten Veblen (1899) developed the concept of **conspicuous consumption:** In other words, families acquire possessions that are visible (conspicuous) and give them a certain status. However, technology and fashion change so rapidly in this century that families have to keep upgrading their possessions to reflect their affluence or to have what others have. In view of these observations, it is somewhat surprising that contemporary sociologists of the family have paid little attention to these processes and dynamics of market forces. As Daly (2003:778) points out, we have given little "attention to understanding how spending behaviours and consumer goods are the basis for the construction of meaning in the everyday experience of family life." In contrast, there are indications that parents who encourage their children to have a savings account are, by the same token, helping them in terms of math achievement (Elliott et al., 2010)—perhaps as a result of the positive effect of delayed gratification on intellectual development. Conversely, it would be important to know what happens later to children and adolescents who are given large allowances and credit cards.

FAMILY POVERTY

Canada is an advanced society technologically; yet poverty, even if diminished—but higher again as a result of the 2008–2009 recession—has persisted, particularly among the working poor. The **working poor** are those whose wages are too low to raise their family above the poverty line determined by the government. When wages are minimal, many families become or remain poor, despite the fact that both parents are employed. Part-time work and minimum-wage jobs are largely responsible for this situation. Statistics Canada calculates a "Market Basket Measure" based on a formula that includes the cost of food, clothes, shelter, and transportation for each region. This formula tells us how much, in theory, a family needs to earn in order to meet its basic needs: Families who earn less are considered disadvantaged, thus the concept of "living below the poverty line," or LICOs, which stands for low-income cut-offs. In 2007, the following poverty lines were established for Canada's major cities for a family of four, from most to least expensive cities to live in (HRSD Canada, 2009):

Vancouver	$31,768	St. John's	28,544
Toronto	31,729	Winnipeg	27,256
Calgary	30,951	Saint John	27,202
Charlottetown	30,527	Regina	26,835
Halifax	29,761	Montreal	26,560

Although the percentage of persons in poverty in general had dropped from 15 percent in 2000 to 10.1 percent in 2007, one can see that poverty touches a large proportion of the Canadian population at one time or another in their **lifespan.** Between 2002 and 2007, 20 percent of Canadians experienced at least one year of low income and 8 percent at least three years (Food Banks Canada, 2009). For instance, 27.8 percent of all children below age 13 had been poor at least once. In addition, nearly 10 percent of children had experienced persistent poverty between 2002 and 2007 (HRSD Canada, 2009).

Especially at high risk for poverty are children who live in mother-headed families, who are Aboriginal, or belong to recently immigrated families. In 2007, well over 40 percent of children in mother-headed families were poor compared with only 11 percent among children living in a couple family (Statistics Canada, 2009j). In Toronto, by some calculations, fully 70 percent of one-parent families are poor (FSAT, 2004). To these statistics, one must add at least another 10 to 15 percent of families and children who hover precariously above the threshold. These vulnerable families constitute the **near poor** (Morissette, 2002). Any crisis can send them tumbling below the poverty level—crises such as a dental emergency, the need for prescription medicine, the birth of an additional child, or the loss of even one of the many part-time jobs these families may hold. At least one third of all families have no liquid assets and cannot survive even a modest spell of unemployment (Ratcliffe and Vinopal, 2009).

Another aspect of poverty is its **depth**—that is, how deep down below the poverty line families are. For instance, in 1999, half of all one-parent families with one child who were poor had incomes of $10,000 or less—this is called deep poverty (United Way, 2001). The profile is similar for recent years. In Toronto, more than $15,000 would be needed on average to lift poor families with children out of poverty (FSAT, 2004). As a result, most disadvantaged families cannot afford some of the basics of life, such as food. As well, fewer low-income families can afford certain expenditures that provide both social, cultural as well as material capital for families—as

TABLE 4.3

Percentages of Household Purchasing Certain Goods and Services by Income Level, 2005

Goods & Services	Income Levels		
	Poorest Fifth	Middle Fifth	Richest Fifth
Children's summer camps	1	6	16
Own vacation homes	2	7	18
Dental insurance plan	2	8	11
Attend live sports events	6	17	34
Accident & disability insurance	4	13	21
Buy sports & athletic equipment	11	36	58
Air travel	9	23	46
Books & other reading material	25	52	75

Source: Adapted with permission from R. Sauvé. table commissioned by R. Sauvé, 2008, from Statistics Canada's Survey of Household Spending.

indicated in Table 4.3. This table shows the differences in lifestyle between the well-to-do and the poor.

SOURCES OF FAMILY POVERTY

Why are there so many disadvantaged families amidst affluence? What are the causes of families' poverty? At the risk of oversimplifying what is a highly complex issue, the sources of poverty fall into three categories: the systemic, or structural, sources at the societal level. Related to these are causes that are rooted in the historic treatment of some groups, or sociohistoric sources, and, finally, the personal ones. Structural and sociohistoric refer to overall social conditions, whereas personal refers to particular status situations rather than attributes and behaviours of the poor. The personal sources are generally fostered by the large-scale socioeconomic or structural causes that generate both the personal sources of poverty and poverty itself. If the economic, historical, and social causes of poverty were eliminated, the personal sources, while not vanishing entirely, would be radically reduced.

Structural Sources of Poverty

In Canada and the U.S., poverty is the result of an unequal distribution of resources among families rather than an overall lack of riches (Ambert, 1998). As we have seen, the gap between rich and poor families has widened in the past two decades (Frenette et al., 2007). The following structural aspects of the organization of our society probably constitute the major causes of family poverty:

- the loss of employment due to the restructuring of the labour market, such as companies relocating jobs "offshore"—that is, to other countries where salaries are extremely low

- the lack of creation of green industries that would open employment opportunities to replace the loss of manufacturing jobs
- low-paying and part-time jobs, especially among women and minority groups, and the lack of a subsidy for minimum wages
- the timidity of our governments (federal, provincial, and municipal) that fail to improve infrastructures that would create jobs
- the greed of some unions in terms of wages and overtime for the "haves" that prevents institutions and companies from hiring additional persons or helping the "have-nots"
- pay inequity by gender (women are paid less than men for comparable job qualifications) and overall inequality
- "welfare for the rich" whereby very high earners pay taxes that are relatively low in comparison to those of more equitable countries such as Sweden and Denmark where poverty is rare
- insufficient social benefits for families

Sociohistorical Sources of Poverty

The sociohistorical sources of poverty are those that have occurred during the history of Canada and have resulted in such inequities that their effects are still felt today. The most salient and painful ones pertain to the centuries of cruel attempts at cultural genocide of Aboriginals, deprivation of territories, and nefarious effects of contacts with Europeans—as described in Chapter 2. Indeed, currently, poverty is probably the most evident social problem facing many Aboriginal families who tend to have the lowest living standard of any other group in the country (CCPA, 2009). Using the same index used by the United Nations Development Programme, which consistently ranks Canada as one of the best places to live in the world, Beavon and Cooke (2003) found that persons designated as "status Indian" and living on reserves would be ranked seventy-ninth.

Canadian Aboriginal peoples suffer from high unemployment rates, substandard housing conditions, and inadequate health care and educational services, which accounts for their having the lowest education, income, and health levels in the country (Frideres, 2000). Although Aboriginals constitute only 3.8 to 5 percent of the population, they constituted 12 percent of those assisted by food banks in 2008 and 2009 (Food Banks Canada, 2009:7). Poverty has also affected their family life, as they have significantly higher infant mortality rates and substantially lower life expectancies (Harrison and Friesen, 2004). Because of poverty, lack of employment opportunities, and generations of family breakdown caused by the residential school system, the suicide rate among Aboriginal peoples is, on average, between two to seven times that of the national population. Other serious problems include alcoholism, substance abuse (even among children), suicide, and delinquency, including more recently the formation of criminal gangs in some communities. Aboriginal men and women constitute a disproportionate share of prison inmates (Statistics Canada, 2005b). And, as we see in Chapter 13, domestic violence is widespread.

Such deeply ingrained problems cannot be remedied in five years as their solution would involve a thoughtful and open-minded reconsideration of the reserve system and of the role of some chiefs and bands in the finances of their group. Other solutions might include programs of monetary incentives for youths and their mothers based on school attendance, delayed childbearing (programs that are being tested in a few large Canadian and American cities), and of the creation of employment opportunities near reserves and Native villages. The greater willingness on the part of some urban Aboriginal practitioners to take advantage of services offered by non-Aboriginal practitioners, such as family support and child psychology, provided that the latter are culturally sensitive, would also be helpful.

Sociopersonal Sources of Poverty

The sociopersonal sources of family poverty are generally the ones favoured for discussion by the public, the media, and policy-makers. These sources imply that individuals who bear certain demographic characteristics, such as single mothers, are responsible for their poverty and for all the consequences flowing from it. An emphasis on the strictly personal aspect of these sources of poverty too often precludes a consideration of the larger socioeconomic causes of poverty and conveniently excuses the lack of political change to remedy the situation. This is why, in decades of budgetary restraint, welfare programs for mothers with dependent children are popular targets of suspicion and cuts: Welfare policies are gendered (Vosko, 2002). It is also why cuts are made to programs geared to help new arrivals better integrate themselves into a difficult labour market.

Divorce and Break-Ups as Risks for Poverty

Divorce is a direct source of poverty or near poverty for women and children, although a sizeable proportion of divorces are themselves caused by economic hardship (Amato and Previti, 2004; Frenette and Picot, 2003:15). Indeed, families under economic pressure are more likely to experience negative interactions, spousal conflict, domestic violence, and child abuse. Any of these problems can lead to divorce and break-ups, as more extensively discussed in Chapter 12. Once separation takes place, the mother and child unit becomes even poorer. Rotermann (2007a) found that, within two years after a separation/divorce, 43 percent of women had experienced a decrease in

The working poor include families in which both parents are employed in low-paying jobs. One parent may even hold two jobs. These families are hovering precariously, just one slippery step above the poverty level. This situation is even worse in the U.S., where these families rarely have health insurance.

household income as had 15 percent of men. In contrast, 29 percent of men and only 9 percent of women had experienced an increase. After divorce, women are more likely to go on welfare (Frenette and Picot, 2003). Although the sex of the person is not specified, 4 percent of all bankruptcies are the result of a marriage breakdown (Sauvé, 2009a).

For those women who were comfortably middle class before divorce and who fall into poverty after, this situation usually is transitory. They are generally able to lift themselves out of poverty, after several months to a few years, through employment, their parents' help, fathers' child support, and especially remarriage and cohabitation.

Births to Single Women and Father Absence as Risks for Poverty

Lone parenting more often than not stems from poverty and leads to poverty (Singh et al., 2001; Thomas and Sawhill, 2005). As we descend the socioeconomic ladder, the number of births to unmarried women increases noticeably—and the same is evident for the males who coproduce these children (Guzzo and Furstenberg, 2007a; Manlove et al., 2008a). Following Wilson's (1987) example, American demographers, such as South (1996), have studied the impact of men's and women's wages on marriage formation for all races. They found that both men's and women's marriage rates rise with each additional thousand dollars that men earn. Poverty is not the only source of nonmarital births because most single women and men who are poor do not have children. However, disadvantaged adolescents who hold low educational and vocational expectations are more likely to engage in risky behaviours leading to pregnancy (Clark et al., 2006). They may also feel that they have little to lose by engaging in unprotected sex that might lead to pregnancy. This attitude is well expressed by a student:

> "I am 28 and had my son at 16. At the time I was fed up with school and my mother and I didn't care to work and I thought the baby would be fun to have. I didn't go out of my way to have one but I certainly took no precautions. . . . It didn't end up being the rose garden I had wanted. . . . I was on welfare for many years . . . and bored. I went back to school at 23 and it has been a struggle."

In contrast, whether they are poor or not, youths who are pursuing their education and who maintain reasonable expectations of finding a decent job after college or postsecondary training, or who already have achieved these goals, are generally motivated to avoid pregnancy.

In the short term, lone motherhood makes relatively little economic difference in the life of an already impoverished teenager or young woman. But once an already disadvantaged young woman has a child, her maternity entrenches her poverty or makes it last longer, and her chances of marrying decrease. Such mothers also spend more time on welfare than divorced mothers do (Cooke, 2009). Another study has found that, once in poverty, a mother who remains single can expect to spend 5.1 to 6.9 years in that state because she is not likely to receive much support from an equally impoverished father. Morissette and Zhang (2001) report that lone parents have a 16 percent probability of being poor for at least four years, compared with 3.5 percent for couples with children. And, even more recently, through the Canadian

INTERVIEWING IS EASIER SAID THAN DONE

Kathryn Edin and Laura Lein (1997) wanted to resolve the discrepancy reported in large surveys showing that single mothers' expenditures are higher than their incomes. They interviewed 214 welfare-reliant and 165 wage-reliant, low-income mothers several times in order to track their unaccounted sources of income as well as types of expenditures. During the first meeting, the researchers asked mothers to detail all their monthly expenses. Edin and Lein point out that it was crucial to ask about expenses first and sources of income later. In their very first trial interviews, respondents who had talked about their incomes first had then adjusted their expenses downward to fit the reported income. Once the mothers had claimed that they spent nothing on clothes, for instance, it was impossible to make them retract, even if the interviewer saw the clothes on them! Thus, the order in which the questions are presented is extremely important in surveys.

Edin and Lein also emphasized that interviewers must listen carefully to the meanings that respondents attach to questions and words. For instance, the researchers learned that, when responding to large multiple-choice survey questions, most of the single mothers acknowledged receiving "child support" only when it was collected by the state. As a result, Edin and Lein found that the total value of money or gifts the women actually received from their children's fathers far exceeded what they reported in official surveys under the rubric of child support.

National Longitudinal Survey of Children and Youth, it has been shown that, of those children who were two to five years of age and in poverty in 1994–95, 43 percent were still in a low income in 2002–03 (Statistics Canada, 2005a).

In the future, it may become more difficult for such young women and their children to exit poverty, both because of the educational requirements of the new economy and lower social assistance payments (Hofferth et al., 2001). As well, when the putative fathers are equally disadvantaged educationally, there is little chance that they will contribute to support the children. There are also indications that, in dangerous neighbourhoods, teen mothers' own mothers are frustrated by the uncooperative and menacing peer culture that often engulfs their daughters and sons; consequently, they may not be as supportive as previous generations had been (McDonald and Armstrong, 2001).

This said, older single mothers have lower rates of poverty than in the past because more of them have post-secondary education than in previous decades (Myles and Picot, 2006). For their part, Menaghan and Parcel (1995) find that single mothers who are employed in well-paid occupations provide their children with a home environment equivalent to that available in similar two-parent families. Unfortunately, among the never-married, these mothers are the exception, unless they had their first child later in life, were able to accumulate both social and financial resources, or had a supportive coprogenitor.

For many impoverished young women, having a baby alone may be the only form of social status they can look forward to. Motherhood provides an important source of satisfaction and self-esteem when economic opportunities do not exist.

Young fathers' own social standing among peers may also benefit and they frequently have other babies from different "baby mothers" (Guzzo and Furstenberg, 2007a). From the individual point of view of the young mother, it makes short-term sense to have a child alone because there are relatively few males who could marry her and help support her child, particularly if she is black (see Chapter 7).

On the other side of the coin, it makes no sense for the child who is born in poverty or who becomes at higher risk of poverty. Even when his or her mother exits poverty two to six years later, these few years represent a sizeable proportion of a young child's life (Morissette and Zhang, 2001)—and early poverty is most detrimental to later educational and occupational outcomes. Indeed, whether children in single-mother families have divorced or never-married parents, two salient facts emerge. First, these children are much more likely to be poor than those who live with both parents (Bogenschneider and Corbett, 2010). Second, having a single mother who is a member of an ethnic minority places children at an extraordinary risk for poverty because of discrimination (Statistics Canada, 2009j). As well, single mothers, even when not poor, are less likely to accumulate net assets (Morissette, 2002). Thus, one can be concerned that the near future will result in a larger proportion of poor elderly women who have been single mothers most of their lives and have never received any support from the men who coproduced their children.

Difficulties Encountered by Recent Immigrants as Risks for Poverty

In general, recent immigrant families have more difficulties making ends meet than older immigrants and Canada-born persons of the same educational level or even with a higher education. There are four general reasons for this. First and foremost at the societal level is the fact that recent immigrants arrive in an economy that has changed drastically in terms of labour market opportunities, as explained in the outset of this chapter. Second, and consequently, recent immigrants have higher unemployment rates. For instance, in 2006, recent immigrants with a B.A. had an **unemployment** rate of 11.4 percent, thus much greater than that of Canadian-born persons with a B.A. (Statistics Canada, 2007a). Recent immigrant women have a higher unemployment rate at 13 percent. As well, persons aged 15 to 24 had even greater rates at 17 percent compared with 11 percent among Canadian-born youth.

The third source of economic liability for recent immigrants resides in **language difficulties** (and also explains in part the first source above). Immigrants who speak neither English nor French or who use neither in their work earn less and the former have higher unemployment or are employed in occupations that bring lower incomes (Boyd and Cao, 2009). As indicated by Statistics Canada (2009k), such persons are less able "to convert their educational qualifications into higher earnings." This may also be reinforced by the fact that recent immigrants who arrive here as adults and settle in **ethnic enclaves** earn lower incomes than warranted by their educational levels (Warman, 2007).

Finally, although more educated on average than the remainder of the Canadian population (because of Immigration Canada's point system), immigrants who have earned their degrees abroad before arriving have higher unemployment and lower salaries than comparable Canadians (Fong and Cao, 2009). In other words, the accreditation system disadvantages more recent immigrants, especially those from non-European countries (Ferrer and Riddell, 2008). All of these factors combined lead to lower income and greater difficulties in adjustment for the entire family.

> *For instance, recently I met a 40-year-old concierge working in a high rise condo, earning about $13/hour, who was supporting his wife and sons while his wife was doing her accreditation years to return to the profession she had had in a Middle Eastern country: a physician. This man then left his low-paying job because it was his turn to be supported while he studied for his accreditation: He also had been a physician in his country. In two other buildings, an engineer from an African country is employed as a superintendent, and a former university professor from a South Asian country does the paperwork and answers the phone for a management company.*

It should be added that temporary visa workers, that is, foreign nationals, who constitute 1 percent of all full-time workers in Canada, earn less than other immigrants for the same work (Thomas, 2010). They are not generally included in poverty studies. They are often exploited and easily lose their jobs. The loss of employment, for which they obtained their visa, then, forces them to become "illegals" and often become even more exploited. For instance, they get paid less or, at times, not at all, as they have no legal recourse.

CONSEQUENCES OF FAMILY POVERTY

Overall, poverty creates stressors which then increase distress among mothers and fathers (Orpana et al., 2009). Poverty also contributes to isolating people socially; for instance, low-income Canadians are much less likely to participate in community activities or to say that they trust other people than are other Canadians (Statistics Canada, 2004l). Put differently, poverty deprives families of social capital. It also deprives them of food. Food Banks Canada (2009) reports that in March 2009 alone, 794,738 Canadian residents walked into a food bank seeking help, which is an increase of 18 percent over March 2008—a result of the recession. The following provinces had the largest increases: Alberta saw a 61 percent increase; Nova Scotia a 20 percent one; Ontario, 19 percent; Manitoba, 18 percent, British Columbia, 15 percent and New Brunswick a 14 percent increase. In Alberta and, Saskatchewan, over 40 percent of those who were assisted were children.

Overall, Food Banks Canada (2009:13) estimates that at least 2.7 million persons will experience what they politely call "household food insecurity" during the year. This is nearly 9 percent of the population. In all provinces, between 32 percent (in Alberta) and 71 percent (in Newfoundland and Labrador) of those who approach food banks are on social assistance, indicating that government assistance is insufficient. It may not be surprising, therefore, that low income is related both to poorer health and a lower life expectancy (McIntosh et al., 2009). But poverty affects mothers, fathers, and children differently, in part because of gender roles (mothers versus fathers) and in part because of life stage: Children are affected early in their life course, whereas fathers and mothers are affected as adults, although many had also been poor as children.

For Mothers

Impoverished mothers who live in neighbourhoods with a high concentration of poverty, especially when criminality is added, are particularly vulnerable to failure as mothers because the circumstances under which they raise their children are simply unfair. Their ability to supervise their children is often undermined by the conditions imposed by poverty. In view of this situation, it is not the elevated rates of negative child outcomes that are surprising, but the fact that they are not higher. That so many of these mothers' children grow up to be decent citizens is a tribute both to the resilience of some children and to their mothers' extraordinary diligence and devotion.

These mothers, who are both poor and live in low-income areas, are deprived of the resources that a middle-class woman takes for granted in raising her children. In addition, they often lack credibility in their children's eyes, due to their poverty and, in some cases, due to their never-married status, as described recently by the following student:

> "*What made me the most unhappy between ages 10 and 14 is the conscious struggle I went through because of my mom* [who had her first child nonmaritally at age 18]. *I loved her but didn't pay her any respect and obedience and my brother didn't* [either]. *We had big mouths and we knew that we could get away with murder because what could she do all alone with us? . . . I got pregnant twice and had two abortions before I turned 17. I felt guilty about my mom but I wanted to have fun. . . . My brother had babies . . . and did time. . . . At 18 I finally got my act together probably because my mom was a good woman, she worked so hard and she wanted me to get an education. I wanted the respect she never got and I am no unwed mother, I tell you.*"

As Cook and Fine (1995:132) note, low-income mothers have few childrearing options and cannot afford to make errors. In many neighbourhoods, they have to be more strict and vigilant because "errors" lead to delinquency, drug addiction and trafficking, early pregnancy, and even death. Therefore, success in socialization goals is seen in terms of "sheltering their children from the pitfalls of self-destruction, such as drugs, crime and cyclical government dependency" (Arnold, 1995:145). Loftier goals, such as the development of children's verbal and reading skills, are a luxury in such environments. The basic tasks of feeding, housing, and shielding their children, and especially their adolescents, from danger are at the forefront of these mothers' thoughts and energy. When Alisha, a student, was small, her mother emigrated from Jamaica to Baltimore, where Alisha and her two younger brothers joined her. Alisha was then 10 years old and was 13 when the family relocated to Toronto. In both cities, they lived in poor neighbourhoods. She recalls her life in the Baltimore "ghetto":

> "*In the morning, we were often late for school and I had to get my brothers ready because my mother had left a long time ago; she had to commute to her job. . . . After school, we'd go back home minding our own business and careful to stay away from the older boys as my mother had told us to do. We'd get something to eat and then watch TV and my mother would come home around 8:00. When it was dark in the winter months we used to be real afraid alone and sometimes Jamal would disobey and leave the apartment and get into trouble*

with the boys down the hall. I was so scared that my mother would blame me. . . . During weekends my mother would take us grocery shopping and then we'd stay home. We didn't have friends because my mother was afraid that we'd run with the wrong crowd. . . . We were not doing well at school and when we got to Toronto we were put back two years. I was so lonely in Baltimore . . . my mother was no fun to be with because she was real strict with us because she was afraid we'd go wrong or we'd get killed."

As they become single parents, many women and their coprogenitors perpetuate and even create poverty. But this occurs more in countries that have very limited profamily and prochild social policies. For example, in countries such as Sweden, single mothers' poverty rates are not much higher than that of married mothers. Why? First, Sweden and other European countries provide adequate subsidies and child care arrangements that allow mothers to be employed, whatever their marital status. A second reason why the poverty rate in single-mother families is not much higher in some countries is that most first-time single mothers are older: Rates of single teen childbearing are very low, thus further reducing the potential for poverty.

For Fathers

The effects of poverty on men as fathers have been less extensively studied than those on mothers, in great part because fathers are often absent in indigent families. Fathers are affected by poverty differently, depending on the place they occupy in their families of procreation. In this respect, at least four categories of economically disadvantaged fathers exist:

1. fathers who are part of two-parent families and are gainfully employed (their salaries are low and they may have to combine two jobs, or their work is seasonal)
2. unemployed fathers in two-parent families
3. separated or divorced fathers with minimal income or who are unemployed
4. men who have fathered children and do not reside with them, who are either unemployed or earn inadequate wages

The first two categories of fathers are the most negatively affected by poverty, particularly when they are unemployed. They experience a great deal of pressure, even if only from within themselves, to support their family more adequately. They may be working two jobs, in itself a source of stress and a potential for ill health. Society defines fathers as the chief breadwinners and this assigned role can be a heavy psychological burden on the shoulders of a disadvantaged man. His self-esteem may be badly bruised; he may feel that he has little control over his life or that he is failing his children and wife. In stark contrast, a man who earns a decent income is proud of his ability to support his family and his psychological health is positively affected (Schindler, 2010).

For a married man, unemployment becomes a source of friction, general tension, and irritability between husbands and wives. Men feel diminished, experience psychological duress due to their unacceptable status and their humiliating and fruitless job searches, and may react more abrasively and withdraw emotionally from their wives or partners. These behaviours may undermine the spousal relationship and contribute to conjugal instability. Wives and partners may become resentful of their lack of financial resources and, when employed, may complain that they are shouldering the entire family's economic burden.

For their part, divorced or separated fathers who are too poor to contribute child support may distance themselves from their children. Their ex-wives may also prevent these men from seeing their children, either because they fail to support them or they are a "bad example" or a "bad influence." They are "deadbeat dads." Others were abusive before. As for those men who have fathered children nonmaritally, do not live with them, and are too poor to support them (which may well be a majority of adolescent mothers' boyfriends), very little is known as to how poverty affects them as fathers.

For Children

Child poverty denies human beings the chance of developing adequately and securely from the very beginning of their lives. However, not all children are affected in the same way and, in fact, despite the high risk factor that it creates, most poor families are resilient. Thus, how children are affected is contingent upon a **combination of factors**, including characteristics of the child, the family, the environment, and especially the length and timing of poverty (Conger et al., 2010; Schnittker, 2008).

Mounting evidence shows that, in terms of IQ development and school achievement, the most devastating impact occurs when children begin life in poverty (Pagani et al., 1997). Thus, **early child poverty** is the most detrimental in terms of a child's future adult status in society (Duncan, 2010). This is in great part because homes that are disadvantaged are more likely to be less stimulating cognitively (Eamon, 2002). **Persistent** poverty, particularly when it begins early, is also related to negative life course outcomes (Wagmiller et al., 2006). Young children who live in persistent economic hardship are more at risk of developing more problems, particularly at the cognitive level, than those whose poverty is temporary (NICHD, 2005). In turn, the latter have more problems than children who have never experienced disadvantage. Early disadvantage tends to be related to higher levels of antisocial behaviour when a child is very small and this level remains higher when they are 12 to 13 years old; this behaviour decreases but remains higher on average than that of children who were never poor (Strohschein, 2005).

Children who experience poverty at any point are three times more likely to be poor as adults than children who have never been disadvantaged, and are also more likely to earn less—even when the economy is flourishing. That is, the consequences of child poverty and its attendant misfortunes may far outlast the initial period of poverty and may be lifelong. The **depth of poverty** also exerts a dramatic effect on children's abilities and performance: Children in families with an income that is 50 percent below the poverty level are at a great disadvantage. Overall, children born into indigence or who are poor for many of their formative years are denied the opportunity to actualize their abilities, to receive a good education, often to live in a safe neighbourhood, and even to be fed adequately (McIntyre et al., 2002). In turn, these cumulative disadvantages can later produce deficits in employment and health well into adulthood: Malnutrition and stress caused by poverty imperil health and well-being in midlife and old age, and ultimately reduce life expectancy (Evans, 2004). Characteristics of the environment, such as a detrimental neighbourhood (high crime rate and proportion of poor families, pollution), quality of schools, presence of antisocial peers, as well as racial/ethnic segregation of disadvantaged minorities are also key factors and are discussed in the next chapter (see Evans, 2004).

Family characteristics such as family structure (one versus two parents), parental education and mental health, and functioning such as warmth and parental monitoring of child's activities, particularly during adolescence, are also key elements that mediate the effect of poverty on children. At their negative level (e.g., low maternal education and lack of parental supervision), all of these variables represent risk factors: The greater the number of risk factors accompanying poverty, the more negative the effect. At their positive level (e.g., maternal warmth, stimulating activities), these variables offer resilience against the potential negative effects of poverty (Kim-Cohen et al., 2004). As well, when disadvantaged mothers have to increase their work hours, children, particularly adolescent sons, may suffer negative consequences in terms of their school behaviours (Gennetian et al., 2008).

Child characteristics also have to be considered. Any problematic child characteristic, such as low birth weight, deficient cognitive abilities, or difficult temperament and hyperactivity can combine with poverty to produce additional negative effects for the child, both currently and in the future (Ambert, 1998). In contrast, a similarly frail child raised in an economically secure family generally has a more positive life course (McLoyd, 1998). As well, children with qualities such as a more outgoing temperament are less affected by deprivation (Kim-Cohen et al., 2004).

FAMILY RESEARCH 4.2

National Longitudinal Survey of Children and Youth (NLSCY)

This ongoing large-scale research program has already begun to give us a deeper knowledge of the role that poverty plays in a child's developing life. The NLSCY has been conducted by Statistics Canada and Human Resources Development Canada every two years since 1994/95. It follows a representative sample of thousands of children aged newborn to 11, in all provinces and territories, into adulthood. In each family, the person considered most knowledgeable about the child answers a set of questions designed to provide socioeconomic and general health information about himself or herself, the spouse or partners, and the child, including the child's health, general development, and social environment. When the children were 10 to 13, both parents and children provided information. At older ages, children answered questions themselves. Were the data for all these family members analyzed jointly, much information could be gathered on families rather than just on individuals.

The most visible and consistent deficit related to poverty is that disadvantaged children, on average, have lower IQs, academic skills, and school achievement, and have more behavioural problems than non-poor children (Willms, 2002b). On average, therefore, poor children repeat grades, drop out of school, and become unemployed or enter dead-end jobs more often than children who have never been poor. Thus, one can see why it is so important to prevent early childhood poverty, both for the short and long term. A recent longitudinal Canadian study illustrated how low income affected adolescents' chances of going to university, not so much because of the high tuition fees as generally believed. Rather, the reason rested in a peer group with little interest in schooling, lower academic performance in high school, lower marks, and lower parental expectations than is the case for higher-income youths (Statistics Canada, 2007b).

Disadvantaged children have more frequent accidents than other children because their surroundings are less safe and they are less well supervised; they are also less healthy and witness violence at home more often (Moss, 2004). As well, their mental health problems far outstrip those of other children (Carey, 2001). Disadvantaged children are more often identified by teachers than other children for behavioural problems. Even if one reduces this figure by half to account for possible teachers' prejudice against disadvantaged children or their parents (or against minority children or children in single-parent families), the difference remains substantial and is confirmed across the world.

As illustrated in the following student quote, disadvantaged children often stand out from others in a multitude of ways that are psychologically painful. For instance, some live in a housing project and may be ashamed of it. They may not want to let their peers know about their predicament and may not invite them home. Further, poor children are unlikely to have the pocket money, clothes, and cellphones that their schoolmates take for granted. They may be unable to participate in extracurricular activities with their peers, which can lead them to be ostracized and even steal or engage in other acts of criminality to compensate. All or any of these visible social stigmas are humiliating and painful to bear, although they may be less so in a school where a great proportion of the children are equally poor. In fact, low-income children in economically mixed schools are less popular than more affluent children (Pettit et al., 1996).

"What I recall as having been the most painful between the ages of 10 and 14 is that we were poor. At least that's when I realized that we were poor, until then I guess I had not noticed and I had had other problems on my mind [her father's drinking and violent outbursts]. *At that age kids can be cruel and they found out that I lived in a dump and even the other little scums as poor as me would pick on me to make themselves look superior. My mother was trying very hard to raise us well and always sent us to schools in the other neighbourhood. That's probably why nobody found out or made me notice* [that she was poor] *until that age. . . . There were so many days when we were hungry, what can I say, my father drank every bit of money we could get. . . . I am ashamed now to think that I dreaded it when parents had to meet the teachers because my mom looked so tired, so old, her clothes were so out of style. She was so so tired and so so sad and often so ill but she hung on for us. . . . What I recall as having been the happiest time since 15? It's when my mom and older brother told my father to leave*

and dumped all his stuff outside and she got a better job and my brother got off school for a year to help her. We moved to a better place, I mean not rich but better and things started picking up from there. We were still poor but we were on our way and didn't have to tiptoe around my father." [When this autobiography was written, the siblings were in university and doing well.]

CONCLUSIONS: THE COSTS OF FAMILY POVERTY

When all the consequences (both short term and long term) of family poverty are considered, it becomes obvious that it is much more economically advantageous for a society to invest in families and children to prevent child poverty—a topic to which we return in the last chapter of this book. Otherwise, society has to keep paying throughout the decades for poverty's multiple, recurring consequences. This means that subsequent generations will pay for the current societal neglect of poor children. They will pay in terms of remedial schooling, illness, mental hospitals, juvenile courts, prisons, drug rehabilitation programs, and, later on, unemployment and medical care in old age—to name only a few of the long-term economic costs on society of child poverty (Bogenschneider and Corbett, 2010). Not to omit here the fact that children, especially those of single mothers who are unsupported by their coprogenitors, too often repeat the parental pattern of poverty in their own adult lives (Scaramella et al., 2008).

Today, people live in a society and in an era in which the economy, broadly defined, is probably one of the most determining features of family life, along with gender, although people are rarely conscious of this effect as they go about their daily activities at home. The economy and its accompanying technology determine job and income availability, which, in turn, have an impact on family life and even family formation and structure. These same larger, structural forces contribute to poverty, which then creates a fertile ground upon which personal sources of poverty (such as divorce and single parenting) can grow. In turn, the personal sources of poverty reinforce the effect of the larger economic forces that cruelly bear down upon the poor. When detrimental neighbourhoods are added to this cauldron of forces, there is, on the one hand, a potent recipe for an enormous range of familial problems, and, on the other hand, an even wider range of familial resilience, survival, and success against all odds, but often at a price.

Summary

1. Economic and technological developments have contributed to the current profile of families. Manufacturing has become a less important source of good entry-level jobs for youths with only a high school education. The service sector has expanded to provide jobs that require high educational credentials, and yet others that pay little and are part-time. The latter are often held by women, particularly minority women. As a result of the changes in the economy, the gap between poor and rich families has widened.

2. Economic changes have had the following effects on families: They have resulted in an

increase in feminine employment and in two-income families, a continued domestic division of labour along gender lines, a reduction of familial as well as individual time, the rise of consumerism in family life, and, as seen in Chapter 10, the fact that young adults remain at home with their parents longer and delay marriage.

3. The dual-income family creates a second work shift for mothers. The main question asked concerning the effect of parental employment is gendered: Is maternal employment detrimental to children? Recent studies have found no such important detrimental effect. However, the possibility remains that when both parents work extremely long hours, children are deprived of adult attention and may not be adequately socialized.

4. The structural and sociohistorical sources of family poverty are reviewed, with special attention devoted to poverty among Aboriginals. The three main sociopersonal sources of family poverty discussed are divorce, the formation of families by single women with absent fathers, and difficulties encountered by recent immigrant families.

5. After divorce, many women's income plummets, and a good proportion become poor, as they have to support their children on a reduced budget. Families formed by single mothers are both a result and a source of poverty: A majority of the mothers and fathers are from poor families. However, a substantial proportion escape from poverty. Recent immigrants encounter more difficulties on the labour market than earlier cohorts. The reasons behind this are explained.

6. The consequences of poverty for mothers reside in the difficulties inherent to raising children within a very negative environment, particularly for those who live in high-risk neighbourhoods. Men have not been studied in terms of how poverty affects them as fathers. We know that their unemployment becomes a recurrent source of friction within the family and that divorced fathers who cannot afford to pay for child support often become alienated from their children.

7. The consequences of poverty for children are more numerous and more severe when they are poor during their early childhood, when they are poor for a long period, and when they live in an unsafe neighbourhood with a high ratio of delinquent peers. Poor children are particularly affected in the domain of cognitive development, school progress, and conduct problems.

8. It would be economically advantageous for society to eliminate child poverty. Poverty is related to familial problems, but it also highlights familial survival and success against all odds.

Analytical Questions

1. Given the structural economic forces discussed at the beginning of the chapter, what could the government do for the future of our country in these domains so that families are not further burdened?

2. Analyze the two-way relationship between poverty and the formation of families by single mothers.

3. Above all, what role do men play in this economic causality path?

4. Within the family itself, how can parents alleviate the negative effects of poverty on their children?

5. What other social policies would prevent family and child poverty?

Suggested Readings

Ambert, A.-M. 1998. *The web of poverty: Psychosocial perspectives.* New York: Haworth. This book focuses on the consequences of poverty for neighbourhoods, schools, families, mothers, and childrearing, as well as child and adolescent outcomes. It also contains a chapter on the reciprocal effects of poverty and genes.

Bradbury, B. (Ed.) 2000. *Canadian family history.* Toronto: Irwin Publishing. Sections of this book contain several articles on feminine employment and the gendered division of labour in the late 19th and 20th centuries.

Duncan, G. J., and Brooks-Gunn, J. (Eds.) 1997. *Consequences of growing up poor.* New York: Russell Sage Foundation. The various articles present state-of-the-art information on the consequences of child poverty.

Hochschild, A. 1989. *The second shift.* New York: Avon. The author documents the disproportionate amount of work that employed mothers do, their exhaustion, and, often, the strain that the father's not sharing in housework brings to the dual-income marriage.

Suggested Weblinks

Canadian Council on Social Development provides information on policy aspects related to various issues, including the economy.

www.ccsd.ca

National Council on Welfare is an advisory group to the government. Its site includes data, such as social assistance statistics.

www.ncwcnbes.net

Raising the Roof is an action website on homelessness.

www.raisingtheroof.org

Statistics Canada's website, particularly through The Daily, regularly provides information on the economy and families.

www.statcan.gc.ca

In the U.S., **The Urban Institute**'s website offers special sections related to the economy.

www.urban.org

The Annie E. Casey Foundation includes the Working Poor Families Project as well as Kids Count.

www.aecf.org

CHAPTER 5

Impacts of Neighbourhoods and Housing Conditions on Family Life

"We lived in three different places since my birth moving each time to a bigger better house. The first was a rented semi-detached that I lived in until I was 5, then we moved to a semi-detached we owned on a better street also downtown and then we moved to where we are now when I was 12 in our own house with three bathrooms and a big yard."

"My parents bought a three story semi-detached house downtown one year before I was born and we still live in the same house today. My family occupied only two rooms, a kitchen and a washroom. Every other room in the house was rented [to pay for the mortgage]. In four years, we started taking up more rooms for ourselves."

"I grew up on a farm that we still own. We could see the neighbours' farmhouses but we could not see the neighbours themselves. Except for the road turning into a near highway with more traffic coming through, nothing has changed much. Some neighbours have died and some farms have been sold but we know everyone even though we do not see them often. I like the feeling of community and I miss it here where I live during the school year. Everyone is in a rush and no one knows who lives where."

"My family has always lived in a two-bedroom apartment except that we have not lived in the same one all the time. I think we have lived in eight different ones. According to my mother we have moved because we were evicted once, we couldn't afford the rent. Then the other times we moved because the neighbours were either too noisy or too rough or too criminal. Now that we are older we are thinking of buying a townhouse just north of here [beginning of a middle-class suburb]."

Housing and neighbourhoods constitute a family's first immediate context. As the students' quotes well illustrate, families' economic conditions and lifestyles are expressed through their dwellings and surroundings. Families' daily lives—and, in turn, their children's opportunities, health, and behaviour—are affected by these surroundings. Although rarely encountered in family textbooks, the study of neighbourhood effects on families is a domain of sociological inquiry with a long tradition. This tradition has recently been renewed and has become particularly visible in studies by researchers for Statistics Canada and in sociologically oriented sections of child development publications. It is a field inspired by the Chicago School of Sociology (Park and Burgess, 1925) and by current concerns about the difficulties families encounter in American inner cities—problems that are replicated to some extent in many Canadian cities (Kohen et al., 2002a). In this chapter, the discussion is extended to an entire spectrum of families' housing conditions.

TYPES OF URBAN AND SUBURBAN AREAS AND FAMILY LIFE

During the past two decades, the largest urban areas in Canada have experienced three phenomena. First, a greater proportion of the population now lives beyond the boundaries of cities in successive rings of suburbs that combine to form metropolitan areas. Second, suburbs have evolved and many have become cities themselves. As well, cities' and suburbs' new housing is now growing vertically with condos, often high-rise, but also with compact townhouse developments.

Overall, about 25 percent of Canadians surveyed report having experienced problems with their neighbourhoods (Orpana et al., 2009). Although most Canadians, especially the affluent, find their neighbourhoods safe, the issue of security is ever present (Peters, 2002). Security essentially means being away from property crime, violence, and drugs. As a result, many families, especially in middle-class and affluent areas, now opt to enrol their children in supervised activities after school, rather than allow them free play time on the streets of their neighbourhoods. In the past, children had the potential of turning a set of streets into a community because they played outside and established links between families, as described by this student who grew up in the 1970s:

> "I also remember how much fun I used to have playing on our street. When my family moved into our house, the housing area was new and just starting to develop and many young families also moved into the area. The street was full of kids in the same age group, and we would get together and play games such as hide-and-seek, and almost everyone would play. There used to be something to do almost every night, especially in the summer. If it wasn't baseball, it was football or road hockey. As I now realize today, it was the kids of this age group which linked our street together, and as we got older we spent less and less time with each other."

Children's role as informal community organizers and links between families may have eroded (Torres, 2009). As well, as seen in Chapter 3, the advent of video games, the Internet, and cell phones, along with television, has changed children's patterns of play and social interactions. Generally, couples with children have more contact than others with their neighbours, and the level of contact is higher in areas that have detached homes. Provincially, families living in the Maritimes and Saskatchewan have the most interaction with neighbours, while Québécois have by far the least (Kremarik, 2000a). Perhaps contact can be explained by having lived in the same area for several years, as may be the case in the Maritimes, but it is difficult to explain the Quebec difference in this respect. However, Québécois are equally less likely than other Canadians to engage in community activities (Jones, 2000). They also feel less connected to their local community (Shields and Tremblay, 2005).

AFFLUENT NEIGHBOURHOODS

While there are many studies comparing families in low-income neighbourhoods with those in average or middle-class areas, very little information exists on family life itself in affluent or upscale neighbourhoods. As Marks (2000:613) points out, affluent families are part of **family diversity**, yet they are rarely studied. Rather, they tend to be positively stereotyped in view of their economic and social capital advantages or, yet, to be analyzed as the oppressing class.

In well-to-do areas, a majority of households have incomes well over the $125,000 level. These families hold assets in the form of real estate, stocks, bonds, and businesses. They own or manage a majority of the means of production in society. Their heads are heirs, investors, and top executives of large corporations (at the upper-upper class level). Others are bankers, successful stockbrokers, highly educated persons in the top echelons of the civil service, as well as owners of smaller private corporations (at the lower-upper class level). The neighbourhoods of the affluent are also home to scholars, physicians, lawyers, and entertainers at the upper-middle-class level. These families together account for about 15 percent of the population.

Many parents at that class level do not necessarily worship material possessions and do not particularly value such extrinsic rewards as fame, wealth, and big houses over interpersonal relations and community service. The values they pass on to their children do not centre on the acquisition of material possessions and they may, in fact, be concerned about giving too much to their children at the material level. These parents provide their children with as many educational and developmental opportunities as possible but do not push them to be competitive.

At the other extreme in this group of affluent families are parents who, above all, value social and material success; the pressure to work, acquire, and consume depletes their energies to the detriment of interpersonal relationships. These parents are over involved in high-paying jobs. As a result, they have very little time for their children and are minimally involved in their upbringing, so that the children feel isolated (Luthar and Becker, 2002). Further, they are teaching values that are materialistic and competitive. Children are put on a "treadmill" of acquisitiveness and they measure their sense of self by what they have. Because these well-to-do areas are more "private" and there is a greater distance between houses, children and parents are also less likely to exchange services with friends or to feel connected to a social community in their neighbourhood (Myers, 2000).

One can therefore hypothesize that the first group of adolescents whose parents are not disproportionately invested in materialistic and status-related rewards should have a higher level of social conformity, lower anxiety, and feel more connected to family and community than the other group of adolescents (Kasser, 2002). At the adult level, studies of physical and mental health show a positive correlation between neighbourhood income and well-being (Diener and Biswas-Diener, 2002). Nevertheless, one has to emphasize the fact that the rich are a heterogeneous group of families and that their family dynamics will be related to the lifestyle they adopt and the degree to which they emphasize values that are, or are not, purely materialistic and competitive.

The few studies that have appeared on families who live in affluent neighbourhoods are American and focused on young adolescents living in suburbs. As Luthar (2003) points out, we do not know if these results apply in all regions and to adolescents who live in affluent neighbourhoods within cities. Luthar and Becker (2002) have found that a higher proportion of these affluent suburban teens suffer from anxiety and depression, and use alcohol, marijuana, and other illicit drugs more than disadvantaged inner-city students do. They are also less supervised in their home, as young as age 10 to 12, perhaps because parents rely on the relative safety of their neighbourhoods (Luthar, 2003).Thus, a segment of relatively affluent adolescents spends their time in cars, at various "hot spots," or partying with drugs in otherwise empty homes, and even engages in gang activities leading to break-ins and thefts. Hence, one should not err in the direction of attaching an aura of superiority to a district simply on the basis of material affluence and lack of visible street criminality. An affluent neighbourhood is not automatically a "good" one in which to raise children. Obviously, family studies would benefit from an injection of research on affluent families, both in rural and urban Canadian neighbourhoods.

LOW-INCOME NEIGHBOURHOODS

An area is defined as low-income when at least one of every five households, or 20 percent, fall under the poverty level (Statistics Canada, 2004a). For instance, in 1999 in Toronto, the 12 neighbourhoods with the lowest incomes had poverty rates of 29 percent or higher (United Way, 2001). Obviously, not all disadvantaged persons live in a low-income area. However, these areas do not tend to be favoured by middle-class persons (Frenette et al., 2004). Indeed, advantaged persons seek to live in areas that meet their needs and standards (Boyle et al., 2007). Overall, low-income areas have a detrimental effect on family life and on individuals' opportunities, even when families are well functioning or are not poor (e.g., Xu et al., 2009). In Montreal, Toronto, and Vancouver, low-income families moving into a low-income neighbourhood tend to remain locked in for an average of five years (Statistics Canada, 2004a). Families that are started in these disadvantaged areas may remain in them even longer.

When Social Problems Are Added

Often, but not always, low-income areas suffer from visible cues indicating the breakdown of social order (Ross et al., 2001)—cues such littering, graffiti, loitering, harassment, crime, and even violence. As indicated in Family Research 5.1, residents perceive this situation. Generally, many of these neighbourhoods experience a *multiple* concentration of disadvantages, each feeding on the other: poverty, deteriorated housing, violent criminality, as well as drug trafficking, and single-parent households. The predominant factor related to high rates of violent crime in cities across Canada, as is the case in the U.S. and European countries, is low income, that is, when a high proportion of residents living in a neighbourhood are disadvantaged (Charron, 2009; Fitzgerald et al., 2004; Savoie, 2008).

Children who are exposed to violence in their neighbourhood are more likely to develop conduct problems later (McCabe et al., 2005) and their parents are more likely to feel depressed (Kim, 2010). These residents' health is poorer on average (Hou and Myles, 2004). Their life expectancy is five years lower for men and 1.6 years lower for women than in the highest-income areas (Wilkins et al., 2002). This deficit in life expectancy is especially salient among Aboriginals (Maxim et al., 2003). As well, violence in disadvantaged areas is related to early reproductive behaviour in both genders and lower rates of school completion (Harding, 2010). Neighbourhood disorder produces noxious results on residents' health (Hill et al., 2005).

Measuring Respondents' Perception of Problems in Their Neighbourhoods

Ross and Mirowsky (1999) designed a 15-item scale to measure respondents' perception of neighbourhood problems. Respondents are given statements and indicate the extent to which they agree with them. Examples are:

- Vandalism is common in my neighbourhood.
- There is too much drug use in my neighbourhood.
- There is a lot of crime in my neighbourhood.
- In my neighbourhood, people watch out for each other.
- People in my neighbourhood take good care of their houses and apartments.

For each question on this and similar surveys, respondents are given choices ranging from "totally agree" to "totally disagree."

Each response is scored so that computers can make calculations, just as in multiple-choice questions on a test. For instance, totally agree = 5, and totally disagree = 1, if the scale is a 5-point scale. Some scales range from 1 to 7 while others have choices from only 1 to 3. A larger range allows respondents to give answers that are closer to their feelings. With only three choices, respondents are very restricted in the choice of answers, and this may introduce a bias in the results—i.e., the results may not be as valid.

Sociologist Robert Sampson and colleagues (2002) suggests that social disorganization follows when a community is no longer able to maintain **social control** or to supervise youth peer groups. For instance, both in Montreal and Regina, neighbourhoods with a high proportion of youth and low income show higher crime rates (Savoie et al., 2006; Wallace et al., 2006). As well, the concentration of female-headed households not only means that children may be less well monitored when their sole parent is employed, but also that large numbers of unattached young males roam the district with few responsibilities and too much free time on their hands. A heavy concentration of out-of-school and unemployed young males generally precludes effective social control of their activities and those of male children who grow up imitating them. Toronto has a few such areas, which, unfortunately, make the news on practically a daily basis. "Mayhem's ground zero," hails the *Toronto Star* (Doolittle, 2009). Turf wars between rival gangs have resulted in successive murders in several cities.

These young males, neither responsive to their mothers' demands nor to their children's needs, are the most important element of community disorganization (see Luster and Oh, 2001). Furthermore, the absence of responsible adult males in households often leads to the perception of women and children as more accessible targets for theft and sexual assault. Many adolescents become easier recruits for delinquency, as they are less supervised. As seen later in Chapter 10, there is a correlation between low supervision and delinquency. This is illustrated in Figure 5.1 on the following page. (The purpose of Figure 5.1 is to allow the reader to visualize what correlations look like; a further definition appears in the Glossary.) In some areas of

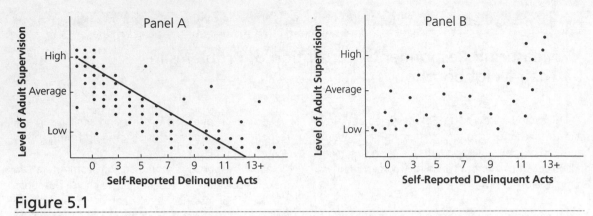

Figure 5.1

Correlation between Adult Supervision and Number of Delinquent Acts

Each dot represents an adolescent who is placed on the diagram depending on how many delinquent acts he or she reports and how well supervised he or she is by adults (parents, teachers, neighbours, etc.). When the dots fall in a well-ordered pattern, as in Panel A, this is an indication that a good correlation exists. The straighter the line, the higher the correlation. However, in Panel B, there is no correlation because there is no pattern: The dots are scattered, which means that there is no relationship between level of adult supervision and self-reported delinquent acts. Panel A describes reality (more or less), while Panel B is presented only to illustrate what a lack of correlation looks like.

Toronto, for instance, youth gangs kill a shocking number of other males of their own race—assured that the numerous eyewitnesses to their crimes will not report them to the police out of fear of retaliation: This is a reversed form of social control. The *Toronto Star*'s Moira Welsh (2006) captures well this situation:

> "*Some of their* [youth's] *mothers work 14-hour days and when their sons say they are at the Boys and Girls Club playing basketball, they believe them.*" *Later on in her text, an underground arms dealer admits being afraid of his young clients:* "*These kids aren't very smart and they're not afraid of getting caught. It's like they think they're in a movie. . . . Boys in their early teens get power by being so vicious that brutal men fear them.*"

As a result, there is a culture of silence that pervades entire neighbourhoods because no one wants to be caught "snitching." Violence continues and more mothers' children die. These same young men, by the time they are 21, often have one to three small children by different "baby mothers." There are indications, however, that a good school, even in a detrimental neighbourhood, can deflect some of these problems (Chapter 6).

Risk Factors for Children in Low-Income Areas

The wording of this subtitle is important: "Risk factors" mean that there is a higher probability that problems will arise for families in low-income areas than in other areas (Nathers and Rivers, 2006). But, as indicated in the title of two books, *Good Kids from Bad Neighbourhoods* (Elliott et al., 2006) and *City Survivors* (Power, 2007), it certainly does not imply that the majority of families are malfunctioning or yet "pathological." Nevertheless, parents in these areas are aware of these risks, for only 35 percent of Canadians with low income agree that their neighbourhood is an excellent place in which to raise their children. In contrast, a majority of middle-class and affluent families have a positive image of their neighbourhood in this respect (Peters, 2002).

But for those who are trapped in an area with a high rate of criminality, often violent, and especially those who live in a high-rise where gangs rule, the dangers are real, and parents can become helpless. In some cases, there may be selection processes that have taken place so that a certain number of less well functioning parents drift to these areas (Boyle et al., 2007). In such cases, children experience heightened risk factors: from their parents, their own predispositions, from the area, and from the interaction between all these variables.

The Risk of Inadequate Mainstream Socialization

Thus, one can see how children in neighbourhoods that are both poor and beset by social problems, especially when their parents are also poor, may be less adequately socialized; that is, many may not be taught the social skills needed in the workplace or in their personal lives, or general habits expected in mainstream society (Wilson, 1996). For instance, even when their families' socioeconomic status (SES) is taken into account, children as young as four and five years of age who live in poor neighbourhoods have lower verbal skills and more behavioural problems than children whose neighbours are more comfortable financially (Kohen et al., 2002a). A good-natured student from a very deprived family and neighbourhood describes the difficulties she encountered in Grade 1 when she went to a religious school out of her area. This touching quote well illustrates a young child's own resilience, maturity, and ability to plan strategies to overcome disadvantage:

> "Going to school for the first time was supposed to be a wonderful experience and I had so much looked forward to it: at last I was going to have something special that my four younger brothers and sisters didn't have. But things turned out differently than expected. . . . I was always late in the morning because my parents never got us up on time and we were too tired because we had watched TV late, even the babies. Then I would often fall asleep at my desk so that I missed out on a lot of things and most of the children seemed to know what to do and I didn't and I didn't know what to ask my parents to buy for me and they had other things on their minds anyways; for them my being at school was just one fewer child in the house but as far as the rest was concerned they were hopeless. Then I dressed differently than the other children or my clothes were dirty because we didn't have a washing machine in the apartment and my mother had to go to the laundromat. . . . I tried to fit in by copying the other children's behaviours and even watching what their parents did for them when they picked them up. Slowly by the end of grade 1 I had learned my way around school in terms of expected behaviour and I've wanted to be a teacher ever since."

Where large housing developments are located, and fear and mistrust reign, parents cannot establish links among themselves and collectively monitor the whereabouts and activities of one another's children (Chung and Steinberg, 2006; Ross et al., 2001). Thus, parents in such areas are deprived of adequate power of supervision over their children and even good parenting practices may not prevent child antisocial behaviours (Simons et al., 2002). Indeed, studies have shown that community adversity affects adolescents' mental health; in some cases, a favourable family environment cannot even compensate for the negative impact of the neighbourhood (Wickrama and Bryant, 2003). Steinberg and colleagues (1995) point out that parenting is "more than the individualistic process that contemporary society makes it out to be." It is a group phenomenon. **Collective efficacy** refers to those social ties within the community that facilitate the collective supervision and socialization of children concerning shared norms and behaviours (Odgers et al., 2009; Sampson et al., 1999). This also overlaps with the concept of the **effective** or **caring community** (Bould, 2004). In such a community, parents are involved in school activities, supervise their children's behaviour and associations, and get acquainted with other children's parents (Coleman and Hoffer, 1987:7).

Kupersmidt and colleagues (1995) compared children with familial vulnerabilities living in relatively low SES areas to similar children living in somewhat more affluent neighbourhoods. They found that the latter neighbourhoods served as a protective shield against the development of aggression in high-risk children. These areas do not tolerate street and school aggressiveness. Therefore, children are less likely to associate with difficult peers so that inadequate parental supervision is not as detrimental as it would be in a low-income area. Thus, it seems that a certain percentage (a **critical mass**) of low-income neighbours increases the risk for behavioural problems and subsequent school difficulties. In contrast, a critical mass of affluent neighbours raises a child's chances of completing high school. Research indicates that low-income neighbourhoods begin producing a negative effect on the development of a child's IQ by age three, above and beyond the family environment (Klebanov et al., 1998). Overall, there is a larger concentration of negative child outcomes in low-income areas (Mather and Rivers, 2006). Moves to higher-income areas seem to result in a lower crime incidence and improvements in health (Katz et al., 2001; Ludwig et al., 2001).

The Risk of Inadequate Supervision and Protection

It is apparent, then, that many poor children in unsafe areas are at risk of not being as adequately supervised as children in other neighbourhoods. They may have peers who belong to gangs that largely escape the supervision of responsible adults. Moreover, these neighbourhoods are also disproportionately populated by single-parent families. On average, children from such families are less well monitored (Fischer, 1993), particularly when mothers' educational level is low (Quane and Rankin, 1998). Single mothers are frequently beset by problems that worry them and that take away attention and time that could be devoted to their children. However, as emphasized earlier, supervision by parents in individual families may no longer be a sufficient element (Baumer and South, 2001). Rather, it is a collective level of supervision that is necessary (Sampson, 1997).

Finally, children and adolescents who live in areas of poverty are more at risk of being inadequately protected; many mothers feel powerless in controlling teen daughters whose deviant peers are at the centre of their lives (McDonald and Armstrong, 2001). Lack of collective supervision leaves children free to roam buildings and streets that are unsafe. It also allows them to be prey to negative opportunities that may be too difficult to resist, particularly because they are exposed to peers who may engage in deviant activities. These children are not sufficiently protected from bullying, sexual abuse, substance abuse, delinquency, and early pregnancy. In the following excerpt, a non-white student describes her childhood neighbourhood:

> *"My area had developed a reputation of being full of poor non-white crime-related people. . . . I lived in a large dirty very unsafe apartment with thirteen floors that had no security or superintendent. . . . I specifically remember one night when our family was home and we heard people yelling and scuffling at the front door and in the hallway, it was intense and loud. . . . I peeked out of the mail slot and saw two guys fighting, they looked about 18 but I knew they were much younger than that. As I continued to look I saw more guys were fighting, it had turned out to be a huge gang fight. . . . In the morning as I left to go to school . . . there was blood all over the walls and on the doors, pieces of clothing and knives were all over the floor. I wasn't as much horrified by the blood, it was the violence of such young people that had got to me. It was a sight and a feeling that I would never forget."*

This student later reminisces on the contrast between her old and new neighbourhoods:

> *"Well at this age the happiest moment I remember was when we moved away from the apartment and into our new house. . . . I remember finally being able to feel the freedom to play out in the streets whenever I wanted. In the summer we would stay outside until eleven o'clock and I wouldn't be scared. . . . That was something we wouldn't even think of doing at the apartment, so it was nice to know I could be safe."*

Well-Functioning Families in Low-Income Areas

The focus of research and social policies is on poor families and their problems; consequently, very little is known about the majority of families that succeed despite all the risks surrounding their lives. Poor neighbourhoods still contain a majority of families that are not exactly poor but may be forced to remain where they are because they do not have the means to move, because of discrimination or because they feel more at ease with people of their ethnic background. Therefore, poor areas contain both poor and non-poor families that function well.

High levels of parental monitoring are particularly protective for children in poor neighbourhoods that are beset by social problems (Pettit et al., 1999). These families try to protect their children from the negative influences that pervade their area. Their tasks are numerous—they have to keep their adolescents in school and ensure that they make good grades. This is difficult to achieve in areas with a high dropout rate and the presence of gangs whose lifestyle may appear exciting to a teenager from a good family, "where nothing ever happens." Parents also have to delay or prevent early sexual activity that could lead to premature parenting (Moore and Chase-Lansdale, 2001). Then, they have to shelter their adolescents from the attraction of drugs and criminal activities. They also have to orient their youths toward the job market, a difficult task when many neighbours are unemployed.

How do parents manage? Many succeed only by controlling their children's activities outside the home. They may take them to public libraries, to swimming pools and parks, or to lessons at church. Many children (and even adolescents) are kept at home after school hours and during weekends. Overprotection is necessary to weed out negative influences and physical dangers. Choosing schools away from the neighbourhood is also an adaptive response. Indeed, children and adolescents who are exposed to violence in their area have better mental health outcomes when they perceive receiving moral support from parents and siblings and when they are more attached to their school (Ozer, 2005). In other families, mothers sacrifice their own needs for companionship (see Burton and Jarrett, 2000). A student describes his reaction to his parents' efforts to keep him safe in a high-risk area:

> *"At the time I didn't appreciate having to be home early and not going in the schoolyard to play ball with the other guys. My parents were afraid that I would get into drugs, that I would get a girl pregnant and whatever. I don't know if any of this would have happened but I know that it did happen to most of my old buddies so now I can appreciate their devotion and the fact that they put up with the fuss I stirred up."*

Some of these parents help organize support groups, crime prevention patrols, and other constructive activities in their immediate neighbourhood. Furstenberg et al. (1994:243) appropriately write of the "supermotivation" that such parents, often single mothers, need in order to protect their children and to create opportunities for them. Overall, neighbourhoods constitute contexts for families and children. But their effect on child development and behaviours is not as important, generally, as are family resources and functioning. These have a greater impact on children's genetic predispositions than neighbourhoods. However, negative areas constitute incredible forces, largely via peer groups, which dilute familial resources and capital, hence effect. Deleterious areas amplify and reinforce vulnerabilities rather than create them directly (Dupéré et al., 2008; Kohen et al., 2008).

ETHNICITY AND RACE IN NEIGHBOURHOODS

Often, immigrant families settle in areas where they feel comfortable at first, which may mean neighbourhoods that "contain a relatively large number of people from the same ethnic background" (Murdie and Teixeira, 2003:137). According to Statistics Canada, the number of neighbourhoods that are largely populated by non-white groups has increased from a mere six in 1981 to 254 in 2001. A "*visible-minority neighbourhood*" is so defined by Statistics Canada *when more than 30 percent of the population is from a particular group other than white or Aboriginal* (Hou and Picot, 2004). Such an area is more likely to exhibit minority concentration, which is not the same as ethnic diversity (Hou and Wu, 2009).

More than 60 percent of these neighbourhoods are Chinese, primarily in Toronto and Vancouver. Nearly a third are South Asian, and only 13 percent are primarily black. Blacks are often less segregated from whites than Chinese are—which is a reversal of what takes place in the U.S. (Myles and Hou, 2004). Perhaps one reason why black families are less concentrated geographically is that the black population in Canada is more fragmented than are other non-white minority groups: It is fragmented by language, culture, and geographic origins (Owasu, 1999). For their part,

Aboriginal families are found in higher concentration in Winnipeg, Regina, and Saskatoon, where they tend to live in low-income neighbourhoods (Binda, 2001).

However, in Vancouver, Toronto, and Montreal (cities containing the majority of recent immigrants), black families are also more likely to live in neighbourhoods with a low SES. Hou and Milan (2003) have actually found that neighbourhoods that have larger proportions of blacks are characterized by lower SES, and this association has increased since 1986. This phenomenon has also been observed for Southeast Asians in Toronto and Vancouver. However, when black families' income rises and, especially when they buy a home, they generally exit minority neighbourhoods (Myles and Hou, 2004). In contrast, among the Chinese, home ownership leads to the formation of ethnic enclaves, as has been the case for Italians and Jews (Balakrishnan et al., 2005).

This situation was predicted by Logan et al. (2002), who foresaw that segregation *by choice* would become more prevalent among ethnic groups with high levels of capital. These enclaves are often in suburbs, especially around Vancouver and Toronto. However, these tendencies do not (yet) result in racial segregation as it exists in the U.S., for instance; rather, what we have is segregation by income first (Balakrishnan et al., 2005). The lower incidence of residential segregation of blacks than that of Chinese may be one of the reasons why blacks have high rates of interracial unions compared with Chinese Canadians (Milan and Hamm, 2004).

HOMELESS FAMILIES

The number of homeless people, particularly families, has increased greatly, especially in the late 1990s following welfare cuts and increases in rents. Currently, in Toronto, each night, over 5,000 persons are homeless: About 90 percent sleep in 64 shelters (Chiu et al., 2009), and over 300 children are born to homeless women each year (Ogilvie, 2010).

The Sources of Homelessness

The homeless are the most destitute among the poor. A majority have either been poor all their lives or poised at the margin of poverty. However, this may not necessarily apply to the homeless who are recent immigrants as the latter may actually have fewer problems than others (Chiu et al., 2009). Families are homeless because of a lack of affordable housing. They can no longer pay rent and are evicted while others have left their homes because of domestic violence or family breakdown.

Among adolescents, running away is a contributing factor to homelessness, although many, particularly among immigrants, simply have no one (Chiu et al., 2009). Runaways generally have a conflictual relationship with their parents, although this does not unavoidably involve bad parenting (Shane, 1996:5). Many youths from foster care also run away. Neighbourhood victimization, school suspension, and delinquency are also precursors, particularly among females (Tyler and Bersani, 2008). Whatever the causality, homeless youths' mental health is more precarious (Taylor et al., 2004) and they experience more problems with their parents

(Wolfe et al., 1999) as well as far more drug use than at-home youth (Mallett et al., 2005). But compared with the other homeless, youths do not uniformly originate from the disadvantaged class, although a majority do. A student from an affluent and educated family describes her former street life after she was "kicked out" by parents who had, until then, tolerated all her drug- and sex-related activities:

> "*I went and stayed at various friends' houses. I continued this for some weeks, but I soon ran out of friends. When one lives nowhere, on the street, one loses common ground with one's old companions. They want to talk about things they've done or seen. You're more concerned with basics. A shower for the first time in days. Some socks. Perhaps eating or actually washing your clothes. Frankly, you turn into a bum. 'Hey, what's happening man? Like, can I have your clothes, shoes, underwear, food, money, cigarettes? Cool! Blankets! Like, I've been sleeping in this stairwell, you know. It's not so bad, ya don't get caught or nothin, ya just gotta get out before the mall opens in the morning. Ya got a smoke?' . . . I spent nine months as a street kid. My experiences were, for the most part, fun. I think this is partly because I knew that I could always go home. I still don't know why I kept it up for so long. . . . It's a complete sub-culture and many kids simply don't want to leave even if they do have somewhere to go.*"

In addition to poverty, mental illness, disabilities, and addictions contribute to continuing homelessness once it has begun (Chiu et al., 2009). In the case of youth, those with fewer behavioural problems when leaving home or who decrease their problems are more likely to feel closer to their parents (Milburn et al., 2005). Parents who try to protect their homeless young adults often experience high levels of stress as a result (Polgar and North, 2009). A great proportion of homeless adults have never married; most others are either separated or divorced. Most have no relatives or even friends who can take them in during hard times, possibly because their own families are equally poor or because they have lost touch with them. The magnitude of the personal problems many suffer from may have worn out their welcome with their families or depleted the support the homeless person could receive from them. It is also possible that many of their families are equally maladapted. At the very least, the personal problems of many of the homeless certainly prevent their reintegration into society at large.

Psychiatric problems as well as various addictions are endemic and contribute to social isolation. Moreover, the decades-old deinstitutionalization of people with mental illness, without the safety net of community care that had been promised by politicians, has exacerbated the problem: Too many families are unable to shelter and care for their relatives with mental illness. For many former patients of mental institutions, the streets become their only recourse. Domestic violence is also often a cause of homelessness for women and their children, and may serve to isolate them from at least a part of their family. In fact, homeless mothers often have a long history of victimization. Once homeless, a mother's mental health easily deteriorates. In other words, homelessness is a risk factor for emotional disorder and general ill health (Carey, 2004). Nevertheless, many mothers develop coping mechanisms in order to keep their young families together and reduce the effect of the daily stressors they encounter.

The Effects of Homelessness on Mothers and Children

Most children who are homeless live in shelters with their mothers. As many of these women have been abused and/or suffer from emotional problems, their children are doubly affected (Gewirtz et al., 2009). Once in shelters, mothers encounter many difficulties in fulfilling their parental role. For instance, they no longer have control over the daily routine of their family life, whether it is bedtime or other rituals. They may, however, receive practical help as well as recourse to mental health agencies. Mothers often report a sense of becoming closer to their children while in the shelter (Lindsey, 1998). A woman student on welfare describes her experience:

> *"The most painful event in my life occurred two years ago after my husband left me with my two preschoolers. I became very depressed, didn't do much of anything and ended up evicted. I had no family here and we ended up in a shelter. I got even more depressed, was briefly hospitalized, my children were in foster care, and back into the shelter where I finally bounced back or else I was going to lose the children. A social worker helped me find a job and daycare and then a small apartment. But it had been a nightmare: we couldn't sleep, the children were totally out of it and went berserk, it was awful."*

In order to separate the effects of homelessness from those of poverty, studies have compared homeless children in shelters to disadvantaged children who live in their own home (e.g., Schteingart et al., 1995). The two consistent disadvantages of homelessness reside in health and education. In terms of **health**, homeless children are ill more often than other poor children. Their incidence of respiratory infections is especially elevated as a result of crowded conditions and the sharing of inadequate sanitary facilities. One can also presume that noise, overcrowding, and parents' distress depress children's immune systems so that they easily catch viruses.

The second domain in which homeless children are at a particular disadvantage is **schooling**. Their disadvantage in this domain stems from a variety of interlocking causes: They change schools, are sick more frequently than other children, and have higher rates of absenteeism. The crowded conditions in which they live are not conducive to homework, and may even deprive them of sufficient sleep. Their parents may be too distressed or emotionally unbalanced to help and guide them. Older children may not want to go to school because they fear the ridicule of peers who, even though poor themselves, at least can claim a permanent address. Frequent school changes isolate homeless children socially, lead to disengagement from school, and even to falling in with a crowd of antisocial peers. Moreover, schools are unprepared to address these children's multiple problems as many of them have been in at least two different shelters.

RURAL AREAS AND FAMILY LIFE

The rural population (farm and nonfarm) is decreasing and accounted for 19.7 percent of the Canadian population in the 2006 census. The farm population itself included only 2.2 percent of all Canadians or just over 684,000—although these percentages are higher in the Prairies, particularly Manitoba where the population is 35 percent rural and 11.5 percent farm (Statistics Canada, 2008d). The lives of rural families have undergone substantial change in recent decades because of increased proximity to urban areas, technological development, and economic uncertainty. In some regions, particularly when rural life involves the seasonal fishing or lumber industries, young people migrate to larger cities, thus leaving many rural communities populated by seniors and middle-aged householders. This phenomenon is especially relevant to Newfoundland and Labrador, where fully 42 percent of the population is rural, largely coastal.

In other cases, rural areas grow into towns or suburbs and become populated by young families who have recently moved to a new housing subdivision: Fathers and mothers commute to work in the nearest city or even metropolitan area, sometimes an hour or more each way. These couples are generally willing to tolerate long commutes to remain in their towns where housing and land prices are lower and where they feel that it is easier to raise a family away from the hectic pace of the big cities. Rural areas offer families a better chance of being members of a true community. Indeed, in smaller rural communities over 50 percent of individuals know all their neighbours versus only 16 percent in cities (Statistics Canada, 2005c). Greater social cohesion may offer family members advantages from which urbanites do not benefit.

Of course, many rural residents make their living without relying on nearby cities. However, when rural family members lose their jobs, it is more difficult for them than for urbanites to find another occupation at reasonably close proximity. This stems in part from the fact that rural areas are less diversified at the economic level: They contain a higher proportion of blue-collar workers than do urban zones (Anisef et al., 2000). White-collar workers with more education tend to move out of rural areas so that this selective out-migration reduces the diversity of human resources available to all rural families. In areas with fewer than 5,000 persons, young people, especially women, leave home much earlier than other youth (Beaupré et al., 2008). There are fewer alternatives in rural areas, including health care and care of the elderly (Morris, 2004).

Farm Families

Farm families constitute a tiny minority of the total population, even though they feed the entire country and many other parts of the world as well. Farm productivity increased tremendously in the 20th century: In 1946, about 1.2 million Canadians worked on farms as a main job while only 346,205 did so in 2001, and even fewer in 2006, down to 327,055 (Statistics Canada, 2008c)—a 5.5 percent decrease in just five years. In 1931, one in every three Canadians lived on a farm; by 2006, only one out of every 46 did (Statistics Canada, 2008e). In some parts of Canada, especially near expanding suburbs that form a ring around large cities and metropolitan areas, farmland is rapidly disappearing. This creates a multiplicity of problems in terms of lack of preservation of the environment, availability of fresh produce, and general well-being, not to omit a cultural loss because farm families are part of our **diversity** (Josey, 2008).

Children growing up on farms are not only more involved in the family's economy, but when small, they also benefit from the lessons of the natural environment and helpful relationships with neighbouring families.

As well, the median age of farm operators has increased to 52 and 50, respectively, for men and women: 40.7 percent are 55 and older. The **aging** of the farm population is particularly evident in British Columbia where 13.5 percent of farm operators are over 65. Such numbers have deep implications for the well-being and care of senior couples and elderly widowed persons in rural areas, as they may not necessarily have adult children living in close proximity.

Farmers are far from being a homogeneous category as they vary in terms of their economic circumstances: Some are tenants, and others are migrant workers; some own small acreage and are struggling financially, and others are involved in large-scale agribusiness and ranching. Moreover, there are differences in the farming lifestyle, depending on the crops produced—from grain to cattle in the Prairies and the west, to fruit, vegetables, and wine-grapes in southern Ontario, to dairy products in Quebec and Newfoundland.

The level of technology utilized also determines the daily activities of farm families, from the Amish and Mennonites, who often do not have recourse to fuel- or electricity-propelled machinery, to others in which computers dictate levels of feed, fertilizers, and pesticides. Farm families also vary with respect to their degree of isolation. Many farms cluster along well-travelled rural roads, yet others are more remote and connect with neighbours in their area only via long drives, a ferry, the telephone, and for a few, the Internet and cellphone.

Kinship and Gender Roles

Farm families tend to be patrilineally oriented because property is generally acquired via a son's inheritance. In fact, his parents frequently live nearby. Consequently, although grandparents play a more salient role in rural families than in urban ones, paternal grandparents are particularly important (King et al., 2004). This is in contrast to the usual urban situation where maternal grandparents play a larger role. The trajectory of inheritance is a long one across the two generations and involves decades of shared familial work, which leads both to family cohesiveness and stress. This situation can become problematic when middle-aged parents begin to think about their wills. If they decide the inheritance should favour the son who is interested in farming, then the bulk or even the entirety of the estate has to go to him if he is to survive at all economically. Perhaps very little can be passed on to the other children—a situation that may create sibling conflict later on in life (Taylor and Norris, 2000).

Despite the hazards of farming, Swisher and colleagues (1998) found that marital and familial conflict was less frequently reported by farm men than non-farm men in Iowa. However, when conflict exists, it is particularly detrimental because farm families are units of production. Thus, conflict threatens the normal pattern of kinship interdependence. Non-farmers, in contrast, establish more obligations based on friendship and can escape, to some extent, from the negative impact of family conflict. The potential for conflict and the experience of stress is especially great for a daughter-in-law in multi-generation farm families. This is more so when she feels left out of decision making and perceives her relationship with either of her in-laws as deficient.

Farm machinery does not require as much physical strength to operate as before, thus many wives work in the fields and even prefer this lifestyle to staying home. However, wives are more likely to be fully involved on vegetable farms, on those that have a mixture of crops and livestock, and on organic farms than on those where mechanization is very heavy and intensive crop production exists—perhaps a matter of gender roles (Hall, 2007). Children raised on farms are initiated in the use of large machinery early in life. It is not uncommon for 12- to 15-year-old boys to drive combines alongside their fathers in the fields—even though they do not qualify for a driver's license.

The 1996 census enumerated nearly 67,000 farms that were operated jointly by a husband and a wife—or 24 percent of all farms in Canada (Silver, 2001). Farm couples devote more time to their livelihood than do other Canadians—as much as 108 hours a week on large dairy farms. Couples share their long hours, but husbands put far more time on farm work while wives do a much larger share of the housework. This division of labour, however, is more egalitarian on small than on large farms. As well, when young children are present, wives do somewhat fewer hours of farm work but much more housework than their husbands or than wives without young children (Silver, 2001).

Farm Families' Adaptation to Economic Crises

By 2006, 48 percent of farm operators held a second job. At the lowest farm income level, 60 percent did so (Statistics Canada, 2009m). In fact, more and more farmers have a job other than farming as their primary employment. In order to respond to economic and environmental challenges, others are diversifying into new crops, new products and livestock (llamas, for instance), and even on-farm processing of produce (Bessant, 2006). These entrepreneurs tend to be families that are more attached to their farm and where both spouses see their agricultural work as their main occupation and branching out may be a way of retaining family members in full-time farming (Barbieri et al., 2008).

Researchers have found that mothers who have to seek off-farm employment not only benefit their families financially but they also gain personal and occupational skills as well as make new social contacts. However, most miss their previous lifestyle and long to return to work alongside their husbands (Elder et al., 1994b). In some families, even adolescents increase their off-farm employment hours or leave school and take a job in order to help the family financially or to be self-supporting, thus minimizing family expenditures. In other families, both boys and girls increase their on-farm economic activities or work for relatives. Thus, children and adolescents living on farms are far more **familialized** than urban children. A student explains how her contribution to her family's economic survival as an adolescent had shaped her sense of self:

> *"Between the ages of 10 to 14 I recall being very happy because I really felt that I was important in my family. I helped my mother with cow milking before I went to school and we enjoyed each other's company. After school, I helped my father feeding the same cows and cleaning up. It was dirty work but it was meaningful because we all had to pitch in as we were afraid to lose the farm."*

Economic pressure, however, can lead parents to become more preoccupied with survival and less involved in parenting. When adolescents transgress, these parents are more likely to react harshly and with hostility. This situation occurs less frequently when the parents' relationship has remained warm and supportive (Simons et al., 1994b). In families that experience serious economic pressures, husbands often become more hostile toward their wives, and wives become more depressed. The quality of the marriages decline, both because of the wives' depressed moods and the husbands' increased hostility. Overall, these family dynamics in the face of economic hardship are similar to those of many poor urban families.

Vacation Areas

Many rural areas near lakes, rivers, oceans, or skiing facilities have been transformed into vacation spots for urbanites while still serving as a primary home for regular residents. Thus, cottages, condos, hobby farms, or other forms of rural property develop where city families can choose their lifestyle and replenish their relationships, as described by a student:

> *"I was especially happy there* [at the cottage] *because my family was always around, and there was a certain air of freedom that we could not find anywhere else. This is probably due to the fact that the cabin had no electricity or hot or cold running water. So essentially we were roughing it. We received water from a manual pump in the kitchen, and we got light from oil lamps and warmth from blankets and each other. We never knew or cared what time it was or what anyone else was doing, just as long as our little world was happy, and we only had guests on the rare occasion. It seemed like a different world because we were the only ones*

[in the area] *with no means of communication, such as telephone, radio, televi-*
sion, or close neighbours to rely on. . . . For instance, we counted on catching fish
at least three dinners of the week, so it became a matter of survival."

This quote is interesting from yet another perspective: It illustrates the lifestyle
contrasts that may exist between urban families on vacations and neighbouring rural
families. The former at times embrace a temporary frugal lifestyle, whereas the latter
often have to struggle to avoid it. In many areas, rural families make a living by
offering goods and services to these tourists and cottagers.

Ownership of a second residence in the countryside is generally related to a
higher income and some level of wealth. About 7 percent of Canadian households
own a vacation home. Of these, only 26 percent are owned by married families with
children. However, many other children have free access to such homes via their
grandparents or other relatives (Kremarik, 2002). Others rent cottages or condo
units. It would be interesting to study the organization of family time and dynamics
as families shift from urban residence to vacation home. This is yet another element
of family life for which no research exists.

FAMILIES' HOUSING CONDITIONS

Much has already been said in this chapter about families' housing conditions. But
the focus so far has been on the external conditions. In this section, we look at the
quality of the interiors in which families live. Not only are families affected by their
neighbourhood surroundings, but their functioning is also related to the size of the
lodging, the state of its maintenance, the personal space it allows, how close it is to
other buildings, and the level of noise.

The state of **maintenance** or deterioration of a dwelling can have an impact on
family atmosphere as well as on health. Old houses often contain asbestos or paint
laced with lead—hazards for young children that have been related to intellectual
and behavioural deficits. The houses and apartments in which low-income families
live may be poorly ventilated in the summer and inadequately heated in the winter,
and the plumbing may have so deteriorated that leaks frequently occur. Such situations occur mainly in rental housing and in poor neighbourhoods, thus further
adding to the diminished state of well-being of the disadvantaged. As well, in many
cities, dilapidated housing is one of the correlates of higher crime rates. In France, it
also correlates with higher feminine mortality—either because women in poor health
can only afford this type of housing or because of the general impact of this housing
and area on their health (Mejer and Robert-Bobée, 2003).

Overall, the burden of **housing costs** has increased since the 1970s. This burden
has become particularly difficult for renters, compared with homeowners: In 2001,
19 percent spent over one half of their income on rent compared with 6 percent of
owners who spent that much on their mortgages and condo fees (Statistics Canada,
2004c). This burden is particularly heavy for single-mother and minority families
with three or more children. Two-thirds of Canadians own their home; ownership is
most common in the Maritime and Prairie regions (about 75 percent), while Quebec

has the lowest rate at 58 percent (Lefebvre, 2003). Before the Second World War, ownership hovered around 45 percent. The Canadian rate of ownership is similar to that of the U.S., lower than that of Ireland and Spain, and higher than that of France and Germany.

Home ownership tends to be the rule among top-earning families, but what is of particular significance among the more affluent is that ownership occurs early on in family formation and remains stable thereafter. Young couples coming from high-income families are often helped by their parents. (This is referred to as the intergenerational transmission of wealth.) In contrast, home ownership occurs later in the family life cycle among other social groups, including the middle class. For instance, in 2006, 77 percent of higher-income persons aged 20 to 34 were homeowners; and, of those aged 55 to 64, 90 percent were homeowners. In contrast, among low-income persons, only 19 percent of young adults aged 20 to 34 owned a home and 55 percent of those aged 55 to 64 did (Hou, 2010).

Thus, at the higher-income levels, children grow up in homes that are owned by their parents, whereas children in other families reach this goal at a later age or never. What is important to recall here is that home ownership inequality has increased. In 1971, among young persons, 31 percent of those in lower incomes owned their homes compared with 38 percent among top earners—not a huge difference. But, by 2006, only 19 percent of low-income young persons were homeowners versus 77 percent of the same-age top earners (Hou, 2010). Thus, low-income persons are much less likely to be homeowners now than in 1971 while top earners are more likely to be so—reflecting the increasing gap between rich and poor discussed in Chapter 4.

The "Mansionization" of Housing

In addition, the **size** of the family home has been increasing steadily at a time when the number of persons living in the average household has decreased from 3.7 persons in 1971 to 3 in 2000 (Statistics Canada, 2002b). Between 1951 and 1996, homes passed from having 5.3 rooms to 6.1 rooms and even the most modest new homes now have two and even three bathrooms. Currently, among the well-to-do, particularly the new rich, the tendency is to build homes with over 5,000 square feet. This phenomenon is often referred to as the "mansionization" of housing; others call them "monster" homes or McMansions.

This tendency toward extremely large homes would make an interesting study: The space per capita is vast and family members may be scattered throughout the house with only minimal contact with one another. There is less sharing of familial space (Clark, 2002), a factor that may contribute to feelings of loneliness (Pappano, 2001). Researchers might focus on how families who live in large dwellings (where each member has his or her own separate suite, often on different floors) develop mechanisms that contribute to family cohesiveness and interaction as opposed to isolation and interpersonal distance. Such families may have more clearly delineated boundaries within their system than others: The parents on one side and each child separately on the other side. Currently, very little is known about how family space contributes to increasing or eroding intimacy as well as parents' ability to socialize their children.

Condos: The New Trend

Condominiums (or strata in B.C.) have existed for several decades in North America (and in Europe before this, with different names). But it is only in the late 1990s that this mode of housing really became more prevalent in Canada as a result of climbing prices of detached homes, immigration, and lack of available space in large cities. This is also ecologically friendly housing in the sense that 300 households can live vertically where, before, only 10 might have. As well, condo living may be ideal for extended families that do not want to live together but would want to be close to one another: Indeed, I am aware of several instances where an adult couple lives on one floor and their aged parents on another or in an adjacent building.

Unfortunately, there is no information on family life in condos as it is not a topic that has been researched—perhaps because this is not a lifestyle that university professors generally choose! Even Statistics Canada cannot tell us how many people or households live in condos because such residents fall under the rubric of "apartment" or "multi-unit" dwellers. Condo residents may be owners while others are tenants of owners who live elsewhere, whether in the same city, elsewhere in Canada, or abroad. For instance, in some areas of Toronto, over 60 percent of condo residents are tenants: For non-resident owners, condos are simply an investment. In certain cities such as Toronto and Vancouver, a great proportion of condo residents are from China, Taiwan, South Korea, Iran, and Russia.

It is regrettable that researchers, especially urban sociologists, are missing out on the opportunity of studying basic issues of family life in condos—and such issues abound as can be gleaned via letters posted on a Canadian website providing information for condo owners. This is another example of research lagging behind new realities. Sociologists would want to know how resident families and couples differ, if at all, from families living in single-unit or "regular" housing. What adaptations or constraints does condo living require of or places on couples and parents? What are specific issues that arise, if any? Are condo dwellers less or more inclined to participate in neighbourhood, school, and other civic activities that would provide social capital to children and parents alike? How do condos facilitate immigrant families' integration to Canadian life in view of the close proximity of neighbours compared with other type of housing? This is only a sample of the questions that sociologists and psychologists could address.

Mobile Homes

At the other extreme of housing conditions are mobile homes, which, in 1996, represented about 1 percent of private dwellings. Although 57 percent are located in rural areas, others can be found in small cities and towns (Kremarik and Williams, 2001). Mobile homes are more likely than other dwellings to house smaller families and single people. Families living in such homes have on average a lower income and over half of the adults have not completed high school (MacTavish, 2007). In fact, mobile homes are convenient for lower-income families because they are less expensive to acquire and cost less to heat, for instance.

However, dwellers often lack sources of community support and may be marginalized (Notter et al., 2008). Their homes are built less solidly and require more repairs and maintenance than other dwellings; as well, more are hazardous during stormy weather. As a result, a larger proportion of mobile homes are in poorer condition than other types of residences. Although well over 300,000 Canadians live in mobile homes, there is no research on family life and community dynamics in this alternative type of residence. Some harbour resilience while others shelter domestic abuse and child maltreatment (Notter et al., 2008).

Family Privacy

Family privacy is both a characteristic within the family itself and a situation of the family toward the rest of the world (Coontz, 2000:284). Family life is much less public than it used to be when homes were designed with front porches, for instance. Now, the family has retreated inside or to the backyard. Families have become more individuated, as individualism is closely related to the concept of privacy. Nock (1998b) emphasizes that technological change has contributed to the notion of privacy. For instance, air conditioning (the windows of the house are closed); few, if any, trips to the laundromat (most homes have washers and dryers); and even a reduction in neighbourhood grocery shopping (as online shopping increases in popularity and as many families shop in larger malls or superstores where they go by car). All these factors have enhanced privacy and separation from one's immediate neighbourhood.

In modern societies, the **social construction** of what proper family life should be dictates that parents need some privacy and children need a place where they can do homework, play games, talk on the phone, and interact among themselves. In fact, so well accepted is this ideology that many researchers believe that children need space that is their own and that they can control and where they can "individuate," in psychological terms—all of which are social constructs of the type of society we live in rather than human necessities.

The separate space occupied by each family fulfills certain functions, but it can also be problematic. As reviewed by Berardo (1998), family privacy allows couples to resolve their problems without external pressure. It serves to protect family members against the pressures of the external world. In this sense, privacy functions as a buffer as well as a protection. In contrast, public exposure and revelations are probably some of the elements that contribute to the rapid and successive divorces and repartnerings often occurring among film, sports, and entertainment personalities. On the other side of the coin, as each couple and each family leads its life separately, they have few points of comparison that would allow them to improve their family functioning or even appreciate how good it is compared with that of others. Privacy also means that abuse and neglect can go on for extended periods of time without external detection and/or intervention. Therefore, privacy can camouflage problems and prevent victims from seeking help, as is the case in some instances of elder abuse.

Overcrowding

Overcrowding is the opposite of privacy and is often, but not always, a result of poverty (Rizk, 2003) and the lot of renters rather than owners (Engeland et al., 2005). Renters have on average a lower income than owners and more are poor.

In 2008–09, 87 percent of those who had recourse to a food bank lived in rented accommodations (Food Banks Canada, 2009:8). Overcrowding is not generally a valued state, so that Canadian-born or raised families do not accept it as a fact of life and may find it highly stressful. Therefore, when too many family members congregate in too little space, the following is likely to happen.

First, parents may not be able to spend time alone; the level and quality of their communication and intimacy may suffer. Second, personal hygiene may become problematic when the facilities have to accommodate too many persons. Third, contagious illnesses, such as colds and flu, may spread more easily in families living in cramped quarters, so that work or school days are frequently missed. Moreover, neither children nor adults may get enough sleep; as a result, their physical and mental health may be affected. Fourth, the noise level may distract children and prevent them from doing schoolwork, particularly when the television is on at all times in the small dwelling. (Here, one can see that technology exacerbates the impact of our ideological preference for private space.) Children with an attention deficit disorder may be particularly affected in this context.

Finally, family members unwittingly compete for scarce space so that conflict may arise; in some families, siblings may quarrel more, parents may yell at them and tell them to "shut up," and the atmosphere is one of exasperation. Particularly affected both by overcrowding and dilapidated housing are Aboriginal families (Engeland et al., 2005). Those living on reserves are even more affected. For instance, in 2006, 28 percent of First Nations people lived in homes that needed major repairs—including 44 percent of those on reserves—compared with only 7 percent of the non-Aboriginal population (Gionet, 2009).

Nevertheless, some families do cope well in cramped quarters. These are often immigrants who were used to very little space in their home country because of weather, culture, war, or poverty. In fact, their crowded situation in Canada may be an improvement over what they had at home. Others came from high-density areas, such as Hong Kong, where small apartments are the norm, or Cuba or Moscow, where several families may share a few rooms. Again, these new Canadians may adapt well to their new situation as it compares favourably with what they left behind and, at any rate, they expect to do better in the near future. Tolerance of overcrowding therefore depends on cultural norms and the family's stage in the life course. Although immigrants also prefer new and spacious housing, 44 percent of recent immigrant households have to live in housing that both needs repairs and is too small (Engeland et al., 2005).

RESIDENTIAL MOBILITY

Between 2001 and 2006, 41 percent of the total population had moved. Half of these moves took place within the same municipality (Statistics Canada, 2007d). Turcotte and Vezina (2010) show that 14 percent of persons between the ages of 25 and 44 in Toronto, Montreal, and Vancouver had moved from the core city to the periphery between 2001 and 2006 because they had become parents. Over 1.5 million Canadians moved in 2004 alone (Statistics Canada, 2005d). Some provinces, particularly Newfoundland/Labrador, have had historically high rates of outmigration, both to the U.S. and Ontario, as well as Alberta more recently, because of the degradation of the fishing industry and the seasonal nature of the work available to young people. In contrast, Europeans change residence far less frequently.

Kremarik (1999) has estimated that, when Canadian adults move, 60 percent improve the quality of their lives, whether they move to a larger home or a better area, or relocate for a better job. However, although one-parent families are more likely to move, fewer than half are better off as a result. In general, low-income people have similar rates of residential mobility as others, and do gain from moving—but much less so than persons with more education who move.

Moving from one home to another and, particularly for children who are already in school, from one neighbourhood to another, is an important transition in a family's life. It does it require adjustment to a new interior spatial configuration and functioning. As well, all the members have to become acquainted with a new neighbourhood, town, and even province. A family move does not benefit its members equally (Audas and McDonald, 2004).

Several studies have documented that the number of moves experienced by children and adolescents correlates with lower school achievement and rates of high school completion, and even with behavioural problems and early sexuality (see South et al., 2005). Adolescents' friendship networks also suffer (South and Haynie, 2004). This may be related to the fact that school-age children in separating and divorcing families move the most. By 2006, for instance, 57 percent of Canadians who were in a separated family had moved within the past five years as had 45 percent in divorced families compared with 34 percent for those in married families (Statistics Canada, 2007d). Thus, children of separating parents are already at risk of poor school performance and, by moving, acquire another risk. When divorced families relocate, they tend to go from being owners to renters because their economic situation has deteriorated. Consequently, the adjustment that children and adolescents have to make may be too demanding: They incur four losses simultaneously—their old family structure, their school, their former peer group, and their house. As well, adolescents who move may have difficulties integrating themselves into existing peer groups. As a result, they may be attracted to new peers who are more delinquent, thus accounting in part for their higher rates of delinquency and violence (Haynie and South, 2005).

Adjustment may be particularly difficult when a move leads to an unstable neighbourhood where the social control of youths is largely nonexistent. In such contexts, an adolescent from a family that has just suffered a breakup may be particularly susceptible to opportunities for delinquency (Sampson, 1997). School performance suffers with mobility, but this impact applies more to one- than to two-parent families. Children in one-parent or stepparent families seem to suffer from any mobility (Tucker et al., 1998). The reason is that such families face more adjustments and have less social capital that can be devoted to children to counterbalance the potentially negative impact of moving. A male student describes part of this dilemma:

"The most painful thing that happened to me was when I had to move. I lost all my friends and had to leave my school but the worst . . . was coming to a new school with new kids. They aren't very nice in Grade 6 if you don't wear the

same clothes as them or have as much money, etc. This was truly one of the hardest periods of my life. I remember going into the cafeteria at lunch and having to sit by myself or with some other losers who were in the same position as me. I was bothered and picked on by a lot of people because I was small and it took me a long time to adjust to my situation. Of course I eventually made friends but I never quite made it with the people who I most wanted to be friends with."

(As an aside, it is interesting to note that the student labelled other children in the same situation as "losers." This evaluation reflects cultural norms of what is entailed in being successful in one's peer group.)

When a family relocates in order to enhance a father's position on the job market, the mother may not benefit. She may actually have to abandon her own job, and if the move takes the family to another province or even to the U.S., she may lose her social support network. Nevertheless, spouses who move because of the relocation of the chief breadwinner generally experience wage growth (Audas and McDonald, 2004). But children have to adjust.

Elder's (1995) developmental or life course theory offers a new perspective on this situation. What is an advantage for the father becomes a dislocation in the children's lives: The two generational stages in the life course of a family do not mesh and the goals of one are incompatible with the needs of the other. However, this disparity in the life-course timing of the family members can be mitigated in several ways. Husbands can compensate to some extent for their wives' loss of social support, and may even accept a promotion requiring relocation only after their wives have also found a new job. It is still rare that a family moves to meet a wife's career opportunities. The reasons rest "in prevailing labor market inequality and gender ideology" (Shauman, 2010:390). However, women with a great deal of human capital may be in a position to prevent a family's move.

As far as children are concerned, a harmonious home as well as the continued or even increased involvement of both parents in their lives is an important stabilizing element (Stoneman et al., 1999). Mothers' involvement helps, but the combined paternal and maternal involvement mitigates the disruptive effects of mobility on children more effectively (Hagan et al., 1996). When only one parent is involved, the social capital from which children can draw on may not be sufficient during a transition period. When neither parent is involved, because of financial or career pressures or because of personal problems, children are at high risk of failing to integrate themselves in a positive way in their new neighbourhood and school.

CONCLUSIONS: THE MEANING OF NEIGHBOURHOOD AS CONTEXT

Children and unemployed youths are often the most visible persons in a neighbourhood, the ones who are the most influenced by its social climate, and the ones who affect it most heavily. For many children and youths, the streets are a nexus of same-age sociability and of links between families. In other neighbourhoods, the homes and the backyards fulfill this purpose; close acquaintances and friends often come from other areas to visit. Thus, a family's social life may be located within its spatial framework or neighbourhood or may extend to other areas and may even include several residential spaces. This is one of the reasons why neighbourhood effects on child development and youth achievement are not generally as salient as family and genetic effects.

Neighbourhood structure and housing conditions not only have an impact on people's lives but also reflect a society's values concerning social diversity. This chapter reinforces and extends the findings presented in Chapters 3 and 4 on ethnic and economic inequalities. It also serves as a link between these chapters and the next one on education and religion, two institutions that constitute additional contexts influencing family life—in some cases, limiting family members' opportunities and, in other cases, enhancing them.

Summary

1. Neighbourhoods constitute families' first immediate, external context. Urban areas vary widely, ranging from metropolises to small towns, and include a great variety of suburbs. The types of families residing in these various areas differ by social class, race, and household composition.

2. Affluent neighbourhoods are described with an emphasis on the fact that little research exists on families who are well-to-do. Neighbourhoods that are poor and to which social problems are added present several risk factors for children. First, they may receive inadequate mainstream socialization: There is no effective community helping children develop the social and academic skills needed for the current labour market. Instead, there is a critical mass of low-income neighbours, a factor that is related to behavioural problems and low school achievement. Parents' conscientious childrearing is often defeated by the negative peer context and adult example. Second, children may not be adequately supervised, and third, may therefore not be protected from the dangers of their areas.

3. Disadvantaged areas nevertheless contain a high proportion of families that function well and are resilient. But the task facing parents of successful children are enormous, as they have to be far more vigilant than similar parents in middle-class areas. These parents have to ensure their children's physical safety, moral development, school success, and conformity to norms amidst a social climate that provides opposite models and opportunities.

4. Canadian minority groups are not as segregated as they are in the U.S., particularly blacks. However, Chinese families are becoming more segregated by choice.

5. Entire families have joined the ranks of the homeless and are generally found in shelters. Poverty, lack of subsidized housing, domestic violence, mental illness, and addiction are some of the key forces leading to homelessness. Family life is severely disrupted in shelters, and mothers encounter many difficulties in the fulfillment of their parental duties. Homeless mothers are often depressed as a result, and the general health of both mothers and children suffers. Compared with poor children living at home, homeless children have more health- and school-related problems.

6. Rural areas vary in their settings and in the employment opportunities they offer to families. Farm families are now in the minority and many are severely stressed economically.

Today, most farm couples combine off-farm work with farming to make ends meet. In most farm families, adolescents contribute to the family economy. Patterns of farm inheritance lead both to family cohesiveness and stress. Rural areas also contain vacation neighbourhoods for city families, another topic on which little research exists.

7. The state of maintenance of a dwelling can have an impact on family atmosphere and health. Three types of housing trends are discussed: mansionization, condo dwelling, and mobile homes. Family space connotes privacy in detached homes and the trend is toward larger space (square footage) at a time when family size is relatively small. There are problems related to overcrowding but one has to consider that certain cultures tolerate tight living space better than others.

8. A family's residential mobility does not benefit its members equally. Children and adolescents who experience many moves are more likely to suffer from school difficulties and disruptions in their social networks. Particularly affected are children in one-parent families.

9. Neighbourhood structure and housing conditions affect families' lives and reflect society's values concerning social diversity.

Analytical Questions

1. How can the theme of the effective community help determine social policies that could improve the lives of children and parents living in high-poverty areas where social problems may exist?
2. How different are well-functioning families living in high-risk areas compared with those living in middle-class neighbourhoods?
3. Given what you have read in this chapter, is the building of "social" housing developments in certain areas of town a good social policy? (Support your answer with the help of research results.) If your answer is no, what might be a better solution?
4. Suggest at least three research questions that are lacking concerning rural families and housing conditions in general.
5. Draw up a correlation diagram showing a relationship between numbers of moves in young adults' past lives and school achievement.

Suggested Readings

Conger, R. D., et al. (Eds.) 1994. *Families in troubled times: Adapting to change in rural America*. New York: Aldine de Gruyter. This book reports the results of the Iowa Youth and Family Project on various aspects of family life on farms.

Kazemipur, A., and Halli, S. S. 2000. *The new poverty in Canada: Ethnic groups and ghetto neighbourhoods*. Toronto: Thompson. This book focuses on the links between poverty and ethnicity. It also offers comparative material from the U.S. and European countries.

Paquette, K., and Bassuk, E. L. 2009. "Parenting and homelessness: Overview and introduction to the Special section," *American Journal of Orthopsychiatry*, 79, 292-298. This article presents a good overview and is accompanied by several articles on the topic of parenting and homelessness.

Wilson, W. J. 1987. *The truly disadvantaged*. Chicago: University of Chicago Press. This book is a historically grounded classic that is still very relevant and influential in the U.S. It presents an interesting perspective for Canadian students.

Suggested Weblinks

Statistics Canada regularly presents statistics on neighbourhoods, home ownership, the rental market, and housing conditions.

www.statcan.gc.ca

Canadian Centre for Policy Alternatives includes much material that pertains to neighbourhoods. Particularly important is the article by Sheila Black (June 2010) entitled "Ontario's growing gap: The role of race and gender."

www.policyalternatives.ca

www.growinggap.ca

Greater Toronto Urban Observatory also includes many articles on various topics related to neighbourhoods and inequalities, particularly that by J. David Hulchanski et al.: "Toronto divided? Polarizing trends that could split the city apart, 1970 to 2005," which appeared January 2010, and documents the increasing gaps in income between Toronto neighbourhoods over 35 years.

www.gtuo.ca

www.urbancentre.utoronto.ca/cura/

www.children.gov.on.ca

In the U.S., the **Urban Institute** is an economic and social research organization focusing on problems confronting the nation and the search for appropriate social policies. One concern is poverty, both rural and urban; another is neighbourhoods.

www.urban.org

Condoinformation.ca is a practical Canadian website designed to inform and help condo owners. Its contents include a chapter entitled "Are condos family friendly?"

www.condoinformation.ca

These suggested weblinks are also very relevant to Chapters 4 (on families' economic situations) and to Chapter 14 (on policies).

CHAPTER 6

Roles of Educational Institutions and Religious Participation in Family Life

"Between the ages of 14 to 18 the hardest part was school, school, school. I was not a good student, not motivated and a shit disturber, it seems I did my best to be the worst. . . . I ended up suffering for this and dropped out and [moved] back in at my parents' pleadings so that I was still in high school at age 20. . . . It wasn't all my fault because the school was the pits, the teachers didn't care, they just gossiped about their divorces and whatever and the students were more or less like me so we all deserved each other except that our parents didn't deserve this and it took them four years after that to convince me to go to a community college from where I enrolled here."

"High school was my best experience, better than my friends because my teachers were supportive and I got involved in about 10 clubs and participated in various contests and won and my parents were proud of me. It was an exciting time for all of us because both my parents volunteered, my father as a coach, and my mother helped organize many school functions. They were well liked by all the teachers and even the students and it was just great, I felt at home everywhere I went."

"For sure the cornerstone of all my values and of my life for that matter is my faith in God. We're very religious by today's standards in the younger generation and at times I used to be teased by kids in high school about it so I like the freedom of university life in this respect. The only problem is that university life says nothing about religion. I haven't had a single prof in sociology who even went so far as to say a single word about it."

"I get along reasonably well with my parents now that they accept my lack of interest in religion and a few other deviances on my part. But I've never been religiously inclined and I don't feel I miss out on anything."

Education and religion are key cultural and social institutions that have an impact on family life. In view of the salient role that education plays in children's outcomes, it will not surprise the reader to learn that students' autobiographies contained a great deal of material about their experience with child care and school systems. In fact, schools are the second most frequently mentioned source of past misery, after peers—and they are not often referred to as a key source of happiness. For its part, religion plays a dominant role in the lives of only a minority of students. For the majority, it is a matter of membership and general beliefs rather than active participation. However, in recent years, more and more of my students have come from Asian and Middle Eastern countries; these students mention religion as a central theme in their lives more often than most other students. In this chapter, the focus is on religiosity rather than religion per se, in order to link this with the lived experience of families.

THE EDUCATIONAL SYSTEM: AN OVERVIEW

Although schools existed over 2,000 years ago in ancient Greece and Rome and later in China and Japan, they were the prerogative of a select group. The remainder of the child population worked alongside adults. In Western Europe and North America, primary school attendance became compulsory between 1840 and 1890. Middle-class children were the first to benefit, whereas working-class and rural parents had some difficulty adjusting their economic circumstances to the loss of their children's labour and wages. Therefore, several decades elapsed, well into the first part of the 20th century, before mass schooling spread to all social classes equally. Quebec lagged particularly in this respect because of its rural economy. For instance, in 1891, the census revealed that 41 percent of the Quebec population was illiterate compared with 18 percent of the Ontario population.

Yet, the first infant school and the first daycare opened in Montreal in 1828 and 1858 respectively; all were charitable organizations for poor children. In English Canada, the first child care facility opened in Toronto in 1857 (Prochner, 2000). But these developments spread very slowly, in part because there was not a sufficient number of poor wage-earning mothers serving as a base for charitable childhood education centres. From the 1920s to the 1950s, the focus of early education was on children's emotional and social development, while from the 1960s until now, the focus shifted to intellectual development (Varga, 1997). Currently, the emphasis of governments regarding early education is on preparing children from disadvantaged families for a schooling system that is becoming more and more oriented toward a global, technological labour market (Pitt, 2002).

In Canada, the majority of children now begin school earlier than they did 30 years ago. Currently, most attend kindergarten, and a substantial proportion participates in preschool programs. Moreover, about a third of preschool children whose parents are employed are in daycare centres, some as young as six weeks old. Therefore, the educational function traditionally assigned to families has been taken over by institutions at younger ages. However, parents have to be more involved in their children's grade-school and high-school education than they might like to be or can afford to be in view of other time constraints in their own lives. Parents have to do far more planning than was the case in the 1960s, for instance (Sweet and Anisef, 2005). After parents, schools have traditionally been considered the main agent of socialization. In essence, the educational system pursues family goals of gender-role differentiation and of the social integration of children in society and its economy (Reynolds, 2004). In other societies, particularly Muslim ones, schools emphasize religious scriptures and children's integration into the faith of the country.

This chapter focuses on child care, as well as on primary and secondary schooling as contexts for families, parenting, and children's outcomes. Post-secondary education is becoming a more important context for family life than in the recent past, as more students attend university while living at home and need more parental assistance than was the case just a few decades earlier (Bouchard and Zhao, 2000). However, research is lacking in these respects concerning family issues. We follow the life course and begin with child care.

CHILD CARE: QUALITY AND OUTCOMES

Child care generally refers to the care given to a child by a person other than his or her primary caregiver—and the primary caregiver is usually defined as the mother (see Chapter 1). Overall, Canada suffers from a lack of government-funded child care facilities, and waiting lists are very long, especially for subsidized care. Further, Canada does not have a national strategy for early childhood education and care (Friendly et al., 2002). Quebec has the best system of inexpensive daycare but there are not enough places to meet the demand, as indicated in Table 6.1: In 2008, only 18.6 percent of all young children could be accommodated in **regulated** child care in Canada and 20.3 percent of those aged zero to five (Beach et al., 2009).

We already know that 77 percent of mothers with a child aged three to five are working, so we see the inadequacy of this situation. Parents have recourse to a variety of other child care arrangements, from alternating shifts between mothers and fathers to non-regulated care in another individual's home or care by relatives,

TABLE 6.1	**Percentage of Children Aged 0–12 and 0–5 for Whom There Was a Form of Regulated Child Care Space in 2008**	
	Aged 0 to 12	Aged 0 to 5
Canada	18.6%	20.3%
Newfoundland / Labrador	16.2	9.9
New Brunswick	9.2	17.3
Prince Edward Island	22.2	41.0
Nova Scotia	11.6	22.1
Quebec	**36.1**	**25.0**
Ontario	13.6	19.6
Manitoba	15.5	20.6
Saskatchewan	6.3	9.1
Alberta	13.7	17.4
British Columbia	15.4	18.3
North West Territories	20.5	23.3
Nunavut	11.2	20.2
Yukon	27.9	28.3

Source: Adapted with permission from Beach et al., 2009, Table 9.

especially grandmothers, or a nanny or at-home sitter. Young children who have a multiplicity of non-parental child care arrangements tend to have more behavioural problems (Morissey, 2009): It is probably too difficult for them to adapt to a variety of rules that are often inconsistent. Compared with the 1960s, proportionally more children are in centres than with female relatives, because the latter tend to be employed. As well, affluent families are the least likely to choose care by relatives.

Child care of **high quality** includes a low child-to-caregiver ratio allowing for more adult-child interaction. The availability of activities, toys, and educational materials, as well as space, are other indicators of quality. Nutritious food and an age-appropriate structuring of daily activities, including naps, are other important elements. More and more, an integrated educational component is a requisite of a good child care system. But particularly important are caregivers' qualifications (Mashburn et al., 2008). We should consider staff's low salaries as an indicator of quality: Low salaries lead to high turnover rates, thus instability in children's lives. In Canada and the U.S., caregivers' salaries are much lower than those in Europe, and their turnover rate consequently is around 40 percent per year. In 2006, the median full-time salary of Early Childhood Educators was $25,100 and $27,366 for those with the ECE credential (Beach et al., 2009). These are low salaries for persons who take care of our children—this country's most important investment. In Canada, non-profit centres generally provide better quality child care, and have better trained staff and lower turnover (Friendly, 2000). Caretakers who are more adequately trained and are satisfied with their working conditions provide a more optimum environment for children (White and Mill, 2000).

The Effects of Child Care on Children

Poor-quality care has been related to child disadvantages in the domains of cognition and language, as well as social and emotional adjustment (McCartney et al., 2010). Some of these results are found in follow-up studies of children after they have begun school (Belsky et al., 2007). Unfortunately, research on the effect of nonfamilial care on children has until now largely failed to take **family characteristics** into consideration. It is entirely possible that some of what are believed to be negative consequences of daycare centres are actually results of other activities the children are involved in or of certain family characteristics, such as a mother's low educational level or a detrimental housing situation (NICHD, 2004; Scarr, 1998). Naturally, to some extent, parents choose or are forced to accept a quality of care corresponding to some of their own characteristics, including income (Kohen et al., 2002b; Singer et al., 1998). But this is less the case in Quebec than in other provinces because of indirect subsidies. In studies that have controlled for family variables, the quality of daycare centres still produces a small but evident difference in terms of language, cognitive development, and overall adjustment (McCartney et al., 1997).

A review of large-scale studies of hundreds of centres that was carried out in the U.S., Bermuda, Sweden, and Holland concludes that the differences found in children raised at home versus in daycare do not have persistent consequences. Furthermore, daycare centres have no major impact on children's development when the children come from average homes. However, children from disadvantaged homes, for whom quality child-care programs may supply missing elements in their lives, benefit from quality daycare, particularly in terms of school achievement later on (Votruba-Drzal et al., 2004). But children from high-SES families probably derive the same benefits they would obtain at home, at least at the educational level. However, as seen in the case study on p. 103, such children could benefit when their parents do not read to them or do not have enough time to talk with them—as indicated in a Toronto study (Rushowy, 2004).

Several studies find that children in daycare centres are more self-confident, assertive, expressive, and helpful, as well as less timid in new situations than children in other types of care (Clarke-Stewart, 1992). But other studies also report that many of the children in nonmaternal care are less polite, agreeable, and compliant with mothers' or teachers' requests, and more irritable, aggressive, and boisterous (Belsky et al., 2007; NICHD, 2003). These results are particularly evident for children who have been placed in care when very small and spend long hours in this setting. By age 15, these children still have a somewhat higher score on externalizing problems (Lowe Vandell et al., 2010). However, a restructuring of daycare educational ideologies that would foster cooperation and responsibility might redress the situation (Maccoby and Lewis, 2003).

Small children who have too much **peer contact** or spend too many hours with a large group of peers may develop more externalizing problems (McCartney et al., 2010). Children who have too little adult attention early in their lives may be at a deficit in terms of social adjustment, especially when they are more socially fearful by nature (Watamura et al., 2003). We already know from other studies on large family size that such children are at a disadvantage in terms of language skills and intellectual development (Marks, 2006). Overall, the long-term effects of parenting seem to predominate over those of nonparental care (Belsky et al., 2007). There is nevertheless one important question that is still being debated: Are children who are in daycare for over 30 hours a week from an early age less influenced by parents' teachings and other family characteristics than children who are in care for fewer hours?

In comparison to the numerous studies of children in child care centres, not enough research has been carried out on at-home child care by non-relatives in terms of its impact on children. The following student quotes reflect the wide variety of conditions that small children can encounter:

"At first I didn't like being separated from my mother but the lady was so nice. She took in two other children who were more or less my age and she gave us such a great time. She really loved children and looking back on that I wonder where she got all her ideas because she had dropped out of school after Grade 9. She used to take us on long walks and we went to the park where we collected 'treasures' such as pine cones, leaves, bugs and she taught us things and then she had all these story books from the library, always different ones. It was never boring and we all learned to read with her and count, and when we got to school I was placed in Grade 2." [woman student]

"What I hated the most [during ages four to five] *was this old woman who came home to babysit us each morning. She was like an old witch, nice with my*

Good child care centres are a society's investment in the stability of families and in the future of their children. Child care that is affordable contributes to parents' and children's well-being. It also contributes to job creation and satisfaction. Quality child care centres are thus functional for families, children, and the economy.

parents but a real sulk as soon as they were out. She had nothing to do with us for the entire day except to feed us and stuff her own face. She knitted and watched TV and ate some more. . . . My parents noticed that we were becoming withdrawn and shy and my mother became concerned. We were too small to tell her much . . . but my mother probably guessed that something was wrong and found another woman." [male student]

Early Childhood Education for Children in Low-Income Families

Children from low-income families are often unprepared when they enter Grade 1 and consequently fall behind at each subsequent level. Many such children repeat grades and then drop out of school to join the ranks of the unemployed and underpaid. Programs such as Head Start, which was created in the U.S. in 1965, raise the level of disadvantaged children's school readiness (Dearing et al., 2009). Much of the research on this topic is American, but its results apply to the Canadian situation. Indeed, expanding early childhood education for all families and also with the purpose of helping disadvantaged children should be a key element in all provinces. Furthermore, an Aboriginal Head Start program was initiated in 1995 for northern and urban communities and was expanded to include reserves in 1998 (Goulet et al., 2001; Mayfield, 2001). By 2002, 16 percent of six-year-old Aboriginal children had attended a preschool program locally developed to meet the culture and the needs of the community (RCAP, 1996; Statistics Canada, 2004k). The following conclusions about children who have participated in Head Start are distilled from the research of

Barnett (1998), Brooks-Gunn (2003), Love et al. (2005), and Raver and Zigler (1997):

1. Children experience a short-term boost in IQ scores that may last for a few years.
2. Once they are in Grade 1, these students do better than comparable students not previously enrolled in Head Start.
3. Only a small group is eventually placed in remedial "special education."
4. Only about one-fifth are eventually retained in a grade, compared with one-third of a control group that did not attend Head Start.
5. More Head Start children graduate from high school.
6. More of these children are eventually employed than those children in the control group.
7. Children show an improvement in family interaction, health, and nutritional status, as well as socioemotional adjustment.

More recent research indicates that the positive effects on cognition and school achievement are still evident at age 15 (Lowe Vandell et al., 2010). Some of the above results may in part be related to the fact that quality Head Start programs generally provide positive parent-teacher contact that encourages mothers to help their children remain motivated and to read to them, for instance (Raikes et al., 2006). Moreover, some of these programs have reduced abuse and neglect over the children's life span to age 17 (Reynolds and Robertson, 2003). When children arrive in Grade 1 free of behavioural problems, not only are they more attentive in class and better able to learn but they also impress their teachers and peers more favourably (Ladd et al., 1999). Teachers, in turn, expect more of them, and these higher expectations carry through the rest of their school years, even though their initial IQ gain eventually disappears. As Entwisle and colleagues (1997:18) remind us, "It is key to realize that only modestly better achievement in the first couple of grades might be enough for children to avoid retention or Special Education."

Full-day programs carry longer benefits than half-day ones: The longer children stay in a quality school daily and the less they miss school, the better they do on aptitude tests. Similarly, a longer school day seems to raise reading and math scores (Frazier and Morrison, 1998). Most experts now agree that disadvantaged children who are segregated in poor neighbourhoods would do far better if they were to start preschool as early as possible, even at age two (Kagan and Neuman, 1998). They also agree that such an early intervention should extend through grade school to build on the initial progress and to involve other aspects of these families' lives (Reynolds and Temple, 1998). Such an extension would prevent the loss of early gains, a situation that currently occurs as a result of the low-quality school environments in which disadvantaged children find themselves after Head Start. What is needed is a program such as "Beyond 3:30," which was initiated by the Toronto Community Foundation, whereby children stay in school until their parents return while engaging in interesting activities and receiving remedial help (Daubs, 2009).

Head Start programs are thus an excellent **investment for a society** that has a large pool of disadvantaged families (Rushowy, 2004). It is an investment in education, in children's present and future, in families, and in a society's economy. Inasmuch as such programs are both remedial and preventive, they are cost effective and save taxpayers enormous burdens in the long run, in terms of lower rates of delinquency, unemployment, ill health, and even adult criminality (Bogenschneider and Corbett, 2010). For instance, children's reading proficiency begins early and this advantage carries over into post-secondary education (Statistics Canada, 2006a). The precursors of school readiness are already established between the ages of three to five (Statistics Canada, 2006b). For example, nine-year-old children whose scores are high in math, vocabulary, and attention span already had developed these skills by age five (Statistics Canada, 2009n).

The Effects of Child Care on Parents

Child care should also be studied in terms of its effects on parents, particularly on their well-being. Care that is too expensive reduces parents' well-being as well as that of the entire family. If too great a proportion of the domestic budget goes into child care, it depletes resources that could be utilized for other aspects of family life, such as better housing, nutrition, and leisure activities. Furthermore, expensive daycare may prevent some parents from having a second child, or, when a second baby arrives, one of the two parents (generally the mother) may be forced to leave her employment. Thus, indirectly, via the expenses required, child care may reduce parental well-being—hence the importance of inexpensive child care in Quebec.

There is a second path via which child care can lessen parental well-being: Low-quality care not only has a negative impact on children's development, but parents worry about their child as they attend to their job during the day (Erdwins et al., 2001). Mothers especially may feel insecure and guilty. In other instances, the child is well cared for, but by relatives or sitters who exact a psychological price from parents, particularly mothers, by being intrusive or quarrelsome. Also, parents may feel that their child needs more attention, but they may be afraid of antagonizing relatives by making additional requests.

Thus, child care availability, affordability, and quality are key ingredients in parents' well-being. From a societal perspective, quality and affordable child care increases productivity, lowers employee stress and absenteeism, and offers a wider pool of potential workers. It also contributes to a healthier family situation. When both parents can be employed because they have access to quality child care, this contributes to prevent poverty. From this perspective, child care is especially important for young single mothers, both in terms of jobs and as an educational tool in the care of their children. As well, care for children with special needs is essential, including for their parents' well-being in all social classes, with an emphasis on vulnerable families. Hence, child care availability should be a prime target of social policies directed at improving family life.

SCHOOLS AND FAMILIES

Schools and families are intersecting environments in the unfolding lives of children (Crosnoe, 2004). For one, schools constitute a key context for child development and family relations. In turn, family characteristics, such as their SES, dictate to some extent the type of school children attend. From the perspective of rational theory, schools that serve as an effective community can add resilience to a child whose family is experiencing a stressful situation, such as divorce (Leon, 2003). Schools that create a prosocial environment, as perceived by children, contribute to their health and behavioural outcomes (Ma and Zhang, 2002). Other key school variables are fair and consistent discipline, safety, extracurricular programs to encourage physical activity, school commitment, and parental involvement.

Teachers play an important role in children's lives and may counterbalance or exacerbate negative familial environments (Forehand et al., 2002). In terms of motivation and behaviours at school, good and supportive teachers can be even more influential than parents (Wentzel, 2002). More studies are needed to see which type of school social capital can be beneficial to children, and at what age, over and above the social capital available from their parents (Dufur et al., 2008). In normal situations, the more schooling children receive, the larger their cognitive growth. Years of schooling tend to increase IQ levels, and absence from a good school for a prolonged period results in lower scores. Further—and to pursue a theme just discussed—in terms of social capital, when the number of pupils is too high and/or the teachers are indifferent, children from homes with less capital become particularly at risk developmentally (Parcel and Dufur, 2001). This may be especially so for immigrant adolescents whose command of English or French is not yet fully developed (Anisef and Kilbride, 2003).

Vulnerable children who attend schools with relatively few difficult students are less likely to associate with peers who reinforce their own negative tendencies: Their opportunities for negative behaviours are reduced (Cleveland and Wiebe, 2003). In contrast, female teens who attend schools with a large percentage of disadvantaged students are more likely to become pregnant than if they attended a school with a different SES profile (Manlove et al., 2002). As well, when a school is predominantly populated by students from single-parent families, children's test scores are significantly reduced, largely a function of poverty (Bankston and Caldas, 1998). For their part, children from female-headed families who attend a school where most peers have two parents, and have therefore more resources, are positively affected in their test scores. In contrast, children from two-parent families who attend a school where most families are headed by lone mothers do less well in test scores (Pong, 1998).

In the following subsections, we investigate family variables that promote or impede school success. Five interrelated variables are discussed: parental involvement, social class, family–school compatibility, antisocial behaviour, and minority-group status.

Parental Involvement

Parental involvement in education is related to children's achievement and fewer behavioural problems (Nokali et al., 2010). It is a key concern of teachers who expect parents to support them and to prepare children for school. In Aboriginal communities, it is recommended that schools involve Elders and other members as well as parents to ensure cultural continuity (Goulet et al., 2001). Education textbooks emphasize the "partnership" that exists between teachers and parents. Yet, the word partnership implies equality, and this is generally not what teachers seek: Teachers approve of meetings with parents only when they, and not parents, initiate them (Steinberg et al., 1996:129). Moreover, the concept of parental involvement implies that it rests solely on parents' motivation. Yet, there are several elements that either encourage or discourage parents from being involved, such as teachers' attitudes and mothers' workload (Pena, 2000).

Parents can involve themselves directly in school activities—for instance, by volunteering—or they can closely follow their children's education from home by showing interest, maintaining high expectations, and supervising homework (Mandell and Sweet, 2004). In this respect, maternal supportiveness has been found to be even more effective than paternal in terms of fostering school readiness among young children (Martin et al., 2010). Overall, parental participation and empowerment is related to children's school performance and interpersonal relationships (Ma and Zhang, 2002—see Family Research 6.1). All in all, research indicates that parents can have a positive effect on raising their children's school achievement, as well as educational expectations and personal aspirations (Trusty, 1998).

FAMILY RESEARCH 6.1

How to Study Parental Involvement

Ma and Zhang (2002) used the 1998 data from the Canadian Cross-National Survey on Health Behaviours in School-Aged Children (HBSC) to examine the effects of some aspects of school experience on health and behaviours of students enrolled in Grades 6 to 10. About 10,000 students participated in the survey during school time. Health behaviours were measured with questions pertaining to the use of drugs, recent medical treatments and injuries, exercise habits, hygiene, and eating patterns. Other questions addressed interpersonal relationships, self-esteem, and the ability to make new friends.

For its part, parental involvement was measured by the following statements:

- If I have problems at school, my parent(s) are ready to help me.
- My parents are willing to come to school to talk to teachers.
- My parents encourage me to do well at school.

Other statements pertained to the quality of the child-parent relationship:

- My parents understand me.
- My parents expect too much of me.
- I have a lot of arguments with my parents.
- What my parents think of me is important.

Parents' Higher Social Class and Involvement

Building on Coleman's (1988) **theory of resources,** Lareau (2003) demonstrates how parents' social class equips them with an unequal set of resources that can differentially affect their ability to be involved in their children's education. Her sample consisted of black and white families at the upper-middle-class executive or professional level. These parents have the competence to help when their children encounter difficulties with the curriculum. They feel self-confident with teachers and do not hesitate to request changes that could benefit their children or to question teachers' decisions. At the negative level, it is not uncommon for such parents to flatly reject teachers' suggestions concerning children's behavioural difficulties. This situation is described by a student teacher who is doing her practicum in a new upper-middle-class neighbourhood where parents are upwardly mobile and are extremely busy with their careers:

> *"Right now I can't wait to get out of that school because some of these parents aren't used to money and what comes with it and they treat you as if you were their maids. Most kids are fine but we have a few bad apples and the parents are high on denial, perhaps because they are never home to see what's wrong with their precious children. There's nothing that their Danny Boy or whoever can do wrong, yet the boy is a regular delinquent. Oh no, he doesn't steal, how dare we complain, accuse him of this! More or less they tell us to learn manners, which they don't even have themselves. It ruins your life as a teacher."*

In their own social networks, upper-middle-class parents often have access to professionals, such as psychologists and other teachers whom they can consult on school matters. These parents are also better equipped to meet teachers' requests, because they have more material and cultural resources at their disposal (Jaeger, 2009). They can provide their children with educational supplies, computers, tutors, art or music lessons, and even summer camps (Ertl, 2000). Lareau (2003) mentions that these parents often bring work home from the office that expands children's horizons, gives them some preparation for the adult world of employment, and may serve as an incentive for homework. One student explains this:

> *"I've always wanted to be a family doctor because my father sells pharmaceuticals to them and he used to bring his samples home to show us at dinner time and it was very educational. But at a later time my mother returned to school to get her advanced degree in social work and the cases she'd talk about at home started to fascinate me. So I figured that I could be a social worker in a hospital context because I like both areas. So that's what I am studying for."*

Educated parents are also more likely to read to their children and spend time with them, although this frequency is much lower when mothers are employed full-time and as children get older (Cook and Willms, 2002). Above all, middle-class parents engage in a process of **concerted cultivation** (Lareau, 2003). That is, they deliberately stimulate the development of their children's cognitive and social skills by fostering larger vocabularies, familiarity with abstract concepts, and negotiating abilities. They enrol their children in an array of organized activities. (Indeed, both Aboriginal and other Canadian children who participate in extracurricular activities do better in school and in their relations with friends—Statistics Canada, 2004k). All of this gives children an advantage with institutional representatives, raises their sense of entitlement, and transmits habits that will be useful for higher education and on the individualistic, competitive labour market later on (Knighton and Mirza, 2002). In contrast, in working-class and disadvantaged families, children experience a socialization pattern that includes more free time, clear boundaries between parents and children, parental directives, a more simple speech pattern, and lower expectations of personal entitlement.

This concerted education, although western in origins, can be observed in educated families of most ethnic groups. However, because a smaller proportion of blacks and Aboriginals are middle class, as is the case for other Aboriginal groups elsewhere, this parenting style is less often encountered among them. This places children at a disadvantage in schools—but not necessarily in their personal relationships. For instance, Baker (2001:45) points out that Samoan children in New Zealand are disadvantaged by the school system because they are taught at home not to question their elders, and their learning style is of the "passive" type. In contrast, the process of concerted education stems from the individualistic and competitive nature of middle-class western education and places additional demands on mothers (Pitt, 2002; Wall, 2004), as seen in Chapter 1. It is in itself an ideology supported by the technological and capitalist infrastructure of society.

Barriers to Low-Income Parents' Involvement

Disadvantaged parents generally value education as much as their wealthier counterparts do. But they often have low achievement expectations for their own children because several problems stand in their and their children's way that prevent the actualization of their values. These obstacles then lower their aspirations. Indeed, studies indicate that parental expectations are key predictors of school achievement, starting in Grade 1. Entwisle et al. (1997:93) point out that raising **parents' expectations** could affect performance indirectly for several years after Grade 1. As we have seen, programs such as Head Start often lift parents' expectations, which in turn contributes to their children's success.

Disadvantaged parents encounter several problems that prevent them from actualizing their high value for education. First, they often lack the skills to help their children when they have school problems (Kralovec and Buehl, 2001). This was well illustrated by a student describing her Grade 1 experience in the previous chapter (p. 129). Second, they often feel intimidated or stigmatized by teachers, as discussed by a mature and already well-educated student on welfare:

> *"Currently, one of my worries is my daughter's school, rather, her teachers. They know that I am a single mother on welfare and it does not matter to them consequently that I have as much and even more education than they have. I can't talk to them, any of them, because they have subtle ways of putting me down, of making me feel that I am not a competent parent and person because I am poor. I wanted to get them involved in making sure that the children spell correctly . . . well, what a mistake because they can't spell themselves! But, of course, I am the problem: I am poor. Who am I? How can I have an opinion about my daughter's education, least of all spelling?"*

Third, teachers make more frequent requests for involvement from disadvantaged parents, but these requests are often negative, in part because poor children have more learning or behavioural problems (Sui-Chu and Willms, 1996). In fact, when children's grades are low, parents have more contact with the school. Otherwise, low-income parents attend parent-teacher conferences far less frequently. Often, lack of child care prevents them from doing so. Others may not have a flexible work schedule that would allow them to participate in school activities such as volunteering, which would give them the opportunity to become informally acquainted with teachers and other parents. Such activities would, in turn, give their children an advantage within the system—an "inside track." Aboriginal parents too often feel out of place and do not feel welcome by teachers (Poonwassie, 2001).

A fourth aspect of a family's low position in the class system that affects parents' expectations and children's education resides in the fact that, when these parents want to help their children with school work, they often meet resistance because the youngsters lack confidence in their competence. A female student, reminiscing on her own experience growing up in a disadvantaged family, makes this point:

> *"When I look back on that period what I regret the most is the way I treated my mother; just because we were poor I felt that she was not as good as other mothers and whenever she'd try to help me with homework, I'd turn to her and give her my most despising look. Not only [did] I hurt her a lot and made her feel useless as a mother but I made her feel worthless as a person because even then she was more educated than I am now especially when it comes down to writing proper sentences."*

A male student recalls how his negative view of his mother as a woman deprived him of much needed help:

> *"I always refused my mother's help with my homework because I felt that as a woman she didn't know much of anything. I was a guys' guy and always resisted any suggestion for improvement from my mother and I felt that it was her fault that we were poor and that if she had been any brighter, my father would not have left her . . . . Now I see how much better off I would have been with a better attitude."*

Nevertheless, among school students, Mandell and Sweet (2004) have not found any difference by social class in the level of mothers' involvement in their children's homework. However, the gendered division of labour and child care that focuses on mothers presents a serious roadblock in parental involvement. The intensive mothering that society and schools now expect cannot easily be fulfilled by women on low incomes who may be struggling to simply feed their children (Hays, 1996). The child as a project is often out of these mothers' reach, their best intentions notwithstanding (Wall, 2004).

Families' Social Class and Children's Achievement

As indicated in Figure 6.1, children from families of higher socioeconomic status (SES) do better in reading, writing, and mathematics (Lipps and Frank, 1997). This observation holds internationally (Willms, 2002b). As well, university attendance is still related to social class (Knighton and Mirza, 2002). Thus, inequalities in achievement

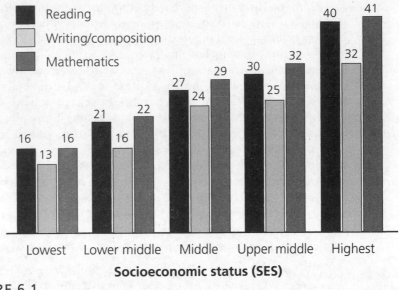

FIGURE 6.1

Percentages of Children Ranked Near the Top of Their Class by Their Teachers (by SES)

Source: Human Resources Development Canada and Statistics Canada, National Longitudinal Survey of Children and Youth, 1994–95; Lipps and Frank, 1997.

continue over the life course (Anisef et al., 2000; Pallas, 2002). Further, children who attend schools with a greater percentage of students from higher SES backgrounds do better academically (Frempong and Willms, 2002).

Pong (1998) found that, at the group level, high parental participation in educational activities alleviated the economic deficit by providing a positive community effect on the school and its students. Students did better when parents' participation was high, in general, even though their own individual parents may not have been involved. The same findings applied for the extent to which parents were acquainted with one another. When parents knew many other parents, they served as sources of information and reinforcement for one another. This helped them create a positive climate within the school for the benefit of all students. These results support Coleman's (1988) theory of social capital and the positive effect of an effective community above and beyond a family's social class and structure. However, Crosnoe (2004) found that there is overlap between social capital available in families and schools: Students who receive more emotional support from their parents then benefit more from the socioemotional resources of school.

Family-School Compatibility

Although Canada is a multicultural society, the structure of its economy rests on skills and education. On the one hand, a larger dose of cultural diversity in the contents of the curriculum and in the school climate would contribute to the academic success of minority-group children (Manning and Baruth, 2000). This said, however, children are more successful at school and better adjusted to its requirements when family life is similar to the skill set required by the school system. Children in families that have a **schedule**—where they eat breakfast, where rules are followed, and where educational activities are encouraged—are more easily integrated into the school system. Households with no employed adults are less likely to provide such a structure. In homes where everyone gets up whenever he or she wants, does not dress until later or not at all, eats meals whenever hungry, watches unlimited hours of television, and where reading material is absent, daily life is a world apart from school routine and goals. Children from these families may experience more difficulty fitting in at school, as well as have more trouble learning, because the two lifestyles clash.

Several researchers have emphasized the differences that exist between children of diverse social classes in terms of **summer activities**. Middle-class children benefit from summer activities that are compatible with school routine. For instance, many attend special camps. In contrast, disadvantaged children often spend their vacations in pursuits that increase their distance from what is required for school performance. A knowledge vacuum is created and they have more difficulty in readapting themselves to school work once classes resume. Not surprisingly, these children lose a few points on the IQ scale as well as on tests of mathematical ability during vacations. A student inadvertently explains this linkage:

> "What I like best to remember at this age [11–14] was my summer camps. I used to go to these camps that were basically for gifted children and we did a lot of science experiments and maths along with the usual crafts & physical activities . . . And when it was time to go back to school I always did better than the others, my science project was ready and I had more time to play hockey so I was not put down as a geek. I also liked showing off to my parents with everything I had learned and they were proud of me. All of this has helped me to this day."

Entwisle and colleagues (1997) tested children and examined their school grades at the beginning, middle, and end of the school year. They found that, although disadvantaged children begin the school year with lower scores and less knowledge than those from more affluent families, they gain as much proportionately. In other words, some of the yearly difference in test scores between poor children and children of higher SES is caused by summer loss for the former. A student describes her frustration:

> "I hated school because the other kids were so much more advanced than me, they'd come back to school with all kinds of stories about their summer activities and camps and special classes and they'd be rearing to go while I had spent all my summer watching TV babysitting and it'd take me until Christmas until I'd be caught up with the others, well some of the others. I was always last and later I had to take summer school to help my grades. It's been tough because I didn't have the same opportunities that the other students had."

Schools and Antisocial Behaviour

But there is another aspect of school/family compatibility that has to be taken into consideration. It resides in the fact that a substantial proportion of youth criminality occurs on school grounds. In fact, 27 percent of violent crimes involving youth and

20 percent of drug offences occur on school property in large cities (Savoie et al., 2006). Thus, schools can be an area where deviance-training takes place (Snyder et al., 2008). A student inadvertently sheds some light on this situation:

> *"Right now what's most stressful to me is my kid bro, he's 16 and more than a handful and my mom doesn't see it this way because he brings in money and I can't believe that my mom doesn't see where it comes from [drugs]. He also got a gun that goes down well in his baggy pants, he's a real delinquent but I think my mom's afraid of him and to tell the truth I am too. He brings his gun to school and he's going to hurt someone some day. He got a girl he gives bling-bling [to], she loves him, it sickens me because one day she be left with kids and him dead. So the school cant do a thing, he skips most of it, but he a real bad influence and the teachers are afraid of him. So he's the king of the castle until he ends dead. I know lotsa mothers like my mom that sort of know that their boy is packing and in shit but they're afraid of them and they get food on the table and bling-bling around their neck, ya know such a 'good son.' He treats me bad and my mom too."*

School is also the place where bullying begins. In Ontario, about 13 percent of high-school students are worried about being harmed or threatened at school—and more so in Toronto (Paglia-Boak et al., 2010).

Many studies have found that a school climate, "the feel" of a school as perceived by teachers and students, is related to children's behavioural outcomes (Lawrence, 2007). Schools with a more engaged and interested staff have lower rates of students' problems; in contrast, a school that feels less safe or has a lot of vandalism will have higher rates of student behavioural problems (Gottfredson et al., 2005). In a study by Fitzgerald (2009), school social capital and school disorder were measured and compared with rates of students' self-reported delinquency. They found that Toronto schools that had the least **social capital** (low student attachment, low teacher involvement, fewer activities) had rates of violent delinquency that were 53 percent higher than in schools with the highest level of social capital.

Students' own characteristics as well as those of their families also predicted violent behaviour, as described by the student above. But similar students attending schools with low disorder and high social capital are much less likely to become offenders (Fitzgerald, 2009). Therefore, good schools, attentive parents, and secure neighbourhoods all combine to reduce difficult behaviours and, together, constitute a tripartite zone of **effective**, collective socialization. However, one can also see that the sudden influx of a critical mass of difficult teens in a previously good school can demoralize teachers, lower social capital, and "contaminate" more fragile students:

> *"I'd describe myself as not so happy, about 2 [out of 5]. My placement is at that same high school where I graduated just four years ago and although it was not as good in the last two years, I don't recognize it. The students have no attention span, a whole bunch of them disrupt classes, talk out of turn, laugh at you, intimidate you. I heard that a lot are delinquent and there is certainly drugs going on, but the worst part is that some of the really good teachers we had have retired early because they could not cope with this; some of the new ones that have arrived have 'adjusted' and couldn't care less, and the few other good ones left don't smile anymore, they are like scared and scurrying around, totally discouraged. I am totally discouraged myself because I know that I couldn't cope with this; I don't want to be a parole officer!"*

Minority-Group Children

Family and school compatibility may be particularly challenging for minority-group children. For instance, as indicated in Table 6.2, a study of 15-year-olds' reading achievement in five provinces shows that those who attend the French school system in English-speaking provinces have much lower scores than those who attend the English school system (majority language). In provinces that are predominantly English speaking or mixed, French-speaking children often attend schools that are of lower academic quality than their English counterparts, except in large cities. Moreover, many of these francophone children live in a family that may no longer be technically fluent in their French language (Statistics Canada, 2004e).

For their part, immigrant adolescents who arrive without sufficient Canadian language skills often acquire them more rapidly than do their parents and may have to act as cultural brokers or translators for them (Anisef and Kilbride, 2003). One of the consequences of this situation is that, while these parents generally hold high educational aspirations for their children, they are not in a position to become involved with the school system or to help their adolescents with homework, even though they may be highly educated themselves. Furthermore, the Anisef and Kilbride study group also encountered immigrant youths who resisted conformity to "the culture, values, and established norms of the mainstream society" as coping mechanisms (2003:245). The end result is often conflict with parents and failure at school. This may be compounded by the fact that parents are struggling to make ends meet and are unable to be as supportive as they might have been in their country of origin. However, here as well, immigrant parents' economic means, own level of education, and high expectations all combine to facilitate school achievement.

In terms of Aboriginal families, village- or band-controlled schools value their children's culture more and understand their family dynamics better. For instance, Wall and Madak (1991) have found that high-schoolers who attended tribal schools reported that their teachers and parents held higher educational aspirations for them than did Natives who attended regular public schools. In the latter case, cultural heritage may be substantially diluted and staff may lack an understanding of Natives'

TABLE 6.2	**Reading Averages of Students in French and English School Systems by Province**		
	English School Systems	French School Systems	Provincial Average
Nova Scotia	522	474	521
New Brunswick	512	578	501
Quebec	543	535	536
Ontario	535	474	533
Manitoba	530	486	529

Source: Adapted with permission from Statistics Canada, *The Daily*, March 22, 2004.

family processes. These two factors combine to place children at a disadvantage in terms of school achievement. However, the fact that Aboriginal languages are still being lost in these schools remains a major problem in the cultural continuity of families (Nicholas, 2001). As well, a reverse problem exists when a Native language is taught at school but parents no longer speak it (Paupanekis and Westfall, 2001).

Further, family characteristics (parents' education, employment, and marital status) do not necessarily have the same impact on school success on reserves as they do off reserves and in the population at large (Ward, 1998). Reserve Native parenting style is less supervisory than is the case in the rest of society, because it is their custom to rely on assistance from their **extended kin** or community for child supervision. For these parents, then, how well their children do in school may depend more on the social capital the community makes available to children than their own socialization practices. As well, many Native parents have been alienated from their education and that of their children because of historical factors, and would need to be reintegrated into the educational system (Poonwassie, 2001). This reintegration is particularly important for Natives who live off reserves, especially in cities such as Winnipeg where they are concentrated in disadvantaged areas and may no longer benefit from the support of their original community.

Ideally, when an Aboriginal village controls the school, parents and other community members can voice their concerns and have a greater impact on the curriculum (Ward, 1998). When a school has a very high proportion of Native students, the students are more likely to participate in extracurricular activities and to develop an attachment to their school. Both variables, in turn, prevent drop out, which is an enormous problem among Aboriginals (Mackay and Miles, 1995). However, in some cities such as Winnipeg, students are often placed in classes for "special needs" children, which in effect pathologizes their history of discrimination (Binda, 2001). This situation prevents Native families from accumulating human capital that could be passed on to the next generation and allow them to become integrated at the economic level.

PRIVATE EDUCATION

We look at two different alternatives in children's education: private schools and home schooling.

Private Schools

Semi-private institutions include public schools that are religious in nature, such as the public Catholic school system in many provinces. Then, there are also schools that are sponsored by religious groups—whether Jewish, Mennonite, Muslim, or Mormon—that do not receive taxpayers' subsidies (Seljak, 2005). Next are private schools that focus on academics and are a means for certain families to raise their children within an exclusive environment. CAIS (2009) reports 81 such independent schools in Canada with an enrolment of 40,813 students and a teaching staff of 4,863. Students who attend these schools tend to have higher occupational and social class outcomes later on than students in public schools. This result remains even after family selection factors are controlled (Brewer et al., 1999). A third type of school, often called the alternative school, serves children whose parents are ideologically opposed to certain tenets of mass schooling (i.e., competitiveness, individualism), children who have not adapted to regular schools because of behavioural, emotional, or intellectual challenges, or, yet, children with careers. Some of these alternative schools are publicly funded to meet certain students' needs while others are entirely private.

Parents expect that private schools will pass on their values as well as their lifestyles to their children, whether religion- or class-inspired. From this perspective, such schools serve as an **extension of the family** far more than public schools can:

"I had a wonderful adolescence! My parents put me in this wonderful private school in Grade 7 and I just bloomed. It was like one very large family that sheltered us from the bullies we had had at the public school. I was a nerd and there certainly was no problem with this at this school. I was actually encouraged to read, explore new fields, ask questions, and tag-along [with] the teachers. We were all nerdy and it was just great. Both boys and girls were like that so that even dating was not a problem even though the teachers and our parents all made us understand that this was a stage of life that could wait. So we waited. We did not have to conform to the 'peer culture' (some Culture!) at other schools. We never envied them and all of us grew up to be very well rounded, sociable, and athletic nerds. If we had gone on to public high schools, we would have grown up screwed up or most of us would have given up being intelligent just to fit in."

The staff of a private school are hired on the basis of academic qualifications and indirectly on how well they conform to the school's ideology, which in turn reflects parental ideology. The compatibility between the two is particularly evident in the preceding student quote. Parents and teachers encouraged their adolescents along similar lines of intellectual, moral, and social development. Bibby (2009) has found that students in religious schools hold ideas and values that diverge on some dimensions from those held by other youth. They are less likely to be tolerant of homosexuality, uphold honesty and hard work more, and are more concerned about world poverty. Students attending Sikh, Muslim, and other non-Christian schools would be less likely to live in Canada if they had a choice, which may bring complications in terms of integration into their new country later on.

Home Schooling

Home schooling is where the worlds of children and parents are most intertwined. It is the most clear-cut example of parental resistance to the defamilialization and institutionalization of children, discussed in Chapter 3. Home schooling is currently considered somewhat unusual. Yet, when one examines human history, home education has always prevailed until recently. Parents who resort to home schooling are reacting against the quality, philosophy, structure, and functioning of the formal educational system. Others, especially in the U.S., home-school for religious and moral reasons, while many are responding to what they perceive to be dangerous peer influences (Smith, 1993).

Both in Canada and the U.S., home schooling has been growing each year (Luffman, 1998). The timing of this growth is somewhat paradoxical: It occurs while most married families have two wage earners. Yet, most home teachers are mothers, so that they in effect have to forgo paid employment. In 2000–2001, there were between 60,000 and 95,000 registered home-schoolers in Canada (Ray, 2001). Over 60 percent are elementary-school students. In Ontario, only 8 percent are high-schoolers compared with 45 percent in Alberta and Saskatchewan (Luffman, 1998). In the U.S., there are approximately one million home-schooled children.

Home-schooling parents do not generally function in a vacuum (Brabant et al., 2004). To begin with, every province supervises home-schoolers for compliance with the *Education Act*—although some parents fail to register their children with their local school board. In some provinces, students can use public school libraries and other resources. Both in Canada and the U.S., national, state, and provincial organizations exist for the purpose of offering instrumental and moral support to families involved. Similarly, several relevant magazines are published; jointly, they probably reach most home-schooling parents.

Objections to home schooling, especially by the educational establishment, largely fall into three broad categories: (1) worries that the education provided may not meet national standards, (2) concerns that "zealot" parents may brainwash their children ideologically and religiously, and that (3) children will lack peer contact, will not develop appropriate social skills, and may become socially isolated.

In order to examine the validity of the first objection, Brabant et al. (2004) and Mayberry et al. (1995) have summarized the social profile of the parents of home-schooled children in Quebec and the U.S., respectively. The majority are white and tend to engage in occupations at the professional and technical level more than is the case nationally. The educational level is quite high, especially in Quebec. On average, the familial income is higher, situating them at the middle- to upper-middle-class level. Overall, these parents are educationally qualified, even though they have not generally been trained as teachers.

Interestingly, research fails to find any significant relationship between fathers' educational level and home-schooled children's achievement scores (Ray and Wartes, 1991): The children of parents with a high school education are doing as well as those with parents who graduated from university, which is the opposite of what occurs in regular schools. What probably counts for children's achievement in home schooling is parents' unusually high involvement and motivation. The children perform at the national average and frequently exceed it on standard tests. Many accelerate while being home schooled and enter higher education at a younger age. The only home-schooled student I ever had explains her experience. Although it is on the idyllic side, it nevertheless makes interesting points:

"I never attended school until I entered university. [When] my younger brother . . . left to do his last two years at a private school, I came here . . . my parents are researchers and we lived up north in the bush really and both my parents wanted their career and neither wanted to go at it alone and be separated. We partnered

with a private school when I was in grade 6 and they sent us video tapes of two classrooms so we could see other children and we sent them tapes of our lives here and talked about our lives and did questions and answers from both sides and we visited the school each January and some came here to visit us on field trips. We made friends like that and still have them. We learned a lot and our parents were great teachers and also used us as assistants so we would grow up to be socially responsible. We were all crazy about books and came back from our annual January trips to California and BC with crates of books and also videos. A lot of people were afraid that we would grow up maladjusted but I don't think that there is anything wrong with being 'stuck with your parents' and not having a peer group. Unlike many other children, we had no worries, no anxieties, no fears. We also were very active physically with hiking, canoeing and swimming in wet suits in summer and skiing and skating in winter."

As to whether parents brainwash their offspring and offer them an education that is, for instance, so religiously oriented that it closes the door to children's options in the future, there is no direct research that could answer this critique scientifically. However, it would seem that "brainwashed" children would not do very well on the standard tests they have to take to enter college or that researchers have given them. Yet, we have seen that the contrary happens, although there are certainly exceptions to that rule. Parents themselves have an answer to this objection. They point out that secular humanism taught in public schools does brainwash children into values and beliefs that go against their principles.

In terms of growing up socially inept and isolated, as well as emotionally maladjusted, the tests that have been carried out indicate normal development. However, it can be argued on the basis of other material presented in this chapter that the potential for maladjustment exists for too many children who attend regular schools. As we will see in Chapter 13, studies unanimously indicate that children are often bullied and victimized by peers. These statistics and experiences actually lead many parents to begin home schooling. Children who are home schooled generally have at least one sibling. They also meet peers who are in similar circumstances; they know children in the neighbourhood and many participate in extracurricular activities, such as sports teams and Scouts, which put them in frequent contact with regularly schooled peers. At the high school level, many home-schooled teens have jobs like other youths. Overall, although home schooling is unusual, it does not appear to produce negative effects, and perhaps quite the opposite occurs (Rothermel, 2000).

RELIGIOUS PARTICIPATION AND FAMILY LIFE

Religion constitutes one of the most important cultural domains in most societies. In Canada, it still plays an important role in the lives of a substantial proportion of families, even though its institutional role and moral authority have declined, as is the case in most western societies (Bibby, 2002). Its impact on family life is therefore likely to be more obvious among the observant, hence the focus on religiosity. New arrivals to Canada are often very religious and family studies do not yet adequately reflect this reality (Biles and Ibrahim, 2005). As is the case in Europe, their level of religiosity may contrast with that of the remainder of the population (Westoff and Frejka, 2007).

The Factor of Religiosity

How is the importance of religion to a family or to some of its members measured? A great deal of controversy revolves around this matter, as one can well imagine, because religiosity is difficult to define and measure and so, especially, is spirituality. Religiosity is more community focused and organized, with specific beliefs, while spirituality is more subjective and personal (Koenig et al., 2001). The two may be related but one does not necessarily follow the other (Taylor et al., 2004). In this chapter, the focus is on the *communal aspect*.

The most obvious and commonly used **indicator** of religiosity is attendance at religious services (see Family Research 6.2). Generally, phone or door-to-door surveys ask questions such as: "Did you, yourself, happen to attend church, mosque, or synagogue in the last seven days?" This is actually a Gallup survey question (Smith, 1998). (However, Canadian Social Surveys now include the word "meetings"— Statistics Canada, 2004l). The first problem with these and similar questions resides in how well they reflect the increasing religious diversity in Canada.

For instance, among Sikhs and Hindus, religious ritual is often focused on the home and in a variety of practices; thus the question asked will fail to tap their level

---

FAMILY RESEARCH 6.2

What Can Be Done with a Question on Religiosity?

Statistics Canada conducts an annual General Social Survey from a sample of 10,000 Canadians. Since 1985, two questions about religion have been included. One question concerns religious affiliation and the other pertains to religiosity, that is, the frequency of attendance at religious services or meetings. Clark (1998) first controlled for or took into account income, family structure, education, age, sex, and employment because it is well known that these variables are related to various aspects of well-being. Then, with these controls in the background, the researchers still found that persons who attend religious services or meetings weekly are half less likely to feel stressed and 1.5 times more likely to have a very happy marital relationship than those who do not

attend religious services at all. Weekly attendees' marriages are also far more likely to last. Overall, weekly attendees hold more conventional family values and adopt better health practices.

It would be interesting to break down the results by religious affiliation, given that Canada is such a diverse society: Would these results apply equally well for Chinese religion, Hindus, Sikhs, Buddhists, or Muslims? As well, there are more indicators of religiosity that could be included, such as frequency of reading religious books, watching/listening to religious television/radio, and prayers (Atkins and Kessel, 2008; Taylor et al., 2004).

of religiosity, even though they do have gurudwaras and multi-use temples (Banerjee and Coward, 2005). Further, for many, attendance at temple or mosque functions may be more a matter of maintaining their culture and of networking within their group than being religiously observant. Tapping into Chinese religiosity is even more complex because it focuses on home altars, temples, festivals, and Chinatowns. As Lai et al. (2005:100) point out, "since Chinese religion is so completely intertwined with daily life, culture, and family, one could argue that the many Chinatowns are themselves the most accessible public expression of Chinese religion in Canada."

In 2001, about 20 percent of the adult Canadian population attended religious services on a weekly basis, down from about 67 percent in 1946 (Clark, 2003). In 2008, 31 percent of women and 26 percent of men attended religious services at least once a month (Statistics Canada, 2010a). The monthly rate in the U.S. is 45 percent, thus much higher. In Canada, there are regional as well as immigration-related differences. Monthly attendance ranges from 53 percent in Prince Edward Island, 36 percent in Ontario, and 25 percent in Quebec and British Columbia. Table 6.3 illustrates the fact that attendance has declined among the Canadian-born but has increased among immigrants, except in Quebec—probably as a result of the strong secular effect of that province or a selection effect among future immigrants themselves. The increase of religious attendance among immigrants may stem from a change in the countries of origin of immigrants (Chapter 2). More Filipinos attend Catholic churches, as is the case in Toronto. In addition, mosques as well as Hindu and Sikh temples have been erected during the past decade and facilitate attendance (McDonough and Hoodfar, 2005).

Considering all the religious indicators together, but particularly attendance at services, women are more religious than men, the older more than the younger,

| TABLE 6.3 | Change in Religious Attendance by Place of Birth in the Three Largest CMAs: Percentages of Those Who Attend at Least Once a Month* |

	1989–1993	1999–2001	Difference
Montreal			
Canadian-born	26%	17%	−9%
Born outside Canada	44	40	−4
Toronto			
Canadian-born	31	28	−3
Born outside Canada	44	50	+6
Vancouver			
Canadian-born	19	21	+2
Born outside Canada	35	39	+4

Source: Adapted with permission from Statistics Canada, General Social Survey; Clark, 2003.
* For the population aged 15 and over.

"conservative" Protestants more than "liberal" Protestants, and the married more than the single and divorced (Presser and Stinson, 1998). In the U.S., black families attend religious services and participate in other religious activities far more frequently than do white families, except Latinos (Aldous and Ganey, 1999). There is a greater mixture of secular and religious functions in the black community (Lincoln and Mamiya, 1990). As well, in terms of giving money to charities and volunteering time, Canadians tend to give more of both to religious organizations (Grona, 2009).

Parents' and Children's Religiosity: The Socialization Aspect

Parents transmit their beliefs to their children by their teachings and their example. Attendance at church, synagogue, temple, or mosque is itself a powerful socialization situation (Pearce and Thornton, 2007). The example set by mothers who are warmly accepting of their children is particularly powerful in the transmission of religious beliefs (Bao et al., 1999).

Myers (1996) tried to see what characterized religious parents who were the most successful at transmitting their beliefs to their children. Parental religiosity was measured in 1980, when the offspring were still living at home and thus under direct parental influence. In 1992, the children, who by then had reached adulthood, were interviewed. Highly devout parents had children who, on average, were less similar to them than were the offspring of parents who were either moderately religious or not religious. In other words, the religious standards of many devout parents may have been too high to emulate; hence their children became only moderately religious later on—or rebelled against religious practice—thus becoming less similar to their parents in this dimension. Two students describe pertinent but totally different experiences:

> *"One constant source of unhappiness throughout childhood and adolescence was religious observance. My parents are extremely religious. . . . I hated having to go to church weekly and say family prayers and having to go to religious school . . . even the teachers thought that my parents were overdoing it. My parents and I fought constantly over religious issues and even theological matters. The end result is that I am religiously atheist."*

> *"My parents are not religious at all so that we never had religion in our lives but I am about to get married and it would have been nice to have had a church wedding because it is less commercial and has more meaning and my future husband and I have decided that it would be better to raise our children in a religion because that way it would give them a feeling of belonging. They would also get raised with better values. I think that children need this in our type of world because no one teaches morality any more."*

As all studies were largely carried out with Christian and Jewish respondents, it would be important to know how these factors would play out among Buddhists, Hindus, Sikhs, and Muslims, for instance—although their immigrant status and home culture are variables that may be even stronger factors than religiosity alone. Myers also found that parents who both agreed on religious or secular beliefs had been more successful at transmitting them, which makes sense because children learn better in a consistent environment. In families characterized by high marital happiness, offspring were more likely to resemble their parents in religious beliefs—whether these beliefs were orthodox, moderate, or lukewarm. This is related to other findings described in Chapter 9, indicating that a harmonious parental relationship constitutes a positive child socialization context.

THE ROLE PLAYED BY RELIGIOSITY IN FAMILY LIFE

Does religious participation fulfill any role in family life besides the transmission of beliefs and related behaviours? What does religiosity do for the family and its members? Religious beliefs can be analyzed as a form of capital—**religious capital** as Iannaccone (1990) calls it—from which families can, in theory, draw cohesion as well as strength. Participating in a congregation may constitute a form of **social capital** in the guise of informal networks of social support. The following discussion is based on studies of Christians and to some extent Jews. I would hypothesize that the research described below applies equally well to other religions, but with differences pertaining to matters related to gender roles and marital quality (see Bramadat and Seljak, 2005). The issue of **cultural capital** may even be more salient in other religions, especially for recent immigrant families.

Religiosity Correlates with Well-Being

A substantial body of literature indicates that religious involvement and strength of beliefs are related to general feelings of well-being (Clark, 1998) as well as psychological and physical health, including lower adult mortality (Hummer et al., 1999). This benefit may manifest itself as early as adolescence (Crosnoe and Elder, 2002). Religiosity provides internal coherence; it serves as an explanatory platform that enables persons to make sense of everyday life and its adversities. It offers guiding principles of action, and makes people less individualistic and more duty bound.

Religiosity serves as an internal and external **agency of social control** (Durkheim, 1951); hence, religious commitment lowers health risks such as alcoholism, drug addiction, and precocious sexual activity, and may serve to prevent depression and anxiety (Ellison et al., 2009). In fact, religiosity is related to children's prosocial behaviours (Bartowski et al., 2008). It may deter drug use and delinquent behaviour among adolescents, in part because religious adolescents are less likely to associate with peers who use drugs (Johnson et al., 2001). Adolescents who are more religious view delinquent actions as morally unacceptable and tend to select a peer group with a similar commitment. As a result, their level of delinquency is lower than that of non-religious adolescents, hence facilitating parental socialization (Simons et al., 2004). Other studies show that private religious practice among adolescents, or the degree to which their religion is internalized, is related to fewer behavioural problems in environments in which violence is often witnessed and victimization occurs (Pearce et al., 2003). Finally, let's mention the many studies indicating that family religiosity is related to a later age of onset of sexual behaviours among adolescents (Manlove et al., 2008b).

Religious participation contributes to extend a family's social network and sources of social support. Frequent churchgoers have somewhat larger social networks than others and enjoy more frequent person-to-person contacts. They are also more involved in their community (Jones, 2000). They receive more help and report feeling cared for and valued. Therefore, religious participation becomes an important social resource for families (Bramadat and Seljak, 2005). This was expressed by a student above. Below, a complementary perspective is presented by yet another student:

> "My mother is a concern to me at this stage because she is 65 and widowed and unemployed [but not poor]. But I think that her church activities and all the friendships she's made there help her a lot and will sustain her for some years to come. Sometimes I even go with her because I like meeting all these people of all ages. Anyway, my mother says that religion keeps her in good health and she is far from being a zealot."

Religiosity Relates to Marital Quality and Stability

Adults who declare a religious affiliation are more likely to see marriage as a lifetime commitment than adults who profess no religious affiliation (Stanley et al., 2004). This may apply to same-sex couples (Oswald et al., 2008). They are also less likely to engage in extramarital sex. Couples who hold beliefs that are more religious experience higher conjugal satisfaction and quality (Lichter and Carmalt, 2009; Treas and Giesen, 2000; Tremblay et al., 2002). Couples who regularly attend church together have a lower rate of divorce than those who attend infrequently or not at all (Fincham and Beach, 2010; Provencher et al., 2006). However, couples in which only one spouse attends are even more likely to divorce than couples who never attend (Vaaler et al., 2009). The latter finding can probably be explained in terms of religious similarity, or homogamy, described in Chapter 7: Couples who differ in religious matters have one potentially large source of conflict. In contrast, couples who attend church together benefit from the sharing of a social and spiritual activity that reinforces their solidarity. They may also benefit from exposure to more **altruistic values** than non-churchgoers, and this would in turn contribute to a less individualistic pattern of marital interaction (Pearce and Axinn, 1998). A student expresses this sociological observation within the context of his intimate relationship:

> "My problem right now is that my girlfriend is not religious and this worries me a lot because I know from my parents' experience that sharing beliefs and especially [going to church] . . . give a couple a lot in common. Above all I am concerned that my girlfriend may miss out on the importance of values that help keep a marriage together, like learning how to be committed and think in terms of the good of the relationship and not just about your own personal desires."

Similarly, mutually shared religious beliefs strengthen marital stability as religions tend to be pro-marriage rather than pro-divorce. Amato and Rogers (1997) report that frequent church attendance may reduce the likelihood of divorce through a reduction in marital problems. Why would couples who attend church frequently experience fewer marital problems? Their explanation is congruent with the ones just presented. They reason that church attendance, or even shared at-home devotional activities, allow for the internalization and thus acceptance of norms of behaviour that encourage couples to get along (Ellison et al., 2010). They also refer to the social aspect of church attendance: It serves as a **support group** as well as a control group or an effective community. Vaaler et al. (2009:930), for their part, note that more religious people are less prone to divorce because their level of marital satisfaction is higher, their likelihood of engaging in domestic violence lower, and "they perceive fewer attractive options outside the marriage than their less religious counterparts." As well, parents' religiosity influences adult children's attitudes toward divorce (Kapinus and Pellerin, 2008). The sum of these studies therefore indicates a salutary effect of religiosity on the quality of the marital relationship as well as on the stability of the family unit.

Religiosity Scaffolds the Parental Role

Religious beliefs strengthen parents' involvement with their children, even when the latter become particularly difficult and stressful. Pearce and Axinn (1998:824) surmise that "exposure to religious themes such as tolerance, patience, and unconditional love" through religious activities constitutes a resource that helps parents and children maintain a good relationship. Mother-child similarity in religiosity strengthens the bond between the two. Some studies indicate that, especially among African Americans who are disadvantaged, religious parents use fewer coercive methods with their children than non-religious parents (Wiley et al., 2002). Overall, research shows that religious mothers experience a higher quality of relationship with their children (Pearce and Axinn, 1998), and that religious fathers, whether married or divorced, are more involved in their role (King, 2003b).

In a study of five European countries, Gans et al. (2009) found that religious individuals were more likely to engage in supportive behaviours toward elderly parents. Adolescent mothers who attend church services have been found to be less abusive and had children with fewer internalizing and externalizing problems by age

Worshipping together constitutes a form of social capital. Religious participation can also be the basis of an effective community, which contributes to child and adolescent socialization, and buttresses the parental role.

10—as religiosity increased social support and served as a protective factor (Carothers et al., 2005). But it is possible that a genetic selection process occurs as well to explain this correlation.

Following a **family developmental perspective**, Stolzenberg et al. (1995) demonstrate that people often become more religious with age. But the addition of children to the family unit further enhances this increase in religious participation (Nock, 1998c). In contrast, as childless married adults age, their religious participation does not increase to any great extent. One explanation may be that adults with children seek religious membership and participation in order to become better anchored in the community and as a means of social support in their parenting role. Along this line of reasoning, another student projects a greater role for religion later in her life:

> *"Right now I don't go to church often but I intend to become active again as soon as I have children, just as my parents did. I think that a bit of religion is very helpful to children: it teaches them values other than what they see on TV. The few times I go to church I am always struck by how civilized people behave and it gives you a warm feeling of humanity."*

One could perhaps speculate that many parents need religion nowadays in order to feel more secure in their role in a very demanding and confusing world. Conventional families form the mainstay of organized religion. Such parents may get gratification for their role within the context of religion, which would serve as a compensatory mechanism for the blaming and disempowerment they receive from so many quarters. Wilcox (2002:791) concludes: "The irony is that religious institutions, generally taken to be carriers of more traditional mores, seem to be showing some success" in fostering paternal involvement in times of change. Parents may also use religion as an agent of socialization and as a source of support for their children. In this respect, it is interesting to note that Canadian youths leave home significantly earlier when they never attended religious services as teenagers (Beaupré et al., 2008).

Limitations of Religion for Nonconventional Families

Organized religions, which have been culturally developed by men over several millennia or centuries, support gender stratification (Sered, 1999). It follows that families headed by women and men who are strongly aware of inequalities based on gender may not find spiritual sustenance and stability in religion as much as do other families. Furthermore, most religions frown on nonmarital forms of sexuality, and individuals who regularly attend religious services are less favourable toward nonmarital sex. Depending on the religion, churchgoers may also strongly disapprove of homosexuality.

Therefore, while faith and religiosity are very positive for the faithful's well-being on many levels, they are less so for the well-being of those who engage in nonconventional forms of family life, such as families headed by same-sex couples. Religious communities by and large exclude these couples so that these families are deprived of a powerful instrument of child socialization and a powerful source of family stability. There are indications that many gays and lesbians are deeply religious but fear rejection, as explained in a student autobiography:

> *"My lover and I both come from religious families and this has probably contributed to our mutual attraction. We're basically both moderately religious but we can't go to church. I suppose we could go separately and I could even join the choir . . . and he might volunteer in the child care. But we can't do this because we'd stick out like sore thumbs and we might even be discouraged from participating. We could go with my parents but what if they were ostracized as a result? I'm sure that there must be other gays out there who are religious but Bob and I don't mix much with the gay community because we're a monogamous couple."*

(It is probably not a coincidence that this couple is planning to adopt children; their values are mainstream.) In many areas, various congregations are opening their community to homosexuals and have been at the forefront of gay rights issues. As well, churches located in downtown areas may be more accepting of diversity than those in suburbs or in rural areas. But overall, one can conclude that religious establishments do not serve the entire spectrum of families equally well, although some congregations are far more proactive than others in this respect. As well, religion is heavily influenced by regional cultures and even political situations. For instance, depending on cultural origins and time periods, Muslim women may dress in an occidental manner while others wear a head scarf and even the burqa.

CONCLUSIONS: THE BALANCING ACT OF FAMILY FUNCTIONS

Children and adolescents attending educational facilities and child care centres come to school from their families and return to their families when the school day is over. Their parents must manage this institutional link and remain vigilant so that the best interest of their child is well served. This is an especially difficult role for families because school systems serve the economies in which they are nestled and economies are currently largely driven by a relentless technological and globalized marketplace. Many families are unable to compete and even survive within the harsh realities of this context.

In particularly deficient schools, parents have to supplement their children's education. As well, when schools harbour a critical mass of antisocial children, parents have to step in, if they can, to protect and even shelter their children. Thus, although schools have taken over some of the functions previously fulfilled by families, schools have also forced an extension of family functions into the public domain. Furthermore, depending on family structure and place within the social class system, schools create a host of demands on parents.

Thus, to return to the discussions in Chapter 3, the educational system often expands family functions and may even burden the family system and, more specifically, mothers. For families that are religiously oriented, however, religion seems to scaffold parents in their socialization role—support for the parental role and support for adolescents and youths who wish to lead a life devoid of lifestyle risks. Therefore, at least for religious families, the practice of their faith generally strengthens their ability to fulfill their functions in a society that often provides pressures against this goal.

Summary

1. After parents, schools are a main agent of child socialization. Children today begin school earlier, and for many, this experience includes child care other than parental. Among the several types of non-parental child care available are centres or mini-schools, women who take one or several children into their homes, care by relatives, and care by a nanny. Poor-quality care has been related to disadvantages in cognition, language development, as well as social and emotional adjustment. Questions are arising concerning potentially negative effects of very long hours, too much peer contact, and too little interaction with adults. Child care availability, affordability, and quality are key ingredients in contemporary children's development and in their parents' well-being. Head Start programs benefit poor children living in disadvantaged areas, as they prepare these children for school, both cognitively and behaviourally. Some Aboriginal groups have initiated Head Start programs.

2. Parental involvement in their children's education contributes to school success. However, parents' social class largely determines the extent as well as the effectiveness of their involvement. Parental social capital benefits children's access to social as well as material resources that help them increase their adaptation to school. Overall, children from higher-SES families do better academically, as do children who attend schools with greater percentages of students from higher-SES backgrounds. Middle-class parents engage in the process of concentrated cultivation. Disadvantaged parents value education as much as others but practical problems often prevent this valuation from translating into higher aspirations and then achievement for their children. Incompatibility between family life and school routines often prevents children from adapting successfully. Incompatibility increases in schools that have a high proportion of antisocial students. The summer activities of low-income children are often incompatible with learning, and they usually return to school even further behind higher-income students. Family and school compatibility in the guise of band-controlled schools is especially important for Aboriginal children. Immigrant adolescents, in particular, face challenges in this respect.

3. Private schools are selected by parents who can afford them and who expect that their own values will be reinforced. Private schools, particularly religious ones, constitute an effective community that enhances children's academic abilities. Home schooling is another system that parents turn to in order to ensure the passage of their values to their children as well as their educational success. It is a growing phenomenon, and concerns for home-schooled children's well-being and academic success do not seem to be warranted.

4. Religion plays an important role in the lives of many Canadian families. The most commonly used indicator of religiosity is church or temple attendance. About 20 percent of Canadians attend religious services weekly and 31 percent at least monthly. Americans' church attendance is higher.

5. Parents transmit their religious beliefs to their children by their teachings and example, but the overall religious climate in a society also contributes to child socialization in this respect. Parents' marital happiness may also be a factor contributing to the transmission of their religious values to their children. Overall, religious involvement seems functional in terms of health, psychological well-being, marital stability and happiness, as well as child socialization. Religiosity supports the parental role. However, some religions are less supportive of nontraditional families.

6. While the educational system often increases the functions that families have to fulfill, the religious system may offer a supportive framework for the fulfillment of family functions.

Analytical Questions

1. What would be some methodological difficulties involved in the study of the effect of child care on child development?
2. Why do you think that school officials and even some researchers are worried about home schooling? (Note: The question is why they are worried, not what they are worried about.)
3. How could the school system be reformed to meet the needs of families of immigrants as well as low income families?

4. Religion and especially religiosity are rarely discussed in family textbooks. Why do you think that this is so?
5. What role does religiosity play in families that are not Christian or Jewish? (You will need to use other sources or your own personal experience/observations to address this question.)

Suggested Readings

Bramadat, P., and Seljak, D. (Eds.) 2005. *Religion and ethnicity*. Toronto: Pearson Education. This collection of articles presents an overview of more recent ethnic groups in Canada and their religious organizations.

Castellano, M. B., Davis, L., and Lahache, L. (Eds.) 2000. *Aboriginal education: Fulfilling the promise*. Vancouver: University of British Columbia Press. This book contains a series of research articles, some of which originally served as a basis for the 1996 report of the Royal Commission on Aboriginal People. The articles, however, were not intended to have a focus on families.

Entwisle, D. R., Alexander, K. L., and Olson, L. S. 1997. *Children, schools, and inequality*. Boulder, CO: Westview. The researchers marshal an impressive array of data to study the effect of schooling on children as well as the effect of social inequalities (parents' social class, for instance) on children's progress and test scores.

Houseknecht, S. K., and Parkhurst, J. G. (Eds.) 2000. *Family, religion and social change in diverse societies*. New York: Oxford University Press. This collection of articles focuses on religion and the family in various cultural contexts of social change. It includes sections on gender as well as on economic factors.

Suggested Weblinks

Canadian Child Care Federation provides news, information, and links to other sources regarding child care practice and issues.
www.cccf-fcsge.ca

Childcare Canada. Childcare Resource and Research Unit. Combination of scholarly and practical material.
www.childcarecanada.org

Various associations for home schooling include:
Ontario Federation of Teaching Parents

www.ontariohomeschool.org

Canada Homeschooling
http://homeschooling.gomilpitas.com/regional/Canada.htm

Association of Canadian Home Based Education
www.flora.org/homeschool-ca/achbe/index.html

National Homeschooling Info
http://homeschooling.about.com

CHAPTER 7

Couple Formation and Sexual Relations

OUTLINE

"The most painful aspect of my life at this age [about 21] *is that I don't have a steady boyfriend. I haven't had one in two years and I am worried that life is passing me by."*

"I rate myself as very happy . . . . Before I broke up with my boyfriend of two years I had no life. I was entirely wrapped up in a relationship that denied my identity . . . . It's freedom now and time for me to use it to mature."

"I live with my boyfriend and I really like it for now but I worry about the future. I am 23 and want to get married one day but the way I see it, he likes it just fine the way it is and won't want to commit himself to something more serious."

"In 10 years from now I realistically see myself living with a partner but it will not be the one I am with now as you can guess [this lesbian student is currently living with a woman at least 15 years her senior who supports her financially but is very controlling and possessive]. *This relationship has left me with some 'emotional' baggage I have to get rid of before I can contemplate another relationship and I plan on living on my own for some years after school is over."*

"What has made me the most unhappy in the past years has been the gay social scene. I really hated every minute of it. . . . What has made me the most happy in the past year has been getting out of the gay social scene and finding my lover who just feels the way I do. [This student lives with his parents.]

"I am still a virgin and it has its inconvenience socially [popularity]. *. . . I am proud of myself because I have stuck to my principles and my parents' and one day the full discovery of sex will be a very exciting experience to share with my husband. It will add something to our marriage and he will know that I have waited for him."*

The preceding students reveal how they feel about dating, cohabitation, being partnered, and sexuality—all main topics of this chapter. These quotes were chosen to reflect the variety of personal experiences and expectations in student populations. This chapter starts with the chronological beginning of life as a couple: Individuals select partners, become couples, and initiate sexual relations. Sexual identity is also discussed. For most of these topics, there is now far more Canadian research than used to be the case just a few years ago.

DATING

Dating is an American institution that emerged after the First World War. To this day, nowhere is dating as ritualized among adolescents and students as it is in the U.S. and only to a slightly lesser extent in Canada. In addition, nowhere else does it exist at the preadolescent level. Even U.S. researchers seem to accept the ages of 13 and 14 as "developmentally appropriate" for the onset of dating (Longmore et al., 2001)—even though many parents may disagree. When it began, dating was revolutionary because it replaced the traditional *courtship* system as a prelude to marriage: It represented a shift in terms of control over couple formation—from parents to the youths involved.

But this social invention has also evolved over time. The period of adolescence has lengthened and age at marriage was delayed in order to consolidate education and career at the upper and middle echelons of the class system. As a result, dating was separated from marriage as a goal. Its purpose became recreational and sexualized. In fact, today many youths, particularly males, are simply more interested in "hooking up" than in dating (Bogle, 2008; Hamilton and Armstrong, 2009). Other youths move in together rather than date. Later on, we will see that Internet dating is changing the shape of dating itself, if not necessarily its purposes.

Heterosexual Dating

Children as young as age five are at times asked if they have a girlfriend or boyfriend yet. They learn, perhaps too young, that a couple culture pervades North American social life, which later makes it difficult for individuals to feel that they "belong" if they do not have a steady date or partner. Thus, steady dates represent a measure of social and personal predictability and security in a youth's social life. But when concerns about being a couple occur early in a child's life, they may supplant other experiences and sources of self-definition. Not surprisingly, research indicates that young adolescent females who are romantically involved are more vulnerable in the emotional and academic realms than are older adolescents (Brendgen et al., 2002; Joyner and Udry, 2000). Dating often becomes a form of social pressure and a key source of status, although this may be diminishing (Bibby, 2002:180). Dating also serves the function of socializing youths, both positively and negatively, for the role they will play when they cohabit or marry.

Women tend to invest more in their dating relationship than do men (Sacher and Fine, 1996). This pattern of **gender roles** in the emotional domain is pursued at all levels of romantic relationships. The greater female investment stems in part from their socialization, which has taught them to be nurturing and understanding of others (Onyskiw and Hayduk, 2001:382), and to depend on males. Females also perceive that they have access to fewer desirable alternatives outside their relationship than do males. Students' autobiographies indicate that this situation exists across social class and ethnicity:

> *"The most painful experience at this stage has occurred three months ago when I broke up with my boyfriend of three years. . . . I should have broken up with*

him two years ago . . . but I was afraid to be left alone, that I wouldn't be able to go out without a boyfriend, that I couldn't find another one, but now I realize that I have wasted two years of my life, and that's terrifying."

This perception of a lack of alternatives contributes to reinforcing women's tendency to work harder at relationship maintenance, even if this is to their detriment. Studies confirm that dating interactions are nonegalitarian, at least at the beginning (Laner and Ventrone, 1998). This pattern is pursued into pre-wedding relationships (Humble, 2003) and spousal relationships, as discussed in Chapter 9. However, in terms of **social exchange theory**, females with the most desirable resources (often defined by males as attractiveness) can "afford" doing less maintenance work, as their alternatives may be more numerous and desirable than those of their date.

Same-Sex Dating

It is not yet possible to provide solid information on same-sex dating because little research exists on this topic. To begin with, gay youths are not readily accessible for research purposes (Anderson, 1998). Not only do many shun publicity so as to avoid stigmatization but they also constitute a small minority. Furthermore, there is not always a clear-cut demarcation between homosexual and heterosexual self-identity, particularly among youths.

This being said, one can presume that "dating" may fulfill emotional functions for homosexuals similar to those among heterosexuals. Same-sex dating may, however, be difficult in terms of high school popularity as well as social acceptance in colleges and universities located outside key metropolitan areas. The high school environment is often anti-gay, as it is at some universities. As a result, gay youths may be harassed, which in turn can lead to mental health problems.

Gay adolescents and young adults, then, might not be able to date as do their heterosexual peers for fear of being socially stigmatized. Or, they may not yet know how to recognize a potential partner, may not have access to enough potential partners to find an appropriate one, while others may rely on sexual minority youth groups to find partners (Elze, 2002). Further, for many, "coming out" (revealing their sexual identities) may occur only when they reach adulthood.

Internet Dating

Internet dating has greatly increased recently and deserves attention in family textbooks. What is written here about this new phenomenon is tentative because it is too soon to expect extensive research to have been carried out in this domain. We do not even have estimates, but it is obviously widespread if one judges from the proliferation of Internet sites for the purpose of meeting dates, sexual partners for all types of relationships and marital partners. There are ethnic sites, same-sex sites, sites pertaining to match people with certain conditions, such as HIV. Internet dating, as well as chat rooms, also contributes to enlarging both the structure and the meaning of dating itself.

There are several important issues that require urgent research, even though this approach to relationship formation is evolving rapidly (Wilson, 2009). For instance, when one meets someone in person rather than on the Internet, a chain of dynamics begins: A face-to-face interaction develops, and one can immediately "test" certain realities, such as physical appearance, voice, facial expressions, and general demeanour. Online, in contrast, one starts with a description that may or may not be accurate, even when pictures are attached. Then, emails may be exchanged, additional pictures may follow, a phone call may result. The face-to-face interaction arrives only after one has already developed an impression, an image, of the other, and even after an online relationship has progressed.

A second difference is that Internet and "speed dating" involve a multiplicity of potential partners; it is akin to a buffet as opposed to a sit-down dinner! What does it do to a person to have access to so many potential contacts? Does it take a shorter or a longer time to concentrate on one person, to commit to one person? Do Internet daters run the risk of never committing themselves to a relationship? And how solid is this commitment when one knows that there are so many others "out there" that one could try? Do new Internet partners go through the same phases of acquaintanceship and attachment as others do when they meet face to face? Are the relationships as successful, as happy, as long? Do they result more in cohabitations or in marriages? These are only a few of the questions that could be studied.

DATE AND PARTNER SELECTION

Dates and now "hook ups" are largely selected from schools, neighbourhoods, part-time work sites, and social clubs to which adolescents or their parents belong. Parents, siblings, and their friends may also constitute a source of dates, particularly in some religions or ethnicities among whom marriage within the group is preferred. Overall, **propinquity**, or physical proximity, is the first rule that explains how adolescents choose dates and, later on, partners. In young adulthood, proximal availability continues to be an important factor, but its scope broadens to include the worlds of higher education and employment. Thus, the new phenomenon of Internet dating defies the first rule of partner selection.

As they age, young adults generally become more selective and the pool of eligible dates narrows because each individual then tries to select only certain types of persons (Sassler, 2010). This is called **assortative mating**, which refers to choosing a date or partner on the basis of certain traits. When two persons choose each other on the basis of some elements of similarity, this is called **homogamy**. The term **endogamy** is used when people date, cohabit, and marry within their own status group or with persons who are similar to them in terms of basic social characteristics. Homogamy leads to compatibility of interests, values, and lifestyle. Endogamy and homogamy make sense, both from a functional perspective and exchange theory: Similarity of lifestyle, values, and interests gives couples a larger pool of experiences they can share and activities they can engage in together. It strengthens mutual feelings, "we-ness," and companionship—key elements in modern relationships—and lowers the risk of divorce (Kalmijn et al., 2005).

Elements in Partner Selection

Race and even **ethnicity** are usually the first two elements that are considered in partner selection. Even "hook ups" largely involve same-race selection, albeit far less so than dating (McClintock, 2010). Although intermarriage (exogamy) between whites and other groups is now widely accepted at the attitudinal level in Canada, only 3.9 percent of married and cohabiting couples are racially mixed. For instance, in the 2006 census, there were 247,600 couples involving a white person with someone who is from another group, or 3.3 percent of all couples; in addition, there were 41,900 couples involving members of two different non-white groups or 0.6 percent of all couples. Japanese Canadians, who have been in Canada for many generations, were overwhelmingly intermarried at 60 percent (Milan et al., 2010; Statistics Canada, 2009p). In contrast, South Asian and Chinese Canadians have, so far, been the least likely to intermarry, at 18 and 9.5 percent, respectively. It is, however, expected that their rates will increase over time (Lee and Boyd, 2008).

In 2006 in Canada, a much larger proportion of black men than black women who were in unions were in mixed ones (Milan et al., 2010). This creates a serious imbalance for black women, which has been called the "new **marriage squeeze**" (Crowder and Tolnay, 2000). Black American women college students do not approve of interracial encounters, in great part because they are disadvantaged in this domain (Childs, 2005). They are also concerned about black men's reluctance to commit themselves to exclusive relationships (McClintock, 2010). In the U.S., black/white unions are far more common in casual hook ups and simple dating. Both in Canada and the U.S., mixed unions involving a black person are more common among cohabiting than among married couples (Batson et al., 2006). Such unions are also less stable. A black student expresses her frustration:

> *"My older sister is tall and slim and has great features and she just married a nice black guy and our parents are so proud of her. I admit, they're a lovely couple but this leaves me nowhere because I don't have her looks and I haven't met a decent black guy who isn't interested in just sex (and I apologize for being so crude but I guess I'm really angry) or white girls. They seem to think that black girls are there just to make kids for them.... I'm not bold enough to look at white guys and I'm afraid that if I got a white boyfriend his family and friends would be very disappointed and this would reflect badly on our relationship. Lots of my girlfriends are in the same spot but it doesn't make me feel any better. I don't think that people understand this."*

As the number of Canadians who belong to minority groups increases, interracial marriages will also increase over the years. Indeed, Kalbach (2000) has found that, at least for ethnicity, the Canadian-born have higher exogamy rates than the foreign-born. Further, white interethnic marriages are the norm rather than the exception among Canadian-born groups from northern and western Europe. In general, however, intermarriages involve partners who, except for race or ethnicity, are very similar in terms of religion, education, lifestyle, and values (Yancey, 2002).

Social class, or socioeconomic status (SES), as well as **educational** endogamy, is widespread. This is partly explained by the fact that the proximity factor is driven by parents' social class, which dictates where children live and which schools they attend (Nelson and Robinson, 2002). Even at work, people are attracted to one another because of common interests and shared topics of conversation that are partly related to their class-linked resources, including education and leisure activities. When the partners are discrepant, the more common scenario involves a woman in a relationship with a man of higher income.

In terms of **education** alone, there is an even greater trend than 30 years ago toward homogamy, especially among the university educated (Hou and Myles, 2008). Inasmuch as higher education is related to better salaries, as seen in Chapter 4, educational similarity at the top contributes to the increasing gap between the rich and the poor. However, in terms of gender, men are more advantaged than women in this respect because 68 percent of university educated men marry homogamously but only 53 percent of similar women do (Hou and Myles, 2007). One has to keep in mind here that men and women with university degrees are still a minority in Canada, although this minority is increasing among younger cohorts. In contrast, cohabitors, whether in Quebec or in the rest of Canada, have a lower level of educational homogamy (Hamplova and Le Bourdais, 2008).

Religious endogamy is related to marital quality but less so than a generation ago (Myers, 2006). Religious similarity is more important in some groups, including the Jewish and other non-Christian faiths, especially Sikhs, Hindus, and Muslims, than among Protestant and Catholic groups. Statistics Canada (2006c) reports that people who are highly religious, are older, or are immigrant and belong to communities that are religiously homogeneous, are less likely to marry someone of another religion. In 1981, 15 percent of couples were interreligious and, by 2001, 19 percent were—not a huge increase. Nearly half of these unions were between Catholics and Protestants, which are the two largest religious groups in Canada. Sikhs, Hindus, and Muslims have the lowest interreligious marriage rate and it is even lower now than it was in 1981 when fewer persons of these religions lived in Canada. Muslims who marry out tended to have a Catholic partner and represented 4 percent of Muslim couples. About 17 percent of couples in which there was one Jewish person were interreligious in 2001, up from 9 percent in 1981. However, substantial proportions of these marriages are remarriages.

A preference for **age** homogamy also exists. In 58 percent of couples, the spouses are no more than three years apart in age while 24 percent have a spouse who is four to six years older. However, when there is an age difference, norms favour an "older man-younger woman" situation: While 36 percent of Canadian couples include a male who is older by three years, only 6 percent of couples include a woman who is more than three years older than the man (Boyd and Li, 2003). When men marry at an older age, or remarry, they usually do so to women considerably younger than they (Wu et al., 2000). The **age gap** increases with subsequent remarriages. Thus, the older men are at marriage, the larger the age difference (England and McClintock, 2009). Because there is a double standard of aging, men are generally less receptive than women to the idea of marrying someone older than they (Buss et al., 2001), and they value good looks in women when seeking a partner (Abu-Laban and McDaniel, 2004). Overall, large age differences tend to be found more often among the foreign-born, non-white minorities, cohabitations rather than marriages, and lower-income groups (Boyd and Li, 2003).

The principle of homogamy or assortative matching is somewhat less important among same-sex couples (Jepsen and Jepsen, 2002). Homosexuals are nonconformists in at least one area of their lives—their sexuality (Bell and Weinberg, 1978). This may well lead them to be nontraditional in other domains, including the criteria that dictate choice of partners. Further, as a minority, they may have to cast a wider net than do heterosexuals because suitable mates may not be readily available. Thus, because of necessity or rejection from their ethnic group, gays and lesbians who belong to minority groups have high rates of interethnic and interracial partnering (Milan et al., 2010).

The qualities that men and women seek in a partner have been converging in recent decades, although males still value **physical appearance** more than women (Buss et al., 2001; Carmalt et al., 2008). In a study of newlyweds, both spouses behaved more negatively toward each other when they had rated the wives to be less attractive than the husbands (McNulty et al., 2008). Physical attractiveness is a more important element of mate selection among males (Fisman et al., 2006). Hence, partner selection among gay men may be more influenced by physical appearance than is the case among lesbian women. There is, in fact, a certain obsession about "partner-shopping . . . for Mr. Right only if he is also Mr. Buff—muscled and perfectly toned" (DeAngelis, 2002). This theme is developed by the gay student quoted at the outset of this chapter and pursued by another one:

> *"What was so hard for me is that I am not Mr. America, I am small framed and . . . I look a bit older so that I don't appeal to males who are looking for a well built body and especially an adolescent type. I am not particularly sexy. I am just a plain guy with plain habits and the bar and club scene was very hard on me. Another problem is that I am not the promiscuous type and there is no way, but no way, that a gay guy is able to find a partner if he is not willing to do a lot of compromising in this respect. Maybe things will be better when guys like me can meet partners in a more normal environment like at school or whatever. Maybe then the gay scene will evolve from muscles and flesh (the meat market) to personalities and feelings."*

In contrast, many lesbians are less concerned about femininity and general appearance (Krakauer and Rose, 2002). Therefore, the principles guiding partner selection may differ for male and female homosexuals.

ROMANTIC LOVE

In Canada and western countries in general, couples "fall in love," or, at the very least, one of the two does. Being "in love" has been the main overt reason to marry for over a century (see Shumway, 2003). It is still a key dimension in young adults' values concerning a relationship, particularly among females and heterosexuals (Meier et al., 2009). Failing to keep this love alive has led to many divorces and separation. The "fact" that people need to be romantically linked to marry represents a specific **social construction** of the marital relationship that does not exist universally (Noller, 1996).

However, romantic love is not new historically: Since time immemorial, some couples have married for romantic reasons or had other relationships that fulfilled that purpose. Romantic love, called **courtly love** during the Middle Ages, often involved relationships that did not include physical sexuality. The noble lady who was the object of a knight's courtly dreams was usually married and his attention, which was fashionable then, did not constitute a risk to her marriage. In turn, courtly love had itself been influenced by Greek and Roman concepts found in the philosophies of Ovid and Plato. Hence, the term "platonic" love. There was also the phenomenon that can be called **passionate friendship**, a totally platonic but intense relationship between a man and a woman who were often married to others (Harris, 2002). The term reserved for this relationship in French is *amitié amoureuse*.

In other words, there have been many types of romantic love throughout the centuries and not all were related to marriage or sex. More recently, romantic love has been associated with the development of individualism in western societies, which was particularly anchored in Great Britain and the U.S. Since the last half of the 20th century, romantic love has become the necessary ingredient in the decision to marry and in the definition of what constitutes marital happiness. As marriages develop and children arrive, romantic love is often replaced by more practical forms of love or companionship. The reverse may happen in arranged marriages in which love may grow and romance may flourish after.

COHABITATION

Cohabitation is referred to as a *common-law union* in Canada. After one to three years of coresidence, the partners are as legally protected as are married couples in terms of health care insurance and support, but not residence ownership. As indicated in Table 7.1, the proportion of all couples living common-law

TABLE 7.1 | **Proportion of Cohabitational Couples for Selected Countries and Regions**

Country	Year	As % of All Couples
Canada	2006	18.0
Quebec	2006	35.0
Other provinces/territories	2006	13.0
United States	2000	8.2
Sweden	2000	30.0
Norway	2000	24.5
Iceland	2000	19.5
Finland	2000	18.7
Mexico	2000	18.7
New Zealand	2001	18.3
France	1999	17.5

Source: Adapted with permission from Statistics Canada, *The Daily*, October 22, 2002b; Girard, 2008.

is far higher in Quebec than it is in other provinces. But, overall, a higher proportion of Canadians now choose common-law rather than marriage as a *first* union (Le Bourdais et al., 2000).

A cross-cultural perspective on family structure compares the prevalence of cohabiting couples in various western countries with Sweden as a baseline: This country has a longer history of consensual unions. Table 7.1 shows that Quebec and Sweden have equivalent proportions of cohabiting couples. When Quebec is excluded, only 13 percent of Canadian couples are common-law. Hence, the cohabitation rate for the rest of Canada more closely resembles the American rate than the Quebec one (Kerr et al., 2006). Further, the phenomenon is mainly a Quebec one (Belleau, 2007) rather than a French one because, in France, the percentage of cohabiting couples is lower than that of Quebec. As well, francophones in other provinces have cohabitation rates similar to those of the rest of the population (Laplante et al., 2006).

It should also be added that Québécois marry even less than people in France: In 2001, France had the same marriage rate as that of Canada at 5.0 per 1,000 population compared with 2.7 for Quebec (Girard, 2008). Quebec constitutes a specific "francophone" cultural phenomenon related to its own evolution rather than to its cultural attachments to France. Reasons that are generally given for Quebec's low marital rates include a reaction to centuries of dominance by the Church's teachings on nuptiality, chastity before marriage, and high fertility.

Further, when studying Canadians' attitudes to living common-law, the 2001 General Social Survey found that those most willing are young people aged 15 to 25, francophones, the non-religious, and those born in Canada (Milan, 2003). Within each of these categories, there is a substantial **gender difference**: As reflected in Figure 7.1, women are much less willing than men (Belleau, 2007). In Latin American countries, where consensual unions have a long history, educated women are less often found in such unions than in marriage (Martin, 2002). Cohabitations are more likely to result in marriage when the male partner has economic resources (Smock and Manning, 1997). When educated women have children, they are more likely to be married. This class phenomenon is also observed in Latin American countries (Martin, 2002).

At least in the short term, in the life course of young couples, cohabitation is delaying marriage because cohabitants are less likely to be actively searching for a marital partner than others. However, among young adults aged 20 to 29, the proportion of those who are neither cohabiting nor married has increased—a trend that was already noticeable by 1996 (Bélanger and Dumas, 1998). *This means that fewer adults are living in unions than in the past*; therefore, it is not only cohabitation that is delaying marriage but also a **longer period of singlehood**. For instance, from 1981 to 2001, the proportion of 25- to 29-year-old Canadians living in a union of any type decreased from 64 to 45 percent for men and from 73 to 57 percent for women (Statistics Canada, 2002b). A longer period of singlehood results from the necessity of pursuing an advanced education, establishing oneself in the employment sector, and getting settled economically (Beaujot and Bélanger, 2001)—all of which take a longer time than was the case 20 years ago. In turn, coresidence with parents contributes to delaying marriage, a phenomenon also found in Japan (Raymo, 2003). A longer period of singlehood is also a result of the fact that sexual relationships outside marriage are now more socially acceptable.

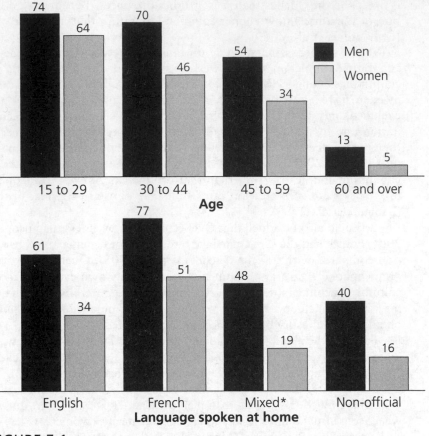

FIGURE 7.1

Percentages of Canadians Who Are Willing to Live Common-Law by Age and Language

Source: Statistics Canada, General Social Survey, 2001; Milan, 2003.

*Mixed refers to any combination of English/French and/or unofficial language.

Relationship Stability and Types of Cohabitation

Some individuals choose cohabitation because it requires, in their opinion, less sexual faithfulness than marriage (Bibby, 2004). Further, fewer cohabitants than married persons feel that it is very important to have a lasting relationship to achieve a happy life (Milan and Peters, 2003). Overall, the **role demands** of cohabitation are weaker than those for marriage. In other words, it is easier to enter into a cohabitational than a marital relationship because it is *less institutionalized*. For the same reason, it is easier to dissolve because there are fewer barriers against dissolution—whether legal, economic, or social—than is the case for marriage (Johnson's structural commitment, 1999).

More than 50 percent of all cohabitations end in dissolution within five years (Milan, 2000), a phenomenon that is also noted in Latin American countries. In North America, instability has even increased in recent years, in great part because fewer such unions result in marriage than in the past (Bumpass and Lu, 2000). Thus, cohabitations are not as stable as marriages—and this is true in all western societies (Wu, 2000). Further, they tend to dissolve more rapidly (Provencher et al., 2006). Cohabiting couples are less tolerant of differences between them than are married couples (Hohmann-Marriott, 2006). They also have more conflict and are less committed (Marcussen, 2005). As well, fewer cohabitants who break up attempt reconciliation than married couples do (Binstock and Thornton, 2003).

However, in a society such as Sweden where cohabitations are more **institutionalized,** such unions last longer. This is also the case for Quebec compared with the rest of Canada (Le Bourdais and Juby, 2002). It is estimated that 55 percent of Quebec women aged 30 to 39 who opted for cohabitation as a first union go through a separation, compared with 66 percent among women in the other provinces (Turcotte, 2002). Nevertheless, no matter how one looks at these numbers, they are far higher than the 30 percent Canadian divorce rate after five years of marriage.

Cohabitations are not a homogeneous category, so that stability depends in part on the reasons why a couple cohabits and how quickly the relationship is transformed into a marriage (Brown, 2004a). The term "stability" includes cohabitations that last and others that are transformed into a lasting marriage. The latter are forming a smaller proportion of all cohabitations than before in Canada. For instance, in the 1970s, about 50 percent of cohabitants went on to marry their partner within five years. This compares with only about 30 percent in the early 1990s (Turcotte and Bélanger, 1997). Thus, **"trial" marriages** are more rare than was the case just 20 years ago. Today, couples do not need this "excuse" to cohabit and do not need to be concerned about marriage as the "next step." In fact, probably fewer than 50% of couples begin their union with marital intentions (Guzzo, 2009a). In Quebec, cohabitation is more a substitute than a prelude to marriage (Belleau, 2007).

A large proportion of young couples who cohabit now begin living together rather quickly after the onset of dating, with little thought of permanency and least of all of marriage (Sassler, 2004; Wu, 2000). As some say, "it just happened" (Stanley and Rhoades, 2009). One would expect very high rates of eventual dissolution, as a short acquaintance is a precursor to divorce among the married. It may well be that instability is in the very nature of casual and/or **rapid-onset cohabitations**, which are more akin to "glorified" *dating* than to other types of cohabitations. Unfortunately, they may also be more painful and complicated to end than dating is, and this may be why many simply "slide" into marriage. More research is needed to define the various characteristics and trajectories of types of cohabitations, including those that are entered into as a precursor to marriage (Bianchi and Casper, 2000).

Sexual availability motivates many persons to cohabit rather than to continue dating (Sassler, 2004). A woman student expressed this in her autobiography:

"Right now I'd rate myself as being fairly unhappy and it's because I have found out that my boyfriend I live with lives with me just so that he can have sex that he knows is safe. . . . That means that I have wasted the past 18 months of my life that I could have better spent looking for a better guy and also one that

*would have accepted me as a whole person and not just as a sex machine. . . .
Now I have to think about ending this relationship but it's hard you know
because I am really attached to him."*

Living together also results when one or the other dater is looking for an apartment (Sassler, 2004). Cohabiting is then a form of savings: Sharing an apartment is less
expensive than maintaining two separate ones. Adults who divorce may also find similar economic advantages in cohabitation, especially in view of the fact that many
divorced men have to support a child who lives elsewhere. It is a matter of convenience
and **economies of scale**, even though cohabitants are more likely than married couples
to keep money separately, especially when one or the other has previously divorced
(Heimdal and Houseknecht, 2003). Young couples who are engaged often find cohabitation similarly convenient for financial reasons, as described by a student:

*"We're getting married this summer and we're both looking forward to it. We've
lived together for one year because we could not afford the wedding and we felt
that paying for one apartment as opposed to two would help us financially for
when we get married. I would not however have lived with him had we not been
engaged. That's a good way to get burned."*

Relationship Aspects

As we see later, cohabitants have more frequent sexual intercourse than married
couples (Yabiku and Gager, 2009). In part, this is because cohabitations are of
shorter duration and the frequency of sex is generally higher earlier on in unions of
any type. This result may also stem from the nature of cohabitation itself: These
relationships are more individualistic and may be more invested in sexuality, while
marriages may be more characterized by a greater general commitment. Indeed,
although low sexual frequency is related to union dissolution, it is more so among
cohabitants than married couples (Yabiku and Gager, 2009). Although married
spouses are usually happier with their relationships than are cohabitants (Nock,
1998a), when cohabitants plan to marry, the quality of their relationship is not
much different from that of a married couple that has been together for the same
duration. In Quebec, couples who cohabit for several years are more similar to married ones in terms of relationship satisfaction—which suggests that more studies
should be carried out on couples who have been together for many years (Lachance-
Grzela and Bouchard, 2009).

Cohabitation is less institutionalized so that couples may feel freer to invent
their relationships outside the mould of traditional expectations and gender roles.
Yet, recent studies are not unanimous: Some do not find a more **equal division of
labour** within cohabitation than within marriage while others do (Wu, 2000). Generally, young cohabiting women do less housework than married ones (Smock and
Gupta, 2002). Women who cohabit feel less secure in their relationship; consequently, they are less willing to sacrifice their employment opportunities and to
invest as much in housework as do married women (Seltzer, 2000). Matters may be
different in countries such as Sweden that have higher gender equality (Batalova and
Cohen, 2002).

In a study carried out by Aquilino (1997), **parents** felt closer to their married children than to their cohabiting ones, even though they were involved in social activities with both (see also Eggebeen, 2005). Parents may invest less emotion in their adult children's cohabitations as they perceive or worry that these relationships may not last (Hoggerbrugge and Dykstra, 2009). In contrast, in-laws loom larger in a marriage because it is a more family-oriented institution.

Cohabitants are **less faithful** to their partners sexually than married persons, even after controlling for personal values regarding extramarital sex (Treas and Giesen, 2000). Forste and Tanfer (1996) report that cohabiting women are more likely than married women to have had another sexual encounter since the beginning of their relationship. In fact, they are even slightly less faithful than dating women. The above authors agree that their data support the view that, in many cases, cohabitation is selective of **less committed** individuals: Cohabiting men especially are often less committed to their relationship and partner than are married men (Stanley et al., 2004). This sentiment is expressed by a divorced man during an interview and by his former cohabiting partner at a follow up, and then by a student in her autobiography:

"No, I don't know if I'll get married [to the woman he lives with]. . . . *Right now I am not even sure that she's the right woman for me so that I prefer to take it easy; I have a wait-and-see attitude at this point."* At the follow-up interview two years later, this couple had separated. He was casual about it, but the woman was very upset: *"He should just have dated me, I mean, you don't start living with someone if you don't love them . . . it's dishonest. It's even worse because I have two small children. I mean, it's not a game you play with children."*

"I have lived with two different guys and that's it! No more! It's always the same thing: We just play at being married because they don't want to do anything except play. They couldn't get married because . . . the usual line is 'I'm not ready for such a commitment.'"

What these quotes, as well as one of the chapter's openers (with the recurring themes of "play" and lack of commitment), well illustrate is that cohabitation can serve to delay commitment and give a longer time lead during which to find a better alternative. Many cohabitants, perhaps more male than female, remain in a **permanent state of availability**. In other words, they are still "playing the field." In terms of exchange theory, the committed partner has less power because the relationship is more important to him or her than it is to the partner who has less invested. As a result, the partner with more invested is unhappy, may feel depressed, harbour regrets, and feel more insecure and less in control of his or her life (Brown, 2002). Furthermore, in view of the fact that marriage is still the most valued conjugal state in our society, one partner often wishes to transform the cohabitation into a marriage. Therefore, cohabitation may be problematic for many young and middle-age adults, particularly women, as expressed by yet another student:

"I would rate myself low on happiness currently because I have lived with my boyfriend for two years against my parents' wishes [after one year of dating] *and when we talk of marriage, he always says that we're too young for this, he is 29 and I am 25. Or he'll say, you know, marriage is 'serious business' and this*

makes me feel that he sees what we have as being of a lower quality. I love him and we're well suited but I'm afraid that he'll leave me if I put a deadline for marriage. But how long can I wait? I think that women are getting short changed when they agree to live together."

In fact, women who cohabit serially are at high risk of never marrying and, if they do, of divorcing (Lichter and Qian, 2008; Sassler, 2010). There is also evidence that entry into cohabitation does not provide the same protective benefits against depression as does entry into a marriage (Lamb et al., 2003). However, overall, Wu et al. (2004) did not find significant health disadvantages related to cohabitation. But entry into cohabitation heightens a woman's risk of physical abuse (Brzozowski and Brazeau, 2008; Sev'er, 2002) and even spousal homicide (Ogrodnik, 2009). Kenney and McLanahan (2006) have found that there is more conjugal violence among cohabitants than among married spouses. This is probably because cohabitants who are violent are less likely to be selected into marriage while married persons who suffer from violence are more likely to divorce. As a result, the married population has a lower rate of conjugal violence than the cohabiting population.

For Older Adults

For older adults who have already been married, cohabitation may carry far fewer risks than it does for younger adults. For those who are widowed or divorced, an eventual marriage may not be as important because they have already reached this goal before. Cohabitation may be more advantageous psychologically and in terms of relationship satisfaction (Hansen et al., 2007; Wu, 2000). It then becomes a substitute to marriage, a relationship in its own right with a similar level of commitment (King and Scott, 2005). In fact, in later life (after age 60 perhaps) the double standard of commitment that often exists among young and middle-aged cohabitants may disappear entirely because, in terms of exchange theory, males may need a partner as much as or even more than females. Hence, older males are likely to be more committed than younger males because they need a spouse more: We know, for instance, that after widowhood, older men do not adapt easily to the loss of their wives and are more helpless than are widowed women (Lee et al., 1998). In fact, King and Scott (2005) have found that older cohabitants have higher levels of relationship quality than younger cohabitants.

Men generally benefit highly from living with a partner (Cooney and Dunne, 2001). In comparison, widowed and divorced women in later life are often hesitant to relinquish their newly acquired independence or to replace a deceased spouse whom they loved. They may also be afraid that a marriage will soon return them to the role of nurse for an ailing husband. Such women may welcome a new form of partnership and may find cohabitation functional. Others may actually look for an emotional and sexual relationship that does not involve the sharing of a dwelling—thus maintaining their independence. The economic benefits of cohabitation may be even more important among the older generation (Chevan, 1996): It offers the advantage of economies of scale while, at the same time, it may allow the partners to protect their respective children's inheritances.

HETEROSEXUAL MARRIAGE

Marriage, particularly a good and equitable marriage, carries many benefits for the spouses. It is, above all, highly beneficial to children, whether it is equitable or not between the parents. There is a school of thought whose proponents argue that what is important is not family structure (one versus two, married versus cohabiting parents), but healthy **family processes**. It is certainly true that positive family dynamics explain a part of children's positive outcomes; however, the fact remains that *healthy dynamics are more likely to occur in married families or perhaps long-term cohabitational families* (Bibby, 2004). As well, even though unachievable for many poor women, marriage carries high positive symbolic value (Edin and Kefalas, 2005).

As indicated in Figure 7.2, the yearly rate of marriage per 1,000 population has diminished substantially since 1941, its peak year, in part because of the low marriage rates in Quebec where cohabitation is so frequent; in part because a proportion of persons cohabit and will never marry; and also because the aging of the population

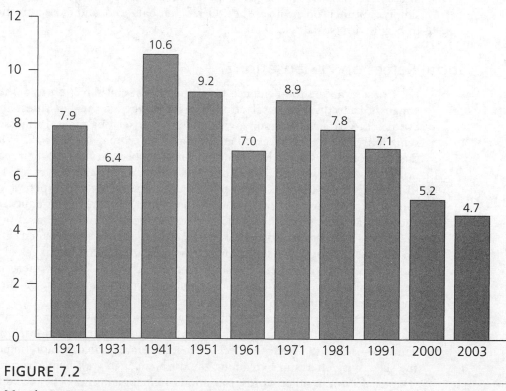

FIGURE 7.2

Marriage Rates per 1,000 Population, 1921–2003

Source: Statistics Canada, Selected Marriage Statistics 1921–1990. Cat. 82-552. *Canadian Social Trends*, 68, 2003, p. 27; Statistics Canada, 2007e. Adapted with permission from Statistics Canada.

means that fewer people of marriageable age are present. **Quebec** has a large population and its low marriage rate, 2.9 in 2007, contributes to reducing the overall Canadian rate (Girard, 2008:64). The rate at which Quebec singles marry is nearly half that of Canada, France, Sweden, and Italy. Marriage rates are especially high in the U.S., at 7.5 in 2003. As seen in Figure 7.2, the rate was 4.7 in Canada, from a high of 6.0 for PEI, 5.2 for Ontario, 5.6 for Alberta, 4.9 and 5.0 for Manitoba and Saskatchewan respectively.

Research shows that both married men and women, compared with men and women in any of the other marital status categories, do better in the domains of physical and psychological well-being and longevity (Waite and Gallagher, 2000). They have lower rates of emotional problems, are healthier physically, and live longer (Coombs, 1991)—although the latter result may be equally a consequence of married people generally having higher incomes, which in turn is related to better health and lower mortality. However, in a study of 17 western countries and Japan, Stack and Eshleman (1998) have found that being married is 3.4 times more closely tied to happiness than is cohabitation. Their results indicate that marriage, rather than cohabitation, increases both financial and health satisfaction, which in turn increase happiness. (See, also, Bierman et al., 2006.) Naturally, the question that arises here is: Does marriage contribute to well-being (social causation) or does it simply capture people who are healthier, better balanced, and more attractive partners to begin with (social selection)?

Social Selection or Causation?

Let's first examine the evidence favouring the **social selection** hypothesis, which suggests that there is a selection into marriage of the healthiest individuals. Studies indicate that persons who suffer from serious mental illnesses, such as schizophrenia, are less likely to marry, particularly men (Link et al., 1987). Highly dysfunctional persons either do not marry or, when they do so, their marriages do not last, after which it becomes difficult to remarry (Forthofer et al., 1996). Very ill persons as well as persons who are intellectually incompetent do not get selected into marriage as frequently as others. As well, the educated tend to choose marriage more than the less educated (Schoen and Cheng, 2006). Overall, therefore, a selection process takes place, particularly among men. Once people are married, another selection process is activated: The marriages of disturbed, incompetent, or antisocial persons are less likely to last, as these individuals become very difficult spouses with whom to live. Psychological balance certainly contributes to marital stability.

Nevertheless, most people still marry at least once, whether they are well balanced or not, and a certain number of well-balanced persons choose not to marry. This means that the positive effects of marriage are probably more important than the selectivity effects in explaining the differences in well-being by marital status (Daniel, 1996). In other words, **causation** often explains far better the differences in well-being between the married and the non-married (Wu et al., 2004). Marriage helps adults stabilize their personalities, gain self-esteem and personal security, and develop competencies and a sense of responsibility that were not required as single persons, particularly among men (Nock, 1998a). Warm and supportive relationships enhance happiness, psychological well-being, physical health, and consequently longevity (Martikainen et al., 2005).

Married men are more often regularly employed than other men, which provides them with greater personal stability (Daniel, 1996). When they change jobs, it is more to increase their economic gains than is the case among single and divorced men (Gorman, 1999). Further, when his wife is employed, which has become the norm, a husband is now far better off financially than he would be as a single man. Married couples with an employed wife have an income advantage of at least $15,000, on average, over married couples with a wife who is not gainfully employed (Sauvé, 2002). Therefore, men are generally far more secure with a wife than without because married couples are more likely to pool their resources than are cohabiting couples. As Lerman (2002:6) puts it, "The presence of more than one potential earner helps diversify the risks arising from unemployment, lost wages, or shifts in demand for various occupations."

Moreover, married adults are more likely to maintain a healthy lifestyle than nonmarried adults. The former eat at home more, stay out late less, use alcohol and illegal drugs less, and are better organized to take care of their basic needs (Bachman et al., 1997). A cohesive marriage is an important social resource and brings an *informal element of social control* into the lives of individuals. This may be the reason why married people drink less than cohabitants (Horwitz and Raskin White, 1998). Furthermore, Horney et al. (1995) as well as Laub and colleagues (1998) have found that when a person who engages in illegal activities enters into a good marriage with a prosocial partner, the marriage eventually contributes to the cessation of illegal activities by the criminal.

Are Marriage Benefits Gendered?

Some literature indicates that marriage may be more advantageous to men than to women—even though women want it more than men (England, 2000). Health has generally been used as the key indicator. What has been found is that there is a larger difference between the scores of well-being of married men compared with divorced and never-married men than there is among similar women, although the male gap has narrowed (Liu and Umberson, 2008). Why would marriage benefit women less? To begin with, once children arrive, women have more responsibilities than men, particularly when both spouses are employed, and they suffer from more work interruptions than men. Therefore, for many women, marriage becomes a mixed blessing. However, for both genders, the self-rated health of the divorced, separated, and widowed has worsened in the recent past and it may have worsened more for women than men, although women still cope better in this respect (Liu and Umberson, 2008).

It should be noted that no study has yet compared married men and women with **cohabiting** ones in terms of the diverse facets of well-being. Neither do studies exist on the relative responsibilities of cohabitants who have children. The

Marriage formation, happiness, and stability are important elements in the social organization of western societies: They contribute to couples' well-being and productivity as well as to their children's positive outcomes, both currently and in the long term.

quotes presented earlier highlight problems of emotional security, powerlessness, and unhappiness among young cohabiting women who were not engaged to their partner. There were clear indications in these quotes that the benefits of cohabitation are gender specific among the young: They may favour males even more than marriage does and this may well be more so when children are present. However, the following hypotheses deserve to be tested: Women may be as advantaged by cohabitation as men in cultures where the phenomenon is more widespread, such as Quebec and Sweden. As well, both genders may be equally advantaged when they cohabit later in life after a divorce or widowhood and after children from previous unions have become independent. Such advantages are not likely to exist, however, among groups for whom cohabitation is not sanctioned, such as people of Hindu or Muslim faith.

The **quality of the relationship** is an important determinant of well-being. All in all, marriage is beneficial to adults, but a troublesome marriage negates some or all of these benefits, particularly for women. Second, the benefits accrued in marriage and even cohabitation may differ for men and women depending on the domains studied—emotional well-being, physical health, happiness, or security. These gendered benefits may also differ depending on ethnicity and the stage of the life course or age of the person. For instance, it is not clear whether marriage is more or less beneficial among young than middle-aged persons. Finally, the benefits of marriage depend on the time or cohort period that serves as a context for marriage. For example, more recent cohorts of women seem to benefit from marriage less than preceding cohorts, and this would be especially so for career women. But, here again, one has to consider the dimensions of personality and life that are measured in these studies because it is possible that more recent cohorts of researchers favour some aspects of life (i.e., independence) over others.

It is also possible that research may not have focused on all the benefits of marriage for women. Marriage has advantages for women, especially over their lifespan, in terms of wealth accumulation, and this effect is particularly evident after retirement age (Wilmoth and Koso, 2002). In this respect, marriage is also functional for men and should continue to be so as married men tend to earn more than single men (Beaujot, 2000) and as most wives are employed and many earn more than their husbands. Financially, marriage is advantageous to both genders, so long as it lasts. The fact that on some issues (particularly the division of labour at home) women are generally at a disadvantage compared with men does not mean that marriage is no longer functional for a majority. What it means is that marriage could become more functional for women than it now is, with the help of changes in our values in terms of gender roles and with increased social investment in child care centres, for instance (Beaujot, 2000). The benefits of cohabitation need to be similarly studied, with a distinction between committed versus non-committed ones, and in comparison with happy versus less well functioning marriages.

SAME-SEX MARRIAGE

In 2000, Parliament enacted the *Modernization of Benefits and Obligations Act* which extended benefits and obligations to common-law couples, be they of opposite sex or the same sex. In 2001, the Netherlands became the first country to legalize same-sex marriage and was followed by Belgium in 2003. British Columbia and Ontario did so in 2003, and Canada followed suit in 2004.

Between June and December 2003, about 2,000 same-sex couples, including 600 Americans, have married in Ontario and British Columbia (Statistics Canada, 2007e). It is difficult to establish numbers and rates of same-sex marriage for Canadians because many gays from other countries have come here to marry, especially Americans. In Quebec, same-sex marriage is more frequent among men (Girard, 2008:65). The 2006 census enumerated 45,345 same-sex couples of which 7,465 or 16.5 percent were married (Statistics Canada, 2007h).

The movement among gays and lesbians to form families and be recognized legally by both civil and religious authorities as married couples invites consideration of one particular **ideological contradiction**. Marriage is defined as a sexual, economic, social, and emotional partnership involving obligations as well as rights. Commitment is a key aspect of the institution and so is fidelity. Some gay groups are ideologically committed to "open contracts"—that is, a relationship that includes extramarital outlets (Sullivan, 1995). This is a contradiction in terms because marriage is meant to be a committed and exclusive relationship. It could be argued that homosexuals and heterosexuals who espouse this definition of marriage should cohabit because their marrying would weaken the elements of commitment and fidelity in the institution of marriage. Of course, this does not mean that some degree of infidelity may not occur as it does among some heterosexual marriages.

However, one can expect that, generally, "lesbigay" partners who marry are a select group who have been together for many years and wish to legalize their commitment to each. Indeed, the couples whose marriages were celebrated at City Hall in Toronto in 2003 and 2004 generally fit this profile. In British Columbia, in 2003, the average age at first marriage between men was 43.9 years and 41.6 years between women compared with 31 years for men and 29 years for women in heterosexual marriages (Statistics Canada, 2007e). Thus, it could be argued that homosexuals who intend to marry share a commitment to monogamy and fidelity. It would also be important that a similar cultural consensus concerning the unacceptability of same-sex extramarital infidelities emerge in the public at large. Otherwise, a **double standard** would develop: one for heterosexual marriage and one for gay marriage.

SEXUAL RELATIONS

The focus of studies on sex has been on measuring attitudes toward premarital and extramarital sexual intercourse and frequency of intercourse. Measuring the frequency of sexual intercourse alone may represent a **masculine bias** in the research and may also misrepresent the level of sexuality among heterosexual and lesbian couples (Patterson, 2000; Rothblum, 2002). There is more to sexuality than penetration: Mutual masturbation, kissing, and caressing are important elements of sexuality (and affectivity) among couples. Thus, the incidence of sexuality in general is likely to be far higher among some groups than depicted in the statistics on intercourse.

The study of sexuality is influenced by **social constructions**. To begin with, sexuality is a prime concern in western countries, as illustrated by the contents of television programming, advertisements, online material, literature, as well as magazines and newspapers. People from non-western cultures and especially previous centuries might well view our focus as an obsession. Sex, especially in the form of intercourse, has come to be defined as a primary need. While it is indeed a basic human "instinct," its absence in a person's life cannot be equated with the consequences of being deprived of air, food, or light. The psychological consequences of abstaining from sex much depend on how we construct its meaning and importance.

Attitudes about nonmarital sex have become more permissive. Bibby and Posterski (2000) found a gender difference both among adults and adolescents concerning the propriety of having sex before marriage. While the majority of adolescents (82 percent) agree that sex before marriage is acceptable when people love each other, this acceptance declines to 48 percent among females but remains fairly high at 68 percent among males when "people like each other" (Bibby, 2001). Only 5 percent of females but 20 percent of males approve of sex on a first date. This **gender divide** means that many young women actually have sex at a time when they are not emotionally ready for it, as explained by a woman student:

> "I got conned into having sex when I look back on my first experience [age 16]. . . . [H]e told me all the things he knew I wanted to hear, but none were true . . . and I felt really cheap after . . . plus it was very, very painful, you know, I cried out and it was humiliating. . . . I lied and told my friends it had been great but I stayed away from guys for a year after that."

Adolescent Sexuality

We do not have precise information as to the average age when young Canadians begin having **sexual intercourse**. However, in a national survey, Rotermann (2008) reports that, in 2005, about 33 percent of 15- to 17-year-olds had had intercourse as had about 66 percent of 18- and 19-year-olds. Another national survey of over 10,000 students in grades 7, 9, and 11 carried out in 2002-03 presents similar results, as detailed in Table 7.2. These are lower percentages for females than in 1997 (Rotermann, 2008). The proportion of teens who had had intercourse before age 15 also fell from 12 to 8 percent between 1997 and 2005 (Rotermann, 2008).

Among those who had intercourse in grade 9 (23 percent of all males and 19 per cent of all females), fully 40 percent of these males and 29 percent of these females had had three or more partners. Rotermann found that 33 percent had had more than one, with males reporting multiple partners more often. In other words, some 15-year-old youths are quite experienced: They constitute over 10 percent of all adolescents their age. It would be paramount to have more information on this group, which is at risk for many problems, including STIs. Adolescents who have **multiple partners** and do not practise safe sex tend to consume alcohol more and have lower school achievement and a more difficult parent-child relationship (Perkins et al., 1998). They are also less likely to receive a great deal of supervision;

TABLE 7.2	Description of High Schoolers' Dating and Sexual Activities for Grades 9 and 11, for Males and Females, in Percentages			
	Grade 9		Grade 11	
	M	F	M	F
No. of **boy/girlfriends** past year:				
None	42%	37%	38%	32%
One	26	30	36	40
Two+	32	34	28	27
Ever had intercourse	23	19	40	46
If yes: No. of intercourse partners:				
One	45	53	43	54
Two	15	19	21	18
Three+	40	29	36	28
Reason for **not** having had intercourse: not yet ready	29	40	12	30
Ever had oral sex	32	28	53	52

Source: Boyce et al., 2006. Adapted with permission from Tables 3, 5, 6, 7, and 8.

permissive maternal attitudes about sexuality are equally related to having multiple partners (Miller et al., 1999).

As seen in Table 7.2, in both grades 9 and 11, a greater proportion of students had had **oral sex** than intercourse. In contrast, a few decades ago, oral sex was considered a more intimate step to take and generally followed intercourse. Indeed, the recreational or "fun" aspect of sexuality, as opposed to the relationship aspect, is often one of the highlights of early teen parties. In 1980, an older student wrote:

> *"Today I am upset because my twelve-year-old daughter went to a party this weekend and the spin the bottle game found her in a closet with the target boy masturbating each other. The reason I found out was the telltale semen on her dress. When I was her age, we'd spin the bottle and kiss. Things have changed and I am very, very concerned about what this does to these children's frame of mind when time comes to get into a real relationship."*

Over twenty years later, in 2004, a female student wrote on the same theme:

> *"My thirteen-year-old sister tells me everything because she thinks I'm cool. She was supposed to go to a sleepover at some girlfriend's house but they ended up at this boy's party, her age, not supervised and they drank quite a lot and then spinned the bottle among other things and each girl had to suck the boy's you-know-what. She thought it was both hilarious, mature, and 'yukkie.' It's her first sexual experience and I don't think it's a good start and I am very worried about her."*

FAMILY RESEARCH 7.1

Are Results on Teen Sexuality Valid?

You may ask, especially if you belong to a cultural group that does not allow early adolescent dating (Zaidi and Shuraydi, 2002), if these research results are "for real"? In other words, is it a sample that represents the entire population of Canadian adolescents? And was that study well carried out? First, let's recall that Rotermann's results (2008) were essentially the same. Second, the Boyce et al. sample is a very large one: The study was carried out in a representative stratified sample of schools, and the methods are entirely credible. "Active parental/guardian consent was obtained for all study participants. The students were guaranteed anonymity and sealed their surveys in individual envelopes for return to the researchers" (Boyce et al, 2006:60). As you can imagine, nearly 20 percent of students did not return the parental consent, nearly 9 percent were absent on that day,

and 5 percent refused to participate, so that there was a response rate of 67.7 percent—which is very good.

However, Alberta and British Columbia did not participate and neither did private and religious schools. It is difficult to ascertain how this might have affected the results. As well, it is possible that the 25 percent who refused to participate or whose parents refused may have been very different: These students might have come from families that were either malfunctioning or, more likely, where parents objected to this study on moral grounds—which might have excluded from the study adolescents whose parents had a different set of values and who, as a result, delayed sexual activities for later. If the latter were the case, then the actual proportions of adolescents having oral sex and intercourse would be lower.

Spin-the-bottle is a "game" with a content that has been evolving over the decades toward a purely genitalia focus among some early teens.

Not shown in Table 7.2 is the fact that, in grade 7, the proportion of students who reported having had no *steady* **girlfriend/boyfriend** for the past year (42 percent of males and 46 percent of females) is fairly close to that of ninth graders. However, 18 and 15 percent of these seventh graders reported having had three or more "steadies," which is higher than older students. The authors conclude that "adolescent relationships have been characterized as serially monogamous and of short duration" (Boyce et al., 2006). There is a complementary explanation. It may be that many seventh graders are more inclusive in their definition: They may include as a "steady" a peer they have a crush on, or one who regularly talks with them or walks home with them, something that an older student would simply describe as a friend. In fact, in their autobiographies, I rarely encountered students who mentioned having had a steady boyfriend or girlfriend by grade 7. This generally occurred, when it did, one to three years later:

> *"I was nuts about this girl in my class . . . I lived for the moment she would look at me. . . . She was this big thing in my life and I was crushed when she started walking home with another boy. It was puppy love for me and all of this was more in my mind than real."*

> *"What made me the most happy between the ages of 11 and 14 was this 'boyfriend' I had in grade 6. He and I used to be on the same school bus and after a while he started to sit with me. I was in heaven! He was soooo cute, at least I thought so. Everyone called us an 'item' but we never even talked on the phone or go out together but having a 'boyfriend' certainly raised my status among my classmates. Now I can't even remember how it ended."*

In contrast, students recalled word for word "how it had ended" with real boyfriends or girlfriends. They always mentioned this as having been the most, or one of the most, painful aspects of their lives at ages 15 to 19 or even older.

Issues of Control and Consequences

Simply mentioning when first sexual intercourse takes place camouflages an important reality: the degree of **voluntariness** and desire for the experience. In the Boyce et al. (2006) study, 17 percent of females in grade 9 and 28 percent in grade 11 had been pressured into sex, while the percentages for males were 7.7 and 11 percent. There is also a great deal of difference by gender in the quality of the experience at first intercourse among adolescents. In part, this may stem from the fact that sexuality is more goal oriented toward intercourse—and rather quickly—which may be more a male than a female vision of sexuality, as mentioned earlier (Schwartz and Rutter, 1998:94). While males describe their first intercourse as exciting and satisfying, more females report fear, anxiety, embarrassment, and even guilt. Two women students' recent memories are presented:

> *"The first time I had sex was both most exciting and most painful."*

> *"I did not enjoy my first sexual experience at all because I was not ready for it and that's why I mention it here because it became something I regretted for a long time after and made me feel dirty. It took me three years after that, until*

with my boyfriend, to consider it again and the experience was so different because I felt loved."

For many adolescents, sexuality is a positive experience. And, overall, mental health issues arise only in certain contexts. Therefore, several variables have to be taken into consideration when evaluating the impact of adolescent sexuality. Ann Meier (2007) has found that when adolescents are sexually active and others are aware of it, a relationship breakdown can be very embarrassing and humiliating. This can, as a result, affect their mental health, particularly when the relationship was not a committed one: Sex without commitment may induce greater regrets among girls than boys. In fact, females in the Boyce et al. (2006) study were more likely than boys to give "love for the person" as the reason for having had first intercourse: 39 percent of grade 11 males compared with 60 percent of the females (Table 7.2).

In a country as diverse religiously and culturally as Canada is, one should carefully consider the possibility that, for youths whose parents are new arrivals from countries that segregate the sexes, particularly girls, engaging in adolescent sexuality may carry negative consequences in terms of guilt, relationships with peers and parents, and difficulties finding a mate later. In fact, a young woman's life could be in danger as a result of the shame she could bring to her family (honour killings) or she could be shipped "back home" and be forced into an arranged marriage. It should be noted that, for Canadians in general, persons who have had a high number of sexual partners are not considered as desirable dates and partners (Garcia, 2006).

One problem concerning sex among adolescents is the high rate of sexually transmitted infections, particularly for those who begin intercourse by age 13 (Rotermann, 2005). Let's just take one instance, chlamydia, an infection that does not have overt symptoms and generally goes undetected but can lead to infertility or tubal pregnancy. Although its incidence has decreased over the years, young women aged 15 to 19 are far more likely to contract this disease than their older counterparts (Health Canada, 2000).

Early Teen Sexuality

Besides gender, the following variables contribute to a later sexual initiation: higher parental social class, two-parent family, school achievement, and religiosity (Mendle et al., 2009). Parental caring and monitoring are key elements (Longmore et al., 2009). Both high-quality parent-child relations and less permissive parental attitude toward early sexuality delay initiation (Davis and Friel, 2001). Among girls, engaging in sports is related to postponement of sexual activities (Manlove et al., 2002). In contrast, teens who engage in risky behaviours such as alcohol and drug use, who have been sexually abused, and who mature early physically are more likely to begin sexual intercourse at a younger age than other teens (McKay, 2005). Even smoking is related to earlier sexual initiation (Garriguet, 2005). There are two trajectories in the explanation of these links. One is the selection process: Students who smoke, drink, or do drugs are more likely to be at least somewhat different than others who do not in terms of willingness to go against certain rules and this may, for many, include sex. The second trajectory concerns the fact that both alcohol and drugs lower inhibitions and can easily lead to unplanned sex.

Young teen girls who have a boyfriend who is six years older or more than they are have a higher chance of beginning intercourse than other girls with a same-age boyfriend (Kaestle et al., 2002) and to acquire an STI (Ryan et al., 2008). Garriguet (2005) reported that girls whose self-concept was weak at ages 12 and 13 were more likely than those with a strong self-concept to have had intercourse by age 14 or 15 while the opposite was true for boys! The latter's early age was more related to low income and a poor relationship with parents.

Some of these factors continue to exert an influence among college and university-age groups. For instance, religious attendance is significantly related to lower rates of sexual intercourse among nonmarried students (Uecker, 2008). It is also related to the number of sexual partners (Barkan, 2006). As well, patterns of sexuality and relationships initiated during adolescence are precursors to behaviours in young adulthood. For instance, casual sex in adolescence is related to cohabitation rather than marriage later (Raley et al., 2007).

The Role of Peers

Were it not for general **peer pressure** and, in many instances, rape or psychological coercion, perhaps a majority of young women would initiate oral sex and sexual intercourse later than they currently do (Abma et al., 1998). Even some males obviously feel pressured as well as "left out":

> *"I always felt left out in high school just because I didn't get laid. I was the only guy still a virgin at graduation.* [This was probably his perception based on peer boasting rather than a fact, or else his 'crowd' included sexually active peers.] *The counsellor told me there was nothing to worry about and he was right but to a 16-year-old that's not what you want to hear."*

Several studies indicate that a student's peer group is a key ingredient in early sexual initiation. The Boyce et al. (2006) study shows that very few students who think that their friends have not had sex report having had intercourse themselves. However, when most of their friends are perceived to have had sex, then they themselves also report having had intercourse. This is quite a "correlation" indicating a peer influence or a choice of peers based on similar values and behaviours. Sieving et al. (2006) found the same results in a longitudinal study: High-schoolers who perceived that they would gain their friends' respect by having sex themselves were also more likely to have initiated intercourse in the 9 to 18 months that elapsed between two interviews. (See, also, Boyce et al., 2008.)

As well, sixth to eighth graders who have a boyfriend/girlfriend initiate intercourse earlier. Females who have an older boyfriend are much more likely to become sexually active than others (Marin et al., 2006). Therefore, parents and schools who are able to convince young adolescents to postpone dating are, by the same token, helping them delay intercourse and attendant risks at that young age. This would require that an effective community exists in schools because students' perceptions of their peers' sexual experience is such an important element (Hampton et al., 2005). Families' and schools' social capital may also play a different role for male and female students (Smylie et al., 2006). From what I have gathered throughout the years from the autobiographies, delayed dating would also be a relief to students who feel left out when they do not date while their peers do or are perceived to be so doing. Many students could recall that, in order to enhance their status within their peer groups, they invented stories of dates, sex, "pot," and later "rave" weekends, from grade 6 through the end of high school.

> *"I was convinced that I was the only one in my class who didn't have sex, so I made up all kinds of stories and this was easy for me to do because we had a cottage and we went there nearly every weekend and no one could check. I have had pictures of me with some girls on the ski slope to prove everything but these girls were just children of my parents' friends."*

> *"All the girls in my class had sex so of course I said that I had it too except that it was all a bunch of lies because I was well supervised by my parents and they were good at communicating with me why I should wait and do things that were more enriching at that stage of my life . . . the funny thing about this is that a couple of my friends told me years later that they were still virgins and that they had lied as well so we all felt so happy to know that we were not the only ones [not having had sex] and now looking back on all of this trauma, I suspect that most of our friends and classmates were making up similar stories and this means that we were all living in a fantasy world that didn't exist except that we were creating this world together, one big deception that is so hurtful and throws so many kids to the wolves so to speak and they are not ready for this."*

In other words, a collective delusion often takes place. And this delusion of a perceived, but not real, situation still affects many students even in university.

Sexual Identities and Sexualities

Sexuality may be somewhat more fluid, both in terms of identity and practices, than heretofore realized, and because of cultural changes. For instance, at some point in their life course, but not necessarily throughout their entire adult years, a number of persons identify as **homosexual**. Based on the fact that younger Norwegians are less attached to "fixed identity structures, more so among women than men," Andersson et al. (2006:81) ask how homosexuals should be identified: Should respondents be asked how they identify themselves or is it better to measure sexual practice? With three large American data sets, Black et al. (2000) estimate that possibly as many as 30 percent of gay men and 46 percent of lesbian women have been or are married heterosexually. Similar results have been obtained in Sweden and Norway (Andersson et al., 2006). In fact, until now, a good proportion of lesbians, especially those older than 30, have discovered their identity later in life (Morris et al., 2001). Some may identify as bisexual and many do not engage in genital sex (Rothblum, 2002).

The carefully designed studies carried out by Laumann et al. (1994) indicate that 2.8 percent of men identify as gay and 1.4 percent of women identify as lesbian. These figures are similar to the rates for men and women who have exclusively same-sex relationships: 3 percent for men and 1.6 percent for women. In the Black et al. (2000) analyses, 4.7 percent of men and 3.5 percent of women had had at least one same-sex experience since age 18. But only 2.5 percent of men and 1.4 percent of women had engaged in *exclusively* same-sex activities over the year preceding the survey. In the U.S., more women reported having had sex with a same-sex partner during the previous year in 2002 than in 1988, probably as a result of better accessibility to opposite-sex partners and greater social tolerance. Still, in 2002, about 3.35 percent of women and men reported having had sex with a same-sex person in the previous year (Butler, 2005). In 2006, 1.5 percent of young adults identified as homosexual and 1.55 as bisexual (Meier et al., 2009).

All these numbers are presented to document the fact that, whether one uses self-identity or behaviours as a measure, homosexuality is a minority phenomenon. Lesbians and gays at times appear to be more numerous than they are because they disproportionately live in large metropolitan areas in most countries (Andersson et al., 2006). In Canada, this means Vancouver, Toronto, and Montreal (Statistics Canada, 2007h). This concentration gives them higher social visibility (Black et al., 2000), allows them to advocate for equality, and gives them media exposure. Furthermore, there is a tendency among homophobic persons to exaggerate the size of the homosexual population in order to sustain their "worst-fear" scenarios and prejudices. And, among some homosexuals, there is a tendency to inflate the numbers for political and social purposes. Hence, many misleading "facts" abound.

This being said, a number of individuals identify as **bisexual**, but there is little research on their family lives (Biblarz and Savci, 2010). Some have sex both with men and women while others have sex only with persons of their own sex or even with the opposite sex. Bisexuality is an identity and, especially, a practice that has far more complex ramifications and risks (Engler et al., 2005). In the Boyce et al. (2006) study of high schools, about 5 percent of female and 2.5 percent of male students reported some attraction to the same sex or both sexes, or about one such student in each classroom.

Perhaps as many as one-third of all teens in some groups may experience sexual violence before reaching adulthood (Saewyc et al., 2008a). One of the results is teenage pregnancy. Teens who are gay, lesbian, or bisexual, who are more at risk of being stigmatized and less well protected sexually, are also more often violated and physically abused, both currently and as children (Balsam et al., 2005). The younger they are when their sexual identity develops, the higher the rates of victimization (Corliss et al., 2009). A surprising result is that females have much higher rates of pregnancy (Saewyc et al., 2008b). Many of these teens have more partners and begin sex even younger than others; they are thus at greater risk for a multiplicity of problems, in great part because they have little adult guidance in this respect.

More recently, the term **transgendered** has been used to refer to individuals who are born into one sex but, from very early in their lives, have never felt comfortable in this designation. They may, later on, receive hormonal and even surgical treatment in order to be reassigned to the other sex. On March 13, 2010, CNN presented one such case in a documentary entitled *She Was Named Steven*. Several transgendered persons have been or are still married to an opposite-sex persons (that is, to a person of the sex other than the one they were born into or raised into). Transgender is not the equivalent of cross-dressing, which may be an occasional lifestyle that people of one sex engage in for personal gratification. Overall, there is practically no research on transgendered persons and their family lives (Biblarz and Savci, 2010).

Marital and Cohabitational Sexual Relations

Interestingly enough, conjugal sex is not as popular a topic of research as is sex outside of marriage! The few studies on marital sexuality tend to focus on the following questions: How often do couples have intercourse? What factors differentiate those with a high frequency compared with those with a low frequency?

Frequency of Sexual Intercourse and Aging

There is agreement that the frequency of sexual intercourse in marriage diminishes with age (Laumann et al., 1994). This downward trend is illustrated below in percentages provided by Call et al. (1995):

19 to 24 years of age:	11.7 times per month
30 to 34 years of age	8.5 times per month
50 to 54 years of age	5.5 times per month
65 to 69 years of age	2.4 times per month

But Call and colleagues caution the reader that averages are not the best measure of couples' sexual activity after age 50: Couples who stop having sex depress the overall average. For instance, for respondents older than age 75, the average stands at about once a month. But when only those who have sexual intercourse are considered, the average rises to three times a month.

The question to address here, however, is how to untangle the effect of age from that of marital duration. In other words, as couples age, so does their marriage and habituation could be a factor reducing frequency. Call et al. (1995) have done the calculations to answer this question. First, they found that age is the main variable. Second, if habituation has any effect at all, it occurs early in the marriage. That is, couples' frequency of sex was highest during the first two years of marriage, regardless of age. After two years, or what is called the **honeymoon period**, the frequency of sex declined sharply. The researchers explained that, if habituation kept producing an effect, sex would then keep diminishing in frequency as the marriage continued, which is not the case.

The same phenomenon is observed in remarriages. The frequency of sexual intercourse is high at the beginning of the relationship, no matter the age, and drops after the initial period. After that, it becomes a matter of age rather than length of marriage. Generally, couples who are younger at marriage or remarriage have a higher frequency of sexual intercourse than couples who are older. It is possible that, in a few years, this section will be rewritten to include references to the effect of sexual enhancement pills such as Viagra on older couples' sexual lives. We are beginning to hear anecdotes from lawyers who are seeing more divorces stemming from older men who have discovered "the fountain of youth" and discarded less attractive wives to "trespass into younger pastures."

Frequency of Sexual Intercourse and Cohabitation

Laumann and colleagues (1994), Call et al. (1995), and Yabiku and Gager (2009) find that cohabiting couples have sexual intercourse much more often than married couples. For instance, Laumann and colleagues report that only about 7 percent of married men mentioned having sex four or more times a week compared with nearly 19 percent of cohabiting men. The women's reports were similar. The reader may then perhaps conclude that, at least as far as sex is concerned, cohabitation is more enjoyable. Is it?

Unfortunately, most long-term cohabiting unions tend to last, at best, for the same duration of time as the honeymoon period in marriage (Milan, 2000). Therefore, it is entirely possible that a higher frequency of sex among cohabitants simply reflects the fact that they are mainly honeymooners. When the couple remains happy together, most then go on to marriage and, at least at the beginning, may maintain a higher frequency of sex. So far, there have not been sufficient numbers of cohabiting couples at older ages whose relationships have remained intact for 10 to 25 years to compare with married couples of the same age. However, it appears that sex plays a more important role in cohabitation than it does in marriage and constitutes a larger part of the mutual attraction (Yakibu and Gager, 2009). Nevertheless, the frequency of sexual intercourse must also diminish with age among cohabitants who remain together. Longitudinal research is needed in this domain, comparing couples consisting of two men, two women, and heterosexual partners (Patterson, 2000).

Frequency of Sexual Intercourse and Relationship Quality

Couples with a higher frequency of sexuality experience a happier relationship and greater conjugal stability (Yabiku and Gager, 2009). The more vital couples are, the more likely they are to remain interested in each other, and this interest generalizes to the sexual aspect of their relationship. Couples who get along better and share a higher level of companionship are inclined to be more physically affectionate, which leads to a desire and opportunity for sexual activities. Another complementary process is also at play: Having intercourse leads to a greater satisfaction with the marriage and the partner. Sex is a valued activity, and when it is satisfying, it increases a person's sense of well-being and appreciation. The partners feel rewarded. In contrast, when frequency diminishes too much or sex becomes less pleasant, the overall relationship may be negatively affected. As well, when a couple quarrels a great deal or is more distant, this in turn depresses marital satisfaction and contributes to a decrease in sexual activity (Call et al., 1995). One actually encounters both processes when studying how divorced couples' marriages deteriorated. One woman put it this way about her ex-husband in my study on divorce/remarriage:

> "He always wanted sex more than I did and he was always mortally offended that I didn't. But he was always so mean to me otherwise that I had developed a sense of physical, you know, I felt repulsed at the thought of even touching him. I mean, you can't just separate the two. He used to call me a cold bitch, frigid, and that explained it all [her lack of interest in sex] in his mind. But, you know, my husband [remarriage] will tell you that I am a very physical woman [laughs]. If someone, your husband, is wonderful to you, it goes without saying that sex comes easily."

The next respondent, also remarried, is explaining why he stayed so long with his ex-wife even though he did not like her much:

"Don't take me wrong here, I am not a pervert [we both laugh] *but sex is the answer. We didn't get along well at all and didn't share much, but our sex life was great. It's difficult to explain but it was a nice release at the end of a hard day at work and even at home. That's why I stayed: I had a lot to lose here."*

Extracouple Sexual Relations

Generally, no matter the type of union they are in, males engage in extracouple sex more than women, as indicated in the percentages provided by Blumstein and Schwartz (1990). The respondents were men and women who reported at least one instance of extrapartner sexuality:

Husbands	11 percent
Wives	9 percent
Male cohabitants	25 percent
Female cohabitants	22 percent
Gay unions	79 percent
Lesbian unions	19 percent

In the 1994 study by Laumann and colleagues, the results were essentially similar. Whatever their marital status, most men and women reported having had only one sexual partner in the past year (67 and 75 percent, respectively). Of those who were married, 94 percent had been monogamous compared with 75 percent of the cohabitants. (More recently, Whisman et al., 2007, report an annual rate of infidelity of about 2 percent.) As well, persons whose first union was cohabitational have had more sexual partners than those whose first union was marital. However, over recent decades, there has been an increase in infidelity, particularly among older men and the younger cohort aged 18 to 25 (Fincham and Beach, 2010).

This said, there is general agreement in the various reliable sources of statistics and several salient conclusions emerge. First, heterosexual men and women are more faithful than are homosexual men. Second, among gay unions, men are less monogamous whereas lesbian women are more. And third, married spouses have the lowest rate of infidelities. Cohabiting couples are far less monogamous, but there is little difference between men and women (Treas and Giesen, 2000). In fact, in the U.S., attitudes toward extramarital affairs have become less accepting in recent decades (Thornton and Young-DeMarco, 2001). There is actually a great deal of consensus among western countries that extramarital infidelities are unacceptable. For instance, Swedes who are very liberal in other domains of sexuality nearly unanimously disapprove of conjugal infidelities: 96 percent compared with 94 percent among Americans (Widmer et al., 1998). In 2009, 85 percent of Canadians disapproved of marital infidelity (MacQueen, 2009).

Internet Infidelities and Pornography

The least that can be said is that married couples are *more sexually faithful than portrayed in the media*. This stems in great part from the fact that many commercial enterprises catering to various sex trades/businesses want to promote the idea that "everyone is doing it," that "infidelity is natural," to make **money**. This media bias also stems from the other fact that **media "personalities"**—generally actors, some sports figures, entertainment persons—are far more likely than the remainder of the population to have extramarital affairs and to divorce; as well, television soap characters also portray such behaviours.

A new outlet for infidelities now resides in online dating services, especially those catering to extramarital affairs. Douthat (2008) asks the question whether "pornography is adultery?" Indeed, some research indicates that spouses who are unfaithful are three times more likely to have used Internet pornography than others who have not been unfaithful—which rather contradicts those who promote the idea that pornography and infidelities "save marriages" by providing a sexual outlet. As well, statistics indicate that online pornography is far more watched by males than females at all age levels, including student populations (Douthat, 2008). Pornography is a billion-dollar industry, constituting a vast market, and there are thus various research questions that arise in how porn contents can affect people's expectations regarding sexuality and faithfulness once in a committed relationship (Fincham and Beach, 2010:639).

CONCLUSIONS: THE CHANGING PROFILE OF COUPLES AND SEXUALITY

The past three decades have brought about changes in cultural attitudes and practices concerning sexuality and couple formation. Despite these many changes, marriage is still the preferred type of union, especially among heterosexual women. Gays' recourse to this institution confirms its desirability.

Changing trends are not equally shared by all ethnic or religious groups in Canada, especially among recent arrivals whose cultures still emphasize marriage and restrict sexuality within its boundaries, particularly for women. Thus, the new "lifestyle alternatives" practised by so many Canadian-born citizens constitute a difficult environment for others who prefer to wait until the right person comes along and for immigrants from different cultural backgrounds, and especially for their children. Textbooks that emphasize the changing aspects of family life in Canada may inadvertently misrepresent reality—when "changing" refers only to liberalization, especially in the domain of sexuality, rather than cultural diversity (values, religion) under our large Canadian roof.

Summary

1. Dating as an institution originated in the U.S. and replaced traditional courtship. Women tend to invest more in their dating relationship than men do. Same-sex dating and Internet dating are discussed. More research is needed on these topics.

2. The choice of heterosexual dates (and later, partners) at first follows rules of propinquity. Assortative mating becomes more prominent later on, and the term homogamy is used to refer to couples who are similar to each other in some characteristics.

Homogamy becomes endogamy when couples partner themselves within their own group. Endogamy takes place largely along lines of race, social class, religion, and age. Research is needed on partner selection among homosexuals.

3. Romantic love is examined historically and within the context of the western world.

4. Cohabitation has increased in Canada from 6 percent of all couples in 1981 to 13 percent in 2006; however, the largest increase took place in Quebec, where 30 percent of all couples cohabit. Women are less favourable than men to cohabitation. This type of union is less stable than marriage. Its relationship aspects, issues of commitment and fidelity, and its ramifications for older adults are presented.

5. Marriage is discussed as an institution that provides advantages to the partners in terms of well-being. A certain degree of social selection in marriage explains some of this well-being; but social causation is a more important explanation. Marriage is more of a mixed blessing for women than for men.

6. Same-sex marriages became legal in Canada in 2004.

7. Issues of gender are first introduced regarding sexuality. The study of adolescent sexual relations largely centres on factors related to onset, delayed initiation into sexual intercourse, multiple partners, and oral sex. Variables that contribute to later sexual initiation are high parental social class, a two-parent family, school achievement, religiosity, and parental supervision. The role of peers is emphasized. There are degrees of voluntariness and desire in the experience.

8. Homosexual and bisexual identities are discussed as well as transgendered situations.

9. Within a marriage or a remarriage, couples' frequency of sex usually peaks during the first two years. It then diminishes but remains stable in subsequent years, only to be gradually affected by age. Cohabiting couples experience higher rates of sexual intercourse, but there are no studies on long-term cohabiting couples. Frequency of sexual activity is related to marital happiness. Contrary to myths, a majority of married couples are sexually faithful. Cohabitants are less faithful. Least monogamous of all are same-sex male cohabitants. Lesbian cohabitants are less monogamous than wives but slightly more than cohabiting women.

10. The role of the media, online infidelities, and pornography is mentioned as well as how these can affect conjugal relationships.

11. The new changes in couple formation are not shared equally by all ethnic or religious groups in Canada, especially among recent arrivals.

Analytical Questions

1. What makes dating an American institution even at this point in time?

2. Cohabitation has increased in Canada. Yet, as we see in Figure 7.1, there is a large difference by gender in terms of willingness to live common-law. What are the implications of these two seemingly contradictory trends?

3. If you were entirely free to choose your own union type, which would you prefer: cohabitation or marriage? Examine the reasons behind your choice.

4. Does same-sex marriage endanger the institution of marriage?

5. Discuss the notion that sexuality is a largely male construct in our society.

6. If this chapter were written in a Hindu or Muslim country, how different would it be?

Suggested Readings

Cate, R. M., and Lloyd, S. A. 1992. *Courtship*. Newbury Park, CA: Sage. This text covers the history of courtship, discusses its functions, and traces the development of the relationship. It also looks toward the future.

Laumann, E. O., et al. 1994. *The social organization of sexuality: Sexual practices in the United States*. Chicago: University of Chicago Press. This book presents survey results on sexual practices in heterosexuality as well as homosexuality, and in married as well

as nonmarital sex. This book covers everything you ever wanted to know about sex, but does it within a carefully executed sociological analysis.

Wu, Z. 2000. *Cohabitation: An alternative form of family living*. Toronto: Oxford University Press. This review book provides a comprehensive discussion of all aspects of cohabitation and can be useful both for this and the next chapter.

Suggested Weblinks

PFLAG (Parents, Families and Friends of Lesbians and Gays) has several chapters across the country.

www.pflag.ca

SIECAN (Sex Information and Education Council of Canada) also supports the *Canadian Journal of Human Sexuality*.

www.sieccan.org

CHAPTER 8

Patterns of Family Formation and Planning

"I come from a single-parent family and I wouldn't recommend it to anyone. My poor mom had too much of a hard time raising us three all alone, with no help and no respect from anyone."

"My father left my mother before I even knew he existed so that I haven't missed out on much. The only drawback is that we weren't very well off, but outside of this I often think that I may just end up a single mother too one day if the right man doesn't come along. Beats not having children and besides I am very much like my mother and I would do very well thank you."

"I had an abortion two years ago and that was rather draining emotionally because it would have been nice to have had the baby, but it would also have ruined my plans for school and perhaps getting married. So now I am thankful for it."

"Abortion is much easier than birth control." [from a student who had had three abortions]

"I hope to have had two children by then [in 10 years]. *I guess it would be too much to think of having three because I'll need to keep my job."*

"I don't see children on the horizon. I've got too many plans for my life and all that I can fit in there is a wife to share these projects with. Children are too time consuming nowadays."

These students' reflections on some aspects of family structure and planning set the tone for this chapter in which we look at family formation, including alternative modes such as adoption and recourse to reproductive technologies. Family formation has different starting points: marriage and cohabitation (including same-sex), and single parents. *Although adults are present in this chapter, its focus is on children's well-being* within the various alternatives for family formation.

OVERVIEW OF FAMILY STRUCTURE

The 2006 census indicates that the proportion of families comprised of a mother, father, and at least one dependent child has continued to decline while other forms of family structure are increasing. This parallels the steep decline in marriage rates in the 1990s described in the previous chapter. This decline is in part driven by the exceptionally low rate of marriage in Quebec, which had dropped to 2.9 per 1,000 population by 2007, compared with 6.9 in 1980 (Girard, 2008).

In Table 8.1, we see that married-couple families constituted 68.6 percent of all families in 2006. This is down from 83 percent in 1981—a substantial change. At the same time, the proportion of cohabiting families increased from 5.6 percent in 1981 to 15.5 percent in 2006. The proportion of one-parent families remained stable. In Quebec, only 54.8 percent of families fall into the married category, compared with 68 to 74 percent for most of the other provinces. However, the less populated Nunavut, Yukon, and Northwest Territories also have a low rate of families headed by married couples, perhaps as a result of the greater poverty of these regions as well as cultural dislocation.

Looked at from a **child focus**, in 2006, 66 percent of children below the age of 15 lived with married parents (compared with 81 percent in 1981), 15 percent lived with common-law parents (compared with 4.5 percent in 1981), while 18.3 percent were with a lone parent versus 12 percent in 1981 (Statistics Canada, 2008h). First Nations and Métis children were far more likely to live in a lone-parent family: 37 and 31 percent, respectively (Gionet, 2009). From a **father perspective**, between 1995 and 2006, the proportion of married fathers in Quebec has significantly decreased, from 62 to 48 percent. In contrast, in other provinces, the decline was much smaller, from 81 to 79 percent. Similarly, the proportion of fathers in common-law unions substantially rose in Quebec, from 26 to 40 percent, while the increase was small in other provinces (Beaupré et al., 2010).

| TABLE 8.1 | Distribution of Canadian Families by Marital Status and Provinces/Territories, 2006 Census |

	% Married	% Cohabiting	% One-Parent
Canada	68.6	15.5	15.9
Newfoundland and Labrador	73.6	10.9	15.5
Prince Edward Island	73.2	10.4	16.3
Nova Scotia	70.1	13.0	16.9
New Brunswick	69.4	14.2	16.3
Quebec	**54.8**	**28.8**	**16.6**
Ontario	74.0	10.3	15.8
Manitoba	72.2	10.8	16.2
Saskatchewan	72.6	10.8	16.6
Alberta	72.9	12.8	14.4
British Columbia	72.3	12.2	15.1
Yukon	**55.7**	**23.6**	**20.7**
Northwest Territories	**51.1**	**27.5**	**21.6**
Nunavut	**41.0**	**31.3**	**27.6**

Source: Statistics Canada, 2007g; adapted with permission from Statistics Canada; percentages by Ambert.

FAMILY FORMATION VIA MARRIAGE

In Chapter 4, we saw that children living with their married parents have the lowest poverty rate. In Chapter 12, the effect of parental divorce and remarriage will be studied. The overall conclusion from these various sources of information is that children benefit more unequivocally than adults from their parents' marriage. However, children who experience a conflictual parental marriage benefit less than children living with a well-balanced single parent (Jekielek, 1998). On the whole, highly conflictual marriages do not last long because of the acceptability of divorce as an alternative. Even among those who divorce, at best one-third have highly conflictual marriages and many of those are childless. Therefore, a relatively small proportion of marriages are detrimental to children and an even smaller proportion of divorces are beneficial to them (Amato and Booth, 1997). Conflict aside, even when parents do not judge their marriage to be the happiest, children still benefit from it. What is important to children above all else is **family stability** and the care they receive from their parents—not whether their parents are madly in love with each other. The latter is an adult perspective.

In a society with a nuclear family system, children who have **two parents**—whether natural or adoptive, whether of the same or opposite sex—are at an advantage because they have two rather than one person **invested** in their well-being, responsible for them, and acting as **authority figures**. Additionally, two parents provide a greater repertoire of behaviours, attitudes, and knowledge from which children can draw and learn. In James Coleman's theory, two parents constitute a greater source of social capital, which then translates into more human capital for the children. With two parents, children have an alternative when the other has less time, is ill, or is otherwise preoccupied. Two parents can also provide moral support to each other in their coparental duties, and this benefits children.

Infant mortality is lower in married families, and this advantage is even found in Scandinavian countries, where there is less poverty among single mothers and where cohabitation is more institutionalized than it is in Canada (Oyen et al., 1997). Children also benefit from marriage in terms of economic security, school achievement, emotional stability, prosocial behaviour, supervision, and later on as adults, in terms of work (Cooksey et al., 1997; Langille et al., 2003).

Inasmuch as the institution of marriage contributes to the emotional stability and overall well-being of adults and children, it becomes an institution beneficial to society. It produces a great deal of social capital and serves as an **agency of social control** (Laub et al., 1998). For instance, children in two-parent families on average get more education and are less often on welfare (McLoyd, 1998). Later on, they pay more taxes. From a societal point of view, marriage contributes to the successful socialization of citizens, which does not mean, however, that a majority of children in other forms of family are less adequately socialized. It means that proportionally more children from married families are successfully socialized.

FAMILY FORMATION VIA COHABITATION

Family formation through cohabitation occurs when a couple cohabits before or just after the birth of their child; or when a mother begins cohabitation before or after the birth of a child with a man who is not the father. In other cases, cohabitation occurs as a form of repartnering after a conjugal dissolution. A large proportion of cohabitations involve children (Seltzer, 2000). In 2006, 15 percent of Canadian children aged 0 to 14 lived in common-law households—including in Quebec, where 29 percent lived in such households. When Quebec is excluded, the Canadian rate falls to 8.2 percent of children. In many cases, however, one of the two spouses is the child's stepparent.

Cohabiting couples with their own children have a higher level of stability than others and are more likely to marry. However, even children whose parents cohabit will experience more **instability** than those whose parents marry before they are born (Smock and Greenland, 2010), and this holds true in most countries, including Sweden, Norway, and the U.S. (Osborne et al., 2007). Marcil-Gratton (1998) found that 60 percent of children born to cohabiting parents had experienced family disruption by age 10, compared with 14 percent of those children whose parents had not cohabited. Overall, children are more likely to experience a parental divorce when their parents began their union as cohabitants or when a single mother cohabits and then marries. In some families, there is a "revolving door" situation, whereby serial partners succeed one another over the years. In a nutshell, children born to cohabiting parents are not at a large advantage compared with those in one-parent families, especially when a mother cohabits with a man who is not the children's father. One can hypothesize that longer cohabitations that are stable benefit children as much as a marriage.

However, when a single mother begins to cohabit, **family poverty is reduced** by as much as 30 percent, which benefits children—although this benefit is often of short duration because of the fragility of these unions (Raley and Wildsmith, 2004). This advantage is also mitigated by the fact that male cohabitants often earn less than married men. Thus, parental cohabitation does not make children well-off, but less poor (Morrison and Ritualo, 2000). Better-off cohabitants tend to marry when or before they have children, although this is less the case in Quebec. *Repeated cohabitations* may prevent young people from building *shared* capital or assets as couples as well as for their children later.

Results are contradictory as to whether children living with their own parents have fewer or more behaviour and emotional problems depending on whether the parents are married or cohabiting (Brown, 2002; Manning, 2002). Brown (2004b) has documented more problems among adolescents whose biological parents are cohabiting. However, much of the literature on children in cohabitations is complicated by the fact that perhaps a majority, when they are adolescents, have a stepparent and have been part of a familial transition (Bumpass and Lu, 2000). Manning and Lamb (2003) have found that *family instability rather than structure* is a more important factor for adolescent well-being. More research is needed on small children whose mothers cohabit with a man who is not the natural father. These couples are generally quite young and often disadvantaged. Unemployment is common. Such mothers are in a precarious situation both conjugally and economically (Brown,

2002). In some instances, the mothers themselves enter into these unions for short-term benefits and do not commit themselves to marry a man whose economic situation is unstable. In other instances, the mothers are the most committed partner but they are in a weaker bargaining position because they have a child who does not belong to the partner. Thus, the selection factor in cohabitation certainly accounts for some differences in children's well-being (Brown, 2002).

The potential instability of these women's unions and the instability of the level of support they receive result in stressors that can disrupt their parenting activities (Beck et al., 2010). The mother's partner is not as likely to compensate for this neglect as a married father or even stepfather might do because the partner's attachment to the children is often low. Physical abuse is also more likely (Gelles, 1989). Girls are at risk of being sexually abused (Gordon, 1989); this is especially so in homes where males are transient. In instances where the mother is obviously sexually active with a series of men, the transmission of poverty, early pregnancy, and behavioural problems may become an intergenerational characteristic of these families. A student dramatically explains this:

> "*What made me the most unhappy at this age* [0 to 5] *is the same for all the other ages to this day. You see, we never lived with our fathers* [her two siblings have two different fathers] *for long and the men my mother lived with took from us the time and attention my mother could have given us without them. Sometimes, they even took the money too. . . . I remember the times when my little brother's dad used to reject me and my other brother because we weren't his. . . . This* [other] *man beat us up and my mother when he drank. . . . We had to move often because my mother would get a bad reputation so we had to change school. I never had friends. . . . This was the year* [14] *when I ran away and lived in a shelter and where I got my first break in life. . . . My two brothers got their first 'breaks' with the police . . . they both have babies, not me.*"

After divorce, cohabitation instead of remarriage may bring in a less involved stepparent (Manning and Lamb, 2003). Further, when a divorced father cohabits, he visits his children less often than a father who is remarried (Cooksey and Craig, 1998). This may be less evident in Quebec and in countries where cohabitation after divorce is more prevalent. Nevertheless, at this time in North America, cohabitation is not a situation that signals investment in children as much as does marriage, although there are many exceptions. **Commitment** and stability are at the core of children's needs; yet, in too many cohabitations, these two requirements are absent, which may have consequences well into adulthood (Teachman, 2003): Commitment in a parental relationship is an important value that is transferred to children and affects their own subsequent relationships (Ryan et al., 2009:950).

SAME-SEX-PARENT FAMILY FORMATION

At least 3,000 same-sex couples are raising children in Canada today. The 2001 census revealed that 15 percent of households headed by lesbian couples had children, compared with 3 percent of households headed by gay couples (Statistics Canada, 2002a). These numbers underestimate the situation to some extent. They also omit lesbians and

A structural-functional analysis suggests that society would benefit if all family types were equally supported. Children in same-sex-parent families need stability and security, as do other children, in order to grow up to become fully functional members of society.

gays who are single and have a child living with them, as well as those who are married heterosexually and have a child at home: Black et al. (2000) estimate that over 28 percent of all American lesbians and 14 percent of all American gays have children living with them. But even these numbers omit those whose heterosexual ex-spouse has custody of their children following a divorce. Thus, overall, more gays and lesbians have children than is apparent in the general statistics.

Although this is slowly changing, a majority of children in same-sex couples were born to a mother-father unit that ended in divorce and the lesbian or gay parent obtained custody. A similar situation exists in Sweden and Norway (Andersson et al., 2006). Thus, a majority of these children have another parent who is heterosexual. There are instances when both partners bring children from previous relationships. These situations are similar to those of stepparenting among heterosexuals, but they may also differ depending on whether the children came from a heterosexual marriage or from another lesbian union.

Tasker and Golombok (1995, 1997) initiated a longitudinal study comparing children of single lesbian mothers and heterosexual mothers. The children were, on average, 9 1/2 years old, and were re-interviewed 14 years later. The young adults with a lesbian mother reported a better relationship with her and with her partner than did young adults whose mother was heterosexual and brought in a stepfather. The children of lesbians even had a better relationship with their fathers. Hence, there is a possibility that such children experience a less difficult time before and after their parents' divorce compared with children who have two heterosexual parents: There may be less parental conflict, jealousy, and feelings of personal rejection, perhaps because a mother's female partner does not "compete" with a father. However, a divorce between two same-sex parents may be no less difficult, a topic which deserves research.

More and more lesbian couples give birth via donor insemination or adopt (Gartrell et al., 2000). In order to share motherhood more equally, one can donate a fertilized egg to the other partner who will carry it to term (Dondorp et al., 2010). Some gay couples also adopt (Ross et al., 2009). In the U.S., particularly California, several have had recourse to surrogate mothers. Gay couples can also cooperate with lesbian couples in producing children (via donor insemination) and raising them jointly, an arrangement that allows children to have parents of both sexes. Same-sex couples who have a child have to do far more **planning** than heterosexual couples, both before and after a child's arrival. They may, for instance, arrange for a cooperative childrearing environment with another homosexual couple of the opposite sex. In lesbian couples where one of the two women has given birth, the biological mother typically assumes greater responsibility for the care of the child and at first enjoys a closer relationship with this child than the co-mother (Bos et al., 2007). Other studies show an equivalent attachment to both mothers as the child ages (Goldberg et al., 2008). Upon the arrival of a child, lesbian and gay couples experience transition issues in their relationships equivalent to those of heterosexual couples (Biblarz and Savci, 2010; Goldberg et al., 2010). Some research shows that they receive less support from friends who are not planning on having children and more from their families (DeMino et al., 2007)—which used to be the contrary in the past when families had difficulties accepting their adult children's homosexuality.

Studies of planned families of *lesbian* couples indicate that their children are as well adjusted as children in heterosexual families (Bos et al., 2008; DeMino et al., 2007). The same result applies to children raised by solo lesbian mothers (Golombok and Badger, 2010). Indeed, in a follow-up study of lesbian couples who had used a fertility clinic, the 10-year-old children were receiving as much affection and discipline from each mother—as perceived both by the children and both parents—compared with a heterosexual sample (Vanfraussen et al., 2003). Another study comparing lesbian and heterosexual mothers, some single, some in couples, found no difference in children's development around age seven, even though all had been produced by donor insemination—which is certainly an additional complication in a child's self-definition (Chan et al., 1998). Overall, as parents, lesbian mothers are similar to heterosexual mothers; it is not their sexual orientation that emerges as an important variable but their **identity as mothers** (Bos et al., 2007). Similar results have been obtained for children adopted in gay/lesbian homes (Averett et al., 2009). Healthy family processes are key to children's well-being, whether in same-sex or heterosexual families (Strohschein, 2010).

Children with experiences of homophobia are more distressed (Gartrell et al., 2005), and they have more behavioural problems, especially in the U.S. compared with countries where there is a greater acceptance of lesbigay relationships (Bos et al., 2008). Children living in same-sex-parent families are often teased by peers and shunned by their peers' parents, and thus their lives may be more stressful (Morris et al., 2001:151). Yet they do not seem to grow up disadvantaged emotionally and may even possess certain strengths of character such as tolerance of diversity, empathy, and contentment (Gartrell et al., 2005; Goldberg, 2007; Patterson, 2000). However, other evidence points to difficulties experienced by adolescents who feel embarrassed by their parents' homosexuality, a situation which may be attenuated in later cohorts (DeAngelis, 2002).

Children of homosexual parents usually adopt heterosexual identities (Bailey and Dawood, 1998). Bailey et al. (1995) compared adult sons who had spent many years with their gay father to sons who had lived only briefly with a gay father. The rate of homosexuality among the offspring with longer contact with their father was not higher. A small research by Costello (1997) found that many homosexual partners consciously avoid pressuring their children to conform to their sexual preference. Nevertheless, young people raised in same-sex-parent families are more tolerant of same-sex experimentation, and they develop a homosexual identity more often than do children in other families—whether heredity and learning are interrelated causal factors is impossible to evaluate at this point (Stacey and Biblarz, 2001).

Tasker and Golombok (1995) found that, when mothers had had more lesbian partners and were more open about their sexuality when the children were young, there was a greater likelihood that, as young adults, these children would have a homosexual identity. However, we do not know to what extent a mother's serial same-sex relationships pose developmental problems similar to those found among children whose heterosexual mothers have had serial relationships, particularly multiple cohabitations (Dunifon and Kowaleski-Jones, 2002).

FAMILY FORMATION BY SINGLE PARENTS

Single-parent families are of interest to sociologists because the cultural values of most societies dictate that children should have two parents rather than one. Second, families that deviate from this norm often differ from two-parent families in other ways as well, especially in economic circumstances (Wu and Schimmele, 2003). But contrary to what is often believed, single-parent families do not represent a new phenomenon (Lynn, 2003). In 1941, for instance, they accounted for 14 percent of all families. In the past, because life expectancy was shorter, large proportions of children lost one parent and then another to death. What has changed over time is the **composition** of such families: By the 1970s, a majority of these families had divorced rather than widowed parents. As the years went by, a larger proportion of nonmarital one-parent families occurred as sexuality outside marriage became more acceptable and as single mothers increasingly kept their babies rather than have them adopted.

The number of **births** to unmarried mothers has increased continuously since 1921, when only 2 percent of all Canadian births were outside marriage. This number reached 5 percent of all births by the end of the Second World War, nine percent in 1971, 14 percent in 1981, and 27 percent in 1991 (Belle and McQuillan, 1994). There were over 1.4 million single-parent families in 2006, or 16 percent of all families with dependent children (refer to Table 8.1). *A majority are headed by a female parent, generally a divorced one.* In Canada, 25 percent are headed by a single woman as a result of a nonmarital birth, compared with 35 percent in the U.S. Using children as the unit of analysis, in 2001, 18 percent of Canadian children and 28 percent of American children lived in one-parent families. As is the case in the U.S. and Caribbean nations, far more black Canadian children aged 0 to 14 (46 percent) belong to one-parent families than other Canadian children (Milan and Tran, 2004).

When a single mother is employed, not only is she the sole wage earner for herself and her child, she is also far more likely than a male worker to earn a low salary and to fall behind in her loan and housing payments (Pyper, 2002). She generally earns less than an employed divorced mother, even though the latter does not earn as much, on average, as a male breadwinner. Therefore, the economic disadvantage of women in general is especially detrimental to single mothers' families, both divorced and never married, but particularly the latter.

Among adolescents, the U.S. birth rate for single mothers is more than double the Canadian one. Consequently, Americans more than Canadians have held a moral and social problems-oriented discourse on this issue (Caragata, 1999). However, not all these families suffer from adversities, and a proportion do not differ from two-parent families in any meaningful way. The main problem with the generic concept of "single parenting" is that it actually is a **gendered** one because women, not men, give birth. As well, women do the caring work, have financial responsibility, and are blamed by society for their poverty and their children's problems—and by the welfare system in particular (Ambert, 2006). This is related to what has been called the feminization of poverty (Brady and Kall, 2008). **Older single mothers by choice,** however, are rarely studied. They represent a select group of more educated women. Their children are generally positively affected (Golombok and Badger, 2010; Jadva et al., 2009a).

Teen Birth Rates and the Structure of Teen Parenthood

Teen pregnancies, live births, and abortions have all declined in the past decade and, in all cases, the rates are higher for adolescents aged 18 and 19 than for younger ones. In 1996, there were 22 births per 1,000 women aged 15 to 19 versus 14 in 2007. This compares with the low Swedish rates of 7.7 and 5.7 and the high American rates of 53.5 in 1996 and 41.9 in 2006 (McKay and Barrett, 2010). Below are the teen birth rates per 1,000 women aged 15 to 19 for the year 2007 in Canada (Statistics Canada, 2009s):

For Canada as a whole	**14.0 births per 1,000 teens**
Newfoundland and Labrador	17.0
Prince Edward Island	17.0
Nova Scotia	16.5
New Brunswick	19.8
Quebec	9.7
Ontario	10.8
Manitoba	31.9
Saskatchewan	35.2
Alberta	20.9
British Columbia	10.7
Northwest Territories	35.7
Nunavut	116.7

Quebec, British Columbia, and Ontario have particularly low teen birth rates, in part because of urbanization and the availability of abortion. For Canada as a whole, nearly half of pregnant adolescents give birth because they, their parents, or their boyfriends prefer to have a baby or object to abortion on moral grounds. As well, many realize that they are pregnant or accept that fact too late in the gestation period to have recourse to an abortion. Since 1974, the proportion of teens choosing or being able to access an abortion has climbed steadily, while the proportion of those giving birth has declined accordingly. Teen mothers are now less likely than in the past to have subsequent children while still so young. Those who do are highly concentrated in low-income neighbourhoods and among Aboriginals and, in the U.S., among blacks (Guzzo and Furstenberg, 2007b; Rotermann, 2007b).

The Structure of Adolescent Parenting

In 1974, only 10 percent of teens who gave birth were single, but now about 80 percent are and it is this fact that led to the concept of "teen" pregnancy. Thus, "teen" pregnancy and births are **historically grounded social constructs**, and are a concern for policy-makers (Bonell, 2004). Births to single teen mothers *have never represented more than 20 percent of nonconjugal Canadian births.*

The causes and consequences of adolescent motherhood are similar in all western countries and the structure of this motherhood—generally associated with poverty (Chapter 4)—contains the seeds of disadvantage, often for several years (Turner et al., 2000). It is difficult in our society to be both an adolescent and a mother or a father. Adolescence is socially constructed as a period during which children acquire rights and independence as well as formal education, whereas motherhood involves assuming responsibilities and being tied down. The two may conflict to the girl's detriment, but particularly to the infant's disadvantage, and this is often problematic for the entire kin group, especially for mothers and siblings (East and Jacobson, 2000), as illustrated in the following quote from a resilient student:

> "My sister had her first baby at 15, the second at 16, and the third at 18. She 'loves' babies but we've always had to take care of them and now she lives in our basement. I really resent her because sometimes I have to write a paper and there are these babies that I have to babysit. And now guess what, my brother's girlfriend is pregnant too and she's only 17. My mother should have never set a precedent by helping my sister."

Many young mothers at first bask under the sun of family attention and love for the baby, peer support or curiosity, as well as the young father's temporary interest. For many, the baby represents someone who will love them unconditionally. The transition to motherhood is overlaid with the usual transitions that adolescents in this society make as they become more independent from their parents. Teen mothers thus experience a double transition. But it is more likely that many adolescent mothers had long emancipated themselves from their parents and had done this earlier than comparable girls who led a more normative life course. This premature disaffection from parental rules may actually have been one of the immediate causes of their becoming sexually active and pregnant. As well, when these young women have many friends who also have babies, they are more likely to have subsequent children (Raneri and Wiemann, 2007).

Further, because they initiate life course transitions, adolescent mothers are more likely than older women to experience multiple transitions, such as successive cohabitations and separations (Luong, 2008). These transitions make lives, including those of small children, less stable and more vulnerable—a situation that too often becomes intergenerational (East et al., 2007). Little is known about how women who mother on their own most of their lives and then become **single grandmothers** experience their personal development, identity, health, and old age (Kasper et al., 2008).

There are several paths to adulthood among adolescent mothers (Oxford et al., 2005). Those who complete high school and, especially, those who go on to pursue some post-secondary education are not much different from other mothers when they reach their thirties. Luong (2008) suggests that other resources and **characteristics** of these young mothers may account for their education and ability to support themselves and remain out of poverty. This may relate to teen mothers' socioemotional development. From Montreal, Serbin and colleagues (1998) report that childhood aggressiveness is related to early pregnancy and dropping out of school. Before having a baby, adolescent mothers average more instances of suspensions, truancy, drug use, and fighting in school than other adolescent girls. Among poor teens, psychological distress is also related to a pregnancy (Mollborn and Morningstar, 2009). Thus, single parenting is part of a non-normative life course for a number of adolescents who were problematic children long before becoming pregnant (Woodward et al., 2001). Even though these adolescents are still antisocial and impulsive, as are many of the fathers, they now have the responsibility of a helpless baby and some will have additional children from other partners (Guzzo and Furstenberg, 2007a).

The **babies' fathers** often have a background similar to that of the young mothers. For instance, Moffitt et al. (2002) found that young men who are highly antisocial produce nearly three times the percentage of babies than do more prosocial young men by the time they reach the age of 26. Woodward et al. (2006) have obtained similar information about young fathers (and mothers) in New Zealand, including characteristics such as novelty seeking tendencies, as well as early drug use. Fathers with a history of incarceration are more than twice as likely to have had children by two or more partners (Carlson and Furstenberg, 2006). For these young men, the practice and meaning of fatherhood is very different from that of other fathers. Guzzo and Furstenberg (2007a) have calculated, for the U.S., that one out of six poor black men aged 34 to 45 have had a child from three or more different women—a pattern of **"serial" fatherhood**. These men are also less likely to spend time with their children and some of these children are more at risk (Bronte-Tinkew et al., 2009). As well, most alarming is the fact that recent cohorts transition from one birth with one mother to another more quickly and at a higher rate than in the past (Manlove et al., 2008a). Multi-partner fertility is belatedly receiving research attention south of the border (e.g., Sinkewicz and Garfinkell, 2009).

Children Born to Single Mothers

Poverty, especially when it is intergenerational, is one of the key causes of single motherhood that is related to deficits in children. Therefore, general consequences for children born to single mothers overlap with the effects of poverty (Chapter 4). However, the consequences for children of having a single mother depend greatly on:

- mother's characteristics: income, education, mental health, maturity, social conformity, social support
- parenting quality: warmth, involvement, supervision, expectations

- father's characteristics: number of other children elsewhere, contribution, involvement, and relationship with mother (Shook et al., 2010)
- child's characteristics: birth weight, health, abilities, and temperament

On average, children of single mothers are more likely than children living with both parents to exhibit behavioural problems including hyperactivity, aggressiveness, fighting, and hostility, especially when the mother was an adolescent (Pogarski et al., 2006). They are also more at risk of becoming young offenders (Willms, 2002b; Zeman and Bressan, 2008) and of repeating this pattern of family structure (Hofferth and Goldscheider, 2010). Emotionally, they are more at risk of suffering from depression, anxiety, and other disorders, as well as having relationship problems, in part due to their difficult behaviours. On average, they do less well in school and repeat grades more often. Adults who have spent part of their childhood in a single-mother-headed family are more likely to have a child nonmaritally, particularly during adolescence, to have achieved lower educational levels, to be unemployed, and to do less well economically than those adults who have spent their entire childhood in a two-parent family. They are also at greater risk of having a criminal record for violent and serious property offences and to have marital problems and divorce.

Outcomes for the children of adolescent mothers are more negative than those for children of older mothers (Letourneau et al., 2007). In turn, outcomes for the babies of difficult teen mothers are more negative than for the babies of conforming mothers (Stevens-Simon et al., 2001), as explained by a mature student:

> "I had my only child when I turned 17 and although I had a lot of support from my mother our family situation became precarious because I was too young and saw my son as a doll that I could leave behind when I went out with my friends or at other times I would take him out with me at all hours. The friends I had were not very good as you can imagine and we were all school dropouts. The clincher in all of this is that I didn't nurture my son, he had no regular life and became hyperactive and out of control by age 2. He was no longer a live doll and I often resented him. He is now 13 and the problems are endless. . . . I have no life because of him . . . [but] when he was small he had no life and no luck because I was an irresponsible adolescent who only wanted to have a good time."

Thus, difficult adolescent mothers are often unable to meet even basic child needs and use harsher parenting techniques (Berlin et al., 2009:1416; Lee, 2009). As a consequence, their small children are more frequently brought to hospital emergencies because of injuries that suggest both neglect and abuse (Serbin et al., 1996).

However, some previously difficult teens change for the better after the birth of their child. They may, however, have much catching up to do in terms of acquiring habits necessary for the survival of a young parental unit. The corollary is that parenting by older and well-balanced adolescents is less detrimental for all involved and may actually be based on a rational decision. Adolescent mothers' educational level is the best predictor of small children's outcomes (Clark, 1999; Serbin et al., 1998). As already mentioned, young mothers who are able to remain in school and continue on to higher education probably possess other positive characteristics—such as maturity and emotional stability—that are also helpful in their parental role. It would be interesting to know the characteristics of children's fathers that are helpful in promoting better outcomes.

As well, studies in behaviour genetics contribute to explaining the linkages between adolescents' early sexuality, early childbirth, and their children's subsequent behavioural difficulties. Indeed, there are indications that certain genes, which are also related to problematic and antisocial behaviours, at least create a frailty in some children. This frailty then interacts with a less than optimal environment to result both in difficult behaviours and early sexuality, which then lead to early childbearing, and in turn to the new children's own vulnerabilities (Mendle et al., 2009). In other words, an environment of poverty would affect more negatively those children with frail genetic predispositions inherited from their difficult young parents (Ambert, 1998).

DELAYED PARENTHOOD

The age at first birth is increasing in Canada and in many countries of the world: For women, it is 27.7 years—28.5 in Ontario and British Columbia (Statistics Canada, 2004i). As well, the proportion of women who have their first child at age 30 and over has increased spectacularly: They represented nearly half of first births in 2006 compared with 24 percent a decade earlier. Births to women aged 35 and over now represent 11 percent of all first births compared with only 4 percent in 1987 (Statistics Canada, 2008h). In 2006, 9 percent of the women aged 40 to 44 were mothers of at least one child aged 0 to 4 compared with 4.3 percent in 1986 (Vézina and Turcotte, 2009).

As indicated in Figure 8.1, women who give birth for the first time after age 40 are, on average, more educated—and this higher educational level is one of the contributing factors to delayed parenthood (Rajulton and Ravanera, 2006a). These women are also more likely to be urban, immigrant, and professionals, incurring another delay for career formation (Toronto and Vancouver have the highest rates). They have higher incomes (Vézina and Turcotte, 2009). Naturally, a delay in the transition to marriage also accounts for later parenting and lower fertility (Jones, 2007).

Overall, the results are mixed but generally indicate a lower level of parenting stress, greater nurturing, and fewer interparental childrearing conflicts among older than younger first-time parents (Cebello et al., 2004). This is expressed in the following student quote:

> *"In 10 years from now? I will probably be thinking of getting married and having children but not before. I want to do like my parents and have children late when there is more time for them and more money. I just don't envy people my age who are getting married. I wouldn't be a good mother, not until I am older, satisfied with my life, more experienced, have seen the world. My parents did all of that and then after gave so much more of themselves to us, they had more time for us than my friends' parents who were much younger had because they were struggling financially and were often impatient with their lives and their children."*

Heath (1995) replicated the positive results of late parenting and added that late-timing fathers are more nurturing and hold higher behavioural expectations for their

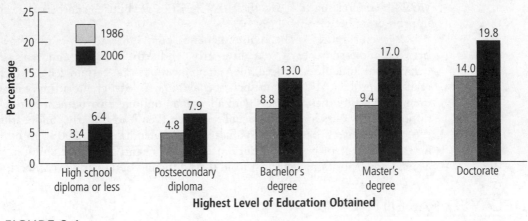

FIGURE 8.1

Proportion of Women 40- to 44-Years Old Who Were Mothers of Young Children by Educational Level, 1986 and 2006

Source: Statistics Canada, censuses of populations 1986 and 2006. Reprinted with permission from Statistics Canada. Vézina and Turcotte, 2009.

children than young fathers. Late-timing fathers are often more positive about their role, more involved, and more satisfied with their marital relationship. Older parents often feel more competent, and their self-esteem is less tied to the vagaries of parenting. Greater personal maturity during the transition to parenthood implies a more stabilized sense of self, one that is less easily bruised by "failures" in the exercise of the parenting role. Older parents offer more material and social capital to their children as well as a more stable marital union (Lockhead, 2000; Martin, 2000).

However, late-timing mothers are more likely to suffer from hypertension during pregnancy, to have a caesarean section, and 17 percent of their children are born pre-term compared with 11 percent of other children (Statistics Canada, 2008h). Older mothers are also more likely to have recourse to fertility treatment and, consequently, to have multiple births. Further, as illustrated in Figure 1.1 (Chapter 1), delayed parenthood decreases the number of generations present in a family. One also has to consider that many of the postponed first births may be so for only one of the two spouses: One of them may already have had children from a previous relationship.

FAMILY PLANNING, BIRTHS, AND FERTILITY

Family planning refers to individuals' or couples' decisions concerning the number and spacing of children they desire. Family planning still remains particularly problematic for adolescent women whose first intercourse is not voluntary. People's family planning intentions change over time, depending on circumstances such as health, finances, and work requirements. Only 7 percent of Canadians aged 20 to 34 do not intend to have children (Stobert and Kemeny, 2003). However, 12 percent of those who have no religious affiliation wish to remain childless. Men generally want to have slightly fewer children than women—2.28 versus 2.46. The **desired fertility** is therefore higher than the **achieved** one, as indicated below. Many individuals are unable to achieve their ideal family size because of financial problems, instability in conjugal relationship, and the difficulty of linking production with reproduction (Beaujot, 2004; Beaujot and Muhammad, 2006). Couples who have reached the goal of one son and one daughter stop childbearing more often than those who have two same-sex children. For example, some couples with two or three girls "try one more time" in order to have a son.

Births and Fertility

Fertility or birth rates refer to the number of births per 1,000 women during their fertile years (ages 15 to 44). The **total fertility** rate, which is an estimate, *refers to the lifetime average number of children per woman*. Currently, it stands at **1.66** in Canada (for 2007), which is well below the 2.1 children needed per woman for population replacement (Statistics Canada, 2009q). Rates are lower in Newfoundland/Labrador, highest in Saskatchewan at 2.3 and Nunavut at 2.97. As well, Aboriginal women have a much higher fertility rate: 3.4 among the Inuit, 2.8 among Natives who are status Indians, 2.4 among the Métis, and 2.0 among non-status Indians (Beaujot and Kerr, 2004).

In Canada, family size began declining after the 1880s, as illustrated in Figure 8.2, and stood at 4.6 children in 1901, down to 3.5 by 1921, then dropped to a further 2.6 in 1937 during the Great Depression (Milan, 2000). This decline continued throughout the decades, only to reverse temporarily during the **baby boom** of the late 1940s and 1950s. Indeed, after the Second World War, there was a sharp increase in fertility, in part because of the social and economic optimism then generated. This increase was also fuelled by a return home of soldiers and young women who had been employed during the war. Thereafter, the downward trend resumed and has continued to this day with an upturn after 2000, in part because the 25 to 34 age group has been increasing in terms of first births during this decade (Beaupré and Cloutier, 2007).

While over half of women currently aged 65 to 69 have had three children, fewer than a quarter of women in the 35 to 39 age group have (Bélanger and Oikawa, 1999). Women who have their first child when they are younger than 25 years old are the most likely to have a third one. Those who are over 30 when their first child is born are the least likely to have a third one. Thus, smaller family size is in part related to a greater proportion of women than before waiting until later to have their first child. However, *among women who have at least one child, the average number of children was 2.4 in 2003*.

Recently, most western European nations have experienced fertility rates below the 2.1 replacement value needed to maintain a population. There has also been a rebound in some by 2006, notably in the UK at 1.84 births and Sweden at 1.85, in

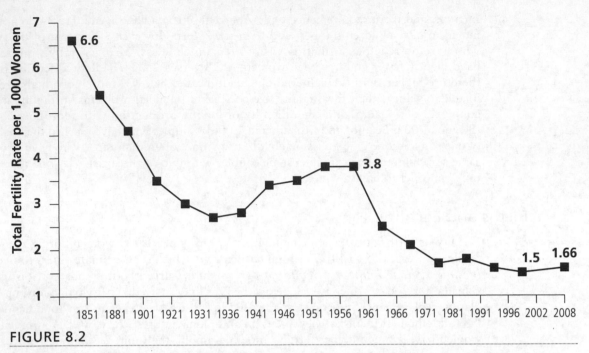

FIGURE 8.2

Total Fertility Rate per 1,000 Women Aged 15 to 64, 1851–2008

Sources: Milan, 2000; Statistics Canada, 2004i; Statistics Canada, 2009q. Adapted with permission from Statistics Canada.

great part again because of a surge among the older groups of women. France's fertility has risen in 2006 to 1.8 (Girard, 2008). Several European nations have a rate at or below 1.4: Spain, Greece, Austria, Germany, Italy, and Russia. As well, the more economically advanced Asian countries had very low fertility rates in 2005: Japan, 1.25; South Korea, 1.08; Taiwan, 1.12; Singapore, 1.25; and Hong Kong, 0.97. In comparison, China's fertility rate is around 2.0, South America's 2.7, and Africa's 5.3 (Beaujot and Kerr, 2004). The American rate was 2.1 in 2006—the exception in the western world.

The very low fertility rates experienced in all western societies and in others as well, such as Japan, is a result of the combination of industrialization, urbanization, individualism, female labour force participation, and later age at marriage (Jones, 2007; Krull and Trovato, 2003a). Parents respond to the economic situation by increasing the number of wage earners in their family unit and decreasing childrearing costs. Indeed, children are less useful to the family unit and more costly in industrialized and technological societies (Zelizer, 1985). In contrast, families tend to be larger in horticultural and agricultural societies or in the countryside more than in the urban zones of these societies. Agrarian children contribute to the familial economy in ways that are often substantial. In these same societies, large families, particularly those with many sons, are a source of masculine pride.

Childlessness by Choice

For its part, *involuntary infertility*, or the inability to conceive, affects approximately 15 percent of all couples. Although precise statistics do not exist for Canada, this trend is largely the result of delayed childbearing among current cohorts who then have difficulty conceiving when they finally try to do so during their less fertile reproductive years. Involuntary infertility may lead to "feelings of guilt, anger, frustration and depression, and to marital disputes" (Baker, 2001:129). Eventually becoming a mother erases earlier distress (McQuillan et al., 2003). Women are generally more affected than men emotionally because, until now, the onus has been placed on their reproductive role. It is only recently that medicine has discovered that men are equally implicated and **male infertility** is now widely recognized. Men may be infertile for many reasons: Some do not produce sperm or not enough, or the sperm's mobility is too low; in other cases, the quality of the sperm is compromised. Infertility can be genetic or related to stress, including heat stress in the scrotum region, or environmental (pollutants, for instance), and can also result from obesity or other health reasons.

It is difficult to know at which point in their life course women, or couples, reach the decision to remain childless, which is certainly facilitated by the recognition that women can occupy roles other than that of mother (Wu and MacNeill, 2002). Thus the same sociocultural factors that have lowered fertility are implicated in **childlessness by choice**. Women and couples who choose this alternative tend to have higher incomes (Smock and Greenland, 2010). Although childless couples are more likely to divorce, controlling for number of years in a marriage, they experience greater marital satisfaction on some dimensions of their relationship than do parenting couples (Twenge et al., 2003). Childless couples retain a more egalitarian division of household labour, for, as we see in Chapter 9, the transition to parenthood leads to more traditional roles between husbands and wives. A couple alone has far less housework and does not have a schedule revolving around children. Consequently, the spouses do not have to renegotiate the terms of their relationship concerning who does what after the arrival of the first child, as is the case among couples who form a family. Childless couples have more freedom for work and leisure and fewer economic constraints. Their sexuality may be more spontaneously expressed. Their life choices as individuals are more numerous. As for the effect of childlessness at older ages, it largely depends on attitudes (Koropeckyj-Cox, 2002).

Abortion

Induced abortion is an extreme form of birth control and occurs after other methods have failed or because no precautions were taken. In 1969, a law was passed allowing abortions to be performed by a qualified medical practitioner in a hospital after approval by a Therapeutic Abortion Committee. In 1988, the Supreme Court gave women more freedom in this domain. Abortion clinics outside of hospitals existed only in Quebec (initiated by Dr. Henry Morgentaler) but, by 1995, other clinics were in existence in all the other provinces, except Prince Edward Island. In the U.S., therapeutic abortions became legal in 1973, with the famous Roe v. Wade case. The topic of abortion has remained mired in political minefields and emotional rhetoric far more in the U.S. than is the case in Canada. However, the fact that abortion is legal does not necessarily make it equally accessible in all parts of Canada. For instance, it is still not available in many rural and northern regions, where women have to travel long distances for this purpose (Peritz, 2010).

Abortion rates increased dramatically after 1969, then dropped and stabilized at a lower level in the early 1980s, and increased again after the 1988 Supreme Court decision. Between 1990 and 2001, the rate rose slowly from 14.6 to 15.6 per 1,000 women aged 15 to 44 years and then declined to 13.0 by 2006 (Statistics Canada, 2004f, 2009r). The Territories, Nunavut, and Quebec had the highest abortion rates in 2006. In terms of age, the rates are as follows:

Under 15	1.2 per 1,000 women
15 to 19	14.2
20 to 24	**25.8**
25 to 29	18.7
30 to 34	12.6
35 to 39	8.2
40 and older	2.9

Abortion to adolescents constitute fewer than 20 percent of all abortions in Canada and have declined from 22.1 abortions per 1,000 teens in 1996 to 14.2 in 2006 (McKay and Barnett, 2010). Overall, abortion rates have declined worldwide: Fewer unintended pregnancies are occurring, because of contraception availability. However, unsafe abortions are not declining (Singh et al., 2009). But there are also countries where abortions are used routinely, more or less replacing birth control measures. For instance, in Armenia, Azerbaijan, and Georgia (former Soviet countries), women have on average three abortions in their lifetime (Sedgh et al., 2007). In Canada, about 35 percent of abortions are repeat procedures, generally a second one, compared with about 48 percent in the U.S. (Fisher et al., 2005). A history of physical or sexual abuse by a male partner is associated with repeat abortions as is a higher tendency to be nonmarried, with more children, and a member of a non-white group.

The decision to terminate an unwanted pregnancy, while not lightly made, rarely leads to serious and lasting psychological distress, as expressed by a student:

> *"My boyfriend didn't want a baby so I had an abortion and I really hated myself for it eventually. I hated him because he could have left me with the baby; my parents would have helped. But he had said that no man should be forced to be a father against his will and that one day I'd ask for support when he couldn't afford it or the child would bounce up and sue him. . . . So it broke up the relationship. . . . Now with hindsight I know I am better off all around."*

When abortion is accompanied by a great deal of lasting distress, there generally are preexisting emotional problems. In fact, among adolescents, the long-term consequences of childbearing are more detrimental than those of abortion (Fergusson et al., 2007). Further, children who were unintended at times suffer from negative outcomes and may receive less parental investment than intended children (Barber and East, 2009; Hummer et al., 2004). Others parents consciously compensate by lavishing resources and love on these "unexpected gifts," as explained by a student:

> *"I am an 'accident' of birth and I arrived when my last older sister was 19 and my parents thought that my mother who was then 45 couldn't get pregnant. After a period of shock and readjustment to their plans of living happily in an empty nest home, my parents were overjoyed, felt that they had been given a new start in life, and gave me so much love and attention that I was even spoiled compared to what the older ones had received but I am glad that they* [older siblings] *thought that this was a hoot."*

This being said, however, it is quite likely that abortion can result in lasting distress when the woman's moral beliefs, or those of her family, are opposed to it. Therefore, abortion is both a matter of conscience and practicality. But the matter of conscience is often both ignored in research and over-emphasized among politically conservative groups.

REPRODUCTIVE ALTERNATIVES

For women and men who are infertile, medical advances now offer a wide range of reproductive alternatives generally labelled "reproductive technologies." The issues surrounding these technologies are sociologically interesting beyond the relatively small number of persons who have recourse to them. First, for medical researchers, biologists, and geneticists, discoveries represent progress as well as a source of income. However, governments are not given a chance to evaluate the social merits of these discoveries before they are implemented. Second, critics argue that children may become commodities themselves, made to order in a catalogue. Better-off women and couples are advantaged in this process (Rothman, 1999). Third is the issue of rights. These technologies are creating children who will have needs and rights separate from the wishes of their parents (McWhinnie, 2001). They are created specifically so that persons can become parents, often secretly, at a time when current ideologies are promoting children's needs to be informed of their background.

Donor Insemination

Donor insemination is a relatively simple and accepted procedure that was practised by the end of the 19th century. Newer techniques exist, such as intracytoplasmic sperm injection or ICSI. ICSI is more successful because semen does not always contain sperm and the clinic may be able to extract it from the father. At that point, the procedure is similar to an IVF discussed below. Although sperm donors are occasionally friends or relatives, organized donor insemination now predominates: Males donate their sperm to a physician or to a sperm bank. In this instance, the husband is not the biological father; he is technically the social father and, in lesbian couples, only one of the two mothers is the biological parent (Chabot and Ames, 2004). Prospective parents can also request "designer" sperm by choosing a donor with certain characteristics, such as high IQ.

One potential complication resides in the child's being half-adopted: Should parents divulge to the child his or her biological background? After all, only one parent is not biological and this factor can easily be kept secret. Indications are that most heterosexual parents do not tell their child about his or her different genetic origins (Brewaeys et al., 2005)—as is the case in the estimated 5 to 8 percent of children who are the result of an extramarital "slip" (McWhinnie, 2001). Unfortunately, many parents confide in other people and this creates the risk of the child learning about it from someone else (Golombok et al., 2002). Therefore, several European countries have legislated children's right to know the donor after age 18. At the same time, these donors are protected against any legal and financial duty toward child and mother and are not obligated to meet the child. However, this law has had the effect of substantially reducing the number of sperm donors (Janssens, 2006).

As well, one can wonder about multiple donations by the same man within a narrow geographic area. The possibility exists, however remote, that two half-siblings of the opposite sex could meet and have a child who may then suffer from a birth defect. In France, only two or three donations per man are allowed.

In Vitro Fertilization and Transplantation

Another step in reproductive technologies occurred in Great Britain in 1978 with the birth of the first test-tube baby, Louise Brown. Her mother's egg was fertilized in vitro (in a test tube) by her father's sperm, and was then implanted into her mother's womb. Other kinds of IVF then followed, each involving a degree of biological distancing and pushing the boundaries of the "nature" of parenthood:

- The mother's egg is externally fertilized by donor sperm and then transplanted into her uterus. The birth mother is the biological mother, whereas her spouse is the social father.
- A donor's egg is fertilized by the father's sperm and then transplanted into the wife's uterus. The wife becomes a nonbiological birth mother to her husband's and donor's biological child.
- A donor's egg is fertilized by a donor's sperm and transplanted into the birth mother's uterus. Neither the birth mother nor the birth father are biological parents. They are very similar to adoptive parents, except that the mother has carried the baby and given birth.

The last technique has recently been applied for women over age 55; one birth mother in India was 72 years old. These cases have raised many questions concerning the future of a child who may be left orphaned at a young age. But it has been pointed out that older men often have children without encountering social disapproval (Schwartz and Rutter, 1998); older women, the argument goes, are discriminated against simply on the basis of their gender (van den Akker, 1994).

The rate of success of both ICSI and IVF are low, and many mothers discontinue treatment because of stress, financial problems, and health issues (Rajkhowa et al., 2006). Yet, IVF and ICSI carry risks of premature delivery, miscarriage, multiple births, low birth weight, and a small risk of birth defects even to single

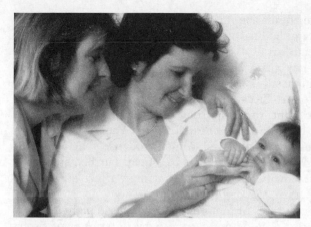

Lesbian couples generally use IVF. The same donor may be used for both women. In other cases, one woman can carry to term the other's fertilized embryo. These approaches are used to reinforce genetic bonds and equalize the situation of motherhood.

infants (Bonduelle et al., 2005; Hansen et al., 2005; Ombelet et al., 2006). In turn, low birth weight is associated with an increased risk of cerebral palsy and developmental delay (Stromberg et al., 2002). However, other studies attribute these differences, not to the treatment, but to pre-term births (Middelburg et al., 2008). But the highest risk is that of **multiple births** of high order. One can recall here the "Octo-Mom" of 2009 fame whose physician transplanted too many embryos. Indeed, because implantation frequently fails, there is a higher chance of pregnancy when two or more embryos are transplanted. Sweden, for instance, allows only one transfer in order to decrease maternal and child health risks associated with multiple births.

Overall, children's development seems to be proceeding well (Golombok et al., 2002). This is especially so when informed earlier rather than later of their origins (Javda et al., 2009b). Mothers whose embryos have been implanted are not negatively affected by their experience in terms of their parenting skills subsequent to the birth of one baby. Parents who searched for their children's donor and half-siblings generally report a positive experience (Freeman et al., 2009).

Couples wishing to delay parenthood or when one is to have radiation therapy can freeze their embryos so that they may have children of their genetic background when they are in their late thirties or early forties—a relatively safe procedure (Pelkonen et al., 2010). However, there have already been cases in France and the U.S. of the death and divorce of the potential parents and legal issues arose (Ciccarelli and Ciccarelli, 2005): Who has the right to these embryos?

Surrogate Mothers

A surrogate mother is a woman who carries a baby to term and relinquishes the child to the married couple or, more rarely, gay couple who contracts with her, generally for medical expenses and a fee to compensate for her time. However, following the *Assisted Human Reproduction Act* of 2004, payments other than medical expenses are not allowed in Canada. Surrogacy is the oldest and most controversial reproductive alternative and dates back to the Old Testament. Traditionally, the surrogate is inseminated with the father's sperm: Therefore, such women are actually biologically related to the child. This is called **genetic surrogacy**. Other surrogate mothers carry a woman's ovum fertilized by either the father or a donor; such surrogates are not biologically related to the child: This is called **gestational surrogacy**. These two situations can carry vastly different consequences for all parties concerned, both legally and emotionally (Ciccarelli and Ciccarelli, 2005).

Attitudes toward this phenomenon are not entirely positive in the population at large (van den Akker, 2007). It can be analyzed both from class and feminist perspectives, although there is a great deal of overlap between the two perspectives on this particular topic. Couples or gay men who avail themselves of a surrogate's services are unavoidably well off financially, whereas the surrogate is usually of modest to average means, albeit not poor (Ciccarelli and Beckman, 2005). Even though many surrogates enjoy being pregnant, there is a social class gap between the parties involved, and this is seen as exploitative (Rothman, 1999). Feminists point out that this "rent-a-womb" arrangement exploits women and uses their bodies, although until now, another woman (the mother) has benefited. Further, surrogacy with embryo transplant involves medical treatment that may affect a woman's health.

However, there have been many cases of a mother carrying her daughter's baby because the daughter had no uterus or could not carry a baby to term, or of sisters doing the same, including here in Canada. In South Africa, for example, a mother carried all her daughter's children; in other words, she gave birth to her three grandchildren. In 2005, a surrogate in the U.S. gave birth to quintuplets and declined the agreed-upon payment so as to help the parents financially. The motives in these cases are purely altruistic. Therefore, although surrogacy is questionable from some analytical frameworks, it can also be analyzed from an altruistic perspective. Many surrogates describe their act as a gift to another woman.

Studies of surrogates and intended mothers reveal that, as the pregnancy advances, both the intended mothers and the genetic surrogates show more anxiety than surrogates who are not genetic (van den Akker, 2007). However, this anxiety does not last after the birth. Intended mothers were more attached to the fetus than the surrogates: "Surrogates are developing constructive coping mechanisms towards the baby following delivery, thereby minimizing any potential feelings of loss at relinquishment" (van den Akker, 2007). Being well treated by the intended parents is key to surrogacy treatment (Hohman and Hagan, 2001). However, it was also found that surrogates receive less social support, including from their parents and partners. It is suggested that everyone would benefit if these surrogates received more social support during and after the pregnancy. Overall, long-term research is needed to follow-up on the relationships formed and the resulting outcomes, including for the surrogate mothers and their own children. At this early stage of research, there are no indications that small children, intended parents, and their relationships are negatively affected by this type of family formation (Golombok et al., 2006; 2007).

FAMILY FORMATION VIA ADOPTION

The main difference between children who are the result of assisted reproduction and those who are adopted is that the former are created to provide children for people, generally couples. In contrast, adopted children already exist but their parents are unable to care for them. In all cases, however, children's needs are the same. In the late 1990s, 1.2 percent of Canadian children under 12 years of age had been adopted

(Vanier Institute of the Family, 2002). In the U.S., 2.5 percent of all children under 18 are adopted (Adoption Council of Canada, 2003). However, we have no information on the proportion of the entire Canadian population that is adopted—the estimate is around 2 percent—nor how many children are adopted each year. But we do know that Ontario alone has about 150,000 adoption registrations (Beaute, 2009). Although many adoptions involve adults who are already related to the child, the focus here is on *non-kin adoption* because the issues that surround it allow for a deeper sociological analysis of family formation within a social constructionist perspective.

The Social Construction of Adoption

Adoption is found in all cultures, at times known as child "borrowing" (Arnett, 2008; Miller, 2005:183). In North America and other societies of European origin, family is equated with biology and this cultural bias leads to ambivalence concerning adoption—even though, in general, a majority of Canadians and Americans express favourable views toward adoption in public opinion surveys (Miall and March, 2005). Yet, adoption is now rarely offered as an option to young single women who have an unplanned pregnancy (Caragata, 1999).

In more recent years, advances in the fields of **genetics** and **medicine** have given rise to a "genetic consciousness" that reinforces negative stereotypes of adoption. What Lebner (2000) includes under the rubric of medicalization and geneticization of our life stories—of our medical risks based on our parents' histories—increases adoptive parents' anxieties when they do not have a full account of their adopted children's background. Yet, these anxieties are only rarely justified because, for the majority of human beings, the environment is far more influential than genes in the domain of health. Further, very soon, a person's own genetic profile will be mapped for preventive medicine and treatment purposes.

Biological motherhood is often considered superior to adoptive motherhood, even by a few feminists (Chesler, 1989). This alliance of biology with feminism presents an anomalous situation at the ideological level because feminist theories generally reject gender roles based on biological constraints (Rothman, 1989). We have all heard the well-known feminist slogan that "biology is not destiny." Arlene Skolnick (1998) rightly criticizes this "new biologism" as a cultural phenomenon with policy implications. As well, Rothman (1989:39) points out that "we can recognize and appreciate the genetic tie without making it the determining connection."

The more recent development of **reunions** of adopted children with their birth mothers well illustrates the theme of the social construction of adoption. Search-movement activists have depicted the psychological need to search as a universal one, although not every adoptee has this need and will feel "incomplete" without a reunion (Wegar, 1997). What "incomplete" entails is also a social construction but it is **compelling imagery**: It has high value in current popular psychology. This presumed universal need to locate one's biological roots has arisen from our concerns over genetic connectedness. This need is then packaged within other very modern themes such as "the need to find oneself," freedom, choice, human rights, and the presumed personal problems and "repression" of those who do not search. It is a need that has been created by our culture and then has become real and quite salient in many adoptees' lives. Thus, the recognition of the social construct aspect of this phenomenon is not synonymous with shrugging the **created need** aside. Bartholet (1993) points out that the search movement has inadvertently contributed to further stigmatize adoption and particularly adoptive parents as well as adult adoptees who are not interested in finding their birth parents. This is well illustrated in a student's autobiography—she had been adopted along with her non-biological siblings:

> *"Last year ... my sister [age 19] was reunited with her birth mother. ... My parents were apprehensive because my sister has always been a more easily influenced child than me and my brother. The school counsellor had put it in her head that she'd feel 'whole' only after she was able 'to make peace with her past.' Lisa and me had long arguments over this because we were both adopted within a month of our birth and I said, 'What past? Our past is here.' You may ask, Am I not curious about my birth family? Only to the extent that I could finally tell my physician that there is or there is not breast cancer or heart problems or diabetes in my background. ... I have had parents practically from Day One and I don't see what finding a woman who is supposed to be my mother just because I got a set of genes from her and she carried me would do for me. ... So my sister located her birth mother and she doesn't look a thing like her and the woman is not sure who the father is on top of it all ... my sister is still recovering from the shock of these discoveries and she even thinks that the Children's Aid located the 'wrong mother' because she has it in her mind that she should have looked just like her."*

Adopted Children's Development

Therefore, because of this need, one should really expect adopted children to develop many problems of a serious nature, in addition to the fact that more adopted children have various disabilities, 12 percent versus 5 percent among biological children. Nevertheless, difference in adjustment between adopted and non-adopted persons are generally small (for reviews, see Miller, 2005; Sharma et al., 1998). However, several studies have also indicated that adopted **adolescents** have slightly more problems and conflict with parents than non-adopted ones (Miller et al., 2000). Rueter and colleagues (2009) observed interactions in various types of adoptive and biological families and did not find that parents interacted differently with their adolescents; rather, on average, the adopted adolescents themselves were more conflictual.

The deficits and strengths that are found largely depend on the methodology used, the type of adopted children in the sample, the comparison group, and the outcomes measured. For instance, adoptive mothers report more child problems, whereas adoptive fathers' and adopted children's reports are more similar to those in biological families (Lansford et al., 2001). But, overall, adoptees and their parents do not show any consistent deficit that would warrant concern (van Ijzendoorn et al., 2005). This may be in part related to the fact that parents of adopted children provide health care interventions more often than do other parents (Bramlett et al., 2007). Two studies of young adult adoptees concluded that whatever differences existed between them and non-adopted adults were small; as well, these differences were not identical in both studies (Feigelman, 1997; Smyer et al., 1998). Borders et al. (2000) focused on adoptees who ranged from 35 to 55 years of age compared with a similar group of non-adopted adults. Both groups were experiencing their adult years similarly, but adoptees had a slightly lower level of self-esteem and a slightly higher level of depression. One study has shown that adopted children fare equally well across a variety of family structures—when they are only children, have younger or older adopted siblings, or have younger or older biological siblings (Brodzinski and Brodzinski, 1992). However, adoptions of multiple siblings also have a higher rate of failure (Smith et al., 2006).

Parents often experience more stress when they adopt **older children** (Bird et al., 2002): Older children often have special needs or suffer from problems related to difficulties in their original families and/or foster placements (Selwyn et al., 2006; Smith et al., 2006). They may also have had more problematic parents than children adopted at birth and thus have inherited more difficult predispositions (Miller et al., 2000). Therefore, older children who are adopted bring with them genetic, emotional, and contextual baggage that may make it more difficult to form an attachment to their adoptive parents and to be parented successfully (Barth and Miller, 2000). One problem that is encountered is ARND or alcohol-related neurodevelopmental disorder and, at a more severe level, FAS or fetal alcohol syndrome, which are caused by alcohol drinking during pregnancy (Buxton, 2004).

Overall, adopted children experience a wide range of outcomes and adjustment in life, as do non-adopted children. But, although adopted children may feel as loved and as accepted by their parents as non-adopted children, their peers and even adults often openly express doubts to them on this topic (Leon, 2002) and so do the media. This situation is similar to that of children of gay and lesbian parents who become more distressed after they encounter questions about their type of family (e.g., Gartrell et al., 2005).

The "Real" Child–"Real" Parents Dilemma

An adopted respondent in March's (1995a:656) study said that outside the family, people *"never believe that your adoptive parents love you like their parents love them. Because you aren't biological."* One of my students recalls returning home one day quite distressed and asking her mother, *"Is it true that you can't love me as much because I am adopted?"* Another student reported that, upon learning she was adopted, her peer on the school bus shrieked, *"Oh, you poor poor child! You don't have any real parents."* Yet another student recalled the following causality chain:

> *"When I was 6 one day I proudly told one of my friends that I was adopted. To me, this had been a source of joy because I had always been told by my parents how much they had wanted me. . . . My little friend didn't say much and with hindsight I gather that she probably didn't know what I was talking about. The next day she and another girl turned around me in a funny way and my friend finally said, 'My mom feels sorry for you.' I was puzzled and asked why. 'Because you're 'dopted [sic] and you don't have real parents. You're not their real little*

girl and you don't look like them.' I didn't understand any of this at first but it sounded awful and I started bawling out and the teacher had to call my mother to come and console me. It did the trick but I never thereafter talked about being adopted to any other child until I was in university. It didn't change my feelings about my situation at home but this incident definitely made me feel different, more socially anxious, and less self-assured."

This theme of not being a "real" child and not having "real" parents is an excellent example of the social construction of adoption and is a recurring one in the autobiographies of students who have been adopted and in the emails sent in 2006 as a result of an online paper. It is not the adoptees' theme but that of others that is forced upon them, as a woman who is both an adoptee and the adoptive mother of two children, now young adults, explains:

"I have suffered much more questions and comments by other mothers and teachers than my [adoptive] mother ever had . . . peers being tactless and thinking that adopted children are not 'real' too often happened to my daughter but not so much to my son because I think that boys are so busy playing games and being active that they don't have time for this nonsense."

This stigmatization is discriminatory and may constitute a heavy mental burden on adoptees (Leon, 2002). Children are especially vulnerable to what their peers think. If their peers present them with questionable notions of their adoptive status, then these children are at risk emotionally. This may explain why, in some studies, adolescence is the time when adopted children begin to show a higher rate of behavioural problems compared with other children (Miller et al., 2000). A mother with an adopted daughter and a biological son recalls that:

"when both children were in the school system, it became known that one was adopted and the other 'real' or one was . . . 'not natural.' Our daughter [who up to that point had delighted in having a little brother] was devastated . . . she changed in a very short time: she became teary, moody, sensitive, touchy, and later on rebellious . . . and felt like the 'fifth wheel in this family.'"

For other children, the fact that their adoptive status is questioned by peers and significant persons in their lives may push them to rebel against their parents, as one adopted adult put it:

"The way I see it, society provides adopted children with loopholes or excuses that may encourage them to become maladjusted without taking any responsibility for their attitude themselves. . . . In order to excuse my own behavior, I started . . . diminishing the benefits of their values and ways of living (after all, they [her parents] were successful and I was becoming an asshole), and just saying in effect, well, I am becoming myself and if you don't like it, just shove off."

Adoptive parents are more likely to be white, older, educated, and to have a higher income than biological parents. They invest more resources in their children, whether economic, social, or interactional than do biological parents (Hamilton et al., 2007). At least one study has found that the transition to parenthood was easier for them than for biological parents (Cebello et al., 2004). A birth mother concluded her email by saying that:

> *"the best solution is to embrace the adoptive parents ... because they have loved and raised and paid for this child ... I did cringe when I saw this 60 Minutes segment of a girl being reunited with her birth mother and the poor real* [adoptive] *mother was just an onlooker and it was a love story between girl and birth mother ..."*

The Diversity of Adoption

Stepchild Adoption

We do not have information about stepchild adoption in Canada. However, over 50,000 American stepchildren are adopted by their stepparents, generally a stepfather, each year (Flango and Flango, 1994). Although there are a few similarities between regular adoptions and adoptions by a stepparent, there are important differences as well as motives specific to each situation (Ganong et al., 1998). The main reasons for step-adoptions after divorce reside in a desire to be a "regular" family, to legitimize the roles and relationships within the reconstituted family, and to sever the ties with the nonresidential parent, particularly when the latter does not contribute child support or is uninvolved with the child (Marsiglio, 2004). The nonresidential parent either consents to the adoption or the case can go to court. A judge will rule in favour of the adoption only if the nonresidential parent is deemed unfit or if it is in the child's best interest to sever the relationship. A better model might be that of the *British Children Act* of 1987, whereby stepparents can have responsibilities for children without obliterating noncustodial parents' responsibilities and rights (Mason, 1998). The long-term consequences of stepchild adoption have yet to be studied but are certainly related to the initial age of the child at adoption (Schwartz and Finley, 2006).

Transracial and Transnational Adoption

We do not have solid information on transracial adoption in Canada. The U.S. 2000 census indicates that 17 percent of adoptions are transracial (Adoption Council of Canada, 2003). Overall, there is absolutely no indication in the American research literature that black children adopted by white parents turn out much differently than those adopted in black families, a result replicated in Great Britain (Bagley, 1993; Silverman, 1993). Vroegh (1997) reports from a longitudinal study that, by adolescence, these children are still well adjusted and enjoy a high level of self-esteem—as is the case for children born to interracial couples (Stephan and Stephan, 1991). Most interracially adopted black children grow up identifying as black, and most parents conscientiously promote their children's African-American heritage (Vroegh, 1997). This does not prevent them, however, from at times feeling out of place in a totally white environment.

In Canada, the adoption of Native children by non-Native parents has been and continues to be an issue, in great part because cultural genocide indeed took place in the recent past as it did in the U.S. However, in the U.S., the First Nations represent a smaller proportion of the population than in Canada and are less visible politically so that this topic is less researched. But, again, we do not have statistics on transadoptions of Native children in Canada. Currently, the numbers seem to be relatively small—despite the large number of these children in foster care.

As the number of young children available via foster care and especially private agencies declined, international adoptions increased. Canadians have recently adopted between 1,535 (2006) and 2,220 (1998) children internationally each year (Adoption Council of Canada, 2007). Quebec and Ontario are the provinces with the most transnational adoptions (Ouellette and Belleau, 2001). There has been a preponderance of girls over boys: 68 percent and 32 percent respectively (Adoption Council of Canada, 2003). This sex ratio imbalance in part stems from the fact that so many children originate from China where most of the available children are female because of the one-child family policy and preference for male children.

Over 70 percent of the children are younger than five years of age, so that Canadians who wish to adopt infants often find international adoptions, if not easier, at least faster and more likely to result in a young child than would be the case within their country. However, adoption of children who had been very deprived in their country of origin often leads to stressful parenting, especially when behavioural problems emerge (Judge, 2003). Older age at adoption and pre-adoption adversity are related to lower levels of adjustment later, including in a sample of Chinese little girls adopted by Americans (Tan, 2009). Age and deprivation among Romanian adoptees have also been related both to improvement and persistence or even development of problems (Beckett et al., 2006). Yet, overall, international adoptees experience only slightly more emotional and behavioural problems than other children (Juffer and van Ijzendoorm, 2005).

Open Adoption and Opening Adoption Records

The trends are moving toward opening the process of ongoing and future adoptions as well as opening the records of past adoptions with vetoes for persons who do not want to be found, as has been done in Ontario on June 1, 2009. Reports from several countries indicate that privacy is rarely invaded, which has been a fear expressed by some adoptees and birth parents (Carp, 2008)—hence the veto document that can be placed in the files.

Grotevant and McRoy (1998) have categorized adoptions along a continuum ranging from confidential to mediated and then to fully disclosed. Confidential adoptions provide anonymity but generally disclose parents' backgrounds. In the mediated category, the adoption agency may transmit pictures, letters, and gifts, or even arrange meetings between parents without full identification. In the fully disclosed category, both parties know each other's identity and may meet. Many single mothers now relinquish their infant only under circumstances that allow them greater control over the adoption process and even access to the child. At the extreme continuum of openness, biological parents more or less enter the adoptive parents' family system as they exchange regular visits and participate in decision-making concerning their child's health.

Studies on the outcomes of open adoption are still embryonic, but, overall, many indicate that most of the adoptive and biological parents are satisfied with their relationship with one another (Grotevant et al., 2008; Ge et al., 2008). However, McRoy et al. (1998) found that semi-open (or mediated) adoptions might be more functional than fully open ones. For instance, in fully open cases, adoptive parents reported feeling burdened by meetings with birth parents. Berry et al. (1998) and Frasch et al. (2000) noted that, in nearly half of the open adoptions, the level of contact between the two families had decreased after four years. Along these lines, the 1987–1992 longitudinal study by Grotevant and McRoy (1998) of 190 adoptive families and 169 birth mothers indicated that openness does not threaten adoptive parents' sense of entitlement to parenthood. However, it does not necessarily ensure that birth mothers will be successful in their grief resolution or that children's curiosity will be satisfied when they reach adolescence.

At least two studies have found no difference on measures of child adjustment between open and confidential adoptions (Berry et al., 1998; Grotevant and McRoy, 1998) or between physical versus letter contact with birth relatives (Neil, 2009). The concept of boundary ambiguity leads to the possibility of problems when children are attached to two sets of parents, as is the case in foster families (Leathers, 2003), or when children have been adopted at older ages (Logan and Smith, 2005). Further, Kohler et al. (2002:100) concluded that adolescent "preoccupation with adoption is not an inherent outcome of confidential adoptions." They also found that adolescents who were extremely preoccupied with their adoption felt somewhat more alienated from their parents—although one can only offer hypotheses concerning the direction of causality.

Reunions with Birth Parents

Today, search for birth parents or biological siblings is legally encouraged and records are more accessible than in the past. Registries exist in which birth parents as well as children and even siblings can enter information and indicate for whom they are searching. One example is the Canadian Adoptee Registry Inc. on the Internet. Mothers and daughters are the most common clientele. This **gender difference** may be the result of women being more biologically involved in reproduction and birthing and because women are socialized to be more nurturant and family oriented than males. In some instances, young women search for their birth parents only after they have become mothers themselves. Others do after their parents' divorce (Tieman, 2008). Similarly, **birth fathers** are less commonly involved (Passmore and Feeney, 2009). They are often not known and more difficult to locate, in great part because only a small fraction of the adoption records list a father's name (Beaute, 2009).

The few existing studies on the topic of reunion indicate that a majority of adoptees who have been reunited with their biological family see this as a positive experience (March, 1995a), although March (1995b) also documents many cases of rejection. In most instances, the adoptee acquires a stronger sense of being their adoptive parents' child and, although at times apprehensive at first, adoptive parents are generally at peace with the situation. Even birth fathers recognize the adoptive fathers as the real one (Passmore and Chipuer, 2009). However, a mismatch between the respective motivations and expectations of the two parties may develop over time (Gladstone and Westhues, 1998), especially when there are vast differences between adoptees and birth parents (Passmore and Feeney, 2009), as experienced by a birth mother who had adopted her four stepchildren and was then reunited with her birth daughter:

> *"After several long weekend visits, matters started spoiling. It was obvious that she wanted all my and my husband's attention ... so she started sniping at the [adolescent] children, at talking against them, at trying to make alliances with one against the others ... having temper tantrums."*

Another reunited birth mother had a different perspective and felt that her daughter was too attached to her adoptive parents: *"I feel used because she has found me and now she knows her background. ... All I am for her is a background, a piece of information."*

More recent research has included reunions initiated by birth mothers and various effects on adoptive parents (Petta and Steed, 2005). One should also mention that it is very difficult to study birth mothers and their families. As a result, only those who search or who are reunited can be studied. As well, adoptees who do not search are usually not studied either, which certainly biases the results. As a last note I will mention that no research exists that would describe and explain the impacts of reunions on the spouses and children as well as families of birth parents.

FOSTER FAMILIES: FAMILY RESTRUCTURING

Fostering is really a form of family restructuring rather than family formation and it is far more common than adoption. The number of children in need of foster care far exceeds the availability of suitable families. In 1999, there were nearly 66,000 children in care, at least 20,000 of whom could be adopted (Ross, 2000; Vanier Institute of the Family, 2004). In the U.S., well over 524,000 children are in the foster care system at any point in time in comparison to 200,000 in the 1980s; of those, about 120,000 are awaiting an adoption that may never come (Ross, 2006). One of the problems is that a great proportion of foster children have at least one sibling, yet many siblings are fostered separately because it is too difficult to find families willing to take in more than one child at a time. As a consequence, these children face a second loss after that of their parent(s): They are deprived of the social support they could provide one another. However, large age disparities may lead teens to wish to be placed separately from their younger siblings (Drapeau et al., 2000). In many cases, some siblings fare better separately, especially when one is abusive or suffers from behavioural problems that affect the other(s).

Poverty is the main reason why children end up in foster care and this is especially relevant for First Nations children who are disproportionately represented in the system (Fluke et al., 2010). Along with poverty, homelessness is a prominent factor (Zlotnick, 2009). Most other reasons, such as parental incarceration, drug and alcohol addiction as well as mental illness, child abuse and neglect and domestic violence, also have poverty in the background. Children with fetal alcohol syndrome (FAS) or who need special attention because of delinquent behaviours are also found in the system. Therefore, it is not surprising that children who have been in foster care and group homes generally have more negative outcomes than other children, particularly in terms of delinquency, mental health, and adult criminality (Lawrence et al., 2006; Viner and Taylor, 2005). A meta-analysis showed that adopted children, particularly those adopted at older ages, have more learning problems at school than others (van Ijzendoorn et al., 2005). However, these children did better than those left in foster care, including biological siblings who were not adopted. Adolescents and young adults who are later incarcerated too often suffer from FAS, a situation that is only beginning to be recognized. Indeed, foster care children are a select group (Berger et al., 2009): These children were neglected or abused in their families and the placement represents an additional dislocation (Harden, 2004).

There is little research on children's and parents' lived experience with foster care. Some children call their foster parents "Mom" and "Dad," whereas their biological parents may be referred to by name or as the "other mother." Some foster children believe that they are much better off than in their parents' homes and are even grateful to have been removed from the home when they were small. Others rebel against their foster family and the fact of being in foster care (Whiting and Lee, 2003). Length of care brings greater closeness and a sense of identity with the foster family. On the other hand, regular contact and hopes of reunification with the natural family decrease closeness with foster parents (Leathers, 2003; Moyers et al., 2006). Children who are to be reunited with their original families do better when their parents visit them regularly (McWey and Mullis, 2004). In the U.S., slightly over half of children are reunited with their parents; however, nearly a third eventually return to foster care, often within one year (Connell et al., 2009; Wulczyn, 2004). Children who had suffered from severe neglect are likely to come from more dysfunctional families and are less often reunited (Barber and Delfabbro, 2009).

Foster care does not always work out well and for a variety of reasons, including the scarcity of homes, the lack of support, training, and supervision received by foster parents, as well as children's age and past difficulties, experiences of abuse and neglect (Eggertsen, 2008). Neglected children are less likely to be successfully reintegrated with their family of origin than physically maltreated children, even though they are younger (Bundy-Fazioli et al, 2009; Marquis et al., 2008). A proportion of foster care parents are violent at one time or another as a result of frustration and many more report having been aggressed by the youth in their care (Ringstad, 2009). Foster care within the family may result in less dislocation for children and mothers and may demand less adaptation from children (Lawrence et al., 2006; Metzger, 2008). However, relatives and, especially, grandparents, are generally not as well compensated financially or emotionally supported and this may create severe stressors. Finally, there is very little social support for youth leaving foster care upon or before legal maturity (Collins et al., 2008; Kaplan et al., 2009).

CONCLUSIONS: FAMILY FORMATION ALTERNATIVES IN CONTEXT

The evidence points to marriage as being the current optimal form of family formation for children and, to some extent, adults. Overall, one can conclude that what is the best combination for the healthy development of any child is having at least two parents who are committed to each other and especially to the child, with whom the child enjoys a warm relationship, and who have access to a minimum of resources and support (Strohschein, 2010). As well, the research is unanimous to the effect that married fathers invest far more in their children than either cohabiting or single fathers (Cooksey and Craig, 1998; Doherty et al., 1998). An exception are gay fathers who parent by themselves or with another man (Mallon, 2005).

What about single mothering? Under the current economic and political system, absolutely nothing in the extensive research literature recommends solo motherhood for adolescents and adults alike. For established and mature adults, however, single parenthood may well be a positive alternative for parent and child. This alternative is socially advantageous when an adult, generally a woman, adopts a child who would not otherwise have a family. A feminist analysis suggests that women (and men) should not have to depend on marriage and should have the option of forming one-parent families that function well and contribute to society's social capital (Coontz, 2000). Thus, **single parenting** could become a far better alternative for children and adults in the future under the following circumstances:

1. If young males were socialized to be nurturing and equally responsible for their offspring, then even children in single-mother families would have two parents invested in them and supporting them.

2. If women earned incomes equal to those of men, then the poverty rate of families headed by women would diminish substantially, and so would children's problems.

3. If social reproduction was valued by society and if what is now unpaid work was remunerated, mothers and their children would have more options.

4. Once all these conditions are in place, delaying childbearing until attainment of greater maturity would be the last necessary ingredient to making single parenting more functional for children and their parents than it currently is.

Thus, overall, while much of the research literature documents the disadvantages that single mothering *on average* brings, disadvantages are not inevitable (Ruspini, 2000). Rather, they are tied to the economic structure of our societies, thus to deprivation, lack of a supportive community, and the culture of feminine inequality that pervades all domains of life (Vosko, 2002). Nevertheless, I would be derelict in my duties as a researcher were I to romanticize single parenting as an alternative to free women from marriage—for, indeed, as a few feminists have pointed out, women end up paying the price, not society nor the fathers (Folbre, 1994; Walby, 1997).

Cohabitational parenting and single-mothering currently present a risk element for women and their children, especially within the context of poverty. *Ultimately, family processes are more important than family structure for child outcomes. But the point bears being reemphasized: Positive family processes are more likely to be found in committed marital structures, whether heterosexual or gay.* Thus, it could be argued that educated individuals who promote the equivalency with marriage of solo parenting and even cohabitation, without taking the current cultural and economic systems into consideration, may actually be promoting a perspective that is linked to their advantaged social situation: They are not the ones who will ever suffer from the consequent problems.

Summary

1. Recent changes in family structure in Canada include a decrease in marriage and increases in cohabitational and one-parent families. A longer period of singlehood and more cohabitation among young cohorts are delaying marriage.

2. Marriage as an institution is advantageous for children and society. Children who live with their married parents have the best outcomes of all categories of children. The only exception occurs in highly conflictual marriages. These, however, are a minority, as most end in divorce. Further, a marriage that is not quite satisfactory to the parents still usually benefits children.

3. Cohabitations involving children have increased. Children of these unions are more similar to those in single-parent than married families. Although cohabitation boosts a mother's income, cohabiting couples are less economically secure than married couples. Small children's well-being is less well served by such unions, particularly when a mother cohabits with a man who is not their father.

4. So far, most children who are raised in same-sex-parent families were born in a mother-father family where divorce occurred. But more and more, same-sex couples are having children by donor insemination and adoption. Overall, the results indicate that the public's concern for these children is unwarranted: They grow up normally, but are affected when homophobia occurs.

5. Nonmarital fertility has increased dramatically since the 1960s. Although one-parent families are not a new phenomenon, their composition has changed over time and most are now the result of divorce. Nonmarital teen births have increased and then stabilized at a lower rate. The life course of adolescent mothers generally contains more transitions, and a proportion of them, as is the case for fathers, are truant, aggressive, and use drugs. The babies' fathers tend to come from the same background as that of mothers. Children born to single mothers tend to be the most disadvantaged in their outcomes, but much depends on mothers', fathers', and children's characteristics. Maternal education is a key factor.

6. There has been a general decrease in fertility in all industrialized countries, and Canada's current fertility rate of 1.66 is no exception. Various factors have contributed to this decrease, including urbanization and later age at marriage.

7. As the age at first birth is increasing, a greater proportion of first births are to women aged 35 to 45. There are mainly advantages for children, except in terms of physical health.

8. Childlessness by choice has also increased while abortion rates have declined. Half of abortions are sought by women in the 20- to 29-year age bracket.

9. New reproductive technologies range from various forms of donor insemination, embryo implantation, and surrogate motherhood. Children's and donors' rights are discussed, as are other ethical considerations. With fertility treatment, multiple births have greatly increased. They do not represent an ideal developmental context for children, particularly while they are in the womb.

10. Adoption is an alternative form of family formation that has been socially constructed as less "natural" than biological parenting. The literature on the consequences of adoption for children tends to be divided between studies that show no disadvantage and those that indicate small deficits. The latter may be created by the less than optimal social climate surrounding adoption, particularly in children's peer groups.

11. Stepchild adoption is the most common type of adoption. Transracially adopted children succeed as well as others and identify with their own racial group.

12. In terms of open adoption, the research is largely positive, as is the case for reunions of adopted children with birth parents. In this case, reunions can have consequences for the child, the birth parents, and the adoptive parents. However, samples do not include children or birth parents who are not reunited.

13. Foster children generally have poor outcomes, mainly because of prior neglect or abuse and because of the dislocation in their young lives as they are shifted around.

14. Currently, marriage is the pattern of family formation that is in the best interest of children. Single parenting could become a more appropriate alternative with cultural and economic changes at the systemic level.

Analytical Questions

1. It is said in the media that cohabitation is replacing marriage. Discuss the pros and cons of such a statement.

2. Some often believe that, for children, cohabitation and single parenting are equivalent modes of family life to that of parents' marriage. Yet, the research literature across the world points to a different conclusion. How can you reconcile these two perspectives?

3. Children in same-sex-parent families fare as well as other children, contrary to what many people think. Explain why this is so. (The answers are not necessarily all in the text.)

4. The teen birth rate was far higher in the 1950s than it currently is. How can this be, given the statistics presented in the text?

5. Currently, the Canadian fertility rate stands at 1.66, while the American one is at 2.1. This is a relatively large difference. What factors can explain it?

6. Discuss the "nature" of parenthood within the context of adoption and reproductive alternatives.

Suggested Readings

Beaujot, R., and Kerr, D. 2004. *Population change in Canada*, 2nd Ed. Toronto: Oxford University Press. This comprehensive overview of population trends in Canada includes a great deal of discussion on fertility and family composition.

Booth, A., and Crouter, A. C. (Eds.) 2002. *Just living together*. Mahwah, NJ: Erlbaum. This collection of articles well documents the diversity of cohabitation and the need for research on children and adults who live in cohabitational units.

Cahn, N. 2009. *Test tube families: Why the fertility market needs legal regulations*. New York: New York University Press. This book covers many issues regarding reproductive technologies as well as related rights and duties.

Wong, J., and Checkland, D. (Eds.) 1999. *Teen pregnancy and parenting: Social and ethical issues*. Toronto: University of Toronto Press. This small volume presents a well-balanced and critical series of analyses and policy suggestions on the topics outlined in its title.

Wu, Z. 2000. *Cohabitation: An alternative form of family living*. Toronto: Oxford University Press. This text presents a comprehensive review of the literature on cohabitation.

Suggested Weblinks

Government websites provide some of the best information on family formation trends. For Canada, consult

www.statcan.gc.c

especially *The Daily*.

For the U.S.:
www.fedstats.gov

For general statistics:
www.census.gov.

The Public Health Agency of Canada has sections on reproduction and related issues.

www.phac-aspc.gc.ca/index-eng.php

Health Canada also has sections on reproductive and genetic technologies.

http://hc-sc.gc.ca

For families formed with the help of assisted reproduction technologies of all sorts, and their effect on the children and parents, see **Centre for Family Research** at the University of Cambridge:

www.ppsis.cam.ac.uk/CFR

For adoption, the **Adoption Council of Canada** provides research as well as general information and links to various services.

www.adoption.ca

For a thorough discussion of the implications of reduced fertility, see R. Beaujot's article, "Delayed life transitions: Trends and implications," at

www.vifamily.ca/library/cft/delayed_life.html

as well as several articles from the **Population Studies Centre** at the University of Western Ontario at

www.ssc.uwo.ca/sociology/popstudies

CHAPTER 9

Spousal Relationships

"Right now, I'd rate myself as somewhat unhappy despite the fact that I just got married, which is what I wanted to do most in my life. It's just that marriage is so different than dating and becoming engaged. We used to do things together, special things, and had all the time in the world to talk. Now we're married and it's just like things are all settled for my husband; he has to work. I work, and I am finishing school and there's no time for the nice things in a relationship. Last year we were equally busy but he could find the time. I know that I may be too romantic and that I have to get used to this, but it is so disappointing."

"The past two years have certainly been the happiest of my life and mainly because I got married and even though I felt I was too young at the time it's the best decision I ever made. It's just the little things that make me happy like when I come home and he has the supper ready for me because he knows I have had a hard day and he knows that I am not used to cooking on a regular basis. What I like best probably is that we have so much to talk about, and we still talk about loving each other after two years but now we're also seriously planning the future as in having children. I can tell him that I am afraid to be cooped up in the house with two kids and no one to talk to and he takes it seriously and he says we'll have to find a way to keep me working and him doing a lot of fathering."

These two women students are at the beginning of their marriages and are of the same age—around 24 years old. Yet, their experience, level of happiness, and the extent to which their conjugal **expectations** are met are entirely different. In their autobiographies, they are fairly similar on many personal aspects, such as personality and values. They have, however, married young men with radically different conceptions of conjugal life. As a social category, men are more powerful agents of the construction of reality than women. This systemic advantage, as we see in this chapter, carries into intimate relationships.

Throughout the last half of the 20th century, the relationship between spouses has become far more diverse than it used to be. To begin with, the explosion of divorce on the familial scene has meant that marital stability can no longer be taken for granted. Couples now enter marriage with a less secure feeling of permanency than was the case in the past, when only death could separate them. Second, the massive re-entry of women on the labour market has resulted in more complex feminine expectations and often more complex forms of masculine cooperation or resistance in terms of the household division of labour. Couples now have to negotiate who does what at various stages of family development, and this situation can result in a tense relationship. Third, couples' expectations of marriage concerning love, sexuality, and companionship have heightened. More is demanded of marriage in terms of relationship than in the past, while, at the same time, couples may be less patient when their expectations are not met (Amato et al., 2007). The cultural focus of marriage as an institution has shifted toward an individualistic axis emphasizing needs and gratification; yet, this has not translated into happier marriages. Rather, **commitment** to marriage as an institution is still a key source of marital happiness and stability, but this is a reality that is often overlooked (Wilcox and Nock, 2006).

The relationship between spouses has also become more **diverse** for the simple reason that it now includes more categories of couples. Today, the term spouse has been extended to all couples involved in living-together relationships, whether cohabitants, same-sex couples, or remarried couples. Despite this diversity, marriage is still the predominant demographic basis of family formation. Even though couples are now delaying marriage, a majority of Canadians still expect to marry at least once. This demographic reality, combined with the fact that comparatively more research exists on the marital relationship than on any other form of partner relationship, means that a majority of the pages of this chapter are devoted to heterosexual marriage.

Finally, it should be pointed out that, perhaps following the individualistic values of the past decades, research on the spousal relationship has been carried out mainly within an individual and psychological perspective, with too great an emphasis on conflict and satisfaction, as opposed to other processes (Fincham et al., 2007b). As well, the research in general fails to situate couples within their familial, social, and cultural contexts (Karney and Bradbury, 2005).

TYPES OF MARRIAGE AND HOW THEY CHANGE

I wanted to begin this chapter with an overall classification of marital relationships, but I could not find recent in-depth studies of marriage types. Rather, I noted three methodological trends in the research on marriage and married life. First, usually sociologists do not themselves interview or even observe couples but have recourse to large-scale surveys designed by other researchers. (This is called "secondary analysis" on p. 28.) Second, these surveys, dominated by multiple-choice questions, do not provide sufficiently complete descriptions, and generally focus on only one of the two spouses. The result is that research on marriage (and on other areas of family life, for that matter) tends to present isolated bits and pieces rather than overall, holistic perspectives. Third, as already indicated, most of the studies reach only one of the spouses or, when both are interviewed, they are not linked to each other in the results but, rather, males and females are analyzed separately as two groups. Consequently, the *couple* perspective is lacking (see Sanford, 2010).

In 1965, using a qualitative approach, John Cuber and Peggy Haroff proposed a typology derived from in-depth interviews with 107 men and 104 women who had been married *for at least 10 years* and had never considered divorcing. The five types of marriage derived from the interview material were named on the basis of their central and distinguishing themes. They represent different configurations taken by the couples' relationships. This typology still applies today in many *western* countries. However, the influx of immigrants from countries that are more patriarchal and, in other cases, where marriage is less a matter of companionship than a matter-of-fact relationship for reproductive and economic purposes requires that sixth and seventh types be added (Arnett, 2008). I have taken the liberty of calling these the "congenial reproductive-familial relationship" and the "cultural reproductive-familial relationship" for want of better terms. We would need research both on cohabitational unions and same-sex marriages to see if they have other types of relationships and which of the ones detailed in the sections below are most frequently encountered among them.

The Vital and Total Relationships

The essence of a *vital* relationship is sharing and togetherness. Couples value their relationship, regularly discuss it, and when alone, often think about it. When they encounter conflict, they resolve it rapidly and move on. Differences are settled easily, even though with much discussion, but without insults or humiliating put-downs, as would take place among the conflict-habituated couples. This type of marriage comes close to conforming to Canadians' perception of an ideal marriage. Yet, it probably typifies only about a quarter of couples who have been married for over 10 years. But when a long-term vital relationship moves to a less involved one, such a marriage may become intolerable to one or both partners, even though it may still be a far better marriage than average. Divorce, rather than adjustment, may follow. The vital marriage probably typifies the first years of a great proportion of western marriages as well as many marriages that are past the childrearing years. In other words, it is not only a type of marriage but, for many couples, it represents a stage in their relationship: the honeymoon.

For their part, couples in a *total* relationship form a minority and are the "stuff of novels." They are in many ways similar to the vital couples—the main difference being that there is more sharing at the intellectual and psychological levels, and more discussions taking place for the sake of sharing their interests verbally as well as physically. In many instances, the couples have professional interests in common and help each other, attend conventions together, and confer on a wide range of issues. Whereas vital couples retain their individual existences, total couples melt into the same existence, like identical twins. These couples' sexual relationships are very important and are expressed in a multitude of settings and forms. Total couples define each other as lovers and best friends. Despite this, some do divorce because they have very high romantic and companionable standards. Experiencing less than what they have had, often after two or three decades, is not tolerable.

The Devitalized Relationship

In a devitalized relationship, the spouses had been deeply in love early on in their marriage, had enjoyed their sex lives, and had shared much together. Over time, the relationship lost its original "shine" and vitality. Now these couples simply take each other for granted but conflict is rare. Most of the time spent together is a matter of duty, to fulfill parental roles, to present a united front to the world, and to take care of each other's careers. These couples are often exemplary parents.

The relationship continues because of their commonly shared duties as well as the absence of conflict. There generally are other rewarding aspects in their lives, in which they invest much. They celebrate anniversaries and appreciate each other as parents or as workers. Some hold values that supersede that of individual happiness and they respect marriage as an institution. Cuber and Haroff found this type of marriage to be common in their sample, and may today constitute about one-third of all marriages of long duration.

However, these couples are susceptible to divorce because this type of marriage is considered less than ideal in our culture and the lack of positive affect takes a toll (Gottman and Levenson, 2000). It is a breach of romantic expectations of marital bliss. The risk of divorce is particularly high in view of the fact that these couples have, in the past, experienced greater companionship and pleasure in each other's presence. They are able to make comparisons with what they had before so that expectations for a happier relationship can arise and strain the status quo. Such expectations can also lead to extramarital affairs which may, or may not, lead to divorce.

The Passive-Congenial Relationship

The passive-congenial relationship may be quite similar to the devitalized relationship, with the exception that couples do not have an early exciting past that has been hollowed out through the years. They harbour deep affection and especially respect for each other and are not disillusioned as are the devitalized couples. In fact, they are quite *comfortable* with their situation. They emphasize what they share, such as their total agreement on a variety of political or religious issues, or the fact that they have similar leisure interests, parenting goals, and social network.

These couples' dating lives were generally uneventful, and a strong element of level-headedness rather than passionate love was at the basis of their decision to marry. For them, marriage is a secure platform from which to explore and develop other deep and even passionate interests, whether in parenting, politics, careers, or even volunteer work. Compatibility of background is important. Many of these spouses believe that society is placing too much emphasis on sex and passionate love. Although some of these marriages end in divorce, the risk is not high because this marriage fulfills many culturally acceptable functions for the spouses and their families. These unions may also be cemented by strong principles and these couples may rate their marital happiness quite highly.

The Conflict-Habituated Relationship

The main characteristics of the conflict-habituated union are tension and unresolved conflict, some of which is overt and appears in the form of nagging, quarrelling, and excessive teasing. The spouses seem to argue for the sake of it. When on their best behaviour, these couples are polite, particularly in the company of others. But they do not conceal their differences from their children and, during the interviews, emphasized their incompatibility and how tense they were in each other's presence. Many of these couples had already been conflictual at the dating stage. What holds their marriage together may be force of habit, lack of alternatives, and the fact that the spouses have personalities that are combative or have been so chiselled by the relationship that they might have difficulty adjusting to a more peaceful situation were they to divorce. In other cases, they cannot afford to divorce because of poverty or shared wealth and/or social position. This category can include marriages in which spousal abuse occurs.

Among young couples today, this type of marriage is more conflictual than conflict-habituated because conflicted relationships are likely to end soon (Gottman and Levenson, 2000). Even in the Cuber and Haroff sample in the early 1960s, this type of marriage was not the most frequently encountered. Today, it might cover well over 10 percent of long-term marriages. This is not a marital interaction that is valued in Canada, although it is far more acceptable in other cultures, especially when people appreciate arguing for the sake of it and when a "macho" code of conduct encourages marital spats in public, especially at the expense of women.

The Congenial Reproductive-Familial Relationship

The congenial reproductive-familial relationship is added to the Cuber and Haroff typology to include marriages that are *more or less arranged*, that is, with the adult children's participation, and do not become emotionally intimate but are cordial. This type can, to some extent, also cover those marriages that are not arranged but have been encouraged for familial, rational, or social reasons rather than for romantic purposes. Cordial reproductive-familial marriages are characterized by a lack of romanticism and affectionate companionship and a focus on tradition or practicalities. The spouses tend to lead largely separate lives: Wives take care of the children and spend their leisure time with other women, often kin. Men are the breadwinners and their family's representatives in the community at large, and they spend their leisure time with other men. The extended family system is generally important and family visits usually result in men and women sitting and conversing separately.

The spouses interact with each other for sexual purposes but with a minimum of romanticism involved, although a degree of affection exists. Wives are faithful sexually while men may or may not be. Spouses also have long conversations when alone or in the presence of their children. These conversations are cordial, may involve a great deal of mutual respect, may be supportive, but their focus tends to be on matters related to the family, children, business, jobs, and forthcoming celebrations. These conversations may involve discussions of the relationship and the functioning of the household. When wives are employed, they may be so in their husband's or kinsmen's businesses or even in a professional setting.

The Cultural Reproductive-Familial Relationship

This type of marriage is similar in structure to the previous one, but it has differences in terms of gender segregation and power. These marriages are arranged or even forced according to cultural norms with the issue of feelings being totally left aside. This is the union of a man and a woman that links two families together and where social and cultural considerations are paramount. The couples spend no time alone together, except for sleep, generally live with at least the husband's family, and the importance of the relationship is within the kin context. These couples are even more gender segregated than the previous type and women are rarely employed in non-familial work. Family honour is paramount. Such marriages may be polygamous. These unions are at very high risk for wife abuse and this abuse may actually be culturally sanctioned. These marriages are imports to Canada. Except for moving into the conflict-habituated or the congenial-reproductive categories, they are much less likely than the previous type to move into another category of relationship.

Marriages Evolve over Time

Most students who have read these pages probably think that only the first two types of marriages would be good enough for them. This expectation is well expressed in the first quote opening this chapter, where the young woman is devastated by what appears to be a rapid passage from a dating honeymoon into a devitalized marriage. Few approve of the conflict-habituated relationship and most hope that their marriage will never become devitalized. Although some see merits in the passive-congenial type, it certainly does not appear "very exciting," particularly in comparison to media portrayals in movies and television dramas. The two reproductive-familial marriages, for their part, are generally encountered among certain immigrant groups and, at least for the time being, are becoming more frequent in Canada.

But marital relationships evolve over time. Marital quality generally diminishes and then rebounds later to some extent; yet some couples have a much higher level of happiness at the outset than others so that the consequences of this decreasing quality has different meanings and effects for different couples (Umberson et al., 2005). Most middle-class couples probably begin at the vital stage, but a great proportion rapidly become conflictual or devitalized. At that point, marital satisfaction plummets and divorce rates soar. In today's cultural climate, only a minority of marriages survive constant conflict. The others make a conscious effort to change or seek counselling. Semi-arranged marriages, for their part, may also evolve into a passive-congenial or even a vital relationship or they may degenerate into a conflict-habituated one, often very early on. Divorce may also follow. Marriages that are more or less forcibly arranged have far fewer opportunities for positive transformation, except into divorce, and that option, when taken by a woman, may lead to difficult consequences because of the cultural context of patriarchy in the groups.

A devitalized marriage can also become a conflictual one over the years. At any point during these sequences, the marriage may break down, particularly when conflict and abuse occur, or when better alternatives present themselves. However, another change that may occur throughout the years consists in a revitalization of the marriage after childrearing is completed. This is illustrated in the following student quote. She had described how the burdens of parenting and jobs had dulled her parents' marriage during her adolescence:

"Since then, my parents' happiness with their marital situation has been steadily rising. The business is great and my father's working less hours, Mary [a problematic adolescent] *has a job, and I'm in college. They're happy with the whole*

family in general and they're like best friends. They're always getting all dressed up and they go out here, there, and everywhere. In fact, as I'm writing this down, they're on their way to Florida for a two-week vacation—both from work and us kids. They're as close as a couple could be and are celebrating their 26th anniversary this year. They've made a lot of plans for the near future and they seem very happy and excited about it. Neither would be whole without the other."

DIVISION OF LABOUR AND INEQUALITY

One very important aspect in the spousal relationship is the household and child care division of labour as well as its perceived equity, an element that was lacking in Cuber and Haroff's typology. When they did their research, gender roles and the domestic division of labour had not yet become salient social concerns. These themes were soon to become far more discussed under the convergence of two western trends occurring in the 1970s: the influence of feminism and the massive re-entry of wives into the employment market, thus placing into question the division of labour that had prevailed up to that point. The domestic division of labour is a perfect example of a microsociological phenomenon (here, domesticity) that is closely related to societal ones (in this instance, the social stratification by gender which pervades society's organization, including the work environment—Doucet, 2009).

A Classification of the Domestic Division of Labour

A classification of the division of labour between spouses has been derived from the sum of the research carried out on this topic. The domestic division of labour involves two elements: who does what and who is responsible for planning or management—in other words, chores and responsibilities or availability. This classification is based on behaviours rather than attitudes because far more couples believe in an egalitarian system than practise it. In other instances, daily necessities force couples to share child care equally, yet this egalitarian practice is not necessarily accompanied by egalitarian beliefs, in particular by husbands. Thus, the gap between attitudes and behaviours makes it preferable to focus on the latter.

The Egalitarian, Nongendered Division of Labour

In the egalitarian, nongendered division of labour, both spouses or partners are employed and participate equally in all aspects of the functioning of the household and in the care of the children. These couples are more likely to be encountered among the vital and total categories, or even the passive-congenial type, discussed earlier. They may grocery shop and cook together, or they may alternate, the husband cooking one week and the wife the next. They may dress the children, get them ready for school, help them with breakfast, and so on together, or they may alternate—one week the father does morning duties while the mother does evening duties. If researchers went into such a household, the hours done by each parent on chores and responsibilities would add up to near identical totals.

Although many childless couples fit this description, fewer couples with children do. The arrival of the first child is generally the structural element that contributes to a shift in the spousal division of labour toward the other end of the continuum (Bianchi et al., 2006). However, this is slowly changing in many western countries (Dribe and Stanfors, 2009). When it is generally the mother who takes a parental leave, this further entrenches the gendering of caring and working (Beaujot, 2000). However, paternity leaves, which are becoming more frequent, probably contribute to consolidating the egalitarian division of labour, especially in Quebec (Ravanera et al., 2009). In Canada, between 2001 and 2006, 80 percent of mothers took a leave of absence and 45 percent of fathers did so (Beaupré and Cloutier, 2007).

The Equitable but Gendered Division of Labour

The equitable but gendered division of labour involves a similar number of hours of work (paid and unpaid) and child care but each spouse does different tasks largely based on what is considered appropriately male or female by this couple. For instance, the father may take care of the outside of the house, and he may cook and do the dishes, but the mother does the cleaning and the child care and buys the groceries. They may both visit with their children's teachers; however, the father participates in coaching while the mother is responsible for sick days.

Researchers observing such a family would again arrive at a comparable number of hours for each spouse, but they would note that fathers and mothers generally engage in different tasks and have different responsibilities. Despite increasing trends in this direction, still relatively few families fit this description. Although gendered, this division of labour is deemed fair by employed mothers, even those who earn high salaries, because what is important to them is that fathers participate equitably.

The Specialist Division of Labour: Equitable and Inequitable

The specialist division of labour may be gendered or not and may be equitable or not: It resides in the recognition that one of the two spouses is better at cooking, while the other is more enthusiastic about cleaning or doing the laundry. One spouse or the other is better at putting the children to bed, while the other is more competent at supervising or helping with homework. In other words, things get done by the partner who is defined by the other or who self-identifies as the most qualified for the job. Some tasks may be occasionally shared or rotated depending on who is present when the necessity arises. Researchers studying such

When both spouses are employed, couples with a companionable marriage are more likely to share equally in terms of housework. In turn, equal sharing of work and responsibilities reinforces mutual feelings of satisfaction and companionship.

families may come up with two vastly different sets of results. In one group of families, both spouses spend the same number of hours on their different tasks. This would be an equitable specialist situation, and is often encountered in lesbian-headed families. Many of these women describe themselves as very conscious of problems stemming from the traditional division of labour and want to make sure that neither of the partners will become the conventional mother.

In the other group of families, one spouse has specialized in minor chores (e.g., washing the car and taking out the garbage) so that the other is left doing everything else on a daily basis. The other could be the wife or the husband, depending perhaps on which spouse earns the most or has the most power in the relationship. Here we see the beginning of inequity and of the potential for dissatisfaction by the spouse who carries most of the burden, generally the wife.

The Husband-Helper Division of Labour

The husband-helper takes *no* responsibility to ensure that dinner is ready, that a babysitter is available, that the children do their homework, and so on. The mother takes all the responsibilities and remains on a permanent state of availability for these duties. In some cases, it can be the reverse and it is the wife who is the helper, particularly if her job is demanding or if she has more power in the relationship. But the scenario that typifies so many Canadian families sees the wife attending to most of the chores and child care responsibilities with some husbandly help. The mother's total number of hours devoted to child care and house chores will constitute 60 to 90 percent, and the father's will constitute the balance, after the work the children may do is factored in (Hofferth and Sandberg, 2001). This is why mothers have less free time than fathers (Sayer, 2005).

This division of labour typifies situations where the wife is not employed, as well as cases of dual-earner couples. In families where the wife is employed, the husband's help is often perceived as fair because she feels that he appreciates her role by offering to pitch in. Husbands of unemployed wives may, however, find their own help very generous and less fair. Thus, fairness in this respect is defined in a gendered way. When there is a discrepancy in perceptions, husbands' beliefs and perceptions are more likely to affect wives' perceptions than the reverse (Wilkie et al., 1998:592)—a reflection of the greater masculine power in society at large. Husbands can generally choose the timing of their help, but wives are more bound to a schedule of tasks that have to be performed on a daily basis. Fathers often choose activities they like. This may be why Larson and Richards (1994) have found that mothers' moods are at their lowest when they engage in housework. In contrast, fathers often feel relaxed and cheerful.

The Complete and Delegated Divisions of Labour

With the *complete division of labour*, the mother does nearly everything and the father either watches television, tinkers with his car, or has a beer with his buddies after work. More often than not, the wife is unemployed or holds a part-time job. If she is employed full-time, her husband may have objected to the decision. In his mind, and perhaps in hers as well, her place clearly is in the home. This division of labour is becoming less frequent but still occurs, particularly at the working-class level. It also characterizes many families that have emigrated from countries where gender roles are patriarchal and the relationships are reproductive-familial.

For its part, the *delegated division of labour* is a phenomenon observed among affluent families that can afford a housekeeper, a nanny, or even a gardener. Although neither spouse actually does the work, and child care consists of engaging in leisure activities with the children and visiting their teachers, the wife is usually responsible for finding, hiring, training, and keeping the help. The wife may or may not be gainfully employed. When she is not, she engages in extensive community and volunteer work, organizes her husband's social activities, travels, and spends time shopping. It should be added that there is no research that looks at couple and family dynamics when a low-wage female employee contributes her labour to the household or takes care of the children in her home (Coontz, 2000).

The Overall Perspective

When all these types of division of labour are considered, the husband-helper and the specialized division of labour are probably still the most common ones now (see Ravanera et al., 2009). Whether the mother is married, divorced, part of a stepfamily, or single, she does most of the housework and child care (Coltrane, 2000)—and she does so even when both spouses are employed, although perhaps less so in Quebec where cohabitation predominates. Furthermore, unless they belong to the egalitarian, equitable, or specialist categories, fathers devote little mental energy worrying about household and children's daily needs or planning activities for them.

All these observations are reflected in the 2001 Canadian census which found that more than three times as many women as men spend over 60 hours a week on housework. Overall, among those who do housework, women and men spend respectively 4.3 and 2.8 hours daily in this activity. In the category of primary child care, 2.4 and 1.8 hours are spent daily respectively by women and men *who engage in this activity* (Statistics Canada, 2004d). Figure 9.1 well reflects this reality. Further, even among dual-career couples, mothers spend more time with their children than fathers, including while engaging in housework and shopping (Silver, 2000).

The Effect on Marital Quality: Overview of Recent Changes

In the 1950s and even in the early 1960s, middle-class wives' employment contributed to reducing marital satisfaction, especially among husbands, because it was then an infrequent and unusual phenomenon (Burke and Weir, 1976). Changes in gender roles at the cultural level had not yet occurred. In those days, there was no social support available to wives engaged in paid work. For their part, husbands suffered a lowered sense of self-worth because wife employment often signalled that husbands earned too little and could not support their families. By the 1980s, a cultural shift had occurred, particularly among women, so that employed wives, especially highly educated ones, were more satisfied with their marriages than housewives (Houseknecht and Macke, 1981). In contrast, husbands who held conventional beliefs about the division of labour and preferred to see wives at home

Average Minutes per Day Spent by Parents on Housework/Shopping

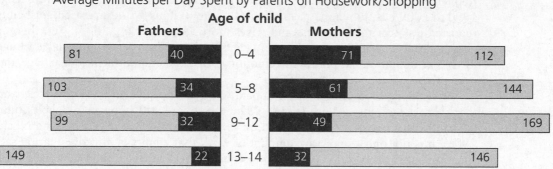

Average Minutes per Day Spent by Parents on Child Care

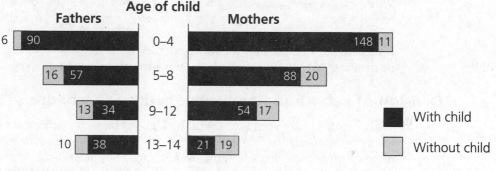

FIGURE 9.1

**Average Minutes per Day Spent by Fathers and Mothers on Housework/
Shopping and Child Care, with and without Child—Both Parents Employed
Full Time**

Source: Statistics Canada, General Social Survey, 1998; Silver, 2000.

reported lower levels of marital happiness when their wives were employed and
earned high salaries (Perry-Jenkins and Crouter, 1990). Although economic necessity
is currently still one of the main reasons why mothers work for pay, it is today a culturally recognized fact that two paycheques are necessary. Therefore, husbands do
not generally feel diminished by their wives' employment, as used to be the case 40 to
50 years ago. Most take it for granted and are as proud of their wives' achievements
as wives are of their husbands'.

At the same time, researchers began to focus on the perception of fairness in the
division of labour as it relates to marital happiness. In the 1990s, wives who were
employed full-time were less satisfied than their husbands and than other wives concerning the equity of the work-family balance (White, 1999). At the close of the 20th
century, researchers were observing a correlation between marital satisfaction and
the perception that the division of labour at home *and* at work is fair. In women's
overall evaluation of the quality of their marriage, the division of labour at home is
much more important, whereas the division of labour at work is considered more

frequently by husbands (Wilkie et al., 1998). An American study of two surveys from 1980 to 2000 has shown that, as husbands' share of housework increased, husbands reported less marital happiness and wives more (Amato et al., 2003). Yet, there is also evidence that it is not egalitarian beliefs and practices per se that make a huge difference in marital happiness, but emotional love and commitment to marriage and each other (Wilcox and Nock, 2006).

Still, the division of domestic and paid work has positive and negative effects on marital satisfaction for both spouses: The effects are still stronger for wives than husbands because equity, as perceived by women, is not reached (Wilcox and Nock, 2006). It is not only the relative amount of work that counts in affecting marital satisfaction but the perception of fairness or equity as well as the feelings that one's overall contribution to the family is appreciated. Perceptions of inequity reduce marital happiness and may lead to divorce, particularly when commitment is low (Frisco and Williams, 2004). Finally, more longitudinal studies are needed to see how the division of labour changes over time within couples—cohabiting or married—and what it looks like among older couples (Szinovacz, 2000). Dush et al. (2008) have found that couples who remain highly satisfied with their marriage over time are also the ones to be the most likely to change by becoming increasingly equitable.

Division of Labour in Remarriages with Stepchildren

With stepchildren present, the division of labour may constitute a more salient aspect of the spousal relationship. Stepchildren who visit often cause an enormous amount of work to stepmothers in terms of cooking and cleaning. In some reconstituted families, fathers tend to contribute more. But in many others, the father simply entertains his visiting children, or he leaves with them after lunch for an outing while his wife inherits a load of dirty dishes. The following is a quote from a woman reminiscing about the problems created by visiting stepchildren in her previous (second) marriage:

> "*His kids kept coming here because he didn't want to visit them at their place, of course, because he hated his ex-wife. We had six kids here at times and his are the rough type; after they'd gone, the whole house was a mess for us to clean and the fridge was empty and I had to pay.*"

This theme of inequity recurred throughout my interviews with stepmothers and was often exacerbated by complaints from the children's mother to the father, which he then passed along. Some mothers complained that the children had not slept enough, had not been well fed, or had watched too much television while at their father's place. The stepmother felt targeted because, after all, she was the one responsible for the smooth functioning of the household.

> "*I feel like a glorified babysitter. I mean, she brings her boys here so that she can have a nice weekend of rest and go out. It's nice for her but I get nothing out of this except work, work, and more work, and the boys order me around like a slave.*" [Their father?] "*Oh, he's so afraid of having further problems with her or that the boys won't want to visit that he says nothing. He pretends it's not there.*" [This stepmother did not intend to "*stick around much longer.*"]

In short, the matter of the division of labour seemed to bring in a great deal of conflict among these couples who had been together for only a few months or years at most. The wife's feelings of inequity may have been greater than in a first marriage with her own children: In a remarriage, the wife is labouring for another woman's children—those of the ex-wife. It would be important to study what develops in this respect when the reconstituted family adds a new shared child.

THE SILENT DIVISION OF LABOUR: EMOTIONAL WORK

Another aspect to the division of labour resides in that, generally, women do more caring as well as emotional or "love" work than men (McDaniel, 2009). Most exceptions to this rule would be found among the vital and total couples. We have seen in Chapter 7 that girls and women who date invest more emotionally in the relationship. They work harder at maintaining it, they initiate more conversations about the relationship, they express their love more often, they divulge more of themselves to their partner in order to show him their commitment, and they plan more of their activities together than he does, often including their wedding ceremonies (Humble, 2003). This pattern continues during cohabitation or marriage. We see in subsequent chapters that females nurture their relationship with their parents, siblings, children, and grandchildren more than males. Thus, all in all, whatever the familial roles they assume, from the time they are very young, females are socialized to become the **kinkeepers**, the expressive partners, and the emotional workers (Erickson, 2005). Were they to be differently socialized, society may lose out because, at this point in time, there are no indications that males are ready to step in and compensate.

According to Hochschild, in *The Managed Heart* (1983), "emotion work" is capital or an asset that women exchange for security in a relationship. In *subordinate* positions, the role occupants tend to rely on emotional capital. There are couples where the husband is subordinate because he wanted the marriage more than she or because she has more alternatives than he. This analysis fits the **exchange theories** outlined in Chapter 1. In general, women have fewer alternatives, either because their maternal investment restricts their ability to work or to find other partners, or because there are many other women competitors "on the market." In other cases, women are disadvantaged because of the double standard of aging (note in Chapter 12 the tendency for men to remarry women younger than their previous wives).

For men, their marriage is a haven, yet for women, it is often both a haven and a source of work and insecurity. Wives are not necessarily more invested in the stability of their marriage than husbands, but they are more invested in its *quality maintenance*. This differential investment is a source of insecurity for women, thus of subordination. It is also a source of marital discontent. Men are not as observant as their wives are concerning the quality of their relationship. They tend to take it for granted, because they are not the emotional worker. However, women get more intrinsic rewards from these relationships—again a matter of gender-role socialization.

For instance, Larson and Richards (1994) observed that wives' moods are more positive when they are with their husbands. Husbands' moods are also more positive when with their wives, but less so. As well, a husband's mood affects a wife's mood far more than the reverse. Indeed, more recent studies show that women are more affected than husbands by marital processes and their spouse's behaviours and mental health (e.g., Du Rocher Schudlich et al., 2004; Kiecolt-Glaser and Newton, 2001; Stimpson et al., 2006). When spouses arrive home unhappy from stressors at work, it is the husband who is more likely to transmit this state of mind to his wife (who is more attuned to his feelings and more dependent on them), than is the case when the wife returns home unhappy. If a husband has any argument at work, this increases substantially the probability that he will have an argument with his wife later on, although both spouses' work stress spills over into their home life (Story and Repetti, 2006). In her autobiography, a mature student explains how deeply affected she is by this situation:

> *"The only reason that I take one course each year is that it gives me something to escape to when my husband comes home in a bad mood because of pressure at work. . . . He wants all of us to feel it or to suffer with him; he takes it out on us. But the few times that I have done this, he laughed it off and walked out. It's so unfair* [when husband ignores wife's bad mood]. *I just hop in my car and come to the library to work on my paper. If I stayed home and went downstairs to type he would follow me and manage to pick a fight."*

Over 30 years ago, reputed sociologist Jessie Bernard (1972) talked of the two separate realities contained within one marriage—what she called a "his" and "hers,"or two marriages in one. This differential still persists today and it is not a phenomenon specific to a particular social class or ethnic group; rather, it applies across the board. For women, it is the quality of emotion work on the part of their husband which is the crucial determinant in their marital quality, probably because his emotional work reflects his commitment (Wilcox and Nock, 2006).

ASPECTS OF SPOUSAL RELATIONSHIPS

In addition to the division of labour, spousal relationships involve elements of happiness or disaffection, communication, as well as potential for conflict and conjugal problems. These elements have a threefold developmental dimension. First, they can be studied throughout the life span of a *couple* well into the later years. Second, within a person's life span, marriages can succeed one another so that the sequencing of marital types, division of labour, commitment, and marital happiness constitutes an important research theme. Third, marital quality can be studied by *cohort*—that is, among couples born and raised in different decades who, consequently, may have different expectations (Amato et al., 2003). Other important aspects of the marital relationship, such as **commitment**, altruism, and forgiveness, receive little attention (Fincham et al., 2007a)—reflecting the values of western researchers in the last half of the 20th century. Indeed, there are suggestions that commitment may prove to be as important a variable as marital happiness, for instance, in the study of marital quality (Amato et al., 2007). Future research may well find that commitment drives marital happiness and success.

Marital Happiness, Satisfaction, and Success

The concepts of marital happiness, satisfaction, and success have been very popular in the North American marriage literature ever since Burgess and Locke began their studies in the mid-1940s (Burgess et al., 1963). The goal of this research is to define what a successful marriage is and compare the characteristics of couples who are satisfied and happy with those of couples who are not. These various concepts are often used interchangeably, but there are different meanings attached to them. Marital happiness is an emotional state and is totally subjective and individual. In contrast, marital adjustment and success, while also subjective, depend much more on how the persons in the dyad perceive how they have achieved their goals, how well they communicate, and how companionable their relationship is (see Family Research 9.1). What makes for a happy marriage changes with the centuries and even the decades as couples' expectations evolve under various cultural influences that provide different **social constructions** of the conjugal relationship. As already pointed out in other chapters, the emphasis on marital happiness as the foundation of a union is rather unique to western countries. In most societies, the notion itself does not even exist.

Not all marital happiness reported by spouses is equivalent because it is a very subjective domain. Loveless, as paraphrased in Carroll and colleagues (2005), has identified three types of marital happiness. One is hedonistic and pertains to the satisfaction of desires. The second is individualistic and pertains to individuals` goals. The third is altruistic: The needs of the other are a primary concern and happiness occurs as a result of fulfillment of this goal. It is also posited that a focus on the first two types of marital gratification to the detriment of the altruistic one prevents

---

FAMILY RESEARCH 9.1

How Is Marital Adjustment Measured?

Several measuring instruments have been devised to quantify marital adjustment and satisfaction. These instruments are generally called *scales* and are used during phone, Internet, and face-to-face surveys designed to evaluate a couple's or even a family's functioning. Among the best-known is Spanier's Dyadic Adjustment Scale, which can be used for couples in general (see Spanier, 1976). The scale contains 32 close-ended questions testing for dyadic satisfaction and happiness, dyadic cohesion (shared activities and communication), dyadic consensus or perceived level of agreement, and perceived agreement on demonstration of affection, including sexuality.

Examples of questions are:

- How often do you kiss your mate?
- How often do you confide in your mate?
- How often do you work together on a project?
- How often do you quarrel?

The methodological issue to be addressed in this type of research is how one would measure marital satisfaction in cultures where husbands and wives lead largely separate lives and where romantic love is not the norm, even though it may happen.

researchers from focusing on marriage "as a social institution that involves important social, intergenerational, and public dimensions" (p. 277). The strictly individualistic view on marriage prevents an analysis of the shared aspects of marriage and of its role in society.

Overall, studying marital happiness is a complex undertaking, for it depends on a multitude of variables and it is impossible to include even most of them in research. The variables that help individuals achieve marital happiness can be found at several levels. Some, including economic situations, are derived from the social context and may help explain the lower marital satisfaction among blacks, who, on average, are less economically advantaged (Aldous and Ganey, 1999; Broman, 2005). Yet, cultural origins are also important because black Caribbean women living in the U.S. have a higher level of marital satisfaction than African-American women (Bryant et al., 2008). Other variables are psychological and involve personality characteristics, communication styles, and coping mechanisms. For instance, Miller et al. (2003) noted that being expressive toward one's spouse ("love" word) promotes marital satisfaction: Expressiveness leads spouses to engage in affectionate behaviours and to interpret their partner's behaviour in a favourable light. Persons who remain unhappily married over many years develop lower levels of overall happiness and life satisfaction as well as lower self-esteem and health. In fact, people in low-quality marriages do less well on these indicators than those who divorce and remarry and even divorce and remain single (Hawkins and Booth, 2005). In contrast, marital happiness increases well-being over time.

One can study what types of couples are happy together and what contributes to their dyadic satisfaction and even success. **Longitudinal studies** indicate to what extent marital happiness at Time 1 predicts happiness at Time 2 and what has happened in the interval to explain change or stability. Currently, researchers are able to predict with reasonable accuracy which relationships will end in divorce and to verify this prediction with a follow-up study of the couples. We do know that marital happiness diminishes after the "honeymoon" period (Mitnick et al., 2009). However, Dush et al. (2008) have also found that couples who begin with a very high level of marital happiness experience a less steep decline over a 20-year period. Overall, at any point in time, only about 20 percent of marriages are unhappy. However, commitment to the spouse and to marriage as an institution may be better predictors of marital quality and stability than marital satisfaction (Wilcox and Nock, 2006).

Communication Issues

Communication is a key component of the conjugal relationship. When couples who have been married for 50 years or more are asked the reasons behind their successful marriage, they unavoidably include "good communication" in their explanation. The quality of communication depends largely on its regularity, predictability, thoughtfulness, sharing characteristic, as well as how well spouses listen to each other. Spouses who are satisfied with their relationships tend to talk with each other about everything, share their thoughts, feelings, and hopes. They enjoy listening to the other and are attentive to the other. Perhaps one of the reasons why women's marital quality is on average lower than that of their spouse is that husbands often communicate less about personal matters and are less interested in these issues—the emotional work mentioned earlier. As a result, women want more companionable communication (Heyman et al., 2009). Positive communication is related to satisfaction in all cultures, as indicated in a cross-cultural study that included Pakistan (Rehman and Holtzworth-Munroe, 2007).

However, there are also signs that inadequate communication may at times be the result rather than the cause of marital distress: Carroll et al. (2006), for instance, have found that negotiation skills are effective only when they are grounded in love and consideration for the spouse—and, they add, commitment to the relationship. They conclude (p. 1029):

> *This distinction calls for therapists and educators to carefully assess whether difficulties in communication are the result of a deficit in the ability to negotiate or in the ability to love on the part of one or both of the spouses. . . . For example, without sustained commitment to one's spouse and marriage, communication skills are likely to falter as a basis for long-term marriage, and without the virtue of justice or fairness, marital problem-solving skills can descend into businesslike negotiations between two self-interested parties.*

As we have seen, women are more invested in their marital and parental relationships than men; also, when there is inequity in the division of labour, it usually favours husbands. In their role of emotional workers, wives are more involved in problem resolution (Gottman, 1998). For all these reasons, wives are generally less satisfied with their current and past marriages than husbands. But more to the point here, wives are compelled to make more demands and express more dissatisfaction to their husbands than the reverse and are therefore in the unpleasant position of initiating more conflict (Kluwer et al., 1997). For their part, men are more likely to withdraw (Christensen et al., 2006). Thus, in terms of quality of communication, women can be more negative than men because they are emotionally more threatened in view of their greater investment in the relationship.

Partner Conflict and Problems

Researchers evaluate the frequency of spousal conflict via self-reports and, at times, observations in homes or in a laboratory. They also investigate the mechanisms used by couples to resolve their conflicts. Thus, most of what is known about marital conflict and resolution comes from *self-reports* as well as spousal appraisals of the other partner's behaviour. The research shows that same-sex and opposite-sex couples engage in similar conflict-resolution mechanisms (Kurdek, 1994). All report a relatively low level of conflict. Lesbian women report using more constructive conflict-resolution styles. They also mention making greater effort to resolve conflict, perhaps because as women they have been socialized to be attuned to a partner's distress more than is the case among other couples that include at least one man (Metz et al., 1994). In this chapter, the focus is on conflict in general: Abuse and violence, as extreme forms of conflict, are discussed in Chapter 13.

Partner Conflict

Marital conflict arises from issues pertaining to the division of labour, communication, lack of attention to each other, finances, sex, children, and leisure time.

Finances involve not only how money is spent but who controls it as well as who earns it. When it exists as an issue for a couple, money becomes a pervasive and recurring source of conflict (Papp et al., 2009). Debt is problematic because it prevents couples from achieving some of their projects and expectations (Dew, 2008). As well, on average, the presence of children increases the frequency of disagreements (Hatch and Bulcroft, 2004).

There is substantial evidence that a genetic component is involved in conflict via personality, temperament, and emotional lability (Harden et al., 2007). Thus, styles of conflict resolution appear to form during the first year of marriage (Schneewind and Gerhard, 2002). Constructive outcomes occur when the communication of the dissatisfaction results in a better understanding of each other's feelings with a mutual search for a solution, including compromise. Egalitarian couples tend to be more responsive to each other's disclosure of dissatisfaction and are more likely to engage in mutually satisfactory solutions. Less egalitarian couples are more likely to avoid discussing their dissatisfaction, particularly with the division of labour. As well, conflicts are least likely to be resolved constructively when, for instance, the husband withdraws from the interaction and thus maintains the status quo: **Conflict avoidance** or withdrawal does not resolve problems and may decrease marital happiness (Christensen et al., 2006). However, were a researcher to ask these "avoiding" couples about conflict, the answer might be that little exists—compared with what the researcher would find among couples containing at least one egalitarian spouse. Thus, a lack of reported conflict in this case simply refers to overt conflict; such couples may actually have a very high level of what could be called covert or simmering conflict, as described by a divorced woman:

> *"My ex-husband always said to whoever would be present that we never had problems or quarrels. That's true, we never fought verbally and certainly not physically. But we could never talk about our disagreements and problems. As soon as I'd mention something, he'd smile, or laugh, or joke and walk away. He just left and things just kept getting bottled up; I mean we couldn't talk about money, about sex, about going out or not, his mother, nothing. Sure, we had no quarrels, we had no communication."*

Forgiveness is a mechanism of conflict resolution that is rarely studied (Fincham et al., 2007a). However, McNulty (2008) has found that it is functional only when it is followed by a change in the misbehaving spouse. Indeed, some spouses continue misbehaving after being forgiven, which results in higher tension in the forgiving spouse—leading McNulty to conclude that spouses should not forgive the constantly misbehaving partner.

Marital Problems

Marital problems are more encompassing than conflict. However, the two overlap in the sense that disagreements and conflict constitute one type of problem reported by spouses. As is the case for the division of labour, there is a **gendered aspect** to marital problems: Wives report problems more than husbands and say that more problems are created by their husbands, both during marriage and after divorce. Further, marital problems affect women's health more negatively than they do men's, although both men's and women's health suffers as a result of marital strain (Hetherington,

2003; Umberson et al., 2006). Not surprisingly, the quality of relationships in wives' own family of origin may have a greater effect on their perception of marital quality (Sabatelli and Bartle-Haring, 2003).

A longitudinal study of married persons spanning the years 1980 to 1992 provided respondents with a list of problems and asked them to indicate which existed in their marriage and which person had the problem: the respondent, his or her spouse, or both. Amato and Rogers (1997) used this information to see if there were specific marital problems that could predict that a couple would be divorced at each subsequent re-interview. They found six problems, at times occurring as far back as nine years earlier, that predicted divorce. These were infidelity, spending money foolishly, drinking or using drugs, jealousy, having irritating habits, and moodiness. However, there might have been other equally good precursors to divorce that had not originally been included in the study. Examples might include problems related to an unequal division of labour, or physical abuse, or lack of commitment to marriage.

Marital Quality through the Decades

The quality of marriages may have declined, at least since 1969. In 1991, sociologist Norval Glenn first showed that the proportion of people reporting their marriages to be very happy had declined between 1973 and 1988. This finding was unexpected because divorce rates had increased during the same period. One would think that the surviving marriages would be happier than in the past when even unhappy couples were forced to stay together. A complementary study carried out by Amato et al. (2003) used data gathered previously through two national phone surveys of couples 55 years of age or younger, one survey in 1980 and the other in 2000.

Members of the 2000 survey reported less marital interaction, more conflict and problems in their marriage, but marital happiness and divorce proneness remained constant. Generally, there was greater conflict and less interaction when both spouses were employed and when there were small children at home. There was also more conflict when the spouses had fewer economic resources and the marriage had been preceded by cohabitation. The researchers concluded that the lives of husbands and wives are becoming more separate and couples are less likely to share activities such as eating meals, shopping, working on projects around the house, visiting friends, and going out for leisure activities (Amato et al., 2003:19).

The Next Time Around: Remarriage

Remarriages are as happy as first marriages, once duration is taken into consideration (Ganong and Coleman, 1994). Yet, remarriages end in divorce more than first marriages. How can this paradox be explained? First, Kurdek (1990) has found that marital satisfaction decreased more in remarriages than in first marriages. Booth and Edwards (1992) suggest that it takes less deterioration in marital quality to precipitate a divorce among remarried than married couples.

Second, in a remarriage, the spouses enter the union with more emotional baggage than in a first one. Their previous union may have raised or depressed their expectations and it may have made them more or less tolerant when expectations are not met (see Chapter 12). So far, the higher re-divorce rate suggests that couples are less tolerant the second time around. Remarried spouses may be less willing to cope with what are considered by others to be smaller disappointments; these disappointments then bring ideas of divorce that might not occur so rapidly in a young couple who has never had to contemplate divorce. Obviously, there are processes involved in the second marital relationship that bring about a dissolution more readily than the first time around. Consequently, remarriages that are successful may require a deeper commitment and a conscious effort to avoid the downward spiralling trend. A re-evaluation of what is and is not important in life is required, as expressed by a remarried man during his interview:

> *"I came to the conclusion that if marriage is to be successful, both partners have to work at it or at least spend time enjoying it. I had to rework my priorities and since I can't imagine myself married to your average Jane Doe, I knew I was in for another career woman and I had to learn to give in a bit. Point of fact, my wife is very similar to my first wife and the reason is obvious: My first wife was fine. It's just that we failed to live our married lives. Now my career's less important, my marriage more. . . . It's a shame that it took a divorce to come to this realization."*

Further, re-divorces occur even more rapidly than first divorces. This rapid breakup may reflect the inability of many remarried spouses to establish a satisfying relationship very early on because of the complications of the structural factors involved. The presence of stepchildren, ex-spouses, and ex-in-laws represents for some couples a force that diverts their attention from the task of building their relationship and hampers their ability to invest in the dyad. A man reflects a similar perspective when trying to evaluate the quality of his remarriage during an interview:

> *"I think it's very difficult to start a remarriage on the right footing even with the best of intentions. There's always someone ready to make you trip over, especially her children. I find it hard to commit to this relationship—and I love her deeply, don't take me wrong here—because her children are so hostile. I can't separate them from her; they come in a package deal. One minute we're happy and I feel that I belong and the next minute they come in, throw stuff around, just ignore me, and it's so awkward."*

Thus, when studying remarried couples' conjugal quality, it would be important to distinguish between those who have dependent stepchildren and those who were childless when they remarried. The latter have a much lower divorce risk.

The Conjugal Relationship in Later Life

Although a proportion of older couples live a conflict-habituated or a devitalized relationship, on average, they experience relatively high levels of marital satisfaction, with a great deal of closeness and little conflict. At this point in time, it is difficult to determine if this elevated level of happiness in later years is the result of the **U-curve phenomenon** or if it is a matter of cohort. The U-curve refers to those studies that have found a dip in the quality of marriages during the childrearing years, followed by an upward trend after children's late adolescence. Such studies imply that the quality of a marriage varies during a couple's life course and is particularly affected by the negative aspects of parenting. So if the U-curve applies, higher marital satisfaction in later years could reflect relief from the stress of active parenting as well as work-related problems.

In terms of a **cohort effect**, older couples who married 40 to 70 years ago began their relationship in a social climate that emphasized more mutuality or duty rather than personal gratification in marriage. These couples may have had lower expectations to begin with in terms of what marriage could do for them, focusing instead on what they can do for the relationship. They may, as a result, have been happier maritally. Rather than being mutually exclusive, it is likely that both the U-curve and the cohort effect are implicated in the longitudinal dynamics of marital quality.

Retirement presents both opportunities and potential strains on the conjugal relationship (Szinovacz and Davey, 2005). On the one hand, it can result in an identity crisis, particularly among men (McDaniel, 2009). On the other hand, it reduces the pressure of commitments related to work, as well as time constraints. Couples can then engage in more activities together and make plans that cannot be derailed because of role conflicts. Indeed, Kaufman and Taniguchi (2006) have found that early retirement is conducive to marital happiness. However, leisure activities become one of the most contentious issues among older couples (Henry et al., 2005). Increased togetherness may be stressful for some, particularly when their entire lives had revolved around parenting and working, and their relationship had become hollow. They may have too much time on their hands and too little to say to each other, and thus some divorces occur at this stage. Many wives dread the day their husbands retire because "he won't know what to do with himself and I'll lose my freedom."

In an in-depth study, Robinson and Blanton (1993) asked 15 couples who had been married for at least 30 years to give their perception of the qualities that had sustained their relationship. The first qualities mentioned were intimacy and closeness, which resulted in the sharing of joys and activities and in mutual support in difficult times. These couples had enjoyed doing things together. They closely resembled the vital couples described earlier. The other quality that made their marriage endure was commitment to the relationship, to the spouse, or even at some points in the past to their marriage and children. The third aspect was communication or the sharing of thoughts and feelings so as to know the other's perspective. The fourth was called "congruence" by the researchers. This refers to the fact that most of these couples had similar perceptions regarding various domains of their lives, from commitment to religious orientation. Finally, the last salient quality was religiosity, which returns us to the contents of Chapter 6 indicating a positive effect of religiosity on the marital relationship and family life in general.

When both spouses live into very old age, one of the two may become frail. Physical impairment, such as difficulties walking, does not diminish closeness between the spouses. But a spouse's **cognitive impairment** lowers the degree of closeness, as perceived by the caregiving spouse (Townsend and Franks, 1997). This spouse also perceives that his or her efforts are less effective. Cognitive disabilities—such as dementia and Alzheimer's disease—bring changes in personality and behaviours that break the pattern of the relationship. In addition, the caregiving spouse becomes more socially isolated because of the demands of his or her new role. A distressed caregiving spouse's health, including memory, may be affected (Mackenzie et al., 2009). It is then more difficult to cope with the conflicts engendered by the new dependency, such as when the afflicted spouse criticizes the efforts of the other, refuses the help offered, or even becomes aggressive. This is more likely to be the reaction of chronically ill husbands (Calasanti, 2004). In contrast, when the frail spouse is supportive of the partner's efforts, the caregiver feels more efficient, less stressed, and is more satisfied with the caretaker role. Similarly, when levels of marital happiness were higher, activity limitations are much less likely to result in negativity on the part of each spouse (Roper and Yorgason, 2009).

SAME-SEX-COUPLE RELATIONSHIPS

Research on the quality of the dyadic relationship among married and cohabiting same-sex partners is scant, and much of what exists is flawed methodologically. To begin with, it is usually difficult to draw large random samples of same-sex couples. Therefore, most of the studies on same-sex couples have been small and many have relied on self-selection (i.e., researchers have placed ads in gay/lesbian newsletters and clubs to solicit couples' cooperation). Obviously, such an approach draws relatively educated couples who maintain links to the homosexual community, may be activists, and are fairly young. Less educated same-sex couples who have little to do with the homosexual subcultures or who are older will not be represented in these samples. Moreover, gays and lesbians have suffered from stigmatization and may not wish to share the intimate details of their lives with researchers for fear of being further victimized or categorized (Nelson, 1996:10). As a result, only couples who are happy together may respond to such ads.

In a large American sample, Kurdek (2008) compared cohabiting gay/lesbian and heterosexual couples with married heterosexual couples, some childless, some with children, and found that all of these relationships worked in similar ways—except that the quality of the relationship may decline more among heterosexual couples (Kurdek, 2008). Gay couples also reported more autonomy from each other in terms of activities, friendships, and decision-making than heterosexual married dyads. Lesbian couples reported more intimacy, autonomy, and equality than heterosexual dyads. (However, the researcher did not present comparisons between gay and lesbian couples.) Both gay and lesbian couples had higher rates of dissolution than heterosexual ones. In countries such as Canada where same-sex marriage is legalized, it would be important to compare those couples who married to a group of similar same-sex couples who are cohabiting to see if the married ones will stay together longer—as is the case among heterosexual couples.

In the domain of conflict, Kurdek (1994) compared gay, lesbian, and heterosexual couples and found little difference in the rank order of frequency of conflict in six global areas: power, social issues, personal flaws, distrust, intimacy, and personal distance. Issues pertaining to intimacy and power were the most frequent sources of conflict among all three types of couples. This is interesting in itself because it indicates that problems related to power are not entirely explainable in terms of gender roles or the patriarchal order, for they exist in same-sex couples as well. For all three types of couples, conflict over intimacy and power was more related to either partner's lower satisfaction with the relationship than other conflict topics. During the one-year duration of this study, conflict over power was the most predictive of later relationship deterioration. These findings are in agreement with those of other researchers for married heterosexual couples. Overall, as herein indicated and as seen in other chapters, there are more similarities than differences in the way homosexual and heterosexual couples live their relationships. The structure and requirements of daily life place similar demands on them.

THE EFFECT OF CHILDREN ON THE COUPLE RELATIONSHIP

The parenting role is a very salient one in adults' self-identity and it is thus surprising how few researchers have examined the effect of parenting satisfaction on marital happiness. In other words, not all adults are happy as parents, particularly when they have serious difficulties with their children. Is it not possible that when parents are happy in their roles this will reflect positively on their marital happiness? Sociologists Rogers and White (1998) found reciprocal effects between marital happiness and parenting satisfaction, both for mothers and fathers. (Parenting satisfaction was defined as parents' satisfaction with their relationship with their children.) They conclude that "success in one family role primes an individual for success in other family roles . . . parents may include their own success as parents as one component of their marital evaluation" (p. 305). Not unexpectedly, when couples have conflict over raising their adolescents, this translates into a decrease in marital satisfaction over time (Cui and Donnellan, 2009). Generally, there is a decrease in love and marital happiness, especially among wives, when children pass through adolescence (Whiteman et al., 2007).

Thus, within a transactional perspective, children affect their parents' relationship (Ambert, 2001). Indeed, most studies show a decrease in marital happiness after the birth of a first child and during the childrearing years. However, one can ask if

The quality of the spousal relationship is one of several key ingredients in a child's development. Parents in a secure and happy relationship transmit similar feelings to their children. Such parents are also more likely to agree in terms of socialization goals, thus again benefiting their children. Therefore, a child's home environment depends in great part on his or her parents' relationship.

this change comes from the parental transition alone or simply the effect of time on marriage because we know that couples' happiness diminishes after the first few years of marriage (Mitnick et al., 2009). It seems that both variables interact because parenting has also been found to carry more costs for marital quality among *younger* couples (Umberson et al., 2005). In fact, Kurdek (2008) may have provided the answer when he found that couples' relationship quality declines rapidly and then levels off. In addition, couples who had become parents saw yet another period of decline. This said, it seems that the transition to parenthood intensifies pre-existing relationship problems. It would be important to know how a couple's level of commitment to each other helps negotiate this transition (Kluwer, 2010).

Children transform a couple into a family with a lesser focus on the couple and more on the parenting role. In fact, parenting couples spend very little time together without their children (Campos et al., 2009). Unplanned births decrease marital satisfaction the most (Lawrence et al., 2008); as well, a child's poor health reduces the probability of parents staying together (Reichman et al., 2004). The division of labour becomes less egalitarian after the birth of a first child (Bianchi et al., 2006) and, as discussed in an earlier section, women do most of the child care. As a result, they are more affected by children than are fathers, and this is one of the contributing factors explaining women's lower level of marital satisfaction. In addition, the simple fact that some infants cry at night has an impact on how parents relate to each other (Meijer and van den Wittenboer, 2007). Children who show a great deal of negativity affect the parental relationship (Schermerhorn et al., 2007). It is also possible that, in remarriage, stepchildren's behavioural problems influence couples more negatively than is the case for shared children (Jenkins et al., 2005b).

THE EFFECT OF THE PARENTAL RELATIONSHIP ON CHILDREN

Researchers are particularly interested in finding a theoretical explanation for the observed link between the quality of parents' relationship and children's well-being. So far, the research has focused on **parental conflict**. This emphasis is understandable in view of the fact that inter-parental conflict diminishes the quality of parenting (Fosco and Grych, 2010). Overall, children who live with openly conflictual parents are often less well adjusted than other children, including those in well-functioning single-parent families. Very young children are affected differently by parental conflict, via their perception (Ablow et al., 2009). For instance, they may perceive that the conflict is their "fault" and that they are to blame, which may translate into internalizing problems (Jenkins et al., 2005b). Marital hostility may prevent adolescents from addressing other developmental tasks; it is also related to internalizing and behavioural problems via various psychological mechanisms such as self-blame and emotional dysregulation (Buehler et al., 2007). Children are more disturbed when the content of the conflict pertains to them. For instance, parents who openly fight about their children upset them more than if they are quarrelling about money. But attentive and warm parenting can mitigate the potentially negative effect of marital conflict (Kaczynski et al., 2006).

Parental disagreement by itself does not affect children negatively (Cummings et al., 2003). In fact, children can learn functional ways of solving human problems by listening to their parents iron out their difficulties in a cooperative manner. However, constant disagreement that is left unresolved or that simmers is detrimental. Continued parental conflict of the hostile type has the most negative effects and can result in a lower quality of parent-child relationship in adulthood (Yu et al., 2010). Children exposed to repeated hostility between parents fail to learn adaptive modes of conflict resolution and this pattern of interaction may spill into their own relationships (Jenkins, 2000).

But, as Fincham (1998:551) correctly remarks, there is more to a marriage than absence of conflict. Above all, "there has been no research on the impact of the spouses' supportive behavior on child development." When parents enjoy a good marriage, the mother's relationship with her small child is warmer and she is more nurturing. Fathering is even more affected than mothering by the quality of the marriage. All in all, when parents get along well, children exhibit far fewer behavioural difficulties than they do when parents are in a conflictual marital situation. The advantage extends to adolescence and adulthood (Hetherington, 2003). Further, a happy parental relationship is related to greater parent-child affection and consensus. Longitudinally, adolescents' negative behaviours tend to increase or decrease after a change in their parents' marital problems (Cui et al., 2005).

Several complementary explanations exist for the correlation between the quality of parents' relationship and their children's outcomes. These are illustrated in Figure 9.2 and discussed in the following sections. But before we examine them, it is important to mention that such a correlation may not be so evident in cultures where the reproductive-familial marriage is the norm—that is, where fathers and mothers, men and women, live largely separate lives; where the marital interaction might revolve around patriarchal authority and kin relationship; and where the relationship is an institutional one rather than one that is largely personal. It is not known what effect, if any, the quality of the marital interaction has on child development or on parenting in these societies, or in Canada, in these types of marriage.

Conjugal Quality Fosters Supportive Parenting

The most frequently mentioned explanation is that the supported and loved mother lives in a warm environment that translates into a close and attentive relationship with her child (arrow from left to centre and then to right in Figure 9.2). In contrast, when conflict exists, parents are stressed, feel unappreciated, and may be less able to transfer loving feelings to their child. Childrearing is disrupted and parents agree less with each other in terms of child care. It becomes more difficult to use authoritative socialization practices (Schoppe-Sullivan et al., 2007). In contrast, a good marital adjustment is related to more effective coparenting (Bonds and Gondoli, 2007). Parents' hostility toward each other often results in harsh parenting and rejecting behaviour toward children. Parents may become so absorbed in their marital problems that they are less available to their children (Sturge-Apple et al., 2006). In some

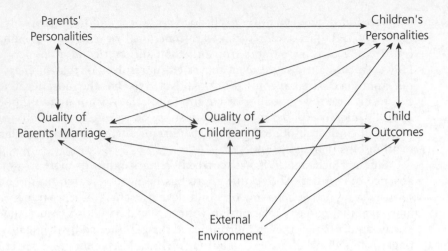

FIGURE 9.2

Variables Explaining the Correlation between the Quality of
Parents' Marriage and Child Outcomes

cases, parents use their children to get at each other, as had occurred to a student
who, in his self-description, grew up to be "out of control":

> *"I was more attached to my father because I always turned to him when my
> mother said no and he usually said yes so that I always ended up doing what
> I wanted. At other times he'd say, 'Ah, don't worry about her, she doesn't know
> what boys are like,' and I think that after a while my mother gave up on me.
> I remember that my father used to just ignore her or would tell her off and I
> didn't mind at the time because I was getting my way. It worked great during my
> adolescence, well, at first, but then it turned sour because I had become way out
> of control and it took my last girlfriend's leaving me before I finally realized
> what had happened to me. She just hated my father and she said I'd turn out just
> like him as a husband and she wasn't going to live with this."*

The Role of Learning and Personality

With the second explanation for the correlation between the quality of parents' relationship and their children's outcomes, the focus shifts on what children can learn in
this context: That quarrelling and even being abused is a normal way of living and of
resolving conflicts. Small children who are already predisposed to hyperactivity, ner-
vousness, or aggression may be especially vulnerable to parental conflict; they may
be particularly susceptible to acquiring maladaptive behaviours by observing and
modelling their parents' conflictual interaction.

This leads us to the third explanation which resides in assumptions about personality and temperament, as shown at the top of Figure 9.2 (Ganiban et al.,
2009): A conflictual marriage may arise because the two parents have problematic
personalities, are difficult to get along with, do not like to compromise, or are

aggressive. Even if only one of the two parents is so, the marriage is likely to be unstable. As well, when parents are too anxious, they may miss out on some cues from each other or their children (Bar-Haim et al., 2007). Further, if a mother is impatient, irritable, and has little tolerance for frustration, she may exhibit these patterns in her parenting practices, and the same holds true for the father. This would explain why, in conflictual marriages, the parent-child relationship is less warm and more erratic and why the babies and children in these families experience more adjustment difficulties, anxiety, and behavioural problems. In contrast, in a peaceful and supportive marriage, there is a strong chance that the parents' personalities are conducive to good relationships, and the child's environment is accordingly regulated (Papp et al., 2004). On the other side of the equation, parental conflict, which can be negative even for infants, affects them differently depending on the infants' own emotionality (Pauli-Pott and Beckman, 2007). Thus, the child's temperament has to be considered as are adolescents' own emotional and cognitive styles (Buehler et al., 2007).

Genes and Within-Family Environment

Thus, the fourth and complementary explanation flows from the preceding one. It resides in joint genetic and environmental considerations. Parents who are aggressive, have little tolerance for frustration, are impatient, or are not easy to get along with not only interact less positively with their children and are less supportive (Trentacosta and Shaw, 2008), but they may well pass at least some of these characteristics via genetic inheritance to their children (Zuckerman, 2005). The result is that some of these babies may themselves be more fussy and irritable. Later, they may become more oppositional, hyperactive, and aggressive than children born to parents who are warm, patient, and cooperative, and who consequently have a stable relationship. In other words, kinship by biology brings some similarities (and differences) caused by genetic factors (Harden et al., 2007).

As well, each person in a family constitutes part of the others' within-family environment. Thus, the behavioural manifestations of parental characteristics become part of the children's environment, both as childrearing styles and as marital styles (Rutter, 2002). At the negative level, children's own behavioural manifestations of their partly inherited traits, such as hyperactivity and aggressiveness, elicit a negative reaction from parents. This reaction then also becomes part of the children's environment. These partly genetically driven environments interact with one another and result in inadequate parent-child relationships as well as negative child outcomes or adjustment.

The Larger Environment Affects Marriage and Childrearing

Finally, as shown in the lower part of Figure 9.2, marriages and childrearing can be strained by the environment imposed upon a family—poverty and neighbourhoods come to mind here as they have been discussed in previous chapters. Children's personalities and outcomes may be indirectly affected by these environmental strains. Further, as they age, children whose parents have a conflictual marriage may be more at the mercy of deleterious neighbourhood, school, and peer influences. A student unwittingly puts her finger on this chain of circumstances when she points out the following:

> *"I stayed home as little as I could between the ages of 10 and 18 because my parents weren't easy to get along with and were fighting all the time, more my father than my mother, and a lot of the time they'd get mad at me or yell at me or it would upset me to see my mother cry. My parents were too busy fighting and maybe it was a relief for them when I was out so that I was on the streets most of the time by [age] 10. Of course, I got into all kinds of trouble but they became aware of little of it and I ran around with much older children. . . . I think that all of this affected my personality because I am somewhat difficult to be with and I don't put up with much. I don't know if I got that from my parents [genes] or because I ran around [with] peers who were like that or because the teachers gave me a hard time (after I gave them a hard time), I don't know. But the fact is that I'd like to have a nice relationship with a male but it's an uphill battle because I tend to fly off the handle."*

CONCLUSIONS: DEFINITIONS OF RELATIONSHIP QUALITY ARE CULTURE SPECIFIC

A spousal relationship consists of several dimensions, from the affective level to its power-sharing aspect. Some of these dimensions tend to be given a greater emphasis in different cultures, at different historical periods, and, within each couple, at different times in their life course. For instance, the romantic or love aspect considered so important in North America is not even taken into consideration in many countries of the world. In other countries, love often develops among a proportion of married couples, but it is not an aspect of marriage deemed necessary. The sexual satisfaction dimension was not given much emphasis in this country 100 years ago, particularly for women. Sex was certainly not something openly discussed concerning marriage. In western countries, romantic love may be considered far more important at the beginning of a couple's relationship, for instance, and so may sexual satisfaction. As time goes by and as the relationship develops, these domains may become less salient than value consensus, shared activities, the division of labour, and parenting.

Culture is a key factor in teaching men and women what to expect in marriage and in determining what constitutes a satisfying conjugal relationship. As culture changes, so do cultural definitions of marital happiness to some extent. Currently, the media are a key source of cultural definitions, including books written by experts and articles in popular magazines, as well as what is depicted in films, on television (particularly talk shows), and the Internet.

The media largely focus on heterosexual dating, cohabiting, and marriage. Thus, the general public inherits the cultural representations that depict ideal partner relationships mainly as opposite-sex couples. Yet, we have learned that there is a great deal of overlap between what makes a homosexual and a heterosexual couple satisfied with their respective relationships. In other words, there is much similarity between gay, lesbian, and heterosexual couples. It would be interesting to gain a better understanding of how and from where homosexuals develop expectations concerning relationship satisfaction in view of the fact that they grow up in a heterosexual culture.

Summary

1. The Cuber and Haroff typology of couples married for at least 10 years includes the vital, the total, the passive-congenial, the devitalized, and the conflict-habituated. To this are added the congenial reproductive-familial marriage and the cultural reproductive-familial one. Changes in marital quality over the conjugal life may lead to conflict and divorce—or revitalization can occur.

2. The spousal division of labour includes not only who does what in the household and in child care but also who is responsible for what. The classification suggested includes the egalitarian and nongendered division of labour; the equitable but gendered; the specialist (which can be equitable or inequitable); the husband-helper (fairly widespread and typical in husband-earner families); the traditional; and the delegated among the more affluent. In general, gender roles dictate that the wife-mother does far more housework and child care and that she remain available for these responsibilities.

3. The effect of this unequal division of labour on marital quality seems to have changed during the last decades of the 20th century along with the evolution of the cultural and economic climate concerning the employment of women. The spousal division of labour becomes a particularly thorny issue for stepmothers of live-in or frequently visiting stepchildren. An important aspect of the spousal division of labour resides in emotional work: Women generally work harder at maintaining the relationship and are more sensitive to its quality and to their partners' moods than are men.

4. The concepts of marital happiness, satisfaction, and success are defined and differentiated. Marital adjustment and success is a predictor of stability. There are reciprocal effects between marital happiness and spouses' satisfaction with their parenting role. The quality of marriages may have been declining since the 1970s as a result of changes in the social context of marriage.

5. Same- and opposite-sex couples engage in similar types of conflict and conflict-resolution mechanisms. Conflict arises from issues pertaining to the division of labour, communication, lack of attention to each other, sex, children, and finances. In marriages, wives are generally less satisfied than husbands and perceive more problems.

6. Older couples experience relatively high levels of marital satisfaction. At this time, it is not known if this is a matter of cohort or of revitalization of marriages after mid-life (the U-curve phenomenon). Qualities that sustain long-term unions are closeness, commitment, communication, and similarity of perceptions and beliefs. The relationship is altered when one spouse becomes challenged, particularly at the cognitive level.

7. The study of the relationship among same-sex couples is still in its infancy and requires methodological refinements. Lesbian couples report more intimacy, autonomy, and equality than married heterosexual couples, whereas male couples report more autonomy. Same-sex couples have higher rates of dissolution than married couples. This may, in part, be due to an absence of barriers, particularly at the legal level, to leaving the relationship. All types of couples, however, experience similar sources of conjugal conflict.

8. Children have an impact on the parental relationship.

9. The parental relationship affects children's development. Parental conflict that is perceived by children is detrimental. Happy marriages are related to healthy child development. This may be explained by the secure environment provided by such parents and the more positive role models presented. Parents' personalities are less problematic in happy marriages. The children may have

inherited easier predispositions; and, finally, external environmental influences affect parents and children.

10. Culture is a key factor in teaching men and women what to expect in marriage and in determining their level of happiness.

Analytical Questions

1. Why did Cuber and Haroff study couples who had been married for a long time rather than newly married ones to arrive at a typology of marriages?

2. Considering the classification of the domestic division of labour, what can be concluded on the basis of exchange theory? (A return to Chapter 1 may help in answering this question.)

3. Which explanation do you prefer for the correlation between the quality of parents' marriage and their children's outcomes? Justify your choice.

4. How does culture play a role in the definition of what constitutes marital happiness? You may want to re-examine Chapter 2.

Suggested Readings

Alford-Cooper, F. 1998. *For keeps: Marriages that last a lifetime*. Armont, NY: Sharpe. The author reports on a study of couples belonging to two cohorts. One was married during the Great Depression and the other during the Second World War. She looks at the problems specific to each cohort of couples as well as their relationships.

Blumstein, P., and Schwartz, P. 1983. *American couples*. New York: Pocket Books. This is a relatively old but still relevant study comparing married, cohabiting, gay, and lesbian couples. Issues pertaining to their relationships are examined comparatively, including sexuality, money, and work.

Schwartz, P. 1994. *Peer marriage: How love between equals really works*. New York: Free Press. The author presents the results of a qualitative study of couples who are in an egalitarian marriage. The relationships are examined, with a focus on compromises and the necessity to radically alter traditional marriage patterns.

Tichenor, V. J. 2005. *Earning more and getting less. Why successful wives can't buy equity*. New Brunswick, NJ: Rutgers University Press. An analysis of qualitative material on gender as a structure, its hidden aspects, power, the household division of labour, and inequity in marriage.

Suggested Weblinks

Canadian Research Institute for the Advancement of Women (CRIAW) presents research, statistical data, as well as activities on issues pertaining to women. Some of these issues are useful with respect to the spousal relationship.

http://criaw-icref.ca

National Council on Family Relations provides several sources and articles on topics related to marriage and spousal relationships. Their major journals, such as *Family Relations* and the *Journal of Marriage and Family*, are accessible on their website.

www.ncfr.org

CHAPTER 10

The Parent-Child Relationship and Child Socialization

If you stay a while in the nursery of a hospital maternity ward, you will see that each newborn is different from the very beginning of life. For instance, you may see Lucia, who cries constantly, even when picked up, and who is agitated and resists feeding. In the next crib, Jack is a total contrast: He sleeps contentedly, nurses avidly, and cries but stops as soon as he is fed or changed. A third baby, Latitia, is small, quiet, does not cry, sleeps most of the time, and drinks little milk.

Each baby needs different types of care. Baby Lucia requires more attention because she calls for more of it with her cries (what is called a child-driven stimulus). In contrast, Baby Jack demands little attention and is easy: All he needs is to be fed, changed, and cuddled. Jack's parents have more free time and feel competent because it seems to them that everything they do for him is rewarded with success. From the beginning of his life, Jack and his parents establish a smooth relationship that is likely to continue in the future.

Lucia's temperament presents at the outset the potential for problems. Her parents may feel less competent and more tense, especially if she is their first child. If they are poor and experience marital conflict, Lucia may constitute an additional challenge. Her parents' reactions may not always be positive because they are already frazzled by other preoccupations. As a result, she might grow up with less positive interactions and may not find interpersonal relations as rewarding as Jack will.

For her part, Baby Latitia arouses her caregivers' concern because of her low birth weight and minimal appetite. At the same time, her parents are likely to feel comfortable because she is an easy baby. If fed regularly, she will eventually thrive and will not make too many demands on them. But when a mother does not know much about infant care, a neonate such as tiny Latitia may deteriorate and waste away because she may not cry enough to indicate that she is hungry.

Our three fictive newborns illustrate some of the mechanisms at the origin of the parent-child relationship, which is studied within a combined interactional-transactional, behaviour genetics, and life course perspective. What emerges from these vignettes are **interactions** or transactions (Clark et al., 2000). On a basic level, each baby has different needs to which parents (generally mothers) respond; this means that infants unwittingly initiate many of the parental gestures that form the cornerstone of the relationship. For instance, a baby who cries constantly may elicit less positive reactions from his or her parents. In turn, this reaction depends on parents' gender, personalities, perceptions, and life circumstances (Crockenberg and Leerkes, 2003). Then, these reactions (being fed, changed, cuddled, or discouragingly ignored) become part of the babies' environment and contribute to the shaping of subsequent behaviours and, later on, their attitudes and beliefs as well as relationships with siblings (Jenkins et al., 2005a).

A small child who is blessed with positive characteristics, such as having a good attention span and low impulsivity, finds it easier to comply with parents' requests as he or she internalizes cultural rules and norms more easily. In turn, this child requires less supervision and less repetition, and receives fewer negative reactions from his or her parents. That child is less frequently disapproved of and scolded. Such children may form stronger attachment to their parents, both as a result of their personalities and of the way parents react to them. This **attachment** then further reinforces their willingness and ability to be socialized. Thus, within the interactional and transactional as well as behaviour genetics perspectives, parents and children interact with and influence one another's behaviours and attitudes (Leve et al., 2010a; Natsuaki et al., 2010). Utilizing the Canadian National Longitudinal Survey of Children and Youth, Elgar et al. (2003) found that maternal depression and children's behavioural problems interacted, one worsening the other over time in a bidirectional pattern. Small children with a negative temperament made it more difficult for parents to coparent together (Yaman et al., 2010).

Thus, from the very beginning, children contribute to the way their parents see them and treat them—albeit unwittingly so. Second, these interactions between parents and children become part of the children's environment (Ambert, 2001). Third, these interactions are in turn affected and shaped by sociostructural variables (Bronfenbrenner, 1979; Lewis, 1997). These include the number of children and adults in the family, the family's economic situation, and how society defines children and good parenting as well as motherhood and fatherhood.

This perspective stands in contrast with usual views on socialization describing children's personalities and behaviours as the product of their parents' childrearing—particularly their mothers'. Although parental practices are indeed important, children and even more so adolescents contribute to the formation of their environment and of their own development. In other words, **children are coproducers** of their own development (Huh et al., 2006). They are co-agents in their socialization process: As we see in Chapter 11, children's genetic background may be nearly as important as parenting (Natsuaki et al., 2010; Rutter, 2002).

The level of **adaptation** required of parents in general after the birth or adoption of a baby is underestimated, particularly by very young couples (Shaffer et al., 2009). In addition, I would hypothesize that the transition to parenthood is probably more difficult for current cohorts of new parents than was the case 40 years ago. Now, many adults have never been close to a baby intimately before they have their own while, in the past, larger families and earlier births offered many role models. As well, as we see in Chapter 1, the intensification of parenting at the middle-class level presents to new parents all manners of requirements in terms of what they have to do and not do (Hays, 1996). The list is long and not always obvious (Wall, 2009). Parents can be intimidated, overwhelmed, and professionalized. As well, the simple shift from that of being a couple to becoming a family with a tiny infant is not without inherent problems. This transition is smoother for couples who were well adjusted before and for those who had planned the timing of their family. Variables that are particularly conducive to a smooth transition are a husband's or partner's expression of fondness for his wife, his attitude of "we-ness," and the private, psychological time the couple retains (Gottman, 1998).

PARENTS' SOCIALIZATION PRACTICES

Socialization practices are methods by which parents ensure child understanding of and eventual internalization of society's rules (Lansford et al., 2009). In the western world, professionals dictate standards by which parents, and especially mothers, should interact with their children. This is part of current trends to standardize and rationalize lives in a postmodern economy, with emphasis on individualism and the development in children of qualities such as independence, self-sufficiency, and academic achievement (Ambert, 1994b; Wall, 2004). Thus, parenting practices and parent-child interactions are **social constructs** (Arnett, 2008) that often contribute to mothers' oppression (Badinter, 2010). North American societies stress "democratic rather than authoritarian relations, including autonomy, psychological well-being, and emotional expressiveness" as the ideal (Pyke, 2000:241). These values are shared by family theorists and clinicians alike. This social construct of proper family relations also makes it difficult for many immigrant children to value their own family's style of interaction, which they see as deficient compared with the model presented to them by television, books, and the Internet (Pyke, 2000). As well, parenting practices may not be equivalent for all children in a family (Rueter and Koerner, 2008).

Much of the vast literature on parents' socialization practices purports to link proper ways of parenting causally to positive child outcomes. This literature generally ignores the role of genes, the dynamics of the interactional perspective, as well as the social construction of motherhood, fatherhood, and childhood. Further, there is no research on "character" and moral or ethical outcomes of children or, for that matter, on parents. In other words, the research does not address the **moral context** of our society. Indeed, morality is a domain that is strangely absent from sociological inquiry. Also absent is the fact that socialization practices support the values of the technological capitalist system (Nadesan, 2002). In the presentation that follows, we begin with Baumrind's (1967) initial typology of parents' socialization practices: authoritative, authoritarian, and permissive styles of parenting. This typology is expanded to meet criteria of cultural diversity.

Authoritative and Authoritarian Parenting

Parents who are authoritative combine warmth, respect for their children's individuality, and psychological autonomy with monitoring of their activities and whereabouts (Gray and Steinberg, 1999). They are firm, yet loving, involved, and make demands for age-appropriate behaviours (Baumrind, 1990). Such parents explain to their children the reasons behind their demands and the consequences of not complying. They insist on obedience and then follow through with enforcement of rules and appropriate punishment. Reasonable punishment, when necessary, increases the effectiveness of reasoning for small children. It may increase their ability to internalize rules of behaviour so that, when older, they will no longer need to be punished (Larzelere et al., 1998).

Warmth and monitoring have been correlated with successful child and adolescent outcomes in all types of family structures in Canada, the U.S., and other western countries (Steinberg and Darling, 1994). More specifically, **monitoring** is related to lower rates of risky sexual activities among adolescents (Miller et al., 1999), fewer behaviour problems among early adolescents (Pettit et al., 1999), and higher academic achievement (Mounts, 2001). Overall, teens whose activities and peers are monitored by their parents are *much* less likely to engage in violent activities than others (Fitzgerald, 2009, 2010). In general, supervision is related to much lower delinquency rates (Statistics Canada, 2007i). Thus, the authoritative pattern correlates the most with good adjustment on all dimensions of development, but its various components (psychological autonomy, monitoring, parental knowledge, warmth, and involvement) contribute in unique and independent ways to diverse child outcomes (Gray and Steinberg, 1999).

However, parental monitoring is often affected when adolescents' problematic and delinquent behaviours increase (Laird et al., 2003). Thus, within an interactional perspective, authoritative parenting cannot prevent all problems, as illustrated here in a male student's autobiography:

> "I had continued to do drugs through Grade 9 and managed to keep a decent average in school. Pete's, John's and my parents had been comparing incidents and behavioural changes for a little while and finally figured that we were doing drugs. The straw that broke the camel's back was when Pete's mother found drugs in his room (I am sure my parents had searched mine). Pete admitted everything, including my participation. What followed was what was most painful to me and that was reality. I had hurt my family, my reputation, and who knows what else during my drug times and now I had to deal with all of this. Firstly, my parents sat down and talked to me. They were crying and told me I was not allowed to see any of those people again, that I was grounded, that I would be much more accountable now, and that I would improve my marks in school to meet my potential."

In this incident, the parents could not detect drug use that was taking place behind their backs. But vigilance, communication with other parents, and then a firm but loving stand contributed to the adolescent's redress—along with his cooperative personality. Thus, again, one sees the interaction between parental efforts and child characteristics. This has led Kerr and Stattin (2003) to advance that it is actually an adolescent's willingness to disclose information to parents that allows them to be authoritative. As well, adolescents' difficult behaviours can discourage parents from engaging and monitoring them (Huh et al., 2006). Still, parental monitoring and control remain important components of adolescents' behaviours (Barnes et al., 2006; Fletcher et al., 2004).

What predominates in the **authoritarian** parenting style is the dimension of control, restriction, and, at the extreme, coercion. Other authoritarian parents are characterized by inconsistency. They are arbitrary and erratic; they tell their children what to do and punish severely and indiscriminately, or they threaten, then harshly punish one day, but fail to follow through the next day. They "order" this and that without explaining why. They are often quick with slaps. They "natter" a lot. This type of discipline is not as effective because children can take advantage of its inconsistencies; it neither stimulates the development of self-control nor does it respect children as persons (Stevenson, 1999). This type of discipline is not so effective for most North American adolescents, perhaps in part because it is not socially constructed as suitable within the broad cultural context. In fact, it may contribute to difficult behaviours (Joussemet et al., 2008). Control and restrictions, however, are better accepted in other cultures, where they are seen as guidance (Gorman, 1998).

"No-Nonsense" Parenting

If Baumrind rewrote her typology today, she would probably include a socialization practice that falls between the authoritative and the authoritarian: no-nonsense parenting, often seen among black Canadians and Americans as well as in Caribbean samples. This style is higher on control than in the authoritative pattern but also involves more warmth and nurturance than is the case in the authoritarian style (Kağitçibaşi, 2007).

This no-nonsense pattern, first described in an ethnographic study by Young in 1974, "represents a functional adaptation to contexts that are more dangerous" (Brody and Flor, 1998:813); it signals to the child that the parent is vigilant and cares. So far, studies have found that this style of parenting promotes black children's sense of competence and regulation, and results in lower rates of detrimental behaviours and attitudes (Brody and Murry, 2001). These findings apply both in one- and two-parent families. This style of parenting is related to black teenagers' better school outcomes and taking personal responsibility—even though these adolescents may find that their parents "hassle" them (Spencer et al., 1996).

Permissive and Uninvolved Parenting

Permissive parents place very few maturity demands on their children, who can behave very much as they wish. Such parents do not actively socialize their children, because they fail to set rules concerning school, behaviour at home, or activities with peers. Neither do they supervise their children. Permissiveness can be combined with either a high level of warmth and acceptance or with disinterest and even rejection.

Subsequent to Baumrind's description of permissive childrearing, another style of parenting was added: uninvolved parents (Maccoby and Martin, 1983). Such parents are either permissive and indifferent or permissive and rejecting. They do not pay much attention to their offspring and do not fulfill their socialization function (Steinberg et al., 1996). Low parental control and rejection are the opposite of support and monitoring. They are a combination that has been consistently related to a host of negative outcomes, including delinquency (Steinberg et al., 2006). Teens raised in such a context tolerate frustration poorly and are more likely than others to be underachievers. They lack emotional control and long-term goals as well as purpose in life. At one extreme, such parents are called **neglectful**: Chao and Willms (2002) refer to them as irresponsible. Others are **abusive**.

The well-known developmentalist Urie Bronfenbrenner (1985) points out that parental permissiveness has more negative consequences than authoritarianism in times when there is cultural and social instability. In such a fluid context, norms of behaviour change rapidly, and a child needs far more guidance than in times when the entire community agrees on what constitutes proper and moral behaviour. Baumrind (1991:114-5) notes that "in a context of social instability, caregivers are required to sustain a higher level of supervision than would be needed in a period of stability." Today, there are more dangers that confront adolescents than was the case 50 years ago. Consequently, "premature emancipation is perhaps a greater threat to mature identity formation than delayed separation from family attachments."

A perfect example of permissive but warm parenting is described by a student whose parents were both professionals. She had initiated sexual intercourse at age 12, had had two abortions, had been "stoned" throughout high school, had sold drugs, and had lived on the streets by choice—all experiences she recalled fondly. Her parents allowed drug use and sex at home and finally bought a condominium to give her more freedom while she was a drugged teenager:

> *"We were allowed to toke in the house and grow pot plants in the basement. . . . My parents were completely straight, but extremely liberal. They allowed all manner of goings on. . . . School at this point was a joke. I was stoned every single day. . . . From age 15 to 18 I simply didn't have any notably painful experiences. This was partly because I was constantly stoned and partly because I was having such an adventurous life."*

The two students quoted in this section shared one problem: drugs. But the two sets of parents' and offsprings' reactions to this problem are dramatically opposite and the results are entirely different. These different outcomes and student appraisals of their situations are not caused just by their parents' socialization practices. They are also the result of environmental factors that both parents and adolescents created as well as of the interaction between parents' and adolescents' shared genetic predispositions (Leve et al., 2010b). In these quotes, one detects some similarities of character traits that each set of parents and their adolescent share. The male adolescent and his parents are more duty bound and emotionally connected. As a young man, he describes himself as cooperative and stable. The female adolescent and her parents are less tied to conventions, less emotionally involved, as well as more individualistic and gratification oriented. As a young woman, she describes herself as unstable, "depressed," and "highly critical" of other people's ways of living.

Additional Parenting Styles

There may yet be at least one other type of parenting style that has not been discussed by researchers. It overlaps somewhat with the permissive, and is tentatively called the **wavering-negotiating** pattern, for want of a better term. Parents who exhibit this style do not guide their children, even their toddlers, or make demands of them. Rather, they consult with their children about every step they undertake, even when the child is very small. When the parents make suggestions, they change them as soon as the child objects or disagrees. Such parents never punish but are very involved and loving. Here are two examples I recently observed:

The mother and a two-year-old boy are getting in line at one of the checkout counters of a large food store. **M:** *You want to follow the lady?* **B:** *No, no, want to leave!* **M:** *If you wait a minute, you'll get to ride the conveyor belt.* **B:** *Want a candy bar.* **M:** *OK, what about this one?* **B:** *No, this one.* **M:** *OK, now let's follow the lady.* **B:** *Want belt right away* [stamps foot]*).* **M:** *Ask the lady* [me] *if she can push her cart.* The conversation went on like this for the approximately three minutes I stood at the checkout counter. When I turned around to leave, the child was on the conveyor belt, to the clerk's obvious dismay.

The mother of a four-year-old girl is trying to buy a blouse in a department store. **G:** *It's ugly, I don't like it.* **M:** *Of course, honey, you're right, but I really don't need a pretty one.* **G:** *This one is nicer* [grabs one from the rack. Note that she is eating ice cream that is running down her hands]. **M:** *All right, I'll try it on if you want.* **G:** *No, I'm tired, I want to see the dollies.* **M:** *All right, sweetie, let's go and see the dollies. The mother patiently follows.*

In all the numerous instances when this pattern of interaction was observed, the mothers appeared well educated and upper-middle class. Mother-child negotiating went on for extended periods and the mothers unavoidably lost each round with a weary smile or sigh. The children never appeared satisfied and, when the mothers finally drew the line somewhere, several of the children threw loud temper tantrums—all in public places and some even kicked their mothers. These observations are anecdotal, but it is my guess that if researchers carried out systematic observations in large food stores and malls in certain middle-class metropolitan areas, they would encounter this pattern regularly. This is not a pattern that less advantaged parents can afford because it would be too disruptive to their lives: As so many researchers point out, working-class parents and poor parents focus on the primary tasks of sheltering, feeding, clothing, and teaching basic skills and values to their children (Lareau, 2003). Misbehaviour is a "luxury" that only better-off families can afford.

The Question of What Constitutes "Proper" Parenting

A particularly sensitive issue when discussing impoverished families as well as families from other cultures is the matter of what constitutes "proper" childrearing practices: the **social construction of proper parenting**. In North America, good parenting is synonymous with the authoritative style with decreasing control as adolescents age (Keijsers et al., 2009). This approach is endorsed by professionals, especially psychologists and social workers as well as child advocates. However, "What may be experienced by adolescents as parental intrusiveness in some cultural groups may be experienced as concern in others" (Steinberg et al., 1992:729). In dangerous neighbourhoods, the disciplinarian or no-nonsense style of parenting may be appropriate to secure compliance and to ensure safety and may be perceived as a form of concern (Lamborn et al., 1996). When peers are problematic, more controlling measures are adaptive and act as a deterrent to detrimental behaviours. Therefore, one needs to evaluate "proper" parenting practices within the context in which they are applied. Rather than value independence and creativity in their children, minority mothers frequently value obedience and respect for authority—as is the case in most countries of the world. The valuation of independence and creativity is a **western phenomenon,** a consequence of education, relative affluence, and safe environments (Arnett, 2008).

There is a related debate among the public as to whether physical or corporal punishment is acceptable. So far, North Americans still largely practice it (Barnett et al., 2005; Bibby, 2004; Durrat et al., 2003). Research documents a relationship between **corporal punishment** and low self-esteem, delinquency, aggressiveness, depression, and other problems (Straus, 2008). However, this research corpus has several limitations. The first rests in a failure to differentiate harsh from mild corporal punishment (Lynch et al., 2006): Corporal punishment is part of a continuum, from mild to harsh, and also from reasoned discipline to vindictive or violent retribution. Second, this research fails to take into consideration the possibility that parents who use harsh corporal punishment and have difficult children who grow up to exhibit problems share a negative genetic background with their children (Leve et al., 2010b). In turn, this heredity interacts with the environment to create both a negative style of parenting, a noxious familial climate, and difficult children.

The third limitation stems from the fact that most studies are not longitudinal; thus, one has no way of knowing if physical punishment "caused" the delinquency, alcoholism, and behavioural problems in some of the adolescents and adults who report having been spanked as children. McLoyd and Smith (2002) have found a longitudinal increase in behavioural problems among children who had been spanked; but this increase nearly disappeared in situations of high maternal support of the child (also, Berlin et al., 2009). Unfortunately, as they point out, "our measure does not reflect the extent to which spanking episodes are or are not preceded by the use of reason to gain the child's compliance" (p. 52). A life course perspective suggests that some of the adults were probably difficult children: Parents of children with behavioural difficulties generally use more disciplinary methods of all kinds, including reasoning, grounding, withdrawal of privileges, and spanking. Thus, parents may have been responding to children who were already problematic and are still so as adults. Similarly, it is possible that troubled young adults recall their parents' behaviours more negatively than they were in reality.

Thus, a fourth limitation of this research is that it rarely inquires about the remainder of the parents' socialization practices. For instance, it rarely considers whether parents are or have been loving or rejecting in their punitive approach. For instance, spanking out of frustration is more detrimental than reasoned spanking (Berlin et al., 2009). As well, this research does not tell us whether children perceive the punishment as a sign of parental rejection or concern (Baumrind, 1994; Simons et al., 1994a). Indeed, in English-speaking western countries, physical punishment is harmful psychologically when the child perceives it as a form of parental rejection or when the overall parent-child relationship is negative (Foshee et al., 2005:339; Larzelere et al., 1998). It is also harmful for adolescents (Lansford et al., 2009). Baumrind (1996) emphasizes that it is not a particular disciplinary practice that is important but the broader parenting context within which it occurs.

In summary, it is unlikely that occasional and fair corporal punishment of young children in itself causes the ills with which it has been associated. Nevertheless, even light physical punishment is not a parenting practice that is appropriate on a *regular* basis or at all (Straus, 2008): It is certainly detrimental for adolescents and children younger than two—particularly when they have difficult temperaments (Berlin et al., 2009; Mulvaney and Mebert, 2007). Young children tend to be more aggressive and less prosocial when their parents are punitive (Statistics Canada, 2005a). **Harsh physical punishment** is dangerous because it is unfairly painful, and is likely to be perceived as an act of rejection and aggressiveness by the victims (Lynch et al., 2006). It may also provide children with an example of a violent style of interaction. There is a subset of parents who use harsh discipline to the exclusion of other approaches (Lansford et al., 2009). Finally, there are no indications that corporal punishment prevents serious antisocial behaviour in North America (Simons et al., 2002). Nor is there solid evidence that banning physical punishment prevents child death, as has often erroneously been concluded from Swedish statistics, what Beckett calls the "Swedish myth" (2005). Several European countries have now made it illegal while, in Canada, a Supreme Court Decision upheld parents' rights to fair corporal punishment, as spelled out in Section 43 of the Criminal Code. But the Court set some guidelines, including the danger of hitting the head, or a child younger than two. This is important because perhaps as many as 40 percent of parents of infants under the age of one do use some physical punishment (Invest in Kids, 2002).

Determinants of Parents' Socialization Practices

How do parents develop their socialization practices (Belsky et al., 2009)? What influences them to adopt one approach over another? Three types of influences come to mind. They are complementary rather than mutually exclusive, and interact with one another: contextual and cultural influences, parents' personalities, and adaptation to their children's personalities and behaviours. Parents' genes affect some of their socialization practices to some extent via personality traits (Burt et al., 2005).

Contextual and Cultural Determinants

Childrearing practices can become ineffective or harsh because of environmentally induced stressors such as poverty, unemployment, marital conflict, and divorce. These stress-inducing circumstances tend to disrupt parental practices and make parents less responsive to children's needs. Stress experienced by mothers because of marital problems or economic hardships often leads to a more erratic, punishing, and disciplinary relationship with their children (Conger et al., 1995). Lenton (1990:173) suggests that harsher disciplinary practices "are explained by insufficient resources and because parents may also experience an erosion of their authority." Thus, the quality of childrearing may change over the life course, not simply in response to the different needs of growing children but also as a consequence of evolving contextual factors.

Parents' beliefs about the proper ways of raising children are also important determinants (Berlin et al., 2009:1416). These beliefs are culturally influenced and may originate from the way parents were themselves raised (Bailey et al., 2009). This transmission stems both from genetic and environmental factors (Kovan et al., 2009). Other parents may be influenced by social constructs of children as naturally good ("If you let them lead the way, everything will be fine"). Yet others have learned that "sparing the rod spoils the child" and behave accordingly. Parents' beliefs and notions can be learned from books, professionals, the Internet, television, or friends. Or, yet, adults who felt unloved as children because their parents were cold and non-expressive may react by becoming warm and supportive parents.

Parents' Personalities and Adaptation to Children

Parents' personalities constitute a key element in how they raise their children (Ganiban et al., 2009). For instance, a wide range of adult personality characteristics can lead to authoritative parenting (Denissen et al., 2009): Parents who are patient, calm, and affectionate, have a sense of humour, or are businesslike may be more inclined to use authoritative or even no-nonsense techniques. In turn, constructive parenting is maintained across generations because of the offspring's positive adjustment that follows (Kerr et al., 2009). On the other hand, think of a man who is easily frustrated, impatient, and impulsive. Such a man is more likely to become a harsh, rejecting, and perhaps abusive parent. There is then a good chance that his children will show some of these partly genetically influenced traits (DeGarmo, 2010). Their irritating behaviours trigger bouts of impulsive punishing, especially when he is under stress. Poor parenting results to a certain extent from parents' difficult personalities and lack of empathy.

A third factor influencing parents' socialization practices is suggested by the interactional perspective: Even if they do not always do so consciously, parents adapt their practices to fit their children's behaviours, personalities, and abilities (Bates et al., 1998; Keijsers et al., 2009). Several studies document this process of adaptation (Huh et al., 2006; Pettit et al., 2007)). For instance, both mild and harsh physical discipline decline with age throughout childhood (Lansford et al., 2009). When hyperactive children are successfully treated with the drug methylphenidate, or Ritalin, their hyperactivity diminishes substantially, and mothers become less controlling (Tarver-Behring and Barkley, 1985). Similar reactions have been observed among teachers (Whalen et al., 1980). In other studies, mothers of cooperative children and mothers of oppositional children were experimentally paired with a difficult child (not their own) and then with a cooperative child (not their own). Both types of mothers exhibited more controlling and intrusive behaviour with the oppositional child than with the cooperative one (Brunk and Henggeler, 1984). In other words, adults may adapt their parenting practices to children's behaviours, or adolescents may determine them (Kerr and Stattin, 2003), as illustrated by this student:

> "I was not an easy child to raise and I think that in the balance of things I had a bigger influence on how my parents raised me than they had on me because I was for ever changing and going through phases of this and that, and I can't imagine that my parents could even figure this out."

Pursuing this interactional line of reasoning, one can see that children and adolescents may influence their parents to become coercive or rejecting, even if they do so unwittingly (Simons et al., 2002). Parents may actually monitor children with behaviour problems more closely than they do children without these problems. Yet, as Simons et al. (1994c:359) point out, "rebellious, antisocial children often punish parental efforts to monitor and discipline while reinforcing parental withdrawal and deviance." Early oppositional and defiant behaviours undermine later parenting practices and nurturance (Huh et al., 2006). In turn, diminished parenting can lead to affiliation with deviant peers and delinquency. It is difficult to monitor the whereabouts of an adolescent who is extremely oppositional (Moilanen et al., 2009). It can be said that children coproduce the parental socialization practices of which they are the beneficiaries or the victims (Lansford et al., 2009). Nevertheless, parenting generally affects child behaviours more than child behaviours detrimentally affect certain aspects of parenting, at least until mid adolescence (Scamarella et al., 2002).

THE PARENT-ADOLESCENT RELATIONSHIP

The parent-adolescent relationship is influenced not only by the social construction of parenthood but also by societal definitions of what adolescence is (Arnett, 2001). In this section, we also examine the limits and contexts of parental influence on adolescents.

The Social Construction of Adolescence

Much research has been devoted to parent-adolescent conflict. In contrast, harmony is much less emphasized in western research. This interest in conflict derives in part from old-fashioned western notions that portray adolescence as being necessarily a period of turbulence—the idea of "storm and stress." At the beginning of the 20th century, the psychologist Stanley Hall was at the origin of this perspective on adolescence as a naturally turbulent stage. Sigmund Freud, who was very influential, reinforced this idea that adolescence is unavoidably a period during which all youths undergo emotional turmoil. Were this textbook written in Africa or in parts of Asia, this discussion on adolescence would either be absent or have a totally different focus (Arnett, 2008).

The beginning of adolescence is generally determined by the onset of puberty—that is, hormonal changes and the development of primary and secondary sexual characteristics. This transition exists in all cultures, even though the age of onset varies depending on life conditions, such as nutrition—a poor diet, for instance, is likely to delay menarches. It is important to underscore that this period of physiological puberty does not give rise to an identical psychological and social puberty throughout the world (Schlegel and Barry, 1991). But, despite the fact that the "storm and stress" ideology concerning adolescence does not apply universally, it still remains a widely held belief and some students confessed to using it to their advantage:

> "Between the ages of 12 and 16 I was the worst for my parents because we were adolescents and we all felt as did our teachers and psychologists that it was natural for us to go through this bad period so we felt all justified in all our bad behaviors and our parents had to put up and shut up because what can you say when psychologists agree with your children? Now looking back on this I truly feel ashamed of what I put my parents through because it was all so avoidable and especially not necessary; it was actually parent-cruelty."

The famed anthropologist Margaret Mead (1928) was the first to document the fact that the problematic type of adolescence, which has become common in most western countries, is a cultural rather than a biological entity. At that time, her research was going against the grain of prevailing social constructions. But in the last four decades, most qualified specialists have reached the same conclusion. "Teenagehood" is a **historical phenomenon** (Modell and Goodman, 1990). Historians Kett (1977) and Demos (1971) have placed the invention of adolescence as a social category between 1890 and 1920—after most middle-class youngsters were pushed out of the labour market and into the school system, separated from the adult world of which they had until then been part (Côté and Allahar, 1994). Adolescent crisis is in great part created by the type of environment that has evolved in most western countries—not by the nature of adolescence in general (Tyyskä, 2001).

This discussion has recently spread to a new issue: That of adolescent brain structure and function. Here again, one has to recall that experience, activities, and responsibilities contribute to brain formation—brain formation is not only a biological phenomenon but a cultural one as well (Sercombe, 2009). Therefore, brain development during adolescence may well differ cross-culturally in terms of its timing and the areas that are favoured.

How Do Parents and Adolescents Get Along?

As stated earlier, much of the literature on the parent-adolescent relationship focuses on conflict, which generally pertains to daily routines rather than key value issues. Nevertheless, 15 percent of adolescents report daily arguments while 40 percent report weekly or more frequent arguments (Bibby, 2001). Adolescents report more conflict than do their parents. Naturalistic studies based on day-to-day reports, such as the one described in Family Research 10.1, show higher levels of daily tension than survey questionnaires do (Larson and Richards, 1994). This information finds resonance in students' autobiographies: Approximately one-third recalled experiencing a psychologically and socially painful adolescence that put a strain on their relationship with their parents. Another third described this period as a happy one both for themselves and their parents; the remaining third recalled an adolescence that included happy as well as unhappy periods. A majority of the adolescents' sources of unhappiness were located at the peer-group level. This was followed by school problems, and much farther down in the hierarchy of stressors were problems with parents. Interpersonal difficulties experienced with parents tended to have resulted from the adolescents' state of mind and transgressions (Keijsers et al., 2009) and particularly from peer-driven stressors. Yet another key aspect of what leads to good relationships between adolescents and their parents is that of personality traits such as agreeableness. As well, Denissen et al. (2009) have found that the effect of adolescent personality increases with age.

Barber (1994:384) suggests that the absence of conflict over controversial topics such as sex and drugs most likely means that, although parents and adolescents differ in attitudes about them, they do not discuss these issues. In turn, this prevents parents from properly advising their children (Keijsers et al., 2009). In Canada, only

Naturalistic Self-Reporting: Daily Activities

In a study conducted by Larson and Richards (1994), adolescents and their parents were asked to carry a pager for one week. (Now, this is done via cell phones.) When beeped, each completed a report indicating what they were doing, where and with whom they were, as well as their thoughts and emotional state at the time of each signal. They were beeped once at random within every two-hour block of time between 7:30 a.m. and 9:30 p.m. This method was called the Experience Sampling Method. Adolescents were sampled from the fifth through ninth grades of a middle- and working-class Chicago suburb. In addition, parents and adolescents filled out many questionnaires about themselves and their family life.

This combination of methods allowed the researchers to study daily activities and accompanying moods of all the family members individually. But above all, it allowed them to compare how each family member felt in the company of the others and how each felt while engaging in various activities together or separately, whether at school, work, home, with peers or coworkers. The researchers could also obtain on-the-spot reports of conflict, contentment, or boredom while family members were together. They could also, for instance, compare how each reported on the same conflict.

8 percent of adolescents turn to parents for guidance about sex (Bibby and Posterski, 2000:172). Another explanation is that parents and adolescents "spend very little time together, often not more than one hour per day of direct interaction" (Demo, 1992:115). While parents' and adolescents' reports on time spent together are somewhat at odds, both mention spending only a few minutes each day talking (Larson and Richards, 1994). In fact, only a minority of adolescents share a meal with their parents on a typical day (CIW, 2010). Yet, family dinners have also been found to promote positive adolescent-parent communication (Fulkerson et al., 2010). Overall, there may be a wide variety of situations that adolescents experience and parents never know about, thus reducing the potential for conflict, but at the same time depriving adolescents of proper guidance. It is at least logical that, when adolescents' behaviours go against parental expectations, they try to carry on as much of their lives as possible without their parents' knowledge (Keijsers et al., 2009).

Larson and Richards (1994) report that adolescents experience less conflict with their fathers than their **mothers**, partly because mothers interact more with them concerning the basics of their daily lives. The household division of labour based on gender places mothers at a disadvantage over fathers in this respect. In this vein, Collins (1990) reviews studies illustrating that, when a mother interrupts her adolescent during a discussion, the youngster subsequently interrupts her even more, but does not do so for the father. Yet, all studies indicate that adolescents are closer to their mothers than their fathers and confide in them more (Nomaguchi, 2008). In married families, adolescents are both more attached to and in conflict with their mothers than with their fathers. They also seek her support and advice more.

Cultural Determinants of Parental Influence

Parental influence or the ability to socialize children and affect their outcomes is a much discussed topic these days, particularly with regard to adolescents. But parental effectiveness does not operate within a vacuum: It is circumscribed by society and the child outcomes it values. Family relationships take place within a distinct cultural context, at a given historical period, and under specific economic conditions (Hareven, 1994a,b).As a general rule, the extent of parents' influence on their children, particularly on their adolescents, varies according to these prevailing sociohistorical conditions (Bronfenbrenner, 1989). In other words, there are **historical eras** or time periods when it is easier for parents to influence their youngsters and others when it is far more difficult to do so. Social change ushers in new influences on children's lives while also reducing the impact of other influences (Adams et al., 2002).

Families' social and cultural contexts have altered drastically and with an extreme rapidity that has no precedent in history. The environment is now controlled by information technology, including the **audiovisual media**. The workplace, schools, homes, and leisure activities have all been affected by these changes and the evolution of the value systems that generally accompanies such transitions. Parents have had to adapt their role within this new context and raise their children accordingly, although much of this adaptation takes place unconsciously (Alwin, 1990). Often, as seen in Chapter 3, the contents of media do not support parental efforts and may even undermine their moral and practical teachings. In contrast, religion, which generally supports parents and upholds their moral authority, used to be a more powerful influence than it is now throughout all regions and social classes. Thus, parents have lost a degree of legitimacy through these two changes alone.

For their part, in western societies, children react to their parents according to what they learn through their environment, including their peer group and the messages they receive from the media as well as from professionals. Children are more aware of their rights than in the past but are not pressed by equivalent responsibilities. They have higher material expectations and requirements. They want more autonomy, and male children in particular are taught to separate themselves from their mothers and the feminine realm. As a result of all these changes, children's and adolescents' receptivity to parental socialization efforts has evolved. Many no longer see their parents as legitimate sources of information or even of authority for their behaviours. While a great proportion of adolescents report that their mothers (81 percent) and their fathers (70 percent) are influencing their lives to quite an extent, only 18 percent say that they turn to them when facing serious problems (Bibby, 2001).

As society evolves, it places a premium on certain specific human outcomes. Thus, parents are emphasizing autonomy and self-reliance in their socialization practices both because of **society's value orientation** toward individuality and because parents who are employed need more self-reliant children (Rossi and Rossi, 1990). Mainstream technological society also values the development of self-esteem and educational achievement (Daly, 2004). Although all of these outcomes are, to some extent, affected by parents, these outcomes are particularly influenced by peer interaction, the school situation, and the media. In contrast, a few decades ago, the development of politeness, obedience, conformity, service to others, and patriotism was given more importance in the socialization of children (Alwin, 2001). These outcomes are more culturally influenced; they are thus subject to direct teaching and example and are more amenable to parental socialization. Therefore, parents were more influential in these respects than is the case for outcomes that are more personality driven, such as self-esteem and the ability to be independent.

The Role of Peers in the Parent-Adolescent Relationship

Today's western parents have less control than in the past over whom their child associates with after a certain age. More peer interactions, especially among boys, take place outside the home than used to be the case and than is the case in most other parts of the world (Schlegel, 2003). When children attend schools outside their neighbourhood, or have a car, or live in a spread-out suburb or in an area where gangs rule, parents cannot monitor what takes place and with whom their child associates.

Peer Groups and Parental Isolation

It is worth emphasizing here that the phenomenon of age-segregated peer groups is typical of only North America and Europe (Schlegel, 2003). It is not a universal situation but more one stemming from urbanization combined with modern education (Arnett, 2008). In North America, particularly, the peer group may support parental teachings, but it may also conflict with parents' values and, as children pass into adolescence, peers' norms begin producing a much greater effect (Masten et al., 2009). Children's socialization is considerably easier when peers and parents agree, and is difficult, at best, when fundamental value contradictions exist between the two systems (Drew et al., 2010). The greater the similarity between parents' values and those of their children's peers, the lower the level of parent-child conflict.

What parent has not heard, "But all the others are going!" "Everybody is doing it," and "Everybody has one." These are powerful and often intimidating messages handed to parents. Thus, each parenting couple and, more and more, each single mother or father has to face what is presented by their child as a normal entitlement among youngsters. Parents are made to feel that, if they do not conform, they will do a grave injustice and deprive the child. This alleged consensus among youngsters allows them to speak with great authority to their parents, because parents are generally more isolated than children when it comes to tactical and moral support. Adolescent groups and subcultures are much more cohesive and less fragmented for each child than are adult subcultures for each individual parent. In reality, there is no such thing as a parental subculture or peer group, and this constitutes a disequilibrium that is detrimental to parents' role. A single mother expresses the situation during an interview in an attempt at understanding how her teenage daughter became delinquent without her noticing it:

> "My daughter has a lot of friends, some I know, some I don't. They talk on the phone on a daily basis . . . they make plans, they exchange clothes, they cover for each other, they watch each other's back against their parents. They come and they go and it's impossible to keep track of all of this. New clothes that she wears are borrowed from Mindy and if I ask Mindy, she'll say, 'Don't I got good taste!' If Mindy's mother calls to find out where she is, all I can say is that they

went to the movies together. That's what I was told. But they actually went to this boy's place. If Mindy's mother calls about clothes, I say that they exchange a lot while in reality they are all shoplifting. So you see you have to be a very, very clever parent to keep track of all of this and to add it all up together to one conclusion: My child is a shoplifter and she's barely 15 and she's screwing around. But don't think for one minute that I added this up on my own; the police did it for me. These girls just protect each other. Protect for what? They're the ones who need protection against each other. Now I tell you that Mindy's mother, Jessie's mother, and I have all been fooled."

Along these lines, Steinberg and colleagues (1995:453) find that, when adolescents' peers have authoritative parents, the latter contribute to positive developmental outcomes above and beyond the adolescents' own parents' authoritativeness: "We believe that this may be due in part to the higher level of shared social control provided by a network of authoritative parents." Yet, in the preceding quote, the parents are exhibiting all the "symptoms" of being authoritative, but their children's delinquent peer group is far more clever and better organized.

Many parents, especially more educated ones, make it a point of knowing their children's friends' parents. **Parent networks** can fulfill several functions both for parents and their children (Knoester et al., 2006). When these are school based, they can contribute to a smoother socialization process, norms that are more closely adhered to, and better-informed parents. It is, however, far more difficult for adolescents' parents than for young children's parents to know their children's peers' parents and form an effective community—at a time when such a context would be the most helpful. As a result, parental knowledge of adolescents' behaviours generally diminishes, particularly when adolescents have high levels of behavioural problems (Moilanen et al., 2009). Problems arise particularly when adolescents have close peers who accept illegal behaviours: These teens are then four times more likely to engage in violent delinquency than others, for instance (Fitzgerald, 2009). There is also the fact that teens who are difficult tend to choose similar peers, which reinforces their problems (Burt et al., 2009). In other words, there is a constant balancing act by parents to counteract negative peer influence when it exists (Chung and Steinberg, 2006).

In addition, parents inherit what one student called "the flak," that is, spillover of maltreatment received by peers. Parents can even be blamed by clinicians for traumas that actually have peers at their source (Ambert, 2001). A student's recollections illustrate this latter phenomenon quite vividly:

"Up to that age [11 years] I had been quite happy at school but then something happened to me, I stopped growing and I became in no time the shortest and skinniest and soon the pimpliest little runt at my grade level. The other boys used to pick on me, hide my coat, steal my lunches, and would never include me in their games. They'd laugh at me openly and the girls started avoiding me too because it wasn't cool to be seen with the most unpopular boy. . . . You can't imagine how many times my mother had to keep me home because I'd start throwing up. I became scared shitless. . . . The funny thing is that my parents had to send me to a psychiatrist and he turned around and blamed them for not being supportive and for whatever else. That's kind of sad when you think that my

problems had nothing to do with my parents. My parents were sort of being made miserable because of this little runt I was and now by this psychiatrist and to this day they have never blamed me and have always been supportive."

THE RELATIONSHIP BETWEEN PARENTS AND ADULT CHILDREN

There are both continuities and changes in the parent-child relationship throughout the various stages of family development, as well as throughout the life course of each family member.

When the Child Is a Young Adult

In North America, full adulthood has traditionally meant financial independence from parents and the establishment of a separate household, usually with a marital partner. However, this life stage is now often postponed. Whereas adolescence as a social construct was the invention of the dawn of the 20th century, young adulthood is the creation of the closing of that century (Côté, 2000). The term **"emerging adulthood"** is now frequently used for the 19 to 35 age bracket (Beaujot, 2006). This term is in itself related to our new economic structure (Côté and Allahar, 2006). It signifies a status somewhere between adolescence and full adulthood (Nelson et al., 2007). Young adults remain home (coresidence) more often than was the case three decades ago and many remain financially dependent on their parents for a longer period of time (Beaupré et al., 2006; Mitchell, 2000). For Canada as a whole, the number of young adults aged 21 to 29 at home has jumped from 27.5 percent in 1981 to 41.1 percent in 2001 and **43.5 in 2006.**

This increasing trend also shows differences between certain census metropolitan areas for the years 2001 and 2006 (Statistics Canada, 2007h, selection from Table 16):

	2001	2006		2001	2006
St. John's	46.3	47.6	Kingston	32.8	36.1
Saint John	38.6	41.9	Oshawa	47.5	53.8
Halifax	30.7	33.2	Guelph	35.2	40.2
Moncton	30.1	30.7	Greater Sudbury	41.3	41.3
Montreal	39.1	39.8	Winnipeg	38.0	42.0
Sherbrooke	26.4	25.3	Regina	32.5	32.9
Ottawa-Gatineau	35.8	41.1	Saskatoon	27.0	28.4
Toronto	54.0	57.9	Calgary	31.8	34.0
Hamilton	48.7	53.8	Edmonton	34.2	34.5
Thunder Bay	43.8	50.0	Vancouver	45.7	50.6
Peterborough	40.1	42.6	Victoria	30.0	33.5
Kitchener	38.7	42.1			

This change is even more obvious among the 25 to 29 age bracket, an age by which youths have nearly all completed their education. In 1981, only 11.8 percent were still at home, compared with twice as many in 2001, or 23.7 percent (Beaupré et al., 2006).

This is a widespread phenomenon in the western world (Ruggles and Heggeness, 2008). In fact, rates of young people up to age 34 who are **single** and have never cohabited are extremely high—as high as 55 percent in Italy, most of whom still live at home (Jones, 2007). This historic context, in turn, postpones **parents' transition** to the empty nest. It also delays grandparenting. Young adults whose parents are still together, as well as those with an employed mother, leave home later because their parents are better able to help them through higher education (Ravanera et al., 2003). Children of immigrant mothers also leave home later (Beaupre et al., 2006).

How to explain this new phenomenon? First, young adults stay home because they remain in the educational system longer and this is costly. Luong (2010) has documented how students' debt load prevents them from accumulating assets while still in their twenties. Second, the development of the service economy and the shrinking of the manufacturing base have resulted in an increase in part-time and **low-paying jobs** for young people without higher education—these jobs force them to remain with their parents for financial reasons (Gee et al., 2003). Thus, coresidence enables better transfers of capital from parents to children (Beaujot, 2004). In contrast, children who leave home too early may be disadvantaged, especially over time.

A third reason for the lengthening dependence of young adults may be related to the finding that they are increasingly endorsing **consumerist values** (Bibby and Posterski, 2000). What were considered luxuries in previous cohorts—cars, home entertainment systems, and computers—have become necessities for current ones, thanks to various marketing strategies that permeate our world (Côté and Allahar, 2006). Consequently, the earnings required to reach such heightened material expectations come later, and in the meantime young adults can afford them only when they remain with their parents. Fourth, in some cities, rents are out of reach for those on low incomes, which makes the parental home comparatively more appealing. This may be one of the reasons why coresidence is so common in some large cities, as seen earlier. A result of high costs and dependence on parents is that young families are now less able to accumulate assets than was the case in the 1980s (Beaujot, 2006:120).

Another change that has occurred in recent decades is that the family may go through **transition reversals**: Approximately one-third of young Canadians aged 20 to 29 have returned home at least once after an initial departure (Mitchell, 2004). This return may occur because of unemployment and other financial problems, or because a relationship has ended (Mitchell and Gee, 1996). This has been referred to as the *revolving-door family* and the "boomerang" children. As Hareven (1994b:448) points out, whereas in the late 19th century, children remained at home to help aging parents or widowed mothers, now "young adult children reside with their parents in order to meet their own needs." As well, coresident children contribute little in terms of housework (Mitchell, 2004). This entire situation represents yet another refutation of the pessimistic point of view of the family's loss of functions. Rather, active parenting is maintained well beyond what used to occur and is even reactivated, often repeatedly after all the children have left home for the first time. As Mitchell (2004:121) points out, mothers have become the new "unpaid social workers" as the welfare state continues to retrench.

When the Child Is a Mature Adult

One key aspect of the *life course perspective* is that it brings attention to the development of the relationship over time as both parents and adult children age and as cohorts change (Martin-Matthews, 2000). For instance, only 8 percent of persons born in 1910 still had a surviving parent by the time they had reached age 60. This percentage rose to 16 for those born in 1930 and it is expected to rise to 23 for people aged 60 born in 1960 (Rosenthal, 2000). As well, there is the fact that more elderly women than men live alone, which may be a factor that motivates their children or even nieces and nephews to be in touch with them. But whatever their age, a majority of adults and their parents report having a good relationship and being in contact with one another fairly regularly, as illustrated in Figure 10.1. Adult children, particularly daughters, often speak with their mothers, although they do so less frequently with fathers (Townsend-Batten, 2002). Generally, the affection that exists between parents and adult children is the chief motivator in continued contact and exchange with parents (Rossi and Rossi, 1990). The more parents and children see one another, the greater affection they have for one another, and vice versa. But these researchers have found that this reciprocity of affectivity does not always apply to fathers. They concluded that "the motivations for interaction between adult children

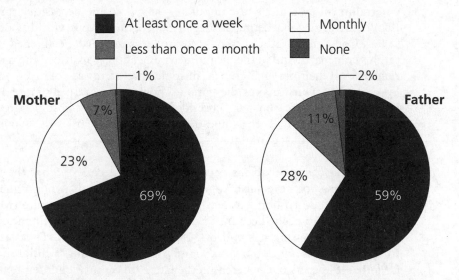

FIGURE 10.1

Frequency of Contact with Mothers and Fathers for Adults Aged 25 to 54 No Longer Living with Parents

Source: Statistics Canada, General Social Survey, 1995; Townsend-Batten, 2002.

and their mothers and fathers are different." Constructive rather than avoidant strategies for conflict resolution between the generations are also implicated in good relationships (Birditt et al., 2009).

Studies tend to present demographic characteristics to explain the quality of the parent-adult child relationship: gender and marital status of parent and child, socioeconomic status, geographic distance, and parents' health status and even religiosity (Connidis, 2010; Lin, 2008a; Townsend-Batten, 2002). The interactional perspective also suggests studies that would look at a child's and a parent's personality characteristics that could affect the relationship. From a life course perspective, other researchers believe that, as adult children mature, their values become more similar to those of their parents because they have lived through similar experiences, such as getting married, having children, and shouldering work responsibilities (Rossi and Rossi, 1990). When children most closely resemble their parents in terms of values and beliefs, they have a better relationship with them, a phenomenon also observed between grandchildren and their grandparents (Giarrusso et al., 2001). In fact, Aldous and colleagues (1985) found that adult children who shared interests and values with their parents were favoured by them. Birth order is a key factor that carries through life in terms of parental favouritism (Suitor and Pillemer, 2007).

Finally, the interactional and life course perspectives accommodate structural variables in the parent-child relationship (Aldous, 1996). For instance, when there is a sharp distinction in professional standing, and therefore income, between father and adult child or mother and child, is the relationship affected? Rossi and Rossi (1990:299) comment that occupational success and social mobility may be attained at the expense of family solidarity and closeness between the generations. What happens, for example, when a child or several children have far surpassed their parents' social status—or, the reverse, when a child or all siblings have drifted downward socially? Do these families become fractured as a result of social mobility or does the generation with the most favourable position help the other? Differences among ethnic groups may exist in this respect, particularly when immigration is involved and parents expect their children to surpass them in occupational prestige.

Parents Help Their Adult Children

In general, parents, especially when they are still in reasonable health, provide a great deal of help to their adult children, including financial (Gee, 2000)—even to their grandchildren (Ploeg, 2003). They are a key resource for adult children with fewer social assets (McIlvane et al., 2007). Parents respond to grown children's needs and problems (Fingerman et al., 2009; Suitor et al., 2006). They provide services such as babysitting, food, clothing, lodging, and gifts in kind as well as cash, and moral support, at least once a month.

As parents age, they often do not or cannot disengage from the problems experienced by their adult children. Pillemer and Suitor (1991) report that a quarter of senior parents mention that at least one of their children is experiencing serious physical or mental health problems or a high level of stress. These children's problems correlate significantly with depression in the older parents, and some studies find that older parents who have to provide a great deal of help to their children feel more depressed. These parents may be particularly worried over children who fail to achieve a reasonable level of independence (Birditt et al., 2010). In addition, when children have problems, they may receive advice that is not wanted or that they are unwilling or unable to put into practice. One can see that, at the very least, the potential for intergenerational ambivalence is high (Connidis and McMullin, 2002a, b). In contrast, parents offer more companionship to children they perceive to be more successful, perhaps because they have more in common with them (Fingerman et al., 2009). Parents over age 65 who have a coresident child usually receive relatively little in terms of household or financial help from that child. In a Dutch study, it was found that a 30- to 40-year-old child's coresidence with a parent was in a majority of the cases dictated by the child's needs (Smits et al., 2010). Overall, the research shows that older parents still contribute a great deal to society via their help to their families as well as volunteer work (Rajulton and Ravanera, 2006b).

Adult Children Help Their Elderly Parents

When elderly parents become much older, generally after age 80, a proportion experience diminished health as well as mobility limitations. At that point, adult children often become parents' key instrumental and social support resources (Connidis, 2010). Nevertheless, the level of family care required by seniors has been overstated. For instance, in 2001, only 4.8 percent of males and 8.3 percent of females aged 15 and over had spent five hours or more a week caring for or assisting a senior (Statistics Canada, 2004b). Caregivers themselves spend an average of 4.2 hours a week on assistance to seniors (Frederick and East, 1999). However, with shrinking social services and the shift away from institutionalized care, demand for family members to provide care for their elderly parents will increase. This shortfall may be especially problematic for those women who are divorced or have been single all their lives and may have fewer social and material resources at their disposal

Social policies concerning adults with special needs are so deficient that even frail elderly parents often have to continue assuming the entire responsibility for the care of their middle-aged children with disabilities. They receive little help, exhaust their meagre resources, and their own health may deteriorate.

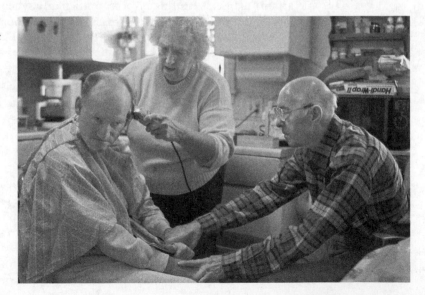

(Abu-Laban and McDaniel, 2004). Aged lesbian women and gay men without partners also need to be studied in this context.

For their part, elderly parents are happier when they give than when they receive, and they accept help more readily when they can contribute something in return (Lowenstein et al., 2007). However, even this parental help may result in feelings of ambivalence in their mid-generation children (Ingersoll-Dayton et al., 2001). When parents require a great deal of support from their children, they are less satisfied with the relationship. In part, this can be explained by the fact that contact with the child is necessitated by the parents' needs rather than by the child's desire to see the parents or by the spontaneity of a visit just to socialize (Silverstein et al., 2010). It is not surprising, therefore, that when older parents are in better health, they report a more positive relationship with their children. Even parents who are in palliative care are concerned about burdening their children (McPherson et al., 2007).

A popular but misleading concept is that of the **sandwich generation**: adults caught between raising their children and caring for frail parents. In reality, only a minority of adults provide care to both generations at the same time (Duxbury et al., 2009; Rosenthal, 2000). Their numbers will increase because more have children late in life. As well, some are grandparents who are caring simultaneously for a grandchild and a parent. Still, one should not downplay the potential for burnout for spouses, generally wives, or daughters who reside with an aged loved one with severe limitations. This situation can be very detrimental to their health. Adult children who help care for a parent are far more stressed when the parent suffers from cognitive-behavioural than physical disabilities (Starrels et al., 1997). In contrast, when the parent's challenges are physical only, the parent-child relationship generally continues to include most of its previous elements. (The same situation occurs when it is a parent who cares for an adult child.)

So far, the research literature has emphasized the stress experienced by adult children, especially daughters, as a result of their role as caregivers of disabled parents. This stress is real and is related to role overload, and more hours result in even greater overload (Frederick and East, 1999). In this respect, the concept of **burden** is frequently utilized. This, in itself, is yet another social construct worth analyzing, because it reflects cultural values about intergenerational relations. For instance, one does not encounter this concept when studying the care that parents give to their children, unless the latter are adults and quite problematic. The reason is that caring for their young children is considered to be part of parents' role. However, when these same parents age and their health falters, help extended to them by their children is analyzed in terms of burden—when in other societies it is simply a duty or an adult child's role. As illustrated in Chapter 2, it is often a male child's role whereas in North America, it is a female child's duty, hence the aspect of **gender inequity** resurfacing once more (McDaniel, 2009).

In great part, the notion of burden arises from the misuse of the word "care." Few adult children actually take care of their parents; rather, they help them (Rosenthal, 2000; Turcotte and Schellenberg, 2007). Not surprisingly, there is also little research showing the positive side of caring for or helping one's elderly parents (Martin-Matthews, 2001). In this respect, Pruchno et al. (1997) have pointed out the importance of distinguishing between caregiving burden and caregiving satisfaction

(Northcott and Wilson, 2008:126). Cranswick (1997) has found that Canadians who help their elderly parents tend to be more positive than negative about this experience, even though a substantial proportion have had to make adjustments in their own lives in order to fulfill this duty, such as sleeping less, changing working hours, and taking fewer vacations. Dupuis and Norris (2001) have found that daughters of parents in long-term care facilities adopt a wide variety of roles/ attitudes in this respect. Robison and colleagues (2009) have shown that negative effects of caregiving largely stem from specific circumstances, in particular low income and lack of community help. Resilience, as Chappell and Dujela (2008) suggest, is a characteristic that deserves more attention as it provides for better adjustment.

Elderly adults who are **childless** are not less happy or in poorer health than those who have living children, although seniors receive more help when they have children (Kohler et al., 2005). What seems to count for the emotional well-being of the elderly is not whether they have children but the quality of the relationship between them and their progeny (Connidis, 2010). For instance, a warm relationship with adult children may increase parental longevity after widowhood. Childless elderly women generally have an economic advantage over other women their age (Plotnick, 2009). This is not surprising because it costs at least $167,000 to raise a child to age 18 and, in addition, childless women are much less likely to have had to interrupt their work years (Canadian Council on Social Development, 2006).

Children's and Parents' Gender

Daughters are far more likely to become their elderly parents' helpers and caregivers than sons (Michelson and Tepperman, 2003). The time demands and emotional costs of help are also higher among daughters than sons (Raschick and Ingersoll-Dayton, 2004). However, when a son has the responsibility for his parents, his involvement is as stable as that of a daughter (Martin-Matthews, 2001). Often, his wife assumes this duty or, at the very least, contributes to it. The key to receiving help resides in having one daughter, and married couples are more likely to respond to the needs of the wife's parents (Shuey and Hardy, 2003). This situation reflects the fact that women are generally assigned nurturing roles in society and learn to be responsible for the well-being of others from the time they are young (Abu-Laban and McDaniel, 2004). Consequently, parents may also expect more help from their daughters than their sons—although the reverse occurs in many other societies, such as China or Japan.

Starrels and colleagues (1997) have found that elderly parents who receive help from their children tend to reciprocate more with sons than daughters and provide less assistance to daughters than sons. Parents seem to appreciate their sons' caregiving more than their daughters' caregiving, perhaps because sons are still more valued and also because it is taken for granted that daughters are nurturing. It is expected that they will help their elderly parents as part of their feminine role. This gender expectation and the greater reciprocity with or recognition accorded to helpful sons may be reasons why daughters experience more stress than sons in their helping role. In general, female caretakers received less help than male ones (McDaniel, 2009).

Gender is a factor not only in who gives help but also in who receives it. As their health deteriorates, widowed mothers in their seventies and older receive more attention from their children than do widowed fathers. Silverstein et al. (1995) report that affection is a stronger motivator for help to older mothers, while expectation of an inheritance is more frequently a factor for assistance to fathers, although this is more the case among sons than daughters. Overall, there is a certain degree of ambivalence in the relationship of adult children to aging parents, and this is especially so among women, toward in-laws, and when the relationship was not optimal during childhood (Connidis, 2010; Wilson et al., 2003).

AN EXTENSION OF PARENTING: GRANDPARENTS

In the 19th century, adults who became grandparents for the first time were often still busy raising their younger children. Today, grandparenting tends to be a separate family developmental stage. As age at marriage is delayed, age at first grandparenting is also going up. In 1995, women were becoming grandmothers on average at age 53.6 and men were becoming grandfathers at age 56.8. As well, 79 percent of all adults aged 65 and over are grandparents and the average grandparent has 4.7 grandchildren (Statistics Canada, 2003f). This is an average that may soon diminish with the reduced birth rate. Indeed, the average 70-year-old grandparent today has 3 to 10 fewer grandchildren than his or her own parents' cohort had. The family tree becomes leaner. Thus, more generations are present in families but with fewer members in each generation. This is called the "bean pole" family because its structure is long and thin (Bengtson, 2001; McPherson, 1998).

The role of grandparents is not rigidly scripted; it is dynamic and fluid (Kemp, 2004; Rosenthal and Gladstone, 2000). It has been qualified as a stabilizing force and as a source of family continuity. Grandmothers enjoy their role more than grandfathers and are also more involved. They have been described as **kin-keepers** and as persons who open the kin system so as to support members in difficulty. The role that grandparents play differs according to their age, health, and ethnic group, as well as the age, gender, and location of their grandchildren. That role may differ for each grandchild; as Mueller and Elder (2003:413) point out, the grandparent-grandchild relationship should be studied within the context of the entire network of family ties.

King and Elder (1995) indicate that the quality of the relationship between grandparent and adult child has a significant impact on the grandparent-grandchild relationship, which may explain why grandchildren are closer to their maternal grandparents (Chappell et al., 2003; Monserud, 2008). Adult children who do not feel close to their parents or who perceive them to be meddlesome are less likely to encourage their children to visit them and to form close bonds with them. Similarly, it is possible that when children feel that their parents are not well treated by their grandparents, they may be reluctant to form close bonds. Parents act as mediators in the grandparent-grandchild relationship. One area of research that should soon be addressed is the family relationships of grandparents who are gay or lesbian (Connidis, 2003b).

Slightly over 40 percent of U.S. grandmothers provide care for at least one grandchild on a regular basis (Baydar and Brooks-Gunn, 1998). **They often babysit** while their daughters are at work. African-American grandmothers fill this role even more than their white counterparts, particularly when their daughters are single. We do not know whether more or fewer grandmothers are babysitting than was the case in the past when fewer young mothers were in the labour force and the necessity for regular child care was less urgent. As well, more grandmothers are now employed themselves, thus precluding extensive babysitting. Some even simultaneously help their older mothers. Grandmothers who have several children and grandchildren have more opportunities to become babysitters. This opportunity increases when a teenage daughter who lives with them has a baby. Grandmothers who simply babysit, and can do so without relinquishing their employment, may even harvest health benefits (Hughes et al., 2007).

Grandparents Who Raise Grandchildren

In 2006, 0.5 percent of all Canadian children were in the care of their grandparents to the exclusion of their own parents, for a total of 28,200 children between the ages of 0 and 14 (Statistics Canada, 2008g). Of course, the real numbers are higher because children aged 14 and over are not included. This is now called the "**skip generation**" household because no parent generation is present (Milan et al., 2009). However, another 181,700 children and a parent also lived with grandparents in an extended family arrangement. All in all, 3.8 percent of all children in this age group share a home with a grandparent, and this occurs more in some groups than others, particularly among Natives: 8 percent of Aboriginal children are in the **care** of grandparents or other relatives (Gionet, 2009). In 1995 in the U.S., 11 percent of grandparents reported that they had raised a grandchild for at least six months in their lifetime (Pearson et al., 1997). In some states, and particularly among African Americans, over a quarter of children in foster care are living with grandparents, generally a grandmother. In Canada, the numbers are more modest, in part because there are proportionally fewer never-married young mothers, and drug addiction is not as prevalent.

Grandchildren live with their grandparents because the child's mother suffers from emotional problems and/or addictions, including alcoholism. In half of the cases, mothers suffer from a multiplicity of problems—not to omit the fact that fathers are absent. Obviously, such grandparents are taking charge of children who have lived in deteriorating family circumstances, a situation well described in this student's autobiography:

More young grandmothers are employed than in the past. Therefore, it is necessary for research to address the issue of change in their roles, particularly as babysitters, in families where two generations of women who are mothers are now employed simultaneously.

"I was raised by my grandparents who took me and my little brother in after my mother flipped after my father left her. We had had a

hard life and all I remember about it is that my parents were scary [they were alcoholic]. *Anyways we were better off with my grandparents and we knew them because they had often kept us over weekends. . . . Now that we're older it's harder on them in a way because my brother grew up with lots of problems but at least I turned out just fine and this just makes up for it. . . . I love them like my own parents and we owe them everything and I am planning on making a lot of money to take care of them because they are getting on in years."*

Generally, grandchildren are thankful for the grandparents' intervention (Dolbin-MacNab and Keiley, 2009). In Canada, grandparents who single-handedly assume the financial responsibility of their grandchildren tend to be younger, healthier, and more educated than grandparents who live with their adult children and grandchildren (Milan and Hamm, 2003). In contrast, in the U.S., those who raise one or more grandchildren tend to be poorer than the average for their age group, more often unemployed, and less educated (Solomon and Marx, 1995). In Strawbridge and colleagues' (1997) longitudinal study, many of these grandparents had experienced negative life events in their own past, such as problems with marriages, finances, and health. The life course of many of these caregiving grandparents had differed from that of other grandparents for several decades, probably as a result of poverty. This is an example of how the consequences of poverty carry through the generations—from the grandparents to their children and their grandchildren, and back to the grandparents again.

Solomon and Marx (1995) used the National Health Interview Survey of 448 American households headed by grandparents to see how this type of family structure affected children's school and health outcomes. Children raised by grandparents were compared with children living with both biological parents and to children in single-parent families. In terms of behaviour at school as well as indicators of school achievement, children in two-parent families had an advantage over the other two groups. But children raised by grandparents were doing better than those with single parents, despite the generally low educational level of these grandparents. In terms of health, there were few differences between children in two-parent and grandparent families, but children in one-parent families were less healthy. Grandparents who raised girls had an easier time than those who raised boys. It should also be pointed out that research should be carried out on how the grandmother-grandfather conjugal relationship is affecting grandchildren (Smith and Hancock, 2010).

Being raised by a grandparent is a reasonable alternative for children, but it is a more problematic one for the grandparents (Burnette, 1999); this is especially so when they are middle-aged and are encountering high demands from several generations as well as employment (Sands and Goldberg-Glen, 2000). In fact, nonretired grandparents who take in a grandchild are far more likely to remain employed (Wang and Marcotte, 2007). Jendrek (1993) has studied the impact that this caregiving role has on grandparents' lifestyles, especially the changes that grandparents have to bring to their own lives, the dreams they have to postpone or abandon altogether, and the physical and emotional demands that such a role places on them to the detriment of their health (Bachman and Chase-Lansdale, 2005). Overall, foster grandparents find themselves out of synchrony with the normal developmental stage of family life: People of their age do not raise children. This anomaly deprives them of moral as well as instrumental support at their grandchildren's schools and in the neighbourhood. Hence, it is not surprising that support groups now exist for foster grandparents; these groups constitute an indicator of changing times (Beltran, 2001).

THE DEATH OF ADULTS' PARENTS

As they age, parents are transformed into patriarchs and matriarchs. When their health falters, their role vis-à-vis their children changes. A transitory period often occurs during which the elderly parent, generally the mother may reside in a long-term care facility. At that stage, the older person may renegotiate her sense of self in terms of what it means to be old and healthy, as one adult describes it:

> *"My mother is 90 and she is totally dependent for her care as she cannot stand up or walk, has Parkinson's in her hands, is in a wheelchair. But she thinks of herself as healthy because she has no illness, no cancer or heart problem, even though she is on medications. She is happy and accepts her dependency with good grace and considers herself lucky. Ten years ago, she would have felt very sorry for a person in her situation."*

Even though middle-aged and young senior adults fully expect their parents to die, this is an event that represents a transition both in their own individual lives and in the life course of their family system (Rossi and Rossi, 1990): The mantle is passed on to the next generation of older adult children who, if they themselves are grand-parents, form a new branch of the family, each with the generations that descend from them. The very large family reunions that used to take place around the now deceased generation become smaller gatherings as the grandparent couples or singles head their own extended families separately from those of their siblings. The families become smaller because the birth rate has declined.

Compared with the past, children and parents have a longer relationship because of an increase in life expectancy (Connidis, 2010). This means that both generations go through family transitions together or witness each other's transitions more often than in the early 1940s, for instance. A century ago, many parents did not even live long enough to see all their children marry (Martel and Bélanger, 2000). Most now do and even watch their children become parents; an increasing proportion see them become grandparents (Silverstein and Long, 1998). Thus, the relationship is not only longer but it also involves more shared life transitions than in the past.

The end result is that adults, particularly females, have a more extended period of time during which to identify with their parents and delay the rupture of the knot by death than in the past. The death of an elderly parent is equally momentous among all ethnic groups, but is expressed differently by men and women (Umberson, 2003). However, this death was probably a more significant passage in previous centuries when people's life expectancy was much shorter: The first generation left young adults and even dependent children orphaned, and the remaining spouses often quickly remarried, especially fathers.

CONCLUSIONS: CONTEXTS AND PERSONALITY ASPECTS IN THE PARENT-CHILD RELATIONSHIP

The parent-child relationship is best examined within the context of the life course of the two generations involved. Out of the child's relationship with his or her parents is born the adolescent relationship and from both flow the adult child-parent involvement, closeness, or conflict and distancing. In addition, the life course is a road that is paved with both risks and successes, most of which originate from the extra-familial environment. Therefore, social and cultural changes as well as economic situations can influence both the quality of parenting (which, in turn, influences child socialization and development to some extent) and of the parent-child relationship. Some of these social forces include peer groups as well as economic and cultural requirements that, for instance, lead to delays in departure of young adults from the parental home.

We consider the effect of personalities both on the quality of parenting and on the parent-child interaction. Parents' and children's personalities influence their behaviours and their subsequent reactions to one another. No longer are children considered a blank slate upon which parents write the script of their offspring's personalities and outcomes. Children are social actors who interact with their parents and contribute to the formation of their destinies. Children's personalities influence their familial environment just as do their parents' personalities. Personalities are the result of the interaction between nature and nurture and, in turn, the familial environment is also the result of this interaction between genetic and environmental forces, which are experienced over the generations. The future in the study of the parent-child relationship lies in the recognition of the combination of sociocultural and genetic influences on family members, a line of inquiry continued in Chapter 11.

Summary

1. The beginning of the parent-child relationship is rooted in the intersection between the infant's personality and needs, the parents' reactions to these needs, the feedback between the two levels of personalities and reactions, as well as the familial environment that they create.

2. The main types of parents' socialization practices are the authoritative, authoritarian, no-nonsense, permissive, uninvolved, neglecting, and even abusive. Socialization practices arise from the combination of (a) cultural and environmental determinants, including poverty and norms about what is considered "proper" parenting; (b) parents' personalities as well as beliefs; and (c) parental adaptation to children's behaviours, needs, and personalities. In this interactional perspective, children contribute to the development of their parents' socialization style. The matter of what constitutes proper parenting is analyzed as a social construct within its context. Research on the consequences of corporal punishment is discussed.

3. The parent-adolescent relationship is largely based on social definitions of adolescence. Adolescence is a social construct dating back to the 1890–1920 period. It is a cultural invention rather than an unavoidable and universal period of stress and turmoil.

Parent-adolescent conflict is generally about minor issues of daily living rather than crucial issues such as sex, drugs, and violence. This apparent paradox may stem from a lack of communication on these issues, the fact that adolescents and parents spend relatively little time daily in direct interaction, and the busy lives of parents. Overall, about one-third of youths have a very difficult adolescence and parent-child relationship.

4. Eras or time periods as well as the human qualities that are valued within each make it easier or more difficult for parents to influence their adolescents. Currently, the media are a key player in this domain.

5. Children's peers affect their relationship with their parents through the peer group spillover effect, the cross-pressures they place, and the relative solidarity of peer subcultures.

6. The timing of the passage into full adult independence is often postponed because of higher educational requirements, lower salaries, higher rents, and consumer expectations. Therefore, young adults often remain home longer than was the case in the 1980s. Furthermore, the family often undergoes transition reversals as some adult children return home. Coresidence is more difficult for parents when adult children remain financially dependent. Within the life course perspective, as children age and acquire new roles, the parent-child relationship generally remains strong, particularly with mothers. Several demographic variables contribute to the frequency of interaction, including the sex of both parent and child as well as geographic distance. Values, attitudes, and lifestyles may also be important variables.

7. Overall, elderly parents help their adult children substantially and are happier when they give than when they receive. Adult children help their elderly parents who become frail or disabled, but few actually undertake their entire care. The weight of care is heaviest when a parent becomes cognitively impaired, because the relationship is entirely altered. The concept of burden is discussed as a social construct. Daughters provide more help, particularly of a personal nature. Childless seniors are not less happy than others but they receive less help than those with children.

8. The grandparent role is not as culturally scripted. Grandmothers are more involved than grandfathers as kin-keepers and a substantial number provide some form of care for at least one grandchild on a regular basis. Some grandparents raise grandchildren who are in their custody. There are attendant stressors to this situation. The children, however, do better than children raised in a single-parent family, but less well than those with two parents.

9. The parent-child relationship has to be examined within the context of the personalities involved and the sociocultural situation in which the family is embedded.

Analytical Questions

1. How is social constructionism utilized in this chapter?
2. What does interactionism help explain in this chapter?
3. Are parents more or less influential in their children's lives than was the case in the 1950s, for instance?
4. Is there a new construction of young adulthood in the making? If yes, what are the consequences on family dynamics?
5. On the whole, which generation of adults benefits the most from the other in our type of society?

Suggested Readings

Alzheimer Society of Canada. January 2010. *Rising tide: The impact of dementia in Canada.* www.alzheimer.ca/english. This report presents statistics and projections to the year 2038 as well as policy implications.

Ambert, A.-M. 2001. *The effect of children on parents*, 2nd Ed. New York: Haworth. This book discusses at greater length the parent-child relationship within a variety of contexts. The theoretical perspective amalgamates interactional, ecological, as well as genetic theories.

Connidis. I. A. 2010. *Family ties & aging.* 2nd Ed. Thousand Oaks, CA: Sage. This book by a Canadian scholar presents an overview of family ties as they evolve in adulthood and particularly in older ages. It includes topics rarely covered elsewhere, such as step-relationships as well as various intimate relationships in later life.

Côté, J. E., and Allahar, A. L. 2006. *Critical youth studies: A Canadian focus.* Toronto: Pearson. This book provides the economic and sociocultural contexts that affect the current life conditions of young people. The focus is on market forces as the main catalyst in youth living conditions.

Crouter, A. C., and Booth, A. (Eds.) 2003. *Children's influences on family dynamics.* Mahwah, NJ: Erlbaum. Collection of articles on this neglected aspect of family life. These articles present several discussions between the contributing authors.

Paul, P., 2008. *Parenting, Inc.* New York: Time Books. A journalistic but well balanced and documented critique of the demands place on parents, particularly mothers, by intensive and commercialized parenting.

Rossi, A. S., and Rossi, P. H. 1990. *Of human bonding: Parent-child relations across the life course.* New York: Aldine de Gruyter. The authors present the results of three-generational research on parents and children and their relationships.

Suggested Weblinks

American Psychological Association
www.apa.org

National Council on Family Relations
www.ncfr.org

Society for Research in Child Development
www.srcd.org

Administration on Aging is a government agency offering information on the care of elderly parents, local resources, and other weblinks.
www.aoa.gov

Canadian Association of Retired Persons (CARP) has websites, information, and chat lines for elderly parents as well as grandparents.
www.carp.ca

Canadian Caregiver Coalition
www.ccc-ccan.ca

Canadian Institute of Child Health
www.cich.ca

Cangrands is a national support and information organization for grandparents raising grandchildren.
www.cangrands.com

National Institute on Aging also has information on elder care, including care by children.
www.nih.gov/nia

National Parenting Center is a centre for parenting information services. It offers information as well as chat rooms, all with the goal of promoting parenting skills.
www.tnpc.com

CHAPTER 11

Sibling Relationships and Situations

At age seven, my family structure became more complex: I inherited four European siblings, whom I had never met, ranging in age from 15 to 21. At the time, I was merely affected by the mixed blessing that such a drastic family restructuring brings to the life of a child and especially that of her 30-year-old mother. I was too little to appreciate how dislocated these fun-loving young people's lives had been. Their mother had died when they were small; my father had left them in the care of two of his sisters and had moved to Canada. When the Second World War arrived, they had to relocate to the southwest of France. Finally, two years after the war was over, they emigrated to Canada where they had to lead a more modest middle-class life shared with small siblings, one of whom had yet to be born.

Besides a large age gap, there were then and remain to this day striking differences between my father's two sets of children. For example, only one in the older group became a professional, whereas all of us younger ones did. We "little ones" had several advantages: We had stable lives and an energetic mother; we benefited from stimulating older siblings and our parents had a very happy marriage. True, we all shared one absent-minded, intellectual father who looked upon all of his children with some sort of "benign" annoyance. Nevertheless, whereas he was absent when the older children were growing up, we in the second group were able to prod him into helping us with our Latin and French homework, in which he would become as involved as we were. This engagement created bonds, stimulated our intellect . . . and led to great marks in school!

Our father had a gift for writing that ran in his family. A strange "coincidence" emerged: We children, so different from one another in terms of personality, life choices, and educational level, share one characteristic—all of us write well; five took up writing as a job in one form or another, and so far four of these have published books (in three different languages). Somehow, this peculiar aspect of my adult family profile is responsible for my awareness of the combined impact of environmental and genetic forces on family dynamics and human development. I have no doubt that some of us were born with this gift, but we would not have been able to develop it had our parents and the tradition in our family not encouraged us in this direction.

This autobiographical vignette—my own—introduces one of the key aspects of this chapter: the combined effect of the environment, including the familial one, and of genetic inheritance in the development of siblings' life course. Almost 80 percent of Canadians have at least one sibling; thus, it is a very important type of familial relationship, which also generally outlasts the parent-child relationship (McDaniel, 2009).

When children reach adulthood, the sibling relationship in industrialized societies, particularly those of western cultures, becomes discretionary. That is, continuing the relationship is a matter of choice and is secondary to the spousal and parent-child ones. In contrast, in other societies, continuation of the sibling relationship into adulthood is the norm and is of fundamental importance for a family's integration into society at large. Sibling relationships, particularly between two brothers or two sisters, may actually be more consequential than their relationship with a spouse, both at the social and economic level (Ogbomo, 1997). Still, in Canada, most adults perceive that they have obligations toward their siblings (Connidis, 2010).

THE SIBLING RELATIONSHIP BEGINS

The transition to a two-child family is one that parents have to help the first-born negotiate (Kramer and Ramsburg, 2002). Children who are between two and four years of age are particularly affected, because their entire life has been spent as their parents' only child. Children who are older are more competent cognitively and can understand the situation better. Parents may be able to appeal to their sense of being "grown up," as explained by this student:

> *"What I like best to remember when I was 5 is the birth of my little sister. I had wanted a brother to play hockey with but you can't be too choosy. What I liked best was that my parents made me feel so important, so grown up to be the big brother. I just loved to take care of her even though the novelty wore off after a while."*

Generally, whether the first-born child recognizes it or not, the birth of a second baby transforms his or her life entirely, as well as that of the family as a system. A new set of interactions is created, those between siblings. Each successive child enters the family at a different moment in its history and contributes to changing its environment (Zajonc, 2001). Furthermore, the family's economic resources available per person diminish with each new child. However, with the arrival of a second baby, the older child generally has a lower chance of experiencing a parental divorce: Happily married couples are more likely to add another child to their family than couples who are not happy together (Myers, 1997).

With the arrival of each baby, parents spend more time interacting with their children altogether, but they have less time for each child individually. After the arrival of the second child, parents can no longer maintain their exclusive relationship with the first-born, a factor that may become paramount in this child's life experience if he or she feels a loss of status as well as affection. The survival requirements of an infant are more urgent and constant than those of an older sibling. As a result, parents give more attention to younger than older children. With the arrival of the second child, the mother-child relationship often becomes less affectionate, particularly if the spacing between the two children is small and the family experiences a reduction in income per person. The mother's parenting style at times becomes more punitive and the older child may feel less securely attached (Teti et al., 1996). As a result of all these changes, the first-born child occasionally suffers from a variety of problems of adjustment, including anxiety, clinging behaviour, bed-wetting, and even aggressiveness.

The child's reaction to the baby's arrival is largely tailored by his or her personality as well as by the steps that parents undertake to reassure and involve him or her. Dunn (1994) points out that small children who are intense and less adaptable react more negatively to the baby's arrival than children with a sunnier and more content disposition. The former may even protest when the mother pays attention to the infant. The following amusing anecdote from a student portrays this situation:

> *"When my little sister was born, I was three, and when my parents brought her home I asked them to return her to the hospital. I did not like to see all the fuss over this little red faced creature that cried all the time. Then one day, seeing that my parents were not returning her, I tried to wrap her in gift wrapping paper and my mother caught me in the act. It's funny to think of this now because we are best friends and often laugh over it. My sister has had my mother tell this story over and over: She just loves it."*

Such an older child's reaction to the newborn often becomes part of the family culture: It constitutes a story everyone loves to hear.

Additional infants benefit from the experience that parents have acquired with their earlier-born children. Many first-born young adults, looking back on their past, feel that their parents acquired a great deal of skills at their expense:

> *"If I could relive my life, I would have wanted to be the second oldest child in my family. I disliked having to be the first to 'test the waters.' I wish that I had had an older sibling whose errors would have served as warning posts on what lay ahead. . . . I was a learning experience for my parents."*

> *"I changed my parents' views on a lot of things. I had to fight to get what I wanted and when my sister reached the same point in life, she didn't have to fight as hard as I did. I was jealous of her for the longest time, but now I have come to learn to deal with it."*

Obviously, the education that the first-born provides parents, while perhaps to the advantage of subsequent children, is often recalled as an injustice by the older child.

Consequences of Children's Spacing

During the newborn's first months, the infant's schedule is quite different from that of the older child, especially if the latter is already at school. With four years or more of spacing between the two children, the parents' relationship with the first-born may continue to be exclusive during a portion of the day as the baby sleeps. With this much spacing, each sibling is in a way an only child, and little competition takes place, especially if the older one likes to play at surrogate parenting:

> *"Surely the happiest memory I have of my mid-teens is when my mother announced that she was pregnant. This took a bit to get used to, you know the idea that your parents are 'doing it' . . . Then the best times arrived with my little sister. Oh how we loved that baby. . . . my mother was happy because she had less work to do as I always volunteered to take care of Kathy. . . . Now Kathy is seven and the brightest kid on the block because we provided her with an adult environment and each one of us in the family taught her different skills. . . . We read*

to her, made her read when she was three and took her skating, biking, rollerblading, swimming. She became incredibly well coordinated. She is also very sociable because despite all the spoiling she got from us older sisters and our cousins, we still insisted on good manners and no temper tantrums or anything of the sort. She had a whole batch of parents to raise her."

In terms of educational achievement, children do less well, on average, when they are closely spaced, and this holds true both for two-children and larger families (Powell and Steelman, 1993). For instance, parents have less individual time for two children who are close in age, because they essentially follow the same routine. When one child is several years older, however, the two children have different needs at different times and receive more individual attention. The older child is an only child longer and the younger child benefits both from having a sibling who is more developed and from parents who have more time for him or her. Much older siblings are more intellectually and socially stimulating for children than siblings closer to them in age (Zajonc and Mullally, 1997): Older children simply know more, as is illustrated in the student quote above. Smaller children tend to look up to them.

Consequences of Family Size

In terms of number of children, those from large sibling groups generally do not do as well at school, on average, as children from small families (Downey, 1995). Neither do they advance as much professionally later on as do adults coming from smaller families. These results become less salient but nevertheless remain when parents' social class is taken into consideration (Marks, 2006): Even upper-class parents provide fewer resources per child in large families than in small families (Fingerman et al., 2009). The concept used to explain this family size effect is the **dilution of parental resources**. In effect, this means that parents have fewer resources for each child individually, whether in terms of time, attention, and even economic means. In fact, mothers are less responsive to their children in larger families (Onyskiw and Hayduk, 2001). Therefore, a large sibling group often dilutes the quality of the home environment available to each child. This occurs even more so when children are closely spaced in a large family, because they interact more among themselves and have less adult attention; they also learn less than they would with one or two much older siblings or alone with their parents. Aggressiveness also appears more often in larger families (Stevenson, 1999), and children leave home earlier than in smaller families (Beaupré et al., 2006).

But, of course, there are plenty of exceptions to the rule and there are large families, particularly well-to-do ones, where all the children do very well at school or become high achievers in their professions later on. These families may benefit from other resources, such as the help of relatives and the presence of a large community of parents' friends and colleagues who contribute to stimulate children's intellectual development and serve as role models. The extended family increases resources and compensates for the dilution of the resources at the nuclear level. These families, in other words, have more **social capital** to offer each individual child.

Further, as Zajonc and Mullally (1997:697) pointedly remark, there are advantages to large family size that are not measured by the research perspectives emphasizing achievement. For instance, it may well be that siblings growing up in a large family are more "affiliative, more affectionate, good leaders, less prone to depression, or otherwise healthier." They may be less individualistic and more cooperative. They are used to sharing everything and adjusting to a far greater number of personalities. They can compromise and overlook frustrating situations. However, the only reasonably recent and large-scale study on this topic has not found any family size advantage in terms of sociability and need to be with others (Blake et al., 1991). Downey and Condron (2004) reported that having one or two siblings was positively related to better social skills; additional siblings did not provide more advantage.

On the other side of the equation, it is equally possible that some siblings in a large family suffer from a lack of individual recognition, feel oppressed by the social pressure within their intimate group, and are hampered by a lack of privacy. Such persons may adapt by growing up to be individualistic and may even distance themselves from the family group. However, despite having had less individual attention, there is no indication that adult children from large families are less attached to their parents nor their parents to them than in small families.

Multiple Births

One aspect of the sibling relationship that is still not sufficiently understood is the relationship that exists between twins and "multiples." As we see later, twins are much studied but are so within the perspective of behaviour genetics rather than simply as an interest in the relationship itself. Twins who are identical are fairly constant in the population: Dissimilar twins, also called dizygotic or DZ, are more related to heredity, thus can run in families (Hoekstra et al., 2008). *Normally*, twins and higher-order births occur in the population at the rate of 1 or 2 percent: one set of twins per 90 births; one set of triplets per 9,000 births; one set of quadruplets per 500,000 births. However, after 1972, triplet births increased by 156 percent, quadruplets by 386 percent, and higher-order births by 182 percent among white women, who constitute the majority of fertility clinics' clientele. In 1995 alone, 57 American infants were born who were quintuplets or sextuplets, although not all survived.

Women who have recourse to fertility drugs have a 25 percent chance of giving birth to more than one baby. Furthermore, women are more likely to release multiple eggs when they are older. Delaying parenthood consequently causes a rise in the number of multiple births. After the 1997 birth of the McCaughey septuplets, the less publicized 1998 birth of octuplets, and in 2009, the "Octo Mom," the medical establishment belatedly began considering the ethical ramifications of such births resulting from fertility treatments that allow the release of several ova or the implantation of multiple embryos. These pregnancies place mothers' lives in serious danger.

Nearly all multiple births have two immediate health consequences for infants: The fetuses have to compete for scarce resources in the womb, and a majority of the infants are born **prematurely** because the womb becomes too crowded. Twins therefore have low birth weight, and babies of higher-order births can have extremely low birth weights—as little as or less than half a kilogram. These infants are then at a far higher risk of neonatal death than singletons. The danger period may last

Twins and higher-order births occur more frequently than in the recent past because of fertility treatment and delayed conception. Their relationship and the relationship they have with their parents and other siblings in the family as well as with their peers need to be researched.

several months, during which the infants are kept in neonatal intensive care units. Prematurely born infants are also far more likely than others to suffer from neurological deficits, whether learning disabilities or muscle coordination problems, although most of them make remarkable progress—and most twins and triplets develop well. For parents, twin and multiple births require a far greater adjustment to parenting than does a single birth (Golombok et al., 2007): more time demands; fewer economic resources available per capita; the necessity to seek and accept help, even from total strangers; and more health-related concerns. All of these factors combined make it imperative that we learn more about the impact that such an event has on the life of an older sibling and on the various sibling relationships that occur in these families compared with those of "regular" ones.

CHILD AND ADOLESCENT SIBLING RELATIONSHIPS

At the personal level, sibling relationships are determined by children's characteristics, their personality similarities and differences, parents' behaviour toward the children, and siblings' perception of such. Given that most of these factors are reasonably stable through each childhood, one can expect a certain degree of stability in the sibling bond. Yet, as children age, relationships can also change (Richmond et al., 2005). As well, the availability of peers as alternate playmates in later childhood and early adolescence is likely to bring change in the relationship. Generally, brothers and sisters whose personalities are compatible or complementary experience greater connectedness than those who are temperamentally incompatible. When one child has an intense or unadaptable personality, sibling interactions are more conflictual. As well, high-activity siblings get in one another's way and their requirements clash quickly and frequently.

Furman and Lanthier (1996) gave personality tests and a relationship questionnaire to 56 triads of mothers and two siblings, one age nine and the other age 11. They found that it was the older child's personality that more strongly affected the distribution of power in the relationship. The dimensions of conscientiousness and agreeableness, particularly in the older child, were strong predictors of harmony and lack of power struggle.

Dunn and colleagues (1994) found that older siblings tend to be fairly consistent over time in their behaviour toward their younger brother or sister: Aggressiveness or friendliness persists. This means that, in some families, younger children spend their entire childhood with a friendly and supportive sibling, whereas in others, they are in a relationship that is hostile, disparaging, and physically aggressive. The impact on child development may be substantial, but it is a question that is rarely raised in research, because theories focus on parental rather than **sibling effect**. *It is* *possible that negative effects that have been attributed to parents and to their harsh or rejecting treatment actually result from the rough handling that a child has received from siblings or from siblings and parents together* (Richmond et al., 2005). Such a possibility makes sense from the perspective of genetics alone: Intolerant and irritable parents may produce some offspring who are like them and may jointly have a negative impact on the sibling who is different from the outset.

In contrast, younger siblings show less stability of behaviour toward their older siblings: They adapt their style of interaction in order to secure the older child's goodwill. The older child does not have to adapt, because it is the younger ones who do. Overall, older siblings tend to be more domineering, and younger ones are forced to be more compliant in the relationship. Putting these variables together, it is therefore not surprising that, in terms of development, the older child usually, but not always, has a stronger effect on the younger one than vice versa (Dunn et al., 1994).

By the time they were 12 or 13 years old, first-born boys in a longitudinal study by Dunn (1996) reported a more distant relationship with their younger siblings than did first-born girls. This difference was, in part, explained as a result of the older boys' growing ties with their peer group. As well, the second-born children were becoming more assertive and more willing to disagree with the older boys, and this in turn contributed to the cooler climate. These pitfalls were less in evidence with older sisters. Indeed, **girls** maintain more intimate bonds with both siblings and peers than do boys (Kim et al., 2006; Updegraff and Obeidallah, 1999). Thus, females begin at an early age their function of **kin-keepers** and emotional workers, as described in Chapters 9 and 10.

For a girl, having an older brother in most societies often represents a precious social resource in male-dominated peer groups. Older brothers who are popular serve as protectors and may also enhance a child's status among peers at school:

> *"It was great having an older brother with so many friends. I remember playing foot hockey with them. I would give all to the game so that my brother would be proud of me.* . . . *After a few games of hockey with the guys, I gained my proud nickname, 'The little green monster.'* . . . *When I was in fifth grade I was known among all the grades.* . . . *It helps to have brothers who are both younger and older than you, since you become familiar with the students."*

Later on, the older brother's social circle may include males who can accompany a younger sister to parties without her having to date. This circle of friends may also be a source of dates.

Another interesting aspect in the study of siblings is that they do not perceive their relationship similarly (Whiteman and Christiansen, 2008). Dunn and McGuire (1994:120) mention that only 23 percent of the siblings in their sample reported a degree of closeness similar to that reported by their brother or sister. This discrepancy may be explained by the age and gender differences among siblings. Smaller children may be more susceptible to feeling left out by older siblings who, for their part, may be more involved with peers and largely ignore the younger ones. Girls may find their brothers less supportive, whereas boys may find it "normal" to ignore their sisters who are "just girls."

Sibling Influence

As we have seen in the previous chapter, peers are a powerful source of influence on children and adolescents. In contrast, sibling influence and pressure are rarely acknowledged in research—as is sibling abuse (Chapter 13). McHale and Crouter (1996) report that preteens spend 33 percent of their out-of-school hours with siblings versus 13 percent with friends. These numbers alone should predict a great deal of sibling influence. What information do researchers have?

Overall, when an older sibling is competent, the younger one is positively affected (Brody and Murry, 2001). Contrariwise, when an older sibling is aggressive, the other tends to follow suit, even at a very young age (Baillargeon et al., 2002). But this is less likely to happen with pairs of older brothers and younger sisters (Williams et al., 2007). Thus, siblings are important agents of socialization to one another in this respect, and probably in many others that have yet to be researched (Garcia et al., 2000). The aggressive interaction style of the older boys in a family trains the younger boys to be equally coercive (Criss and Shaw, 2005). There is a significant level of concordance among boys in a family in terms of delinquency: When one boy is delinquent, there is a good chance that the other one also is. The same has been found for girls (Slomkowski et al., 2001). Furthermore, when one adolescent abuses alcohol, the other is at risk of doing so.

In terms of sexuality, Widmer (1997) reports that older siblings have an effect on the timing of first intercourse among their younger brothers and sisters. Adolescent girls who have a sexually active or childbearing adolescent sister, as well as similar peers, tend to be more sexually active, even when other family variables, such as education, are taken into consideration (Powers and Hsueh, 1997). East (1999) reasons that a birth to a teenager may make it more difficult for mothers to supervise their younger children, as the grandchild increases the new grandmother's workload. Brothers are even more influential than sisters in the timing of sexual intercourse. When older brothers remain chaste longer, their behaviour may reinforce parental teachings on sexual restraint by giving them validity in the mind of younger siblings. However, East et al. (1993) point out that this fraternal influence is less important than parental attitudes and teachings on this topic.

These results together indicate that older siblings act as **role models** for younger ones (Jenkins-Tucker et al., 2001). As well, the sharing of activities leads to an indirect form of influence. An older sibling's treatment of the younger one serves as an incentive to adopt this interactional style in other relationships. These results could also indicate that siblings share an environment that encourages certain behaviours over others, whether at home, school, or in the

Sibling relationships are more important to each child's well-being and development, particularly the younger one's, than is generally believed. Hence, not enough research has been devoted to the sibling role and influence when children are growing up.

neighbourhood. A complementary explanation is that siblings share certain personality characteristics that make them equally vulnerable or equally resilient to life's circumstances.

One also has to mention that siblings do have an influence on the level of happiness of their brothers and sisters. For instance, Richmond et al. (2005) have found that, as sibling relationships become warmer and less conflictual over time, children's feelings of depressed mood also declined. But, when the relationship worsened, children became more depressed.

Siblings Who Share Peers

Sibling influence can be compounded by the sharing of friends. During adolescence, and more in adulthood, siblings' similarity of characteristics seems to increase friendliness and contact as well as the sharing of friends. In turn, frequency of positive contact contributes to an increased resemblance between siblings over the long term, especially with regard to ideas, values, and leisure activities. One would expect that the sharing of a prosocial peer group by siblings enhances their own prosocial behaviours. This, in turn, greatly facilitates parental duties as these prosocial children are probably easier to raise. This network of peers becomes a form of **social capital** to both parents and children. Prosocial peers are also more likely to have authoritative parents; when a group of peers have similarly oriented parents, the burden of supervision is lessened for each individual set of parents, given that they all participate to some degree in the monitoring process (Fletcher et al., 1995). This refers us back to the concepts of the **effective community** and group or collective socialization.

By the same token, when siblings who are already predisposed to deviance share a delinquent or aggressive peer group, this raises the chance that they will commit delinquent acts. Consequently, parents must increasingly monitor such offspring and set more limits on their activities and whereabouts. This demanding level of supervision and alertness may go beyond the abilities of many parents, as indicated in the following passage from a female student's autobiography. It graphically illustrates the family dynamics that may occur during adolescence when siblings are closely spaced, get along well, and encourage one another and peers in activities that parents disapprove of:

> *"The problem with my family at that age is that there were four adolescent children, two boys, two girls, and we actually ran the house. There was nothing that our parents could do to control us. If we wanted some friends over for the night, we'd hide them and my parents would not notice. Anyway, they hated to come in our rooms which were an absolute mess. . . . My brother got a girl pregnant when he was only 15 and my sister became a drug addict at 16. The other two of us turned out all right, which is amazing considering the bad example we got from the other two and the fact that we used to encourage their misbehaviour, side with them, and help them out when in trouble. We had absolutely no solidarity with our parents. It was just among us children, as we were one or two years apart. Our second solidarity was for our friends."*

Supportive Sibling Relationships

The literature on the family is by necessity often oriented toward the study of problems rather than daily dynamics. One of the consequences of this orientation is that there is relatively little research on supportive sibling relationships during childhood and adolescence (Jenkins-Tucker et al., 2001). The major exceptions pertain to brothers and sisters whose parents are conflictual, divorce, or remarry, and to children who have a sibling suffering from a disability. Indeed, sibling support is very important to the 3 percent of Canadian children who have disabilities, as most live at home: Parents usually shoulder the responsibility of caring for or coordinating their care well into adulthood. A cooperative sibling can greatly lighten parents' burden; parents often develop particularly warm feelings for that helpful adult child, as illustrated in this situation:

> *"My older sister is retarded and has some heart problems so that my relationship with her is one of role reversal. She is five years older than me but I take care of her a lot to give some breathing space to my parents. When I was a bit younger . . . once in a while our needs clashed with hers or the demands our parents placed on us because of her. She does look normal and my mother often asked us to take her out with us to see a movie or something of the sort. Jackie loved it but it was different for us because we wanted to be with our friends and felt unpleasantly 'special.'. . .*
>
> *My parents really appreciate what we do for her and for them because they say that they trust that we will take care of her after they are gone, which is the biggest worry that parents of delayed adult children have. My brother and I will take care of her for sure although thankfully our parents are still young. But I think that of the two of us I may end up having to do most of the caring because I noticed that my brother does less than he used to do—he is a male!"*

However, in reality, there is no indication that siblings become the primary caregivers of their disabled brother or sister when parents are no longer able to do so. Many of these disabled individuals have to turn outside the family for help (Pruchno et al., 1996). Siblings of a person with an intellectual deficit develop an obligatory relationship and remain more connected, although not necessarily close to the family. In contrast, siblings of a person with a mental illness are more distant and suffer from more psychological difficulties than others in average families. This is partly the result of a shared genetic vulnerability and of growing up in a more stressful family environment (Taylor et al., 2008).

Seltzer and colleagues' study (1997) also indicates the necessity to help "the mentally ill develop less confrontational behaviors with their siblings." The researchers found that adults had a higher level of well-being and a closer relationship with a sibling with a mental delay than a sibling with a mental illness. Siblings, like parents, are affected more negatively by behavioural and attitudinal problems than by intellectual limitations. In other words, adults who experience better psychological well-being are those whose siblings with mental illness are kept at a distance. This also means that the sibling with mental illness receives less support than the one with mental delay, unless the latter also exhibits difficult behaviours. Horwitz (1993) suggests that therapists should encourage adults with emotional problems to develop mutual relationships with their siblings, given that people are more willing to help someone who reciprocates.

During childhood and adolescence, having a brother or sister with special needs also carries costs (LeClere and Kowalewski, 1994). The literature is quite unanimous in this respect and the previous student quote illustrates this dilemma (Kilmer et al., 2008). The siblings of special needs children generally get less parental attention because so much is demanded for the care of the affected children. The family can less easily pursue leisure activities than other families, and friends cannot be invited home, lest they disrupt the routine of care. When a sibling with disabilities is aggressive toward the helping child or adolescent, the latter tends to be less well adjusted emotionally.

During Parental Conflict, Divorce, and Remarriage

Brothers and sisters, especially older ones who function well, can act as a buffer for their younger siblings at times of marital conflict or divorce, or in the event of a parent's illness or emotional problems. However, so far, the research indicates that this type of sibling support is not always forthcoming—for instance, divorce actually increases negative interactions between siblings (Kim et al., 1999). In fact, a conflictual relationship between parents is more likely to lead to, or be accompanied by, greater sibling conflict (Poortman and Voorpostel, 2009). Conger and Conger (1996:119) find that "it is the actual disruption of marriage rather than the degree" of parental conflict in intact marriages "that most adversely affects relations between brothers and sisters." This effect of divorce on the sibling relationship is one that is infrequently mentioned in the more recent literature on the consequences of marital breakup.

This greater sibling conflict can be explained by a combination of variables. For one, conflict between parents, and even more so the divorce itself, dilutes familial resources so that stress and emotional deprivation pit each child against the other for scarce parental attention. Second, the stressors experienced by parents spill over into their childrearing practices and lead to sibling friction. Third, a portion of divorcing couples may have difficult personalities and their children may have inherited these predispositions so that the children develop conflictual relationships among themselves. Furthermore, the spacing between children has not been considered in these studies: Sibling friction may occur only when there is little age difference among them, because of competition for scarce resources such as parental attention.

Hetherington (1988) finds that the presence of a stepfather is often accompanied by fractious sibling interactions. Children, and especially boys, reaching adolescence disengage more from their siblings in remarried than in married families (Anderson and Rice, 1992). But among those sibling groups that remain cohesive, mutual support reduces the number of problems experienced when they are exposed to parental conflict (Jenkins and Smith, 1990). In families with two children, the presence of at least one girl enhances the chance that a cohesive sibling relationship is established (Conger and Conger, 1996). Thus, once again, children's gender is an important variable.

DIFFERENTIAL PARENTAL TREATMENT

As seen earlier, parents treat children differently depending on each child's age. The focus of this section is on children and adolescents. However, differential parental treatment is probably even more common in adulthood. In fact, Suitor and Pillemer (2000) have found that children's personal problems resulting from their own acts, such as drug use or criminality, are related to a weaker bond with parents. Thus, as children age and make life choices, differential treatment from parents may become more prevalent, although not necessarily more visible to the children themselves.

The younger child is favoured by both parents in some circumstances, yet the older one is in others. It is not uncommon, either, that by adolescence mothers are closer to one identical twin than the other (Crosnoe and Elder, 2002). Furthermore, fathers show more interest in sons, particularly first-borns, and in children who have a more expressive personality (Crouter et al., 1999; see Family Research 11.1 for other aspects of this study). Parents who are stressed by poverty or marital conflict or who are depressed are more likely to treat one child less well than the other. Differential treatment can also involve chore assignments as well as privileges (Tucker et al., 2003).

Birth Order and Developmental Stage as Factors

A longitudinal study yielded high correlations between a mother's treatment of the older child at age two and her subsequent treatment of the younger child at the same age. That is, it appears that mothers treat children in a manner appropriate to each

---

FAMILY RESEARCH 11.1

Parents' Knowledge of Each Sibling's Daily Activities

Crouter and colleagues (1999) wanted to see if parents would be more aware of the older sibling's or the younger sibling's daily life, and whether this knowledge would depend on the children's sex, personality, as well as parents' employment hours. Letters were sent to the homes of fourth- and fifth-graders in 16 central Pennsylvania school districts. The 203 participating families were headed by two parents with at least two children, and the second sibling had to be younger by one to four years.

In a first step, family members were interviewed at home separately; parents and children also filled out questionnaires. Questions were read aloud when children's literacy skills required it. In a second step, both parents and children were interviewed over the phone on several different evenings during a two- to three-week period. Parents and children were queried about their daily activities. An interesting aspect of this research consisted of questions designed to measure parents' knowledge of their children's activities:

- Did child X have English homework today? What was the assignment?
- Did child X watch TV, videos, or movies at home today? What did he or she watch?
- Did child X have any conflict or disagreement with a friend today? Which friend?
- Was child X outside the home at 4 p.m. today? Where was he or she?

age level, so that both children are treated similarly at a given age, yet are treated differently in the present because they are of different ages (Dunn et al., 1986; Whiteman et al., 2003). But the correlations between the maternal treatment of the children at the same age are not perfect. This suggests, first, that mothers adapt their behaviour to each child's individuality and developmental rhythm (Volling, 1997). Second, the later-born child enters the family system at a different point in the **family's life course**. The mother is now a more experienced parent; she may also be busier or more tired when the younger child is two years old than she was when the older one was the same age a few years earlier. This difference in treatment could also be explained by any other factor that may have changed in the child's and mother's lives and environment. For instance, when child B reaches age two, the parents may have separated and the mother may be under more (or less) stress than she was when child A was age two. Her higher or lower level of stress could affect her parenting vis-à-vis the younger child.

To sum up, it seems that mothers tend to treat their children similarly at a given level of child maturity. But they are not necessarily as consistent toward the same child while he or she is growing up because children change with age, and some become easier or more difficult; as well, the parental context evolves. In some families, it is obvious that parents treat their children differently, not simply because of age, but because of birth order: A certain favouritism may exist for a younger child and a more adult relationship with the older one (Suitor and Pillemer, 2007). As well, one offspring may be less adaptive or need more encouragement or structure, as is illustrated in the following student quote:

> *"My parents have always treated my sister differently than they have me. . . . School came easier to her and my parents treated her as the smart one. They were much more concerned about whether I did homework or not and how my marks in school were; I was under much more scrutiny. . . . My sister was allowed to stay up later, go out for longer, do more things, and have more fun."*

Information concerning parenting consistency during adolescence and later ages is lacking. As children grow older, it is quite possible that parents treat them increasingly differently so as to respond to their developmental needs. Children may contribute to this differential treatment as they try to differentiate themselves from their siblings in order to assert their own individuality.

Gender as a Factor

Gender is one of the most important variables in child socialization (Kimmel, 2000). Parents raise boys and girls to assume different roles in society, although families vary in the extent to which they socialize boys and girls differently. Overall, fathers are more likely than mothers to make a distinction between sons and daughters and are generally more involved with sons (Harris and Morgan, 1991). In the student autobiographies, parents are reported as treating sons and daughters increasingly differently as they age. Women students repeatedly complained that adolescent brothers were given much more freedom than they had been allowed at the same age. In some ethnic groups, a slightly older brother or even a younger one chaperones a sister whenever she goes out, especially in the evenings. Causing even more resentment is the fact that these girls have to do more housework, age for age, than their brothers, and some even have to clean up after them:

"In my family, there are two standards: one for my brother and one for my sister and I. We girls do everything in the house and work to pay for school whereas my brother does nothing and works to pay for his car and dates. I really resent it even though I try to rationalize it this way, that my parents come from a non-Christian background, but it does not erase the unpleasant reality. People who immigrate here should leave behind their unpleasant backgrounds and adapt to what families do here which is by and large to treat boys and girls the same."

"My brother gets to go out without even telling my parents where he is going. My sister and I have to tell my parents everything, where we are going, what time we will be home and so on."

The more males are valued in a culture, the greater the difference in parental treatment. (In fact, in some societies experiencing scarcity, sons are given the best food while daughters go hungry.) However, it is possible that, in large families, parents have less time to react to each child's gender and accordingly treat their offspring more similarly than do parents with fewer children. Or, alternatively, they may treat all the boys one way and all the girls the other way. In other instances, fathers feel closer to sons and mothers to daughters because they share same-sex interests, aspirations, and chores.

Developmental Impact of Differential Treatment

The sibling who receives the most favourable parental treatment seems to be doing better than the other (Richmond et al., 2005). Daniels (1987) reports that the sibling who enjoys more affection from the father has more ambitious educational and vocational goals. Children who are more controlled by their mother or perceive receiving less affection than their siblings are more likely to be anxious or depressed. These children also tend to be more difficult.

The Interactional Perspective

Differential parental treatment may not produce the entirety of these reported outcomes (Feinberg et al., 2000). Rather, the interactional perspective suggests a bidirectional causality. For instance, a difficult child may lead parents to become more controlling or, yet, more permissive (Moilanen et al., 2009). Or such children may be treated more harshly (Richmond et al., 2005). It may also be that a more ambitious child attracts paternal attention and encouragement. That is, his or her ambitions create or evoke the favoured attention rather than vice versa. It is also possible that it is the perception and interpretation of differences rather than the actual differential treatment that cause the problems for the child who feels deprived (Reiss et al., 1995). In other words, children may not be adversely affected when their parents give more attention to a sibling if they find that this is justifiable on the basis of a younger sibling's needs, for instance.

In great part, except for gender roles, parents respond to their children according to their personalities and behaviours, as seen in the preceding chapter. Thus,

Bank et al. (1996) find that parents behave differently with a boy who is aggressive and oppositional than with his easy-going sibling. In their experimental study, one group of families had both a difficult and an easy-going boy while the other set of families had two "easy" children. The researchers observed family interactions when the difficult son was present and then when he was absent. The two samples showed different parental treatment of their children when the difficult boy was included. But when only the parents and the easy-going child were considered together, there was no difference between the two samples of families in the way parents treated their children. This result illustrates the impact of a child on family dynamics and on the creation of differential parental treatment. Children may contribute to create the differential treatment they receive from their parents. This being said, however, whatever its origins, differential parental treatment can be related to negative outcomes longitudinally (Shanahan, L., et al., 2008).

Situations That Cushion or Exacerbate the Impact

Volling (1997) makes a distinction between *differential favouritism*, which has negative consequences for family relationships, and *differential discipline*. Among preschoolers, she found that when the older child was disciplined more often than the younger one, the family functioned better than when it was the younger one who was more often disciplined. The reason for this observation is that, in the latter case, parents were not taking into consideration the children's respective developmental levels. They were probably as demanding of the younger as of the older one—a situation that creates difficulties because the younger child has not yet developed the ability to meet such maturity demands.

Differential parental treatment that does not appear fair to children causes jealousy and resentment on the part of the less favoured child, and may well give rise to feelings of entitlement on the part of the preferred child, who becomes the little king or queen. The less favoured offspring may become more distant or express his or her resentment toward the preferred one (Shanahan, L., et al., 2008). These negative feelings may be the result of justified jealousy or, alternatively, it may be the result of the more difficult personality of the less favoured child, who behaves less pleasantly toward siblings and parents alike. As well, negative feelings on the part of parents may spill over into sibling relationships (Jenkins et al., 2005a). Indeed, favouritism by mothers in childhood results in a weaker sibling bond; this perceived favouritism continues to influence the sibling relationship into adulthood. As Suitor et al. (2009:1036) point out, this demonstrates "continuity in family processes across the life course."

McHale and colleagues (1995) as well as Volling (1997) grouped families depending on whether both parents were congruent (displaying more affection for the same child) or incongruent (each parent preferring a different child). Congruent parents predominated. Incongruence tends to occur among couples whose relationship is distressed: These parents at times form a coalition with different children against each other (Kan et al., 2008). When this occurs, the parent-child boundaries melt away while boundaries between parents rise. This situation also makes it difficult to raise children authoritatively. In contrast, parents who get along maintain the boundaries of the parental system and tend to agree on which child needs more support.

Thus, one sees the importance of studying parents' differential treatment in the **context** of other variables, such as marital happiness, number and spacing of off-spring, and marital status (Jenkins et al., 2005b). It is not known, for instance, if differential treatment has a more negative impact in a poor quality environment or in a more privileged environment, or in families that have children of only one sex or of both. Moreover, differential treatment may produce effects that vary according to parental personality, relative parental power within the family, and overall level of parenting involvement. For example, a parent who has little power or who is perceived to be weak may not have the same impact as one who is psychologically strong and is dominant in the family. Siblings may notice it more if they are treated differently by a dominant parent than by a weak one. As illustrated by the following mature student, some children seem to perceive their mother's lower social prominence and "shrug off" her differential behaviours toward them, yet are affected when the father does not treat them equally, however small the slight might be:

"At home, I am in a rather unfortunate situation: Although I am always available to the children and am really their maid, when their father is around I am just as good as not there. They hang on to his every word and find him so interesting. He doesn't even have to ask them to do something, they just do it. One or the other children gets very upset if he doesn't talk to him or her or gives equal treatment. They're like courtesans around a king. Me, what am I? Nothing! So if I yell at one, that one doesn't even notice it. If I give him a compliment, they shrug it off. It has more or less always been like that: My husband is quite the social butterfly, looks good, and is known to a lot of people. In contrast, I am the somewhat mousy wife about whom people wonder, 'Whatever did he find in her?'"

ADULT AND STEPSIBLING RELATIONSHIPS

Personalities and lifestyles are fairly important in determining the quality of adult sibling bonds, particularly in view of the fact that these relationships are largely optional (Connidis, 2007, 2010). Furthermore, the literature on remarriage has been so focused on problems of adult and child adjustment that little attention has been devoted to the new relationships that are formed among children from the merging families. Not only is there little information on the relationship between stepsiblings, but there is equally little on that between halfsiblings (i.e., when new children are born in a remarriage).

Adult Sibling Relationships

Among adults in North America, proximity increases contact among siblings and the potential for both conflict and closeness. When no other family member lives nearby, proximity also increases the exchange of help between siblings (Miner and Uhlenberg, 1997). Different lifestyles and resources can create barriers to closeness (Connidis, 2007). Cicirelli (1996) points out that older persons like to reminisce about the past. They can do so far better with like-minded siblings than with their adult children. Thus, siblings remain important confidants as well as sources of

Although there is some research on middle-aged and older siblings, there is still relatively little literature devoted to sibling relationships during the young adult years, after siblings have established their own families, especially during the years of childrearing. Neither is the role and influence of cousins studied, in part because researchers in western societies do not pay as much attention to the extended family system as perhaps they should.

emotional support, especially after widowhood, but are less central in terms of companionship (Campbell et al., 1999; Connidis and Campbell, 1995). One area of sibling relationship that requires far more research at all age levels pertains to the homosexuality of one sibling, as well as her or his living in a same-sex union (Connidis, 2003b).

We return here to the theme of **gender** in the sibling relationship. Overall, bonds are closer between sisters than between brothers, although there are many exceptions (Spitze and Trent, 2006; Weaver et al., 2004). Further, sisters provide more help to each other as well as to other family members than do brothers (White, 2001); this pattern is more obvious in some ethnic groups than others. For males, a good relationship with their sisters is also important for their morale: Elderly men who have more sisters feel happier and more secure (Cicirelli, 1989). This result probably stems from the greater familial cohesiveness that exists in families that have females and from the nurturing role to which women are socialized. Sisters provide moral support to their brothers and this contributes to the latter's sense of well-being. But sisters do not benefit equally from fraternal support, as brothers have not generally been socialized to be nurturing and supportive. For both genders, ties with siblings are particularly important after widowhood and in periods of crisis (Connidis, 2010).

Siblings are more likely to be supportive of one another when parents are also supportive (Voorpostel and Blieszner, 2008). In contrast, differential parental treatment that was perceived to be unfair when the children were growing up often extends its negative consequences into adulthood and is reflected in the siblings' later relationships. Siblings who were less favoured, or who perceived they were, may feel that they have been cheated and, as they age, may distance themselves from the others. They may find alternative sources of moral support. These relationships may even be more conflictual. In some cases, jealousy continues into old age, even though there never was any factual basis for it—it was simply a matter of perception, which one male student deplores:

"I have never been able to understand why my older brother and sisters are still so jealous of me. It's very painful to me at this age [about 23] because I have never done anything and neither have my parents to attract this attitude. I was sick more often as a child and my parents had to worry about me more. But the older ones had a lot more freedom and they got much more financially: They didn't have to pay for school as I am doing. At my age they all had cars and I don't. I should be the one who is jealous, really. It's just in their heads and it's upsetting because they certainly don't go out of their way to encourage my little nephews and nieces to accept me."

Stepsibling Relationships

Stepsibling relationships have, on average, a greater potential for conflict (Jenkins et al., 2005b). However, remarriages are often brief and stepchildren do not always live in the same household, so that many of these relationships simply do not have the time or the opportunity to blossom. Each set of stepsiblings may simply be an element of curiosity for the other. A nonresidential father's children may feel some degree of animosity toward his new wife's children who live with him. This animosity or jealousy can be provoked by the fact that many nonresident fathers see their own children rarely or do not support them unless forced to by the government:

"My feelings for my father . . . I can't say with 100% certainty that I love him because we have always been his invisible children. . . . I can't stand his wife's children after all those years because they have it all: My father has been very good to them and they've always been in the way, like we can't see him without these two being there and grabbing all the attention."

"So I have a stepsister who is two years older than I am. At first, we hated each other. . . . Now we are not close but we get along quite well now that we don't have to see each other often."

When the remarriage lasts, stepsiblings often become companionable and supportive, and maintain some level of connectedness into adulthood (Anderson, 1999).

"My two stepbrothers were then 2 and 4 years younger than me and they looked up to me so that I soon ended up playing big brother. For a 10-year-old who is rather upset at what has happened to his parents, that was a great thing. We got along famously well and have been a team to this day."

Being a female increases the likelihood of contact between siblings (and we note for the fourth time in this chapter the role that females play in sibling integration and solidarity). The stepsibling relationship is closer when there are no full siblings. Half-siblings and stepsiblings may be better able to bond when the type of solidarity that generally exists between two full siblings, whether biological or adopted, is absent. The former may then serve as substitute siblings and all accept one another as such. Even among older cohorts, more conflict is reported between halfsiblings and stepsiblings than between full siblings, perhaps in part because they have at least one parent they do not share. Halfsiblings and stepsiblings also help one another less in old age than do full siblings.

All in all, in adulthood, the longer stepsiblings have lived together as children, the closer the bond. Having lived with one's mother and stepfather also leads to more contact than having lived with one's father and a stepmother—again indicating the salience of relationships that are maintained by a mother: Halfsiblings who share a mother tend to be closer than those who share a father (Bernstein, 1997).

HOW CAN SIBLINGS BE SO DIFFERENT?

As anticipated through the autobiographical vignette at the beginning of the chapter, we now turn to investigate the question of why siblings can be so different. This issue is linked to the investigation of the role that genes and the environment play in human development.

What Are the Sources of Sibling Differences?

Dunn and Plomin (1990) have documented how dissimilar siblings generally are on at least some important personality characteristics and related behaviours. Everyday experience also presents the reader with many opportunities to observe such differences between two brothers or two sisters who are only one to three years apart. Yet, children in the same family are exposed to a **shared environment** that includes family structure, family routines and events, values and teachings emphasized by parents, as well as the effects of parents' personalities on family functioning (Lemelin et al., 2007). The traditional socialization perspective predicts that this shared environment should make siblings quite similar in terms of personality characteristics, values, behaviours, and even adult lifestyles. Furthermore, each child inherits 50 percent of his or her genetic makeup from the mother and the other 50 percent from the father. Thus, siblings inherit their genetic makeup from the combined gene pool of a same mother and father—hence, one more reason for them to be similar. Why are they not? There are four reasons.

First, siblings are different because each inherits a different **combination** of their **parents' gene pool**. Let's take two sisters, Linda and Jenny. Linda looks like the father physically but is also sociable like the mother; in contrast, Jenny looks like the mother but is shy and reserved like the father is. We should add that the more different the biological parents are from each other, the more likely it is that siblings will be different because they do not inherit overlapping genes. (Think of hair colour here.) In terms of evolutionary survival of the species, it only made sense that siblings be somewhat different so as to create diversity: A family could then adapt better to various environmental situations. Second, siblings are different because of the **nonshared environment**, which essentially refers to environmental influences or experiences that differ for each child, including birth order, peers, school experiences, and accidents and illnesses that affect one sibling but not the other—and the timing of birth in the family life course (East and Jacobson, 2000). As we have seen, even their own relationship can constitute a nonshared experience: Siblings often treat one another differently.

Children's Different Perceptions of Familial Environment

A third reason why siblings are different is that many transform much of their shared or familial environment into a nonshared one. This occurs when siblings, while partaking together of their shared familial environment, such as parental teachings or even divorce, attach **different meanings** (symbolic interactionism) to it because of their individual personalities and what they have learned outside the family. For instance, Dunn and McGuire (1994) compared the impact on siblings of 256 events that had occurred in the families they had observed over a three-year period. These shared events affected the siblings differently in nearly 70 percent of the cases. Thus, only 30 percent of the events produced a common effect.

> Let's take the fictive example of two fraternal twins. Although their parents treat them similarly, twin Bob perceives that he receives less love, whereas twin Harry does not see any difference in the way they are treated. This perceptual gap is the result of twin Bob being more sensitive, anxious, and rebellious than Harry. This perceptual difference produces another consequence: Bob's sense of resentment and then distancing from parents. In effect, because of his reaction, Bob is creating for himself a family climate different from that of his twin.

This divergent family climate will become part of their nonshared environment. In turn, this nonshared environment interacts with each twin's predispositions and will create different ways of behaving toward others, including their parents. For instance, Bob becomes even more rebellious and anxious as a result of the nonshared environment he has in great part created—although he has done so unconsciously.

> Another hypothetical example, that of a disadvantaged family with three daughters, further illustrates this mechanism. One sister is good natured and easily satisfied. She does not feel deprived and makes the best out of a bad situation. The other sister is materialistic, envious, and demanding. Consequently, she reacts to their poverty with stress, dissatisfaction, behavioural problems, and lack of respect for their parents. The last sister is goal oriented and industrious; she is determined to improve her lot.

These three sisters' **perceptions** based on their different personalities lead them to react differently to a shared environment of poverty. In turn, these disparate reactions not only strengthen their personality differences but also create a private environment—that is, one that they do *not* share with their sisters. This nonshared environment contributes to maintaining or even widening the differences among these siblings. Such examples fit very well within the perspectives of interactional theories. In summary, siblings are dissimilar to some extent in terms of personalities, appearance, and physical constitution because of a different combination of genes. (By the same token, however, they are more similar among themselves than to unrelated persons of the same age in their neighbourhood.) As well, psychological traits are influenced by several genes combined (polygene), and the effect of genes can change over time (McCartney, 2003). Second, siblings are also different because of the nonshared environment, such as different friends. And third, their different perceptions of and reactions to their shared environment reinforce their differences and create new ones.

Families That Provide a More Powerful Shared Environment

This said, the fact remains that some families provide more shared socialization experiences for their children than do most other families. This expanded family environment becomes more powerful and can make siblings similar, not necessarily in terms of personalities, but in terms of what is learned, such as leisure activities, lifestyle, beliefs, values, and even the skills they develop. How do parents provide a more comprehensive or powerful shared environment?

To begin with, some fathers and mothers are quite similar to each other as a result of **assortative mating** (Chapter 7). Such parents pass on more similar genes to their children; they are also likely to reinforce each other's teachings and provide a more uniform home climate that leaves less room for differentiation among siblings than when parents hold different views (Feinberg et al., 2005). Second, we can use Thornton and Lin's (1994) theory of **family integration** as an explanation. Parents who engage in many activities with their children, both at home or elsewhere, provide siblings with a more cohesive and integrative learning experience. For instance, parents may take their children along on vacations and to libraries or museums, and they may engage in specific sports activities as a family group. All these activities combined contribute to family integration, which enlarges the children's shared environment. The shared activities also limit the time children spend in nonshared activities and in environments that could lead to different perceptions and learning experiences.

Third, this shared effect becomes even more powerful when parents and children together engage in activities with other parents and their children as a group; the entire family then experiences more shared elements. These activities can include religious worship, sports, communal picnics, and visits to other families' homes. The end result is that parents and offspring interact with others their age within the same context that, in turn, reinforces parental teachings—a matter of **collective socialization**. Fourth, when parents are able to send their children to schools that replicate their own value system and lifestyle, siblings and parents have a more expanded, shared learning environment (Chapter 6). The school becomes an extension of the home, particularly when like-minded parents send like-minded children to the same schools. The school and the family essentially overlap in what the children learn, each agent of socialization reinforcing the other and, in rational theory's terms, offering social closure against the rest of the world. Such a form of social capital may compensate for a child's negative genetic predispositions (Shanahan, M. J., et al., 2008). Or, else, it can reinforce negative predispositions when this capital is a deficit (deviant, for instance), as seen below.

Although each child in such families benefits from the common environment somewhat differently because of his or her personality, the fact remains that these siblings are surrounded by a "wrap-around" lifestyle that is shared by parents, relatives, friends, friends' parents, parents' friends, and even teachers. This shared environment becomes an **effective community** where everyone more or less pitches in and socializes its children similarly. Collective socialization is a far more powerful agent of socialization than isolated parental efforts at home, which can be diminished by different sets of values and behaviours as soon as children step outside. The shared environment becomes a more powerful source of influence on offspring. Siblings then become more similar, not necessarily in terms of personality characteristics, but with regard to lifestyle, education, values, beliefs, and occupational achievement.

One sees such examples among communities of rural Amish and Mennonite families where children who remain home replicate their parents' particular rural and religious lifestyle. As well, collective socialization tends to be the norm rather than the exception in rural areas of economically developing countries (Hewlett and Lamb, 2005; Kitayama and Cohen, 2010). Not only are the villages and settlements smaller, but there are fewer consumerist challenges, and value consensus is higher—not to omit the fact that lifestyles are uniform from one family to the next. At the negative level, such a powerful collective socialization also exists among traditional Mafia families that interact among themselves and where male children learn to engage in illegal activities. This expanded shared environment can also occur by default in geographically isolated pockets of rural poverty or in distant Aboriginal villages deprived of their traditional economies, where all the children fall under the same influences that mould their perceptions and narrow their life alternatives. They consequently grow up to replicate their parents' and their neighbours' poverty, despite having different personalities and innate abilities (Rowe et al., 1999). These abilities may not be allowed to flourish (Ambert, 1998).

SIBLING SIMILARITIES AND DIFFERENCES: TWIN STUDIES

Molecular or biological genetics can occasionally pinpoint exactly which sets of genes are related to specific health conditions, abilities, and certain behaviours (e.g., Guo et al., 2008). However, until this can be done for more behaviours and personality predispositions, geneticists have to rely on sophisticated statistical guesswork. The best natural experiment that life provides at this point resides in twin and adoption situations (D'Onofrio and Lahey, 2010; Leve et al., 2010b; Natsuaki et al., 2010).

Twins as Natural Experiments

The rationale behind research with twins and adopted siblings is to take advantage of degrees of genetic relatedness (Leve et al., 2010a): *Identical twins share all of their genes; fraternal twins and other siblings share about 50 percent. Half siblings and the children of identical twins share about 25 percent of their genes, while the children of fraternal twins and siblings share 12.5 percent.* For their part, stepsiblings and adopted children have no specific genetic background in common—except as human beings (Leve et al., 2010b). The more closely related two persons are genetically, the more likely they are to be similar (Reiss, 2003; see Family Research 11.2). Furthermore, research designs comparing identical twins within a same family allow for the study of the separate and combined role played by genetics, the shared environment, and the nonshared environment. An interesting extension of the twin experimental approach is well illustrated in a research on family conflict: This study included adult pairs of twins of the same sex, their spouses, and one adolescent child

Potential Problems in Twin Studies

The Colorado Adoption Project study compared pairs of adoptive siblings with pairs of biological siblings, including twins, on mild delinquency and aggressive behaviour. For our purposes here, we are interested in the potential problems of twin studies. For instance, one can wonder whether it is valid to assume that twins' family environment is equivalent to that of siblings who are not twins. The equivalency assumption is a necessary one if the results of behaviour genetics studies are to be valid. Yet, one can easily see that parenting two or more same-age children (twins) may create a different familial climate, which would violate the assumption of an equivalent family environment.

Furthermore, identical twins may be more likely to copy each other's behaviour than fraternal twins or even just regular siblings. This situation could artificially increase the genetic influence. Twins, particularly when they are identical, are more likely to share a similar environment, which would again contribute to increasing their similarity (Iervolino et al., 2005). Thus, methodological problems may exist in the research on twins and may reduce researchers' ability to draw solid and generalizable conclusions about the role of genetics and environment in human development. However, studies of twins reared separately in different families do not suffer from this possible methodological complication.

in each unit. This research established that close to 40 percent of the conflict is genetically related (Howitz et al., 2010).

Thus, researchers "experiment" with degrees of genetic closeness and degrees of shared environments: Twins who have been adopted into separate families present an ideal experimental situation. This particular twin research design is illustrated in Table 11.1. This table is fictive in the sense that the numbers are invented for teaching purposes. However, the numbers presented follow the general line of reasoning of such studies. This table focuses on *personality characteristics* because they, along with cognitive abilities, are more likely to be genetically influenced than are lifestyles and activities. The latter depend far more on the available environment, both shared and nonshared (Lemelin et al., 2007). As well, when individuals have extreme characteristics, whether pathologies or gifts, these traits tend to be more heavily influenced by genetics rather than environment (Viding et al., 2005).

Higher percentages in Table 11.1 mean that the twins are more similar. Thus, twins who would be totally similar in terms of personality characteristics would have a 100 percent similarity. As well, if genes were the main source of personality formation, the percentages for identical twins would be close to 100 percent to indicate near perfect similarity whether they were raised together or separately—because they share all their genes. But the highest figure in the table is 80 percent for identical twins raised together compared with 50 percent for those raised separately. This more or less means that around 50 percent of the identical twins' personalities is produced by their genes. Or, looking at twins reared together (Groups 1 and 3), if genes played no role, identical and fraternal twins would be equally similar because, in each set, both share the same environment: But they are not.

TABLE 11.1	Fictive Percentages of Overall Personality Similarity among Identical and Fraternal Twins Who Were Raised Together or Separately*			
	Identical Twins Raised Together (Group 1)	Identical Twins Raised Separately (Group 2)	Fraternal Twins Raised Together (Group 3)	Fraternal Twins Raised Separately (Group 4)
	80%	50%	40%	10%

*The fictive subjects are four groups, each containing 100 pairs of same-sex twins aged 14.

So we also see, in Table 11.1, that the family environment plays a role. For instance, although identical twins are still very similar when they have been raised in different families—by 50 percent—at least 30 percent of personality traits come from the shared familial environment (difference between groups 1 and 2). We also see that even fraternal twins are more similar, by 30 percent, when raised together (difference between Groups 3 and 4).

Interestingly, other studies show that identical adult twins who had been adopted separately and thus raised apart give many similar answers when they are asked to describe the homes in which they have been reared (Hur and Bouchard, 1995:339). Their **perceptions** are more similar than are those of fraternal twins also raised apart. In view of the fact that the homes were different, how can this be? This similarity of perceptions is the result of a combined genetic and environmental effect. To begin with, it is likely that these identical twins' different sets of adoptive parents were reacting fairly similarly to the twins' identical physical appearances and relatively similar personalities when they were growing up. Although living in different homes, the identical twins may then have developed more similar relationships with their two sets of parents and thus naturally perceive these homes more similarly than do fraternal twins (Harlaar et al., 2008). The latter were less alike in terms of appearance and personalities, and consequently elicited **different reactions** from their two sets of adoptive parents.

As the reader can see, these processes are also easily understood through both symbolic interactionism and interactional theories: People create reactions that then become part of their environment, and this environment in turn helps create their personalities and perceptions. All in all, *these studies indicate that genes indirectly play a role in the creation of a person's environment:* Genes and environment, both shared and nonshared, act together. There are also indications that the familial or shared environment marks children more as they get older in some domains while, in others, genes become more important (Haworth et al., 2009).

What about the **nonshared** environment? In Table 11.1, none of the percentages that combine the effect of genes and shared family environment on personalities reaches 100 percent. For instance, we see in Group 1 that genes and family account for about 80 percent of identical twins' personalities. The remaining 20 percent indicates the effect of unique experiences the twins do not share—and this could start even in the uterus. Such unique experiences are likely to be more numerous for twins who are not identical. As well, one can see that siblings who are not twins will be far more affected by their nonshared environments because they have a different age, birth order, classrooms, and peers (Lemelin et al., 2007)—Family Research 12.2.

The Relevance of Parental Influence

Socialization theories indicate that parents are extremely important in the formation of their children's personalities, behaviours, and well-being. Yet, most studies based on this premise find real but only moderate correlations between various child outcomes and parents' socialization practices—which does not mean that they do not count. *Socialization does count, but within its genetic and environmental contexts.* These results combined put into question the validity of many past and current sociological interpretations of the parental role, particularly when it comes to personality development as opposed to behaviours. Traditional research confounds genetic and environmental influences: It studies the family as if it were only an environment and ignores the fact that genes play an important role in the interaction between parents and children. In essence, what in the past has been assumed to be strictly the result of parenting is now better understood as an interplay between parents' and children's genetic predispositions, parenting practices linked to reciprocal gene/environment effects, as well as between all these variables and the general environment in which families are located (Luster et al., 2000: 145).

This perspective meshes well with the interactional-transactional theories that analyze causality from a multidirectional framework. For instance, Jaffee et al. (2003) have found that the less time fathers lived with their children, the more behaviour problems the children had (the role of family structure). But, when fathers exhibited antisocial behaviours, the reverse occurred: Their children had more behaviour problems the longer they lived with their father. These children received a "triple whammy" of risks toward difficult behaviours: genetic (father's predispositions) and environmental (father's poor parenting) and example (Dogan et al., 2007).

Early on, some behaviour geneticists got carried away by the results of their studies: Misled by the fact that siblings are often so different from one another, some concluded, in opposition to the equally misleading socialization theories, that parents and the family environment do not matter: Parents do not influence their children. The reality is that whether siblings are similar or different is irrelevant in terms of parental influence. Parents influence their offspring, both biological and adopted, both similar and different. But they do so within the *limits* set by their children's genetic predispositions, perceptions, and reactions (Reiss, 2003). Parents can, in many circumstances, compensate for children's genetic vulnerabilities and enhance their gifts (Guo et al., 2008; Shanahan, M. J., et al., 2008). Think of it this way: If parents had no impact on their children, they would arrive in daycare or kindergarten totally unsocialized—that is, as small, grunting animals. Yet, quite the contrary is true (Lemelin et al., 2007): Young children who have spent their first four years at home with their parents, even with no television and no peer group, arrive in kindergarten fully equipped with language, skills, beliefs, expectations, and attitudes. These can only come from parental effect or what is called the shared environment (Rutter, 2002).

As seen earlier, some parents are more successful than others at influencing their children, in part because they have more personal resources and the social context they live in is more compatible with their values (Lamborn et al., 1996). Disadvantaged environments often prevent children from benefiting from their genetic strengths and their parents' positive influence—and thus these children frequently do not fulfill their genetic potential (Ambert, 1998; Nielsen, 2006). Further, children unconsciously (and later consciously) filter their parents' teachings through their own predispositions or personalities (Udry, 2003). Rutter (1997:393) correctly puts this into perspective when he points out that parents produce an effect but it is dissimilar or nonshared: It is different for each child because each child is different from birth.

> For example, twin Mia is impulsive, quick to react, and pays little attention to what is said. With the help of her mother, Mia learns to become less impulsive than she would be were she living in a family that provides little structure. In the latter family, she would become more impulsive. Her twin Alan is totally different: He is quiet, shy, and learns quickly. With the mother's help, he becomes more engaging socially, thus less shy. Because he is a quick learner, the mother can teach him many skills, so that Alan learns even better than he would in a family with a less invested mother.

Although both twins remain different, each improves under maternal influence, even though his or her basic personality remains.

Thus, it is false to conclude that, in general, parents and the shared familial environment have no influence, and that, for instance, peers matter more. On the other hand, it is equally false to conclude, as sociologists and psychologists have done, that parents hold the key to their child's development: Both genes and the nonshared environment (siblings, peers, media, teachers, illnesses, traumas) contribute the other keys. Difficult or aggressive peers, for instance, can have a great negative impact (Espelage et al., 2003). Yet, parents' firm behavioural control can be effective against such peer influence (Golombos et al., 2003)—although children's choice of peers may also in part be related to their own genetic propensities (Beaver et al., 2009). As well, one has to consider that certain parental effects on children are derived from their own genes; thus *even the familial environment is partly genetic* (Kim-Cohen et al., 2004).

But, as we have seen when discussing parental influence in the previous chapter, external environmental forces opposing parental influence are today far more powerful in child socialization than they were a century ago: The family then constituted a larger part of a child's environment. As well, the rest of the community tended to hold values that were generally compatible with those reflected in the family, thus providing a larger component of closure from other influences and a more powerful shared environment (Côté, 2000).

Similarly, one has to consider that, via families, various types of cultures will encourage the development of attitudes, skills, and values that are very different. Thus, to give a hypothetical example, twins with similar genetic predispositions may develop even more differently when raised separately, one in Canada and one in an African village. This issue of cultural impact on personality formation is one that is not sufficiently recognized and remains the purview of cultural psychologists (Kitayama and Cohen, 2006).

CONCLUSIONS: THE NATURE AND NURTURE OF PARENTAL INFLUENCE

In western countries, sibling interactions are far more varied and optional than parent-child relationships because they are less scripted culturally. The sibling relationship reflects gender roles whereby females are already kin-keepers. This relationship is also affected by the familial context and later on by the peer network and other social groups. We have also seen that the influence of siblings on one another is underrated: It is quite possible that, at least for the younger child in a family, it is greater than parental influence in many domains of life.

The study of siblings, particularly twins and adopted children, has been directed toward better understanding the role that genes and the environment jointly play in human development. For sociologists, this new knowledge can be utilized to soften long-held views on the presumably all-powerful role that parents play in their child's socialization—and consequently to rectify the blame parents have received when a child turns out "wrong." On the one hand, sociological and psychological theories have overrated parental influence on children's personality development. On the other hand, geneticists' results often lead to the conclusion that parents have relatively little to do in terms of their children's behavioural development. The reality is that parents influence their children, but they do so within a specific context (their culture, social class, neighbourhood, peer group, media), and in conjunction with the genetic material or predispositions inherited by their children as well as their children's interpretations of reality. The latter are also influenced by genetic and environmental factors. Thus, there is a constant interplay between nature and nurture and the diversity of this interplay remains to be studied in societies that are still agrarian and non-western.

Summary

1. The mother-child interaction changes with the arrival of a second infant. The older child's personality and parents' initiatives largely affect the child's adaptation to the arrival. Each new baby dilutes parental resources, but this is particularly so in large families with closely spaced children. In such families, offspring do not do as well at school, on average. There are advantages, however, to being part of a large sibling group, but studies have yet to measure these adequately.

2. Sibling relationships are determined by siblings' characteristics, personality compatibility, and parental behaviours, as well as children's perceptions of how they are treated compared with their siblings. Older siblings tend to be fairly consistent over time in their behaviour toward younger ones, whereas younger ones show less stability because they are the ones who have to adapt to the older's behaviours. It is possible that effects that have been attributed to parental practices are actually the result of the handling a child has received from siblings. Gender plays a very important role in sibling relations, with girls being closer to their siblings than boys. Overall, siblings do not perceive their relationship similarly.

3. Siblings influence one another, particularly older ones toward younger ones. This is documented in studies on aggressiveness, delinquency, early sexual activity, and early childbearing. The sharing of friends contributes to sibling similarity and influence.

4. When a child suffers from disabilities, siblings often help parents care for him or her. However,

adults' well-being is often negatively affected when the sibling has emotional problems compared with physical or mental delay. Although siblings can act as a buffer for one another in times of family distress, the research indicates that divorce and the arrival of a stepparent is often accompanied by sibling disharmony.

5. Differential parental treatment of siblings is in part related to children's age, developmental stage, gender, and child personality. Mothers tend to treat children similarly at a given age, but at any point in time, siblings are treated somewhat differently. We also examine the effects of differential parental treatment.

6. The adult sibling relationship is discretionary in western societies. In North America, proximity increases contact and the potential for both conflict and closeness. Gender continues to be an important variable: Sisters form closer bonds and benefit even brothers. Perceived differential treatment from parents while growing up often contributes to the tone of the adult sibling relationship. Stepsiblings do not usually bond as closely when full siblings are present. The longer stepsiblings have lived together as children, the closer the adult bond.

7. The study of sibling differences returns us to the issues raised by behaviour genetics. This theoretical perspective redressed some of the excesses of long-held socialization theories and meshes with the interactional framework. Despite a shared home environment and genes inherited from the same parents, siblings are different because each inherits a particular combination of their parents' gene pool and has a different nonshared environment, including birth order as well as peer and school experiences. Further, because of their individual personalities, children perceive and interpret their shared environment (such as parental teachings) differently. Certain families are able to extend the shared environment and to make its impact stronger so that siblings become more similar in terms of values, lifestyles, and achievement.

8. In order to study the joint effect of genes and environment on human development, twin and adoption studies are used because they present degrees of genetic closeness. Twins reared apart also present degrees of environmental closeness. Identical twins show more personality similarities than fraternal twins, even when raised separately. The similarity is higher when they are raised together. The totality of the studies indicates that combined environmental forces are generally more important than biology. However, the calculations used by behaviour geneticists have led many to conclude that it is not the shared home environment that is the most important in human development but the nonshared one. They confused a relative lack of similarity between siblings with a lack of parental influence. The fact is that parents influence their offspring, both biological and adopted, but they can do so only within the limits set by the children's genetic predispositions, perception, and reactions.

Analytical Questions

1. Do you think there are advantages to large family size in terms of personality development? Would your answer differ for the 21st century compared with the 19th?

2. Families are becoming smaller (related to lower fertility). Analyze this development from a life course perspective.

3. Why are siblings different from one another? And are they more different from one another than they are from the other kids in the neighbourhood?

4. What role do perceptions play in the distinction of what constitutes the shared versus the nonshared environment?

5. Do you agree or disagree with behaviour geneticists when some rule out parental influence (or the shared environment) as a key element in children's development? Justify your answer.

Suggested Readings

Brody, G. H. (Ed.) 1996. *Sibling relationships: Their causes and consequences.* Norwood, NJ: Ablex. This is a collection of scholarly articles from a wide range of disciplines focusing on diverse aspects of the sibling relationship. Some of the studies presented are longitudinal. Various ages are considered throughout the life span. Sibling influence, family contexts, and behaviour genetics are other aspects surveyed.

Hetherington, E. M., Reiss, D., and Plomin, R. (Eds.) 1994. *Separate social worlds of siblings: The impact of the nonshared environment on development.* Hillsdale, NJ: Erlbaum. As indicated by the title, this collection of articles is largely inspired by behaviour genetics theories. Reviews of the literature as well as new research data are presented.

Reiss, D., Leve, L. D., and Whitesel, A. L. 2009. "Understanding links between birth parents and the child they have placed for adoption: Clues for assisting adopting families and for reducing genetic risk?" In G. M. Wrobel and E. Neil (Eds.), *International advances in adoption research for practice* (pp. 119–143). Chichester, UK: John Wiley & Sons. This article presents a very detailed overview of the various issues pertaining to behaviour genetics in terms of the interplay between nature and nurture or genes and environment.

Suggested Weblinks

Center on the Developing Child has, at the time of writing this text in 2010, a feature explaining nature and nurture as well as another one on Science of Early Childhood.

www.developingchild.harvard.edu

Multiple Births Canada and **Multiple Births** are two websites that provide information, advice, and sources of support for parents of twins, including issues of sibling identity. Many links to other sites are listed.

www.multiplebirthscanada.org

and

http://multiplebirthsfamilies.com

CHAPTER 12

Divorce, Widowhood, and Remarriage

"I really didn't see it coming [his marriage breaking up]. *I guess I was too busy."*

"Oh, I was so unhappy with him, you have no idea. He has no idea either." [The above man's ex-wife]

"My divorce was a pathetic waste, a waste of time and a psychological waste. We could have stayed together; instead we chose to subject each other to all manner of psychological warfare." [This man was happily remarried.]

"Am I better off now? I am not any happier. It's hard to raise children on your own when that wasn't in the planning. But at least I don't have to put up with his constant rejection and abuse."

"I used to think that a woman my age was too old for me. I dated much younger women, you know the stereotypical bachelor. I liked the ego boost these girls gave me. But when the party was over and time came to face life, I went for a woman my age . . . otherwise the life goals, long-term life goals, would have been too different."

"He shares in the upbringing of our children whereas I had to do it all in my previous marriage. He is thoughtful and we plan everything together. In my first marriage, it was all his life; his home was his castle. I was a fringe benefit."

"I love my stepchildren. Now I have a very large family and more grandchildren."

"I'd rather not have my stepsons. Mind you, I care for them and I am attached to them but I never set out to have children, and having someone else's children is a burden; I often resent it."

I have selected these quotes from the thousands available in the files of my longitudinal study on divorce to represent the various stages from divorcing, to repartnering or remaining single, and to stepparenting. These quotes illustrate how divorce is an experience that is both very individual and yet, as we soon see, carries similarities across cases: A first divorce is, at the very least, a marking event in a person's life.

In previous centuries, single-parent families were a common occurrence. For instance, in 1900, 25 percent of all children under the age of 15 had lost a parent to death. Until the Second World War, the death of a spouse remained the leading cause of family disruption, at which point it was surpassed by divorce. It is because of this historical shift that divorce, rather than widowhood, is the main focus of this chapter.

Divorce is a legal institution whose function is to separate spouses who can no longer live together. However, it carries implications for the life course of adults and children alike.

The history of the legalization of divorce in Canada predates that of its colonial overseer, England, where it was only in 1857 that divorce was legislated, mainly on grounds of adultery. Nova Scotia, New Brunswick, and Prince Edward Island respectively enacted divorce laws in 1761, 1791, and 1837, generally on grounds of adultery (Wu and Schimmele, 2009). It was not until 1968 that Canada enacted its first unified federal *Divorce Act*, which was followed by the more liberal or "no fault" act of 1985. But the history of divorce is still unfolding as we now have to consider divorce among same-sex couples (Tyler, 2004).

Although divorce rates have not increased recently in Canada, the number of divorced persons is nevertheless increasing with population growth. In 2007, there were 972,183 divorced women and 712,531 divorced men in the population (Statistics Canada, 2007f). This gender difference stems from the fact that divorced men repartner more and sooner than women and also because women outlive men. There are now more divorced than widowed Canadians (1.7 versus 1.6 million). The divorced account for 5.1 percent of the population versus 4.8 percent for the widowed.

DIVORCE RATES AND TRENDS

The latest estimates by Statistics Canada (2008f) for recently married couples put the risk of divorce at **38 percent** by the 30th wedding anniversary for the country as a whole—ranging from 21.6 percent in Newfoundland and Labrador to 48.4 percent in Quebec, as illustrated in Table 12.1. This compares with an estimated 44 percent in the U.S. (Schoen and Canudas-Romo, 2006). These estimates include persons who are divorcing for the first time as well as others who are divorcing for a second time or more. The probability of divorcing is somewhat lower for a *first marriage* but is higher for a remarriage.

The low rates for the Maritimes may be the result of a higher level of social integration, a more effective community, and demographic variables such as an older population. The higher rates for Quebec may stem from a combination of variables including widespread cohabitation before marriage, lower religiosity, and more liberal and individualistic attitudes.

Calculating divorce rates on the basis of couples who have been married for 30 years is the most accurate measure (Ambert, 2009). With this method, we see that persons who are about to marry have a much higher chance of staying together than of divorcing. However, this statistical method is a recent and sophisticated one that is not used everywhere. Therefore, in order to be able to compare divorce rates over time and across cultures, a less sophisticated method is used: The crude divorce rate based on divorce per 1,000 population.

Table 12.2 presents yearly trends per 1,000 population. We see that rates had already begun climbing before the Second World War, so that by the 1968 *Divorce Act*, divorce was more common, although still rare. Rates then increased spectacularly after the 1968 Act and peaked in 1987 at 3.6 divorces per 1,000 population—compared with 5.2 American divorces in 1981, which was the peak year in the U.S.

TABLE 12.1	Total Divorce Rates, per 100 Marriages, by the 30th Wedding Anniversary by Provinces and Territories			
	1998	2000	2002	2004
Canada	36.1	37.7	37.6	37.9
Newfoundland and Labrador	23.2	22.9	21.8	21.6
Prince Edward Island	26.4	26.9	25.2	29.1
Nova Scotia	28.2	30.4	30.4	30.2
New Brunswick	26.9	31.9	27.2	26.9
Quebec	45.2	47.4	47.6	48.4
Ontario	33.0	34.6	34.9	35.5
Manitoba	30.1	34.6	30.3	30.6
Saskatchewan	31.5	31.4	28.7	27.6
Alberta	39.0	41.5	41.9	41.9
British Columbia	40.0	40.6	41.0	41.8
Yukon	55.2	33.6	43.4	34.5
Northwest Territories and Nunavut	37.5	40.7	31.2	35.5

Source: Statistics Canada, 2002b, 2008f. Reprinted by permission of Statistics Canada.

Thereafter, the rates declined to the point where, in the 2000s, they were equivalent to those of the late 1970s. Similar downward trends are evident in the U.S., although with rates always higher than in Canada.

Cross-culturally, statistics from the United Nations (2008) indicate that Canadian crude rates (2.2) are comparable to those of Sweden (2.2) and are lower than British (2.8) and especially American ones (3.6). The American rates are the highest in the western world but are lower than the Russian ones (4.5).

Before we examine other statistical facts about divorce, several points have to be emphasized to better understand **conjugal dissolution** (cohabitations and marriages that end). Cohabitation is now more common than marriage in Quebec as a first union and after divorce: Currently, 65 percent of Quebec couples are married compared with 87 percent in the rest of Canada (Girard, 2008). In contrast to divorce, when a cohabiting union breaks up, the dissolution does not appear in any statistics. *However, is the breakup of a cohabitation equivalent to divorce?* This is important in order to measure the true extent of conjugal dissolution. The answer is not a simple one. Indeed, including all cohabitations as a form of marriage, for instance, may be misleading and so would be equating their breakup with divorce. In fact, as seen in earlier chapters, many cohabitations last a few months and merely constitute temporary or day-to-day arrangements lacking any long-term commitment as is explicit in marriage. Therefore, at which point should a cohabitation that breaks up be registered in statistics? After one year or two? And how to register these breakups?

TABLE 12.2	Canadian Crude Divorce Rates per 1,000 Population Since 1921	
Years	Numbers	Rates per 1,000 population
1921	558	0.06
1941	2,462	0.21
1961	6,563	0.36
1968*	11,343	0.55
1970	26,093	1.23
1981	67,671	2.71
1985**	61,980	2.53
1986	78,304	2.99
1987*	**96,200**	**3.62**
1990	80,998	2.96
1995	77,636	2.62
1997	67,400	2.25
2000	71,144	2.31
2002	70,155	2.23
2005	71,269	2.20

Source: Adapted with permission from Statistics Canada throughout the years; last one 2008f.

Divorce Act; **Reform of Divorce Laws; ***Peak Year

Another factor to consider is that an unknown number of married couples separate but never divorce. This type of conjugal dissolution may be as significant and consequential as a divorce, yet it does not appear in divorce statistics. It may also be increasing among those who separate and go on to cohabit fairly rapidly after their separation. So, when these two caveats are put together, *at least* one out of every two *unions* ends in dissolution—with lower rates in the Maritimes and Prairies and higher ones in Quebec. The dissolution percentage may continue to rise if younger cohorts continue to enter in greater numbers into cohabitation as a first union.

Statistics are not yet available for **same-sex divorce**. One question that will arise is the extent to which patterns and rates of divorce among gay and lesbian couples resemble those of heterosexual couples. Given that same-sex marriage has only recently become legal, a good proportion of these marriages involves couples who had been in long-term relationships. As such, one could reasonably predict that their divorce rate would be lower than that of married couples who are heterosexual.

However, it should be noted that in Sweden and Norway, gay registered partnerships have higher divorce rates than heterosexual ones; in addition, lesbian partnerships have a 77 percent higher risk than gay ones. Andersson et al.

(2006:96) explain this higher rate among homosexuals by the fact that they are less likely to have children than are heterosexual couples. Also, women's same-sex partnerships may be more at risk of divorce because of a "stronger sensitivity to the quality of relationships" by women than by men "regardless of sexual orientation."

Age at Divorce and Duration of Dissolved Marriages

Another recent trend in divorce rests on the fact that couples are now on average older at divorce than in the past: In 2005, the average age at divorce was 44 years for men and 41.4 for women. This age may rise again to reflect the fact that men and women now marry later—at 29.5 years for men and 26.9 for women in 2005. In Quebec, in 2007, the average at marriage was 32 years for men and 30 for women.

The average duration of marriages ending in divorce in 2005 was **14.5 years** or 1.7 years longer than a decade ago (Statistics Canada, 2008f). In Ontario, it was 13.8 years compared with 16.7 years in P.E.I. Lengthier marriages before divorce are also occurring in other western countries, such as the U.K. (In contrast, between 2001 and 2006, cohabitations that are reported in surveys and are dissolved had lasted 4.3 years—Beaupré and Cloutier, 2007.) As well, Statistics Canada indicates that the highest number of divorces occurs after the third and fourth anniversaries—or 26.1 and 25.8 per 1,000 marriages, respectively. After that, the rate decreases for each additional year married and, by the 40th anniversary, only 1.19 divorces occur per 1,000 marriages.

But we do have to be careful when we consider divorce statistics by duration because, among older persons, a divorce at age 60 or older may be a first one after a long marriage or a second or nth one. For instance, for men 65 to 87 who divorced in 1990–92, the average duration of their first marriage had been 37.8 years, while subsequent divorces occurred after an average of 14 years of remarriage (Gentleman and Park, 1997). The more frequently people divorce and remarry, the shorter each subsequent remarriage (Ambert, 1989).

Multiple (Serial) Divorces

Sixteen percent of divorcing women and men in 2005 had been divorced at least once before (Statistics Canada, 2008f). These rates are lower in Newfoundland (because they have a much lower divorce rate) and Quebec (because the divorced tend to cohabit rather than remarry). The highest rates of serial divorces are in B.C., Alberta, and the Yukon. Therefore, *over 20 percent of all divorces in Canada are a repeat divorce for at least one of the spouses.* Both here and in the U.S., people who divorce many times seem to differ from the once-divorced on some dimensions (Booth, 1999). Some have more personal problems while others are less committed to marriage (Booth and Amato, 2001). For instance, Clark and Crompton (2006) have found that people who experience multiple divorces are much less likely to believe that marriage is important to them and to their happiness. They are not much willing or ready to make adjustments or concessions that could lead to stability, as illustrated in the quotes below:

> *"Women expect too much out of marriage. I sure as hell can't live out their dreams."* [Man in his fourth marriage]

> *"My wife says I have to work at our marriage. I don't agree with her. Marriage is supposed to be pleasant and if it isn't, well, it's not my problem."* [Man in his third marriage]

In comparison, most respondents who had divorced only once expressed feelings of hurt, guilt, and even regret (Ambert, 1989). While interviewing persons who had divorced several times within a short time span, I often had the impression that their marriages were part of the throw-away culture: If it's of no use, then get rid of it. However, the serially divorced did not all unavoidably differ from those who had divorced only once. Some had simply had the misfortune of remarrying a "divorce-prone" spouse. Moreover, there are persons who make a mistake early on and divorce in their twenties, remarry, have children, and divorce again in their forties or fifties. There is no research comparing such persons who divorce a second time after years of stability with those, such as in my study, who had divorced two to four times within 15 years or less. One can reasonably assume that the former may be more stable and more responsible spouses and parents than the latter.

Number of Children Involved

The number of dependent children involved in a parental divorce was 36,252 in 1998—the total number of divorces had been 69,088. The numbers are probably equivalent today. Strohschein et al. (2009) have estimated that about 20 percent of the 1984 birth cohort of Manitoba children had experienced their parents' divorce by age 18. For their part, Juby et al. (2005b) estimated that nearly 30 percent of Canadian children also born in 1984 had experienced the dissolution of their parents' *marriage or cohabitation* by age 15. The 2009 CAMH study obtained a self-report of about 24 percent of students in grades 7 to 12 who lived with a single parent or no parent (Paglia-Boak et al., 2010).

These numbers of children whose parents divorce may seem surprisingly low. One has to consider that only about half of couples who divorce have children. This is due to the fact that a good proportion of divorces occur within the first few years of marriage. As well, only about a third of couples who dissolve a cohabitation have children (Beaupré and Cloutier, 2007). Further, the divorced who have children do not have as many, on average, as couples of their age who remain married. It is not clear whether this is because couples who have a stable marriage are more likely to add a second or third child to their family or if a larger number of children inhibits divorce, at least during the children's young years (Vanderschelden, 2006). But what we know is that the presence of children at home is related to a lower divorce rate (Clark and Crompton, 2006). Paradoxically, in remarriages, the presence of a woman's children from a previous union increases the risk of divorce (Teachman, 2008).

For Canada, there are no estimates of the number of children who experience multiple parental separations, including cohabitations. We know, however, that children who live in cohabitational families are more likely to experience a parental separation than children whose parents are married. Céline Le Bourdais and her colleagues (2004) have found that Quebec children whose parents cohabit have a three-fold chance of going through a parental separation compared with children in married families; the risk for the remainder of Canadian children was nearly five times greater than that of children with married parents. Similar results have been found in the U.S. (Osborne et al., 2007). The research indicates that such **multiple familial transitions** correlate with declining well-being in children and an increase in behavioural problems (Fomby and Cherlin, 2007).

Who Is Responsible for Children After Divorce?

A substantial increase has occurred in the number but not the proportion of fathers who have physical custody. In 1986, 15 percent of custody awards went to fathers exclusively but only 8.5 percent did in 2002. However, in 2003, 42 percent were **joint legal custody**, while 49.5 percent went to mothers—an all-time low for mothers (Statistics Canada, 2004j). But in most of these instances, children still live with their mother. Although joint legal custody may involve children living on alternate weeks or months with each parent, it generally simply involves equal rights of access and decision for both parents while the children remain with one parent. For their part, children prefer equal time with each parent as do young adults retrospectively (Fabricius, 2003). Mothers prefer sole custody, but are favourable to joint custody when they perceive their ex-husbands to be good parents and when the post-marital relationship is not conflictual (Wilcox et al., 1998). In this respect, in February 2005, the Ontario Court of Appeal ruled that joint custody should not be granted when parents cannot communicate effectively with each other about the care of their child(ren).

Custodial fathers compared with custodial mothers are more likely to be remarried or have another adult living with them (Goldscheider and Sassler, 2006). Overall, custodial fathers have fewer resident children, and fewer young ones, than custodial mothers (Beaupré et al., 2010; Rapoport and Le Bourdais, 2006). Fathers who have young children or many tend not to seek their custody (Drapeau et al., 2000). Residence with their children tends to result in a better father-child relationship and contributes to fathers' mental health (Arendell, 1995). Resident fathers experience fewer feelings of lack of control over their paternal situation than nonresidential fathers. But resident fathers are more likely to find their role constraining—they have less freedom and more demands placed on them. So far, it is difficult to conclude how living with a father compared with a mother relates to children's development. There are indications that heterosexual single fathers may be somewhat less hands-on, less supervisory, and perhaps less warm than mothers. As a result, their adolescents may have higher rates of delinquency (Biblarz and Stacey, 2010:16).

Both in terms of numbers and the social construction of motherhood, **noncustodial mothers** are nonnormative (Walker and McGraw, 2000). Among them are mothers who relinquish custody because of financial hardship and a few who do so in order to have more freedom or to remarry someone who does not want children at home. In other cases, the father has won custody after a lengthy and often costly legal battle. Other mothers are involuntary noncustodial as a result of ill health, mental problems, drug addiction, incarceration, child neglect, or because the child has been kidnapped by the father. In the U.S., nonresident mothers maintain more frequent telephone, letter, and extended visitation contacts with their children than nonresidential fathers (Stewart, 1999b). But, overall, this is one instance when adolescents are closer to their fathers (King, 2007). However, both sets of nonresident parents tend to engage largely in leisure activities with their children (Stewart, 1999a). Furthermore, neither mothers nor fathers pay all the child support they owe.

In the U.S., nearly 30 percent of fathers never visit their children (Amato et al., 2009) compared with about 15 percent in Canada, while another 25 percent do so only irregularly (Marcil-Gratton, 1999). As well, parents in common-law unions that dissolve with children are far less likely to provide child support than formerly married ones (Child Support Team, 2000). Some researchers suggest that there is something in the structure of being a nonresidential parent that inhibits active parenting as well as economic support for children outside of marriage (Gaudet and Devault, 2006; Manning et al., 2004). The presence of "new" children is a barrier (Smock and Greenland, 2010). Other barriers include the geographical distance and duration of separation (Manning and Smock, 2000). Low income is a key factor mitigating against active parenting because it often places severe constraints on a father's time, resources, lodging, and availability (Sinkewicz and Garfinkel, 2009; Swiss and Le Bourdais, 2009). Overall, only a minority of nonresident fathers (whether divorced, separated, or single) display high levels of involvement (Carlson, 2006). This is especially evident among single fathers after their relationship with the mother ends and even more so after she repartners (Tach et al., 2010). (See also Family Research 12.1 below.)

As well, new theories suggest that children's characteristics play a role in these parent-child dynamics (Ambert, 2001). For instance, recent studies indicate that fathers are less likely to be closely involved with nonresident adolescents who have behavioural, mood, and academic problems (Hawkins et al., 2007). Such adolescents may discourage their fathers from getting involved, may be aversive, and may place obstacles to visiting with them. In turn, in a causality feedback perspective, this means that these same adolescents then have less support, which may compound

FAMILY RESEARCH 12.1

The Pitfalls of Measuring Father Involvement

Carlson (2006:150) hypothesizes that, when adolescents are interviewed about the level of their fathers' involvement in their lives, they may hold a different standard for fathers who live elsewhere compared with those who live at home. They may have higher standards for live-in fathers and describe as "close" their relationship with a nonresident father for less involvement on his part than do adolescents for their resident fathers. "This is an important area for future research." Indeed, were it true that children's standards differ, then their answers might not be comparable in the two types of families.

their problems: Research is unanimous to the effect that children do far better cognitively and behaviourally when their father remains an active parent (Allard et al., 2005). Amato and Gilbreth (1999) suggest that children of divorce have better outcomes when nonresidential fathers are more than "Sunday daddies" and participate more fully *as parents*—that is, when they provide emotional and practical support, make behavioural demands, place limits on what can be done, and administer consistent discipline.

FACTORS CONTRIBUTING TO DIVORCE

Multiple, interlocking factors have contributed to the rapid rise of divorce in Canada and other western countries in the second part of the 20th century. These same factors have contributed to the maintenance of relatively high rates of divorce into the 21st century as well as to increasing rates of cohabitation. Below, various cultural and demographic contributing factors are discussed, and then linked to the personal reasons people give for divorcing.

Sociocultural Factors

As seen in previous chapters, sociocultural factors are broad social and cultural variables that affect several aspects of people's lives and influence the ways in which families perceive and experience their relationships. Divorce rates were already inching upward in the early 20th century as a result of **secularization trends**, the **liberalization of norms** concerning individual choice, and **lower religiosity**. This is often referred to as the desacralization of marriage. For many, marriage has become an individual choice rather than a covenant before God and this change has contributed to the acceptance of its temporal nature (Cherlin, 2004). These sociocultural trends later came to influence the passage of **more liberal divorce laws**. In turn, easier divorce laws, such as those promulgated in 1968 and 1985, are followed by an increase in divorce (see Table 12.2). Such laws signalled the normalization of divorce, which then lost its stigma and became more socially acceptable. These cultural and legal factors have made it easier for people to be less attached to marriage as an institution and consequently to turn to divorce as a solution.

The trends toward **individualism** that began two centuries ago have resulted in an emphasis on rights rather than duties. When individualism is coupled with an ideology of gratification, particularly sexual and psychological, where people are encouraged to be "happy" and "fulfilled," it follows that spouses' mentality about their marriage is affected. Marriage is less likely to be seen as an institution centered on mutual responsibilities and is more likely to be based on the pursuit of happiness and companionship. More is demanded of marriage in terms of **personal gratification**. As Amato (2007:309) puts it, in individualistic marriages, spouses view the marriage as valuable as long as it meets their needs for self-actualization: "If the marital relationship no longer meets these needs, then spouses feel justified in jettisoning the relationship to seek out new partners who better meet these needs." As a consequence of these trends, Canadians and most Westerners have developed a **lower threshold of tolerance** when their marriage does not meet with their expectations for personal fulfillment. All things considered, while more is expected of marriage, couples are also less tolerant about its challenges and less willing to shoulder the compromises it may require.

Demographic Factors

Given the cultural variables facilitating divorce, we now look at *demographic factors through which vulnerability to divorce is expressed.* We have seen in Chapter 4 how poverty multiplies individual risks in general, reduces life opportunities, and increases stressors. All of these factors have a negative impact on the marital relationship. Thus, **low-income** couples are at a higher risk of divorcing (Amato and Previti, 2004; Pryor and Rodgers, 2001). This risk is very present among couples on welfare (Frenette and Picot, 2003:15). But we have also seen that divorce contributes to poverty. This means that divorce and poverty are two variables that reinforce each other in the causality chain. On the other side of the equation, a **very rapid upward social mobility** where the acquisition of money and status is a prime mover is also a risk factor. This may be because such a pursuit of materialism takes time away from relationships or reflects individualistic values that are incompatible with a good conjugal life—which refers us back to the cultural factors mentioned earlier.

Youthful marriage or cohabitation also increases the risk of divorcing or breaking up (NCHS, 2010; Provencher et al., 2006). Couples who marry during their teens and even early twenties generally have low incomes and **low educational** levels, which are contributing factors for divorce (Clark and Crompton, 2006). Moreover, they often marry for reasons that differ from those of couples who are more mature. They may also lack the maturity and experience to cope with the demands of a marital relationship. Their personalities have not yet stabilized so that their needs may change and upset the balance of their new marriage.

Another demographic factor related to divorce is **solo motherhood**: Mothers who have children without a partner are more likely to be young and poor and to cohabit before marrying—thus combining many risk factors for divorce when they later marry (Luong, 2008). **Remarriages** are a risk factor for divorce, in great part because of a higher propensity to have recourse to divorce and because of the complexities of reconstituted families. Relationships are more difficult to negotiate and negative family processes are exacerbated in stepfamilies (Jenkins et al., 2005b). This risk factor is becoming more salient: In 2000, 33 percent of all marriages had at least one partner who had been previously divorced and, of these, well over a third included two previously divorced persons (Statistics Canada, 2006d). Further, families with a resident stepfather are less stable than families with a resident stepmother (Marcil-Gratton et al., 2003).

The **sex ratio**: Men are more likely to divorce when there is a high proportion of unmarried women with them in the labour force and the same occurs for women who work in domains with a male preponderance (South et al., 2001). These conditions raise married persons', especially men's, chances of sexual infidelity and of forming new relationships. Similarly, when there is a sex ratio imbalance favouring men in a particular ethnic group in a city, this group may also have higher rates of serial cohabitation and divorce (Harknett, 2008).

Parental divorce correlates with lower marital commitment among some children once adult and this is then reflected in higher divorce rates later (Li and Wu, 2008; Whitton et al., 2008). One study has even found that this occurs especially when the parental marriage had a low level of conflict—such parents may divorce simply because they are less committed to marriage and may transmit this value to their offspring (Amato and DeBoer, 2001). As well, as indicated in Chapter 6, low religiosity is related to lower marital happiness and a higher propensity to divorce (Clark and Crompton, 2006; Tremblay et al., 2002). Furthermore, religious and to some extent racial heterogamy are also risk factors, perhaps because of a lack of shared values or the burden of racial discrimination (Jones, 2010).

Cohabitation prior to marriage has been until now a strong risk factor to a first divorce (Clark and Crompton, 2006; Marcil-Gratton et al., 2003) and for a remarriage (Xu et al., 2006). For its part, **serial cohabitation** represents a particularly high risk for divorce (Lichter and Qian, 2008). But there is recent evidence that cohabiting with a future spouse may not increase the risk of divorcing (Teachman, 2008), but only when cohabiting follows an engagement or official commitment (Stanley et al., 2010). However, this does not lower the risk of divorce (NCHS, 2010). This link between prior cohabitation and later divorce may diminish as cohabitation becomes more prevalent and lasts longer before marriage (Hewitt and de Vaus, 2009). Even so, in Quebec, children born to parents who have cohabited before their marriage are 3.96 times more likely to experience their parents' divorce (and 5.71 times in the rest of Canada) than children whose parents have not cohabited before marrying (Marcil-Gratton et al., 2003). As well, in a study of 16 European countries, Liefbroer and Dourleijn (2006) found that, as a result of selection, cohabitation before marriage is related to a higher risk of divorce only in countries in which cohabitation is a small minority, such as Spain and Italy, or when it is a majority phenomenon, such as Norway and Finland.

How Does Cohabitation Before Marriage Increase the Risk of Divorce?

It used to be believed that living together before marriage would teach people both to avoid marrying the wrong person (and probably it does for some) and practise relationship skills. In this process of "trial marriage," it was reasoned, a future marriage would become stronger and divorce less likely. It did not turn out this way. Why not? Because, until now, there has been both a double process of selection into premarital cohabitation as well as one of causality that have resulted in higher divorce rates following premarital cohabitations.

The first part of the *double* process of **selection** is this: Some individuals select themselves into cohabitation because it requires, in their opinion, less sexual faithfulness than in marriage, or because cohabitation is viewed as an alternative to the lifelong commitment assumed by marriage. This situation occurs even in countries such as Sweden and Norway where cohabitation is widespread (Wiik et al., 2006). Cohabitation is easier to get into and easier to get out of than marriage. Therefore, there is less reason to "work" at maintaining a relationship that may never have been viewed as a lifelong commitment to begin with. However, many such less committed couples drift into marriage, and may not be ready for the required commitment. As a result, they have a higher chance of divorcing.

The other part of the process of selection exists at the level of personal attributes. For instance, Hohmann-Marriott (2006) reports that couples who cohabit have somewhat less positive problem-solving behaviours and are less supportive of each other on average than those who have not cohabited before marriage. This may extend into marriage. As well, cohabitants have, on average, lower income and religiosity than married couples, two risk factors for divorce. As we have seen in Chapter 6, there is a correlation between religiosity and marital happiness as well as stability. If couples who are both less religious and less committed to each other and to the institution of marriage cohabit and then go on to marry, it is not surprising that they will have a higher divorce rate—a phenomenon that is particularly relevant to Quebec where religiosity is very low and cohabitation is generally chosen as a first union.

Second, not only is there a selection process, but there is evidence of a **causality effect**. That is, the experience of a less committed, and at times less faithful cohabitation, shapes subsequent marital behaviour (Dush et al., 2003). Such couples continue to live their marriage through the perspective of the low commitment, and even lack of fidelity of their prior cohabitation. Others simply learn to accept the temporary nature of relationships (Smock and Gupta, 2002). The result is a marriage at risk. This is especially so when children were born during a prior cohabitation (Tach and Halpern-Meekin, 2009). Cohabitation may also reduce religiosity, an important factor of stability (Eggebeen and Dew, 2009).

Therefore, people both select themselves into cohabitation, especially serial cohabitations, because of personal and demographic characteristics. In turn, cohabitations that *lack commitment* shape subsequent marital behaviours in ways that may be detrimental to marital relationships. Hence, the increased divorce rates. However, if cohabitation becomes more institutionalized, both as a prelude to marriage and as a relationship in itself, its behavioural contents will evolve so that commitment, sexual fidelity, and feelings of security may be equivalent to those found in marriage. Were such a point reached, the experience itself of cohabitation may promote, rather than weaken, future marital commitment. For instance, in Australia where cohabitations are now of longer duration, this new development may be reducing the risk of divorce (Hewitt and de Vaus, 2009). However, even in Sweden and Norway, cohabitants with no intention of marrying their current partner report a far less committed relationship than those with marital intentions (Wiik et al., 2009). This is also what the most recent U.S. statistics indicate (NCHS, 2010).

One important caveat is necessary: More young people as well as more post-divorce adults engage in **serial** cohabitations than was the case in the past, at times accumulating many such relationships over the years (Sassler, 2010). Just as persons who divorce multiple times seem to differ on some key dimensions compared with the once-divorced, one should expect that future research will find similar results for serial cohabitants—for we already know that serial cohabitants who marry have higher divorce rates than those who had cohabited only with their eventual spouse (Lichter and Qian, 2008). In other words, the process of selection and of behavioural shaping will continue to characterize serial cohabitants.

In conclusion, when a **committed** couple decides to cohabit, one can reasonably expect that, within the current social context, their relationship will last, especially when they marry (Jose et al., 2010). However, couples with a history of multiple cohabitations will continue to be a risk factor for divorce and cohabitation breakups—and, one could hypothesize, a risk for the children they may have. Children suffer from their parents' multiple conjugal transitions as they are then less likely to have a home and parental environment that is child oriented (Cherlin, 2009).

Reasons People Give for Divorcing

When asked what led to their divorce, people mention "irreconcilable differences," "didn't get along," "no longer loved each other," fighting and quarrelling about money, children, and their relationship. In the U.S., Amato and Previti (2004) found that infidelity was the reason most often given. Frequently mentioned also are physical abuse, mental cruelty, religious differences, and alcoholism. Drug addiction, gambling, mental illness, criminality, "he's never home," and child-related problems, such as the stress of caring for a child with a disability, are occasionally mentioned. Domestic violence as one of the reasons for divorce is less often mentioned than in the past in Canada and in other Western countries (de Graaf and Kalmijn, 2006). This finding is consistent with studies showing a decline in conjugal violence between 1993 and 2004 (Laroche, 2007; Statistics Canada, 2006d).

A proportion of couples who eventually divorce threaten to do so or talk about it for a few acrimonious months or years before finally separating. Generally, one of the two partners is more active in this process. In most cases of divorce, one spouse wants out far more than the other (Hopper, 2001). One spouse is happier with the relationship (Waite and Gallagher, 2000). Often it is the husbands who are surprised when their marriage breaks down (Hetherington, 2003). Women generally find more problems with their marriage than husbands do and decide to divorce more often than men, even though they are the ones who carry the larger burden afterwards. Already in 1956, William Goode had explained this apparent contradiction:

> "Women have been socialized to be the expressive and emotional partner. For their part, many husbands disengage from or avoid discussions pertaining to marital problems. Conflicts are thus not resolved and this situation often leads to divorce. We suggest, then, that in our society the husband more frequently than the wife will engage in behavior whose function, if not intent, whose result, if not aim, is to force the other spouse to ask for the divorce first. Thereby the husband frees himself to some extent from the guilt burden, since he did not ask for the divorce. A by-product of this process frees him still more: the wife's repeated objections to this behavior will mean that there are family squabbles, and one almost constant result of repeated family squabbles is a lessened affection between husband and wife." (Goode, 1956:136–137)

Many of the results and insights of Goode's pioneer study are still applicable. Today, though, the dynamics described by Goode can also be initiated by women, particularly when they stand to lose relatively little and gain much from the divorce. Women who would fit Goode's explanation are more likely to be young, financially independent, and marriageable.

In the study I conducted, there were several cases in which a casual and unplanned extramarital affair, such as those occurring at out-of-town conventions, caused an enormous blow-up when the other spouse accidentally learned of it; separation was practically immediate. I refer to these as "**accidental**" or "**useless**" divorces (Ambert, 1989). These divorces may never have otherwise occurred because the relationships were sound and both ex-spouses reported a high level of marital happiness (see Family Research 12.2). Infidelities plant seeds of doubt and insecurity that are too difficult to overcome for persons who may have fewer psychological resources or may have other alternatives.

The Factors Contributing to Divorce Are Linked

The personal reasons or explanations that people give for their divorce, as seen above, actually flow from the sociocultural and demographic factors discussed earlier. For instance, without an emphasis on individualism and gratification, people would not divorce as often because they "fell out of love." In countries where marriage is embedded within a context of family solidarity, these reasons would be considered frivolous. In a society where divorce is more difficult to obtain and less acceptable, or

---

FAMILY RESEARCH 12.2

Asking Both Ex-Spouses about Their Past Marital Happiness

You may recall reading in Chapter 9 that few studies examine the marital happiness of a couple. Generally, only one spouse is interviewed and then husbands and wives are compared as two separate groups. But these husbands and wives are not married to each other. Therefore, little can be said about the couple. The same problem occurs in studies of divorce. In order to compensate for this deficit, I have interviewed both ex-spouses and their new spouses when my respondents had remarried. This allowed me to derive a classification of ex-couples depending on both ex-spouses' reported level of marital happiness in their past marriage:

High happiness ex-marriages	13%
Mid-level happiness ex-marriages (mixture of near high and average)	52%
High unhappiness ex-marriages	35%

At the time, these results surprised me, but they have since been replicated in the U.S. In other words, in only one-third of the cases did both ex-spouses recall having been very to fairly unhappy in their past marriage (Amato et al., 2007:245-6). Furthermore, at least one divorce in 10 occurred to couples in which both partners had been happy or very happy (Ambert, 1989). Analyses at the couple level could shed light on many issues that, until now, have been studied with only one or the other spouse as the basis.

where marriage may represent the only legitimate means of forming and maintaining a family or obtaining economic security, only reasons such as abuse and abandonment are tolerated. Therefore, before people decide to divorce on particular grounds, a social and cultural climate has to exist that offers a legitimate framework for their reasons. It should also be added that many psychological characteristics such as difficult temperaments, higher distress, inability to communicate, among others, are also related to high divorce rates (Markman et al., 2010). But even these variables can increase divorce only within societies that facilitate divorce legally and culturally.

THE AFTERMATH OF DIVORCE FOR ADULTS

We have already seen that poverty increases the risk of divorce. In turn, divorce also increases the risk of poverty for a large proportion of women and their children and so does the dissolution of cohabitations (Avellar and Smock, 2005; Hay, 2009). Rotermann (2007a) found that, within two years after a separation/divorce, 43 percent of women had experienced a decrease in household income compared with 15 percent of men. In contrast, 29 percent of men and only 9 percent of women had experienced an increase. As well, men who divorce are more likely to exit welfare while women are more likely to go on welfare (Frenette and Picot, 2003). Even three years after divorce, women's household income remains below what it had been during marriage and far below their ex-husbands' current income. However, as more women are employed and earn better salaries, this income decline is less painful than before, even though it is still evident. As well, in a decade when most families have two breadwinners, men who divorce lose far more economically than in the past, especially those married to a high-earning wife. As child support payments become better enforced, economic factors may contribute in the long run to dissuade some men from ending their marriage.

Divorce drastically reduces many adults' mental and physical health, often over the life course (Hughes and Waite, 2009).Alcohol abuse increases among divorced men and mothers with young children. A large study found that the negative effect of divorce on psychological well-being especially affected parents of young children, particularly women. Parental strains, economic problems, and the stressors of having to maintain contact with the ex-spouse are explanatory factors (Williams and Dunne-Bryant, 2006). Depression among divorced women as well as a general feeling of being less healthy often occur (Wu and Hart, 2002). Rotermann (2007a) reports even more depression among men after divorce.

Many divorced persons admit that they are not any happier while others are even unhappier than during their marriage. In fact, Waite et al. (2002) have found that even unhappily married people were not necessarily happier five years after their divorce than those who had remained married. Another study found that persons in high-distress marriages were happier after divorce whereas those who had been in relatively comfortable marriages were unhappier (Amato and Hohmann-Marriott, 2007). Divorce generally involves a period of stress, instability, loneliness, hurt feelings, and often hostility. That period of transition is often related to health problems (Dupré and Meadows, 2007). Longer studies are needed to see whether these effects diminish over time. One also has to consider that some effects, both for adults and children, may not appear until later in life (Hughes and Waite, 2009). As well, recent research suggests that some of the negative effects of a divorce are continued two generations later among grandchildren (Amato and Cheadle, 2005).

However, one should keep in mind that marital conflict is a significant risk for mental and physical problems so that remaining in a bad marriage can have an important negative impact on the immune system (D'Onofrio and Lahey, 2010). Thus, a stressful marriage produces noxious effects (Choi and Marks, 2008). Leaving such a marriage may increase well-being (Waite et al., 2009). However, Rotermann's (2007a) longitudinal study included bad marriages, and episodes of depression were still more prevalent after divorce.

Factors Associated with Adjustment

There is a great deal of diversity in the post-divorce experience. Nevertheless, the ex-spouse who has the least personal, financial, and social resources, while at the same time having the most responsibilities, encounters more difficulties and may take longer to adjust, especially when he or she has not initiated the divorce. The ex-spouse who has ample resources adapts more successfully. This does not mean, however, that he or she is less hurt than the other. In fact, the stronger person may suffer the most, yet be able to overcome the pain more effectively. Often, as soon as separation or divorce occurs, a relationship that was rather placid becomes conflictual; it is during this period that women are at greater risk of being assaulted and even killed by their former partner (Fleury et al., 2000; GSS, 2000). This may be particularly so for cohabiting women who leave (Sev'er, 2002).

In a nutshell, *adjusting to divorce is easier when* a couple does not have dependent children and does not share many assets, such as a house. The division of assets constitutes one of the most rancorous aspects of divorce. A brief marriage is also easier because the spouses have had less time to invest in the relationship and less time to build a shared network of friends and to become habituated to being married.

For a *woman*, adjusting to divorce is easier when she is under age 35: A younger age gives her a much higher chance of remarrying and of having a family in her second marriage. It is also easier when she has been employed throughout her marriage or, at the very least, fairly recently: Her economic situation will be less precarious and she may have a work-related social network.

In contrast, divorce is much more stressful and requires a great deal of adjustment, at least for *one spouse*, when a couple has children who still live at home; a couple jointly owns a home and shares other assets; the marriage was long and many habits have to be changed; a couple is older, thus less flexible, and perhaps no longer employed; there is a loss of financial resources and economic status; a husband and wife share all their friends; one or both spouses is in ill health, an alcoholic, or a drug abuser. As well, when respective families take sides, each ex-spouse then loses half of her or his extended kin group. A loss of friends makes adjustment more difficult because social support deteriorates at a time of emotional need.

Changes in Ex-Spouses' Social Networks

Persons' social networks after divorce are rarely studied. In order to modestly remedy this lack of information, I am using qualitative data from my longitudinal study of divorce (Ambert, 1989). With divorce, many couples lose the in-law kin system, so that each ex-spouse now has a reduced kin network. Women become single mothers and their supportive network generally becomes smaller. In my research, more women than men reported losing friends after separation, particularly in long-term marriages during which friendships had been shared as a couple. Mutual friends remained with the ex-husband more often than with the ex-wife. Two women explained this situation thusly:

> "His wife [a friend's wife] feels more secure with Paul I think than with me. As a single woman, I am a threat to her. . . . I just never realized that she'd be so jealous the minute her husband looked at me."

> "My ex-husband is more fun to be with because he has more money to do things and go out."

However, very few women had lost those friends whom they had already had before their marriage or had maintained separately during the marriage. The workplace became an important source of moral support at that time. As pointed out in the next quote, in a couple-oriented society, social support is more readily extended to coupled individuals and, after divorce, to men, unless women have a strong, independent network of female friends. Married men seem less threatened by their divorced male friends than married women are by their divorced women friends.

Women reported a sharp decline in social activities involving friends they had while married: fewer phone calls, visits, outings, and movies, for instance. Men reported either little change or an increase in visiting, particularly being invited over for dinner and for outings when their children were with them. Custodial fathers definitely received more offers of help from friends and colleagues, and even from their children's teachers, than custodial mothers. Friends seem to presume that a father needs more help because it is relatively unusual for men to have sole physical custody of their children. They received far more sympathy than custodial mothers.

At Time 2, and particularly Time 3, of the follow-up, three and six years later respectively, a great proportion of respondents had remarried. These remarriages provided an excellent opportunity to see if changes in social networks had occurred. Remarried women had seen a substantial increase in their social activities involving new friends. This increase was more salient for women who had lost their friends to their ex-husbands. The change had been practically instantaneous for many. One woman sarcastically put it this way:

> "Remarriage puts a woman back where she belongs; she's no longer a threat to other women, no longer a temptation to their husbands. But I also think that socially a woman has value because of her married status; I could feel it. I mean, I felt so bitter about it when I was divorced, it was so obvious. From a couple's point of view a divorced woman is more than useless, and all adults are couples so that leaves you nowhere." [Now?]"I am part of a couple again."

When adults remarry or repartner, they gain another set of in-laws; then, they often acquire each other's friends and this explains in part their increased social network and activities. Again, to paraphrase the last woman's quote, this increase is also in part explained by the fact that, for other couples, a couple is a safer and more valued unit for friendship than a divorced individual. The **status** of marriage or *of being part of a couple* certainly enhances a person's social acceptability. Therefore, adults who need friends less (the married) have more, while those who could benefit from friends' social support, such as divorced mothers and the poor, often have fewer. These are social inequities based on gender and coupling status. We need similar research for cohabiting couples who separate.

WHAT ARE THE EFFECTS OF DIVORCE ON CHILDREN?

In a nutshell, although most children do not experience developmental problems, divorce is certainly a strong risk factor and a source of stressors. Divorce is, above all, an emotionally **difficult transition** and, as Kelly and Emery (2003:359) point out, it can "create lingering feelings of sadness, longing, worry, and regret that coexist with competent psychological and social functioning." Connidis (2003a) remarks that relationships are changed after divorce and have to be renegotiated many times over the years; the effects are felt across several living generations within a family.

Although average differences are not huge, children whose parents are divorced (and even after they are remarried or re-partnered) are *more likely* than children whose parents remain together to suffer from depression, anxiety, and other emotional disorders; exhibit behavioural problems including hyperactivity, aggressiveness, fighting, and hostility; become young offenders; do less well in school and do not remain in school as long; and experience more relationship problems and instability, in part due to their behavioural problems (Cavanagh et al., 2008; Furstenberg and Kiernan, 2001; Oldehinkel et al., 2008; Sun and Li, 2008). The negative consequences of divorce are particularly apparent within the context of poverty (Côté et al., 2003).

Adults whose parents divorced during their childhood and teen years, compared with adults from intact two-parent families, tend to have a child out of wedlock more often, particularly during adolescence; achieve lower educational levels; be more often unemployed and do less well economically; have higher cohabitation rates; enter into a first union earlier; have more marital problems and divorce more; are more likely to have lost contact with their father and to report a less happy childhood (Amato, 2003; Hetherington, 2003; Martin et al., 2005; Provencher et al., 2006; Williams, 2001c).

As well, a study by Boyd and Norris (1995) has found that children of divorced parents leave home earlier than others. They leave home in even greater numbers when their custodial parent remarries and more so when both parents remarry. (We have no information about cohabitation; however, the results are probably similar or more salient.) A consequence is that it becomes too expensive to continue their education. This, in turn, leads to lower occupational skills and higher unemployment. Frederick and Boyd (1998) have shown, on the basis of Statistics Canada data, that

80 percent of men and 84 percent of women aged 20 to 44 who lived with their two parents when they were 15 years old had completed high school. This compares with figures ranging from 65 to 73 percent for those whose parents had divorced, including those whose parents had remarried.

As indicated in Table 12.3, when children who have experienced their parents' marital dissolution reach adulthood, their relationship with their parents is less likely to be warm. Amato and Booth (1997) have found that adult children of divorce fare even less well in this respect than children whose parents remained in an unhappy marriage. Longitudinal studies following children up to age 33 indicate that, when emotional problems develop, the effect of parental divorce may last and can even intensify (Cherlin et al., 1998). Because these studies were longitudinal, the researchers were able to measure other family and child characteristics that could have influenced the development of emotional problems. Yet, even after they had considered these other influences, their results still showed that the divorce itself had increased the likelihood of emotional problems, including later on in adulthood. Divorce even contributes negative effects two generations down to grandchildren (Amato and Cheadle, 2005).

However, children whose parents divorce after a low-conflict marriage are more likely to divorce in adulthood than those whose parents' marriage was conflictual—probably because a low-conflict marriage ending in divorce transmits an attitude of lack of commitment to marriage in general (Amato and DeBoer, 2001).

A new couple's risk of divorcing is even higher when their two sets of parents had divorced during their childhood or adolescence (Amato, 1996). However, there is little information on the effect of multiple parental divorces on children. But we know that the more **marital transitions** parents experience, the less well adjusted children are in some domains of life (Amato and Sobolewski, 2001). Some of the hardships caused to children stem mainly from their own parents' first divorce. Remarriages end more quickly than first marriages, thus children may not have had the time to bond with their temporary stepparent to suffer from this loss. However, repeated divorces affect adults, which in turn may affect their ability to parent adequately (Hetherington, 2003). Moreover, multiple divorces may constitute

TABLE 12.3 | **Recalled Childhood Quality for Men and Women Who Experienced Parental Structure Change Versus Those Who Did Not***

	Men		Women	
	No change	Change	No change	Change
Very happy childhood	93%	74%	91%	71%
Very close emotionally to mother	92	83	87	76
Very close emotionally to father	73	53	75	49

Source: Statistics Canada; Williams, 2001c. Reprinted with permission from Statistics Canada.

* Includes all individuals who began life with two parents (biological or adoptive).

a **socialization experience** for children who see their parents divorce so rapidly and so often: They may fail to learn adequate conflict resolution techniques. Such children may learn to quarrel or to give up without resolving differences. They may also learn to think that marriage is a personal choice of a temporary nature. In turn, they could later on experience more difficulties and instabilities in their own marital lives.

In summary, most children survive their parents' divorce quite well developmentally, even though they may be worried, stressed, and unhappy. Pedro-Carroll (2001) points out that *one has to differentiate between distress and disorder*. Most children of divorce experience a certain level of distress, which often lasts for over a decade. For instance, they miss the other parent and, when little, they may feel that they are partly to blame for the divorce; some desperately try to get their parents together again; they are sad; some cry a lot while others lash out and develop temporary behavioural problems. But, despite their distress, most still function well, that is, do not experience "*disorders*" (Laumann-Billings and Emory, 2000). Indeed, whatever statistics one reads concerning the negative outcomes of children of divorce, they do *not* apply to *all* these children (Corak, 2001). Rather, what these statistics indicate is that children of divorced parents have a greater risk of developing problems or of not reaching their full potential than children whose parents remain together. One needs to add that a parental remarriage often contributes another set of stressors and of risks, as we see later.

THEORIES EXPLAINING HOW DIVORCE AFFECTS CHILDREN

Several theories explaining the negative consequences of divorce for children receive support in the research. These explanations are complementary rather than mutually exclusive, because *each fits some children better than others*. These theories largely explain the contexts that divorce creates for children.

Economic Explanation

As documented in Chapter 4, a majority of children experience a reduction in their standard of living after divorce and many become poor. Poverty contributes to amplifying the negative effects of divorce on the mother-child family unit, on the father-child relationship, and on children's life chances. When all variables are considered, post divorce poverty is at least as strong a source of lower cognitive ability and school achievement as is the divorce itself (Strohschein et al., 2009). In some European societies, particularly Norway and Sweden, the **social safety net** compensates greatly so that single-mother families have a (low) rate of poverty that is close to that of two-parent families. Thus, in countries with a more equitable income distribution, the negative consequences of divorce for children do not disappear but are less pronounced than they are in Canada, the U.S., and the U.K.

A 20 to 40 percent income loss for women and children after divorce leads to many **concurrent changes**. To begin with, a great proportion of Canadian women and their children move after separation, often to more crowded and dilapidated housing, where there is more noise and pollution. Children and their mothers may be less healthy as a result and more stressed (see Kohen et al., 2008). The neighbour-hood may be less safe, have more children who are equally poor, who do less well in school, and engage more in delinquency. Having to adjust to a new and often more difficult peer group can create a great deal of problems—loneliness, bullying, school avoidance, and delinquency (Chapter 5).

The sudden, reduced standard of living is often accompanied by a less than plentiful diet, fewer clothes, and little pocket money. In a consumer-oriented society, such a downfall may be felt acutely by children, particularly in the age group of 10- to 16-year-olds. All of these changes are a lot to ask of children, including adolescents who are also undergoing physiological puberty, which, in western societies, carries socioemotional risks (Hines, 1997).

Disruption of Parenting

The economic theory is not in itself sufficient to explain divorce effects: Living in a breaking-up family still produces an independent negative effect of its own (Wu, 1996). Thus, a second theory that also receives a great deal of research support sees parenting behaviours as either a direct causative variable or as a mediator variable (Osborne and McLanahan, 2007). In a nutshell, this theory posits that parents who divorce or break up experience a great deal of stressors and have to adjust to a new lifestyle that gives them less social support as individuals and as parents. Moreover, the custodial mother may have to work long hours to make ends meet. When she returns home, she may be tired, preoccupied, and have less time to devote to her children. As a result, children of divorced mothers who are poor or near poor may receive less attention, guidance, supervision, encouragement, and affection than other children. Parenting skills and availability suffer. Many become less tolerant of misbehaviour and are more prone to have screaming fits, while others become depressed and withdraw from their children (Forgatch et al., 1996). Divorced parents tend to be preoccupied or busy, which means less time for children—less time for advice, for love, and for monitoring. Sons often become defiant, disobedient, disrespectful, and even abusive (Hetherington et al., 1992).

Amato and Gilbreth (1999) suggest that children of divorce have better outcomes when nonresidential fathers provide emotional and instrumental support, make behavioural demands, place limits on what can be done, and administer consistent discipline. When nonresidential fathers remain **active parents,** as opposed to "Sunday daddies" or their children's "pals," they complement and reinforce custodial mothers' socialization efforts. Children receive the same message of support and authority from both parents, an ideal situation rarely achieved. Basically, what counts in child outcomes is neither the custodial arrangement nor the frequency of visitation, but the **quality of parenting** and parents' psychological functioning (Wallerstein, 1998). However, we know that ex-husbands are more likely to remain involved if they feel supported by their ex-wives in their parenting role (Sobolewski and King, 2005).

The Role of Parental Conflict

The third theory overlaps with the second theory to some extent. It focuses on parental conflict both during marriage and after divorce. Conflict is so detrimental that children who remain in a conflict-ridden family have more negative outcomes than those whose parents divorce to eliminate the tension (Amato et al., 1995; Yu et al., 2010). Parental conflict is particularly painful when adolescents or children hear their parents fight about them: They feel caught in the middle. In at least one study looking at situations of high parental conflict, boys who were in regular contact with their nonresidential parent tended to have more problems than boys for whom this contact was limited (Amato and Rezac, 1994). As expressed in the following male student quote, conflict is extremely painful for children of all ages, both while parents are married and after the divorce:

> *"When I was 11, my parents separated. This has been the most difficult period of my short life until now and it still hurts to this day. But when I was 11 it was worse because my life became so different. My sister seemed to cope better but I just couldn't stand the fighting. They'd fight over the phone about everything and when my father would pick us up for the weekend they'd go at it some more and I'd be shaken up for the entire weekend and it would start all over when he would drop us off and on top of it all, they used to talk against each other and say awful things about each other in front of me. To this day, my skin crawls when I know that they'll talk to each other which is rare now that we're older. My sister's wedding was a nightmare of tension and as far as I'm concerned I'll just elope one day because I just couldn't go through with it. I have been a nervous wreck since that time* [age 11]."

In fact, Buchanan et al. (1996) have found that the worst thing that can happen to a child is that his or her parents remain locked in conflict after divorce. In such cases, divorce fulfills no positive function for the child; rather, it exacts a heavy price for which there is no compensation. Parental conflict also means lack of authoritative and guiding parenting. In contrast, low parental conflict after divorce may shield children from the stressors of divorce. Fewer marriages ending in divorce than in the past are highly conflictual (Kerr and Michalski, 2007). But, as we saw, low-conflict marriages that end in divorce appear to have a strong negative effect on children, whereas divorce for high-conflict couples may have a beneficial effect (Booth and Amato, 2001). But, in many cases, "intense anger and conflict is ignited by the separation itself and the impact of highly adversarial legal processes" (Hopper, 2001; Kelly and Emery, 2003:353). Overall, there is research consensus that pre- and post-divorce conflict is detrimental to children but that the divorce itself contributes an additional source of potential problems (Hanson, 1999). We also need research to separate the effect on children of parental conflict within marriage and that following separation: Parental conflict following separation/divorce may be a separate cause of some children's negative outcomes.

Although this concept is not new (Gardner, 1987), we are now hearing about an extreme problem that has recently been "discovered": **Parental alienation** occurs when one parent more or less brainwashes a child against the other parent and effectively prevents that parent from seeing the child and the child from loving that parent. The child may in fact come to reject the hapless parent (Gagné et al., 2005). The consequences for the child's future mental health can be dire.

Preexisting Child Conditions

A fourth explanation has evolved from longitudinal studies of children who were in intact families at the time of the first interview, or Time 1. Throughout the years, some of these children's parents divorced. This allowed the researchers at subsequent stages of the study to return to what they had observed at Time 1 and compare the behaviour and mental health of children whose parents stayed together to those of children whose parents eventually divorced. Two of these studies found that long before the divorce occurred, children of divorce already exhibited more problems than children whose parents stayed together (Block et al., 1988). This led these authors to warn that some of what is interpreted to be consequences of divorce may have actually existed before the divorce or have been consequences of conflict within the marriage.

Subsequent studies, however, have established that the functioning of children and adolescents often changes negatively after their parents' separation, even when researchers control for the child's predivorce characteristics or difficulties (Aseltine, 1996; Morrison and Cherlin, 1995). In other words, the pre- and postdivorce differences "can be attributed to parental divorce and its accompanying disruption of family processes" (Forehand et al., 1997:157). This conclusion is reaffirmed by Cherlin and colleagues (1998) whose data indicate that predivorce characteristics cannot entirely explain children's problems after divorce. Nevertheless, it appears that, in many cases, children are already more difficult before the divorce, which makes sense, considering that their parents may have been fighting or were at the very least preoccupied. Exiting a dysfunctional marriage may actually decrease children's antisocial behaviour (Strohschein, 2005).

Genetic Influence

A fifth theory relates to the genetic inheritance of problematic predispositions. A proportion of people who divorce or end a cohabitation do so because they are temperamental, conflictual, or impulsive individuals who pass on these predispositions to their children via genetic inheritance. The children are then both predisposed to being problematic and live in a home environment that is conflict-ridden, disorganized, and fosters their negative predispositions. When divorce happens in these situations, the home conditions may worsen, thereby exacerbating the children's existing problems in a circular or feedback model of causality (Guo et al., 2008). In these cases, negative effects of divorce are caused both by the environment that divorce produces and genetic frailties passed on to the next generation (D'Onofrio et al., 2007).

Offspring of divorce "are more likely to have an interpersonal style marked by . . . problems with anger, jealousy, hurt feelings, communication, [and] infidelity" (Amato, 1996:638). These interpersonal behaviours may be both learned and genetically transmitted. Indeed, Hetherington (2003) found moderate correlations between parents' personality risks and offspring's personality risks. Genetic transmission would be particularly relevant to the offspring of parents whose divorce is caused by alcoholism, mental illness, and difficult personality characteristics (Rutter, 2002). When children are already genetically vulnerable, the environment created by the divorce exacerbates their vulnerabilities. They receive less attention, monitoring, and guidance, so that their genetic liabilities often find a fertile ground upon which to grow (Horwitz et al., 2010). In contrast, children who have more positive predispositions and also have more stable parents are far less likely to develop problems after divorce—and their parents are also less likely to divorce to begin with.

WIDOWHOOD AND BEREAVEMENT

There were 1,261,100 widowed women but only 312,357 widowed men in Canada in 2006 (Statistics Canada, 2007f). At all age levels, women are more likely to be widowed than men and this difference widens after age 55. In fact, 45 percent of all women aged 65 and over are widows. Looked at differently, in 2001, 61 percent of senior men lived with a spouse or partner compared with only 35 percent of senior women (Statistics Canada, 2002b). As well, widowed men remarry or begin cohabiting far sooner than do widowed women, even within the younger age groups (Wu, 1995).

Widowhood is therefore a **gendered stage** that affects women far more than men. Widowed women are also more likely than their male counterparts to become poor, especially elderly women who are living alone. However, they may have long-term friendships and are more likely than men to acquire new acquaintances (Martin-Matthews, 1991). Because widowhood occurs later in life than it did even 50 years ago, most young children are spared the loss of a parent by death. In Bibby's (2001) survey of adolescents, only 3 percent had a deceased parent while 25 percent had parents who were no longer living together.

The death of a partner requires much readjustment in addition to the great emotional pain it brings. Age, health status, and level of independence may prolong or shorten bereavement. Adaptation to widowhood also depends on the income that is available, as a drop in income may add a tremendous burden to the afflicted person (Statistics Canada, 2004o). Having been the caregiver for the deceased spouse also affects bereavement (Larkin, 2009).

Among seniors, the loss of a spouse is often followed by some mental confusion, helplessness, depression, and general physical vulnerability, as well as a loss of interest in life. Health care costs generally rise following widowhood (Prigerson et al., 2000). The length of the grieving period depends on personal resources, the social support received, and how well prepared the bereaved spouse was for the death. With a long terminal illness, the spouse often begins mourning before death occurs. The loss of a spouse may bring feelings of relief and newly acquired freedom among older women (Hurd, 1999).

The quality of the relationship is also an important element in the grieving process, but may produce different results. Spouses who took care of an ailing partner are often vulnerable (Schulz et al., 2008). Some may be relieved by the death of a partner who has made their lives miserable, whereas others may feel guilty. When a good relationship existed, some spouses are inconsolable for a long period, yet others are thankful for the years they shared. Others are angry (Carr and Boerner, 2009). At least one longitudinal study has found that happy marriages are associated with more traumatic grief symptoms (Prigerson et al., 2000). Another study found that men and women who had been quite dependent on their spouse during marriage experienced a great deal of personal growth in widowhood (Carr, 2004).

Consequences of a Parent's Death for Children

In terms of outcomes, in most western countries, children and adolescents of widowhood do as well as those in two-parent families or, at the very least, far better than children of divorced and single parents (Biblarz and Gottainer, 2000; Provencher et al., 2006; Steele et al., 2009). This is not to say that children do not grieve and miss their deceased parent. But they benefit from several social, familial, and personal advantages over children of divorce (Teachman, 2004). First, they are less likely to have been subjected to parental conflict before the death and are certainly not affected by it after. Second, the remaining parent is often left in a more favourable economic situation and may also be helped by life insurance benefits so that poverty occurs less frequently. This relative economic security also protects children from a host of accompanying stressors, such as having to move and change school. Third, following death, there are social rites of bonding through which sympathy is bestowed upon children, which is quite a contrast to what happens to children in cases of parental divorce.

Fourth, the remaining parent's task of grieving, of caring for the children's own pain, and of behaving as a proper widow or widower delays his or her re-entry on the mating scene. Children are not faced with a parent who is suddenly unavailable because of the demands of his or her social life. There is no immediate competition for the parent's love. A fifth element protecting children of widowhood is that a good proportion of the deaths occur to couples who had a stable marriage. Thus, the personalities involved may not have included so many parents with difficult personalities as may be the case in situations of divorce (Simons et al., 1996). Consequently, the children themselves have greater chances of being stable individuals.

Children of widowhood may also adapt better to their parent's remarriage later because this loss makes them more receptive to acquiring a substitute parent. Bereaved children no longer have another parent, whether visiting or custodial, whose place seems to be usurped by a stepparent. No visitations are involved; there is only one home, one set of rules, and one family. With peers and teachers, a formerly widowed parent with children and a new spouse more easily pass for a "real" family.

REMARRIAGE AND REPARTNERING

Remarriage has become less common because of the increasing tendency to cohabit after divorce, especially in Quebec (Beaupré, 2008). Wu and Schimmele (2005) have estimated that, 10 years after a divorce or breakup, 59 percent of women and 72 percent of men are repartnered. Remarriage is now more likely to occur after a cohabitation.

Those separated from a cohabitation repartner more quickly, followed by the divorced, and then the widowed (Sweeney, 2010). Remarriage is more common among immigrants than Canadian-born citizens. As well, cohabitation rates after divorce are lower for women than men (Belleau, 2007:15). Rates of remarriage decline with age for both genders but more acutely so for women because men prefer younger women (England and McClintock, 2009; Sassler, 2010).

The Aftermath of Remarriage for Spouses

Although remarriages are as happy as first marriages, controlling for the number of years married, remarriages after a divorce have a higher rate of dissolution (Sweeney, 2010). Remarriages that are preceded by cohabitation are even less stable, although this finding is not unanimous (Teachman, 2008; Xu et al., 2006). Why are remarriages less stable? First, remarriages include persons who have already proven that they can divorce; they may be more accepting of divorce as a solution and more ready to have recourse to it a second time. Second, spouses in remarriages may be less willing to compromise and may become disenchanted more rapidly. Third, there are fewer norms that guide these relationships, making it more difficult for the spouses to feel secure within their respective roles. Fourth, the structure itself of remarriage is a more complex one when children are brought in along with ex-spouses and ex-in-laws (Teachman, 2008). Indeed, remarriages without children from previous unions or only with children born to the union have a rate of divorce equivalent to that of first marriages.

A remarriage after divorce generally enhances the quality of adults' lives, emotionally, socially, and financially—the latter especially for women, but not as much as is the case for a first marriage (Sweeney, 2010). Many mother-headed families exit poverty through remarriage (Wilmoth and Koso, 2002). However, one should not ignore the fact that many divorced and widowed middle-aged and older women may prefer to remain single. These women's level of well-being should be quite high. When a remarriage or cohabitation endures, it may far outlast the first marriage. After years of remarriage or cohabitation, many spouses even forget that they have been married to someone else, particularly when there were no children from the first union.

Adjustment to Remarriage and Stepparenting

In Canada, the term "stepfamilies" includes both marital and cohabitational: One-half of stepfamilies are remarriages. In Quebec, nearly 75 percent of all stepfamilies are common-law unions whereas fewer than 45 percent of stepfamilies are common-law in Ontario, the Prairies, and B.C. Looked at differently, in 2001, 12 percent of *families* composed of a couple with children were stepfamilies, for a total of 503,100. Of these stepfamilies, 50 percent included only the mother's child(ren) from a previous union; 10 percent included only the father's child(ren); 8 percent consisted of both spouses' children from previous unions; and 32 percent included a child born to the union in addition to the children born from previous ones (Turcotte, 2002). About 10 percent of all Canadian *children* under the age of 12 are living in a stepfamily.

When neither spouse has children, adjustment to remarriage is no different than in a first marriage. It becomes more complex with stepchildren, and the complexity increases when there are both live-in and visiting stepchildren. The period of readjustment takes several years before a stepfamily is stabilized. However, we have no research data concerning cohabitational stepfamilies compared with married ones. Being a stepparent is not a role one expects to occupy and for which one is prepared, and it is not an institutionalized one (Cherlin, 1978). With stepchildren, the newlyweds have to adapt to two key roles simultaneously, parent and spouse, while these two roles are generally initiated separately in first unions. Stepparenthood is also a vilified role when one thinks of the "wicked stepmother" in fairy tales. The role is considered inferior to that of mothers. No norms or rules guide the behaviour of a "good" stepparent, as is the case for a good parent. Each stepparent more or less has to reinvent the role and the relationship, which can be both an advantage and a disadvantage. These remarks also apply to stepparenting in same-sex marriages (Nelson, 1996). Overall, the quality of parent-children relationships remains lower in stepfamilies over the years (Ward et al., 2009).

The New Spouse and the Ex-Spouse

In 2002, 34 percent of all marriages included at least one spouse who had been previously married and nearly 46 percent of remarriages are remarriages for both spouses (Statistics Canada, 2006d). A remarried person whose spouse has children may need to relate to the children's other parent—the "ex." Relatively little research exists on this complex relationship, so I have borrowed from my fieldwork. It is obvious from the quotes that follow as well as from the entire research data that a husband's ex-wife or a wife's ex-husband is not overly popular among current wives and husbands:

> *"We don't socialize. It's strictly business for the children's sake. I didn't marry my husband to acquire his ex-wife or her new husband, and my husband certainly does not want to be saddled with my ex-husband and his girlfriend. No. These relationships are nice on a TV screen but not in real life."*

The new husband or wife often resented the help the spouse has to give his or her ex, especially financial help. Noncustodial fathers frequently expressed serious concerns about their ex-wife's new partner who had become their children's live-in stepparent. They worried about the way the new stepfather treated the children, the example he provided, as well as the potential for sexual abuse:

> *"My ex-wife's husband is a burden to me in a way* [he is an alcoholic]. *I told my wife, my ex-wife, that she's got to be very careful never to let the girls alone with him. She was offended but she got the point. I just don't trust him."*

In some instances, the new wife and the ex-wife have to cooperate in order to raise the children and to arrange visitation schedules:

> *"We have a lot of planning to do to arrange her children's visits. . . . So we have a lot to talk about. But I think she must appreciate me because I don't have to have his children over as often as I do especially so since I have three of my own, so actually I babysit for her. She doesn't* [interfere], *not exactly, but what can you expect with so many children, it's a real interference even if they're quite good."*

Remarriages are as happy as first marriages; they are, however, more fragile and likely to end in another divorce. The structural complexity of remarriages—including the presence of children belonging to each partner—certainly contributes to their instability.

Overall, the study unearthed a great deal of uneasiness about the possibility of having a close relationship with the ex, in part because of the threat of instability in the new marriage. For instance, a man's ex-wife more easily accepts his new wife when the latter has not been involved with him in an adulterous relationship. Obviously, boundary maintenance is a key element in the success of remarriages.

What Are the Effects of Parental Remarriage on Children?

This question is complicated by the fact that many divorced parents, perhaps nearly half, cohabit but do not remarry (Marcil-Gratton et al., 2003). There is no research on the effect on children of that type of parental repartnering. Until now, the research on remarriage has looked at the gender and, to some extent, the age of children at parents' remarriage. It is only recently that studies have focused on the fact that, when the custodial parent remarries, the child becomes a stepchild. This familial restructuring requires a great deal of adjustment on their part (Juby et al., 2005a). As well, in a third of stepfamilies, a new child is born who is the couple's shared child. Therefore, at some point after one of their parents' repartnering, many stepchildren become half-siblings (Marcil-Gratton et al., 2003).

Stepchildren do not generally have better outcomes than those who remain with their divorced parent, except perhaps financially while they live at home (Brown, 2004b; Tillman, 2008). Rather, they tend to have higher rates of problems, including delinquency (Savoie, 2007; Statistics Canada, 2007i; Zeman and Bressan, 2008). However, parental cohabitation rather than remarriage seems to be associated with more child problems (Brown, 2006). This may stem from a lower stepfather investment in situations of cohabitation and the biological father's lesser involvement after the mother's repartnering (Guzzo, 2009b). In contrast, there is a correlation between high stepfather involvement in remarriage and mothers' reports of fewer behavioural problems among children (Amato and Rivera, 1999).

When girls had a close relationship with their single mother, they are more likely to fare poorly in the remarriage. They miss the attention their mother lavished on them and may resent the intruder. For them, the remarriage constitutes a loss. As adults, estrangement from fathers also occurs more often among daughters than sons, and many daughters interpret this distancing to be the result of their father's remarriage (Ahrons and Tanner, 2003). In fact, 57 percent of young women and 30 percent of young men in remarried families leave home at a younger age than average (Beaupré et al., 2008). Moreover, stepdaughters are more at risk of being abused sexually by their stepfather or their mother's boyfriend than are daughters in intact families (see Giles-Sims, 1997). This may stem from the fact that roles are more blurred than in biological families. Further, stepfathers have a low involvement in child care, which increases the risk for sexual abuse, even among fathers (in Giles-Sims, 1997). Stepfathers often become acquainted with the child only when she is older and can be perceived as an object of sexual attraction. It should be added, however, that children in stepfamilies (and in single-parent families) have higher rates of several types of victimization (see Chapter 13).

Boys adjust better than girls to being a stepchild, perhaps because they are at home less or because many benefit from the presence of a stepfather. Nevertheless, Pagani et al. (1997) have found that boys living with a recently remarried parent were the most hyperactive at school of all categories of boys aged 12 to 16. This latter result was replicated in the U.S. by Coughlin and Vuchinich (1996), who documented higher rates of early delinquency among boys who had lived in either a single-parent or stepparent family at age 10. We have also seen that youth on average leave both home and school earlier when their parent remarries: Aquilino (2005) has found that remarried parents and stepparents are less inclined than other parents to feel that they have to support their children once they are older.

Overall, younger children usually adapt better, especially when they have always known the stepparent (Hofferth and Anderson, 2003). Many children and adolescents have a close relationship with their resident stepfather and this relates to better outcomes, especially when they also maintain a supportive relationship with their nonresident father (King, 2006). Many boys are advantaged by the addition of an authoritative (not to be confused with authoritarian) adult male role model in the family. Others, however, resent the intrusion of one more authority figures in their lives at a time when they may be seeking autonomy from their family (Hetherington and Kelly, 2002). Even small children benefit when a resident stepfather is involved with them (Bzostek, 2008). Yet, on many measures, young stepchildren still fare less well than other children (Kerr and Michalski, 2007).

One can hypothesize that a **parental cohabitation**, rather than remarriage, may be even less functional for stepchildren, especially when it takes place rapidly after parental separation (Juby et al., 2007). Cohabitation may bring additional stressors to children's lives when it heightens a mother's or father's sense of insecurity and dimishes the quality of her or his parenting. Cohabiting stepparent families bring far more boundary ambiguity than married ones (Brown and Manning, 2009) and probably result in far less support from kin, at least at the outset—and this might be especially so with multiple prior cohabitations that each resulted in fertility (Bronte-Tinkew et al., 2009). Indeed, in general in Quebec and the rest of Canada, about 15 percent of second-born children become a half-sibling to an older child, that is, a child from another father (Duchesne, 2007). Overall, the research has consistently shown that children who live with their original *married* parents have fewer behavioural problems than other children, including children who live with their own cohabiting parents (Hofferth, 2006; Kerr and Michalski, 2007)).

Recent research indicates that **new children** born to blended families may have more problems than children living with their still-married parents (Halpern-Meekin and Tach, 2008). "New" children born to a family reconstituted via cohabitation are over twice as likely as children born in an intact family to have their parents separate (Marcil-Gratton et al., 2003). Children in a remarriage, whether they are stepchildren or a new child born to the remarriage with stepchildren, have on average less positive outcomes than children whose parents have never divorced (Halpern-Meekin and Tach, 2008; Hofferth, 2006; Mac Con, 2006). These results are fairly consistent throughout the western world (Marks, 2006). At this point, no solid explanation exists because this research is very new.

Studies of young adults whose custodial parent's *remarriage has endured* have shown that these offspring were strongly attached to their family and benefited emotionally from it. It is thus possible that some of the positive effects of a parent's good and lasting remarriage do not appear until later in adulthood (see Sun and Li, 2008). Adult children remain more attached to stepparents they have lived with than to other stepparents, even after their parent divorced again (Schmeeckle et al., 2006).

GRANDPARENTING AFTER DIVORCE AND STEP-GRANDPARENTING

There are three separate situations in terms of grandparenting after divorce: Grandparenting when one's adult child divorces; grandparenting after one has divorced at some earlier point, often long before the grandchildren arrive; and divorcing after one already is a grandparent. The available research pertains only to the first two situations, particularly the first one.

Maternal grandparents often help their divorcing children, especially daughters, both emotionally and instrumentally, particularly in terms of child care. But many other grandparents lose touch with grandchildren after a divorce because the custodial parent moves too far away or is not cooperative; others because their son, who is the visiting parent, more or less relinquishes his responsibilities. Such grandparents often experience a sharp decrease in well-being (Drew and Silverstein, 2007). This is yet another example of how adult children's marital or parental transitions create related transitions in the older generation: In the latter instance, grandparents lose their grandchildren.

Grandparents' visitation rights have been legalized in the Yukon and four provinces: Alberta, British Columbia, New Brunswick, and Quebec (Campbell and Carroll, 2007). In theory, in-laws, who are one's children's grandparents, should be a prime source of help. However, in my study, fewer than 20 percent of custodial parents actually talked to their former in-laws in a week's time, had visited them in a month's time, or had received some help from them (Ambert, 1989).

Some 60 percent of respondents talked of former in-laws who were hostile toward them; 35 percent of the respondents felt that their former in-laws projected their negative attitude, either verbally or behaviourally, to their *grandchildren*. The most prominent difficulties were situations in which the ex-in-laws openly accused the custodial parent of having caused the failure of the marriage (48 percent). The second difficulty most frequently mentioned was ex-in-laws' comments concerning custodial parents' fitness as parents (46 percent). These accusations, gossips, and remarks ranged from stating that the parent was "unfit," was a "bad" mother or father, did not spend enough time with the children, left them alone too much, and was unfair or cruel to the father (or mother). These accusations were often extended to other areas of life, such as "poor money manager," "sexually loose," or "unable to hold down a job." Or grandparents would ask their grandchildren: *"Does she go out? Whom with?" "Is she home when you come home from school?" "Does she drink?"* One 14-year-old girl shouted at her mother, *"Grandma says you sleep with anyone so I don't see why you can tell me that I can't go out tonight!"*

Even when words were not spoken, grandparents' refusal to talk to or see the other parent was a behavioural indicator that did not go unnoticed by the children. It has been suggested that, where relevant, grandparents should visit their grandchildren at both their homes, and many do. Such visits contribute to legitimize the children's two-home nuclear family. Grandchildren would retain a psychologically intact family and would not feel torn between the two sides of their kinship group. It is regrettable that not enough research has been carried out on grandparenting after an adult child's divorce (Henderson and Moran, 2001), particularly on those who are helpful, even financially.

Another gap in the research exists in terms of grandparents who have themselves divorced. Divorced or remarried grandparents have a lower frequency of contact with their children (Uhlenberg and Hammill, 1998). Therefore, they, and especially grandfathers, are less involved with their grandchildren than nondivorced ones. But, in part, a good relationship between parents and grandparents compensates for the negative effect of divorce in the older generation (King, 2003a). In other words, these studies confirm the long-term consequences of divorce on family life later on and across generations (Connidis, 2003a).

For its part, step-grandparenting is a role that is even less culturally delineated than that of regular grandparenting, although at least 12 percent of Canadian families include a step-grandparent. A step-grandparent is created when an adult child remarries a person who has children. But a person may also marry a grandparent (who may be widowed or divorced) and thus becomes a step-grandparent to his or her grandchildren. Only the first situation has been studied, however so little.

The step-grandparent relationship may become particularly useful and close if a young child has more or less lost contact with one set of grandparents, generally on the father's side. A functional substitution can then take place. However, when stepchildren do not accept their parent's remarriage, they may not wish to participate in family activities that include the stepparent's kin. It is particularly easy for a child to avoid contact with step-grandparents when it is the nonresidential parent, generally the father, who remarries. The child usually spends little time with his or her father, even less with the stepmother, and none with her kin.

In my research, stepmothers often went to see their own parents when their husband's children were visiting. In part, there was the desire to allow the stepchildren to receive as much attention as possible from their father without interference from the stepmother and her own children. In some cases, women knew that stepchildren and their mother resented them and they preferred to distance themselves from the situation. Thus, in many instances of nonresidential fathers' remarriages, the stepmother and her kin effectively remain in the background. Her parents are step-grandparents in name only, and the termination of her marriage to him affects them very little as step-grandparents.

On the other hand, it may be easier for children and adolescents to accept a step-grandparent when they rebel against having a stepparent at home. This is a less threatening and far more benign relationship. When the remarried custodial parent visits with the new in-laws and brings the children along, the latter may indirectly acquire a sense of normalization of family relationships. Thus, step-grandparents may contribute to the integration of the reconstituted family and fulfill the same functions as actual grandparents (Attar-Schwartz et al., 2009; Connidis, 2010).

CONCLUSIONS: THE FAMILIAL AND SOCIAL IMPLICATIONS OF DIVORCE

According to Furstenberg and Cherlin (1991:28), divorce creates a **structural ambiguity** in that "the social and psychological tasks of divorce directly collide with the normal expectations of parenthood." Divorce represents a solution to conjugal unhappiness and misery. But *what is a solution for adults is not necessarily one for their children* (Beaujot, 2000). We also saw that the same can be said of remarriage and, especially, repartnering. Nevertheless, results on the effect of divorce on children have to be interpreted with caution. First, not all children are affected by their parents' divorce, whether positively or negatively. Some children had no problems before and acquire none after. Others had problems before and have the same or worse ones after. Yet others do better after the divorce of highly conflictual parents. Second, among children who are affected, the magnitude and duration of the effect differ greatly. There is also a great deal of difference in terms of the domains of life that are touched. For instance, some children are affected emotionally, others behaviourally, and still others in terms of school performance. The impact on the most affected touches on all these and other fronts. In many cases, the effects are lifelong. In general, it can be said that most marital status transitions are detrimental to children, if only temporarily—whether it is from marriage to single parenting to divorce to cohabitation or to remarriage and another divorce (Formby and Cherlin, 2007).

Contrary to expectations from various opposite corners of the ideological spectrum, "the increase in marital instability has not brought society to the brink of chaos, but neither has it led to a golden age of freedom and self-actualization" (Amato, 2000:1282). Apparently, neither has remarriage or repartnering after divorce become a cornucopia of blessings, especially for children.

Summary

1. At 2.2 per 1,000 population in 2005, the Canadian divorce rate is half that of the American one. Rates vary by geographic region. Marriages last on average longer and take place at an older age than a few decades ago. Serial divorces have increased. Indications are that individuals who divorce several times within a decade may have deficits in terms of personality that translate into difficulties in getting along and being committed to the relationship. Fewer than half of divorces include children. Joint legal custody is now more frequent, although children nearly always live with their mothers.

2. The sociocultural factors related to a high divorce rate are multiple and interlinked. They include the secularization of society; the desacralization and deinstitutionalization of marriage; the liberalization of norms and divorce laws; individualism; and a lower threshold of tolerance for marital failings combined with a high level of expectation of marital life.

3. At the demographic level, the first four years of marriage are the most vulnerable to divorce. Besides poverty, additional demographic risks include youthful marriage, solo mothering, remarriage, prior cohabitation, and parents' divorce. Selection and causality effects of cohabitation help explain its relationship to divorce. Reasons for divorcing vary, but the most commonly mentioned are irreconcilable differences, conflict, and falling out of love.

4. The many factors associated with an easier adjustment to divorce among adults include a couple having no dependent children and no shared assets; a marriage that has been brief; and each spouse retaining friends individually. Women who are younger and have remained employed are advantaged in the process of adjustment. After divorce, changes occur in ex-spouses' social networks.

5. At the individual level, children exhibit a wide range of effects of divorce, from being very negatively affected to benefiting from it. On average, however, children whose parents divorce experience higher rates of behavioural, emotional, and achievement problems, even into adulthood, than children raised by their two parents. The main theories explaining these negative consequences focus on the diminished family income and even poverty that too often follows divorce; disruption of parenting behaviours as a result of stressors; parental conflict both before and after divorce; and genetic inheritance of difficult personalities in some families. Preexisting negative child attributes and behaviours also contribute to problems after divorce, but problems specific to divorce arise as well.

6. Early widowhood is far less common than it was even in the 1920s. But widowhood is more common among women than men in middle age and after. It is a gendered stage. The stages and length of bereavement vary. In the long term, children of widowhood have outcomes similar to those whose parents remain together.

7. Excluding Quebec, approximately 70 percent of men and 58 percent of women who divorce eventually remarry. The structure of a remarriage is often more complex and related to higher divorce rates. The relationship between, say, a man's wife and ex-wife is generally difficult and there are no norms that guide interaction. Although remarriage usually raises parents' level of well-being and a mother's familial income, children benefit differentially from remarriage. For many, it requires even more negative adjustment than had been the case for divorce. For others, there are few benefits but no disadvantages. Still others, particularly adolescent boys, may benefit from the presence of a stepfather. Grandparenting after divorce and step-grandparenting are discussed.

8. Divorce and remarriage are adult institutions that often create a structural ambiguity

that collides with the requisites of effective parenting. The factors associated with

divorce and remarriage may evolve over time.

Analytical Questions

1. What relationships would you establish among the reasons people give for their own divorce and the sociocultural factors related to divorce?
2. How can young women organize their lives to prevent some of the negative consequences of divorce for themselves later on, if it ever occurs?

3. Of the theories meant to explain the negative effects of parental divorce on children, which would particularly apply to children whose parents have remarried and why?
4. Some politicians, especially south of the border, want to return to a time when divorce was difficult to obtain. What do you think the consequences would be? What, rather, should be done?

Suggested Readings

Cherlin, A. J. 2009. *The marriage-go-round. The state of marriage and the family in America today.* New York: Alfred A. Knopf. An analysis of a problematic duality in family life: On one hand, Americans emphasize personal choice and individualism in relationships. On the other hand, they value marriage, which is based on commitment. This duality translates into higher divorce and remarriage rates. Cherlin discusses divorce and remarriage as well as their impact of children.

Mandell, D. 2002. *"Deadbeat dads": Subjectivity and social construction. Toronto:* University of Toronto Press. This research on a small group of seven fathers includes thorough discussions, information, and a well-balanced perspective on the payment/nonpayment of child support after divorce.

Matthews, A. M. 1991. *Widowhood in later life.* Toronto: Butterworths/Harcourt Brace. The author discusses bereavement and how people rebuild their

lives following the death of a spouse. Comparisons are brought by gender with other marital statuses and by the presence or absence of children.

Moore, W. 2009. *Wedlock: The true story of the disastrous marriage and remarkable divorce of Mary Eleanor Bowes, Countess of Strathmore.* New York: Crown Publishers. A captivating and well-documented story that highlights the stark inequalities and legal burdens faced by married women in 18th-century England—with a focus on wife abuse and the risks that attempting to divorce could bring to a woman.

Northcott, H. C., and Wilson, D. M. 2008. *Dying and death in Canada,* 2nd Ed. Peterborough, On: Broadview Press. The authors present a historical and social overview of dying in Canada, including its social construction. This book also examines the context of social institutions and the effects of death on families.

Suggested Weblinks

BC Council for Families provides articles on a wide range of topics, including stepfamilies.
www.bccf.bc.ca

Bureau of the Census. For the U.S., use the website's search engine to find information on divorce.
www.census.gov

BC's Justice Education Society and **Bountiful Films** created an online resource for children 6 to 11 whose parents are breaking up.
www.kidsBC.ca

Parenting After Separation Program in B.C. A practical website for divorcing parents.
www.ag.gov.bc.ca/family-justice/help/pas/index.htm

Statistics Canada contains information relevant to this chapter, some of which can be found through the Search option.
www.statcan.gc.ca

CHAPTER 13

Family Violence, Abuse, and Neglect

A 16-year-old rapes his 15-year-old girlfriend in his car on the way back from the movies. He felt that they had been going out long enough and it was time "to go all the way." (Abstract from student autobiography)

A police officer brings a 14-year-old girl back home after finding her doing drugs with two older males at a strip mall. It's 3 a.m. She lives in an affluent suburban home. Her parents did not know that she was out. (Abstract from student autobiography)

A 10-year-old girl has been fondled, kissed in the genital area, and convinced to "touch" the genitals of her father's best friend. He is "part of the family," and often babysits the two children, a boy and a girl. One day, he forces the girl to practise oral sex on him when the boy, age 11, walks in. He later tells his parents who call the police. (Abstract from student autobiography)

A man stalks his wife after she leaves him for battery. Despite a restraining order preventing him from coming within 300 feet, he savagely stabs her as she returns home from work. She leaves two children. (Canadian newscast)

Social workers are called to a home where they find five children ranging in age from two to 10 in a filthy and barely furnished home. The children are hungry and cold, and the level of functioning of all but the oldest one indicates delay due to neglect. The two parents involved have been out on a crack-induced "trip" for three days. (American newscast)

A man is beaten up by his gay partner so severely that he requires emergency surgery. The battering has been going on for two years. (American newscast)

What these vignettes share in common is either violence or neglect. In order to form a more complete picture of abuse and neglect afflicting Canadian families, to these situations one can add sibling violence and peer abuse—which are the most common types of maltreatment—and the less well-known child-to-parent abuse (Duffy and Momirov, 2005). In 2001, family violence in general constituted one-quarter of all violent crimes reported to the police (Statistics Canada, 2003b). In this chapter, various forms of family violence and neglect are analyzed as reflections of cultural norms that foster such behaviours. However, not everyone in our society is equally vulnerable to being an abuser and/or a victim: Social inequalities by class, race/ethnicity, marital status, and especially gender and age come to the fore. Females of all ages are more likely to be abused (DeKeseredy and Dragiewicz, 2007; Sev'er, 2002). Hence, feminist theories are particularly relevant.

DATING AND COURTSHIP VIOLENCE

While family violence and partner abuse have finally become more socially and politically visible, dating abuse is only beginning to emerge in the public consciousness. For a substantial segment of Canadian youths, dating is a fertile ground upon which to continue their aggressive behaviours toward their peers. For others, particularly among males, it is an opportunity to discover a new arena in which to exercise **power**. Few incidents of courtship or dating violence are reported to authorities or to parents, but DeKeseredy and Kelly (1993) and Johnson (1996) estimate that over 20 percent of women students are assaulted in a broad sense each year. More recently, Statistics Canada (2010b) has found that, between 2004 and 2008, police-reported dating violence has increased by over 40 percent, with eight out of 10 victims being women. The highest rate of *reported* dating violence involved women in the 30 to 34 age bracket. Many youths actually consider acts of violence a normal part of the "excitement" of the dating process:

> *"We both have strong personalities and don't let people walk all over us and that goes for each other. I don't mind punching him in the stomach or kicking his legs if he's too fresh and he does the same, except that he's bigger and it hurts more. My mother gets on my nerves about this because she says, 'If that's the way the both of you behave now think what it's going to be like in 5 years.'"*

Other women students are not so complacent:

> *"I'd rate myself as unhappy at this point because I have to decide if I'll stay with my boyfriend of three years. Once in a while he calls me names but recently he's grabbed me and shoved me in the car and once against the wall another time and I am afraid that I'll end up a battered wife."*

Indeed, dating violence predicts domestic abuse later on, whether it occurs in cohabitation or marriage. Perhaps the most surprising aspect of courtship violence, as is the case for spousal abuse, is that both men and women are involved in inflicting harm (Swinford et al., 2000), often within a same couple, especially among younger partners (Renner and Whitney, 2010). However, women sustain most of the injuries (Warner, 2010) and much of the violence carried out by women is in self-defence. In contrast, men are more likely to use violence as an exercise of power or as an attempt to regain control (DeKeseredy and Dragiewicz, 2007).

Date Rape and Sources of Dating Violence

Date rape is an issue that has belatedly received attention. In Canada, DeKeseredy and Kelly (1993) found a 28 percent sexual abuse rate among female university students, albeit within a broad definition. Here as well, most of these student victims never report anything to the authorities, as is the case for the following young woman:

> *"The most painful event in my entire life is having been raped. Wayne* [name changed] *was a good friend. I had known him for a long time. One winter day I decided to call Wayne from school. He invited me to come over to watch movies . . . When I got to Wayne's apartment everything seemed to be running smooth. We were watching movies. Wayne then suggested that I check out his bedroom, so, out of stupidity and perhaps curiosity, I went. He then locked the door and raped me. I really did try to fight him off but he's a football player. . . . I couldn't tell my parents, and they still don't know."*

The situation of date and even acquaintance rape became more complex in the 1990s with the arrival of readily available chemicals that, when dropped in a woman's drink, secure her full "cooperation." The woman cannot later recall much of what occurred. These situations happen on campuses as well as in bars and nightclubs where the purpose is to meet members of the opposite sex. They include gang rape, even in college fraternities in the U.S. Gang rape is the ultimate in terms of a "power trip" and **male dominance**. These instances well illustrate young males' readiness to circumvent decency and legality in order to secure their own sexual gratification and to be able to justify their acts.

The sources of dating violence are still debated. Most studies have turned to psychological and familial explanations while excluding extra-familial and cultural influences. This omission of influential factors at the sociocultural level distorts reality and prevents us from acquiring a full understanding of how particular behaviours emerge (Sev'er, 2002). For instance, in certain peer groups, including professional athletes who have been much in the news in recent years with respect to violence, the **social construction of masculinity** includes violent attitudes in general, and particularly toward females. It also involves a mentality of sexual entitlement (Hartwick et al., 2007). Thus, a feminist perspective indicates that, among heterosexual couples, the overall gender stratification provides an open-door policy for violence against women. This type of cultural climate is reflected in the media. As well, much pornographic material, to which many men and boys are exposed, contains graphically detailed violent sex. Similarly, as we soon see, children engage in a great deal of peer abuse that can easily be transposed into dating relationships. This construction of masculinity should also be related to the fact that too many males, particularly disadvantaged, as seen in Chapter 8, feel entitled to have babies they rarely support.

Studies on childhood exposure to interparental violence as the key factor in the origins of dating violence are inconclusive: Some find a relationship between the two but others do not (Foshee et al., 2005). The least that can be said is that exposure to parental violence during adolescence and young adulthood certainly constitutes a risk factor. So does prior abuse in childhood (Wekerle et al., 2009). Furthermore, on average, males who engage in dating violence were more aggressive as boys and more likely to have committed delinquent acts and used drugs than other males (Capaldi and Clark, 1998; Simons et al., 1998). Many exhibited behavioural problems as children and may still be out of control; the same pattern occurs among some abusive females. These results corroborate those of other researchers who report two categories of abusers among the married: those who limit their abuse to the home and those who are violent in other contexts as well (Delsol et al., 2003).

VERBAL AND PSYCHOLOGICAL ABUSE OF PARTNERS

Verbal abuse consists of repeatedly addressing one's partner with epithets, foul language, using berating and demeaning put-downs, and threatening and criticizing, even in public (DeKeseredy, 2000). Its purpose is to dominate, to exercise power, and to show who is "the boss." It is also used to rationalize or excuse one's bad behaviour by demeaning the other. Calling one's date an "idiot" once is unfortunate but it does not constitute verbal abuse; however, if such a behaviour is a pattern, then it is abusive. Verbal abuse marks the **erosion of civility** and sets a precedent upon which physical abuse can be added in the relationship. Indeed, physical abuse is generally accompanied or preceded by verbal insults and attempts by one partner or both to intimidate or control the other. Males particularly tend to practise both types of abuse in severe cases of psychological and physical assaults (Hamby and Sugarman, 1999).

Verbal abuse is quite salient in music videos favoured by youths, and it is nearly always directed against women because, in a subtle way, culture defines women as legitimate targets of male violence. The words bitch and ho are widespread in a growing segment of younger cohorts; they are often used as soon as a quarrel erupts. It is not unusual to hear young couples calling each other foul and demeaning names; such insults were rarely overheard just decades ago. These exchanges represent a dangerous escalation, a lack of civility, part of what Garbarino (1995) refers to as the "toxic" environment surrounding families raising children.

Psychological abuse is often reciprocal, underreported, and its effects on the parties are underestimated (Follingstad and Edmundson, 2010). Renzetti (1997) has discovered among same-sex couples that this type of abuse is often tailored to fit a partner's vulnerabilities. Coercive control can occur without physical violence with damaging consequences (Anderson, 2008). During my study on divorce, ex-spouses, particularly ex-wives, frequently mentioned that such verbal violence had been a pattern in their past marriage:

> One woman who was obese was repeatedly called a "fat slob" and a "pile of lard" by her husband. He would tell her to "move your fat ass" or order her to "sit on your god-damn fat ass, I have something to tell you." At the dinner table, she had to eat like a bird lest he observed to the children, "There goes your mother, stuffing her fat face." Or he would yell, "You're just adding one pound of lard to your fat ass." The more he emphasized her weight, the more she ate, and the larger she became, until her health was threatened.

This tailoring of verbal abuse can focus on facial features, body shape, clumsiness, lack of mental agility, as well as unemployment and financial difficulties: One ex-wife had repeatedly taunted her unemployed husband in front of their children as *"good for nothing"* and *"you're no real man."* Verbal abuse can also take the form of threats and become a form of psychological blackmail:

> One divorced woman recalled that her ex-husband used to threaten to tell her children that she had given up her first-born for adoption—disregarding the fact that the infant had been his and he had not wanted him (this was before they married). Another was constantly threatened by her ex-husband of losing custody

of her children: She suffered from bouts of depression, and the threats, which terrorized her, merely increased her sad condition. One ex-husband was threatened by his ex-wife of legal exposure if he did not "cough up" more monthly support; at some point in the past, he had defrauded his former employers in order to meet his wife's extravagant demands but had never been caught. Now that she was his ex-wife, she used his illegal past activities as leverage to get more money.

Psychological abuse can turn into physical abuse and even life threatening situations. Renzetti (1997:74) writes of two women with physical disabilities:

"Their partners would abandon them in dangerous settings (i.e., an isolated wooded area) without their wheelchairs. Another woman who was diabetic stated that her partner would punish her by forcing her to eat sugar."

Emotionally abusive relationships often lead to physical violence (Frye and Karney, 2006). In 2004, the prevalence of physical violence was 34 percent for females and 26 percent for males in emotionally abusive relationships but 1 percent when there was no emotional abuse (Brzozowski and Brazeau, 2008).

Verbal and psychological abuse is an issue that is particularly important among adolescents who begin dating at an early age, as described in Chapter 7. Young girls are easy prey to being manipulated, ordered around, having their whereabouts controlled, and may even consider their boyfriends' possessiveness and extreme jealousy as proof of love. Thus, the dating process may have negative effects on the personal development of some teenagers and on the dynamics of their intimate relationships later. There is little research on these aspects of dating.

SPOUSAL AND PARTNER PHYSICAL ABUSE

Spousal or partner physical abuse covers quite a range of acts, so that one has to exercise caution when interpreting statistics. The Conflict Tactics Scale (CTS) devised by Straus (1979) is commonly used and includes the following acts, in ascending order of severity:

Threw something at spouse; pushed, grabbed, or shoved spouse; slapped spouse; kicked, bit, or hit spouse with fist; hit or tried to hit spouse with something; beat up spouse; choked spouse; threatened spouse with a knife or gun; used a knife or a gun on spouse.

However, this and similar scales have several drawbacks. For instance, it is not a valid instrument for determining whether an act is committed in self-defence or what its consequences are. Most acts of violence committed by intimate partners *tend to be at the less severe end of the scale.*

In a 2004 survey, 7 percent of Canadian women and 6 percent of men reported that they had experienced spousal abuse *in the past five years*, with a higher proportion for previous than current unions. In contrast, 21 percent of Aboriginal persons in Nunavut and the Northwest Territories reported spousal abuse (Paletta, 2008). As well, approximately 75 percent of spouses who report having been a victim of violence also admit to having been an offender (Laroche, 2007:72). Data from the

1999 and 2004 General Social Survey also show a decline in the overall rate of *self-reported* spousal victimization (Brzozowski and Brazeau, 2008). In 2004, 44 percent of female victims reported having been **injured** compared with 19 percent of male victims; 14 and 11 percent of these injuries resulted in hospital services (Laroche, 2007:93). As well, 34 percent of females feared for their lives compared with 10 percent of males (Brzozowski and Brazeau, 2008).

In 2007 alone, there were 40,165 incidents of spousal violence reported to the *police*—which probably represents only about a third of actual occurrences (Taylor-Butts, 2009). In these statistics, the word "spousal" includes a current as well as an ex-spouse, whether by marriage or cohabitation. These numbers *have been declining* since 1998 but are still extremely high in the Northwest Territories and Nunavut, followed by Saskatchewan (because of the elevated Aboriginal rates), and lowest in the Maritimes. *Over 80 percent of victims are women*; 71 percent of physical abuse took place between current spouses and 29 percent between former spouses, generally before the union was terminated (Laroche, 2007:40). Although rare in Canada, nearly half of all family homicides are spousal. However, spousal homicides have declined since 1978 by more than half. Between 1998 and 2008, there were 753 such homicides: The victims were women in 80 percent of the cases. Common-law partners, both men and women, were more likely to be victims than married partners (Ogrodnik, 2009). Of the 753 homicides,

- 41 percent of the victims were cohabiting;
- 35 percent were married to the perpetrator;
- 24 percent were separated;
- 2 percent were divorced from the perpetrator.

Johnson distinguished between two types of interpartner violence. The first is a matter of self-regulation and is situational or reactive (Johnson and Leone, 2005). The second pertains to power and control; it is what Johnson called intimate terrorism. This type of violence, generally against women, is less frequent but predominates among victims who seek refuge in shelters (Laroche, 2007:170). This type of violence may be a reason why some women are at risk of being battered when they try to separate or after they have separated from their boyfriend or husband (DeKeseredy, 2009). As a result, women often have to seek a restraining court order (Duffy, 2004). Yet, some are killed. This is a reflection of a patriarchal ideology concerning intimate relations and abuse of women (DeKeseredy and Dragiewicz, 2007).

Men who lack the material and status ability "of expressing and maintaining power within their intimate relationships may engage in violence as a means of reestablishing their domestic position" (Anderson, 1997:668). The cultural framework allows them to have recourse to violence as an ego booster. Men in stressful occupations may compensate against their partners while others in physically violent occupations, such as the police and the military, may use the techniques at home (Melzer, 2002). Furthermore, among some groups with different cultural backgrounds, the prerogatives of patriarchy include violence against female kin—in order to keep them "in line" and to save the family's honour (Sev'er, 2002). This may include murder or honour killings (Sev'er and Yurdakul, 2001).

Many batterers are actually quite pathological. But here as well, one has to consider that *pathology is culturally influenced* or even created. In our society as in many others, pathology can lead to interpersonal violence or abuse. As was the case for dating, both men and women who engage in spousal violence are more likely than nonviolent spouses to have been involved in delinquency and to have been considered troublemakers when adolescents (Giordano et al., 1999). University-educated women are often victims of spousal abuse for a longer period because they do not report it out of shame (Johnson, 2003).

Often, once a wife becomes a target of abuse, she is at risk of becoming a repeat victim—about three times each year. This is particularly the case when physical injury results (Brookoff et al., 1997). Women are even attacked during pregnancy, which, of course, does not show in the CTS (Sev'er, 2002). However, in 1999 in Canada, over 60 percent of violence was not repeated during the following year (Laroche, 2007:84). Therefore, it would be important to have longitudinal studies showing the evolution of the beginning, continuation, or cessation of incidents of violence within couples.

The fact that wives also commit acts of violence does not mean that they are more violent than or even as violent as husbands or dates. Quite the contrary, as seen earlier. Women who are truly and forcefully violent and abuse their male partners are still the exception. Above all, women may fear painful retaliation if they hit their partners. They attack with far less force and energy than men. They are often less muscular, tall, heavy, and strong, thus the results of their aggressiveness are generally inconsequential physically and their partners may not even take these assaults seriously.

Rape is another aspect of spousal violence (Duffy, 2004). Men who are very violent toward their wives often combine physical battering with sexual assault. This is the ultimate way of establishing one's power over the other. Browne (1997) points out that women whose partners are sexually aggressive are also at a higher risk of suffering more severe physical aggression than women with male partners who are physically but not sexually violent.

Factors Related to Spousal Abuse

Spousal abuse, as with dating abuse, is facilitated by our **culture of violence** and particularly by ideologies of masculine dominance over women. As pointed out at the outset of this section, spousal abuse is in large part the result of a desire to control women, although women are not exempt from this motive (Migliaccio, 2002). Within this broad cultural context, other factors come into play. For instance, a proportion of dating and domestic violence is committed under the influence of **alcohol** or other substances (Brzozowski and Brazeau, 2008). This is reported by one-half of Aboriginal victims of spousal violence compared with one-third in the rest of the victimized Canadian population (Statistics Canada, 2006e). Many batterers and even their victims construct alcohol as a socially acceptable excuse for violence. It is part of the **social construction of masculinity** (Peralta et al., 2010). The belief that men batter because drinking "pushes" them to it is so well ingrained in the collective mentality that cases have even been thrown out of courts because "he was so drunk that he didn't know what he was doing." Alcohol facilitates abuse because it de-inhibits control. When both the batterer and the victim have been drinking, they may not even notice the presence of their children. In other cases, alcohol use follows a battering incident rather than precedes it. Alcohol and drugs are involved in a majority of the cases when the police are called, perhaps because women are more afraid of the violence and, if they have also been drinking, they may be less inhibited and less inclined to excuse their partner (Brookoff et al., 1997).

Cohabiting couples have the highest rate of partner violence and cohabiting women often suffer more severe abuse (Brown and Bulanda, 2008; Brownridge and Halli, 2001). Both in Quebec and the rest of Canada, even men have a much higher risk of being victimized in cohabitations than in marriages (Laroche, 2007:121). These facts undermine the claim of those who portray marriage per se as a "licence to hit." Magdol et al. (1998) have reported that, in a group of 21-year-olds, cohabitants were even more likely than daters to be abusive. We do not know what causes the relationship between abuse and cohabitation: Is it the structure of short-term cohabiting, with its lesser commitment and absence of norms to guide the relationship? Or do some individuals with a tendency for aggressiveness channel themselves more into cohabitation than marriage?

Very **low-income** couples and women with relatively little schooling are at an increased risk for partner violence (DeKeseredy, 2009). A lack of social control may in part explain the following (DeMaris et al., 2003): Poor couples who live in **disadvantaged neighbourhoods** are more at risk of spousal abuse (and, as seen later, child abuse) than similar couples who live in economically secure environments (Miles-Doan, 1998). The presence of social problems in some neighbourhoods and lack of an effective community described in Chapter 5 are highly applicable to partner violence (Browning, 2002). In contrast, the absence of visible violence in relatively comfortable areas may act as a deterrent against domestic abuse. In fact, poor neighbourhoods exhibit higher rates of violence of all sorts, and this includes spousal abuse. Children in low-income households witness physical violence twice as often as others (Statistics Canada, 2003e). However, this should not be taken to mean that domestic abuse never occurs among the more affluent. It does.

Few studies focus on ethnicity. Yet, in the U.S., one study indicates substantial levels of cohabitant and spousal abuse among blacks (Uzzell and Peebles-Wilkins, 1989). Domestic violence among **oppressed minorities** may have sources compounding those among whites (Baskin, 2003). For instance, blacks are differentially located in society because of their devalued colour. Prejudice and discrimination may be internalized among a segment of black males, who then demean black women and express their general rage toward them rather than projecting it elsewhere (Crenshaw, 1994). One cannot overlook the fact that, in some countries with a more rigid patriarchal structure, women as a group are more likely to be abused—and this pattern is pursued once they settle in Canada (Sev'er, 2002). In a study in Egypt, Yount and Li (2009) report that half of the wives justified wife beating, especially rural women and dependent wives. The variables of resources and cultural beliefs are central.

Aboriginal spousal violence deserves special mention. The consensus of the sparse research on this topic is that it is extremely high. However, as pointed out in the 2006 Department of Justice report, no one knows how high (Chartrand and

McKay, 2006): from 25 percent of women and 13 percent of men (Patterson, 2003) to as high as 90 percent among women in other studies—compared with 7 percent in Canada in general. Complicating the issue of gathering information is the fact that under-reporting is even more widespread among Aboriginals than among other Canadians because more Aboriginals are victims of someone they know (Statistics Canada, 2006e). Therefore, fear of reprisals and ostracism within the community is widespread as well as a lack of hope that anyone can do anything to prevent it (Lane et al., 2002; Stewart et al., 2001). This results in what is called the "normalization of violence."

In turn, the high rates of Aboriginal spousal violence are related to widespread childhood and youth abuse, including sexual victimization (Hylton, 2002). Most of this violence occurs at the hand of other Aboriginals (Statistics Canada, 2006e). As mentioned, this has resulted in a normalization of domestic violence in some communities (Lane et al., 2002; Stewart et al., 2001). Thus, overall, females have extremely high rates of victimization (Levan, 2001) along with youth (ANAC, 2002). These forms of brutalization as well as high criminal rates are interrelated and result from past colonization of Aboriginals and their culture, as detailed in Chapter 2 (ANAC & RCMP, 2001; Chartrand and McKay, 2006). In turn, this becomes a form of internal colonization.

The Effect of Spousal Violence on Children

We have already discussed, in the previous chapter, the effect that parental conflict has on children. We saw that it is an important factor in the negative outcomes of children before and after divorce. Here, we explore what happens to children when they watch or hear their father beat their mother or both parents throw projectiles at each other and engage in mutual slapping and punching, with much yelling and name calling. Some effects are immediate (Minze et al., 2010); others are delayed until certain life transitions occur; and many are long lasting (Sev'er, 2002). One immediate effect is fear, an urge to run away or to help the victimized parent. Children may throw themselves between parents, and older sons may try to fend off a father. Many children are injured in the process (Brookoff et al., 1997). Other children call for neighbours' help or even the police. A few others take the abuser's side, as explained by an older woman student:

> "Ever since I can recall, my father always beat up my mother and in those days (1960–70) women had to put up with it. I used to hide when it would start and then I would run to my mother and hug her and kiss her and cry with her. As a result, I have always been a sad child and to this day I tend to be anxious and easily pessimistic. But perhaps the saddest part is that my older brother never felt sorry for my mom. He used to tell her like my father did, 'That serves you right, next time do as he says.' My brother used to kiss my father's ass and really worship the ground he walked on. He grew up just like him and he often beat me up too and a couple of times he slapped my mother.... [He] beat up his ex-wife and he's tried it on many women but he's such a hypocrite: At work he's a model citizen."

On average, children of abused mothers have more behavioural and psychological problems and exhibit less interpersonal sensitivity (Moss, 2004). Other long-lasting effects include lower psychological well-being in adulthood, increased risk for depression, as well as poor parent-child relationships (McNeal and Amato, 1998; Russell et al., 2010). These consequences may be exacerbated by the negative effect of battering on the mothers themselves. Women who are repeatedly abused have high rates of sleep disorders, depression, illness, and even suicide attempts. These severe maternal symptoms are likely to disrupt mothers' ability to parent and, consequently, negatively affect at least some aspects of many children's personal development (Zerk et al., 2009).

The greatest negative impact of interparental violence occurs in those families where parents are the most violent toward each other and engage in the entire spectrum of abusive activities (McDonald et al., 2009). By the age of 18, offspring from these dysfunctional families have generally been exposed to *other* adversities, including poverty, divorce, parental alcoholism, and even criminality and childhood abuse. Once these contextual circumstances are controlled for, the direct negative effect of interparental violence is substantially reduced but does not disappear entirely (Fergusson and Horwood, 1998). The Canadian follow-ups from the National Longitudinal Survey of Children and Youth showed that children who had witnessed some physical violence (parents, siblings) at home were more aggressive at the time, especially boys, and that their chances of being aggressive and/or anxious were still higher two and four years later (Statistics Canada, 2003e).

The matter of the **intergenerational transmission of violence**—that is, from witnessing parental violence to committing dating and partner violence later on—is much discussed. Pertaining to Aboriginals, McGillivray and Comaskey (1999:72) pointed out that witnessing violent parental behaviour "begins the process of brutalization and violent coaching that may lead to a transgenerational cycle of intimate violence and to offending outside the family setting." But the evidence is not unanimous, and some researchers do not find more violence in the family background of spousal abusers than nonabusers (Delsol et al., 2003). Others point out that "the most typical outcome for individuals exposed to violence in their families of origin is to be nonviolent in their adult families" (Heyman and Slep, 2002:860). Even researchers who support the cycle of violence theory recognize that "the mechanisms by which violence is transmitted appear to be complex and multidimensional" (O'Keefe, 1998:41). As well, certain children are more **resilient** than others because of an easier temperament and higher cognitive abilities (Martinez-Torteya et al., 2009).

O'Keefe distributed questionnaires to 1,012 high school students in the Los Angeles area. She asked them about parental violence, their own dating experience, their attitude toward dating violence, and the type and frequency of violence they witnessed in their community and at school. She then centred her research on the 232 students who reported a great deal of interparental violence in order to see what would characterize those who followed the parental example. She found that 51 percent had never inflicted violence against a dating partner, but 49 percent had done so at least once. As well, 55 percent reported having been victimized at least once. Among males, those who had inflicted or been the victim of dating violence tended to be of lower socioeconomic status and reported more exposure to community and school violence. Among females, those who had followed the parental example or who had been victimized were characterized by exposure to community and school violence, poor school performance, and having been abused as a child.

Therefore, the exposure to a high level of parental violence places youths at a great risk of committing similar acts and/or being themselves victimized. But there are **other risk factors** at the social level that increase the likelihood of such occurrences in the students' own lives (Onyskiw and Hayduk, 2001). The variable of exposure to **community and school violence** is particularly significant because it appears as a risk factor for both genders. Conversely, the protective factors that intervene to prevent the transmission of violence across the two generations are higher SES and low community and school violence. Thus, O'Keefe's results on dating violence confirm those of studies finding more spousal and child abuse in disadvantaged areas where other types of violence exist. These results also help to understand the higher rates of abuse in Aboriginal communities.

Same-Sex-Partner Violence

Same-sex-partner violence is as much a matter of power and control as it is in heterosexual couple violence, except that gender or patriarchal ideologies are not an issue. The rate of violence among same-sex couples is higher than that among heterosexuals (Cameron, 2003). Indeed, gays, lesbians, and bisexuals suffer more from partner abuse than do heterosexuals (Balsam et al., 2005). In Canada, in 2004, 15 percent of gays and lesbians and 28 percent of bisexuals reported being victims of spousal abuse compared with 7 percent of heterosexuals (Beauchamp, 2008).

Bars have been important in the social lives of homosexuals, leading to alcohol-related problems, including partner abuse. However, as happens among heterosexual couples, alcohol is merely a facilitator and is utilized as an excuse, both for one's actions and for those of the abuser by the victimized partner (Renzetti, 1997). Renzetti also found that partner abuse often went hand in hand with child abuse, particularly toward the child of the victimized partner. These cases, however, have been documented only among lesbian couples whose children were from a previous marriage.

Thus, one major drawback of the literature on same-sex domestic violence is that it does not study its effects on children. Lesbian and homosexual couples who have children together represent a new phenomenon and it will take a few years before these children are grown. However, it is reasonable to assume that same-sex couples who are involved in physical abuse are less likely to have children than similar heterosexual couples. Most same-sex couples cohabit, and cohabitation is more fragile than marriage. Thus, same-sex couples who do not get along and quarrel violently probably separate even before the thought of having children occurs to them. Moreover, reproducing children is a far more complicated project to carry out among homosexuals than among heterosexuals. It is not something that happens accidentally, for instance. Therefore, it is possible that a process of **social selection** is at work: Those who decide to have children and are then able to achieve this goal may be a select group of more stable and devoted couples than are average heterosexual couples. Consequently, they would not fall prey to deviances, especially spousal abuse, that could endanger their relationship and their children's well-being. This hypothesis deserves to be tested empirically.

CHILD ABUSE AND NEGLECT BY PARENTS

Physical violence as well as sexual abuse of children are generally investigated separately and are then partitioned between adult perpetrators versus peer and only recently sibling perpetrators. Unfortunately, this partitioning prevents a more comprehensive understanding of the role of maltreatment in general in a child's life course (Finkelhor et al., 2009). Indeed, often children who are distressed by prior victimization then become at greater risk for re-victimization by yet other sources (Cuevas et al., 2010). In Canada, Children's Aid Societies were given the right to remove abused or neglected children from their homes for the first time in Ontario in 1893. In 1998, the incidence of cases *investigated* by welfare agencies was estimated to be 21.5 per 1,000 children—40 percent of which constituted neglect, particularly failure to supervise (Health Canada, 2001). Another estimate of child physical abuse at home yielded a rate of nearly six cases per 1,000 children for 1993 (Kaplan et al., 1999). The Ontario Health Supplement Study found that 31 percent of male and 21 percent of female respondents aged 15 and over reported some abuse that had occurred while they were growing up (MacMillan et al., 1997) and 31 percent of adolescents in Bibby's (2001) study reported that a close friend had been physically abused at home.

It is customary in textbooks to begin discussions of child abuse with abuse by parents, even though, as they enter the school system, children are far more likely to be maltreated by their siblings and peers (right part of Figure 13.1). Only very small children are maltreated mainly by their parents or a caregiver (left part of Figure 13.1)—more by fathers than mothers for assaults, and more by fathers in terms of neglect when they are absent. But the latter situation is never entered in the statistics. AuCoin (2005) reports that, according to police data, children who are physically assaulted within the family are so by a father in 44 percent of the cases, mothers 21 percent, and brothers 15 percent. Figure 13.1 presents a reasonable estimate of the overall sources of child abuse up to age 16 in terms of who tends to maltreat children the most frequently.

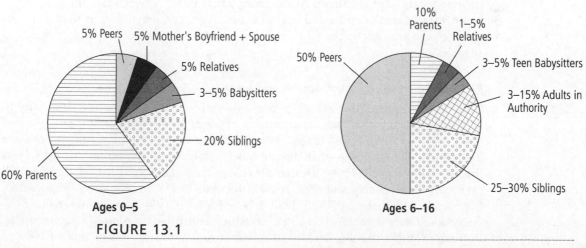

FIGURE 13.1

Estimates of the Main Sources of Child Maltreatment up to Age 16

Child Abuse by Parents

In 2007, there were 41,000 reported cases of physical violence against children up to age 18, of which 9,000 were family related: 5,300 were caused by a parent, generally a father (Nemr, 2009). At the extreme of child abuse are child homicides by parents. Ogrodnik (2009) reports 336 cases of a child killed by a parent between 1998 and 2008, with an equal number of boys and girls. The perpetrator was a father in 65 percent of the cases. *(The term "father" includes stepfathers and live-in mothers' boyfriends.)* Infants are at a higher risk of fatal abuse from their mothers up to age four months, from their fathers between four to 10 months, and from their step-fathers or mothers' boyfriends from 10 to 25 months.

There are, unfortunately, many methodological problems in surveys intended to measure child abuse by parents. First, when children are very small, they cannot report their own abuse; at a slightly older age, many may not know what constitutes abuse. As adolescents and adults, problems of recollection set in, and are exacerbated by current states of mind and relationships. Further, parents are not likely to report all of their own abusive behaviours, and abuse that comes to the attention of authorities represents the tip of the iceberg. As well, what the researchers include in definitions of abuse makes it often impossible to compare the results of various studies. Finally, emotional abuse is too frequently overlooked (Egeland, 2009).

Further, with toddlers and preschool-age children, it is often difficult to distinguish a *first* occurrence of abuse from an accidental circumstance. For instance, day-care workers or kindergarten teachers may notice bruises or a child who is limping. The child may not be able to establish a cause and effect between these physical symptoms and the fact that he or she was punched or thrown against a piece of furniture the day before. Parents generally explain that the child fell into the bathtub, off the toilet seat, or down the staircase. These explanations are plausible because nearly all small children sooner or later have such accidents and some children are more accident prone than others, particularly when they are active as well as impulsive (Schwebel and Plumert, 1999). Trocmé et al. (2003) describe the injury aspect of various forms of child abuse. At the more lethal level, between one-third and one-half of deaths due to abuse and neglect could have been prevented, as these children had already been brought to the attention of law enforcement and child protection agencies.

Factors Related to Child Abuse by Parents

Child abuse and neglect are more common in low-income families, especially in **neighbourhoods** with a high concentration of **poverty** and **violence**. It is possible that child abuse is more easily detected among the poor—particularly those who are clients of social agencies—than among other income groups who may also harbour this problem (Appell, 1998). Despite this cautionary remark, a true relationship still exists between poverty and child abuse (McLoyd, 1995). In fact, three decades ago, Garbarino and Sherman (1980) had already found that living in a high-risk neighbourhood correlated with child abuse, even after controlling for family characteristics. In these neighbourhoods, the lack of an effective community means that each set of parents, or each single parent, is more socially isolated, lacks support, and is deprived of elements of social control (Bogenschneider and Corbett, 2010:795). Were all these missing elements present, parents would be prevented from lashing out at their children as often and cruelly as some do.

Many studies link parents' daily stressors and psychological distress to distant, rejecting, and punitive parenting. McLoyd (1995) shows that, among single mothers, the adverse effects of poverty increase maternal depression and, in turn, punishment of adolescents. All in all, the daily stressors of poverty exacerbate difficult temperaments and may activate predispositions to violence, while simultaneously inhibiting controls against violence. In conditions of poverty, coping mechanisms are unduly taxed by daily irritants that cumulate to form an explosive situation. Depending on the temperament of the individuals affected and the characteristics of the child who is targeted, either explosive or apathetic behaviours may result (Elder et al., 1994a). Poverty aside, a parental history of severe mental illness and especially antisocial behaviour may increase the risk of child abuse (Walsh et al., 2002).

Consequences for Children of Abuse by an Adult

The literature on child abuse unavoidably focuses on children's developmental outcomes rather than on their current suffering, struggles, and small victories—as researchers could not ethically study these children without intervening to help them. Hence, the everyday life of these children is not well documented. What is known is that, on average, children who have been or are abused do less well in school (Eckenrode et al., 1993), are more frequently delinquent (Sternberg et al., 1993), have more peer-related problems (Howes, 1988), and are less reciprocal in their relations (Salzinger et al., 1993). Understandably, they become hyper-vigilant to danger and threat, and as a result are often more aggressive and tend to attribute hostile intent to others (Dodge et al., 1990). They frequently experience conflict with authority figures (Stouthamer-Loeber et al., 2001). As adults, they are also likely to suffer from psychological problems (MacMillan et al., 2001).

In other words, these children share some of the characteristics mentioned earlier about children who witness interparental violence. Fathers who abuse their wives physically are more likely to abuse their children (McDonald et al., 2009). In turn, abused mothers use harsh punishment more often than nonabused mothers. Women who have been abused as children have a higher chance of marrying an abusive husband. Together, these factors mean that child abuse often **coexists** or overlaps with spousal abuse and related difficulties (Moylan et al., 2010). As well, it can be said that witnessing parental violence is an indirect form of abuse (Finkelhor et al., 2009). This combination of factors may explain the similarity between the long-term effects of child abuse and those of interparental violence. It also makes it difficult to determine the effects specific to child abuse alone.

However, children who have been abused generally fare less well than those who witness interparental violence (see Margolin, 1998) and they are also at risk of being abusive later on in romantic relationships (Swinford et al., 2000). Miller et al. (2002) have found that harsh parenting is related to greater anxiety among young children of low SES than children of high SES. Thus, when children are small, low SES makes them even more vulnerable to the consequences of ill treatment. Children who have mental disabilities that are invisible, particularly those suffering from fetal alcohol spectrum disorders (FASD) are frequently victimized by their parents and all their kin (Chudley et al., 2005; Petersilia, 2001). This is particularly prevalent among Aboriginals who, later, often become offenders and inmates in the penal system (Fraser and McDonald, 2009).

Instead of becoming aggressive, adults who have been abused as children at times become depressed, withdrawn, and addicted to drugs (McCauley et al., 1997). Others may become warm and particularly altruistic. Certain types of abuse and degree of severity affect personal development, whereas other types of abuse affect subsequent parenting behaviours or interpersonal relations. Still other patterns of abuse are linked to antisocial behaviour or are causally linked to all such negative outcomes. However, the initial "causative" factor (the abuse) may be outweighed by personality resilience, happy circumstances in the person's life course, and a general lack of subsequent stressors. As well, various types of abuse may coexist: For instance, emotional abuse is not as often studied and in itself surely contributes negative effects (Wekerle et al., 2009).

Therefore, the path between a variable believed to be causal and its resulting outcome depends on many other factors along the life course, including SES (Zielinski, 2009). **Protective factors** must exist for severely abused children who turn out well, whereas risk factors must exist for children who are not abused but go on to become abusive as adults (Schultz et al., 2009). These protective and risk factors may be found at the individual level (the child's personality and genetic inheritance—Jaffee et al., 2005), at the family level (supportive siblings or one parent who is warm); or at the societal level (prosocial schools and neighbourhoods).

Do Abused Children Become Abusive Parents?

Just as is the case for interparental violence, one of the consequences of child abuse that is much studied and debated involves its reproduction in the next generation. As it turns out, abusive parents themselves, compared with nonabusive parents, have, on average, been more frequently abused or harshly treated as children (Pears and Capaldi, 2001). Abusive parents, especially those who are sexually exploitative, lack empathy for their child and entertain unrealistic expectations of what the child can do for them (Bert et al., 2009). Despite these parental drawbacks, most abused children do not grow up to be abusive, although severe and persistent child abuse probably always leaves long-term traces of psychological misery.

The **transmission rate** of family violence across generations has been estimated to be about 30 percent (Möhler et al., 2009). Abuse is not unavoidably transmitted because, as just mentioned, several factors enter into play in the chain of transmission. This includes the meaning that people attach to having been abused: Some children who are beaten interpret this as justifiable punishment, yet, because it has hurt them, decide later on to utilize other forms of punishment with their own children. Attachment to a partner and children as well as the perceived disapproval of friends and relatives concerning family violence also prevent individuals who suffered or witnessed violence in their families from committing it themselves. In other instances, a spouse intervenes and resocializes the potential abuser into utilizing more appropriate punishment.

Although some violent parents are more at risk of transmitting this pattern than others, the mechanisms through which this occurs are still poorly understood. In this respect, Simons and colleagues (1995) propose that a **parent's antisocial orientation** may well be a mediating factor in the transmission of violence to the next generation. Thus, it is possible that abusive parents who have other antisocial characteristics are more likely to transmit various abusive and violent behaviours to their children than adults who, except for being abusive parents, are otherwise prosocial (Frick et al., 1992). Antisocial parents might abuse their spouse, pick fights with others, or engage in criminal activity, for instance. In other words, they provide a stronger negative socialization experience for their children. In a small core of families, it may also be that physical abuse as well as other antisocial activities are transmitted across generations by genetic heredity—that is, parents pass on to their children severe predispositions for aggressiveness or for other partly genetically influenced traits, such as low self-control or high impulsivity (see Jaffee et al., 2005; Jespersen et al., 2009). However, heredity does not mean unavoidability and does not excuse the behaviours. Most people born with a predisposition to aggressiveness are not condemned or forced to act it out. But they are more likely to act it out when their environment encourages violence.

In a previous section, we have seen that exposure to community and school violence represents risk factors in the transmission of violence. We have also noted earlier that spousal and child abuse more frequently occur in poor neighbourhoods, along with many other forms of violence and antisocial behaviours. It is therefore quite likely that children who were abused *and* still live in a high-crime area will be more at risk of reproducing this pattern of violence in their own families than similar children who grow up in peaceful neighbourhoods where visible violence is practically nonexistent.

Is Child Abuse by Parents Decreasing?

Child abuse was brought to the public's attention only in the 1960s by doctors who coined the concept of the *battered-child syndrome* (Kempe et al., 1962). It is therefore impossible to estimate how widespread it was before that date. According to Finkelhor and Jones (2006), the period between 1998 and 2004 saw a decrease in the rate of child abuse. All estimates are lower than reality, but the increases recently apparent in statistics and social work caseloads may reflect the fact that society has become sensitized to child and wife battery as well as sexual exploitation, so that more cases are now reported than in the past (Trocmé et al., 2005). Therefore, social agencies are swamped by **reported cases** at a time when the rate of occurrence may be lower than in those days when no one spoke about the problem and it was more widely practised.

Demographic changes alone are consonant with the notion of a decrease. Families have fewer children and especially fewer unplanned children than in the past. They are less burdened demographically and are less overcrowded. Parents, particularly mothers, spend fewer hours per week with their children, a situation that lowers the potential for child abuse—but not neglect. Women now have their first child when they are older and more mature, and can put their children's needs ahead of theirs. Parents are more aware of some of the literature on child development, at least at the middle-class level, and may try to avoid any situation that could traumatize their children. Furthermore, parents certainly perceive that there is a greater likelihood that they could get caught and punished severely, including losing their children, and this perception may act as a deterrent.

However, there are three caveats. Child abuse may soon increase when children who are violent toward their peers become parents later on. As well, child neglect may be on the rise because parents often suffer from role strain and spend too many hours employed away from home. Third, one of the reasons that may have contributed to a decrease in child abuse—parental fears of being labelled as abusers—may have contributed to lower the authority of parents in general and have led to a reluctance on their part to intervene in some domains of their children's lives. This situation would leave youths unsupervised and unprotected, which are forms of neglect.

Child Neglect by Parents

Neglect involves not so much what parents do to their offspring but what they fail to do; it is a passive form of maltreatment. Straus and Kaufman-Kantor (2005:20) have defined it as "behavior by a caregiver that constitutes a failure to act in ways that are presumed by the culture of a society to be necessary to meet the developmental needs of a child and which are the responsibility of a caregiver to provide." Neglect includes failing to feed children, not clothing them adequately in cold weather, allowing toddlers to roam outside without supervision, failing to keep dangerous substances and firearms out of their reach, and not sending them to school. At the more psychological level, neglectful parents fail to give their children a chance at getting an education or they neglect them emotionally by ignoring them most of the time and not interacting with them. Other parents fail to reprimand their children and their adolescents when they engage in antisocial or badly inappropriate behaviours.

Neglect is a situation that is less easily detected and less reported than abuse. For instance, adolescents are neglected when they are given all the freedom they want to experiment with sex, alcohol, drugs, and even criminal activities. Not surprisingly, many of these youths do not define their parents as neglectful; they often see them as being "understanding" and "cool." Their parents may actually define themselves along the same lines. Adolescents are far more likely to complain about supervisory than permissive parents, even though the former are more invested parents. Although child neglect, particularly at the adolescent stage, is less discussed than child abuse, it is more common than child abuse (Health Canada, 2001). It may carry consequences that well-intentioned persons do not think of linking to it.

In the U.S., child neglect accounts for nearly half of child deaths related to maltreatment (McCurdy and Daro, 1994). Physical child neglect is related to parents' drug addiction and mental illness (Marquis et al., 2008). Above all, it stems from **poverty** as well as the stressors and social isolation created by poverty (Wulczyn, 2009). When families are forced to remain in or move to a poor neighbourhood with social problems, children are immediately at risk of physical and psychological harm as well as bad example. The dangers are so numerous that parents have to be extremely vigilant, which is not a normal state—for parents or for children (Garbarino et al., 1991). Therefore, it is easy for such parents to not be vigilant enough, although they may be doing everything they can. Pelton (1991:3) points out that poverty sets up a double standard of parenting "in that we implicitly ask impoverished parents to be more diligent in their supervisory responsibility than middle-class parents, because greater protection is required to guard children from the dangerous conditions of poverty than from the relatively safer conditions of middle-class homes and neighbourhoods."

When parents are under stress or hold jobs that keep them away from home a great deal of the time, children go unsupervised. In other societies, such as Scandinavian, leaving children home alone has not been, until now, a problem. But this is often not the case here due to the potential risks involved and because professionals have become hyper-vigilant, thus frightening parents. Leaving children alone, then, becomes child neglect unless parents supervise their children's activities by phone, for instance, and set strict rules of safety and behaviours to be followed during their absence. Dangers are less likely in a "good" area because the neighbourhood offers fewer harmful activities for children to engage in and because the presence of other supervising parents helps (Kupersmidt et al., 1995). In a dangerous area, however, such neglect can have serious consequences: It can lead to peer abuse and excessively premature motherhood, for instance.

Children often suffer from abuse and neglect together or from physical and emotional neglect combined (Ney et al., 1994). This overlap makes it nearly impossible to attribute specific effects. The consequences of neglect range from insecurity to aggressiveness toward peers, behaviour problems, and lack of school readiness (Eckenrode et al., 1993). In general, neglectful families function less adequately than other families. They often receive less social support from their immediate kin network, and mothers perceive their children to be more difficult (Harrington et al., 1998). Yet, in spite of all these and their own problems, children who are neglected do not necessarily perceive their family differently than other children. They may have no basis for comparison, particularly if other families around them are similar to theirs. In other instances, children do not wish to report neglect to social workers because they fear being placed out of their homes (Gable, 1998).

CHILD SEXUAL ABUSE BY ADULTS

Sexual abuse is the commission of a sex act without a person's consent or when a person is too young or immature to understand what is asked of or done to him or her. This broad definition involves inappropriate touching as well as penetration for the perpetrator's sexual gratification. Most of the sexual offences reported (81 percent) are of the less severe form (Brennan and Taylor-Butts, 2008). The incidence of child sexual abuse is even more complex to estimate than that of physical abuse because of the elements of victims' shame or ignorance, perpetrators' complete secrecy, and lack of visible physical cues.

As indicated below, of all cases of sexual assaults and other sex-related crimes reported to the police in Canada, a staggering 61 percent have youth younger than 18 as victims (AuCoin, 2005):

0–5 age group: 1,261 reported cases or 8 percent of all reported cases

6–10 age group: 2,251 reported cases or 15 percent of all reported cases

11–13 age group: 2,556 reported cases or 17 percent of all reported cases

14–17 age group: 3,284 reported cases or 21 percent of all reported cases

It is estimated that 90 percent of sexual offences are never reported to the police. However, it is not known whether adult victims underreport more or less than child/youth victims. Girls constitute 85 percent of reported occurrences and 13 is the peak age for girls (Statistics Canada, 2003c). Adolescent girls who work have a high risk of being harassed sexually as have women in their twenties and thirties (Fineran and Gruber, 2009). Overall, the consensus is that about one out of every four females is sexually abused before she reaches age 16. A late-1980s American national survey revealed that 27 percent of the women and 16 percent of the men interviewed reported having been sexually abused as children (Finkelhor et al., 1990). Although no question was asked about this topic, the female students' autobiographies revealed a range from 15 to 25 percent, depending on the year; rare instances surfaced among the less numerous male students. In the U.S., *substantiated* cases of child sexual abuse have declined by a third between 1992 and 1999 (Jones et al., 2001).

Who and Where Are the Sexual Abusers?

Turning to Table 13.1, we see that, for the youngest victims, the abusers are more likely to be a relative. As children age, they become prey to peers and strangers. The focus has often been on fathers as the sexual abusers—especially on TV talk shows. But we have to take four facts into consideration. First, where it says that a "parent"

TABLE 13.1 Perpetrators of Sexual Assaults and Offences Against Children Reported to Police Services, by Age and Gender of Child, 2003

Ages	0–5		6–10		11–13		14–17	
Sex of child	F	M	F	M	F	M	F	M
Perpetrators	%	%	%	%	%	%	%	%
A parent	26	17	15	11	11	10	10	9
A sibling	13	18	17	16	10	8	4	6
Other family	11	14	14	11	9	7	6	6
Friend, etc.	36	38	39	46	53	57	52	57
Stranger/unknown	13	12	17	17	18	18	28	23

Source: AuCoin, 2005. Adapted from Tables 1 and 3 with permission from Statistics Canada.

was the abuser, in 95 percent of the cases it was the "father." Second, the term "father" includes stepfathers, mothers' live-in boyfriends, as well as foster fathers. Third, these fathers together are involved in 9 to 26 percent of these sexual crimes whereas friends/acquaintances account for 36 to 57 percent. Fourth, it is possible that sexual abuse committed by fathers of very young children is underreported when it is not visible, even to mothers.

Other perpetrators within the family include older sisters' boyfriends, siblings, grandfathers, uncles, and cousins. Children are also sexually abused by fathers' friends; in foster care, daycare, and group care institutions; by babysitters and coaches; as well as by peers. A majority of the **perpetrators are males**, but victimization by a mother, a sister, or a female babysitter, as well as a stepmother, occasionally occurs. In the students' autobiographies, only four cases of father-daughter incest came to light in about 1,500 autobiographies. It is possible, however, that students did not want to discuss it because it was too painful and private—but I doubt this because a great deal of other very sensitive material was divulged. Rather, such cases probably occur more in school-age and clinical samples than in university student samples, because this is a type of abuse that carries the most serious consequences (see also Hyman, 2000). Three of the four reported cases had occurred in immigrant families in which many problems coexisted or who originated from patriarchal societies (Duffy, 2004).

In a clinical intervention for 50 adolescent girls who had been sexually abused, the fathers had been the offenders in 16 percent of the cases, whereas stepfathers and mothers' boyfriends had been in 32 percent of the cases (Morrison and Clavenna-Valleroy, 1998). Over half of these girls' mothers also reported having been sexually abused as children, an extremely high rate that coincides with a high rate of these mothers' partners having abused their daughters. This **double female victimization** relates to other research findings showing that a proportion of women who are abused as girls marry partners who abuse them and may also abuse their daughters. The abuse carries from one generation to the next through the transmission of risk factors and victimization from mother to daughter. In fact, children who live with an abused mother are over 12 times more likely to be sexually abused (McCloskey et al., 1995).

Once again, children from **low-income** families are more likely to be victimized than others. As well, among Aboriginals, this is a form of victimization that is more prevalent but about which no one speaks (Hylton, 2002). This brings us back to Chapter 6, where we saw that a proportion of girls who became mothers by age 15 had been coerced into sex, and most were poor. Further, males who have been sexually abused as boys are more likely to impregnate a teenager at some point in their lives (Rosenberg, 2001). In addition, Chapter 5 indicates that, in areas with a high level of poverty, children may be less well supervised and more at risk of victimization. The presence of transient male adults in a family combined with overcrowding can also contribute to explain this difference in child sexual abuse by social class.

It should be added that police-reported sexual assaults against youth under the age of 13 occur the most frequently *between 3 and 7 p.m. after school* and, we presume, before the return home of parents (AuCoin, 2005; Brennan and Taylor-Butts, 2008). In contrast, the 14-to-17 age group is victimized more frequently between 1 and 5 p.m. (related to truancy from school and homes that have no adult presence), as well as between 10 p.m. and 2 a.m. (AuCoin, 2005).

Consequences of Sexual Abuse for the Child

The consequences for the sexually abused child are generally analyzed within a psychogenic model of trauma: The more severe the abuse, the more negative the consequences. Probably the most dramatic results follow **incest**, particularly if a father, mother, sibling, or grandfather is the culprit. The child is at his or her most vulnerable within these situations because of daily availability, longer duration, and more extensive harm (Fischer and McDonald, 1998). Perhaps worst of all is the reality that the child is emotionally attached to and trusts the abuser. The abuser should be the protector and an agent of socialization but instead becomes the tormentor.

> *A student devoted many pages detailing the sexual abuse she began suffering at age six when her grandparents were babysitting her. Although her grandmother was nearby in the kitchen, the grandfather regularly coerced the child into performing oral sex in the family room because "it made him feel good and he used to tell me that I was his special girl." The poor little girl gagged and gagged and had to submit to further indecencies. "At the time I was convinced that I was special and he had me promise not to tell anyone so that I was essentially isolated and didn't know any better." As she grew up, she became more and more repulsed and begged her mother to find her another sitter. The abuse stopped when she was 10 years old. By early adolescence, she feared men, and by late adolescence, she had to seek therapy because sex disgusted her. She began suffering from depressive episodes. "I will never let any old man babysit my children."*

The conjugal unit and even the entire family can be destroyed by incest. Mothers may leave the perpetrator, although cases of mothers who turn against their daughters are not unheard of in clinical practice or among delinquents and street kids. In these instances, the daughter is seen as the trespasser within the conjugal subsystem; yet, in reality, it is usually the father or boyfriend who initiated the coalition with the daughter. When mothers are not supportive or do not believe the daughters, the latter risk becoming very depressive, even during treatment (Morrison and Clavenna-Valleroy, 1998). Mothers who have been sexually abused themselves when they were children experience greater emotional distress than other mothers when they learn of their child's abuse. This maternal turmoil in itself reflects the long-term effects of child sexual abuse; as well, these mothers are forced to relive their own abuse, which is very traumatic for them.

The Life Course Perspective

Within a life course sociological framework, sexual abuse constitutes an inappropriate sexual socialization. Sexual contact with an adult focuses the child on his or her own sexuality from a less than healthy perspective very early on in life. The abuse constitutes a precocious initiation into sex. This may explain why, among those who go on to be abusers themselves, they had been focused on masturbation at an earlier age than others (Jespersen et al., 2009). This life course brings a **premature foreclosure in identity**: The young child begins to define herself in terms of sexuality and perhaps material gains. This may open the door to deviant opportunities and close the door to a normal life course. In turn, these "opportunities" may lead to early sexual relations with older peers and pregnancy (Roosa et al., 1997). These children are often re-victimized (Barnes et al., 2009). They have more sexual partners among older peers, and are at greater risk of contracting sexually transmitted infections and becoming homeless. The same path may lead to prostitution, both female and male (Kingsley and Mark, 2000). As adults, those who have been sexually abused when children have higher rates of serial partners, unwanted pregnancies, abortions, and STIs (Boden et al., 2009; van Roode et al., 2009). They are also more likely to become victims of intimate partners later on (Daigneault et al., 2009).

As Browning and Laumann (1997:557) explain, adult sexual contact with a young girl "seems to provide access to sexuality without cultivating the emotional and cognitive skills to manage sexual experiences." The girls' (or boys') subsequent deviant behaviour often arises from the fact that their **self-perception** has been distorted as a result of the abuse. Some of these children may grow up believing that others have the right to their body or that early sexuality is normal. As we have just seen in the previous case study, this is actually one of the discourses that child abusers hold with their victim. They explain that the act is "normal" or that the relationship is a "special" one in order to convince the child to be victimized and, later on, to justify the abuser's behaviour. Browning and Laumann (1997) find that, when child abuse does not give rise to an early, risky sexual life, the victims are less likely to experience adverse outcomes later in life. The authors conclude that the long-term effects of child sexual abuse are probably indirect through the negative life course that they often generate; *redirecting sexual trajectories* at an early age might cancel most of the severe and long-term negative consequences of sexual abuse.

Most children who are sexually abused do not follow a deviant life course. Parental or peer support, personal strength, and appropriate therapy may be instrumental in resocializing children and helping them build their lives constructively. Still, many such children develop emotional and behavioural problems, both as children and later on as adults. As illustrated in the student vignette, depression is a common sequel that can appear as early as adolescence. Sexual abuse may trigger problems in a child who may not otherwise be at risk, or it may increase pre-existing problems, even later on in life. Studies show that adult sex offenders who abuse children have had particularly high rates of sexual abuse in their past (Jespersen et al., 2009).

Many children grow up to forget or repress the abuse. For instance, Williams and Banyard (1997) followed up men and women who, in the early 1970s, had been examined in a hospital emergency room for sexual abuse. After 17 years, 38 percent of the women and 55 percent of the men had no recollection of the abuse. Widom and Morris (1997) found similar numbers when they followed up court-substantiated instances of child sexual abuse that had taken place 20 years earlier. Perhaps children who grow up to forget have particular strengths. Perhaps the fact that the abuse has been forgotten means that, at the time, it had not been vested with tragic overtones by the child who may not even have realized what was happening to her or him. This would go counter to claims that any sexual gesture toward a child is traumatic. The actual fact is that we have no proof of the effect, if any, of certain types of sexual encounters with children—even though they are morally reprehensible. Above all, perhaps children who grow up to forget are more likely to have had a normal life course, as a result of an early parental intervention (Browning and Laumann, 1997).

SIBLING VIOLENCE

In this section, sibling violence is divided between physical and sexual: Psychological abuse was covered to some extent in Chapter 12. But, in either case, these are neglected topics of research, both in terms of their incidence and consequences (AuCoin, 2005). Negative consequences often ensue for the child who is victimized (Kiselica and Morrill-Richards, 2007). We also have to consider that the abusive child is allowed to socialize himself or herself into a role that may repeat itself later on in other aspects of life and against other victims such as dates and spouses or even children.

Sibling Physical Violence

Straus and colleagues (1980) sampled 1,224 pairs of siblings ranging in age from three to 17 years. Pushing and shoving were the most frequently mentioned acts of physical violence at the less serious end of the continuum. At the other extreme, 14 percent reported having beaten up their sibling and 5 percent reported using a gun, either to threaten or to hurt. This survey took place in 1975. The level of violence among children in general has since risen, and, because adult presence at home has diminished, these figures could be higher today. The result that sister pairs were the least aggressive of all sibling pairs is probably still true today. But here as well, one can expect higher frequencies than in the 1970s because there has been an increase in violence perpetrated by girls. The main difference is that families are now smaller so that children have fewer siblings than in the 1970s.

The media, the public, professionals, and researchers have all paid a great deal of attention to child abuse by parents when, actually, sibling abuse is more common (Wallace, 1999). This selective inattention to sibling abuse stems from widespread beliefs that it is simply part of growing up. It is considered normal. Siblings hurt one another so frequently that no one pays much attention to it (Wieke, 1997). Parents are concerned, however: They do not like the name calling, fighting, shoving, slapping, and hair pulling, but generally do not intervene (Perozynski and Kramer, 1999). Frequently heard comments from parents run like the following:

- "It drives me crazy; they're always at it."
- "I'm always afraid they'll really hurt each other one day, but it's better to let them resolve their problems on their own."
- "Parents shouldn't interfere in their children's lives; they have to learn on their own."

This type of reasoning leads to the conclusion that sibling violence is not "real" violence that one has to prevent, when, in reality, it is the most common form of intimate abuse (Button and Gealt, 2010). These parents' beliefs about nonintervention are reinforced by the lack of professional concern. Because of this widespread **adult tolerance**, children are far less likely to report sibling abuse to their parents or other authority figures than is the case for abuse by adults. The stronger of the two siblings is encouraged on this path because he or she benefits from advantages over the other and no one intervenes. As a result, later on, adults who are asked about victimization in their past of ten fail to equate sibling beatings with assault. Strangely, when perpetrators and victims of sibling aggression become adults, they are more accepting of

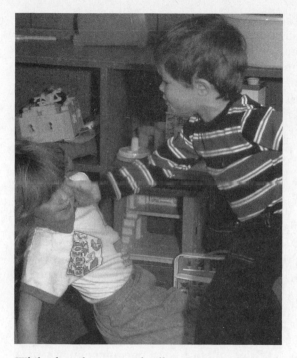

While abuse by peers is finally receiving serious attention (the phenomenon of "bullying"), sibling violence and abuse still remain to be studied in-depth and recognized socially.

this type of abuse (Hardy et al., 2010). Once more, this leads to the under-representation of sibling violence in official surveys. Further, it is only recently that a few studies have been able to look at the developmental consequences of everyday sibling abuse: It is related to behavioural problems, above and beyond genetic inheritance and parental treatment (Natsuaki et al., 2009).

However, not all families experience sibling abuse (excluding, here, the usual quarrels) or tolerate it. For instance, in a large sample of high-school students, Button and Gealt (2010) found, as have others, that sibling victimization occurs more in families where there are other forms of violence. Thus, there are high rates of **co-occurrence** of several types of abusive and problematic behaviours. This means that sibling violence is often part of a family's culture and perhaps genetic background. In turn, sibling violence is also related to increased odds of delinquency, aggression, and even substance abuse. Sibling violence does not occur randomly.

Sibling Sexual Abuse

The following student quote serves as an introduction to a topic that is equally overlooked: Sibling sexual abuse or sibling incest, which is probably more common than parent-child incest:

> *"The most painful time in my life was the period between the ages of 6 to 10: My brother was six years older than me and my parents counted on him to babysit me. . . . At first I did not understand what was happening to me, however difficult this is to explain with hindsight, but my brother got me into performing intimate acts for him and later on after a year of this his best friend used to come over and they would both share me. This is all I can write here because this is very painful. This went on for two years until I became strong enough to resist and threaten to tell my parents which of course I never did because I was too ashamed. At school I was ashamed too because I saw this boy. . . . Now I harbour intensely negative feelings about my brother who seems to have forgotten all about these years. . . . It would kill my parents if I told them. I went into therapy when I got to this university and have come to terms with the situation, which is not to say that I accept it but I can live with it and go on with my life. But I know that I will be very very careful with my own children later on in life. Very careful."*

Sibling incest is a mainly brother-to-sister initiated or coerced phenomenon, but incest between siblings of the same sex also occurs. We are not talking here of "playing doctor," which many small children engage in out of curiosity and from which they have to be distracted and directed to other more prosocial activities. (These incidents can also be used by parents to explain what is inappropriate touching.) As is the case for all types of sexual abuse, sibling incest is found more in clinical than in survey populations. This would indicate that it results in serious psychological consequences for many abused brothers and sisters. As well, sibling sexual abuse may perhaps occur more among already vulnerable and malfunctioning families. Such families simply cannot supervise their children because of various burdens (DiGiorgio-Miller, 1998). It can also result from the way parental roles are carried out. Visible extramarital affairs and open sexuality between parents that children observe, for instance, are related to sibling incest: Children may copy what they see.

O'Brien (1991) compared adolescent sex offenders whose victims were siblings with other adolescent sex offenders whose victims were children outside the family. Adolescents who had sexually abused a sibling had done it more often and for a much longer period of time (one year) than adolescents who had abused a child out-side the family, because of the availability of the little brother or sister at home (as illustrated in the student quote). As well, their sibling victim was much younger, between four and nine years of age, than the victims of the other abusers. This young age allowed for greater accessibility, because a small child can more easily be coerced than an older child. The frequency of the abuse resulted in nearly half of the sibling cases progressing to anal or vaginal penetration. This occurred rarely when the vic-tim was not a sibling, for it is easier to progress to penetration within the context of long-term availability and within the privacy of home.

In families with sibling incest, O'Brien uncovered a phenomenon we have already encountered for child sexual abuse by a father or a stepfather, where both mother and daughter have been abused: Parents of incest perpetrators, particularly mothers, had been more often abused sexually as children than was the case among the parents of the other sex offenders; and 42 percent of the incestuous offenders had been abused sexually, although generally outside the family. Thus, in these families, many parents had themselves been vulnerable during their childhood. Further, some of their sons had also been sexually abused, and of those many had gone on to abuse their siblings. The **transmission** from one generation to the next was one of **vulnera-bility** for sexual victimization in many of these families.

PEER ABUSE

As we have seen in Figure 13.1, older children are more likely to be abused by their peers than by anyone else. Examples of cruel, destructive, and even violent peer behaviours are mentioned in the newscasts on a weekly basis, and in some cases, they result in murder or suicide. Peer abuse is a situation that severely depletes a child's social capital outside the home and often endangers the development of his or her human capital. It also affects family dynamics. In 2010 in Canada, there were at least three lawsuits by the parents of a traumatized child against schools for allegedly fail-ing to protect their child against bullying (Hammer, 2010).

A conservative estimate might be that a minimum of 20 percent of children are *seriously* abused by peers during their young lives—and this does not refer to normal conflicts, disagreements, and teasing. Most adolescents are both victims and abusers, although not necessarily at the same time. Most children bully at one point but few do so persistently (Pepler et al., 2008). In Ontario, 29 percent of grade 7 to 12 students reported being bullied *at school* during the current academic year, which was a decrease since 2003 (Paglia-Boak, 2010).

In the autobiographies, students recalled far more peer maltreatment that they described as having had detrimental and *lasting* consequences on their development than was the case for maltreatment by parents. That is, these peer experiences had affected them negatively for several years, often up to the present time (Ambert, 1994a). Further, such mentions increased as time went on. In the autobiographies as well as in magazines, one reads about students who had been happy and well adjusted, but quite rapidly began deteriorating psychologically, sometimes to the point of becoming physically ill and incompetent in school or even delinquent. For many, the impact of peer maltreatment leads to avoidance of school (Kochenderfer and Ladd, 1996). In other instances, it contributes to poor school performance (Hodges et al., 1997) as well as anxiety and depression (Egan and Perry, 1998). As one student recalls it (see also another similar case on p. 299), even school work can be disrupted, as young victims become too distraught and often too fearful to focus on anything else:

> *"The years between 12 and 16 were the worst in my life. I was surely the most unpopular boy at my school. There was a group of boys with some girls too who used to pick on me and no one would have dared be nice to me after that. They'd steal my lunch, force me to hand over my pocket money, they'd laugh and snicker when I passed by. . . . It got to the point where I felt so terrorized that I couldn't even pay attention to what the teacher said in class and my marks suffered and of course my parents weren't too sympathetic because they hadn't a clue that this was going on until I got really sick with chronic stomach problems, but by then the years had gone by and my life had been ruined. I feel insecure to this day and always sit at the back to avoid being noticed."*

Peer abuse is not merely a psychological situation created by a victim and an abuser because of two sets of personality characteristics. Nor is it merely a consequence of a victim's parents' childrearing practices, as was often described in the literature (Finnegan et al., 1998). Rather, peer abuse is influenced by the **clique** structure of schools and by what children have learned elsewhere, including the media—whether television, video games, or the Internet—and siblings. For instance, Espelage and colleagues (1996) find that adolescent bullies watch more violent television, are more difficult at home, spend less time with adults, and have more exposure to gang activities than other children. Being a bully also negatively affects school performance (Ma et al., 2009) and may persist into young adulthood as does victimization (Pontzer, 2010). A third had a single parent and another third lived with a stepparent. Thus, it would seem that *serious bullies* escape adult influence and control, especially when it comes to social bullying (Brendgen et al., 2008:26). Their family structure is burdened in terms of its ability to provide supervision. Instead, they surround themselves with negative virtual (as in videos) and real role models.

The **culture of violence** in the society at large is implicated along with reduced social control. This is well illustrated in the fact that bisexuals and homosexuals are more often abused by their peers when in school (Balsam et al., 2005). Peer abuse is a situation created by opportunity. It is, above all, a cultural phenomenon and a reflection of a lack of an effective community, including lack of school supervision

(Wienke Totura et al., 2009). And it is now given additional outlets with cellphones and Facebook.

Peer Sexual Harassment and Abuse

Sexual harassment, mainly by boys toward girls, is a particularly pernicious form of abuse that may begin early. It generally goes undetected, may even be approved of by boys' parents (*"he's all boy"*), and some girls may be led by their peers into believing that it is flattering (*"he likes you, silly"*) or simply the normal price one has to pay for popularity. It is the forecaster of date and partner abuse. Many adolescents and even preadolescent girls are coerced into sexuality by male peers (Chapter 7). The degree of coercion ranges from outright rape to subtle pressure in a relationship where the girl is afraid to lose her date. Adolescents are particularly at risk when they score high on scales of conformity to peers (Small and Kerns, 1993): They become vulnerable because they need their peers' approval more than a less conforming adolescent does. While many girls are not raped, they nevertheless do not want sexual intercourse but comply because of peer pressure (Laumann, 1996). Some of this pressure comes from female peers who may already be sexually active or pretend to be. This creates a **cultural climate** that is very potent; a teenager eager for peer acceptance will follow suit.

Victimization from severe forms of sexual abuse, rape, or coercion into unwanted sexuality is more likely to occur to adolescents who live in neighbour-hoods that have a high rate of social problems and whose parents cannot supervise or protect them adequately. Girls from single-parent families, particularly when they are disadvantaged, as well as those who have parents who suffer from alcoholism, for instance, are at a higher risk of sexual victimization in general, including by peers (Moore et al., 1989). Peer sexual abuse, as is the case for peer abuse in general, is very much a **crime of opportunity**. It is done by and occurs to children and adolescents while they are unsupervised by adults, whether at school, at home, in an abandoned building, or in a car (AuCoin, 2005). Peer sexual abuse is the result of media influences and disengagement from adults, including teachers and parents—in other words, a generalized lack of an effective community.

ABUSE OF PARENTS BY CHILDREN

Two additional types of familial abuse exist: Ill treatment of parents by their young children and adolescents as well as the abuse of elder parents by their adult offspring. The literature is thin concerning both topics, particularly that pertaining to young children. Why is this? Perhaps because we tend to socially construct children as victims (Gallagher, 2004a, b). Perhaps because we fail to understand that children are social actors and make choices (Ambert, 2001). Or perhaps we view parents as more powerful than they are and, at times, we stereotype them as the natural abusers of their children.

Physical Abuse of Parents by Young Children and Adolescents

Already in 1979, Harbin and Madden used the phrase, "battered parents." Yet, the topic has largely remained taboo both for families and mental health professionals. Estimates of children who have physically assaulted their parents range from 1 to

16 percent (Laurent and Derry, 1999). As well, the relative absence of research on this topic is perplexing in view of the fact that small children are generally more physically aggressive than older ones (Onyskiw and Hayduk, 2001). They spend more time with parents, especially **mothers**, thus giving them more opportunities for abuse. In fact, the few studies are unanimous to the effect that mothers are the most common victims (Gallagaher, 2004a; Nock and Kazdin, 2002; Straus and Ulma, 2003).

Violent young offenders often target their own families. Those who aggress their parents are more likely to belong to gangs and associate with peers who own guns (Kennedy et al., 2010). Several teens in one of my studies repeatedly yelled at their mother that she was "stupid" and even a "bitch." (If the mothers were the ones doing the name-calling, *they would be censured.*) A few mothers were bearing bruises from the beatings received at the hand of a teenage son. The mothers were single and poor; one was in a wheelchair. The latter was also called a "scumbag" by her 16-year-old son. One can also witness severe physical assault of mothers by children as young as age three (Straus and Ulma, 2003). These observations are made in public areas—such as sidewalks, parks, and subway platforms—for everyone to see, a sign that children do not fear public condemnation in this respect: There is an *entitlement mentality* among some children and adolescents when it comes to mothers. This stems from our social construction of motherhood.

I observed the following scene in a subway train. A well-dressed mother, age 25 to 30, walked in with an equally well-groomed little boy, age four or five. The little boy was screaming at his mother at the top of his lungs:

B: *You hurt my feelings!*

M: (bending down to soothe him) *I'm so sorry, honey, I apologize.*

B: *I hate you, I hate you!* (He was red in the face with rage and was hitting his mother with his fists.)

M: (softly) *Again, I'm sorry honey; it won't happen again.*

B: *You're stupid.* (He kicked her with his booted foot.)

The mother had tears in her eyes. The boy was not in the least bit deterred by the staring disapproval from passengers as he continued punching and yelling. I doubt that anyone had ever told him that this was wrong. The cases observed in public involved higher-SES mothers with small children: The few studies on this topic point out that this is mainly an upper-middle-class phenomenon as well as a white one— at least, up to this point in time. It may be related to parenting permissiveness where proper boundaries of authority and right versus wrong are absent (Gallagher, 2004a; Laurent, 1997; Paulson et al., 1990). Gelles (1997:112) points out that clinical observations of abusive adolescents reveal deficiencies in the authority structure of families whereby adolescents have been granted too much control and decision-making power (see Chapter 10). Studies also indicate that the young abusers tend to be more difficult oppositional children, who stress parents, and who are very demanding of them. Such children burden their familial environment and, as a result, their parents become less competent at setting limits (Nock and Kazdin, 2002).

In Massachusetts, between September 1992 and June 1993, nearly one-third of all restraining court orders issued were requested by parents against children, mainly by mothers against sons (reported in Gelles, 1997). In a 1996 British Crime Survey, one in 10 mothers reported having been assaulted by her children—some of these offspring were over age 18 (Mirrlees-Black et al., 1996). Among American university students, some mutuality of parent and young adult violence exists: There is some continuity of behaviour from parents who have physically maltreated their children to the children who then maltreat parents (Browne, 1998). But the other studies reported have not found this, although such cases certainly occur.

Abuse of Elderly Parents by Adult Children

Overall, neglect and abuse of seniors remains poorly understood by the public (Roger and Ursel, 2009). Rates range from 2 to 10 percent depending on studies (Sev'er, 2009). In general, seniors have the lowest rate of victimization and, when they are victims of crime, the perpetrator is usually someone they know, too often a family member (Vaillancourt, 2009). Women outlive men, and one of the consistent findings on elder abuse within the family is that most victims are women (Biggs et al., 2009; Krienert et al., 2009). Until now, explanations for elder abuse within the family have emphasized the elderly person's caregivers: The line of reasoning is that the frustrated and burdened caregiver lashes out at the frail dependent parent. However, elderly parents are often abused by an adult child who lives with them because of that child's own dependency (Carp, 2000). In that case, the adult child depends on the parent financially or for shelter, because he or she is unemployed or is mentally delayed, physically challenged, or emotionally disturbed. Indeed, after discharge from hospital care, 85 percent of unmarried adult children who are mentally ill move in with their elderly parents (Greenberg et al., 1993). The potential for abuse certainly exists.

Hence, researchers may have placed too much emphasis on the dependence of the elderly as a source of abuse; the elderly who have a dependent and physically stronger spouse or child living with them should be considered at particular risk (Carp, 2000). Other explanations propose that elder abuse is spousal abuse "grown old" or that it stems at least in part from prejudicial attitudes and beliefs toward the elderly (Harbinson, 1999). Elder abuse in general is more frequent because seniors who are dependent on institutions and non-family care are often abused—although we have no objective statistics on what often amounts to torture of defenceless persons.

Police-reported data for the year 2007 showed that **men** are the most frequent perpetrators of violence

Elderly parents who are abused by their adult children rarely report the situation. They feel ashamed and may fear retaliation. They are often socially isolated and have no one in whom to confide.

against an older family member—80 percent of such cases. Older men were more frequently victimized by their adult children whereas older women were as likely to be abused by their spouse or adult children (Vaillancourt, 2009). As well, younger seniors were more frequently victimized by family members than those aged 85 to 98 who are probably more often victimized within institutions: They are too isolated or in ill health to report it (Turcotte and Schellenberg, 2007). Indeed, a study in Michigan showed that, when elders move into a nursing home, their risk tripled (Page et al., 2009). In the 1999 General Social Survey, 7 percent of seniors reported emotional abuse, while 1 percent reported financial abuse and another 1 percent physical or sexual violence (Dauvergne, 2003). Medical abuse is at times perpetrated when the caregiving adult child does not seek assistance for a sick or suffering elderly parent—to safeguard the entirety of the inheritance or precipitate its occurrence. Material forms of abuse by adult children are motivated by greed, personal debts or addictions, or the financial demands of an adult child's spouse or children. Material abuse includes siphoning off parental revenues, walking out with parents' possessions, or controlling the parents' house (Biggs et al., 2009).

> A woman I was interviewing on a totally different topic casually remarked, *"But we're lucky because we can get quite a bit of money from my mother-in-law. She doesn't need it because she's in a seniors' home."* Thinking of my own parents, so generous with us after we had our own children, I said, *"Oh, it's nice of her to give it to you."* *"No, no, my husband is her power of attorney and only child and he has figured that she can get on with much less, so we might as well take it now when we can use it."* I was at first speechless and then asked if the mother had long to live and if she had dementia. No, the older lady was fine mentally, didn't know any of this, but was physically dependent even though she could live a long life. To which I responded that perhaps they could use her money to allow her to have better care and more enjoyment out of life. They were actually stealing from the helpless elderly woman. You may ask and the answer is yes: Something was done about it, but it took a lot of time and persistence to put a stop to this exploitation because it was considered "normal," an opinion shared by the son's lawyer.

Elder abuse has very **low visibility**: In fact, parents may be less likely to report abuse than would a maltreated adolescent or even a child (Payne and Gainey, 2006). Actually, perhaps as few as 5 percent report it (Tatara, 1993). Elderly parents may be ashamed of their situation and may have no one else to turn to for help. An attempt to report the abuse might fail and result in dreaded retaliation. Moreover, while abused children grow up and may eventually denounce their parents, the elderly parent dies with the secret. Thus, abuse of elderly parents is a relatively easy act to commit and can have even less social visibility than abuse of school-age children. The elderly who are most at risk are often socially isolated: They are no longer connected to their social networks, such as church, work, or even friends. No one may notice the abuse, and physicians who see bruises may be told that the senior person fell, something that occurs quite often in old age. (The parallel with small children is obvious here.) It is not known if the model of the intergenerational transmission of violence is a valid explanatory framework for elder abuse. As well, this perspective does not address larger sociological issues of society's role in preventing the abuse of frail elders.

CONCLUSIONS: THE LARGER CONTEXT OF FAMILY VIOLENCE

The literature on neglect, and particularly physical and sexual abuse, is one largely oriented toward the psychological sources of maltreatment of a family member by another. One cannot deny that these sources are present. However, violence within the family is a reflection of violence within society, including its colonization by the media. To begin with, difficult and out-of-control temperaments that lead to abusive situations would not be so prevalent in a society where civility, altruism, and a sense of communal responsibility were the valued forms of interaction. Second, within such a civilized and less competitive-aggressive environment, even impulsive persons would learn to respect others rather than maltreat them.

Other larger sociocultural forces that are implicated in family violence include discrimination and poverty, particularly among Aboriginals, and the fact that the family is the only institution that is single-handedly responsible for the well-being of its dependent members—whether children, the disabled, or the frail elderly. The family fulfills too many functions—particularly too many caregiving functions—while it receives too little social support from the very complex, expensive, and competitive society in which it lives. In other words, we have come full circle, and these remarks return us to the discussion on multiple family functions in Chapter 3.

Five salient themes emerge from this chapter. Females of all ages are the most frequent victims of all types of violence. Males are the most frequent offenders. Several types of violence often co-exist within one family (because of an amalgam of genetic predispositions and difficult environments, such as poverty). Both offender and victim roles are, in some families, transmitted intergenerationally. Finally, violence in one's environment, whether neighbourhood or school, is often a key factor in the transmission of violence to the next generation.

Summary

1. Few incidents of courtship violence are reported to authorities and many youths consider such incidents a normal part of the dating process. Both sexes participate in this phenomenon; however, women sustain most of the injuries. Most of the studies of the origins of dating violence fail to consider extra-familial influences. Indeed, violence and abuse are greatly affected by the sociocultural context in which families live, including the social construction of masculinity. Date rape is the ultimate form of violence in terms of patriarchal dominance.

2. Verbal and psychological abuse of partners is not as easy to measure as physical abuse. It has also been less researched. It is quite salient in music videos favoured by adolescents. This form of abuse is often tailored to fit partners' vulnerabilities.

3. At the spousal level, along with cultural influences, physical violence by a partner is a situational matter as well as an issue of power. It covers a wide range of acts from mild to lethal. Cohabiting couples have the highest rate of partner violence. Poor couples, particularly those living in unsafe neighbourhoods, are more at risk of partner violence. Domestic violence among oppressed minorities may have causes that do not exist among whites. Same-sex-partner violence is as much a matter of power and control as it is in heterosexual couple violence, except that gender is not an issue.

4. On average, children of abused mothers have more behavioural and psychological problems. However, the intergenerational transmission of violence depends on many variables, and only a minority of these children grow up to repeat the pattern in their own families. Factors that contribute to transmission include high levels of interparental violence as well as exposure to community and school violence.

5. Statistics are presented on child and adolescent abuse, but these are merely estimates. Children who have been or are abused, on average, have more behavioural problems, particularly in terms of aggressiveness. Abused children are often surrounded by a climate of violence. Child abuse and neglect are more common in low-income families, especially in areas with a high concentration of poverty and violence. Approximately 30 percent of abused children grow up to repeat this pattern with their own offspring. Many variables enter into the risk of transmission. Parental stress often precipitates abuse, including stress caused by a child's disruptive behaviours. In some families, heredity may be a factor.

6. Child neglect is more widespread and involves not so much what parents do to their offspring as what they fail to do. It ranges from malnutrition to failure to supervise properly, and is not as easily detected nor as reported as abuse. Physical neglect is particularly related to poverty and has many consequences.

7. There may have been a decrease in child abuse by parents in the last two decades of the 20th century, although there has been an increase in reporting. However, child neglect has probably increased.

8. Child sexual abuse tends to occur more within the family among girls and outside the family among boys. A proportion of women who are abused as girls marry partners who abuse them or their daughters. Again, children from low-income families are at a higher risk of sexual abuse. The consequences for the child depend on the nature of the abuse and who the perpetrator is. Father-daughter incest is probably the most damaging. Sexual contact with an adult prematurely focuses the child on his or her sexuality, and this focus in turn often initiates a series of events in the life course of the child that deviate from the norm of other young persons' life courses. Sexual abuse is analyzed as an inappropriate sexual socialization.

9. Sibling violence ranges from mild to severe and is fairly common. Relatively little attention has been paid to it, and parents rarely intervene even though many are concerned. Children rarely report it. Sibling incest is predominantly a brother-to-sister situation. It is reported more in clinical than in survey populations: It may happen more in families that are malfunctioning in other respects.

10. Abuse of children by their peers is probably the most common form of abuse in society. It carries many negative consequences and can be explained by sociocultural factors. Peer sexual abuse also arises out of society's general cultural climate of violence and exploitation of women.

11. A number of children and adolescents assault their parents, particularly their mothers, both verbally and physically, but this topic is not given much attention in research. Among the elderly who are abused by their adult children, most are mothers. Some elderly are abused by their frustrated caregiving children, but perhaps even more are abused by children who depend on them because the adult children have various disabilities. Verbal as well as material forms of elderly parent abuse exist; the latter may be motivated by greed. Elder abuse is a relatively easy act to commit and may be less reported than child abuse.

12. Violence within the family is a reflection of violence in the society at large. It also results from the fact that the family is burdened with functions for which it receives little societal support.

Analytical Questions

1. The intergenerational transmission of violence and abuse is a recurrent theme in this chapter. It is also much emphasized in the media. How are the contents of this chapter different from the media emphases?
2. What role does culture play in partner abuse?
3. Cohabiting couples have high rates of partner violence. Explain why this is so, using information from this chapter and perhaps Chapters 7 and 12.
4. Why is permissiveness a form of child or adolescent neglect?
5. What, for you, is the most salient result of this chapter? Justify your response.

Suggested Readings

Cardarelli, A. P. (Ed.) 1997. *Violence between intimate partners*. Boston: Allyn and Bacon. This collection of research articles focuses on violence in heterosexual marriage and cohabitation, between same-sex partners, and during courtship.

Duffy, A., and Momirov, J. 1997. *Family violence: A Canadian introduction*. Toronto: James Lorimer. This small textbook offers an integrated and comprehensive presentation on violence against women, children, youth, and elders within the family context.

Renzetti, C. M., and Miley, C. H. (Eds.) 1996. *Violence in gay and lesbian domestic partnerships*. New York: Harrington Park Press. Several studies and reviews of the literature form the contents of this book.

Sev'er, A. 2002. *Fleeing the house of horrors: Women who have left abusive partners*. Toronto: University of Toronto Press. This book, although presenting a sophisticated and well-balanced discussion, is easy to read. It is based on a qualitative study of a small group of battered women.

Suggested Weblinks

Canadian Council on Social Development includes a section on violence by partners of immigrant women who belong to visible minorities.

www.ccsd.ca

Canadian Network for the Prevention of Elder Abuse.

www.cnpea.ca

Centre for Research and Education on Violence Against Women and Children.

www.uwo.ca/violence

Health Canada contains a section on violence. This site also contains the **National Clearinghouse on Family Violence** and the **Child Maltreatment Division**.

www.hc-sc.gc.ca

Centre for Research and Education on Violence Against Women and Children

www.uwo.ca/violence

CHAPTER 14

Family Futures and Social Policies

At my publisher's suggestion, the first chapter opened with an autobiographical vignette that was pursued in Chapter 11. This concluding chapter follows up with a personal note as a teaching device. One of my main concerns as a family scholar has been the problems facing families; consequently, I am critical of the lack of social policies that could prevent or alleviate these hardships. But I did not have this critical orientation at the beginning of my research career, even though I was always involved in volunteer work of one sort or another—following my parents' example, as all my siblings have also done. How, then, did this orientation to being critical of social policies arise? The answer: My own development as a researcher was in great part the result of career "accidents"—that is, what I researched. For instance, much marital dissolution is detrimental to children and adolescents. However, long ago, such a conclusion would not have occurred to me because I was (pathetically) libertarian on this subject: I had had an "easy" early divorce after a brief, childless first marriage. In fact, back then, I thought that divorce was "inconsequential" and had "no intellectual interest"—a point of view I expressed to the astonished publisher who wanted me to write a book on this topic!

After a few years of his nagging, I finally relented and agreed to do a book on divorce. I began reading and then interviewed divorced parents and did some semi-participant observation. Although many families were doing well, nothing had prepared me for the problems I was encountering, particularly when these families were poor. The evidence I was gathering and what I was reading went overwhelmingly against my initial beliefs and personal experience.

By then, the students' autobiographies had been going on for years and contained unexpected challenges not well documented or appropriately explained in the research literature. All of this evidence expanded my framework well beyond the realities of my own life. Indeed, long ago, I came to the conclusion that one's personal situation is not necessarily a good base upon which to ground research and draw sound sociological conclusions and related policy implications, although I am sure that there are exceptions. Looking back now, I am relieved that, early on in my career, I was not interested in doing research on topics that pertained to my life. So doing might have influenced the types of questions I would have studied. At the very least, it would have kept me away from important concerns about matters such as poverty and issues of family structure and functions.

This concluding chapter builds on the material presented in the entire book. It opens with a return to the key themes that inform this text and that were initially outlined in the first chapter. The reader is now familiar with the contents of the book and can therefore more meaningfully integrate these themes that have guided the overall context. Future trends in family life are then predicted on a modest scale. Family-related policies are discussed within the context of some of the main themes outlined, as well as some of the problems defined in previous chapters.

SALIENT THEMES REVISITED

The key sociodemographic variables of social class, gender, and race/ethnicity are part of the fabric of the various themes that recur throughout this text.

Social Inequalities and Gender Stratification

It is a key underlying theme that families' major problems are largely, but not exclusively, created by economic, ethnic, and gender inequalities. These stratification challenges are evident as families' struggle to survive economically, or to overcome racial discrimination, or result in difficulties faced by certain parents with regard to child socialization or couple dynamics. Gender inequalities cut across ethnic and class divides. Therefore, gender stratification and roles were in evidence in most chapters. Thus, feminist perspectives influenced the course of these discussions. The text highlighted the extent to which females, at all age levels, are the nurturers and kin-keepers and how much more invested in various couple and family domains they generally are, compared with males. Basic child socialization and care, as well as familial problems and interactions, affect mothers more than fathers, wives more than husbands, sisters more than brothers, and grandmothers more than grandfathers (e.g., Burton et al., 2006).

The gender "revolution," as England (2010) puts it, has stalled in many domains and kin-keeping is one of them. As a result, when social structures fail to meet the needs of fragile families, mothers can be blamed as a political tool (Ambert, 2001; Robson, 2005). Indeed, in their parenting roles, **mothers** are far more subject to moral policing than are fathers (e.g., Knaak, 2005). Furthermore, social inequalities based on gender stratification mean that women are paid less than men for equivalent work (Beaujot, 2000). As well, women often channel themselves into part-time work and less well-paid jobs (with no benefits) because of the unequal household division of labour. This double factor contributes to keeping a large proportion of mother-headed families at or under the poverty level. As well, the types of jobs and the structure of the jobs to which women have access reinforce inequality at home (England, 2010). Other inequalities are created by the fact that, as an institution, the family suffers from its own underprivileged situation. Indeed, compared with other social systems (corporations, army, and political parties, for instance), it is **underfunded** and deprived of resources.

Diversity of Families

The theme of family diversity resides not only at the ethnic level but also at the cultural level, including religion, ideologies, and beliefs. As well, family diversity encompasses structure and modes of family formation: stepfamilies, single-mother-headed units, foster families, same-sex-parent families, and families created by adoption or with the help of reproductive technologies. The theme of family diversity is well captured by social constructionism and its links with inequalities: Not all diversity is socially or culturally acceptable and treated equally. Accepted definitions of what constitutes a family, a "normal" family, a "natural" family, often stigmatize nonnormative ones.

On the basis of available research, two conclusions have been reached with respect to family diversity. First, so long as certain types of families exist and do a good job at loving and raising their children, it becomes functional for society as a whole to support them. Second, because of current socioeconomic conditions, certain types of family structures—namely, single parent and, to some extent, blended and cohabiting structures—are less well equipped than others to invest in children's well-being and future (Hofferth, 2006; Kerr and Michalski, 2007). At this point in time, a child in a stable parental marriage is the context that is the most favourable to that child's development and adult well-being (Halpern-Meekin and Tach, 2008; Mac Con, 2006). Hence, extending the right to marriage to same-sex-parent families has been a step forward and in children's best interest: It is hoped that this right will increase family stability in general. Overall, there is a great deal of *similarity* among diverse types of families because families, as defined in this text, are institutions centred on filiation, reproduction, socialization, nurturance, and the expression of emotions. They are similar in the functions they fulfill.

A Surfeit of Family Functions

The third theme arose from the recurring observation that the family has not lost its functions but, rather, has acquired new ones—in great part because a lack of effective social policies is expanding the range of family care and duties (Beaujot, 2000, 2004). This multiplication of family functions was documented in many chapters, whether we discussed neighbourhood and school quality, peer and media influences, or the lack of adequate care provided by society to its frail seniors. Parents, grandparents, and adult children have to step in to provide care, assistance, guidance, coordination of services, and to exert vigilance over children's activities. Accordingly, we have seen that families are **burdened** with responsibilities imposed by the deficits of the social structure and the poverty of the political culture. This situation in great part explains why single parents as well as poor parents (who are often the same) encounter so many roadblocks to the fulfillment of their responsibilities.

Further, documenting the multiplicity of functions fulfilled by families has led us to question what is often defined as the "decline of the family" in some circles. The new social structure based on the market economy, technology, and cutbacks to helpful policies has bestowed upon the family a new set of responsibilities. Thus, too great a proportion of families are ill equipped to fulfill their functions, particularly in terms of supervising, guiding, educating their youths, and taking care of their frail kin. It is only in this sense that one could think of a decline of the family. This inability of too many nuclear families to care for their members, protect them, and maintain them within a normative life course stems from five major causes.

First, at the juncture of the personal and societal levels of analysis is the absence of an effective community surrounding families, as discussed below. A second cause resides in the **lack of social and political support** that would provide more resources to parents, children, and other family members with special needs—a situation to which we soon return. A third cause, also systemic, refers to those countless families that are forgotten by society and relegated to segregated enclaves. The fourth source of individual families' inability to fulfill their functions is related to the previous ones: Too many families are headed by parents, often young and single, who do not have the financial, educational, and maturity resources to raise children. Finally, at the personal level, parents often become so burdened by their own dramas and the need to make a living for their fractured family that their children are not sufficiently supported, even if only for a brief but crucial period of time. Other families are too burdened with simply making ends meet. Negative consequences can be lifelong, particularly within the context of so many social inequalities.

The Effective Community

We have seen in many chapters that more and more research points to the necessity of having parents supported by a community that cares for its children—all of its children, regardless of social class, race, and parents' marital status and gender. There is convergence among researchers from several disciplines as to the necessity of collective forms of socialization (Frempong and Willms, 2002; Sampson, 1997). An effective community links parents and teachers together and prevents them from being isolated and unaware of children's activities. In turn, within such a context, what children learn at home is reinforced at their friends' homes or in schools. Adolescents then realize that other parents and teachers have expectations similar to theirs. This collectivity lends an aura of legitimacy to their parents' teachings and example and adds credibility to the parenting effort in children's eyes. Furthermore, within the shelter of this effective community and informal social control, there are fewer opportunities for nonnormative behaviours that would take adolescents off the path of prosocial development.

This description of the effective community is one that fits reality less and less, particularly in cities and their new suburbs. Thus, the past decades have seen the **erosion of the community** as a result of urbanization, individualism, dependency on expert knowledge, interest groups, and the technological market economy (Etzioni, 1994). All of these forces have contributed to weaken community that would be so needed in times of cultural changes and increased multiculturalism through immigration and media exposure. As a result, too many problems experienced by families and their children are so intractable.

The Cultural Context

The fifth theme informing the text was particularly evident in Chapter 3, which focused on the cultural revolution constituted by the audiovisual **media** (television, videos, cellphones, the Internet). Concerns about the advisability of exposing children to physical violence, verbal abuse, foul language, exploitative sexuality, and low-quality programming have not been taken seriously by the industries in question. The net effect is that perhaps much of the nastiness, aggressiveness, lack of compliance, and at times lack of morality that is now encountered among some children, adolescents, and even young adults may in great part originate from the media (Garbarino, 1995). Parental roles become far more difficult to fulfill within such a cultural climate—a conclusion that reinforces the previous theme of families' inability to fulfill their functions adequately and to raise their children according to their **values** and not those of a consumerist and competitive society (Côté and Allahar, 2006; Doherty, 2000).

The theme of cultural context was also reflected in the recourse to social constructionism as an explanatory framework. It is the sociocultural context that defines what is proper behaviour and what are masculine and feminine roles. The evolving culture has constructed and reconstructed people's perceptions of the roles of mothers, children, and adolescents throughout the centuries and has done so even more recently, including the concept of emerging adulthood. These are only some of the most salient examples of the role of **social constructs** in family studies encountered in this book. As well, the cultural context was reflected in the chapter on education and religiosity. The cultural context needs to be readjusted to meet with realities that have long existed but have been ignored as problematic, such as sibling violence and abuse of mothers by young children, as discussed in Chapter 13.

WHAT DOES THE FUTURE HOLD?

No responsible sociologist can peer into a crystal ball and predict the future of the family beyond the next five to ten years. The reason for this caution is that rapid change, rather than stability, is the hallmark of our society. We live in a **technology-driven** rather than a socially or morally driven world. The pace of technology is rapidly distancing humanity's ability to control it, plan for it, and adjust to it (Noble, 1995; Talbott, 1995). The family is immersed in a global economy buffeted by the winds of speculation, where profits are paramount, and where the less educated become a surplus population (Rifkin, 1995). Under such circumstances, there is not a great deal of rules; therefore, predictions of the distant future are impossible. A few demographic trends constitute the field's only secure source of predictions for the next decade.

Age Distribution and Fertility

As more seniors live longer and are in better health, they will constitute a larger proportion of the population, because their growing numbers are not accompanied by similar numbers of births at the other end of the age structure. As is the case in many other western countries with a **low fertility rate**, the Canadian population is aging, except for that of the Northwest Territories and Nunavut. For instance, in July 2009, the median age had reached an all-time high of 39.5 years compared with 25.4 years in 1966 (Statistics Canada, 2009t). Persons aged 65 and over accounted for 13.9 percent of the population, and it is projected that this segment will reach 20 percent by 2026 (Turcotte and Schellenberg, 2007). The group that is increasing the fastest is the 85-and-over age bracket. Because of longevity, some families will include more generations than in the past. However, low fertility means that the family takes the vertical or "bean-pole" form: great-grandparents, grandparents, one or two middle-aged children, and a few great-grandchildren. Children will have few uncles, aunts, and cousins. The extended family network will be much less extensive. Thus, a key source of familial support is decreasing.

Unless governments quickly adopt policies more favourable to youths and young families, one can predict that young families will continue having few children and perhaps more couples will choose to remain childless (Lutz et al., 2003). These trends are evident in all western societies as well as in technologically advanced Asian countries such as Japan, South Korea, and even China (the latter because of the one-child family policy). The Canadian fertility rate, currently standing at 1.66 was even lower a few years back and could dip again, especially if environmental pollutants and various lifestyle activities reduce men's fertility and women's ability to conceive and bring to term a viable fetus. Fertility rates also depend on stable marital unions and on the age at first marriage (Beaujot and Kerr, 2004).

Or, yet, fertility could increase slightly if structural conditions that could reduce the costs of having children were put in place (Beaujot and Kerr, 2004)—that is, if policies for accessible and affordable child care were enacted, if the government paid a universal child credit, and corporations and other employers became more family friendly (Beaujot, 2004). A substantial change in social policies that would provide financial compensation for middle-class and low-income parents might serve as an incentive. Adjustment in work hours and the entire production system may be key (Beaujot, 2006:124). Under such circumstances, the interests of adults would compete less with those of children, and parents would find their situation more equitable, especially women, than is currently the case.

Overall, it is difficult to predict which amalgam of policies or cultural change could encourage higher fertility (McQuillan, 2006). It is interesting to note that Torr and Short (2004) have found higher fertility rates among both couples who are "traditional" in terms of the division of labour at home and those who are the most egalitarian. This probably reflects that, when spouses agree on this issue, they are more likely to be satisfied and add another child. In contrast, when one spouse is egalitarian but the other is not, they are less likely to risk another child—at least, the woman will be. But it would be unrealistic to expect any upward shift that might go beyond a rate of two children per woman—even though women desire more children. However, even such an increase would result in positive demographic consequences for several generations to come.

What concerns people in terms of the **aging of the population** is the cost of dependency. However, children are dependents to a greater extent than most seniors are: Most of the elderly live on their own and are in reasonably good health. This being said, however, policies will have to be devised so that the frail elderly are well taken care of and do not become the sole responsibility of families. Beaujot (2004:22) suggests a world that is less centred on work and where family has priority, with work leaves for the caretaking of special-needs children and adults as well as elderly relatives. But such a world also needs to be complemented with one in which consumer aspirations are reduced; however, trends are definitely going in the opposite direction currently.

Cohabitation, Marriage, and Divorce

Will cohabitation rates increase? Probably, at least in the short term, because the current trends in this direction have not yet peaked (Turcotte, 2002). At the same time, marriage rates will dip accordingly among young adults. But over the entire life span, a majority of people will continue to marry at least once, although at a later age. However, this majority will be smaller than in the past. Factors that could halt this trend toward cohabitation are increased immigration from Muslim and Hindu countries or a swing toward greater religiosity—which could also increase marriage and decrease single parenthood (Biles and Ibrahim, 2005). Better economic opportunities for the relatively unskilled might also foster marriage rather than cohabitation (NCHS, 2010). Indeed, because of poverty, marital commitment is often not an option for the less affluent segments of the population (Goldstein and Kenney, 2001).

One also has to consider the possibility that cohabitational relationships may one day become as committed and as stable as marriages. Were this to occur, couples' and children's well-being would be equally well served in both types of unions. From a structural standpoint, cohabitations would no longer be a concern. However, they would remain a concern at the cultural level in terms of values for those who have moral/religious objections to this form of partnering; these objections are more likely to come from persons with strong religious preferences.

What about the divorce rate? Some factors herald lower rates in the future while others herald higher rates. In the balance, the next decade should not bring a marked decline or increase in divorce in Canada. Delaying marriage may act as a preventive measure to those divorces that are related to youthful marriages. Divorce, like marriage and cohabitation, is culturally and economically driven. The media may be influential in this respect: A predominance of individualistic and materialistic values accompanies high divorce rates. Furthermore, the presence of so many adults whose parents have themselves divorced might lead to an increase. We have also seen that marriages that are preceded by *uncommitted* cohabitations are more likely to end in divorce. Thus, a higher level of cohabitation might actually raise the divorce rate. On the other hand, greater religiosity might decrease both cohabitation and divorce. However, there is no indication that any large-scale religious revival is close at hand even though, as seen in Chapter 6, many immigrants are more religious than Canadian-born citizens (Bibby, 2002; Biles and Ibrahim, 2005).

As women continue to make gains on the labour market, the financial burden of divorce for men may slowly increase over time as they will stand to lose more than previous cohorts of men whose wives depended nearly entirely on them (Fry and

Cohn, 2010; McManus and DiPrete, 2001). Whether this trend would contribute to reducing divorce remains to be seen. Were men to behave more equitably at home, and were the cultural assumptions about men's and women's roles changed in society at large, women would be more rewarded by and more inclined to remain in their marriage.

Family Formation by Singles

The rate of births to women who are neither cohabiting nor married has remained stable and has even decreased recently, particularly among adolescents, both in Canada and the U.S. (McKay and Barrett, 2010). This decrease seems to be related to more widespread recourse to contraception and, in the U.S., to a higher level of abstinence. It could be related to a greater emphasis on education and to higher employment rates, which encourage couple formation before the birth of a child.

Let's recall here that nonmarital motherhood is generally neither in the best interest of a mother or a child, at least economically. On the other hand, nonmarital fatherhood is not immediately detrimental to individual men (Nock, 1998a). So long as this **gender-role imbalance** survives, women remain entirely responsible for the reduction of nonmarital fertility. This inequity makes it more complicated to alter the pattern because women's good intentions may be thwarted by men's desire for immediate gratification without consequent responsibilities. It is difficult to predict if this downward trend among adolescents will persist in the face of more permissive sexual attitudes and media influences. Factors that could reduce the rate of births to single women include higher educational attainment, and better job prospects in pockets of poverty for both men and women (Bingoly-Liworo, 2010). As well, a change in cultural values, more adequate utilization of contraception, and male cooperation are also necessary. *Fertility needs to be de-gendered in terms of responsibilities.*

Parenting

Aside from the issue of the gendered role of parenting, there are several other problems facing parents. We have seen that, in English-speaking western countries, childrearing has become professionalized to promote children's acquisition of traits that are valued in our type of society (Alwin, 1986; Arnett, 2008). These traits include individualism, self-esteem, self-sufficiency, and independence (Harkness and Super, 2002). Yet, this "expertise" has resulted in children's lives becoming more structured in terms of extracurricular activities and less spontaneous—and, paradoxically, this promotes dependence—while what is needed is interdependence between the generations (Kitayama and Cohen, 2006).

Parents are encouraged to use an authoritative style by some but a permissive style by others. As a result, many parents, afraid of assuming their role, choose permissive or "negotiating/wavering" styles. These trends are pronounced mainly at the middle-class and upper-class levels, which are the social strata that are the most successfully embedded in the economic system of production and consumerism. Working-class and disadvantaged parents, in general, hold somewhat different values of cooperation, obedience, and familism (the degree to which someone thinks family is important), as do many immigrants. They are also more group oriented and use childrearing practices that fit within the exigencies of their more constrained lifestyles. Sociologist Annette Lareau (2003) calls this the "accomplishment of natural growth" in contrast to the "process of concerted cultivation" enacted by middle-class parents.

However, as middle-class parents, especially mothers, become more stressed by the regimentation of their children's lives, many yearn to return to a situation whereby they and their children can enjoy more free time and especially more family time. As well, as our economy is polluting and depleting the environment of its non-renewable resources in order to meet a spiralling series of consumer "needs," counter-movements of minimalist living and environmental protection are emerging. These movements, along with the limitations of our planet, will eventually have to put the breaks on consumerism and change children's "needs." Further, when one sees the recent trends toward violence and unbridled sexuality in the media, all of which are totally self-centred, one can well wonder whether a backlash may not occur among parents and whether a movement toward a more simple life oriented around the group rather than the individual may not emerge. Thus, at this point, the parent-child relationship and, especially, child socialization and the organization of children's lives may be nearing a turning point: Changes may be needed if adults are going to desire to have any children at all—and be able to raise the ones they have so that a **humane society** rather than a robotic one of atomized individuals emerge.

Children's Well-Being

It is very difficult to predict what the outcomes will be in terms of child well-being in the next decade. This issue is related to the previous one. As well, to begin with, there is still too much poverty in Canada and too many other families are hovering just above this level and, as a consequence, have to limit their expenditures in terms of healthy foods and quality of neighbourhoods. There are several concurrent situations that may not bode well for children's welfare in the near future. The first resides in the consequences of the 2008–2009 recession which has contributed to further erode our industrial employment base while, at the same time, all levels of government have accumulated deficits. These governmental deficits will hamper social programs that are needed to help young families of all types and their children. Children's well-being is largely based on their parents having a solid base in life, on sound schools, on the availability of quality daycare, and on safe neighbourhoods. All of these require government investments.

As well, the new "information" technology and media open so many constructive possibilities for children and their families. Yet, so far, the consumerist aspect has predominated, along with further child/adolescent segregation by age and away from adults in terms of interest and leisure activities. Neither can one ignore the atmosphere of exploitative violence (movies, sports, games) that permeates the media. It is not a coincidence that children/adolescents who are violent have become so with more lethal results to themselves and their communities.

Singlehood in Senior Years

Today, a larger proportion than before of persons 20 to 35 years of age are not part of a couple. Another segment is cohabiting and this number will increase in the near future. We also know that cohabitations do not last as long as marriages (NCHS, 2010; Provencher et al., 2006). These three trends combined, along with divorce, mean that a larger number of elderly persons will be unattached in 20 years and after. Yet, we soon see in Table 14.1 that unattached individuals have higher poverty rates. One can justifiably be concerned that poverty rates will increase among future seniors, especially among women, and that the Canada Pension Plan may no longer be able to compensate.

Families' Natural Environment

In terms of predictions for the near future, it is not too soon to start mentioning the natural environment in family textbooks: Indeed, families depend on the environment for their health, water, food, space, and cultural contents. In turn, the environment depends on families for its survival even though various financial and business concerns often work against this interdependence. Schools are helping to socialize children in terms of issues such as waste, recycling, and composting. Children in turn bring these concerns home. Still, Canadians use far too much electricity, create too much garbage, and use too much water per capita—in fact, we are at the top of the consumption ladder in the world. In addition, the sprawl of our suburbs eats up the best farmland, which is our local source of food.

The Longer Time Frame

The possible trends just presented pertain to a future that is nearly here. Surely within a longer time frame, perhaps 20 years, more momentous changes in family life and structure may take place. Consider the domains of the division of labour at home (more egalitarian?); children's increased or decreased familialization; families' growing dependency on or rejection of technology (virtual sex? robotic companions?); increased unemployment; reproductive modes and technologies (in vitro wombs? cloning?). It is with some interest that I recently reread a passage from a 1973/1976 book where I predicted artificial wombs or *in vitro pregnancies* (Ambert, 1976:207). I then wrote: "People could be socialized to view positively the experience of seeing one's child grow. The father and even the entire family could share in the experience and, at that point, both sexes could contribute equally in the process." I went on to discuss the health advantages for women and fetuses—a situation that would help women whose health is fragile and would replace surrogate motherhood. I was ahead of the times. . .

Most of the changes that will occur in families in general will be largely dictated by techno-economic forces—that is, the combination of technological developments with the structure of the economy, an economy that has become based more on speculation and takeovers than on production and services that could create jobs. However, a point may be reached whereby unbridled technology so saturates life and degrades its humaneness that other societal forces might reassert themselves, including social planning, humanitarian philosophies, religion, morality, and community rather than economic values. What one must not forget is that technology and the market economy are **ideologies**; in theory, such ideologies could be rejected as determinants of people's lives. Rather, people could more judiciously choose technologies that can enhance rather than ruin the environment and family life. This is a choice that humanity will have to make at some point if it is to remain humane.

SOCIAL POLICIES PERTAINING TO FAMILIES

The reader will note that this section is not entitled "Family Policies" because Canada (as well as the U.S. and Great Britain) really does not have a coherent and purposive set of family policies (Beaujot, 2000). In fact, there is no equivalent to a Ministry of the Family, except in Quebec, which is the province that is also the most advanced in this domain. Rather, what we have in Canada are social policies that directly or indirectly affect families. Policies in general and family policies in particular are **social choices**. Such choices are heavily influenced by the ideologies and the values espoused by a political system at a given time. For instance, there are generally vast differences in the policies enacted by a Conservative- versus a Liberal-controlled Parliament (or a NDP one) both at the federal and the provincial levels. There are also vast differences

Government budget cuts will more and more require that the entire care of frail seniors be subsidized by families, thus extending family functions throughout the generations. Adult grandchildren become particularly helpful in this intergenerational chain and contribute to the senior generation's well-being and happiness.

among various western countries because of their ideologies as well as their historical backgrounds (Aysan and Beaujot, 2009; Hay, 2009). In Canada, there are also differences among provinces (Meilleur and Lapierre-Adamcyk, 2006).

Some consequences of planned policies are **unintended** (Bogenschneider and Corbett, 2010). For instance, mothers who are dropped from the welfare rolls because of time limitations may not find jobs. Others may not have enough to eat because their salaries are too low. As well, welfare payments may be set so low that many have to resort to food banks or employment that is unhealthy for one's family. Further, policies aimed at other aspects of social organization or of any of its systems, such as the justice system, can have indirect and unintended consequences for the family. One instance from the U.S. is the incarceration of small-time drug traffickers, which has had devastating results for black families in inner cities. It has led to a severe reduction in the number of young black males available to support their families: For instance, one in 25 white children and one in four black children born in 1990 had a parent who was imprisoned—a huge increase over 20 years earlier (Wildeman, 2009). This has led to an increasing risk among black children and children whose parents have less education, a situation that has echoes in Canada as well, especially among blacks and Aboriginals.

Focus of "Family Policies"

Overall, social policies that can be termed "family policies" largely focus on five areas of family life. These policies generally originate from various ministries at the provincial or territorial level, except for a few domains such as First Nations issues which are more frequently dealt with at the federal level.

1. **Family creation:** An example is the bonus for families that the Quebec government previously initiated at the birth of a child, with a larger amount for subsequent children in order to raise the fertility rate. The bonus was more recently replaced with a different system focusing more on pro-family than pro-natalism (Krull, 2007). Laws pertaining to adoption would also fall in this category: For instance, open adoption records and immigration requirements for international adoptions. Regulations concerning surrogate motherhood, sperm banks, and other aspects of assisted reproduction technologies also fit in this category.

2. **Family reunification or reconstitution:** Examples are the emphasis in the *Immigration Act* on reuniting immigrants with their immediate families. At the provincial level, an example is the emphasis of children's aid societies on returning children who have been abused or severely neglected to their original families.

3. **Childrearing and care:** The legislation of parental leave would fall in this category. Partly paid parental leave is a Canadian social policy that is very useful to parents before and after the birth of a child. It prevents poverty in some families. The *Unemployment Insurance Act* of 1940 (now the *Employment Insurance Act*) was amended in 1971 to allow mothers up to 15 weeks of maternal leave, with a proportion of their salaries paid. In 1990, another 10 weeks were added for either parent and, in December 2000, this was increased to 35 weeks (Marshall, 2006). Currently, mothers can take from six months to a year off. Further,

parents must have worked 600 hours rather than the previous 700 in order to qualify—an advantage for parents who work seasonally. Amendments are being considered for self-employed mothers. However, mothers who work too few hours cannot receive these benefits. Mitchell (2003:16) also found that women with salaries below $20,000 tended to return to work more rapidly than others—probably because their leave benefits are too low to sustain their family.

Between 2000 and 2001, the median maternity leave actually taken increased from six to 10 months. The proportion of fathers who also took some parental leave jumped from about 3 percent in 2000 to 10 percent in 2001. This makes Canada comparable to Holland and Denmark but lower than Sweden (where 36 percent of fathers take some parental leave) and especially Norway where 78 percent of fathers take parental leave. In Norway, fathers' leave is independent of that of mothers and, therefore, does not reduce the mothers' own time off. For very small children, subsidized parental leave may be a more appropriate social policy in large cities than subsidized child care centres (Maccoby and Lewis, 2003). Indeed, Beaujot and Ravanera (2009) suggest that parents would like to spend more time with small children. However, if parental leave is taken only by mothers, the gendered division of child care remains and women may have less access to promotions and salary increases (Beaujot, 2000).

The creation of inexpensive and regulated care centres is especially important here. Quebec has its $7.00 a day system but the waiting list is very long. Ontario begins, in September 2010, offering extended child care before and after kindergarten hours for five-year olds. But, overall, child care spaces are totally inadequate and subject to cuts when government deficits grow.

4. **Caregiving for the frail and elderly:** Governments in the recent past undertook steps toward strong contributions in this domain. However, budget cuts are resulting in increased reliance on family members (Connidis, 2010). The provision of free time to attend to the care of the elderly and the sick, as well as the availability of services such as visiting homemakers, also falls in this category, as does the maintenance of subsidized seniors' homes.

5. **Economic support** includes such initiatives as the Child Tax Benefit, the National Child Benefit Supplement, the Universal Child Care Benefit, and Old Age Security (with its components), as well as the Canada Pension Plan (Hay, 2009). For instance, for 67 percent of senior families, government transfers constitute their principal source of income (Williams, 2003). Without this income, a high proportion of seniors, particularly single women, would be poor. However, as poor children age and move out of the nest, their disadvantaged parents, particularly single mothers, may become even poorer because of the loss of child-related benefits (Krull, 2007). As well, low-income youth would need subsidies to attend higher education: Increases in fees have gone beyond their grasp (Coelli, 2009).

We have seen in Chapter 4 that mothers who have been single all their lives and lived in poverty or barely above that level have received very little attention in terms of research: Will we see an increase in poverty in old age as these women become seniors? In Quebec, the system of support provides more money to families with one as opposed to two parents in order to compensate for the number of parents present

(Krull, 2007). As well, as indicated later in Table 14.1, better Employment Insurance provisions are needed for younger unattached individuals because this group has very high poverty rates (Statistics Canada, 2009j).

Inertia of Political Systems

On the whole, it is safe to advance that our political system makes it very difficult to adopt preventive policies. Social governance needs to be changed to adapt to the needs of Canadian families in the 21st century (Scott, 2005). Preventive policies require a great deal of planning and a certain level of consensus on what family policy means and what the goals are (Bogenschneider and Corbett, 2010). Political will to invest in the future is also a prerequisite. Unfortunately, the future needs of families clash with the current political reality of getting votes and, now, of reducing deficits. **Political expediency** forces the adoption of stop-gap policies to solve a few problems that are identified by public opinion polls. But even remedial policies can take a very long time to produce a visible effect that can be assessed by research and appreciated by the public. In contrast, politicians need immediate or foreseeable results if their party is to remain in power.

Thus, politics conducted on the basis of media appeal and ability to raise huge sums of money from lobby groups to fund campaigns does not favour constructive family policies. Finally, it should be emphasized that social policies pertaining to families should be the object of evaluation or research to ascertain the extent to which the explicit goals have been reached and to seek unintended (negative or positive) consequences (Bogenschneider and Corbett, 2010). But here as well, such necessities do not fit well with the short attention span of politicians.

One should point out that human nature is flawed and even the best family policies cannot eliminate all problems for families and for individuals. Our scientifically focused century often leads us to believe that there is a solution for every problem. This is an overly optimistic notion. Thus, while alleviating poverty is a must, it cannot solve all other problems. Additional structural and cultural factors have to be considered along with individual variables, which include negative genetic predispositions that have yet to be mapped. However, society needs more adequate social policies to offer a **protective structure** for individuals who are challenged at the psychological level. Indeed, countries such as Sweden and Norway could serve as models for Canada, as they have to some extent for Quebec. These social democrat states provide a longer-term approach to welfare, spend more of their GDP on transfer payments, and shoulder a larger obligation to meet the needs of their citizens (Hay, 2009). But even these countries' policies have not, for instance, achieved full parenting equality between men and women nor equity in the labour market; nor have they entirely eliminated the differential outcomes of children in single-parent families.

REDUCING POVERTY

We have seen throughout the text that social inequalities brought by poverty are the root cause of a multiplicity of social problems, family misery, and individual deficits. Poverty prevents and destabilizes marriage and increases the divorce rate. It facilitates social isolation, delinquency, behavioural problems, school dropouts, teenage motherhood, drug abuse and trafficking, as well as human trafficking. These are only a few of the costly human risks related to poverty—overall, *it makes couples and families vulnerable* (Conger et al., 2010). Mothers and their small children, as well as unattached persons (living alone), are particularly affected, as indicated in Table 14.1, which summarizes the 2007 poverty rates for various types of families and individuals (Statistics Canada, 2009i). One has to keep in mind here that poverty cutoffs are a matter of dollars: Families scoring $100 above will not be considered poor, yet such families are in the same predicament as the "truly poor" ones. There are probably as many families near the poverty level as below it. Thus, "poverty" is more widespread than indicated in these statistics alone. As we can also see, the many Canada Pension Plan benefits narrow the gap in terms of income among the elderly (Prus, 2002).

The gendered situation among single-parent families illustrated in Table 14.1 holds across all cultures. It has given rise to the concept of the **feminization of poverty**. Even in Sweden, poverty is transmitted from generation to generation, albeit to a lesser extent, when families have single mothers and/or criminal fathers (Stenberg, 2000). France also has a higher poverty rate among mother-headed families, despite more aggressive *prestations sociales* (Dell et al., 2003). The same can be observed in

TABLE 14.1   **Poverty Rates After Income Tax Cut Offs for Families and Persons in Canada, 2007**

Types of families and persons	%*
ADULTS	
Couples without children	4.7
Senior couples	0.9
Unattached women below 65 years	35.1
Unattached men below 65 years	29.7
Unattached senior women	14.3
Unattached senior men	13.9
CHILDREN **	
In two-parent families	6.5
In male single-parent families	9.2
In female single-parent families	26.6
Immigrant children	33.0
Aboriginal children not on reserves	28.0

Sources: National Council of Welfare, 2009a, b. Adapted with the permission of the Minister of Public Works and Government Services Canada, 2010.

*After income tax cutoffs. Poverty rates before income tax would be higher than shown here because low-income persons receive tax credits which help some rise above the poverty level.

**Below the age of 18.

Quebec despite more progressive policies. In Quebec, the higher rates of cohabitation leave many women financially marginalized when their union breaks up (Meilleur and Lapierre-Adamcyk, 2006). A majority of poor children (54 percent) live in two-parent families because this is the most common type of family. However, children in lone-parent families are disproportionately represented among the poor. Thus, as indicated in Table 14.1, some children are at much higher risk of poverty than others. In 2007, the highest provincial rates of child poverty were in British Columbia at 13 percent and the lowest were in Prince Edward Island at 4.7 percent (National Council of Welfare, 2009b). Poverty rates are much higher in large cities, particularly those where disadvantaged groups are located. For instance, in 2006 for Winnipeg, 46 percent of Aboriginal households were poor and so were 26 percent of households with a child under six (CCPA, 2009).

A Critique of Current Policies

Policies aimed at truly preventing and reducing poverty rather than simply displacing it (to jails, for instance) or shifting it to private agencies and food banks would benefit the entire society (Lindsey and Martin, 2003). Pong et al. (2003) have shown that the gap in academic achievement between children from one- and two-parent families narrowed in those countries that have policies aimed at equalizing economic resources between families. Families should receive welfare payments until they are able to be self-sufficient (Gennetian and Morris, 2003). Welfare payments should be socially constructed as a form of *salary* given to families that have been marginalized by the economy, discrimination, or even their own frailties. It is an investment in the nation's youth and education. Sufficient assistance could lift children and their parents out of poverty and give them better life chances. Society would benefit, even economically, in the next generation. But, then again, the next generation is not generally a priority among politicians.

Adequate welfare payments that raise families above the poverty level can prevent the transmission of poverty, rather than perpetuating it, by enhancing children's cognitive development, which later contributes to their economic success (Duncan and Brooks-Gunn, 1997). In turn, this situation could lower the rates of unmarried motherhood for, as we have seen, this is largely a poverty-related phenomenon. As well, adequate welfare support may actually be correlated with lower homicide rates (DeFronzo, 1997). Such programs are preferable to investing in prison, which are not a remedy.

Low wages also create poverty, and some families living on such wages hold two or three jobs to make ends meet and have recourse to food banks. There is a great deal of political and business-community resistance to raising minimum wages to acceptable levels because this would reduce corporations' profits and affect small employers. This returns us to Chapter 4 where we saw that the ease with which companies relocate their plants and services abroad, where wages are very low, is probably one of the main factors that prevent provincial governments from raising wages more substantially than they do. Under these circumstances, raising the minimum wage might result in layoffs and simply displace poverty from country to country.

However, governments could make up the difference by topping low wages so that they reach a minimum that is sufficient—according to the cost of living in different areas. In other words, monthly wage supplements allow families a release from working overtime or three jobs that prevent some couples from spending enough time together and others from having another child (Nyberg et al., 2010). Such a program has been shown to bring behavioural and school-related benefits to children (Bogenschneider and Corbett, 2010:792). A **guaranteed minimum income** should be provided to all men and women who are employed, including those who work part-time, and extend it to men and women who remain home to care for children or frail family members. Once children are older, their mothers should continue receiving a supplement so as not to become even poorer.

Creating Green Jobs

In Canada, even more than in many European countries, employment is the most important factor to avoiding poverty (Hay, 2009). Nearly seven out of 10 households with no employment are poor. With one wage earner, 21 percent are poor while only four percent are when two or more persons are gainfully employed. Our new economy, based on the service sector, information technology, and financial speculation no longer provides well paid **entry-level jobs** that young people can turn to and then be in a position to establish families they can support (Beaujot, 2006). Our governments need to invest in new industries and technologies that are environment friendly (such as solar energy). Once energy concerns are addressed, other jobs can follow to create new materials that are environmentally neutral, which can go into more durable roads, residences and cars or even clothes and printing paper, as other instances.

At the same time, governments need to enter into partnerships with the private sector to retain jobs here. Each country should be able to provide work for its citizens, above and beyond the ideology of globalization. This is important for Canada because it is a country that is too dependent on the consumerism of other nations, particularly the U.S., for its exports and too dependent on the depletion of its own natural resources (gas, oil, wood, and minerals), the extraction and processing of which pollutes the environment.

In this vein, helping farmers produce more but with better incomes would help provide many jobs for young people with little education. Not all youths have the ability, desire, or means to acquire higher education—hence the economic marginalization of too many (Côté and Allahar, 2006; National Council of Welfare, 2009a). Some are much happier and productive doing manual work. We need a greater variety of jobs even if this means retaining or resuscitating certain industries, such as shoe manufacturing, that can provide basic labour.

Facilitating Adequate Housing

One component of poverty, and even of average income, is the lack of affordable housing, especially in expensive metropolitan areas such Toronto and Vancouver (CBoardC, 2010). We have seen in Chapter 5 that neighbourhoods that have high proportions of low-income families are related to more problematic family dynamics and child outcomes. For instance, Kohen et al. (2002a) have found that disadvantaged children benefit from living in a neighbourhood that has a greater proportion of economically secure residents. In contrast, social housing, as currently designed, tends to increase an area's already existing poverty.

Thus, one suggestion is that poor families receive **subsidies** that would allow them to find lodgings in a range of neighbourhoods. This could be accompanied by subsidies that would offer a proportion of stable low-income families the opportunity to buy a housing unit. Individual development accounts would assist families by providing them with monthly supplements to pay their mortgage and/or a down payment (Boyle, 2002). Options for Homes, for instance, uses innovative financing to make **home ownership** more affordable, even in high-rises (CBoardC, 2010). Habitat for Humanity is another helpful example. These policies would have the triple advantage of mixing social classes, empowering the poor via home ownership, and allowing them to move out of nefarious neighbourhoods. At the same time, governmental costs for building, managing, and maintaining public housing would decrease. Green and White (1997) suggest that home ownership itself forces people to acquire new management skills related to property maintenance, financial planning, and interpersonal functioning that, in turn, may be transferred to more successful parenting practices. Indeed, there are indications that parents who are homeowners become more hopeful and future oriented; their children benefit in terms of adaptive behaviours (Boyle, 2002).

However, it is difficult to know what the effect of such policies would be in terms of the neighbourhoods themselves. First, what would it do to areas that are currently devastated by poverty and even criminality? Would the truly dysfunctional families be left behind in the difficult areas creating ghettoes of even more acute deprivation (Fletcher, 2007)? There is also the possibility, based on an earlier study, that low-income youths moved to higher-income areas may feel excluded; they may react by becoming even more antisocial (Boyle et al., 2007). Or, yet, would policies that help disadvantaged families move out displace problems to areas that are stable, as may have happened in the U.S. (Rosin, 2008)? These two possibilities might be the case if these families do not receive scaffolding support to equip them with coping mechanisms necessary to function in more stable neighbourhoods.

A small example of this possibility occurred in a condo located in a stable neighbourhood in Toronto when a family with two teenagers and one school-age child moved in as renters after having lived in a notorious area of town. The teenagers promptly used the stairwells to smoke, drink, and have sex and began intimidating other residents who tried to put a stop to these disturbing activities. Many other nonresident teens began visiting this apartment and then loitered in corridors and harassed residents. The younger child began playing ball in the unit and the neighbours below developed headaches. Then adults were showing up as guests at all hours of the night. The police became frequent visitors. After a month of hearing complaints from residents and the terrorized janitorial as well as security staff, the president of the board of this condo discussed the issue with two owners of the same race as the new residents. The family was called in and it became very obvious that they were elated at having "escaped" from their "jungle" but had no idea as to how to behave according to the norms of their new area. The rules were explained to them: The teenagers were sneering (as they had always done when confronted with adult authority). After a while, they understood that, if they wanted to stay in this area, they had to change their behaviours. The two owners volunteered to mentor them. They also introduced the family to a new peer group and to adjacent library facilities, among others. The situation improved drastically.

The above case highlights the potential problems of social and cultural gulfs which poverty creates. Although the outcome was positive, it was so only because of extensive informal intervention. This example also highlights the necessity of preventing such social divisions created by poverty and segregation from emerging.

Another problem related to housing pertains to the fact that Aboriginals who live on reserves do not own their homes. A recent agreement between the Nisga'a band and British Columbia may have set a precedent. As well, a reserve near Vancouver has become a free township with property rights. Home ownership would allow for the accumulation of wealth and the transmission of this capital to the next generation as is the prerogative of other Canadians. It would also provide some capital for Aboriginals who move away from a reserve and settle in a city. As owners, inhabitants of reserves would have a stake in maintaining their properties so that the standards of housing that are now so low on many of these communities might rise. With this, other problems might be easier to solve.

Expansion of Child Care Programs

Universal child care would be particularly important in the prevention of poverty and as a remedy when it occurs (Kershaw et al., 2005). The availability of inexpensive and quality child care for the entire population would lower the burdens of parenting in an economy that necessitates two salaries. It is also needed to redress the gender imbalance against women in the domain of child care. Inexpensive and quality child care can also promote the economy of an area (Albanese, 2006). Since the 1990s, the federal commitment to universal child care has wavered along with reduced funding.

We have seen in Chapter 6 that only 20 percent of Canadian pre-schoolers have access to regulated child care (Beach et al., 2009). As a first step, child care should be available to all low-income families, especially the youngest children, because early poverty is the most detrimental for child, family, and society in terms of preventing the formation of skills needed in schools (Duncan et al., 1998). This step has already been widely suggested (Friendly et al., 2006; Pascal, 2009), and it consists of providing care of the Head Start type or enriched care to all children aged one to five in poor and near-poor families, all day long (Rushowy, 2004). (Intensive programs are more effective than half-day ones.)

Two immediate results would follow. First, we know from Chapter 6 that children in such programs develop more human resources, both behaviourally and cognitively, that prepare them for school (Pascal, 2009). Second, since child care constitutes mothers' main roadblock to self-sufficiency, this program would make it easier for mothers to find and retain jobs. For mothers on welfare, pursuing some postsecondary training would be an excellent investment, which current welfare policies do not necessarily encourage, but which extended child care programs could make feasible.

The results of Head Start programs in the U.S. vary depending on their duration (Reynolds and Temple, 1998). When Head Start children soon lose the gains they have made after they enter school, it is because their one-year stay in the program is too limited to overcome the cognitive and behavioural deficits created by poverty. Furthermore, upon arriving in Grade 1, these children are deprived of any support that would perpetuate whatever gains they have already made, and the quality of the school may not be adequate. However, one also has to be cautious in proclaiming institutional child care as the solution to all problems as so much of its results will depend on the quality of the educators, the peer group, and the families involved. As well, too many hours of child care may be difficult for small children in terms of adaptation to all the stimuli involved. There is the possibility that behavioural problems could emerge as a result of prolonged exposure (Belsky et al., 2007).

After-School Care and Improved Schooling

To extend the benefits of early childhood education, a second phase of the program would provide after-school care and tutoring through junior high school (Pascal, 2009). These have been shown to improve academic competence (Mahoney et al., 2005). This would, at the same time, provide children with much needed supervision and reduce opportunities for delinquency. Indeed, physical and sexual assaults against school-age children too frequently occur between 3 and 6 p.m.—that is, between the end of the school day and a parent's return home from work (AuCoin, 2005:68). Such programs could also reduce parenting stress (Barnett and Gareis, 2006). Extended after-school hours already exist in Quebec and are implemented on an experimental scale in some areas in Ontario. One in particular is the Peel District School Board's Early Years Hubs and Readiness Centres, located in areas of need and which involve parents as well (Grieve and Hogarth, 2009). The Pascal report in Ontario (2009) also suggests extended programs during the summer in areas where 15 or more families request it.

As well, the quality of schools should be improved in areas of poverty. This might begin in primary school, and when the "improved" cohort of children moves on, then the program would be extended throughout high school. Each high school at risk should include incentive programs, at least on a trial basis, as exist in some American states and in some cities in Canada on an experimental basis. For instance, adolescents from low-income families could be given a "salary" to remain in school in good standing (no truancy, no disruptive conduct, and all homework done). As well, students who achieve an A or B+ could be guaranteed scholarships for higher education. Such incentives might have the unanticipated result of creating a school and peer culture that values rather than denigrates education. If this were to happen, material incentives would no longer be needed in the next cohort of children.

Consequences and Limitations of Programs

Each one of the preceding policies in isolation is insufficient to lift a sizable number of children out of poverty. It is the total configuration that counts. The financial costs of such multipronged, proactive, preventive policies may appear high initially, but their **long-term results** would make them cost effective. To begin with, welfare

The effects of poverty on children differ, not only because of their familial and personal characteristics, but also depending on the era in which poverty occurs. This boy grew up in a rural area during the Great Depression and may even have been a Home Child.

outlays would rapidly diminish as better-educated parents are able to secure and maintain jobs. At that point, guaranteed income supplements would need to be added. Since low income brings poor health, health costs would certainly be reduced after a while, and so would costs stemming from child abuse and foster care (Pelton, 1997). Over $65,000 a year is needed to maintain a young person in a correctional institution. Thus, within a few years, the costs incurred for law enforcement and penal institutions would fall along with delinquency.

Further, an unintended consequence of enriched programs and school reform in disadvantaged areas might be a further reduction in the rate of family formation by young mothers. This could result from a greater interest of children in school achievement and extracurricular activities generated by school quality and financial incentives toward postsecondary education. As children mature into adolescents who have been supported by appropriate structures since age one, their enhanced educational capital would lead to jobs. College and university fees should be lower to prevent heavy debt load early on in a youth's employment history. In turn, we already know that increased income constitutes an incentive to marriage before procreation and that two-parent families are less likely to become poor.

Not all poverty can be eradicated. Some individuals are not sufficiently gifted by nature and need to be supported because they are in no way responsible for their deficits of human capital. Further, the ideology that has contributed to the initial creation of poverty would still survive. Indeed, poverty is created, as we have seen in Chapter 4, by global socioeconomic forces that include "smart" technology requiring higher educational credentials. It is also created by corporations that are guided by an ever-increasing profit motive for their shareholders, largely disregarding human costs. Currently, repayment of government debts siphon off monies that could be used to help young families. The combined ideologies of racism and sexism also contribute to poverty: Poverty of minority women who cannot find employed males to help support their children. All women are disadvantaged on the labour market in terms of wages.

STRENGTHENING CONJUGAL UNITS: ECONOMIC AND GENDER ROLE FACTORS REVISITED

Another priority of family policies should reside in the encouragement of marriage as an institution and the promotion of happy conjugal relationships (Bibby, 2004). Four caveats exist, however. First, I am not suggesting that divorce be made less accessible: Whether one likes it or not, divorce is necessary. Second, neither am I suggesting that marriage is necessary to all adults. Third, neither is it suggested that cohabitation is inherently detrimental. And fourth, as pointed out at the end of Chapter 8, a time may come when women (and men for that matter) will not have to depend on marriage or cohabitation in order to have a family that is beneficial to themselves and to their children. However, the fact of the matter is that the research clearly indicates that this time has not yet arrived.

As seen in Chapter 8, currently cohabiting partners and their children as well as never-married mothers and their children are family forms that are more related to poverty and problematic child outcomes than are married families. These two forms of family are currently neither in the best interest of the child or the mother, nor do they promote responsible fatherhood. Thus, by encouraging marriage and stable cohabitations, paternal involvement is also strengthened. Research indicates that the latter benefits children. In a nutshell, marriage fosters parental involvement in children, particularly when the marital relationship is positive. So does a stable cohabitational unit—and more research is required in this respect. By encouraging the formation of happy conjugal units and strengthening existing ones, the family would be in a better position to fulfill its customary functions as well as the new ones it has been invested with by current techno-economic changes.

The topic of the formation of marital units relates to the previous section on poverty and to Chapter 4, where we have seen that poverty, including male unemployment and low wages, prevents marriage. For instance, better-off cohabitants are more likely to marry when or before they have children. In contrast, poverty deprives males of their potential ability to support children or even to contribute economically for a couple living on its own, whether married or cohabiting. As a consequence, low-income or unemployed males are not ideal marriage prospects in young women's minds—neither are these men inclined to shoulder family responsibilities. Within the current cultural climate of tolerance, women have no option except to have children in temporary cohabitations or on their own (Pagnini and Rindfuss, 1993). As an additional result, the likelihood of these women ever marrying is reduced. Hence, a great proportion of these children are deprived for life of paternal investment. Furthermore, appropriate childrearing practices are more difficult to sustain under circumstances that involve poverty. Reducing unemployment and providing top-ups for low wages would contribute to the formation of marital units among all ethnic groups in society. Thus, the policies described earlier aimed at reducing poverty would have the secondary advantage of encouraging the formation of marital units or, at the very least, of mother-headed families that have adequate resources.

Inasmuch as economic uncertainty creates or exacerbates conjugal conflict (Chapters 9 and 13), the alleviation of poverty would contribute to the strengthening of the conjugal bond once it is formed. Were marital happiness promoted via cultural and anti-poverty measures, divorce and break-up rates might possibly decrease as a result. More children would be spared the negative effect of parental conflict, divorce, and subsequent poverty. This is not to say, however, that divorce would disappear, because it exists at all social class levels. But conjugal instability is particularly detrimental for poor families and it is a source of poverty in itself.

It should also be reemphasized here that **proper gender-role socialization** that would define boys as equally nurturing as girls, and fathers as equally responsible as mothers, would substantially reduce the gap in paternal investment that currently exists between married and unmarried fathers. Basically, it is the faulty socialization of boys that leads to their later disinvestment as fathers. Were the father-child bond accorded the same importance as the mother-child bond, then a father's relationship with his children would remain, even after his relationship with the mother has ended. In other words, the problematic aspects of nonmarital motherhood are largely created by paternal failures and the social construction of fatherhood.

SUPPORTING THE PARENTAL ROLE

Most "family" functions are actually fulfilled by parents, especially females. The parenting role itself has numerous constitutive elements, not to mention the additional roles occupied by most parents outside the home. Parents are still believed to be the main agents of socialization, even when other agents, such as schools, peers, and the media, often have a great influence on children, particularly during adolescence and in certain neighbourhoods. However, despite this belief in parents' importance, society does not generally support them, although blame is often lavished upon them. Indeed, only 42 percent of Canadian parents of young children agree that "Canada values its young children" (Invest in Kids, 2002). Hence, it is necessary that parents regain an effective moral authority (Doherty, 2000).

Based on these data and those presented in several chapters, parents should be respected and supported by schools, professionals, welfare agencies, and law enforcement personnel (see also Adams et al., 2002). In other words, the parental role should be more adequately institutionalized and more positively **reconstructed socially**. Invest in Kids (2002) also found that parents were not confident in their role and often lacked knowledge, that many were distressed, and too many utilized ineffective parenting practices. Chao and Willms (2002) noted that only about a third of parents are authoritative. All parents should receive training.

But also recall that interactional theories view children as coproducers in their development. Within this perspective, it is suggested that professionals help youngsters cooperate in their upbringing rather than evade their responsibilities (Brody et al., 2004). If children were encouraged from all quarters, including the media, to value their **parents' moral authority**, the family would become a more effective institution, whatever its structure and size. Within such a context, children would more easily accept and internalize norms of behaviour and would be more inclined to cooperate in their upbringing (Ambert, 2001). This means that parental investment and monitoring would be facilitated, with the result that behavioural problems, drug and alcohol abuse, as well as delinquency would diminish substantially.

Faced with often contradictory how-to advice, constrained by a variety of professionals whose blame they fear, and muzzled by media and peer influences, many parents become indecisive, unsure of themselves, and unable to make maturity demands of their offspring. They no longer dare try to pass on their values to their children, give them guidance, or make them accountable for transgressions. Others are disempowered by poverty. Still others, particularly nonresidential fathers, are disaffected because of their familial context. Many adults find it easier to disengage from the parental role and to reduce it to one of being their child's friend (Adams et al., 2002). This role configuration may work well with adolescents who are self-controlled, have an easy temperament, and especially with those who benefit from a prosocial peer group. But adolescents who are blessed with all these advantages are in the minority, so that egalitarian parenting, which is akin to the permissive style discussed in Chapter 10, is often disastrous.

This discussion, however, should not be interpreted as the sanctification of parents *as individuals*; rather, it is a call for the re-institutionalization of parenting. It would be unrealistic to disregard the fact that many adults today are less than ideal parents in terms of the values they pass on to their children, the examples they set, as well as the behaviours they allow. For instance, parents who are excessively oriented toward material gain and acquisition have little time for their children and encourage materialism. A second type of less than ideal parent is those who, either by their example or simply because of permissive attitudes, allow or encourage their children to engage in risky sex, to use drugs, to steal, behave aggressively, or, for boys, act exploitatively toward girls.

The types of adults just discussed may well constitute 10 to 25 percent of the parent population in certain areas. Policies aimed at supporting the parental role do not address all these parents. However, these policies would help conscientious parents and those who want to so become. The ranks of the "less than ideal" parents would, in the long run, thin down as a result of the pressure of the effective community that would arise with the **empowerment of conscientious parents**—who constitute the majority (see also, Steinberg, 2001).

A problem that deserves mention, and flows from Chapter 1, is that parents have entered an era of competitive parenting. Others call it hyper-parenting (Honoré, 2008), or intensive parenting, particularly mothering (Hays, 1996), or "concentrated cultivation" (Lareau, 2003). This is parenting guided by experts to "optimize" children's outcomes ("the best") in terms of skills, particularly academic skills (Bodovski and Farkas, 2008). This type of parenting is demanding, both of parents and of children. It induces insecurity among parents, a sense of never doing enough, and a fear that one's child will miss out on opportunities. Children become managed children as well as **products**. This parenting is costly financially and contributes to the time crunch everyone is in, particularly mothers. It also makes parents feel less secure in their ability to play their role because they are subject to evaluation along norms of productivity. These norms are set by various experts who gain a great deal in the bargain. This is part of the culture of the type of economy we live in: competitive, acquisitive, and driven.

FACILITATING THE CARE OF ELDERS

Persons aged 65 and older account for 13 percent of the Canadian population. Of these, only about seven percent are in a seniors' home at any point in time, generally during their oldest years (after age 85) or when they become very frail and dependent in the last year of life. In 2001, 32 percent of those 85 and older were in an institution. Thus, most seniors are **independent** and live on their own. If we only consider those aged 80 and over, 24 percent of men lived alone and 55 percent of women did in the 2006 census (Statistics Canada, 2007h). Indeed, 77 percent of these elderly women are widowed while 33 percent of men are. Thus, senior women are at greater risk of poverty and social isolation.

In the 2003 Canadian Community Health Survey, of seniors 65 and over not living in an institution, 18 percent needed help for home and grounds maintenance as well as transportation and errands. Another six percent needed help for personal care. A total of 31 percent of older senior women (85 +) were receiving help because of a long-term health problem while only 20 percent of men were because their wives were providing this help (Turcotte and Schellenberg, 2007). However, the help needed was more frequent among older seniors. Despite this help, 18 percent of Canadian seniors still have unmet needs (Busque, 2009).

Among seniors who received assistance because of a long-term health problem, 72 percent received it in part or totally from informal sources such as relatives; 45 percent received it exclusively from such informal sources. As seniors age and their problems become more serious, they receive more assistance from formal sources, whether government, paid employees, or non-government organizations. In 2002, the GSS showed that seniors tended to receive more of their help from informal sources when they had many living children. After spouses, **daughters** provided more in terms of housework and personal care and shared with sons in terms of transportation, shopping, and the payment of bills. Personal care was more often carried out via organizations and paid employees.

The 2007 GSS completed this profile, focusing on **caregivers** 45 years and older and care recipients 65 years and older. Cranswick and Dosman (2008) report that women are more often caregivers than men and do more of the tasks requiring regular assistance (such as meal preparation and medical-related care). These tasks compete with their work schedule. They also point out that wives' care of their elderly husbands is vastly underreported as it is simply seen as part of the household routine. In the same study, caregivers between the ages of 45 and 65 had been providing assistance for 5.4 years while older caregivers had been doing so for an average of 6.5 years. A British study has found that many caregivers had played this role at least twice before. Larkin (2009) used the term "serial carer." Finally, and perhaps surprisingly, they found that caregiving occurs more often when an older person enters a facility. This can in part be explained by the fact that institutions offer a limited range of free services and, in some cases, the caregiving is substandard (e.g., Reid, 2008).

What all this information indicates is a *concern for future seniors* with no or few children—as is becoming more and more the norm. Social inequalities among seniors, with perhaps disastrous consequences for their well-being, will exist, not only in terms of physical assets but also in terms of social capital (Keating and Dosman, 2009). In addition, the number and proportion of seniors are increasing in the population.

Therefore, more seniors will need help from organizations. Informal caregivers, whether spouses, daughters, or daughters-in-law, will need more formal support to carry out their role. Indeed, there will soon be more caregivers who belong to the **sandwich generation** as children are born later and stay home longer. As Duxbury et al. (2009) point out, just over one in 10 Canadians provide some form of help for an elderly person who lives nearby or in another location. This help tends to be given as a labour of love. In 2007, about 1.65 million Canadians aged 45 and over were providing assistance to a parent or a parent-in-law. About 360,000 of these adult children, or 22 percent, were helping a parent who lived at least an hour away by car (Vézina and Turcotte, 2010). This situation required more financial outlays on the part of the adult children and 40 percent of them had to miss work compared with 28 percent of those living closer. Yet, employment tends to mitigate the stress of caregiving (Rubin and White-Means, 2009).

On the other side of the equation, Turcotte and Schellenberg (2007) also show that 23 percent of seniors who are 75 and over do volunteer work in the community. Overall, 31 percent of all seniors engage in **volunteer work** (CIW, 2010). Thus, while nearly 30 percent received help for transportation and errands, another 19 percent provided this same help to someone else and over 10 percent did housework for someone else not living with them. As discussed in Chapter 10, the flow of help is bidirectional throughout families—as seniors also help the younger generations—and is largely based on altruistic and filiation motives (Beaujot, 2006; Rajulton and Ravanera, 2006b).

Our society, therefore, needs to focus on better integrating seniors both in the volunteer section and the workforce—the two aspects of production. As well, more flexible workplaces are necessary so that children and relatives can assist their elderly parents more efficiently and with a lesser sense of burden. As well, the government should institute a **"care leave"** similar to parental leaves after a child is born or adopted for adults who need to take a more hands-on role in the help or care of a parent. This would prevent financial difficulties for the caregivers and reduce the strain of doing two jobs at the same time: Although helping one's frail relatives, as is the case for child care, is an altruistic act, it is also an economic act and *benefits the entire society* (see Funk and Kobayashi, 2009).

CONCLUSIONS: THE FAMILY IN CONTEXT

The family represents an experience lived by all people, making each individual an "expert" on the topic. But as we have seen, this personal expertise is insufficient, for family life has many faces, speaks many languages, harbours a multitude of cultures, and involves different cohorts and dynamics. It entails great happiness and cradles painful dramas. It appears so simple but in its totality it is so very complex.

Family Research and Historical Context

The chapters in this book have highlighted many areas of family life and its relationship with the other social systems that have yet to be researched. Thus, despite the giant steps made by various disciplines in the advancement of knowledge on the family, much is still unknown. History also compounds this problem: Knowledge that is applicable today may no longer be valid 10 to 20 years from now. This is due to the fact that, as the sociocultural context in which families are embedded changes, so do lives in the family. Therefore, many topics of research will need to be revisited as the decades of the 21st century unfold, so that people do not draw conclusions and then implement policies based on results that are obsolete.

Some of the areas that may see change in research results in the near future are the statistical relationships between cohabitation and higher divorce rates. If cohabitants were to become more committed, then it is possible that premarital cohabitation would cease to be related to higher divorce rates. Similarly, if single parents, who are most often mothers, were to receive more adequate social and economic support, their children's well-being might become comparable to that of children in stable two-parent families. On another level, if the media that are accessible to children were regulated in terms of antisocial and materialistic contents, aggressiveness and consumerism might be reduced among children and adolescents. Thus, the results of current studies would no longer apply.

Until a decade or so ago, research pertaining to family life suffered from three limitations, which still exist to some extent. First, studies are often too simplistic when investigating causality. This can be observed in the domains of consequences for children of abuse, parental conflict, and divorce, to name just a few examples. More or less, the conclusions derived tend to bring a simple causality model whereas the reality is that, depending on other environmental and genetic variables, there are several causality paths and different types of consequence for a singular cause. The second limitation is even more widespread: It resides in that most research on family life ignores genetics or, rather, the interplay between genes and environment (D'Onofrio and Lahey, 2010; Plomin et al., 2008). As a result, family studies are deprived of information regarding many aspects of causality and consequences. Indeed, family life is not only a social, cultural, and economic phenomenon but a biological and genetic one as well. Many outcomes so far attributed to parenting, for example, are actually also the result of parents' own genetic makeup, their children's genetic risks or protective factors, as well as the interplay between all these variables together. In turn, the effects of this interplay may change over time—the developmental framework—as families change and as persons age.

The third limitation in family studies is that most of the research has been carried out in western English-speaking countries because these are the ones where sociology and psychology are highly developed. Consequently, we really do not know if the various causality models, whether environmental, genetic, or both together apply to other societies. This question is particularly relevant for small societies where families are interdependent, live in subsistence economies, and are relatively isolated from current sociotechnological developments. In other words, we lack a knowledge base that is humanity wide (Arnett, 2008). Indeed, perhaps what we find for our types of society does not fully apply elsewhere—and we broached this issue in several chapters when discussing various social constructs.

Family Functions and Their Contexts

The research summarized and evaluated in this book does not support the pessimistic view of a family decline and loss of functions. Rather, the research supports pessimism concerning *individual families' ability* to fulfill their ever-increasing functions adequately, particularly that of the socialization of children and the care of frail elders. On the one hand, the family as an institution is highly valued, and exacting demands are placed on it in terms of its responsibilities in many domains. On the other hand, this same sociocultural context generally fails to provide individual families with equivalent moral support and practical help that could allow them to fulfill their functions.

For instance, society is choosing to embrace market capitalism and technology as a value and as a way of life (Côté and Allahar, 2006). Unavoidably, there are high costs to such a choice, and families bear a disproportionate burden in this respect, especially those that are marginalized by poverty and lack of access to the new types of jobs (Phillips and Phillips, 2000). As Blank (1997:198) phrases it, when a society "has chosen a market-oriented economy, it has a responsibility to those who cannot survive in the market on their own." This responsibility should not be displaced onto families. Unfortunately, this is exactly what continues to happen.

Above all, in western societies, the family is a small and relatively isolated unit that is much affected by its various environments. In recent decades, this cultural and socioeconomic context has broadened considerably because of globalization and a more pervasive as well as intrusive technology. At the dawn of this new millennium, families are experiencing change at a rapid pace and are contextualized in a larger world, but receive relatively fewer resources in terms of instrumental and effective moral support. Empowering and assisting families, no matter their structure, is one of the key social challenges of the 21st century.

Summary

1. The three key sociodemographic variables of social class, gender, and race/ethnicity are part of the fabric of the various themes that have recurred throughout this text. These themes are social inequalities and gender stratification, family diversity, the increase in family functions, the importance of the effective community, and cultural contexts.

2. Trends in the very near future of family life include more surviving generations, continuing low fertility, and consequent skewed age distribution toward the elderly; a temporary increase in cohabitation; the maintenance of the current divorce rate; a slightly reduced rate of family formation by single mothers. Questions concerning the parental role and children's well-being are also raised. As well, issues pertaining to a potential increase in poverty among future generations, particularly single mothers, are raised.

3. Areas of family life addressed by policies are presented, and a critique of the political system is offered, including critiques of policies concerning poverty. Suggestions for the reduction of poverty are presented: creation of environment-friendly jobs, especially for youth with no post-secondary education; the creation of better housing strategies for low-income persons; expansion of daycare and after-school programs is suggested. The encouragement and strengthening of conjugal unions through economic and cultural means is then discussed. Another suggestion consists of better support for the parental role, including a valorization and respect of parents. Elder care has to be facilitated and leaves are suggested for employed relatives who help their elders.

4. Many areas of family life are lacking in research; other domains would benefit by being constantly studied as change occurs, because current results may no longer apply. The three main limitations of family research are discussed. The research presented in this book does not support the pessimistic view of a loss of family functions, but does support pessimism concerning individual families'

ability to fulfill these ever-increasing functions adequately. The socioeconomic context in which the family evolves is problematic in terms of families' well-being.

Analytical Questions

1 Why are more and more families unable to meet their diverse functions?
2. The concept of the effective community has been used repeatedly in this text. What could be done to put it into practice and what would be the consequences?
3. Why should marital units be encouraged and strengthened? Why not one-parent families?

4. How does this chapter present a critique of our political system? How could this system be improved for the benefit of families and their members?
5. Relate the sections on the facilitation of elder care to their related sections in Chapter 10—particularly the concepts of burden and care.

Suggested Readings

Baker, M. 2006. *Restructuring family policies: Convergences and divergences.* Toronto: University of Toronto Press. A thorough presentation of Canadian social policies that affect families, including a comparison with other countries.

Beaujot, R. 2000. *Earning and caring in Canadian families.* Peterborough, ON: Broadview Press. The last chapter contains a thoughtful discussion and critique of policies affecting families. Other countries such as Sweden are utilized in a comparative approach.

Crittenden, A. 2001. *The price of motherhood.* New York: Henry Holt. This popular and easy-to-read

book presents many policy suggestions as well as a critique of the current system of gender inequality.

Danziger, S., and Waldfogel, J. (Eds.) 2000. *Securing the future: Investing in children from birth to college.* New York: Russell Sage. This collection of articles discusses policy suggestions that would increase investment in institutions that support children.

Mason, M. A., Skolnick, A., and Sugarman, S. 2003. *All our families: New policies for a new century,* 2nd Ed. New York: Oxford University Press. This text focuses on policy reform and covers a wide range of topics, such as teen pregnancy, child abuse, and divorce.

Suggested Weblinks

American Psychological Association Policy Office presents information on policy activities as well as research. The office coordinates advocacy efforts at the federal level.

http://apa.org/ppo/topic.html

Canadian Policy Research Networks

www.cprn.ca

Centre of Excellence for Child Welfare

www.cecw-cepb.ca>

Future of Children is now published jointly by Princeton University and the policy- and research-oriented Brookings Institution. This site also contains the journal *The Future of Children.*

www.princeton.edu/futureofchildren

Invest in Kids Foundation includes a national survey of parents of young children. The results of this survey are particularly relevant because they can lead to policy changes at various levels in order to revalue the parental role as well as provide parents with the knowledge and support they obviously need.

www.investinkids.ca

Child Trends includes research with the goal of improving children's lives.

www. childtrends.org

National Human Services Assembly includes the Family Strengthening Policy Center.

www.nassembly.org/fsc

Please also see the suggested weblinks at the end of Chapter 5.

Glossary

Assortative mating: Refers to selecting spouses or mates in a nonrandom fashion; marrying persons who have similar given characteristics. The characteristics may be physical appearance, IQ, values, one or several personality traits, or even social class. The opposite of assortative mating is random mating.

Authoritarian parenting: Refers to parental behaviours and attitudes that are predominantly controlling and punishing. At the extreme, they can be even harsh and rejecting. The authoritarian approach does not appeal to a child's sense of reasoning or morality. It is a "do-as-I-say-or-you'll-get-smacked" type of upbringing. Authoritarian parents may also be inconsistent: They may threaten to punish but do not follow through with the punishment.

Authoritative parenting: Combines both warmth and monitoring of children's activities and whereabouts. Authoritative parents make maturity demands on their children. They explain the reasons behind their demands or rules. Once they have explained the reasons and the consequences, they consistently follow through with enforcement of those rules.

Cohort: A group of people who were born around the same time and who therefore go through life experiencing similar sociohistorical conditions. For example, people born during the Great Depression form a cohort.

Correlations: Correlations exist between two factors or variables, such as poverty and violence, when, as one increases or decreases, the other also changes. When both change in the same direction (e.g., both increase), this is a positive correlation. A negative correlation exists when one factor increases at the same time that the other decreases, as in the example of a decreasing number of cases of serious delinquency with an increasing level of socioeconomic status. Correlation is a statistical test, which is schematically illustrated in Figure 5.1 on page 128.

Critical mass: Refers to a proportion of well-functioning families that is necessary in a neighbourhood if that neighbourhood is to remain a good environment in which to raise children. The term can also refer to the proportion of children who are good students that is necessary in a classroom if learning is to take place. Researchers have not yet been able to determine what this exact proportion should be: 30 percent? 40 percent? 60 percent? (This term can also be used to refer to the negative as in "a critical mass of antisocial adolescents.")

Defamilialization: Refers to the fact that children are increasingly being taken care of and socialized by nonfamily members; children spend less time at home interacting with their parents.

Dilution of parental resources: This concept is used to explain the finding that children in large families do less well, on average, than those in smaller families. The rationale is that, in large families, parents have fewer resources to place at the disposal of each child: The resources are scattered over several children, or diluted.

Dysfunction: See *Function*. Dysfunctional behaviours are those that impair a person's functioning and success. They are maladaptive either for society, the family, the person concerned, or all of these. Persons or groups can be dysfunctional for their family or society, for instance.

Effective community: Refers to parents' links to other parents and to members of the community who maintain a prosocial set of values and are in contact with one another. The sharing of values, socialization goals, instrumental help, and collective supervision of children are characteristics of an effective community.

443

Endogamy: When people date, cohabit, or marry within their own social class, race, religion, or even language group.

Ethnic group: A group that is set apart from others because of its unique cultural patterns, history, language, as well as its sense of distinctiveness.

Ethnocentric: Refers to the judgments of social situations and people that individuals make based on their experiences within the culture of their own ethnic or cultural group. It can also be the assumption that one's own way of life is superior to that of other cultures or groups.

Exogamy: The opposite of *endogamy*: marrying out of one's group. Interracial and interreligious marriages are examples of exogamy.

Function: What an institution or group does for society, for families, or for individuals.

Gender roles: Norms or rules that define how males and females should think and behave. Gender roles represent the social definition of what a society constructs as appropriately masculine or feminine in terms of behaviour.

Homogamy: See *Assortative mating*.

Homogeneity: Uniformity; similarity.

Human capital: The entirety of abilities, skills, education, and positive human characteristics that a person possesses or has achieved. Synonymous with human assets.

Hypothesis: A testable proposition or sentence. For instance, "Wives who have been employed all their married lives adjust better to divorce than do homemakers or women who have been employed irregularly." Hypotheses are often designed to test theories.

Indicator: Indicators are used to measure variables, such as conjugal conflict. They are sentences, numbers, or observations that serve to illustrate a variable. Indicators are often coded (given a number) to derive statistics. Indicators of conjugal conflict can be the number of times spouses say they quarrel and how long their quarrels last.

Individuation: A psychological concept referring to the process by which children gain a sense of identity separately from their connection to their parents. This is a western concept.

Institution: A recognized area of social life that is organized along a system of norms (or rules)

regulating behaviours that are widely accepted in a society. Examples of institutions are the family, schools, and the banking system. On a larger scale, institutions include the political, economic, and religious systems of a society.

Longitudinal studies: Consist of studying the same people over time. For instance, people may be interviewed at age 18 and studied again at ages 25 and 35. This research design contrasts with cross-sectional or one-time studies and surveys. Synonymous with panel study.

Macrosociology: The study of the family within its broader sociocultural context to see how global forces such as the class system, the economy, and religion shape family structure and dynamics. In other words, "large" sociology or the study of large-scale phenomena and developments in a society, and its social structure and organization.

Median: The middle number in a set of numbers that are arranged in order of magnitude.

Microsociology: The study of interactions between individuals within specific and generally smaller contexts, such as the family or a group of friends. It is also the study of the internal dynamics of small groups, including the family.

Minority group: This generally refers to a group that is not as large as others. Or it can be a group that is given inferior status and less power in a society because of race, ethnicity, cultural practices, or religion. In Canada, this term generally refers to people other than white and Aboriginal.

Nonshared environment: Generally refers to experiences that differ for each sibling in a family. These can be different school, peer, and street experiences or environment. Within the home, the term refers to experiences that are specific to each child, such as differential parental treatment, the presence of the other siblings, or the chores given to a child because of his or her age or gender.

Polygenic: Refers to a trait, characteristic, or illness that can occur only when several specific genes are present.

Reference group: A group or category of persons whom people look up to, whose behaviour they imitate and emulate, and according to whose standards they evaluate themselves.

Shared environment: Generally refers to the home environment that siblings have in common or share. This could include parental behaviours, teachings, family routines and special occasions, and transitions, such as divorce or the death of a grandparent. It refers to the familial atmosphere. However, this shared environment is often perceived somewhat differently by each sibling, depending on his or her age, gender, and personality: The environment is shared but its impact differs.

Significant others: Persons who play an important role in an individual's life or with whom the individual identifies.

Social capital: A resource that resides in relationships, particularly family and community relations, that benefits child socialization. In Coleman's (1988) theory, social capital refers both to the positive interactions between a child's parents and between the child and his or her parents, as well as the relationships that parents maintain outside of the family that can benefit children or the entire family. Synonymous with social assets.

Social causation: Refers to theories that explain, for example, the high rates of well-being and economic success found among the married compared to the nonmarried, as a result of the benefits of marriage.

Social construct: A socially acceptable definition of a situation held by a group or a society. It is a cultural creation or invention. Social constructs concerning a phenomenon such as adolescence generally differ across history and across cultures.

Socialization: Refers to the process whereby a child learns to think and behave according to the ways of the society and the group into which he or she is born.

Social mobility: The passage from one social stratum to another or from one social class to another. Downward mobility occurs when individuals fall below their parents' stratum (intergenerational mobility) or below the one they have themselves occupied earlier (intragenerational mobility). Upward mobility takes place when individuals achieve a higher socioeconomic status than that of their parents. In other words, they "move up" in the class system.

Social selection: Refers to theories that explain, for example, the high rates of delinquency found among adolescents who suffer from FASD (fetal alcohol spectrum disorder) and low self-control. In other words, some adolescents are being selected into delinquency because they are less well balanced psychologically, and even intellectually, to control their behaviours and to choose pro-social situations.

Socioeconomic status or SES: The ranking of people on a scale of prestige on the basis of occupation, income, and education. SES is often used as a synonym for social class.

Stratification: Refers to the ranking that people occupy in a system. Social stratification can be based on gender, race, or social class. For instance, families that belong to the higher social class have more resources, power, and prestige than the others.

Systemic: Refers to a problem that is built into a system, an institution, or a society. Solutions to such problems often require a restructuring of the institution, a difficult enterprise at best.

Theory: A set of interrelated propositions that explain a particular phenomenon. A theory is a sophisticated explanation that can be tested against facts to see if it fits. A good theory should withstand the test of research.

Bibliography and Author Index*

*The boldfaced numbers are the pages on which these citations appear.

Ablow, J. C., et al. 2009. Linking marital conflict and children's adjustment: The role of young children's perceptions. *Journal of Family Psychology, 23,* 485–499. **276**

Abma, J., Driscoll, A., and Moore, K. 1998. Young women's degree of control over first intercourse: An exploratory analysis. *Family Planning Perspectives, 30,* 12–18. **207**

Abu-Laban, S., and McDaniel, S. A. 2004. Aging, beauty, and status. In N. Mandell (Ed.), *Feminist issues: Race, class, and gender,* 4th Ed. (pp. 100–126). Toronto: Prentice Hall. **83, 188, 305, 306**

Adams, G. R., Côté, J., and Marshall, S. 2002. *Parent/Adolescent relationships and identity development.* Ottawa: Health Canada. **297, 436, 437**

Adler-Baeder, F., et al. 2005. *Marital transitions in military families: Their prevalence and their relevance for adaptation to the military.* U.S. Military Family Research Institute, Purdue University. **77, 78**

Adoption Council of Canada. 2003 and 2007. *Canadians adopt almost 20,000 children from abroad. U.S. Census asks about adopted children.* **244**

Adoption Council of Canada. 2003. International adoptions steady: 1,891 in 2002. Ottawa. <www.adoption.ca>. **239, 243, 244**

Ahearn, L. A. 2001. *Invitations to love: Literacy, love letters and social change in Nepal.* Ann Arbor, MI: The University of Michigan Press. **59**

Ahrons, C. R., and Tanner, J. L. 2003. Adult children and their fathers: Relationship changes 20 years after parental divorce. *Family Relations, 52,* 340–351. **373**

Aird, E. G. 2001. On rekindling a spirit of "home training": A mother's notes from the front. In S. A. Hofferth, N. Rankin, and C. West (Eds.), *Taking parenting public* (pp. 13–28). New York: Rowan & Littlefield. **13**

Albanese, P. 2006. Small town, big benefits: The ripple effect of $7/day child care. *The Canadian Review of Sociology and Anthropology, 43,* 125–141. **432**

Aldous, J. 1996. *Family careers: Rethinking the developmental perspective.* Thousand Oaks, CA: Sage. **16, 303**

Aldous, J., and Ganey, R. F. 1999. Family life and the pursuit of happiness: The influence of gender and race. *Journal of Family Issues, 20,* 155–180. **174, 268**

Aldous, J., Klaus, E., and Klein, D. M. 1985. The understanding heart: Aging parents and their favorite children. *Child Development, 56,* 303–316. **303**

Alexander, A. 1994. The effect of media on family interaction. In D. Zillman, J. Bryant, and A. C. Huston (Eds.), *Media, children, and the family* (pp. 51–59). Hillsdale, NJ: Erlbaum. **87**

Aliaga, D. E. 1994. Italian immigrants in Calgary: Dimensions of cultural identity. *Canadian Ethnic Studies, 26,* 141–148. **47**

Al-Krenawi, A., Graham, J. R., and Al-Krenawi, S. 2002. The psychological impact of polygamous marriages on Palestinian women. *Women & Health, 34,* 1–16. **10**

Al-Krenawi, A., Slonim-Nevo, V., and Graham, J. R. 2006. Polygyny and its impact on the psychosocial well-being of husbands. *Journal of Comparative Family Studies, 37,* 173–189. **8, 10**

Allard, F. L., et al. 2005. Maintien de l'engagement paternel après une rupture conjugale: Point de vue des pères vivant en contexte de pauvreté. *Enfances, familles, générations, 3,* 1–42. **353**

Alwin, D. F. 1986. From obedience to autonomy: Changes in traits desired in children, 1924–1978. *Public Opinion Quarterly, 52,* 33–52. **422**

Alwin, D. F. 1990. Cohort replacement and changes in parental socialization values. *Journal of Marriage and Family, 52,* 347–360. **297**

Alwin, D. F. 2001. Parental values, beliefs, and behavior: A review and promulga for research into the new century. In S. L. Hofferth and T. J. Owens (Eds.), *Children at the millennium: Where have we come from, where are we going?* (pp. 97–139). Oxford, UK: Elsevier. **298**

Amato, P. R. 1996. Explaining the intergenerational transmission of divorce. *Journal of Marriage and Family, 58,* 628–640. **363, 367**

Amato, P. R. 2000. The consequences of divorce for adults and children. *Journal of Marriage and Family, 62,* 1269–1287. **376**

Amato, P. R. 2003. Reconciling divergent perspectives: Judith Wallerstein, quantitative family research, and children of divorce. *Family Relations, 52,* 332–339. **362**

Amato, P. R. 2007. Transformative processes in marriage: Some thoughts from a sociologist. *Journal of Marriage and Family, 69,* 305–309. **353**

Amato, P. R., and Booth, A. 1997. *A generation at risk: Growing up in an era of family upheaval.* Cambridge, MA: Harvard University Press. **219, 363**

Amato, P. R., and Cheadle, J. 2005. The long reach of divorce: Divorce and child well-being across three generations. *Journal of Marriage and Family, 67,* 191–206. **360, 363**

Amato, P. R., and DeBoer, D.D. 2001. The transmission of marital instability across generations: Relationship skills or commitment to marriage? *Journal of Marriage and Family, 63,* 1038–1051. **355, 363**

Amato, P. R., and Gilbreth, J. G. 1999. Nonresident fathers and children's well-being: A meta-analysis. *Journal of Marriage and Family, 61,* 557–573. **353**

Amato, P. R., and Hohmann-Marriott, B. 2007. A comparison of high- and low-distress marriages that end in divorce. *Journal of Marriage and Family, 69,* 621–638. **359**

Amato, P. R., and Previti, D. 2004. People's reasons for divorcing: Gender, social class, the life course, and adjustment. *Journal of Family Issues, 24,* 602–606. **109, 354, 357**

Amato, P. R., and Rezac, S. J. 1994. Contact with nonresident parents, interparental conflict, and children's behavior. *Journal of Family Issues, 15,* 191–207. **366**

Amato, P. R., and Rivera, F. 1999. Paternal involvement and children's behavioral problems. *Journal of Marriage and Family, 61,* 375–384. 373

Amato, P. R., and Rogers, S. J. 1997. A longitudinal study of marital problems and subsequent divorce. *Journal of Marriage and Family, 59,* 612–624. 176, 271

Amato, P. R., and Sobolewski, J. M. 2001. The effects of divorce and marital discord on adult children's psychological well-being. *American Sociological Review, 66,* 900–921. 363

Amato, P. R., Meyers, C. E., and Emery, R. E. 2009. Changes in non-resident father-child contact from 1976 to 2002. *Family Relations, 58,* 41–53. 352

Amato, P. R., Spencer-Loomis, L. S., and Booth, A. 1995. Parental divorce, marital conflict, and offspring well-being during early adulthood. *Social Forces, 73,* 895–915. 366

Amato, P. R., et al. 2003. Continuity and change in marital quality between 1980 and 2000. *Journal of Marriage and Family, 65,* 1–22. **264, 266, 271**

Amato, P. R., et al. 2007. *Alone together. How marriage in America is changing.* Cambridge, MA: Harvard University Press. **254, 266, 358**

Ambert, A.-M. 1976. *Sex structure,* 2nd Ed. Toronto: Longman. **423**

Ambert, A.-M. 1989. *Ex-spouses and new spouses: A study of relationships.* Greenwich, CT: JAI Press. 349, 350, 358, 361, 374

Ambert, A.-M. 1994a. A qualitative study of peer abuse and its effects: Theoretical and empirical implications. *Journal of Marriage and Family, 56,* 119–130. **31, 405**

Ambert, A.-M. 1994b. An international perspective on parenting: Social change and social constructs. *Journal of Marriage and Family, 56,* 529–543. **19, 286**

Ambert, A.-M. 1997. *Parents, children, and adolescents: Interactive relationships and development in context.* New York: Haworth. 15

Ambert, A.-M. 1998. *The web of poverty: Psychosocial perspectives.* New York: Haworth. **107, 117, 121, 229, 336, 340**

Ambert, A.-M. 2001. *The effect of children on parents,* 2nd Ed. New York: Haworth. **15, 21, 275, 285, 299, 313, 352, 406, 415, 437**

Ambert, A.-M. 2006. *One-parent families: Characteristics, causes, consequences, and issues.* Ottawa: Vanier Institute of the Family. <www.vifamily.ca>. 225

Ambert, A.-M. 2007. *The rise in the number of children and adolescents who exhibit problematic behaviours.* Ottawa: Vanier Institute of the Family. <www.vifamily.ca>. 12

Ambert, A.-M. 2009. *Divorce: Facts, causes, and consequences.* Ottawa: Vanier Institute of the Family. <www.vifamily.ca>. 346

Ambert, A.-M., et al. 1995. Understanding and evaluating qualitative research. *Journal of Marriage and Family, 57,* 879–893. 29

ANAC (Aboriginal Nurses Association of Canada) and the RCMP (Royal Canadian Mounted Police). 2001. *Family violence in Aboriginal communities: A review.* Ottawa: Aboriginal Nurses Association of Canada. **50, 388**

ANAC (Aboriginal Nurses Association of Canada). 2002. Exposure to violence in the home: Effects on Aboriginal children. *Conference Proceeding Report.* Ottawa: Aboriginal Nurses Association of Canada. 388

Anderson, A. L. 1998. Strength of gay male youth: An untold story. *Child and Adolescent Social Work Journal, 15,* 55–71. 185

Anderson, C. A., Gentile, D. A., and Buckley, K. E. 2007. *Violent video game effects on children and adolescents: Theory, research, and public policy.* New York: Oxford University Press. 86

Anderson, C. A., et al. 2004. Violent video games: Specific effects of violent content on aggressive thoughts and behavior. *Advances in Experimental Social Psychology, 36,* 199–249. 86

Anderson, E. B., and Rice, A. M. 1992. Sibling relationships during remarriage. In E. M. Hetherington and G. Clingempeel (Eds.), *Coping with marital transitions* (pp. 149–177). *Monographs of the Society for Research in Child Development, 57,* no. 227. 325

Anderson, E. R. 1999. Sibling, half sibling, and stepsibling relationships in remarried families. In E. M. Hetherington, S. H. Henderson, and D. Reiss (Eds.), *Adolescent siblings in stepfamilies: Family functioning and adolescent adjustment* (pp. 101–126). *Monographs of the Society for Research in Child Development, 259, 64,* no. 4. 332

Anderson, K. L. 1997. Gender, status, and domestic violence: An integration of feminist and family violence approaches. *Journal of Marriage and Family, 59,* 655–669. 385

Anderson, K. L. 2008. Is partner violence worse in the context of control? *Journal of Marriage and Family, 70,* 1157–1168. 383

Anderssen, E., and McIlroy, A. 2004. Starting from ten: Part 5. *Globe and Mail.* April 10, A1, A7. 53

Andersson, G., et al. 2006. The demographics of same-sex marriages in Norway and Sweden. *Demography, 43,* 79–98. **208, 209, 222, 248**

Andreasen, M. S. 1994. Patterns of family life and television consumption from 1945 to the 1990s. In D. Zillman, J. Bryant, and A. C. Huston (Eds.), *Media, children, and the family* (pp. 19–36). Hillsdale, NJ: Erlbaum. 79

Anisef, P., and Kilbride, K. M. 2003. Overview and implications of the research. In P. Anisef and K. M. Kilbride (Eds.), *Managing two worlds: The experiences & concerns of immigrant youth in Ontario* (pp. 235–272). Toronto: Canadian Scholars' Press. 159, 167

Anisef, P., et al. 2000. *Opportunity and uncertainty.* Toronto: University of Toronto Press. **53, 136, 164**

Ansen, J. 2000. Nationalism and fertility in francophone Montreal: The majority as minority. *Canadian Studies in Population, 27,* 377–400. 52

Appell, A. R. 1998. On fixing "bad" mothers and saving their children. In M. Ladd-Taylor and L. Umansky (Eds.), *"Bad" mothers: The politics of blame in twentieth-century America* (pp. 356–380). New York: New York University Press. 392

Aquilino, W. S. 1997. From adolescent to young adult: A prospective study of parent-child relations during the transition to adulthood. *Journal of Marriage and Family, 59,* 670–686. 195

Aquilino, W. S. 2005. Impact of family structure on parental attitudes toward the economic support of adult children over the transition to adulthood. *Journal of Family Issues, 26,* 143–167. 373

Arendell, T. 1995. *Fathers and divorce.* Newbury Park, CA: Sage. 351

Arendell, T. 2000. Conceiving and investigating motherhood: The decade's scholarship. *Journal of Marriage and Family, 62,* 1192–1207. 19

Ariès, P. 1962. *Centuries of childhood: A social history of family life.* New York: Knopf and Random House. 18

Arnett, J. J. 2001. *Adolescence and emerging adulthood: A cultural approach.* Upper Saddle River, NJ: Prentice Hall. 294

Arnett, J. J. 2008. The neglected 95%: Why American psychology needs to become less American. *American Psychologist, 63,* 602–614. **10, 75, 239, 255, 286, 291, 294, 298, 421, 440**

Arnold, M. S. 1995. Exploding the myths: African-American families at promise. In B. B. Swadener and S. Lubeck (Eds.), *Children and families "at promise"* (pp. 143–162). Albany: State University of New York Press. 114

Aseltine, R. H., Jr. 1996. Pathways linking parental divorce with adolescent depression. *Journal of Health and Social Behavior, 37,* 113–148. **367**

Atkin, C. 1978. Observation of parent-child interaction in supermarket decision making. *Journal of Marketing, 42,* 41–45. **87**

Atkins, D. C., and Kessel, D. E. 2008. Religiousness and infidelity: Attendance, but not faith and prayer, predict marital fidelity. *Journal of Marriage and Family, 70,* 407–418. **172**

Attané, I. 2006. The demographic impact of a female deficit in China, 2000–2050. *Population and Development Review, 32,* 755–770. **8**

Attar-Schwartz, S., et al. 2009. Grandparenting and adolescent adjustment in two-parent biological, lone-parent, and step-families. *Journal of Family Psychology, 23,* 67–75. **376**

AuCoin, K. 2005. *Children and youth as victims of violent crime.* Ottawa: Statistics Canada. Catalogue no. 85-002-XIE, vol. 25, no. 1. **102, 391, 398, 399, 402, 406, 433**

Audas, R., and McDonald, T. 2004. Rural-urban migration in the 1990s. *Canadian Social Trends, 73,* 17–24. **145, 146**

Aulakh, R. 2009. Forced marriage. *Toronto Star.* November 14, A1, A18. **60**

Austin, E. W. 2001. Effects of family communication on children's interpretation of television. In J. Bryant and J. A. Bryant (Eds.), *Television and the American family* (pp. 377–395). Mahwah, NJ: Erlbaum. **89**

Avellar, S., and Smock, P. J. 2005. The economic consequences of the dissolution of cohabiting unions. *Journal of Marriage and Family, 67,* 315–327. **359**

Averett, P., Nalavany, B., and Ryan, S. 2009. An evaluation of gay/lesbian and heterosexual adoption. *Adoption Quarterly, 12,* 129–151. **223**

Aysan, M. F., and Beaujot, R. 2009. Welfare regimes for aging populations: No single path for reform. *Population and Development Review, 35,* 701–720. **425**

Baber, K. M. 2010. Reconceptualizing gender: A review essay. *Journal of Family Theory & Review, 2,* 88–94. **25**

Baca Zinn, M. 2007. Feminist rethinking from racial-ethnic families. In S. J. Ferguson (Ed.), *Shifting the centre: Understanding contemporary families* (pp. 18–27). New York: McGraw-Hill. **24**

Bachman, H. J., and Chase-Lansdale, P. L. 2005. Custodial grandmothers' physical, mental, and economic well-being: Comparisons of primary caregivers from low-income neighborhorhoods. *Family Relations, 54,* 475–487. **309**

Bachman, J. G., et al. 1997. *Smoking, drinking, and drug use in young adulthood.* Mahwah, NJ: Erlbaum. **199**

Badinter, E. 2010. *Le conflit: La femme et la mère.* Paris: Flammarion. **286**

Bagley, C. 1993. Transracial adoption in Britain: A follow-up study, with policy considerations. *Child Welfare, 72,* 285–299. **243**

Bailey, J. A., et al. 2009. Parenting practices and problem behavior across three generations: Monitoring, harsh discipline, and drug use in the intergenerational transmission of externalizing behavior. *Developmental Psychology, 45,* 1214–1226. **292**

Bailey, J. M., and Dawood, I. 1998. Behavior genetics, sexual orientation, and the family. In C. Patterson and A. R. D'Augelli (Eds.), *Lesbian, gay, and bisexual identities in families: Psychological perspectives.* New York: Oxford University Press. **223**

Bailey, J. M., et al. 1995. Sexual orientation of adult sons and gay fathers. *Developmental Psychology, 31,* 124–129. **223**

Baillargeon, R., Tremblay, R., and Willms, J. D. 2002. Physical aggression among toddlers: Does it run in families? In J. D. Willms (Ed.), *Vulnerable children* (pp. 71–103). Edmonton: University of Alberta Press. **322**

Bakan, A. B., and Stasiulis, D. (Eds.). 1997. *Not one of the family: Foreign and domestic workers in Canada.* Toronto: University of Toronto Press. **25**

Baker, M. 2001. *Families, labour and love.* Vancouver: University of British Columbia Press. **11, 162, 223**

Bala, N., et al. 2005. *Polygamy in Canada: Legal and social implications for women and children—An international review of polygamy.* Ottawa: Status of Women Canada. <www.swc-cfc.gc.ca>. **10**

Balakrishnan, T. R., Maxim, P., and Jurdi, R. 2005. Social class versus cultural identity as factos in the residential segregation of ethnic groups in Toronto, Montreal and Vancouver for 2001. *Canadian Studies in Population, 32,* 203–227. **133**

Balsam, K. F., Rothblum, E. D., and Beauchaine, T. P. 2005. Victimization over the life span: A comparison of lesbian, gay, bisexual, and heterosexual siblings. *Journal of Consulting and Clinical Psychology, 73,* 474–487. **209, 390, 405**

Banerjee, S., and Coward, H. 2005. Hindus in Canada: Negotiating identity in a "different" homeland. In P. Bramadat and D. Siljak (Eds.), *Religion and ethnicity in Canada,* (pp. 30–51). Toronto: Pearson. **173**

Bank, L., Patterson, G. R., and Reid, J. B. 1996. Negative sibling interaction patterns as predictors of later adjustment problems in adolescent and young adult males. In G. H. Brody (Ed.), *Sibling relationships: Their causes and consequences* (pp. 197–230). Norwood, NJ: Ablex. **329**

Bankston, C. L., III, and Caldas, S. J. 1998. Family structure, schoolmates, and racial inequalities in school achievement. *Journal of Marriage and Family, 60,* 715–724. **159**

Bao, W.-N., et al. 1999. Perceived parental acceptance as a moderator of religious transmission among adolescent boys and girls. *Journal of Marriage and Family, 61,* 362–374. **174**

Barber, B. K. 1994. Cultural, family, and personal contexts of parent-adolescent conflict. *Journal of Marriage and Family, 56,* 375–386. **295**

Barber, J. G., and Delfabbro, P. H. 2009. The profile and progress of neglected and abused children in long-term foster care. *Child Abuse & Neglect, 33,* 421–428. **247**

Barber, J. S., and East, P. L. 2009. Home and parenting resources available to siblings depending on their birth intention status. *Child Development, 80,* 921–934. **235**

Barbieri, C., Mahoney, E., and Butler, L. 2008. Understanding the nature and extent of farm and ranch diversification in North America. *Rural Sociology, 73,* 205–230. **139**

Bar-Haim, Y., et al. 2007. Threat-related attentional bias in anxious and nonanxious individuals: A meta-analytic study. *Psychological Bulletin, 113,* 1–24. **279**

Baril, R., Lefebvre, T., and Merrigan, P. 2000. Quebec family policy: Impact and options. *Choices: Family Policy, 6,* 4–52: IRPP. **53**

Barkan, S. E. 2006. Religiosity and premarital sex in adulthood. *Journal for the Scientific Study of Religion, 45,* 407–417. **207**

Barman, J. 2003. Schooled for inequality: The education of British Columbia Aboriginal children. In N. Janovicek and J. Parr (Eds.), *Histories of Canadian children and youth* (pp. 212–235). Toronto: Oxford University Press. **43**

Barnes, G., et al. 2006. Effects of parental monitoring and peer deviance on substance use and delinquency. *Journal of Marriage and Family, 68,* 1084–1104. **287**

Barnes, J. E., et al. 2009. Sexual and physical revictimization among victims of severe childhood sexual abuse. *Child Abuse & Neglect, 33,* 412–420. **401**

Barnett, O. W., et al. 2005. *Family violence across the lifespan: An introduction,* 2nd Ed. Thousand Oaks, CA: Sage. **291**

Barnett, R. C., and Gareis, K. C. 2006. Parental after-school stress and psychological well-being. *Journal of Marriage and Family, 68,* 101–108. **433**

Barnett, S. W. 1998. Long-term cognitive and academic effects of early childhood education of children in poverty. *Preventive Medicine, 27,* 204–207. **157**

Barrow, C. 1996. *Family in the Caribbean: Themes and perspectives.* Kingston, Jamaica: Ian Randle Publishers. **7, 20, 55, 79**

Barth, R. P., and Miller, J. M. 2000. Building effective post-adoption services: What is the empirical foundation? *Family Relations, 49,* 447–455. **241**

Bartholet, E. 1993. *Family bonds: Adoption and the politics of parenting.* Boston: Houghton Mifflin. **240**

Bartowski, J. P., Xu, X., and Levin, M. L. 2008. Religion and child development: Evidence from the Early Childhood Longitudinal Study. *Social Science Research, 37,*18–36. **175**

Baskin, C. 2003. From victims to leaders: Activism against violence towards women. In K. Anderson and B. Lawrence (Eds.), *Strong stories: Native vision and community survival* (pp. 213–287). Vancouver: Sumach Press. **387**

Batalova, J. A., and Cohen, P. N. 2002. Premarital cohabitation and housework: Couples in cross-national perspective. *Journal of Marriage and Family, 64,* 743–755. **195**

Bates, J. E., et al. 1998. Interaction of temperamental resistance to control and restrictive parenting in the development of externalizing behavior. *Developmental Psychology, 34,* 982–995. **293**

Batson, C. D., Quian, Z., and Lichter, D. 2006. Interracial and intraracial patterns of mate selection among America's diverse Black populations. *Journal of Marriage and Family, 68,* 658–672. **187**

Baumer, E. P., and South, S. J. 2001. Community effects on youth sexual activity. *Journal of Marriage and Family, 63,* 540–554. **130**

Baumrind, D. 1967. Child care practices anteceding three patterns of preschool behavior. *Genetic Psychology Monographs, 75,* 43–88. **286**

Baumrind, D. 1990. Parenting styles and adolescent development. In R. M. Lerner, J. Brooks-Gunn, and A. C. Petersen (Eds.), *The Encyclopedia of adolescence* (pp. 746–758). New York: Garland Press. **286**

Baumrind, D. 1991. Effective parenting during the early adolescent transition. In P. A. Cowan and M. E. Hetherington (Eds.), *Family transitions* (pp. 111–163). Hillsdale, NJ: Erlbaum. **289**

Baumrind, D. 1994. The social context of child maltreatment. *Family Relations, 43,* 360–368. **291**

Baumrind, D. 1996. The discipline controversy revisited. *Family Relations, 45,* 405–414. **291**

Bawin-Legrow, B., and Gauthier, A. 2001. Regulation of intimacy and love semantics in couples living apart together. *International Review of Sociology, 11,* 39–46. **78**

Baydar, N., and Brooks-Gunn, J. 1998. Profiles of grandmothers who help care for their grandchildren in the United States. *Family Relations, 47,* 385–393. **307**

Beach, J., et al. 2009. *Early childhood education and care in Canada 2008.* 8th Ed. Toronto: Childcare Resource and Research Unit. **98, 153, 154, 432**

Beauchamp, D. L. 2008. *Victimization amongst gays, lesbians and bisexuals.* Ottawa: Statistics Canada, Canadian Centre for Justice Statistics. **390**

Beaujot, R. 2000. *Earning & caring in Canadian families.* Peterborough: Broadview Press. **25, 26, 201, 260, 376, 415, 424, 426**

Beaujot, R. 2004. *Delayed life transitions: Trends and implications.* Ottawa: Vanier Institute of the Family. **16, 18, 96, 231, 301, 419, 420**

Beaujot, R. 2006. Delayed life transitions: Trends and implications. In K. McQuillan and Z. R. Ravanera (Eds)., *Canada's changing families. Implications for individuals and society* (pp. 105–132). Toronto: University of Toronto Press. **300, 301, 419, 430, 439**

Beaujot, R., and Bélanger, A. 2001. *Perspective on below replacement fertility in Canada: Trends, desires, accommodations.* Paper presented at the International Union for the Scientific Study of Population, Tokyo, March 2001. **191**

Beaujot, R., and Kerr, D. 2004. *Population change in Canada,* 2nd Ed. Toronto: Oxford University Press. **49, 51, 76, 231, 232, 419**

Beaujot, R., and McQuillan, K. 1982. *Growth and dualism: The demographic development of Canadian society.* Toronto: Gage Publishing. **40**

Beaujot, R., and Muhammad, A. 2006. Transformed families and the basis for childbearing. In K. McQuillan and Z. R. Ravanera (Eds)., *Canada's changing families. Implications for individuals and society* (pp. 15–48). Toronto: University of Toronto Press. **231**

Beaujot, R., and Ravanera, Z. 2009. Family models for earning and caring: Implications for childcare and for family policy. *Canadian Studies in Population, 36,* 145–166. **426**

Beaupré, P. 2008. I do. Take two? Changes in intentions to remarry among divorced Canadians during the past 20 years. *Matter of Fact,* Ottawa: Statistics Canada, July 19. **369**

Beaupré, P., and Cloutier, E. 2007. Navigating family transitions: Evidence from the General Social Survey. *Canadian Social Trends,*June 13. **231, 260, 349, 350**

Beaupré, P., Dryburgh, H., and Wendt, M. 2010. Making fathers "count." *Canadian Social Trends, 90,* June 8. **218, 351**

Beaupré, P., et al. 2008. *When is junior moving out? Transitions from the parental home to independence.* Ottawa: Statistics Canada. **136, 178, 373**

Beaupré, P., Turcotte, P., and Milan, A. 2006. When is junior moving out? *Canadian Social Trends,*August. **300, 301, 318**

Beaute, N. 2009. Adoptees can find mom, but not dad. *Toronto Star,* December 10, A1, A16. **239, 245**

Beaver, K. M., et al. 2009. Gene-environment interplay and delinquent involvement. *Journal of Adolescent Research, 24,* 147–168. **22, 340**

Beavon, D., and Cooke, M. 2003. An application of the UN Human Development Index and registered Indians in Canada, 1996. In J. White et al. (Eds.), *Aboriginal conditions: Research as a foundation for public policy.* Vancouver, BC: University of British Columbia Press. **108**

Beck, A. N., et al. 2010. Partnership transitions and maternal parenting. *Journal of Marriage and Family, 72,* 219–233. **221**

Becker, G. S. 1974. A theory of social interactions. *Journal of Political Economy, 82,* 1063–1093. **12**

Beckett, C. 2005. The Swedish myth: The corporal punishment ban and child death statistics. *British Journal of Social Work, 35,* 125–138. **292**

Beckett, C., et al. 2006. Do the effects of early severe deprivation persist into early adolescence? Findings from the English and Romanian adoptees study. *Child Development, 77,* 696–711. **244**

Bélanger, A., and Dumas, J. 1998. *Report on the demographic situation in Canada 1997.*Ottawa: Statistics Canada. Catalogue no. 91, 209. **191**

Bélanger, A., and Oikawa, C. 1999. Who has a third child? *Canadian Social Trends, 53,* 23–26. **231**

Belanger, Y. D. 2008. *Gambling with the future: The evolution of Aboriginal gambling in Canada.* Saskatoon: Punch Publishing. **51**

Bell, A. P., and Weinberg, M. S. 1978. *Homosexualities: A study of diversity among men and women.*New York: Simon and Schuster. **189**

Bell, R. Q. 1968. A reinterpretation of the direction of effects in studies of socialization. *Psychological Review, 75,* 81–85. **15**

Belle, M., and McQuillan, K. 1994. Births outside marriage: A growing alternative. *Canadian Social Trends, 33,* 14–17.**224**

Belleau, H. 2007. *L'union de fait et le mariage au Québec: analyse des différences et similitudes.* Québec: Institut national de la recherche scientifique. Urbanisation, Culture et Société. **191, 193, 370**

Belsky, J., Conger, R., and Capaldi, D. M. 2009. The intergenerational transmission of parenting: Introduction to the Special Edition. *Developmental Psychology, 45,* 1201–1204. **292**

Belsky, J., et al. 2007. Are there long-terms effects of early child care? *Child Development, 78,* 681–701. **154, 155, 433**

Beltran, A. 2001. [A review of several books on] Empowering grandparents raising children: A training manual for group leaders/Grandparents raising grandchildren: Theoretical, empirical, and clinical perspectives. *The Gerontologist, 41,* 559–563. **310**

Bengtson, V. L. 2001. Beyond the nuclear family: The increasing importance of multigenerational bonds. *Journal of Marriage and Family, 63,* 1–16. **68, 307**

Bennett, J. W., and Seena, B. K. 1995. *Settling the Canadian-American west, 1890–1915: Pioneer adaptation and community building. An anthropological history.* Lincoln, NE: University of Nebraska Press. **47**

Berardo, F. M. 1998. Family privacy: Issues and concepts. *Journal of Family Issues, 19,* 4–19. **143**

Berger, L., et al. 2009. Estimating the "impact" of out-of-home placement on child well-being: Approaching the problem of selection bias. *Child Development, 80,* 1856–1876. **247**

Berger, P. L., and Luckmann, T. 1966. *The social construction of reality: A treatise in the sociology of knowledge.* New York: Doubleday. **18**

Berlin, L. J., et al. 2009. Correlates and consequences of spanking and verbal punishment for low-income White, African American, and Mexican American toddlers. *Child Development, 80,* 1403–1420. **228, 291, 292**

Bernard, J. 1972. *The future of marriage.* New York: World. **266**

Bernstein, A. C. 1997. Stepfamilies from siblings' perspectives. *Marriage and Family Review, 26,* 153–176. **333**

Berry, M., et al. 1998. The role of open adoption in the adjustment of adopted children and their families. *Children and Youth Services Review, 20,* 151–171. **245**

Bert, S. C., et al. 2009. The influence of maternal history of abuse on parenting knowledge and behavior. *Family Relations, 58,* 176–187. **394**

Berthet, T. 1992. *Seigneurs et colons de Nouvelle France: l'émergence d'une société distincte au XVIIIème siècle.* Cachan, Éditions de l'E.N.S. **42**

Bessant, K. C. 2006. A farm household conception of pluriactivity in Canadian agriculture: Motivation, diversification and livelihood. *Canadian Review of Sociology and Anthropology, 43,* 51–73. **139**

Bianchi, S. M., and Casper, L. M. 2000. American families. *Population Bulletin, 55,* 213. **193**

Bianchi, S. M., Robinson, J. P., and Milkie, M. A. 2006. *Demographic rhythms in American family life.*New York: Russell Sage Foundation. **260, 276**

Bibby, R. W. 2001. *Canadian teens: Today, yesterday, and tomorrow.* Toronto: Stoddart. **202, 295, 297, 368, 391**

Bibby, R. W. 2002. *Restless gods: The Renaissance of religion in Canada.* Toronto: Stoddart. **171, 184, 420**

Bibby, R. W. 2004. *The future families project.* Ottawa: Vanier Institute of the Family. **192, 197, 291, 435**

Bibby, R. W. 2009. *The emerging millennials: How Canada's newest generation is responding to change and choice.* Lethbridge, Alberta: Project Canada Books. **169**

Bibby, R. W., and Posterski, D. C. 2000. *Teen trends: A nation in motion.* Toronto: Stoddart. **202, 296, 301**

Biblarz, T. J., and Gottainer, G. 2000. Family structure and children's success: A comparison of widowed and divorced single-mother families. *Journal of Marriage and Family, 62,* 533–548. **369**

Biblarz, T. J., and Savci, E. 2010. Lesbian, gay, bisexual, and transgender families. *Journal of Marriage and Family, 72,* 480–497. **209, 223**

Biblarz, T. J., and Stacey, J. 2010. How does the gender of parents matter. *Journal of Marriage and Family, 72,* 3–22. **351**

Bierman, A., Fazio, E. M., and Milkie, M. A. 2006 A multifaceted approach to the mental health advantage of the married. *Journal of Family Issues, 27,* 554–582. **198**

BIFHSGO (British Isles Family History Society of Greater Ottawa). n.d. *Origins of the Home Children sent to Canada.* <www.bifhsgo.ca/home_children_origins.htm>. Accessed March 18, 2010. **46**

Biggs, S., et al. 2009. Mistreatment of older people in the United Kingdom: Findings from the First National Prevalence Study. *Journal of Elder Abuse & Neglect, 21,* 1–14. **408, 409**

Biles, J., and Ibrahim, H. 2005. Religion and public policy: Immigration, citizenship, and multiculturalism—Guess who's coming to dinner? In P. Bramadat and D. Seljak (Eds.), *Religion and ethnicity in Canada* (pp. 154–177). Toronto: Pearson. **26, 172, 420**

Binda, K. P. 2001. Native diaspora and urban education: Intractable problems. In S. K. Binda and S. Calliou (Eds.), *Aboriginal education in Canada* (pp. 179–194). Mississauga: Canadian Educators' Press. **133, 168**

Bingoly-Liworo, G. 2010. The influence of characteristics of men's job on the timing of the first birth in Canada. *Canadian Studies in Population, 37,* 77–105. **421**

Binnema, T. 1996. Old swan, big man, and the Siksika bands, 1794–1815. *Canadian Historical Review, 77,* 1–32. **36**

Binnema, T. 2001. Migrant from every direction: communities of the Northwestern Plains to 1750. In T. Binnema (Ed.), *Common and contested ground: A human and environmental history of the Northwestern Plains.* Norman, OK: University of Oklahoma Press. **36**

Binstock, G., and Thornton, A. 2003. Separations, reconciliations, and living apart in cohabiting and marital unions. *Journal of Marriage and Family, 65,* 432–443. **78, 193**

Bird, G. W., Peterson, R., and Miller, S. H. 2002. Factors associated with distress among support-seeking adoptive families. *Family Relations, 51,* 215–220. **241**

Birditt, K. S., Fingerman, K. L., and Zarit, S. H. 2010. Adult children's problems and successes: Implications for intergenerational ambivalence. *Journal of Gerontology: Series B, 65B,* 145–153. **304**

Birditt, K. S., Rott, L. M., and Fingerman, K. L. 2009. "If you can't say anything nice, don't say anything at all." Coping with interpersonal tensions in the parent-child relationship during adulthood. *Journal of Family Psychology, 23,* 769–778. **303**

Black, D. A., et al. 2000. Demographics of the gay and lesbian population in the United States: Evidence from available systematic data sources. *Demography, 37,* 139–154. **208, 209, 222**

Blake, J., Richardson, B., and Bhattacharya, J. 1991. Number of siblings and sociability. *Journal of Marriage and Family, 53,* 271–284. **319**

Blank, R. M. 1997. *It takes a nation: A new agenda for fighting poverty.* New York: Russell Sage. **90, 441**

Blau, P. 1964. *Exchange and power in social life.*New York: Wiley. **12**

Block, J. H., Block, J., and Gjerde, P. F. 1988. Parental functioning and the home environment of families of divorce: Prospective and current analyses. *Journal of the American Academy of Child and Adolescent Psychiatry, 27,* 207–213. **367**

Blood, R. O., and Wolfe, D. M. 1960. *Husbands and wives. Dynamics of married living.* New York: The Free Press. **12**

Blum, L. 1999. *At the breast: Ideologies of breastfeeding and motherhood in the contemporary United States.* Boston: Beacon Press. **20**

Blumer, H. 1969. *Symbolic interactionism: Perspective and method.*Englewood Cliffs, NJ: Prentice Hall. **15**

Blumstein, P., and Schwartz, P. 1990. Intimate relationships and the creation of sexuality. In D. McWhirter, S. Sanders, and J. Reinisch (Eds.), *Homosexuality/heterosexuality: Concepts of sexual orientation* (pp. 96–109). New York: Oxford University Press. **212**

Boden, J. M., Fergusson, D. M., and Horwood, L. J. 2009. Experience of sexual abuse in childhood and abortion in adolescence and early adulthood. *Childhood Abuse & Neglect, 33,* 870–876. **401**

Bodovski, K., and Farkas, G. 2008. "Concerted cultivation" and unequal achievement in elementary school. *Social Science Research, 37,* 903–919. **437**

Boekhoven, B. 2009. *"Caution! Kids at play?" Unstructured time use among children and adolescents.* Ottawa: The Vanier Institute of the Family. **75**

Bogenschneider, K., and Corbett, T. J. 2010. Family policy: Becoming a field of inquiry and subfield of social policy. *Journal of Marriage and the Family, 72,* 783–803. **13, 68, 71, 112, 119, 158, 393, 425, 427, 430**

Bogle, K. 2008. *Hooking up: Sex, dating, and relationships on campus.* New York: New York University Press. **184**

Bond, J. T., Galinsky, E., and Swanberg, J. E. 1998. *The 1997 national study of the changing workforce.* New York: Families and Work Institute. **104**

Bonds, D. D., and Gondoli, D. M. 2007. Examining the process by which marital adjustment affects maternal warmth: The role of coparenting support as a mediator. *Journal of Family Psychology, 21,* 288–296. **277**

Bonduelle., M., et al. 2005. A multi-centre cohort study of the physical health of 5-year-old children conceived after intracytoplasmic sperm injection, *in vitro,*fertilization and natural conception, *Human Reproduction, 20,* 413–419. **237**

Bonell, C. 2004. Why is teenage pregnancy conceptualized as a social problem? A review of quantitative research from the USA and UK. *Culture, Health & Sexuality, 6,* 255–272. **226**

Booth, A. 1999. Causes and consequences of divorce: Reflections on recent research. In R. A. Thompson and P. R. Amato (Eds.), *The postdivorce family* (pp. 29–48). Thousand Oaks, CA: Sage. **349**

Booth, A., and Amato, P. R. 2001. Parental predivorce relations and offspring postdivorce well-being. *Journal of Marriage and Family, 63,* 197–212. **349, 366**

Booth, A., and Edwards, J. M. 1992. Starting over: Why remarriages are unstable. *Journal of Family Issues, 13,* 179–194. **271**

Booth, A., Carver, K., and Granger, D. A. 2000. Biosocial perspectives on the family. *Journal of Marriage and the Family, 62,* 1018–1034. **23**

Booth, B., et al. 2007. *What we know about army families: 2007 update.* U.S. Army, MWR. **77, 78**

Bopp, M., Bopp, J., and Lane, P., Jr. 2003. *Aboriginal domestic violence in Canada.* The Aboriginal Healing Foundation. <www.ahf.ca>. **51**

Borders, L. D., Penny, J. M., and Portnoy, F. 2000. Adult adoptees and their friends: Current functioning and psychosocial well-being. *Family Relations, 49,* 407–418. **241**

Borrell, K., and Karlsson, S. G. 2002. *Reconceptualizing intimacy and ageing: Living apart together.* Paper presented at the International Symposium on Reconceptualising Gender and Ageing, University of Surrey: Centre for Research on Ageing and Gender, June. **78**

Bos, H. M. W., et al. 2007. Child adjustment and parenting in planned lesbian-parent families. *American Journal of Orthopsychiatry, 77,* 38–48. **223**

Bos, H. M. W., et al. 2008. Children in planned lesbian families: A cross-cultural comparison between the United States and the Netherlands. *American Journal of Orthopsychiatry, 78,* 211–219. **223**

Bouchard, B., and Zhao, J. 2000. University education: Recent trends in participation, accessibility, and returns. *Education Quarterly Review, 6.* **153**

Bould, S. 2004. Caring neighborhoods: Bringing up the kids together. *Journal of Family Issues, 24,* 427–447. **130**

Bourdieu, P. 1977. *Reproduction in education, society, culture.* (Translated). Thousand Oaks, CA: Sage. **13**

Boyce, W. F., Gallupe, O., and Fergus, S. 2008. Characteristics of Canadian youth reporting a very early age at first sexual intercourse. *The Canadian Journal of Human Sexuality, 17,* 97–109. **207**

Boyce, W., et al. 2006. Sexual health of Canadian youth: Findings from the Canadian Youth, Sexual Health and HIV/AIDS Study. *The Canadian Journal of Human Sexuality, 15,* 59–68. **203, 204, 205, 206, 207, 209**

Boyd, M., and Cao, X. 2009. Immigrant language proficiency, earnings, and language policies. *Canadian Studies in Population, 36,* 63–86. **112**

Boyd, M., and Li, A. 2003. May–December: Canadians in age-discrepant relationships. *Canadian Social Trends, 70,* 29–33. **188**

Boyd, M., and Norris, D. 1995. Leaving the nest? The impact of family structure. *Canadian Social Trends, 38,* 14–19. **362**

Boyle, M. H. 2002. Home ownership and the emotional and behavioral problems of children and youth. *Child Development, 73,* 883–892. **431**

Boyle, M. H., et al. 2007. Neighborhood and family influences on educational attainment: Results from the Ontario Child Health Study Follow-Up 2001. *Child Development, 78,* 168–189. **126, 129, 431**

Brabant, C., Bourdon, S., and Jutras, F. 2004. L'école à la maison au Québec: l'expression d'un choix familial marginal. *Enfances: Familles, Générations,* Fall. **170**

Bradbury, B. 1996. *Working families: Age, gender, and daily survival in industrializing Montreal.*Toronto: Oxford University Press. **25, 98**

Bradbury, B. 2000. Gender at work at home: Family decisions, the labour market, and girls' contribution to the family economy. In

B. Bradbury (Ed.), *Canadian family history* (pp. 177–198). Toronto: Irwin Publishing. **74, 97, 121**

Brady, D., and Kall, D. 2008. Nearly universal, but somewhat distinct: The femininization of poverty in affluent Western democracies, 1969–2000. *Social Sciences Research, 37*, 976–1007. **225**

Bramadat, P., and Seljak, D. (Eds.). 2005. *Religion and ethnicity in Canada.* Toronto: Pearson. **175, 176, 181**

Bramlett, M. D., Radel L. F., and Blumberg, S. J. 2007. The health and well-being of adopted children. *Pediatrics, 119S*, S54–60. **241**

Brandáo, J. A. 2003. *Nation Iroquoise: A seventeenth-century ethnography of the Iroquois.* Lincoln, NE: University of Nebraska Press. **37**

Brendgen, M., et al. 2002. Same-sex peer relations and romantic relationship during early adolescence: Interactive links to emotional, behavioral, and academic adjustment. *Merril-Palmer Quarterly, 48*, 77–103. **184**

Brendgen, M., et al. 2008. Linkages between children's and their friends' social and physical aggression: Evidence for a gene-environment interaction? *Child Development, 79*, 13–29. **405**

Brennan, S., and Taylor-Butts, A. 2008. *Sexual assault in Canada, 2004–2007.* Canadian Centre for Justice Statistics Profile Series, Catalogue no. 85F0033M, no. 19. **397, 399**

Brewaeys, A., et al. 2005. Anonymous or identity-registered sperm donors? A study of Dutch recipients' choices. *Human Reproduction, 20*, 820–824. **236**

Brewer, D. J., Eide, E. R., and Ehrenberg, R. G. 1999. Does it pay to attend an elite private college? Cross-cohort evidence of the effects of college type on earnings. *Journal of Human Resources, 34*, 104–123. **169**

Brody, G. H., and Flor, D. L. 1998. Maternal resources, parenting practices, and child competence in rural, single-parent African American families. *Child Development, 69*, 803–816. **288**

Brody, G. H., and Murry, V. M. 2001. Sibling socialization of competence in rural, single-parent African-American families. *Journal of Marriage and Family, 63*, 996–1008. **288, 322**

Brody, G. H., et al. 2004. The strong African American families program: Translating research into prevention programming. *Child Development, 75*, 900–917. **436**

Brodzinski, D. M., and Brodzinski, A. B. 1992. The impact of family structure on the adjustment of adopted children. *Child Welfare, 71*, 69–76. **241**

Broman, C. L. 2005. Marital quality in Black and White marriages. *Journal of Family Issues, 26*, 431–441. **268**

Bronfenbrenner, U. 1979. *The ecology of human development.* Cambridge, MA: Harvard University Press. **285**

Bronfenbrenner, U. 1985. Freedom and discipline across the decades. In G. Becker, H. Becker, and L. Huber (Eds.), *Ordnung und unordnung (Order and disorder)* (pp. 326–339). Berlin: Beltz. **289**

Bronfenbrenner, U. 1989. Ecologial systems theory. In R. Vasta (Ed.), *Six theories of child development* (pp. 185–246). Greenwich, CT: JAI Press. **15, 297**

Bronte-Tinkew. J., et al. 2009. Fathering with multiple partners: Links to children's well-being in early childhood. *Journal of Marriage and Family, 71*, 608–631. **227, 374**

Brookoff, D., et al. 1997. Characteristics of participants in domestic violence. *Journal of the American Medical Association, 277*, 1369–1373. **386, 387, 388**

Brooks-Gunn, J. 2003. Do you believe in magic?: What we can expect from early childhood intervention programs. *Social Policy Report* (Society for Research in Child Development), *17*, 3–13. **157**

Brooks-Gunn, J., Han, W.-J., and Waldfogel, J. 2002. Maternal employment and child cognitive outcomes in the first three years of life. The NICHD study of Early Child Care. *Child Development, 73*, 1052–1072. **101**

Brouillet, F. 2004. *Une dirigeante de société gagne un tiers de moins que son homologue masculin,* 2004. Paris: INSEE. **99**

Brown, J. D, et al. 2006. Sexy media matters: Exposure to sexual content in music, movies, television, and magazines predicts black and white adolescents' sexual behavior. *Pediatrics, 117*, 1018–1027. **88**

Brown, S. L. 2002. Child well-being in cohabiting families. In A. Booth and A. C. Crouter (Eds.), *Just living together* (pp. 173–187). Mahwah, NJ: Erlbaum. **195, 220, 221**

Brown, S. L. 2004a. Relationship quality dynamics of cohabiting unions. *Journal of Family Issues, 24*, 583–601. **193**

Brown, S. L. 2004b. Family structure and child well-being: The significance of parental cohabitation. *Journal of Marriage and Family, 66*, 351–367. **220, 372**

Brown, S. L. 2006. Family structure transitions and adolescent well-being. *Demography, 43*, 447–461. **372**

Brown, S. L., and Bulanda, J. R. 2008. Relationship violence in young adulthood: A comparison of daters, cohabitors, and marrieds. *Social Sciences Research, 37*, 73–87. **387**

Brown, S. L., and Manning, M. D. 2009. Family boundary ambiguity and the measurement of family structure: The significance of cohabitation. *Demography, 46*, 85–102. **373**

Browne, A. 1997. Violence in marriage: Until death do us part? In A. P. Cardarelli (Ed.), *Violence between intimate partners* (pp. 48–69). Boston: Allyn & Bacon. **386**

Browne, K. D. 1998. Physical violence between young adults and their parents: Associations with a history of child maltreatment. *Journal of Family Violence, 13*, 59–79. **408**

Browning, C. R. 2002. The span of collective efficacy: Extending social disorganization theory to partner violence. *Journal of Marriage and Family, 64*, 833–850. **387**

Browning, C. R., and Laumann, E. O. 1997. Sexual contact between children and adults: A life course perspective. *American Sociological Review, 62*, 540–560. **401**

Brownridge, D., and Halli, S. S. 2001. *Explaining violence against women in Canada.* Lanham, NJ: Lexington Books. **387**

Brunk, M. A., and Henggeler, S. W. 1984. Child influences on adult controls: An experimental investigation. *Developmental Psychology, 20*, 1074–1081. **293**

Bryant, C. M., et al. 2008. Marital satisfaction among African Americans and Black Caribbeans: Findings from the National Survey of American Life, *Family Relations, 57*, 239–253. **55, 268**

Bryceson, D., and Vuorela, U. 2002. Transnational families in the twenty-first century. In D. Bryceson and U. Vuorela (Eds.), *The transnational family* (pp. 3–30). New York: Oxford University Press. **75**

Brzozowski, J.-A., and Brazeau, R. 2008. *What are the trends in self-reported spousal violence in Canada?* Statistics Canada, November. **196, 384, 385, 386**

Buchanan, C. M., Maccoby, E. E., and Dornbusch, S. M. 1996. *Adolescents after divorce.* Cambridge, MA: Harvard University Press. **366**

Buchignani, N., and Armstrong, C. E. 1999. Informal care and older Native Canadians. *Ageing and Society*, 19, 3–32. **50**

Buckley, K. E., and Anderson, C. A. 2006. *A theoretical model of the effects and consequences of playing video games*. In P. Vorderer and J. Bryant (Eds.), *Playing video games: Motives, responses, and consequences* (pp. 363–378). Mahwah, NJ: Earlbaum. **86**

Buehler, C., Lange, G.M., and Franck, K. L. 2007. Adolescents' cognitive and emotional responses to marital hostility. *Child Development*, 78, 775–789. **276, 279**

Bullen, J. 2000. Hidden workers: Child labour and the family economy in late nineteenth century urban Ontario. In Burton, P., Lethbridge, L., and Phipps, S. (Eds.) 2006. Children with disabilities and chronic conditions and longer-term parental health. Statistics Canada, *The Daily*, November 22. **71**

Bumpass, L. 2001. The changing contexts of parenting in the United States. In J. C. Westman (Ed.), *Parenthood in America: Undervalued, underpaid, under siege* (pp. 211–219). Madison, WI: The University of Wisconsin Press. **70**

Bumpass, L. L., and Lu, H.-H. 2000. Increased cohabitation changing children's family settings. *Research on Today's Issues*, NICHD, 13, September. **193, 220**

Bumpus, M. F., Crouter, A. C., and McHale, S. M. 1999. Work demands of dual-earner couples: Implications for parents' knowledge about children's daily lives in middle childhood. *Journal of Marriage and Family*, 61, 465–475. **102**

Bundy-Fazioli, K., et al. 2009. Placement outcomes for children removed for neglect. *Child Welfare*, 88, 85–103. **247**

Burgess, E. W., Locke, H. J., and Thomes, M. M. 1963. *The family: From traditional to companionship*. New York: American Book. **267**

Burke, R., and Weir, T. 1976. Relationship of wives' employment status to husband, wife and pair satisfaction and performance. *Journal of Marriage and Family*, 38, 279–287. **262**

Burnette, D. 1999. Social relationships of Latino grandparent caregivers: A role theory perspective. *The Gerontologist*, 39, 49–58. **309**

Burney, S. 1995. *Coming to Gum San: The story of Chinese Canadians*. Toronto: Health Canada (for the Multicultural History Society of Ontario). **57**

Burstyn, V. 1999. *The rites of men: Manhood, politics, and the culture of sport*. Toronto: University of Toronto Press. **86**

Burt, S. A., et al. 2005. How are parent-child conflict and childhood externalizing symptoms related over time? Results from a genetically informative cross-lagged study. *Development and Psychopathology*, 17, 145–165. **292**

Burt, S. A., McGue, M., and Iacono, W. G. 2009. Nonshared environmental mediation of the association between deviant peer affiliation and adolescent externalizing behaviors over time: Results from a cross-lagged monozygotic twin differences design. *Developmental Psychology*, 45, 1751–1760. **299**

Burton, L. M. 1996. Age norms, the timing of family role transitions, and intergenerational caregiving among aging African American women. *The Gerontologist*, 36, 199–208. **18**

Burton, L. M., and Jarrett, R. L. 2000. In the mix, yet on the margins: The place of families in urban neighborhoods and child development research. *Journal of Marriage and Family*, 62, 1114–1135. **132**

Burton, P., and Phipps, S. 2007. Families, time and money in Canada, Germany, Sweden, the United Kingdom and the United States. *Review of Income and Wealth*, 3, 460–483. **102**

Burton, P., Lethbridge, L., and Phipps, S. 2006. Children with disabilities and chronic conditions and longer-term parental health. Statistics Canada, *The Daily*, November 22. **416**

Bushman, B., J., and Huesmann, L. R. 2001. Effects of televised violence on aggression. In D. G. Singer and J. L. Singer (Eds.), *Handbook of children and the media* (pp. 223–254). Thousand Oaks, CA: Sage. **83, 84**

Bushman, B. J., and Huesmann, L. R. 2006. Short-term and long-term effects of violent media on aggression in children and adults. *Archives of Pediatrics and Adolescent Medicine*, 160, 348–352. **85**

Busque, M.-A. 2009. *Unmet home care needs among Canadian elderly*, McMaster University, SEDAP, Research Paper. no. 251, August. <http://socserv.mcmaster.ca/sedap>. **438**

Buss, D. M., et al. 2001. A half century of mate preferences: The cultural evolution of values. *Journal of Marriage and Family*, 63, 491–503. **188, 189**

Butler, A. 2005. Gender differences in the prevalence of same-sex sexual partnering: 1988–2002. *Social Forces*, 84, 421–448. **209**

Button, D. M., and Gealt, R. 2010. High risk behaviors among victims of sibling violence. *Journal of Family Violence*, 25, 131–140. **402, 403**

Buxton, B. 2004. *Damaged angels*. Toronto: Alfred A. Knopf. **241**

Bzostek, S. 2008. Social fathers and child well-being. *Journal of Marriage and Family*, 70, 950–961. **373**

CAIS (Canadian Association of Independent Schools). 2009. *Statistics summary 1998–2009/2010*. <www.cais.ca>. **168**

Calasanti, T. M. 2004. Feminist gerontology and old men. *Journals of Gerontology*, 59B, S305–314. **274**

Calixte, S. J., Johnson, J. L., and Motapanyane, J. M. 2010. Liberal, socialist, and radical feminism: An introduction to three theories about women's oppression and social change. In N. Mandell (Ed.), *Feminist issues: Race, class, and gender*, 5th Ed. (pp. 1–39). Toronto: Prentice Hall. **19, 23**

Call, V., Sprecher, S., and Schwartz, P. 1995. The incidence and frequency of marital sex in a national sample. *Journal of Marriage and Family*, 57, 639–652. **210, 211**

Calliste, A. 2003. Black families in Canada: Exploring the interconnections of race, class, and gender. In M. Lynn (Ed.), *Voices: Essays on Canadian families*, 2nd Ed. (pp. 199–220). Scarborough, ON: Thomson Nelson. **40, 45, 53, 54, 55**

Cameron, P. 2003. Domestic violence among homosexual partners. *Psychological Reports*, 93, 410–416. **390**

Campbell, A. 2005. *Polygamy in Canada. How have policy approaches to polygamy responded to women's experiences and rights? An international comparative analysis*. Status of Women Canada. <www.swc-cfc.gc.ca>. **9**

Campbell, L. D., and Carroll, M. 2007. Aging in Canadian families today. In D. Cheal (Ed.), *Canadian families today* (pp. 117–133). Toronto: Oxford University Press. **374**

Campbell, L. D., Connidis, I. A., and Davies, L. 1999. Sibling ties in later life: A social network analysis. *Journal of Family Issues*, 20, 114–148. **331**

Campbell, R., et al. 2010. "What has it been like for you to talk with me today?": The impact of participating in interview research on rape survivors. *Violence Against Women*, 16, 60–83. **29**

Campos, B., et al. 2009. Opportunity for interaction? A naturalistic observation study of dual-earner families after work and school. *Journal of Family Psychology*, 23, 798–807. **276**

Canadian Council on Social Development. 2006. *Families: A Canadian profile.* <www.ccsd.ca>. **306**

Canadian Forces. 2008. *Annual Report 2007–2008, for the year ending 31 March.***77**

Cantor, J., and Nathanson, A. I. 2001. The media and parents: Protecting children from harm. In J. C. Westman (Ed.), *Parenthood in America: Undervalued, underpaid, and under siege* (pp. 232–241). Madison, WI: The University of Wisconsin Press. **85**

Capaldi, D. M., and Clark, S. 1998. Prospective family predictors of aggression toward female partners for at-risk young men. *Developmental Psychology, 34,* 1175–1188. **382**

Caragata, L. 1999. The construction of teen parenting and the decline of adoption. In J. Wong and D. Checkland (Eds.), *Teen pregnancy and parenting* (pp. 99–120). Toronto: University of Toronto Press. **225, 239**

Carey, E. 2001. Kids' special needs often unmet: Study. *Toronto Star.* November 21. **118**

Carey, E. 2004. Homeless women "crisis." *Toronto Star.* April 13, A1, A4. **134**

Carlson, M. J. 2006. Family structure, father involvement, and adolescent behavioral outcomes. *Journal of Marriage and Family, 68,* 137–154. **352**

Carlson, M. J., and Furstenberg, F. F., Jr. 2006. The prevalence and correlates of multipartnered fertility among U.S. parents. *Journal of Marriage and Family, 68,* 718–732. **227**

Carmalt, J. H., et al. 2008. Body weight and matching with a physically attractive romantic partner. *Journal of Marriage and Family, 70,* 1287–1296. **189**

Carothers, S. S., et al. 2005. Religiosity and the socioemotional adjustment of adolescent mothers and their children. *Journal of Family Psychology, 19,* 263–275. **178**

Carp, E. W. 2008. Does opening adoption records have an adverse social impact? Some lessons from the U.S., Great Britian, and Australia, 1953–2007. *Adoption Quarterly, 10,* 29–52. **244**

Carp, F. M. 2000. *Elder abuse in the family.* New York: Springer. **408**

Carr, D. 2004. Gender, preloss marital dependence, and older adults' adjustment to widowhood. *Journal of Marriage and Family, 66,* 220–235. **369**

Carr, D., and Boerner, K. 2009. Do spousal discrepancies in marital quality assessments affect psychological adjustment to widowhood? *Journal of Marriage and Family, 71,* 495–509. **369**

Carroll, J. A., et al. 2005. Theorizing about marriage. In V. L. Bengtson et al. *Sourcebook of family theory & research* (pp. 263–266). Thousand Oaks, CA: Sage. **12, 267**

Carroll, J. S., Badger, S., and Yang, C. 2006. The ability to negotiate or the ability to love? *Journal of Family Issues, 27,* 1001–1032. **269**

Cartier, G. 2008. City of Quebec 1608–2008: 400 years of censuses. *Canadian Social Trends,* June 3. **38, 39**

Castaneda, C. 2002. *Figurations: Child bodies worlds.*Durham, NC: Duke University Press. **71**

Castellano, M. 2002. *Aboriginal family trends: Extended families, nuclear families, families of the heart.* Ottawa: Vanier Institute of the Family. **50, 181**

Cavanagh, S. E., Crissey, S. R., and Raley, R. K. 2008. Family structure history and adolescent romance. *Journal of Marriage and Family, 70,* 698–714. **362**

CBoardC (Conference Board of Canada). 2010. *Building from the ground up: Enhancing affordable housing in Canada.* Ottawa, March. **430, 431**

CCPA (Canadian Centre for Policy Alternatives). 2009. *State of the inner city 2009.* December 9, Manitoba Office. **108, 429**

Cebello, R., et al. 2004. Gaining a child: Comparing the experiences of biological parents, adoptive parents, and stepparents. *Family Relations, 53,* 38–48. **229, 243**

Chabot, J. M., and Ames, B. D. 2004. "It wasn't 'let's get pregnant and go do it'": Decision making in lesbian couples planning motherhood via donor insemination. *Family Relations, 53,* 348–356. **235**

Chan, R. W., Raboy, R. C., and Patterson, C. J. 1998. Psychosocial adjustment among children conceived via donor insemination by lesbian and heterosexual mothers. *Child Development, 69,* 443–457. **223**

Chandra, A, et al. 2008. Does watching sex on television predict teen pregnancy? *Pediatrics, 122,* 1047–1054. **88**

Chao, R. K., and Willms, J. D. 2002. The effects of parenting practices on children's outcomes. In *Vulnerable children* (pp. 149–166). Edmonton: University of Alberta Press. **436**

Chaplin, L. N., and John, D. R. 2005. The development of self-brand connections in children and adolescents. *Journal of Consumer Research, 32,* 119–129. **86**

Chappell, N. L., and Dujela, C. 2008. Caregiving: Predicting at-risk status. *Canadian Journal on Aging, 27,* 169–179. **306**

Chappell, N. L., and Penning, M. J. 2001. Sociology of aging in Canada: Issues for the millennium. *Canadian Journal on Aging, 20,* 82–110. **25**

Chappell, N., et al. 2003. *Aging in contemporary Canada.* Toronto: Prentice-Hall. **307**

Charron, M. 2009. Neighbourhood characteristics and distribution of police-reported crime in Toronto. *Crime and Justice Research Paper Series.* Statistics Canada Research Catalogue 85-561-M2009018. Ottawa. **126**

Chartrand, L. N., and McKay, C. 2006. *A review of research on criminal victimazation and First Nations, Métis, and Inuit Peoples 1990 to 2001.* Ottawa: Department of Justice, Research and Statistics Division, Policy Centre for Victim Issues. **43, 49, 387, 388**

Chartrand, L. N., Logan, T. E., and Daniels, J. D. 2006. *Métis history and experience in residential schools in Canada.*The Aboriginal Healing Foundation. <www.ahf.ca>. **43, 51**

Cheadle, J. E., Amato, P. R., and King, V. 2010. Patterns of nonresident father contact. *Demography, 47,* 205–225.

Cheah, C. S., et al. 2009. Authoritative parenting among immigrant Chinese mothers of preschoolers. *Journal of Family Psychology, 23,* 311–320. **58**

Cherlin, A. J. 1978. Remarriage as an incomplete institution. *American Journal of Sociology, 84,* 634–651. **371**

Cherlin, A. J. 2004. The deinstitutionalization of American marriage. *Journal of Marriage and Family, 66,* 848–861. **353**

Cherlin, A. J. 2009. *The marriage-go-around.* New York: Alfred A. Knopf. **357**

Cherlin, A. J., Chase-Lansdale, P., and McRae, C. 1998. Effects of parental divorce on mental health throughout the life course. *American Sociological Review, 63,* 239–249. **363, 367**

Chesler, P. 1989. *The sacred bond: The legacy of Baby M.* New York: Vintage. **239**

Chevan, A. 1996. As cheaply as one: Cohabitation in the older population? *Journal of Marriage and Family, 58,* 656–667. **196**

Child Support Team. 2000. *Selected statistics on Canadian families and family law: Second edition.* Ottawa: Department of Justice. **352**

Childs, E. C. 2005. Looking behind the stereotypes of the "angry Black woman": An exploration of Black women's responses to interracial relationships. *Gender and Society, 19,* 554–561. **187**

Chiu, S., et al. 2009. The health of homeless immigrants. *Journal of Epidemiology and Community Health, 63,* 943–948. **133, 134**

Choi, H., and Marks, N. F. 2008. Marital conflict, depressive symptoms, and functional impairment. *Journal of Marriage and Family, 70,* 377–390. **360**

Christakis, D. A. 2009. The effects of infant media usage: What do we know and what should we learn? *Acta Paediatrica, 98,* 8–16. **80, 81**

Christensen, A., et al. 2006. Cross-cultural consistency on the demand/withdraw interaction pattern in couples. *Journal of Marriage and Family, 68,* 1029–1044. **269, 270**

Christensen, C. P., and Weinfeld, M. 1993. The black family in Canada: A preliminary exploration of family patterns and inequality. *Canadian Ethnic Studies, 25,* 26–44. **53, 55**

Christensen, D. 2000. *Ahtahkakoop: The epic account of a Plains Cree head chief, his people, and their struggle for survival, 1816–1896.* Shell Lake, SK: Ahtahkakoop. **36**

Chudley, A. E., et al. 2005. Fetal Alcohol Spectrum Disorder: Canadian guidelines for diagnosis. *Canadian Medical Association Journal, 12,* Supplement 5, S1–S21. **394**

Chung, H. L., and Steinberg, L. 2006. Relations between neighborhood factors, parenting behaviors, peer deviance, and delinquency among serious juvenile offenders. *Developmental Psychology, 42,* 319–331. **129, 299**

Chung, L. 2006. Education and earning. Statistics Canada, *The Daily,* June 23. **96**

Chunn, D. E. 2000. "Politicizing the personal": Feminism, law, and public policy. In N. Mandell and A. Duffy (Eds.), *Canadian families: Diversity, conflict, and change,* 2nd Ed. (pp. 225–259). Toronto: Harcourt Brace. **24**

Ciccarelli, J. C., and Beckman, L. J. 2005. Navigating rough waters: An overview of psychological aspects of surrogacy. *Journal of Social Issues, 61,* 21–43. **238**

Ciccarelli, J. K., and Ciccarelli, J. C. 2005. The legal aspects of parental rights in Assisted Reproductive Technology. *Journal of Social Issues, 61,* 127–137. **237**

Cicirelli, V. G. 1989. Feelings of attachment to siblings and well-being in later life. *Psychology and Aging, 4,* 211–216. **331**

Cicirelli, V. G. 1996. Sibling relationships in middle and old age. In G. H. Brody (Ed.), *Sibling relationships: Their causes and consequences* (pp. 47–74). Norwood, NJ: Ablex. **330**

CIW (Canadian Index of Wellbeing). 2010. *Caught in the time crunch: Time use, leisure and culture in Canada.* **89, 103, 104, 296, 439**

Clairmont, D. H. J., and Magill, D. 1999. *Africville: The life and death of a Canadian black community,* 3rd Ed. Toronto: Canadian Scholars' Press. **45**

Clark, D. J. 2001. *Surfing for seniors: Report of the National Council on Family Relations.* March, F18, F20. **84**

Clark, J., et al. 2006. The role of low expectations in health and education investment and hazardous consumption. *Canadian Journal of Economics, 39,* 1151–1172. **110**

Clark, L. A., Kochanska, G., and Ready, R. 2000. Mothers' personality and its interaction with child temperament as predictors of parenting behavior. *Journal of Personality and Social Psychology, 79,* 274–285. **284**

Clark, S. 1999. What do we know about unmarried mothers? In J. Wong and D. Checkland (Eds.), *Teen pregnancy and parenting* (pp. 10–24). Toronto: University of Toronto Press. **228**

Clark, W. 1998. Religious observance, marriage and family. *Canadian Social Trends, 50,* 2–7. **172, 175**

Clark, W. 2002. Time alone. *Canadian Social Trends, 66,* 2–6. **103, 141**

Clark, W. 2003. Pockets of belief: Religious attendance patterns in Canada. *Canadian Social Trends, 68,* 2–5. **173**

Clark, W., and Crompton, S. 2006. Till death do us part? The risk of first and second marriage dissolution. *Canadian Social Trends, 11,* Summer. **349, 350, 354, 355**

Clarke-Stewart, A. 1992. Consequences of child care for children's development. In A. Booth (Ed.), *Child care in the 1990s: Trends and consequences* (pp. 63–82). Hillsdale, NJ: Erlbaum. **155**

Cleveland, H. H., and Wiebe, R. P. 2003. The moderation of adolescent-to-peer similarity in tobacco and alcohol use by school levels of substance use. *Child Development, 74,* 279–291. **159**

Clio Collective. 1987. *Quebec women: A history.* Toronto: Women's Press. **39, 63**

Clydesdale, T. T. 1997. Family behaviors among early U.S. baby boomers: Exploring the effects of religion and income changes, 1965–1982. *Social Forces, 76,* 605–635. **102**

Coakley, J., and Donnelly, P. 2004. *Sports in society: Issues and controversies.* Toronto: McGraw-Hill Ryerson. **75, 86**

Coelli, M. B. 2009. Tuition fees and equality of university enrolment. *Canadian Journal of Economics, 42,* 1072–1099. **426**

Cohen, P. N., and Petrescu-Prahova, M. 2006. Gendered living arrangements among children with disabilities. *Journal of Marriage and Family, 68,* 630–638. **21**

Coleman, J. S. 1988. Social capital in the creation of human capital. *American Journal of Sociology, 94,* S95–S120. **13, 161, 164**

Coleman, J. S. 1990a. *Foundations of social theory.* Cambridge, MA: Harvard University Press. **13, 102**

Coleman, J. S. 1990b. *Equality and achievement in education.* Boulder, CO: Westview Press. **13**

Coleman, J. S., and Hoffer, T. 1987. *Public and private schools: The impact of communities.* New York: Basic Books. **130**

Coley, R. L. 2001. (In)visible men: Emerging research on low-income, unmarried, and minority fathers. *American Psychologist, 56,* 743–753. **21**

Collins, M. E., Paris, R., and Ward, R. L. 2008. The permanence of family ties: Implications for youth transitioning from foster care. *American Journal of Orthopsychiatry, 78,* 54–62. **247**

Collins, P. H. 1990. *Black feminist thought: Knowledge, consciousness, and the politics of empowerment.* Boston: Unwin Hyman. **296**

Collins, P. H. 1992. Black women and motherhood. In B. Thorne and M. Yalom (Eds.), *Rethinking the family* (rev. Ed., pp. 215–245). Boston: Northeastern University Press. **20**

Coltrane, S. 2000. Research on household labor: Modeling and measuring the social embeddedness of routine family work. *Journal of Marriage and Family, 62,* 1208–1233. **262**

Conger, R. D., and Conger, K. J. 1996. Sibling relationships. In R. Simons and Associates (Eds.), *Understanding differences between divorced and intact families* (pp. 104–121). Thousand Oaks, CA: Sage. **325**

Conger, R. D., Conger, K. J., and Martin, M.J. 2010. Socioeconomic status, family processes, and individual development. *Journal of Marriage and the Family*, 72, 685–704. **16, 116, 427**

Conger, R. D., Patterson, G. R., and Ge, X. 1995. It takes two to replicate: A mediational model for the impact of parents' stress on adolescent adjustment. *Child Development*, 66, 80–97. **292**

Connell, C. M., et al. 2009. Maltreatment following reunification: Predictors of subsequent Child Protective Services contact after children return home. *Child Abuse & Neglect, 33*, 218–228. **247**

Connidis, I. A. 2003a. Divorce and union dissolution: Reverberations over three generations. *Canadian Journal on Aging*, 22, 353–368. **362, 375**

Connidis, I. A. 2003b. Bringing outsiders in: Gay and lesbian family ties over the life course. In S. Arber, K. Davidson, and J. Ginn (Eds.), *Gender and ageing: Changing roles and relationships* (pp. 79–94). Maidenhead, UK: Open University Press. **307, 331**

Connidis, I. A. 2007. Negotiating inequality among adult siblings: Two case studies. *Journal of Marriage and Family*, 69, 482–499. **330**

Connidis, I. A. 2010. *Family ties & aging*, 2nd Ed. Thousand Oaks, CA: Sage. **72, 303, 304, 306, 307, 310, 313, 316, 330, 376, 426**

Connidis, I. A., and Campbell, L. D. 1995. Closeness, confiding, and contact among siblings in middle and late childhood. *Journal of Family Issues*, 16, 722–745. **331**

Connidis, I. A., and McMullin, J. A. 2002a. Sociological ambivalence and family ties: A critical perspective. *Journal of Marriage and Family*, 64, 558–567. **304**

Connidis, I. A., and McMullin, J. A. 2002b. Ambivalence, family ties, and doing sociology. *Journal of Marriage and Family*, 64, 594–601. **304**

Contenta, S., and Monsebraaten, L. 2009. Canada "guest workers." *Toronto Star*, November 1, A1, A6–A7. **76**

Cook, C., and Willms, J. D. 2002. Balancing work and family life. In J. D. Willms (Ed.), *Vulnerable children* (pp. 183–198). Edmonton: University of Alberta Press. **161**

Cook, D. 2004. *The commodification of childhood: The children's clothing industry and the rise of the child consumer*. Durham, NC: Duke University Press. **105**

Cook, D. A., and Fine, M. 1995. "Motherwit": Childrearing lessons from African-American mothers of low income. In B. B. Swadener and S. Lubeck (Eds.), *Children and families "at promise"* (pp. 118–142). Albany: State University of New York Press. **114**

Cooke, M. 2009. A welfare trap? The duration and dynamics of social assistance use among lone mothers in Canada. *The Canadian Review of Sociology, 46*, 179–206. **110**

Cooksey, E. C., and Craig, P. H. 1998. Parenting from a distance: The effects of paternal characteristics on contact between nonresidential fathers and their children. *Demography, 35*, 187–200. **21, 221, 248**

Cooksey, E. C., Menaghan, E. G., and Jekielek, S. M. 1997. Life-course effects of work and family circumstances on children. *Social Forces*, 76, 637–667. **101, 219**

Cooley, C. H. 1902. *Human nature and the social order*. New York: Scribner. **14**

Coombs, R. H. 1991. Marital status and personal well-being: A literature review. *Family Relations*, 40, 97–102. **198**

Cooney, T. M., and Dunne, K. 2001. Intimate relationships in later life. *Journal of Family Issues*, 22, 838–858. **196**

Coontz, S. 1992. *The way we never were: American families and the nostalgia trap*. New York: Basic Books. **81**

Coontz, S. 2000. Historical perspectives on family studies. *Journal of Marriage and Family, 62*, 283–297. **69, 75, 143, 248, 262**

Coontz, S. 2006. *Fact sheet on polygamy*. US: Council on Contemporary Families. **8**

Corak, M. 1998. Getting ahead in life: Does your parents' income count? *Canadian Social Trends, 49*, 6–10. **69**

Corak, M. 2001. Death and divorce: The long-term consequences of parental loss on adolescents. *Journal of Labor Economics, 19*, 682–716. **364**

Corbin, J., and Strauss, A. 2008. *Basics of qualitative research: Techniques and procedures for developing grounded theory*. Thousand Oaks, CA: Sage. **29**

Corliss, H. L., et al. 2009. Age of minority sexual orientation development and risk of childhood maltreatment and suicide attempts in women. *American Journal of Orthopsychiatry, 79*, 511–521. **209**

Corsaro, W. A. 1997. *The sociology of childhood*. Thousand Oaks, CA: Pine Forge Press. **15**

Costello, C. Y. 1997. Conceiving identity: Bisexual, lesbian, and gay parents consider their children's sexual orientation. *Journal of Sociology and Social Welfare, 24*, 63–90. **223**

Côté, J. E. 2000. *Arrested adulthood: The changing nature of maturity and identity*. New York: New York University Press. **105, 300, 340**

Côté, J., and Allahar, A. L. 1994. *Generation on hold: Coming of age in the late twentieth century*. Toronto: Stoddart. **74, 87, 295**

Côté, J., and Allahar, A. L. 2006. *Critical youth studies. A Canadian focus*. Toronto: Pearson. **75, 92, 96, 300, 301, 313, 418, 430, 441**

Côté, S., Tremblay, R. E., and Vitaro, F. 2003. Le développement de l'agression physique au cours de l'enfance: Différences entre les sexes et facteurs de risque familaux. *Sociologie et Sociétés, 35*, 203–219. **362**

Coughlin, C., and Vuchinich, S. 1996. Family experience in preadolescence and the development of male delinquency. *Journal of Marriage and Family, 58*, 491–501. **373**

Cranswick, K. 1997. Canada's caregivers. *Canadian Social Trends, 47*, 2–6. **306**

Cranswick, K., and Dosman, D. 2008. Eldercare: What we know today. *Canadian Social Trends,* October, 47–57. **438**

Crenshaw, K. W. 1994. Mapping the margins: Intersectionality, identity politics, and violence against women of color. In M. A. Fineman and R. Mykitiuk (Eds.), *The public nature of private violence*. New York: Routledge. **387**

Criss, M. M., and Shaw, D. S. 2005. Sibling relationships as contexts for delinquency training in low-income families. *Journal of Family Psychology, 19*, 592–600. **322**

Critchley, K. A., et al. 2007. Building healthy Mik'mac communities in Prince Edward Island. *The Canadian Journal of Native Studies, 27*, 1–17. **38**

Crockenberg, S., and Leerkes, E. 2003. Infant negative emotionality, caregiving, and family relationships. In A. C. Crouter and A. Booth (Eds.), *Children's influence on family dynamics* (pp. 57–78). Mahwah, NJ: Erlbaum. **285**

Crosnoe, R. 2004. Social capital and the interplay of families and schools. *Journal of Marriage and Family, 66*, 267–280. **159, 164**

Crosnoe, R., and Elder, G. H., Jr. 2002. Adolescent twins and emotional distress: The interrelated influence of nonshared environment and social structure. *Child Development, 73*, 1761–1774. **175, 326**

Crotty, M. 1998. *The foundations of social research*. London: Sage. **18**

Crouter, A. C., et al. 1999. Conditions underlying parents' knowledge about children's daily lives in middle childhood: Between and within-family comparisons. *Child Development, 70,* 246–259. **102, 326**

Crowder, K. D., and Tolnay, S. E. 2000. A new marriage squeeze for Black women: The role of racial intermarriage by Black men. *Journal of Marriage and Family*, 62, 792–807. **187**

Cuber, J., and Harroff, P. B. 1965. *The significant American*. New York: Hawthorn. **254, 256, 257**

Cuevas, C. A., et al. 2010. Psychological distress as a risk factor for re-victimization in children. *Child Abuse & Neglect, 34,* 235–243. **391**

Cui, M., and Donnellan, M. B. 2009. Trajectories of conflict over raising adolescent children and marital satisfaction. *Journal of Marriage and Family, 71,* 478–494. **275**

Cui, M., Conger, R. D., and Lorenz, F. O. 2005. Predicting change in adolescent adjustment from change in marital problems. *Developmental Psychology, 41,*812–823. **277**

Cummings, E. M., Goeke-Morey, M. C., and Papp, L. M. 2003. Children's responses to everyday marital conflict tactics in the home. *Child Development*, 74, 1918–1929. **277**

Daigneault, I., Hébert, M., and McDuff, P. 2009. Men's and women's childhood sexual abuse and victimization in adult partner relationships: A study of risk factors. *Child Abuse & Neglect, 33,* 638–647. **401**

Daly, K. 2003. Family theory versus the theories families live by. *Journal of Marriage and Family*, 65, 771–784. **14, 105**

Daly, K. 2004. *The changing culture of parenting.*Ottawa:The Vanier Institute of the Family. **297**

Daniel, K. 1996. The marriage premium. In M. Tommasi and K. Ierulli (Eds.), *The new economics of human behavior* (pp. 113–125). Cambridge: Cambridge University Press. **198, 199**

Daniels, D. 1987. Differential experiences of children in the same family as predictors of adolescent sibling personality differences. *Journal of Personality and Social Psychology*, 51, 339–346. **328**

Danvers, G. D. 2001. Gendered encounters: Warriors, women and William Johnson. *Journal of American Studies*, 35, 187–202. **37**

Darlington, J. W. 1997. Farmsteads as mirrors of cultural adjustment and change: The Ukrainian Canadian experience. *Great Plains Research*, 7, 71–101. **47**

Das Gupta, M., Chung, W., and Shuzhuo, L. 2009. Evidence for the incipient decline in numbers of missing girls in China and India. *Population and Developmental Review, 35,* 401–416. **8, 57**

Das Gupta, T. 2000. Families of Native people, immigrants, and people of colour. In N. Mandell and A. Duffy (Eds.), *Canadian families: Diversity, conflict, and change*, 2nd Ed. (pp. 146–187). Toronto: Harcourt Brace. **25, 44, 48, 49**

Daubs, K. 2009. Tasty idea to keep kids off the streets. *Toronto Star*. November 21, GT8. **157**

Dauvergne, M. 2003. Family violence against seniors. *Canadian Social Trends*, 68, 10–14. **409**

Davis, E. C., and Friel, L. V. 2001. Adolescent sexuality: Disentangling the effects of family structure and family context. *Journal of Marriage and Family*, 63, 669–681. **206**

Davis, K. D., et al. 2008. Nonstandard work schedules, perceived family well-being, and daily stressors. *Journal of Marriage and Family*, 70, 991–1003. **99**

DeAngelis, T. 2002. A new generation of issues for LGBT clients. *Monitor on Psychology*, *33*, February. **189, 223**

Dearing, E., McCartney, K., and Taylor, B. A. 2009. Does higher quality early child care promote low-income children's math and reading achievement in middle childhood? *Child Development, 80,* 1329–1349. **156**

DeFronzo, J. 1997. Welfare and homicide. *Journal of Research in Crime and Delinquency, 34,* 395–406. **429**

DeGarmo, D. S. 2010. Coercive and prosocial fathering, antisocial personality, and growth in children's postdivorce noncompliance. *Child Development, 81,* 503–516. **293**

De Graaf, P. M., and Kalmijn, M. 2006. Divorce motives in a period of rising divorce. *Journal of Family Issues, 27,* 483–505. **357**

Dei, G. J. 1993. Narrative discourses of Black/African-Canadian parents and the Canadian public school system. *Canadian Ethnic Studies*, 25, 45–54. **53**

Dekel, R., and Goldblatt, H. 2008. Is there intergenerational transmission of trauma? The case of combat veterans' children. *American Journal of Orthopsychiatry, 78,* 281–289. **77**

DeKeseredy, W. S. 2000. Current controversies on defining non-lethal violence against women in intimate heterosexual relationships: Empirical implications. *Violence Against Women, 6,* 728–746. **383**

DeKeseredy, W. S. 2009. Patterns of violence in the family. In M. Baker (Ed.), *Families: Changing trends in Canada,*6th Ed (pp. 179–205). Toronto: McGraw Hill Ryerson. **385, 387**

DeKeseredy, W. S., and Dragiewicz, M. 2007. Understanding the complexities of feminist perspectives on woman abuse: A commentary on Donald G. Dulton's Rethinking Domestic Violence. *Violence Against Women 13,* 874–884. **381, 385**

DeKeseredy, W. S., and Kelly, K. 1993. The incidence and prevalence of woman abuse in Canadian university and college dating relationships. *Canadian Journal of Sociology, 18,* 137–159. **381**

Dell, F., Legendre, N., and Ponthieux, S. 2003. *La pauvreté chez les enfants*. Paris: INSEE. **428**

Delsol, C., Margolin, G., and John, R. S. 2003. A typology of maritally violent men and correlates of violence in a community sample. *Journal of Marriage and Family*, 65, 635–651. **382, 389**

DeMaris, A., et al. 2003. Distal and proximal factors in domestic violence: A test of an integrated model. *Journal of Marriage and Family*, 65, 652–667. **387**

DeMino, K. A., Appleby, G., and Fisk, D. 2007. Lesbian mothers with planned families: A comparative study of internalized homophobia and social support. *American Journal of Orthopsychiatry, 77,* 165–173. **223**

Demo, D. H. 1992. Parent-child relations: Assessing recent changes. *Journal of Marriage and Family, 54,* 104–117. **296**

Demos, J. 1971. Developmental perspectives on the history of childhood. *The Journal of Interdisciplinary History, 2,* 315–327. **295**

den Boggende, B. 1997. Alone in the province: The Cobourg ladies' seminary of Burlington Ladies' Academy 1842–1851. *Ontario History*, 89, 53–74. **41**

Denissen, J. J. A., van Aken, M. A. G., and Dubas, J. S. 2009. It takes two to tango: How parents' and adolescents' personalities link to the quality of their mutual relationship. *Developmental Psychopathology*, 45, 928–941. **293, 295**

Derne, S. 2008. *Globalization on the ground: Media and the transformation of culture, class, and gender in India*. London: Sage. **59**

Dew, J. 2008. Debt change and marital satisfaction change in recently married couples. *Family Relations, 57*,60–71. **270**

Dickason, O. 2002. *Canada's First Nations: A history of founding peoples from the earliest times.* Don Mills, ON: Oxford University Press. **39**

Diener, E., and Biswas-Diener, R. 2002. Will money increase subjective well-being? *Social Indicators Research, 57*, 119–169. **125**

DiGiorgio-Miller, J. 1998. Sibling incest: Treatment of the family and the offender. *Child Welfare,77*, 335–346. **404**

Dion, K. K., and Dion, K. L. 2001. Gender and cultural adaptation in immigrant families. *Journal of Social Issues, 57*, 511–521. **25**

Dittman, M. 2002. *Running on Ritalin.* New York: Bantam Books.**87**

Dodge, K. A., Bates, J. E., and Pettit, G. S. 1990. Mechanisms in the cycle of violence. *Science, 250*, 1678–1683. **393**

Dogan, S. J., et al. 2007. Cognitive and parenting pathways in the transmission of antisocial behavior from parents to adolescents. *Child Development, 78*, 335–349. **339**

Doherty, J., Norton, E., and Veney, J. 2001. China's one-child policy: The economic choices and consequences faced by pregnant women. *Social Science and Medicine, 52*, 745–761. **56**

Doherty, W. J. 2000. Family science and family citizenship: Toward a model of community partnership with families. *Family Relations, 49*, 319–325. **418, 436**

Doherty, W. J., Kouneski, E. F., and Erickson, M. F. 1998. Responsible fathering: An overview and conceptual framework. *Journal of Marriage and Family, 60*, 277–292. **22, 248**

Doherty, W. J., Kouneski, E. F., and Erickson, M. F. 2000. We are all responsible for responsible fathering: A response to Walher and McGraw. *Journal of Marriage and Family, 62*, 570–574. **22**

Dolbin-MacNab, M. L., and Keiley, M. K. 2009. Navigating interdependence: How adolescents raised solely by grandparents experience their family relationships. *Family Relations, 58*,162–175. **309**

Dondorp, W. J., De Wert, G. M., and Janssens, P. M. W. 2010. Shared lesbian motherhood: A challenge of established concepts and frameworks. *Human Reproduction, 25*, 812–814. **222**

Donnerstein, E., and Linz, D. 1995. The media. In J. Q. Wilson and J. Petersilia (Eds.), *Crime* (pp. 257–266). San Francisco, CA: Institute for Contemporary Studies. **84**

D'Onofrio, B. M., and Lahey, B. B. 2010. Biosocial influences on the family: A decade review. *Journal of Marriage and Family, 72*, 762–782. **23, 336, 360, 440**

D'Onofrio, B. M., et al. 2007. A genetically informed study of the intergenerational transmission of marital instability. *Journal of Marriage and Family, 69*, 793–809. **367**

Doolittle, R. 2009. Mayhem's ground zero. *Toronto Star.* September 1, A1. **127**

Doucet, A. 2006. *Do men mother? Fathering, care, and domestic responsibility.* Toronto: University of Toronto Press. **19, 21, 22**

Doucet, A. 2009. Gender equality and gender differences: Parenting, habits, and embodiment (The 2008 Porter Lecture). *The Canadian Review of Sociology, 46*, 103–113. **259**

Douthat, R, 2008. Is pornography adultery? *The Atlantic,*October, 81–85. **213**

Downey, D. B. 1995. When bigger is not better: Family size, parental resources, and children's educational performance. *American Sociological Review, 60*, 746–761. **318**

Downey, D. B., and Condron, D. J. 2004. Playing well with others in kindergarten: The benefit of siblings at home. *Journal of Marriage and Family, 66*, 333–350. **319**

Drapeau, S., et al. 2000. Siblings in family transitions. *Family Relations, 49*, 77–85. **246, 351**

Drew, L. M., and Silverstein, M. 2007. Grandparents' psychological well-being after loss of contact with their grandchildren. *Journal of Family Psychology, 21*, 372–379. **374**

Drew, L. M., Berg, C., and Wiebe, D. J. 2010. The mediating role of extreme peer orientation in the relationships between adolescent-parent relationship and diabetes management. *Journal of Family Psychology, 24*, 299–306. **298**

Dribe, M., and Stanfors, M. 2009. Does parenthood strengthen a traditional household division of labor? Evidence from Sweden. *Journal of Marriage and Family, 71*, 33–45. **260**

Drolet, M. 2001. The male-female wage gap. *Perspectives on Labour and Income, 2*, December, 5–11. **99**

Drolet, M. 2003. Motherhood and paycheques. *Canadian Social Trends, 68*, 19–21. **99**

Dua, E. 1999. Beyond diversity: Explaining the ways in which the discourse of race has shaped the institution of the nuclear family. In E. Dua (Ed.), *Scratching the surface: Canadian anti-racist feminist thought* (pp. 237–260). Toronto: Women's Press. **24**

Dubeau, D. 2002. *Portraits of fathers.* Ottawa: The Vanier Institute of the Family. <www.vifamily.ca>. **21**

Duchesne, L. 2007. *Un nouvel enfant d'un autre père.* Québec: Institut de la statistique du Québec. **374**

Duffy, A. 2004. Violence against women. In N. Mandell (Ed.), *Feminist issues: Race, class, and gender,* 4th Ed. (pp. 127–159). Toronto: Prentice Hall. **385, 386, 399**

Duffy, A., and Momirov, J. 2005. Family violence: A twenty-first century issue. In N. Mandell and A. Duffy (Eds.), *Canadian families.* Toronto: Thomson Nelson. **380**

Dufur, M. J., et al. 2008. Capital and context: Using social capital at home and at school to predict child social adjustment. *Journal of Health and Social Behavior, 49*, 146–161. **159**

Dumont, M. 1995. Women of Quebec and the contemporary constitutional issue. In F. P. Gingras (Ed.), *Gender politics in contemporary Canada* (pp. 153–175). Toronto: Oxford University Press. **52**

Dunaway, W. A. 2003. *The African-American family in slavery and emancipation.* Cambridge, New York: Maison des sciences de l'homme/Cambridge University Press. **44**

Duncan, G. J. 2010. Early-childhood poverty and adult attainment, behavior, and health. *Child Development, 81*, 306–325. **116**

Duncan, G. J., and Brooks-Gunn, J. 1997. Income effects across the life span: Integration and interpretation. In G. J. Duncan and J. Brooks-Gunn (Eds.), *Consequences of growing up poor* (pp. 596–610). New York: Russell Sage. **121, 429**

Duncan, G. J., et al. 1998. How much does childhood poverty affect the life chances of children? *American Sociological Review, 63*, 406–423. **432**

Dunifon, R., and Kowaleski-Jones, L. 2002. Who's in the house? Race differences in cohabitation, single parenthood, and child development. *Child Development, 73*, 1249–1264. **224**

Dunn, J. 1994. Temperament, siblings, and the development of relationships. In W. B. Carey and S. C. McDevitt (Eds.), *Prevention and early intervention* (pp. 50–58). New York: Bruner/Mazel. **317**

Dunn, J. 1996. Brothers and sisters in middle childhood and early adolescence: Continuity and change in individual differences. In G. H. Brody (Ed.), *Sibling relationships: Their causes and consequences* (pp. 31–46). Norwood, NJ: Ablex. **321**

Dunn, J., and McGuire, S. 1994. Young children's nonshared experiences: A summary of studies in Cambridge and Colorado. In E. M. Hetherington, D. Reiss, and R. Plomin (Eds.), *Separate social worlds of siblings* (pp. 111–128). Hillsdale, NJ: Erlbaum. **321, 334**

Dunn, J., and Plomin, R. 1990. *Separate lives: Why siblings are so different.* New York: Basic Books. **333**

Dunn, J., Plomin, R., and Daniels, D. 1986. Consistency and change in mothers' behavior to two-year-old siblings. *Child Development, 57,* 348–356. **327**

Dunn, J., et al. 1994. Adjustment in middle childhood and early adolescence: Links with earlier and contemporary sibling relationships. *Journal of Child Psychology and Psychiatry, 35,* 491–504. **320, 321**

Dupéré, V., et al. 2008. Neighborhood poverty and early transition to sexual activity in young adolescents: A developmental ecological approach. *Child Development, 79,* 1463–1476. **132**

Dupré, M. E., and Meadows, S. O. 2007. Disaggregating the effects of marital trajectories on health. *Journal of Family Issues, 27,* 623–652. **359**

Dupuis, S. L., and Norris, J. E. 2001. The roles of adult daughters in long-term care facilities: Alternative role manifestations. *Journal of Aging Studies, 15,* 27–54. **306**

Durkheim, E. 1951 (1897). *Suicide.* New York: Free Press. **13, 175**

Du Rocher Schudlich, T. D., Papp, L. M., and Cummings, E. M. 2004. Relations in husbands' and wives' dysphoria to marital conflict resolution strategies. *Journal of Family Psychology, 18,* 171–183. **266**

Durrat, J. E., Rose-Krasnor, L., and Broberg, A. G. 2003. Physical punishment and maternal beliefs in Sweden and Canada. *Journal of Comparative Family Studies, 34,* 585–604. **291**

Dush, C. M. K., Cohan, C. L., and Amato, P. R. 2003. The relationship between cohabitation and marital quality and stability: Change across cohorts? *Journal of Marriage and Family, 65,* 539–549. **356**

Dush, C. M. K., Taylor, M. G., and Kroeger, R. A. 2008. Marital happiness and psychological well-being across the life course. *Family Relations, 57,* 211–226. **264, 268**

Duvall, E. M. 1957. *Family development.* Philadelphia: Lippincott. **16**

Duxbury, L., Higgins, C., and Schroeder, B. 2009. *Balancing paid work and caregiving responsibilities: A closer look at family caregivers in Canada.* Ottawa: Canadian Policy Research Networks. **305, 439**

Eamon, M. K. 2002. Effects of poverty on mathematics and reading achievement of young adolescents. *Journal of Early Adolescence, 22,* 49–74. **116**

East, P. L. 1999. The first teenage pregnancy in the family: Does it affect mothers' parenting attitudes, or mother-adolescent communication? *Journal of Marriage and Family, 61,* 306–319. **322**

East, P. L., and Jacobson, L. J. 2000. Adolescent childbearing, poverty, and siblings: Taking new directions from the literature. *Family Relations, 49,* 287–292. **18, 226, 333**

East, P. L., Felice, M. E., and Morgan, M. C. 1993. Sisters' and girlfriends' sexual and childbearing behavior: Effects on early adolescent girls' sexual outcomes. *Journal of Marriage and the Family, 55,* 953–963. **322**

East, P. L., Reyes, B. T., and Horn, E. J. 2007. Association between adolescent pregnancy and a family history of teenage births. *Perspectives on Sexual and Reproductive Health, 39,* 108–115. **227**

Easterbrook, G. 2003. *The progress paradox: How life gets better while people feel worse.* New York: Random House. **105**

Eckenrode, J., Laird, M., and Doris, J. 1993. School performance and disciplinary problems among abused and neglected children. *Developmental Psychology, 29,* 53–62. **393, 397**

Edin, K., and Kefalas, M. 2005. *Promises I can keep.* Berkeley, CA: University of California Press. **197**

Edin, K., and Lein, L. 1997. Work, welfare, and single mothers' economic survival strategies. *American Sociological Review, 62,* 253–266. **111**

Edwards, M. E. 2001. Uncertainty and the rise of the work-family dilemma. *Journal of Marriage and Family, 63,* 83–196. **98**

Egan, S. K., and Perry, D. G. 1998. Does low self-regard invite victimization? *Developmental Psychology, 34,* 299–309. **405**

Egeland, B. 2009. Taking stock: Childhood emotional maltreatment and developmental psychopathology. *Child Abuse & Neglect, 33,* 22–26. **392**

Eggebeen, D. J. 2005. Cohabitation and exchanges of support. *Social Forces, 83,* 1097–1111. **195**

Eggebeen, D. J, and Dew, J. 2009. The role of religion in adolescence for family formation in young adulthood. *Journal of Marriage and Family, 71,* 108–121. **356**

Eggebeen, D. J., and Knoester, C. 2001. Does fatherhood matter for men? *Journal of Marriage and Family, 63,* 381–393. **21**

Eggertsen, L. 2008. Primary factors related to multiple placements for children in out-of-home care. *Child Welfare, 87,* 71–91. **247**

Eichler, M. 1997. *Family shifts: Families, policies, and gender equality.* Toronto: Oxford University Press. **24**

Elder, G. H., Jr. 1995. The life course paradigm and social change: Historical and developmental perspectives. In P. Moen, G. H. Elder, Jr., and K. Lüscher (Eds.), *Perspectives on the ecology of human development* (pp. 101–140). Washington, DC: American Psychological Association. **146**

Elder, G. H., Jr. 1998. The life course as developmental theory. *Child Development, 69,* 1–12. **16**

Elder, G. H., Jr., Caspi, A., and Nguyen, T. V. 1994a. Resourceful and vulnerable children: Family influences in stressful times. In R. K. Silbereisen and K. Eyferth (Eds.), *Development in context: Integrative perspectives on youth development.* New York: Springer-Verlag. **393**

Elder, G. H., Jr., Robertson, E. B., and Foster, E. M. 1994b. Survival, loss, and adaptation: A perspective on farm families. In R. D. Conger et al. (Eds.), *Families in troubled times: Adapting to change in rural America* (pp. 105–126). New York: Aldine de Gruyter. **139**

Elgar, F. J., et al. 2003. Antecedent-consequence conditions in maternal mood and child adjustment problems: A four-year cross-lagged study. *Journal of Clinical Child and Adolescent Psychology, 32,* 362–374. **285**

Elliott, D. S., et al. 2006. *Good kids from bad neighborhoods.* New York: Cambridge University Press. **128**

Elliott, W., Jung, H., and Friedline, T. 2010. Math achievement and children's savings: Implications for child development accounts. *Journal of Family and Economic Issues, 31,* 171–185. **105**

Ellison, C. G., Burdette, A. M., and Hill, T. D. 2009. Blessed assurance: Religion, anxiety, and tranquility among US adults. *Social Science Research, 38,* 656–667. **175**

Ellison, C., Burdette, A. M., and Wilcox, W. B. 2010. The couple that prays together: Race and ethnicity, religion, and relationship quality among working-age adults. *Journal of Marriage and Family, 72,* 963–975. **176**

Elze, D. E. 2002. Against all odds: The dating experiences of adolescent lesbian and bisexual women. *Journal of Lesbian Studies, 6,* 17–29. **185**

Emberley, J. V. 2001. The bourgeois family, Aboriginal women, and colonial governance in Canada: A study in feminist historical and cultural materialism. *Signs, 27,* 59–85. **43**

Engeland, J., Lewis, R., and Schellenberg, G. 2005. Evolving housing conditions in metropolitan areas, 1991 to 2001. Statistics Canada, *The Daily,* January 5. **143, 144**

Engelbrecht, W. 2003. *Iroquoia: The development of a Native world.* Syracuse, NY: Syracuse University Press. **37**

Engels, J. W. 1995. Marriage in the People's Republic of China: Analysis of a new law. In M. Rank and E. Kain (Eds.), *Diversity and change in families: Patterns, prospects and policies* (pp. 57–67). Englewood Cliffs, NJ: Prentice Hall. **56**

England, P. 2000. Marriage, the costs of children and gender inequality. In L. J. Waite et al. (Eds.), *The ties that bind: Perspectives on marriage and cohabitation* (pp. 320–342). New York: Aldine de Gruyter. **199**

England, P. 2010. The gender revolution. *Gender & Society, 24,* 149–166. **96, 415**

England, P., and McClintock, E. A. 2009. The gendered double standard of aging in US marriage markets. *Population and Developmental Review, 35,* 797–816. **188, 370**

Engler, K., et al. 2005. An exploration of sexual behaviour and self-definition in a cohort of men who have sex with men. *Canadian Journal of Human Sexuality, 14,* 87–105. **209**

Entwisle, D. R., Alexander, K. L., and Olson, L. S. 1997. *Children, schools, and inequality.* Boulder, CO: Westview Press. **157, 162, 165, 181**

Erdwins, C. J., et al. 2001. The relationship of women's role strain to social support, role satisfaction, and self-efficacy. *Family Relations, 50,* 230–238. **158**

Erickson, R. J. 2005. Why emotion work matters: Sex, gender, and the division of household labor. *Journal of Marriage and Family, 67,* 337–351. **265**

Errington, E. J. 1995. *Wives and mothers, schoolmistresses and scullery maids: Working women in Upper Canada, 1790–1840.* Montreal: McGill-Queen's University Press. **41**

Ertl, H. 2000. Parental involvement and children's academic achievement in the National Longitudinal Survey of Children and Youth, 1994–1996. *Education Quarterly Review, 6,* 35–50. **161**

Espelage, D. L., Holt, M. K., and Henkel, R. R. 2003. Examination of peer-group contextual effects on aggression during early adolescence. *Child Development, 74,* 205–300. **340**

Espelage, D., et al. 1996. Paper presented at the annual meeting of the American Psychological Association, reported in the APA *Monitor,* p. 41. **405**

Etzioni, A. 1994. *The spirit of community: Rights, responsibilities, and the new communitarian agenda.* New York: Crown. **418**

Evans, G. W. 2004. The environment of childhood poverty. *American Psychologist, 59,* 77–92. **117**

Evans, P. M. 1996. Single mothers and Ontario's welfare policy: Restructuring the debate. In J. Brodie (Ed.), *Women and public policy.* Toronto: Harcourt Brace. **25**

Eyer, D. E. 1992. *Mother-infant bonding.* New Haven, CT: Yale University Press. **20**

Fabricius, W. V. 2003. Listening to children of divorce: New findings that diverge from Wallerstein, Lewis, and Blakeslee. *Family Relations, 52,* 385–396. **351**

Farnam, K. 1998. The westlings: Swedish pioneers. *Alberta History, 46,* 10–14. **47**

Fast, J., et al. 2001. The time of our lives . . . *Canadian Social Trends, 63,* 20–23. **89**

Feigelman, W. 1997. Adopted adults: Comparisons with persons raised in conventional families. *Marriage and Family Review, 25,* 199–223. **241**

Feinberg, M. E., et al. 2000. Sibling comparison of differential parental treatment in adolescence: Gender, self-esteem, and emotionality as mediators of the parenting adjustment association. *Child Development, 71,* 1611–1628. **328**

Feinberg, M. E., et al. 2005. Differential association of family subsystem negativity on siblings' maladjustment: Using behavior genetic methods to test process theory. *Journal of Family Psychology, 19,* 601–610. **335**

Fenton, W. N. 1998. *The great law and the longhouse: A political history of the Iroquois confederacy.* Norman, OK: University of Oklahoma Press. **37**

Fergusson, D. M., and Horwood, L. J. 1998. Exposure to interparental violence in childhood and psychosocial adjustment in young adulthood. *Child Abuse & Neglect, 22,* 339–357. **389**

Fergusson, D. M., Boden, J. M., and Horwood, L. J. 2007. Abortion among young women and subsequent life outcomes. *Perspectives on Sexual and Reproductive Health, 39,* 6–12. **234**

Ferree, M. M. 2010. Filling the glass: Gender perspectives on families. *Journal of Marriage and Family, 72,* 420–439. **24, 25**

Ferree, M. M., Lorber, J., and Hess, B. B. (Eds.). 1999. *Revisioning gender.* Thousand Oaks, CA: Sage. **18**

Ferrer, A., and Riddell, W. C. 2008. Education, credentials, and immigrant earnings. *Canadian Journal of Economics, 41,* 186–216. **113**

Fincham, F. D. 1998. Child development and marital relations. *Child Development, 69,* 543–574. **277**

Fincham, F. D., and Beach, S. R. H. 2010. Marriage in the new millennium: A decade in review. *Journal of Marriage and Family, 72,* 630–649. **176, 212, 213**

Fincham. F. D., Beach, S. R. H., and Davila, J. 2007a. Longitudinal relations between forgiveness and conflict resolution in marriage. *Journal of Family Psychology, 21,* 542–545. **266, 270**

Fincham, F. D., Stanley, S. M., and Beach, S. R. H. 2007b Transformative processes in marriage: An analysis of emerging trends. *Journal of Marriage and Family, 69,* 275–292. **254**

Fineran, S., and Gruber, J. E. 2009. Youth at work: Adolescent employment and sexual harassment. *Child Abuse & Neglect, 33,* 550–559. **398**

Fingard, J. 1992. Race and respectability in Victorian Halifax. *Journal of Imperial and Commonwealth History, 20,* 169–195. **45**

Fingerman, K., et al. 2009. Giving to the good and the needy: Parental support of grown children. *Journal of Marriage and Family, 71,* 1220–1233. **303, 304, 318**

Finkelhor, D., and Jones, L. 2006. Why have child maltreatment and child victimization declined? *Journal of Social Issues, 62,* 685–716. **395**

Finkelhor, D., Ormrod, R. K., and Turner, H. A. 2009. Lifetime assessment of poly-victimization in a national sample of children and youth. *Child Abuse & Neglect,* 33, 403–411. **391, 393**

Finkelhor, D., et al. 1990. Sexual abuse in a national survey of adult men and women: Prevalence, characteristics, and risk factors. *Child Abuse & Neglect, 14,* 19–28. **398**

Finnegan, R. A., Hodges, E. V. E., and Perry, D. G. 1998. Victimization by peers: Associations with children's reports of mother-child interaction. *Journal of Personality and Social Psychology,* 75, 1076–1086. **105**

Fischer, D. G. 1993. Parental supervision and delinquency. *Perceptual and Motor Skills, 56,* 635–640. **130**

Fischer, D. G., and McDonald, W. L. 1998. Characteristics of intrafamilial and extrafamilial child sexual abuse. *Child Abuse & Neglect,* 22, 915–929. **400**

Fisher, W. A., et al. 2005. Characteristics of women undergoing repeat induced abortion. *Canadian Medical Association Journal, 172,* 637–641. **234**

Fiske, J., and Johnny, R. 2003. The Lake Babini First Nation family: Yesterday and today. In M. Lynn (Ed.), *Voices: Essays on Canadian families,* 2nd Ed. (pp. 181–198). Scarborough, ON: Thomson Nelson. **43, 44, 50**

Fisman, R., et al. 2006. Gender differences in mate selection: Evidence from a speed dating experiment. *The Quarterly Journal of Economics, 121,*673–697. **189**

Fitzgerald, R. 2009. *Self-reported violent delinquency and the influence of school, neighbourhood and student characteristics.* Statistics Canada. Publication 85-561-M. no. 17. September 15. **166, 287, 299**

Fitzgerald, R. 2010. *Parenting, school contexts and violent delinquency.* Ottawa, Statistics Canada, Canadian Centre for Justice Statistics, Catalogue no. 85-561-M, no. 19, January. **287**

Fitzgerald, R., Wisener, M., and Savoie, J. 2004. Neighbourhood characteristics and the distribution of crime in Winnipeg. *Crime and Justice Research Paper Series.*Statistics Canada Catalogue no. 85-561-MIE. no. 4. Ottawa. **126**

Flango, V., and Flango, C. 1994. *The flow of adoption information from the states.* Williamsburg, VA: National Center for State Courts. **243**

Fletcher, A. C., et al. 1995. The company they keep: Relation of adolescents' adjustment and behavior to their friends' perceptions of authoritative parenting in the social network. *Developmental Psychology, 31,* 300–310. **323**

Fletcher, A. C., Steinberg, L., and Williams-Wheeler, M. 2004. Parental influence on adolescent problem behavior: Revisiting Stattin and Kerr. *Child Development, 75,* 781–796. **287**

Fletcher, J. M. 2007. Social multipliers in sexual initiation decisions among U.S. high school students. *Demography, 44,* 373–388. **431**

Fleury, R. E., Sullivan, C. M., and Bybee, D.I. 2000. When ending the relationship does not end the violence. *Violence Against Women, 6,* 1363–1383. **360**

Fluke, J. D., et al. 2010. Placement decisions and disparities among aboriginal groups: An application of the decision making ecology through multi-level analysis. *Child Abuse & Neglect, 34,* 57–69. **246**

Folbre, N. 1994. *Who pays for the kids?* New York: Routledge. **248**

Follingstad, D. R., and Edmundson, M. 2010. Is psychological abuse reciprocal in intimate relationships? Data from a national sample of American adults. *Journal of Family Violence, 25,* 495–508. **383**

Fomby, P., and Cherlin, A. J. 2007. Family instability and child well-being. *American Sociological Review, 72,* 181–204. **351**

Fong, E., and Cao, X. 2009. Effects of foreign education on immigrant earnings. *Canadian Studies in Population, 36,* 87–110. **113**

Fong, V. A. 2002. China's one-child policy and the empowerment of urban daughters. *American Anthropologist, 104,* 1098–1109. **56, 57**

Food Banks Canada. 2009. *Hunger Count 2009.* <www.foodbankscanada.ca>. **106, 108, 113, 144**

Forbes, S. 2003. "Why have just one?" An evaluation of the anti-polygamy laws under the establishment clause. *Houston Law Review, 39,* 1517–1547. **9**

Forehand, R., Armistead, L., and David, C. 1997. Is adolescent adjustment following parental divorce a function of predivorce adjustment? *Journal of Abnormal Child Psychology, 25,* 157–164. **367**

Forehand, R., et al. 2002. African American childrens's adjustment: The roles of maternal and teacher depressive symptoms. *Journal of Marriage and Family, 64,* 1012–1023. **159**

Foreman, A. 1998. *Georgiana: Duchess of Devonshire.* London: Harper Perennial. **38**

Forgatch, M. S., Patterson, G. R., and Roy, J. A. 1996. Stress, parenting, and adolescent psychopathology in nondivorced and stepfamilies: A within-family perspective. In E. M. Hetherington and E. A. Blachman (Eds.), *Stress, coping, and resilience in children and families* (pp. 39–66). Mahwah, NJ: Erlbaum. **365**

Formbe, P., and Cherlin, A. J. 2007. Family instability and child well-being. *American Sociological Review, 72,* 181–204. **376**

Forste, R., and Tanfer, K. 1996. Sexual exclusivity among dating, cohabiting, and married women. *Journal of Marriage and Family, 58,* 33–47. **195**

Forthofer, M. S., et al. 1996. The effects of psychiatric disorder on the probability and timing of first marriage. *Journal of Health and Social Behavior, 37,* 121–132. **198**

Fosco, G. M., and Grych, J. H. 2010. Adolescent triangulation into parental conflicts: Longitudinal implications for appraisals and adolescent-parent relations. *Journal of Marriage and Family, 72,* 254–266. **276**

Foshee, V. A., et al. 2005. The association between family violence and adolescent dating violence onset. *Journal of Early Adolescence, 25,*317–344. **291, 382**

Fournier, S., and Crey, E. 1997. *Stolen from our embrace: The abduction of First Nations children and the restoration of Aboriginal communities.* Vancouver/Toronto: Douglas and McIntyre. **50, 63**

Fox, B. J. 2001. Reproducing difference: Changes in the lives of partners becoming parents. In B. J. Fox (Ed.), *Family patterns, gender relations,* 2nd Ed. (pp. 287–302). Toronto: Oxford University Press. **19**

Frasch, K. M., Brooks, D., and Barth, R. P. 2000. Openness and contact in foster care adoptions: An eight-year follow-up. *Family Relations, 49,* 435–446. **245**

Fraser, C., and McDonald, S. 2009. *Identifying the issues: Victim services' experiences working with victims of Fetal Alcohol Spectrum Disorder.* Ottawa: Departement of Justice, October 10. **394**

Frazier, J. A., and Morrison, F. J. 1998. The influence of extended-year schooling on growth of achievement and perceived competence in early elementary school. *Child Development, 69,* 495–517. **157**

Frederick, J. A., and Boyd, M. 1998. The impact of family structure on high school completion. *Canadian Social Trends, 48,* 12–14. **362**

Frederick, J. A., and East, J. E. 1999. Eldercare in Canada: Who does how much? *Canadian Social Trends, 54,* 26–30. **304, 305**

Freeman, T., et al. 2009. Gamete donation: Parents' experiences of searching for their child's donor siblings and donor. *Human Reproduction, 24,* 505–516. **237**

Frempong, G., and Willms, J. D. 2002. Can school quality compensate for socioeconomic disadvantage? In J. D. Willms (Ed.), *Vulnerable children* (pp. 277–304). Edmonton: University of Alberta Press. **164, 417**

Frenette, M., and Picot, G. 2003. *Life after welfare: The economic wellbeing of welfare leavers in Canada during the 1990s.* Statistics Canada, Catalogue no. 11F0019, no. 192. **109, 110, 354, 359**

Frenette, M., Green, D. A., and Milligan, K. 2007. The tale of tails: Canadian income inequality in the 1980s and 1990s. *Canadian Journal of Economics, 40,* 734–764. **96, 107**

Frenette, M., Picot, G., and Sceviour, R. 2004. *How long do people live in low-income neighbourhoods? Evidence for Toronto, Montreal and Vancouver.* Statistics Canada, Catalogue no. 11F001MIE, no. 216. **126**

Frick, P. J., et al. 1992. Familial risk factors to oppositional defiant disorder and conduct disorder: Parental psychopathology and maternal parenting. *Journal of Consulting and Clinical Psychology, 60,* 49–55. **395**

Frideres, J. S. 2000. Revelation and revolution: Fault lines in Aboriginal-White relations. In M. A. Kalbach and W. E. Kalbach (Eds.), *Perspectives on Ethnicity in Canada* (pp. 207–237). Toronto: Harcourt Brace. **49, 108**

Friendly, M. 2000. Child care as a social policy issue. In L. Prochner and N. Howe (Eds.), *Early childhood education and care in Canada* (pp. 252–272). Vancouver: University of British Columbia Press. **154**

Friendly, M., Beach, J., and Turiano, M. 2002. *Early childhood education and care in Canada in 2001.*Toronto: University of Toronto, Childcare Resource and Research Unit. **153**

Friendly, M., Doherty, G., and Beach, J. 2006. *Quality by design: What do we know about quality in early learning and childcare, and what do we think? A literature review.* University of Toronto: Childcare Resource and Research Unit. **432**

Friesen, J. W. 1999. *First Nations of the Plains: Creative, adaptable, enduring.* Calgary, AB: Detselig Enterprises. **37**

Frisco, M. L., and Williams, K. 2004. Perceived housework equity, marital happiness, and divorce in dual-earner households. *Journal of Family Issues, 24,* 51–73. **264**

Fry, R., and Cohn, D. 2010. *Women, men and the new economics of marriage.* Pew Research Center, January 10. <http://pewresearch.org>. **420, 421**

Frye, N. E., and Karney, B. R. 2006. The context of aggressive behavior in marriage: A longitudinal study of newlyweds. *Journal of Family Psychology, 20,* 12–20. **384**

FSAT (Family Service Association of Toronto and Community Social Planning Council of Toronto). 2004. *Falling fortunes: A report on the status of young families in Toronto.* Toronto. **69, 96, 106**

Fuchs, V. R. 1990. Are Americans underinvesting in children? In D. Blankenhorn et al. (Eds.), *Rebuilding the nest: A new commitment to the American family* (pp. 53–72). Milwaukee, WI: Family Service America. **104**

Fulkerson, J. A., et al. 2010. Longitudinal associations between family dinner and adolescent perceptions of parent-child communication among racially diverse urban youth. *Journal of Family Psychology, 24,* 261–270. **296**

Fuller, C. J., and Narasimhan, H. 2008. Companionate marriage in India: The changing marriage system in a middle-class Brahman subcaste. *Journal of the Royal Anthropological Institute, 14,* 736–754. **58**

Funk, J. B., Buchman, D. B., and Germann, J. N. 2000. Preference for violent electronic games, self-concept, and gender differences in young children. *American Journal of Orthopsychiatry, 70,* 233–241. **86**

Funk, L. M., and Kobayashi, K. M. 2009. "Choice" in filial care work: Moving beyond a dichotomy. *The Canadian Review of Sociology, 46,* 235–252. **439**

Furman, W., and Lanthier, R. P. 1996. Personality and sibling relationships. In G. H. Brody (Ed.), *Sibling relationships: Their causes and consequences* (pp. 127–172). Norwood, NJ: Ablex. **320**

Furstenberg, F. F. 2005. Banking on families: How families generate and distribute social capital. *Journal of Marriage and Family, 67,* 809–821. **13**

Furstenberg, F. F., Jr., and Cherlin, A. J. 1991. *Divided families: What happens to children when parents part?* Cambridge, MA: Harvard University Press. **376**

Furstenberg, F. F., Jr., and Kiernan, K. E. 2001. Delayed parental divorce: How much do children benefit? *Journal of Marriage and Family, 63,* 446–457. **362**

Furstenberg, F. F., Jr., et al. 1994. How families manage risk and opportunity in dangerous neighborhoods. In W. J. Wilson (Ed.), *Sociology and the public agenda* (pp. 231–258). Newbury Park, CA: Sage. **132**

Gable, S. 1998. School-age and adolescent children's perceptions of family functioning in neglectful and non-neglectful families. *Child Abuse & Neglect, 22,* 859–867. **397**

Gagné, M.-A., Drapeau, S., and Hénault, R. 2005. L'aliénation parentale: Un bilan des connaissances et des controverses, *Canadian Psychology, 46,* 73–87. **367**

Gagnon, A. 1994. Our parents did not raise us to be independent: The work and schooling of young Franco-Albertan women, 1890–1940. *Prairie Forum, 19,* 169–188. **47**

Gallagher, E. 2004a. Parents victimised by their children. *Australian & New Zealand Journal of Family Therapy, 25,* 1–12. **406, 407**

Gallagher, E. 2004b. Youth who victimize their parents. *Australia & New Zealand Journal of Family Therapy, 25,* 94–105. **406**

Galloway, G. 2004. Black population growth dramatic, report shows. *Globe and Mail.* March 10, A11. **53, 54**

Games, A. 1999. *Migration and the origins of the English Atlantic world.* Cambridge, MA: Harvard University Press. **40**

Ganiban, J. M., et al. 2009. Understanding the role of personality in explaining associations between marital quality and parenting. *Journal of Family Psychology, 23,* 646–660. **278, 293**

Ganong, L., and Coleman, M. 1994. *Remarried family relationships.* Newbury Park, CA: Sage. **271**

Ganong, L., et al. 1998. Issues considered in contemplating stepchild adoption. *Family Relations, 47,* 63–71. **243**

Gans, D., Silverstein, M., and Loweinstein, A. 2009. Do religious children care more and provide more care for older parents? A study of filial norms and behaviors across five nations. *Journal of Comparative Family Studies, 40,* 187–205. **177**

Garbarino, J. 1995. *Raising children in a socially toxic environment.* San Francisco: Jossey-Bass. **383, 418**

Garbarino, J. 1999. *Lost boys: Why our sons turn violent and how we can save them.*New York: Free Press. **24, 85**

Garbarino, J. 2006. *See Jane hit.* New York: Penguin Press. **82, 86, 88**

Garbarino, J., and Sherman, D. 1980. High-risk neighborhoods and high-risk families: The human ecology of child maltreatment. *Child Development, 51,* 188–198. **392**

Garbarino, J., Kostelny, K., and Dubrow, N. 1991. *No place to be a child: Growing up in a war zone.*Lexington, MA: Lexington Books. **397**

Garcia, L. T. 2006. Perceptions of sexual experience and preferences for dating and marriage. *The Canadian Journal of Human Sexuality, 15,* 85–95. **206**

Garcia, M. M., et al. 2000. Destructive sibling conflict and the development of conduct problems in young boys. *Developmental Psychology, 36,* 44–53. **322**

Gardner, R. A. 1987. *The parental alienation syndrome and the difference between false and genuine child sex abuse.* Cresskill, NJ: Creative Therapeutics. **366**

Garriguet, D. 2005. Early sexual intercourse. Statistics Canada, *Health Reports, 16,* May. **206, 207**

Gartrell, N., et al. 2000. The National Lesbian Family Study: 3. Interviews with mothers of five-year-olds. *American Journal of Orthopsychiatry, 70,* 542–548. **222**

Gartrell, N., et al. 2005. The National Lesbian Family Study. 4 Interviews with the 10-year-old children. *American Journal of Orthopsychiatry, 75,* 518–524. **223, 241**

Gaspar, D. R., and Hine, D. C. (Eds.). 1999. *More than chattel: Black women and slavery in the Americas.*Bloomington: Indiana University Press. **44, 63**

Gaudet, J., and Devault, A. 2006. Quelles sont les conditions associées à une bonne adaptation au rôle paternel post-rupture?: Parcours paternels et points de vues des pères. *Revue Canadienne de Santé Mentale, 25,* 17–32. **352**

Gauthier, A. H., Smeeding, T. M., and Furstenberg, F. F., Jr. 2004. Are parents investing less time in children? Trends in selected industrialized countries. *Population and Development Review, 30,* 647–672. **104**

Gazso, A. 2010. Mothers' maintenance of families through market and family care relations. In N. Mandell (Ed.), *Feminist Issues,* 5th Ed. (pp. 219–246). Toronto: Pearson Canada. **21, 68**

Ge, X., et al. 2008. Bridging the divide: Openness in adoption of postadoption psychosocial adjustment among birth and adoptive parents. *Journal of Family Psychology, 22,* 529–540. **245**

Gee, E. M. 2000. Voodoo demography, population aging, and social policy. In E. M. Gee and G. M. Gutman (Eds.), *The overselling of population aging* (pp. 1–25). Toronto: Oxford University Press. **303**

Gee, E. M., Mitchell, B. A., and Wister, A. V. 2003. Home leaving trajectories in Canada: Exploring cultural and gendered dimensions. *Canadian Studies in Population, 30,* 245–270. **301**

Gelles, R. J. 1989. Child abuse and violence in single parent families: Parent absence and economic deprivation. *American Journal of Orthopsychiatry, 59,* 492–501. **221**

Gelles, R. J. 1997. *Intimate violence in families,* 3rd Ed. Thousand Oaks, CA: Sage. **407, 408**

Gennetian, L. A., and Morris, P. A. 2003. The effects of time limits and make-work-pay strategies on the well-being of children: Experimental evidence from two welfare reform programs. *Children and Youth Services Review, 25,* 7–54. **429**

Gennetian, L. A., Lopoo, L. M., and London, A. S. 2008. Maternal work hours and adolescents' school outcomes among low-income families in four urban countries. *Demography, 45,* 31–53. **117**

Gentile, D. A., et al. 2009. The effects of prosocial video games on prosocial behaviors: International evidence from correlational, longitudinal, and experimental studies. *Personality and Social Psychology Bulletin, 35,* 752–763. **86**

Gentleman, J. F., and Park, E. 1997. Divorce in the 1990s. Statistics Canada, *Health Reports, 9,* 53–58. **349**

Gergen, K. J., et al. 1996. Psychological science in cultural context. *American Psychologist, 51,* 496–503. **18**

Gewirtz, A. H., et al. 2009. Parenting, parental mental health, and child functioning in families residing in supportive housing. *American Journal of Orthopsychiatry, 79,* 336–347. **135**

Giarrusso, R., et al. 2001. Grandparent-adult grandchild affection and consensus: Cross-generation and cross-ethnic comparisons. *Journal of Family Issues, 22,* 456–477. **303**

Giles, W., and Hyndman, J. (Eds.) 2004. *Sites of violence: Gender and conflict zones.*Berkeley, CA: University of California Press. **25**

Giles-Sims, J. 1997. Current knowledge about child abuse in stepfamilies. *Marriage and Family Review, 26,* 215–230. **373**

Gilgun, J. F. 2005. Qualitative research and family psychology. *Journal of Family Psychology, 19,* 40–50. **29, 31**

Gillis, J. 1996. *A world of their own making: Myth, ritual and the quest for family values.* New York: Basic Books. **14**

Gionet, L. 2009. *First Nations people: Selected findings of the 2006 Census.* Ottawa: Statistics Canada, July 27. **49, 144, 218, 308**

Giordano, P. C., et al. 1999. Delinquency, indentity, and women's involvement in relationship violence. *Criminology, 37,* 17–37. **386**

Girard, C. 2008. *Le bilan démographique du Québec, 2008.* Québec: Institut de la statistique du Québec. **52, 190, 191, 198, 201, 218, 232, 347**

Gladstone, J., and Westhues, A. 1998. Adoption reunions: A new side to intergenerational family relationships. *Family Relations, 47,* 177–184. **245**

Glenday, D. 1997. Lost horizons, leisure shock: Good jobs, bad jobs, uncertain future. In A. Duffy, D. Glenday, and N. Pupo (Eds.), *Good jobs, bad jobs* (pp. 8–34). Toronto: Harcourt Brace. **95, 96**

Glenn, N. D., 1991. The recent trends in marital success in the United States. *Journal of Marriage and Family, 53,* 261–270. **271**

Glick, P. C. 1947. The family cycle. *American Sociological Review, 12,* 164–174. **16**

Goffman, E. 1959. *The presentation of self in everyday life.* New York: Doubleday.**15**

Goldberg, A. E. 2007. (How) Does it make a difference? Perspectives of adults with lesbian, gay, and bisexual parents. *American Journal of Orthopsychiatry, 77,* 550–562. **223**

Goldberg, A. E., et al. 2008. Perceptions of children's parental preferences in lesbian two-mother households. *Journal of Marriage and Family, 70,* 419–434. **223**

Goldberg, A. E., Smith, J. Z., and Kashy, D. A. 2010 Preadoptive factors predicting lesbian, gay, and heterosexual couples' relationship quality across the transition to adoptive parenthood. *Journal of Family Psychology, 24,* 221–232. **223**

Goldscheider, F., and Sassler, S. 2006. Creating stepfamilies: Integrating children into the study of union formation. *Journal of Marriage and Family, 68,* 275–291. **351**

Goldstein, J. R., and Kenney, C. T. 2001. Marriage delayed or marriage forgone? New cohort forecasts of first marriage for U.S. women. *American Sociological Review*, 66, 506–519. **420**

Golombok, S., and Badger, S. 2010. Children raised in mother-headed families from infancy: A follow-up of children of lesbian and single heterosexual mothers, at early adulthood. *Human Reproduction, 25*, 150–157. **225**

Golombok, S., et al. 2002. Families with children conceived by donor insemination: A follow-up at age twelve. *Child Development, 73*, 952–968. **236, 237**

Golombok, S., et al. 2006. Non-genetic and non-gestational parenthood: Consequences for parent-child relationship and the psychological well-being of mothers, fathers, and children at age 3. *Human Reproduction, 21*, 1918–1924. **238**

Golombok, S., et al. 2007. Parenting and the psychological development of a representative sample of triplets conceived by assisted reproduction. *Human Reproduction, 25*, 150–157. **238, 320**

Golombos, N. L., Baker, E. T., and Almeida, D. M. 2003. Parents *do* matter: Trajectories of change in externalizing and internalizing problems in early adolescence. *Child Development, 74*, 578–594. **340**

Goode, W. J. 1956. *Women in divorce*. New York: Free Press. **357**

Gordon, M. 1989. The family environment and sexual abuse: A comparison of natal and stepfather abuse. *Child Abuse & Neglect, 13*, 121–129. **221**

Gore, A. 2006. *An inconvenient truth*. New York: Rodale Books. **72**

Gorman, E. H. 1999. Bringing home the bacon: Marital allocation of income-earning responsibility, job shifts, and men's wages. *Journal of Marriage and Family, 61*, 110–122. **199**

Gorman, J. C. 1998. Parenting attitudes and practices of immigrant Chinese mothers of adolescents. *Family Relations, 47*, 73–80. **288**

Gorman, T. 1997. Canadian television in transition. *Canadian Social Trends, 44*, 19–23. **79**

Gosa, T. L., and Alexander, K. L. 2007. Family (dis)advantage and the educational prospects of better off African American youth: How race still matters. *Teachers College Record, 109*, 285–321. **54**

Gottfredson, G. D., et al. 2005. School climate predictors of school disorder: Results from a national study of delinquency prevention in schools. *Journal of Research in Crime and Delinquency, 42*, 412–444. **166**

Gottman, J. M. 1998. Toward a process model of men in marriages and families. In A. Booth and A. C. Crouter (Eds.), *Men in families* (pp. 149–192). Mahwah, NJ: Erlbaum. **269, 286**

Gottman, J. M., and Levenson, R. W. 2000. The timing of divorce: Predicting when a couple will divorce over a 14-year period. *Journal of Marriage and Family, 62*, 737–745. **256, 257**

Goulet, L., Dressyman-Lavallee, M., and McCleod, Y. 2001. Early childhood education for Aboriginal children: Opening petals. In K. P. Binda and S. Calliou (Eds.), *Aboriginal education in Canada* (pp. 137–153). Mississauga: Canadian Educators' Press. **156, 160**

Grant, A. 2004. *Finding my talk: How fourteen Native women reclaimed their lives after residential school*. Calgary: Fifth House Ltd. **49**

Gray, M. R., and Steinberg, L. 1999. Unpacking authoritative parenting: Reassessing a multidimensional construct. *Journal of Marriage and Family, 61*, 574–587. **286, 287**

Green, R. K., and White, M. J. 1997. Measuring the benefits of homeowning: Effects on children. *Journal of Urban Economics, 41*, 441–461. **431**

Greenberg, B. S., and Busselle, R. W. 1996. Soap operas and sexual activity: A decade later. *Journal of Communication, 46*, 153–160. **87**

Greenberg, J. S., Seltzer, M. M., and Greenlay, J. R. 1993. Aging parents of adults with disabilities: The gratifications and frustrations of later-life caregiving. *The Gerontologist, 33*, 542–549. **408**

Greitemeyer, T. 2009. Effects of songs with prosocial lyrics on prosocial thoughts, affect, and behavior. *Journal of Experimental Social Psychology, 45*, 186–190. **86**

Greitemeyer, T., and Osswald, S. 2010. Effects of prosocial video games on prosocial behaviour. *Journal of Personality and Social Psychology, 98*, 211–221. **86**

Grieve, J., and Hogarth, B. 2009. Opportunity to transform early learning in Ontario. *Toronto Star.* June 16, A19. **433**

Grona, M. 2009. Canada Survey of Giving, Volunteering and Participating. Statistics Canada, *The Daily*, June 8. **174**

Grotevant, H. D., and McRoy, R. G. 1998. *Openness in adoption: Exploring family connections*. Thousand Oaks, CA: Sage. **244, 245**

Grotevant, H. D., et al. 2008. Many faces of openness in adoption: Perspectives of adopted adolescents and their parents. *Adoption Quarterly, 10*, 79–101. **245**

Grzywacz, J. G., et al. 2002. Work-related spillover and daily reports of work and family stress in the adult labor force. *Family Relations, 51*, 28–36. **101**

GSS (General Social Survey). 2000. Family violence. Statistics Canada, *The Daily*. **360**

Guilmoto, C. Z. 2009. The sex ratio transition in Asia. *Population and Development Review, 35*, 519–549. **8, 56, 60**

Guo, G., Roettger, M. E., and Cai, T. 2008. The integration of genetic propensities into social-control models of delinquency and violence among male youths. *American Sociological Review, 73*, 543–568. **336, 339, 367**

Guzzo, K. B. 2009a. Marital intentions and the stability of first cohabitations. *Journal of Family Issues, 30*, 179–205. **193**

Guzzo, K. B. 2009b. Maternal relationships and nonresidential father visitation of children born outside of marriage. *Journal of Marriage and Family, 71*, 632–649. **372**

Guzzo, K. B., and Furstenberg, F. F., Jr. 2007a. Multipartnered fertility among American men. *Demography, 44*, 583–601. **110, 112, 227**

Guzzo, K. B., and Furstenberg, F. F., Jr. 2007b. Multipartnered fertility among young women with a nonmarital first birth: Prevalence and risk factors. *Perspectives on Sexual and Reproductive Health, 39*, 29–38. **226**

Habermas, J. 1987. *The theory of communicative action: Lifeworld and system: A critique of functionalist reason* (vol. 2, translated by T. McCarthy). Boston: Beacon Press. **88**

Hagan, J., MacMillan, R., and Wheaton, B. 1996. The life course effects of family migration on children. *American Sociological Review, 61*, 368–385. **146**

Hall, A. 2007. Organic farming, gender, and the labor process. *Rural Sociology, 72*, 289–317. **138**

Halpern-Meekin, S., and Tach, L. 2008. Heterogeneity in two-parent families and adolescent well-being. *Journal of Marriage and Family, 70*, 435–451. **374, 416**

Hamby, S. L., and Sugarman, D. B. 1999. Acts of psychological aggression against a partner and their relations to physical assault and gender. *Journal of Marriage and Family, 61*, 959–970. **383**

Hamilton, L., and Armstrong, E. A. 2009. Gendered sexuality in young adulthood. *Gender & Society, 23*, 589–616. **184**

Hamilton, L., Cheng, S., and Powell, S. 2007. Adoptive parents, adaptive parents: Evaluating the importance of biological ties for parental involvement. *American Sociological Review, 72*, 95–116. **242**

Hamilton, R. 2005. *Gendering the vertical mosaic: Feminist perspectives on Canadian society,* 2nd Ed. Toronto: Pearson Prentice Hall. **23, 33**

Hammer, K. 2010. Lawsuits question schools' responses to bullying. *The Globe and Mail.* February 17, A7. **404**

Hamplova, D., and Le Bourdais, C. 2008. Educational homogamy of married and unmarried couples in English and French Canada. *Canadian Journal of Sociology, 33*, 845–872. **188**

Hampton, M. R., McWatters, R., and Jeffery, B. 2005. Influence of teens' perceptions of parental disapproval and peer behaviour on their initiation of sexual intercourse. *The Canadian Journal of Human Sexuality, 14*, 105–122. **207**

Han, W.-J., et al. 2001. The effects of early maternal employment on later cognitive and behavioral outcomes. *Journal of Marriage and Family, 63*, 336–354. **101**

Hansen, M., et al. 2005. Assisted reproductive technologies and the risk of birth defects—a systematic review. *Human Reproduction, 20*, 328–338. **237**

Hansen, T., Mourn, T., and Shapiro, T. 2007. Relational and individual well-being among cohabitors and married individuals in midlife. *Journal of Family Issues, 28*, 910–933. **196**

Hanson, T. L. 1999. Does parental conflict explain why divorce is negatively associated with child welfare? *Social Forces, 77*, 1283–1315. **366**

Harbin, H., and Maddin, D. 1979. Battered parents: A new syndrome. *American Journal of Psychiatry, 136*, 1288–1291. **406**

Harbinson, J. 1999. Models of intervention for elder abuse and neglect: A Canadian perspective on ageism, participation, and empowerment. *Journal of Elder Abuse and Neglect, 10*, 1–17. **408**

Harden, B. J. 2004. Safety and stability for foster children: A developmental perspective. *The Future of children, 14*, 31–47. **247**

Harden, K. P., et al. 2007. Marital conflict and conduct problems in children of twins. *Child Development, 78*, 1–18. **247, 270, 279**

Harding, D. J. 2010. Collateral consequences of violence in disadvantaged neighborhoods. *Social Forces, 88*, 757–785. **126**

Hardy, M., et al. 2010. Personal experience and perceived acceptability of sibling aggression. *Journal of Family Violence, 25*, 65–71. **403**

Hareven, T. K. 1994a. Continuity and change in American family life. In A. S. Skolnick and J. H. Skolnick (Eds.), *Family in transition,* 8th Ed. (pp. 40–46). New York: HarperCollins. **67, 297**

Hareven, T. K. 1994b. Aging and generational relations: A historical and life course perspective. *Annual Review of Sociology, 20*, 437–461. **297, 301**

Harkness, S., and Super, C. M. 1992. Shared child care in east Africa: Socioculture origins and developmental consequences. In M. Lamb et al. (Eds.), *Child care in context: Cross cultural perspectives* (pp. 441–459). Hillsdale, NJ: Erlbaum. **20**

Harkness, S., and Super, C. M. 2002. Culture and parenting. In M. H. Bornstein (Ed.), *Handbook of parenting,* 2nd Ed, (pp. 253–280). Mahwah, NJ: Erlbaum. **20, 422**

Harknett, K. 2008. Mate availability and unmarried parent relationships. *Demography, 45*, 555–571. **55, 354**

Harlaar, N., et al. 2008. Retrospective reports of parental physical affection and parenting style: A study of Finnish twins. *Journal of Family Psychology, 22*, 605–613. **338**

Harrington, D., et al. 1998. Child neglect: Relation to child temperament and family context. *American Journal of Orthopsychiatry, 68*, 108–116. **397**

Harris, F. 2002. *Transformation of love.* Oxford, UK: Oxford University Press. **190**

Harris, K. M., and Morgan, S. P. 1991. Fathers, sons, and daughters: Differential paternal involvement in parenting. *Journal of Marriage and Family, 53*, 531–544. **327**

Harrison, T. W., and Friesen, J. W. 2004. *Canadian society in the twenty-first century: A historical sociological approach.* Toronto: Pearson-Prentice Hall. **43, 49, 50, 51, 64, 108**

Hartwick, C., Desmarais, S., and Hennig, K. 2007. Characteristics of male and female victims of sexual coercion. *The Canadian Journal of Human Sexuality, 16*, 31–45. **382**

Hassouneh-Phillips, D. 2001. Polygamy and wife abuse: A qualitative study of Muslim women in America. *Health Care for Women International, 22*, 735–748. **10**

Hatch, L. R., and Bulcroft, K. 2004. Does long-term marriage bring less frequent disagreements? Five explanatory frameworks. *Journal of Family Issues, 25*, 465–495. **270**

Hawkins, D. N., Amato, P. R., and King, V. 2007. Nonresident father involvement and adolescent well-being: Father effects or child effects? *American Sociological Review, 72*, 990–1010. **352**

Hawkins, D. N., and Booth, A. 2005. Unhappily ever after: Effects of long-term, low-quality marriages on well-being. *Social Forces, 84*, 451–470. **268**

Haworth, C. M. A., Dale, P. S., and Plomin, R. 2009. The etiology of science performance decreasing heritability and increasing importance of the shared environment from 9 to 12 years of age. *Child Development, 80*, 662–673. **338**

Hay, D. I. 2009. *Poverty reduction policies and programs.* Ottawa: Canadian Council on Social Development. **359, 425, 426, 427, 430**

Haynie, D. L., and South, S. J. 2005. Residential mobility and adolescent violence. *Social Forces, 84*, 370–373. **145**

Hays, S. 1996. *The cultural contradictions of motherhood.* New Haven, CT: Yale University Press. **19, 20, 21, 70, 99, 163, 285, 438**

Hays, S. 1998. The fallacious assumptions and unrealistic prescriptions of attachment theory: A comment on "Parents' socioemotional investment in children." *Journal of Marriage and Family, 60*, 782–795. **20**

Health Canada. 2000. *1998/1999 Canadian sexually transmitted disease (STD) surveillance report.* **206**

Health Canada. 2001. *The Canadian incidence study of reported child abuse and neglect.* **391, 396**

Heath, D. T. 1995. The impact of delayed fatherhood on the father-child relationship. *Journal of Genetic Psychology, 155*, 511–530. **229**

Heflin, C. M., and Pattillo, M. 2006. Poverty in the family: Race, siblings, and socioeconomic heterogeneity. *Social Science Research, 35*, 804–822. **55**

Heimdal, K. R., and Houseknecht, S. K. 2003. Cohabiting and married couples' income organization: Approaches in Sweden and the United States. *Journal of Marriage and Family, 65*, 525–538. **194**

Henderson, T. L., and Moran, P. B. 2001. Grandparent visitation rights: Testing the parameters of parental rights. *Journal of Family Issues, 22*, 619–638. **375**

Henry, R. G., Miller, R. B., and Giarrusso, R. 2005. Difficulties, disagreements, and disappointments in late-life marriages. *International Journal on Aging and Human Development, 61,* 243–264. **273**

HERI (Higher Education Research Institute). 2003. *College freshmen spend less time studying and more time surfing the net, UCLA survey reveals.*Los Angeles, CA: UCLA Graduate School of Education and Information Studies. **89**

Herrington, D. L. 2009. *Prevention of spousal abuse in the Canadian Forces.* Canadian Forces. **78**

Hetherington, E. M. 1988. Parents, children, and siblings: Six years after divorce. In R. A. Hinde and J. Stevenson-Hinde (Eds.), *Relationships within families: Mutual influences* (pp. 311–331). Oxford: Oxford University Press. **325**

Hetherington, E. M. 2003. Intimate pathways: Changing patterns in close personal relationships across time. *Family Relations, 52,* 318–331. **270, 277, 357, 362, 363, 367**

Hetherington, E. M., and Kelly, J. 2002. *For better or for worse: Divorce reconsidered.* New York: Norton. **373**

Hetherington, E. M., et al. 1992. Coping with marital transitions. *Monographs of the Society for Research in Child Development, 57,* 2–3. **365**

Hewitt, B., and de Vaus, D. 2009. Change in the association between premarital cohabitation and separation, Australia 1945–2000. *Journal of Marriage and Family, 71,* 353–361. **355, 356**

Hewlett, B. S., and Lamb, M. E., (Eds.). 2005. *Hunter-gatherer childhoods.* New Brunswick, CT: Aldine Transaction. **18, 19, 74, 336**

Hewlett, S. A., and West, C. 1998. *The war against parents.* Boston: Houghton Mifflin. **90**

Heyman, R. E., and Slep, A. M. S. 2002. Do child abuse and interparental violence lead to adulthood family violence? *Journal of Marriage and Family, 64,* 864–870. **389**

Heyman, R. E., et al. 2009. Desired change in couples: Gender differences and effects on communication. *Journal of Family Psychology, 23,* 474–484. **269**

Hill, E. J., Hawkins, A. J., Ferris, M., and Weitzman, M. 2001. Finding an extra day a week: The positive influence of perceived job flexibility on work and family life balance. *Family Relations, 50,* 49–58. **103**

Hill, T. D, Ross, C. E., and Angel, R. J. 2005. Neighborhood disorder, psychophysiological distress, and health. *Journal of Health and Social Behavior, 46,* 170–186. **126**

Hines, A. M. 1997. Divorce-related transitions, adolescent development, and the role of the parent-child relationship: A review of the literature. *Journal of Marriage and Family, 59,* 375–388. **365**

Hochschild, A. R. 1983. *The managed heart.* Berkeley: University of California Press. **265**

Hochschild, A. R. 1997. *The time bind.* New York: Metropolitan Books. **100**

Hochschild, A. R., with Machung, A. 1989. *The second shift.* New York: Avon. **99, 121**

Hodges, E. V. E., Malone, M. J., and Perry, D. G. 1997. Individual risk and social risk as interacting determinants of victimization in the peer group. *Developmental Psychology, 33,* 1032–1039. **405**

Hoekstra, C., et al. 2008. Dizygotic twinning. *Human Reproduction Update, 14,* 37–47. **319**

Hofferth, S., and Anderson, K. G. 2003. Are all dads equal? Biology versus marriage as a basis for paternal investment. *Journal of Marriage and Family, 65,* 213–232. **373**

Hofferth, S. L. 2006. Residential father family type and child well-being: Investment versus selection. *Demography, 43,* 53–77. **374, 416**

Hofferth, S. L., and Goldscheider, F. 2010. Family structure and the transition to early parenthood. *Demography, 47,* 415–437. **228**

Hofferth, S. L., and Sandberg, J. F. 2001. Changes in American children's time, 1981–1997. In S. L. Hofferth and T. J. Owens (Eds.), *Children at the millennium: Where have we come from, where are we going?*(pp. 193–229). Oxford, UK: Elsevier. **103, 261**

Hofferth, S. L., Reid, L., and Mott, F. L. 2001. The effects of early childbearing on schooling over time. *Family Planning Perspectives, 33,* 259–267. **111**

Hoffman, F., and Taylor, R. 1996. *Much to be done: Private life in Ontario from Victorian diaries.*Toronto: Natural Heritage/Natural History Inc. **41, 42, 45**

Hoggerbrugge, M. J. A., and Dykstra, P. A. 2009. The family ties of unmarried cohabiting and married persons in the Netherlands. *Journal of Marriage and Family, 71,* 135–145. **195**

Hohman, M. M., and Hagan, C. B. 2001. Satisfaction with surrogate mothering: A relational model. *Journal of Human Behavior in the Social Environment, 4,* 61–84. **238**

Hohmann-Marriott, B. E. 2006. Shared beliefs and the union stability of married and cohabiting couples. *Journal of Marriage and Family, 68,* 1015–1028. **193, 356**

Homans, G. C. 1961. *Social behavior: Its elementary forms.* New York: Harcourt, Brace, and World. **12**

Home Children, 1869–1930. <www.collectionsCanada.gc.ca>. Accessed December 18, 2009. **45**

Honoré, C. 2008. *Under pressure: How the epidemic of hyper-parenting is endangering childhood.* Toronto: Alfred A. Knopf Canada. **437**

Hopper, J. 2001. The symbolic origins of conflict in divorce. *Journal of Marriage and Family, 63,* 430–435. **357, 366**

Horney, J., Osgood, D. W., and Marshall, I. H. 1995. Criminal careers in the short term: Intra-individual variability in crime and its relation to local life circumstances. *American Sociological Review, 60,* 655–673. **199**

Horwitz, A. V. 1993. Adult siblings as sources of social support for the seriously mentally ill: A test of the serial model. *Journal of Marriage and Family, 55,* 623–632. **324**

Horwitz, A. V., and Raskin White, H. 1998. The relationship of cohabitation and mental health: A study of a young adult cohort. *Journal of Marriage and Family, 60,* 505–514. **199**

Horwitz, B. N., et al. 2010. Genetic and environmental influences on global family conflict. *Journal of Family Psychology, 24,* 217–220. **337, 368**

Hostetler, J. A. 1993. *Amish society,* 4th Ed. Baltimore: Johns Hopkins University Press. **70**

Hou, F. 2010. Homeownership over the life course of Canadians: Evidence from Canadian Census of population. Statistics Canada, *The Daily,* June 6. **141**

Hou, F., and Milan, A. 2003. Neighbourhood ethnic transition and its socio-economic connections. *Canadian Journal of Sociology, 28,* 387–410. **133**

Hou, F., and Myles, J. 2004. Neighbourhood inequality and self-perceived health status. Statistics Canada, *The Daily,* September 27. **126**

Hou, F., and Myles, J. 2007. Study: Changing role of education in the marriage market in Canada and the United States. Statistics Canada, *The Daily,* May 18. **188**

Hou, F., and Myles, J. 2008. The changing role of education in the marriage market: assortative marriage in Canada and the United States since the 1970s. *Canadian Journal of Sociology, 33,* 337–366. **188**

Hou, F., and Picot, G. 2004. Visible minority neighbourhoods in Toronto, Montreal, and Vancouver. *Canadian Social Trends,* 72, 8–13. **132**

Hou, F., and Wu, Z. 2009. Racial diversity, minority concentration, and trust in Canadian urban neighborhoods. *Social Science Research, 38,* 693–716. **132**

Houseknecht, S. K., and Macke, A. 1981. Combining marriage and career: The marital adjustment of professional women. *Journal of Marriage and the Family, 43,* 651–661. **262**

Housseaux, F. 2003. *La famille, pilier des identités.* Paris: INSEE. **69**

Howes, C. 1988. Abused and neglected children with their peers. In G. T. Hotaling et al. (Eds.), *Family abuse and its consequences* (pp. 99–108). Beverly Hills, CA: Sage. **393**

HRSD (Human Resources and Skills Development). 2009. *Low-income in Canada: 2000–2007, Using the Market Basket Measure.* Gatineau, Que: HRSD Canada, August. Catalogue no. SP-909-07-09E. **106**

Huebner, A. J., and Mancini, J. A. 2005. *Adjustments among adolescents in military families when a parent is deployed.* U.S. Military Family Research Institute, Purdue University. **77**

Huebner, A. J., et al. 2009. Shadowed by war: Building community capacity to support military families. *Family Relations, 58,* 216–228. **78**

Huesmann, L. R., et al. 2003. Longitudinal relations between children's exposure to TV violence and their aggressive and violent behavior in young adulthood: 1977–1992. *Developmental Psychology, 39,* 201–221. **85**

Hughes, M. E., and Waite, L. J. 2009. Marital biography and health in mid-life. *Journal of Health and Social Behavior, 50,* 344–358. **359, 360**

Hughes, M. E., et al. 2007. All in the family: The impact of caring for grandchildren on grandparents' health. *The Journals of Gerontology:* Series B, 62B, S108–120. **308**

Huh, D., et al. 2006. Does problem behavior elicit poor parenting? A prospective study of adolescent girls. *Journal of Adolescent Research, 21,* 185–204. **285, 287, 293, 294**

Humble, A. M. 2003. *"Doing weddings": Couples' gender strategies in wedding preparation.* Oregon State University: Doctoral dissertation. **185, 265**

Hummer, R. A., Hack, K. A., and Raley, R. K. 2004. Retrospective reports of pregnancy wantedness and child well-being in the United States. *Journal of Family Issues, 25,* 404–428. **235**

Hummer, R. A., et al. 1999. Religious involvement and U.S. adult mortality. *Demography, 36,* 273–285. **175**

Hur, Y.-M., and Bouchard, T. J., Jr. 1995. Genetic influences on perceptions of childhood family environment: A reared apart twin study. *Child Development, 66,* 330–345. **338**

Hurd, L. C. 1999. "We're not old!": Older women's negotiation of aging and oldness. *Journal of Aging Studies, 13,* 419–439. **368**

Hylton, J. 2002. *Aboriginal sex offending in Canada.* Ottawa: Aboriginal Healing Foundation. **388, 399**

Hyman, B. 2000. The economic consequences of child sexual abuse for adult lesbian women. *Journal of Marriage and Family, 62,* 199–211. **399**

Iannaccone, L. R. 1990. Religious practice: A human capital approach. *Journal for the Scientific Study of Religion, 29,* 297–314. **175**

Iervolino, A., et al. 2005. Genetic and environmental influences on sex-typed behavior during the preschool years. *Child Development,* 76,826–840.**337**

Illick, J. E. 2002. *American childhoods.* Philadelphia: University of Pennsylvania Press. **20**

Ingersoll-Dayton, B., Neal, M. B., and Hammer, L. B. 2001. Aging parents helping adult children: The experience of the sandwich generation. *Family Relations, 50,* 262–271. **305**

INSEE (Institut national de la statistique et des études économiques). 2008. Paris, France.

Invest in Kids. 2002. *A national survey of parents of young children*: Invest in Kids Foundation. June. **103, 292, 436**

Jadva, V., et al. 2009a. "Mom by choice, single by life's circumstances . . ." Findings from a large scale survey of the experiences of single mothers by choice. *Human Fertility, 12,* 175–184. **225**

Jadva, V., et al. 2009b. The experiences of adolescents and adults conceived by sperm donation: Comparisons by age of disclosure and family type. *Human Reproduction Advance, 1,* 1–11. **237**

Jaeger, M. M. 2009. Equal access but unequal outcomes: Cultural capital and educational choice in a meritocratic society. *Social Forces, 87,* 1943–1972. **161**

Jaffee, S. R., et al. 2003. Life with (or without) father: The benefits of living with two biological parents depend on the father's antisocial behavior. *Child Development, 74,* 109–126. **339**

Jaffee, S. R., et al. 2005. Nature x nurture: Genetic vulnerabilities interact with physical maltreatment to promote conduct problems. *Developmental Psychopathology, 17,* 67–84. **394, 395**

Jamieson, K. 1986. Sex discrimination and the Indian Act. In J. R. Ponting (Ed.), *Arduous journey: Canadian Indians and decolonization.* Toronto: McClelland & Stewart. **39**

Janssens, P. M. W. 2006. A new Dutch law regulating provision of identifying information of donors to offspring: background, content and impact. *Human Reproduction, 21,* 852–856. **236**

Javed, N. 2008. GTA's secret world of polygamy. *Toronto Star.* May 24, A10, ID1. **7**

Jekielek, S. M. 1998. Parental conflict, marital disruption and children's emotional well-being. *Social Forces,* 76, 905–935. **219**

Jendrek, M. P. 1993. Grandparents who parent their grandchildren: Effects on lifestyle. *Journal of Marriage and Family,* 55, 609–621. **309**

Jenkins, J. M. 2000. Marital conflict and children's emotions: The development of an anger organization. *Journal of Marriage and Family,* 62, 723–736. **277**

Jenkins, J. M., and Smith, M. A. 1990. Factors protecting children living in disharmonious homes: Maternal reports. *Journal of the American Academy of Child & Adolescent Psychiatry,* 29, 60–69. **325**

Jenkins, J. M., et al. 2005a. Change in maternal perception of sibling negativity: Within- and between-family influences. *Journal of Family Psychology,* 19, 533–541. **285, 329**

Jenkins, J., et al. 2005b. Mutual influence of marital conflict and children's behavior problems: Shared and nonshared family risks. *Child Development,* 76, 24–39. **276, 330, 332, 354**

Jenkins-Tucker, C., McHale, S. M., and Crouter, A. C. 2001. Conditions of sibling support in adolescence. *Journal of Family Psychology,* 15, 254–271. **322, 324**

Jensen, A.-M. 1995. Gender gaps in relationships with children: Closing or widening? In K. O. Mason and A.-M. Jensen (Eds.), *Gender or family change in industrialized countries* (pp. 223–242). Oxford: Clarendon. **25**

Jepsen, L. K., and Jepsen, C. A. 2002. An empirical analysis of the matching patterns of same-sex and opposite-sex couples. *Demography, 39*, 435–453. **189**

Jespersen, A. F., Lalumière, M. L., and Seto, M. C. 2009. Sexual abuse history among adult sex offenders and non-sex offenders: A meta-analysis. *Child Abuse & Neglect, 33*, 179–192. **395, 400, 401**

Johnson, B. R., et al. 2001. Does adolescent religious commitment matter? A reexamination of the effects of religiosity on delinquency. *Journal of Research in Crime and Delinquency, 38*, 22–44. **175**

Johnson, H. 1996. *Dangerous domains: Violence against women in Canada.* Toronto: Nelson. **381**

Johnson, H. 2003. The cessation of assaults on wives. *Journal of Comparative Family Studies, 34*, 75–91. **386**

Johnson, J. G., et al. 2002. Television viewing and aggressive behavior during adolescence and adulthood. *Science, 295*, 2468–2471. **85**

Johnson, J. K. 1994. Friends in high places: Getting divorced in Upper Canada. *Ontario History, 86*, 201–218. **41**

Johnson, M. P. 1999. Personal, moral, and structural commitment to relationships: Experiences of choice and constraint. In W. H. Jones and J. M. Adams (Eds.), *Handbook of interpersonal commitment and relationship stability* (pp. 73–87). New York: Kluwar Academic-Plenum Press. **192**

Johnson, M. P., and Leone, J. M. 2005. The differential effects of intimate terrorism and situational couple violence. *Journal of Family Issues, 26*, 322–349. **385**

Johnston, P. 1983. *Native children and the child welfare system.* Toronto: Canadian Council on Social Development, in association with James Lorimer and Company. **50**

Jones, A. 2010. Stability of men's interracial first unions: A test of educational differentials and cohabitation history. *Journal of Family and Economic Issues, 31*, 241–257. **355, 398**

Jones, F. 2000. Community involvement: The influence of early experience. *Canadian Social Trends, 57*, 15–19. **124, 176**

Jones, G. W. 2007. Delayed marriage and very low fertility in Pacific Asia. *Population and Development Review, 33*, 453–478. **78, 229, 232, 301**

Jones, L. M., Finkelhor, D., and Kopiec, K. 2001. Why is sexual abuse declining? A survey of state child protection administrators. *Child Abuse & Neglect, 25*, 1139–1158. **398**

Jose, A., O'Leary, D., and Moyer, A. 2010. Does premarital cohabitation predict subsequent marital stability and marital quality? A meta-analysis. *Journal of Marriage and Family, 72*, 105–116. **357**

Josey, S. 2008. Farmland in GTA is diminishing. *Toronto Star.* September 08. **136**

Joussemet, M., et al. 2008. Controlling parenting and physical aggression during elementary school. *Child Development, 79*, 411–425. **288**

Joy, L. A., Kimball, M. M., and Zabrack, M. L. 1986. Television and children's aggressive behavior. In T. M. Williams (Ed.), *The impact of television: A natural experiment in three communities* (pp. 303–360). Orlando, FL: Academic Press. **85**

Joyner, K., and Udry, J. R. 2000. You don't bring me anything but down: Adolescent romance and depression. *Journal of Health and Social Behavior, 41*, 369–391. **184**

Juby, H., Marcil-Gratton, and Le Bourdais, C. 2005a. *Moving on: The expansion of the family network after parents separate.* Ottawa: Department of Justice, Catalogue no. 2004-FCY-9E. **372**

Juby, H., Marcil-Gratton, and Le Bourdais, C. 2005b. *When parents separate: Further findings from the National Longitudinal Survey of Children and Youth.* Ottawa: Department of Justice. **350**

Juby, H., et al. 2007. Nonresident fathers and children: Parents' new unions and frequency of contact. *Journal of Family Issues, 28*, 1220–1245. **373**

Judge, S. 2003. Determinants of parental stress in families adopting children from Eastern Europe. *Family Relations, 52*, 241–248. **244**

Juffer, J., and van Izjendoorm, M. H. 2005. Behavior problems and mental health referrals of international adoptees. *Journal of the American Medical Association, 293*, 2501–2515. **244**

Kaczynski, K. J., et al. 2006. Marital conflict, maternal and paternal parenting, and child adjustment: A test for mediation and moderation. *Journal of Family Psychology, 20*, 199–208. **276**

Kaestle, C. E., Morisky, D. E., and Wiley, D. J. 2002. Sexual intercourse and the age difference between adolescent females and their romantic partners. *Perspectives on Sexual and Reproductive Health, 34*, 304–309. **207**

Kagan, S. L., and Neuman, M. J. 1998. Lessons from three decades of transition research. *Elementary School Journal, 87*, 365–379. **157**

Kağitçibaşi, C. 2007. *Family, self, and human development across cultures.* Mahwah, NJ: Erlbaum. **27, 71**

Kaiser Family Foundation. 2003. *Sex on TV3.* Menlo Park, CA: H. J. Kaiser Family Foundation. **87**

Kalbach, M. A. 2000. Ethnicity and the altar. In M. A. Kalbach and W. E. Kalbach (Eds.), *Perspectives on ethnicity in Canada: A reader* (pp. 111–121). Toronto: McClelland & Stewart. **187**

Kalmijn, M., de Graaf, P. M., and Janssen, J. P. G. 2005. Intermarriage and the risk of divorce in the Netherlands: The effects of differences in religion and in nationality, 1974–94. *Population Studies, 59*, 71–85. **186**

Kan, M. L., McHale, S. M., and Crouter, A. C. 2008. Interparental incongruence in differential treatment of adolescent siblings: Links with marital quality. *Journal of Marriage and Family, 70*, 466–479. **329**

Kanner, B. 2001. From *Father Knows Best* to *The Simpsons*—on TV, parenting has lost its halo. In S. A. Hewlett, N. Rankin, and C. West (Eds.), *Taking parenting public* (pp. 45–56). New York: Rowan & Littlefield. **82**

Kapinus, C. A., and Pellerin, L. A. 2008. The influence of parents' religious practices on young adults' divorce attitudes. *Social Science Research, 37*, 801–814. **177**

Kaplan, S. J., Pelcovitz, D., and Labruna, V. 1999. Child and adolescent abuse and neglect research: A review of the past 10 years. Part 1: Physical and emotional abuse and neglect. *Journal of the American Academy of Child & Adolescent Psychiatry, 38*, 1214–1222. **391**

Kaplan, S. J., Skolnik, L., Turnbull, A. 2009. Enhancing the empowerment of youth in foster care: supportive services. *Child Welfare, 88*, 133–162. **247**

Karney, B. R., and Bradbury, T. N. 2005. Contextual influences on marriage: Implications for policy and intervention. *Current Directions in Psychological Science, 14*, 171–174. **354**

Kasper, J. D., et al. 2008. Effects of poverty and family stress over three decades on the functional status of older African American women. *The Journals of Gerontology: Series B, 63B*, S201–211. **227**

Kasser, T. 2002. *The high price of materialism*. Cambridge, MA: MIT Press. **125**

Katz, L. F., Kling, J. R., and Liebman, J. B. 2001. Moving to opportunity in Boston: Early results of a randomized mobility experiment. *Quarterly Journal of Economics, 116*, 655–680. **130**

Kaufman, G., and Taniguchi, H. 2006. Gender and marital happiness in later life. *Journal of Family Issues, 27*, 735–757. **273**

Keating, N., and Dosman, D. 2009. Social capital and the care networks of frail seniors. *The Canadian Review of Sociology, 46*, 301–318. **438**

Keating, N., et al. 2003. Understanding the caring capacity and informal networks of frail seniors. *Ageing and Society, 23*, 115–127. **25**

Keijsers, L., et al. 2009. Developmental links of adolescent disclosure, parental solicitation, and control with delinquency: Moderation by parental support. *Developmental Psychology, 45*, 1314–1327. **290, 293, 295, 296**

Kelly, J. B., and Emery, R. E. 2003. Children's adjustment following divorce: Risk and resilience perspectives. *Family Relations, 52*, 352–362. **362, 366**

Kemp, C. 2004. Grand expectations: The experience of grandparents and adult grandchildren. *Canadian Journal of Sociology, 29*, 499–526. **307**

Kempe, C., et al. 1962. The battered child syndrome. *Journal of the American Medical Association, 181*, 17–24. **395**

Kennedy, T., et al. 2010. The clinical and adaptive features of young offenders with histories of child-parent violence. *Journal of Family Violence, 25*, 509–520. **407**

Kenney, C. T., and McLanahan, S. S. 2006. Why are cohabiting relationships more violent than marriages? *Demography, 43*, 127–140. **196**

Keown, L.-A. 2009. *2008 General Social Survey report. Social networks help Canadians deal with change*. Statistics Canada, Publication no. 11-008-X. **84**

Kerr, D. C. R., et al. 2009. A prospective three generational study of fathers' constructive parenting: Influences from family of origin, adolescent adjustment, and offspring temperament. *Developmental Psychology, 45*, 1257–1275. **293**

Kerr, D., and Michalski, J. H. 2007. Family structure and children's hyperactivity problems: A longitudinal analysis. *Canadian Journal of Sociology, 32*, 85–106. **366, 373, 374, 416**

Kerr, D., Moyser, M., and Beaujot, R. 2006. Marriage and cohabitation: Demographic and socioeconomic differences in Quebec and Canada. *Canadian Studies in Population, 33*, 83–117. **191**

Kerr, M., and Stattin, H. 2003. Parenting of adolescents: Action or reaction? In A. C. Crouter and A. Booth (Eds.), *Children's influence on family dynamics* (pp. 121–152). Mahwah, NJ: Erlbaum. **287, 293**

Kershaw, P., Irwin, L., and Hertzman, T. K. 2005. *The BC Atlas of Child Development*. Human Early Learning Partnership, Western Geographical Press. **50, 432**

Kessen, W. 1979. The American child and other cultural inventions. *American Psychologist, 34*, 815–820. **18**

Kett, J. F. 1977. *Rites of passage: Adolescence in America 1790 to present*. New York: Basic Books. **295**

Kiecolt, K. J. 2003. Satisfaction with work and family life: No evidence of a cultural reversal. *Journal of Marriage and Family, 65*, 23–35. **101**

Kiecolt-Glaser, J. K., and Newton, T. L. 2001. Marriage and health: His and hers. *Psychological Bulletin, 127*, 472–503. **266**

Kilmer, R. P., et al. 2008. Siblings of children with severe emotional disturbances: Risks, resources, and adaptation. *American Journal of Orthopsychiatry, 78*, 1–10. **325**

Kim, J. 2010. Neighborhood disadvantage and mental health: The role of neighborhood disorder and social relationships. *Social Science Research, 39*, 260–271. **126**

Kim, J. E., Hetherington, E. M., and Reiss, D. 1999. Associations among family relationships, antisocial peers, and adolescents' externalizing behaviors: Gender and family type differences. *Child Development, 70*, 1209–1230. **325**

Kim, J.-Y., et al. 2006. Longitudinal course and family correlates of sibling relationships from childhood through adolescence. *Child Development, 77*, 1746–1761. **321**

Kimball, M. M. 1986. Television and sex-role attitudes. In T. M. Williams (Ed.), *The impact of television* (pp. 265–301). New York: Academic Press. **85**

Kim-Cohen, J., et al. 2004. Genetic and environmental processes in young children's resilience and vulnerability to socioeconomic deprivation. *Child Development, 75*, 651–668. **117, 340**

Kimmel, M. S. 2000. *The gendered society*. New York: Oxford University Press. **327**

King, V. 2003a. The legacy of a grandparent's divorce: Consequences for ties between grandparents and grandchildren. *Journal of Marriage and Family, 65*, 170–183. **375**

King, V. 2003b. The influence of religion on fathers' relationships with their children. *Journal of Marriage and Family, 65*, 382–395. **177**

King, V. 2006. The antecedents and consequences of adolescents' relationships with stepfathers and nonresident fathers. *Journal of Marriage and Family, 68*, 910–928. **373**

King, V. 2007. When children have two mothers: Relationships with non-resident mothers, stepmothers, and fathers. *Journal of Marriage and Family, 69*, 1178–1193. **352**

King, V., and Elder, G. H., Jr. 1995. American children view their grandparents: Linked lives across three rural generations. *Journal of Marriage and Family, 57*, 165–178. **307**

King, V., and Scott, M. E. 2005. A comparison of cohabiting relationships among older and younger adults. *Journal of Marriage and Family, 67*, 271–285. **196**

King, V., et al. 2004. Relations with grandparents: Rural Midwest versus urban Southern California. *Journal of Family Issues, 24*, 1044–1069. **138**

Kingsley, C., and Mark, M. 2000. *Sacred lives: Canadian Aboriginal children & youth speak out about sexual exploitation: Save the Children Canada*. National Aboriginal Project. <http://dsp-psd.communication.gc.ca/Collection/RH34-12-2000E.pdf>. Retrieved January 21, 2010. **401**

Kirkorian, H., et al. 2009. The impact of background television on parent-child interaction. *Child Development, 80*, 1350–1359. **80**

Kirmayer, L. J., et al. 2007. *Suicide among Aboriginal People in Canada*. The Aboriginal Healing Foundation. <www.ahf.ca>. **49**

Kiselica, M. S., and Morrill-Richards, M. 2007. Sibling maltreatment: The forgotten abuse. *Journal of Counseling and Development, 85*, 148–160. **402**

Kitayama, S., and Cohen, D. 2007. *Handbook of cultural psychology*. New York: Guilford Press. **27, 336, 340, 421**

Klebanov, P. K., et al. 1998. The contribution of neighborhood and family income to developmental test scores over the first three years of life. *Child Development, 69*, 1420–1436. **130**

Kluwer, E. S. 2010. From partnership to parenthood: A review of marital change across the transition to parenthood. *Journal of Family Theory & Review, 2*, 105–125. **276**

Kluwer, E. S., Heesink, J. A. M., and van de Vliert, E. 1997. The marital dynamics of conflict over the division of labor. *Journal of Marriage and Family, 59,* 635–653. **269**

Knaak, S. 2005. Breast-feeding, bottle-feeding and Dr. Spock: The shifting context of choice. *Canadian Review of Sociology and Anthropology, 42,* 197–216. **21, 416**

Knighton, T., and Mirza, S. 2002. Postsecondary participation: The effects of parents' education and household income. *Education Quarterly Review, 8,* 25–32. **162, 163**

Knoester, C., Haynie, D. L., and Stephens, C. M. 2006. Parenting practices and adolescents' friendship networks. *Journal of Marriage and Family, 68,* 1247–1260. **299**

Kochenderfer, B. J., and Ladd, G. W. 1996. Peer victimization: Cause or consequence of school maladjustment? *Child Development, 67,* 1305–1317. **405**

Koenig, H. G., McCullough, M. E., and Larson, D. B. 2001. *Handbook of religion and health.* New York: Oxford University Press. **172**

Kohen, D., Hertzman, C., and Willms, J. D. 2002b. The importance of quality child care. In J. D. Willms (Ed.), *Vulnerable children* (pp. 261–276). Edmonton: University of Alberta Press. **154**

Kohen, D. E., et al. 2002a. Neighborhood income and physical and social disorder in Canada: Associations with young children's competencies. *Child Development, 73,* 1844–1860. **123, 129, 431**

Kohen, D. E., et al. 2008. Neighborhood disadvantage: Pathways of effects for young children. *Child Development, 79,*156–169. **132, 365**

Kohler Riessman, C. 2000. Stigma and every day resistance practices: Childless women in South India. *Gender and Society, 14,* 111–135. **60**

Kohler, H. P., Behrman, J. R., and Skytthe, A. 2005. Partner + children = happiness? The effects of partnerships and fertility on well-being. *Population and Development Review, 31,*407–443. **306**

Kohler, J. K., Grotevant, H. D., and McRoy, R. G. 2002. Adopted adolescents' preoccupation with adoption: The impact on adoptive family relationships. *Family Relations, 64,* 93–104. **245**

Koropeckyj-Cox, T. 2002. Beyond parental status: Psychological well-being in middle and old age. *Journal of Marriage and Family, 64,* 957–971. **233**

Kovan, N. M., Chung, A. L., and Sroufe, L. A. 2009. The intergenerational continuity of observed early parenting: A prospective, longitudinal study. *Developmental Psychology, 45,*1205–1213. **292**

Krakauer, I.D., and Rose, S. M. 2002. The impact of group membership on lesbians' physical appearance. *Journal of Lesbian Studies, 6,* 31–43. **189**

Kralovec, E., and Buehl, J. 2001. End homework now. *Educational Leadership, 58,* 39–42. **162**

Kramer, L., and Ramsburg, D. 2002. Advice given to parents on welcoming a second child: A critical review. *Family Relations, 51,* 2–14. **316**

Kremarik, F. 1999. Moving to be better off. *Canadian Social Trends, 55,* 19–21. **145**

Kremarik, F. 2000a. The other side of the fence. *Canadian Social Trends, 57,* 20–24. **124**

Kremarik, F. 2000b. A family affair: Children's participation in sports. *Canadian Social Trends, 58,* 20–24. **86**

Kremarik, F. 2002. A little place in the country: A profile of Canadians who own vacation property. *Canadian Social Trends, 65,* 12–14. **140**

Kremarik, F., and Williams, C. 2001. Mobile homes in Canada. *Canadian Social Trends, 62,* 14–17. **142**

Krienert, J. L, Walsh, J. A., Walsh, J. A., and Turner, M. 2009. Elderly in America: A descriptive study of elder abuse examining National Incident-Based Reporting System (NIBRS) data, 2000–2005. *Journal of Elder Abuse & Neglect, 21,* 325–345. **408**

Krull, C. 2003. Pronatalism, feminism and family policy in Quebec. In M. Lynn (Ed.), *Voices: Essays on Canadian families,* 2nd Ed. (pp. 245–265). Scarborough, ON: Thomson Nelson. **39, 52**

Krull, C. 2007. Families and the State: Family Policy in Canada. In D. Cheal (Ed.), *Canadian families today* (pp. 254–272).Toronto: Oxford University Press. **425, 426, 427**

Krull, C., and Trovato, F. 2003a. Collapse of the cradle: A comprehensive framework of fertility decline in Quebec: 1941–1991. *Canadian Studies in Population: Special Issue in Honor of Anatole Romaniuc, 40,* 193–220. **40, 232**

Krull, C., and Trovato, F. 2003b. Where have all the children gone? Quebec's fertility decline: 1941–1991. *Canadian Studies in Population, 30,* 193–220. **42**

Kumar, M. B., and Janz, T. 2010. An exploration of cultural activities of Métis in Canada. *Canadian Social Trends, 89.* **51**

Kupersmidt, J. B., et al. 1995. Childhood aggression and peer relations in the context of family and neighborhood factors. *Child Development, 66,* 360–375. **130, 397**

Kurdek, L. A. 1990. Divorce history and self-reported psychological distress in husbands and wives. *Journal of Marriage and Family, 52,* 701–708. **271**

Kurdek, L. A. 1994. Areas of conflict for gay, lesbian, and heterosexual couples: What couples argue about influences relationship satisfaction. *Journal of Marriage and Family, 56,* 923–934. **269, 274**

Kurdek, L. A. 2007. The allocation of household labor by partners in gay and lesbian couples. *Journal of Family Issues, 28,* 132–148.

Kurdek, L. A. 2008. Change in relationship quality for partners from lesbian, gay male, and heterosexual couples. *Journal of Family Psychology, 22, 701–711.* **274, 276**

Lachance-Grzela, M., and Bouchard, G. 2009. La cohabitation et le marriage, deux mondes à part? Un examen des caractéristiques démographiques, individuelles et relationnelles. *Canadian Journal of Behavioural Science, 41,* 37–44. **194**

Ladd, G. W., Birch, S. H. and Buhs, E. S. 1999. Children's social and scholastic lives in kindergarten: Related spheres of influence? *Child Development, 70,* 1373–1400. **157**

Lai, D. C., Paper, J., and Paper, L. C. 2005. The Chinese in Canada: Their unrecognized religion. In P. Bramadat and D. Seljah (Eds.), *Religion and ethnicity in Canada* (pp. 89–110). Toronto: Pearson. **173**

Laird, R. D., et al. 2003. Parents' monitoring-relevant knowledge and adolescents' delinquent behavior: Evidence of correlated developmental changes and reciprocal influences. *Child Development, 74,* 752–768. **287**

Lamb, K. A., Lee, G. R., and DeMaris, A. 2003. Union formation and depression: Selection and relationship effects. *Journal of Marriage and Family, 65,* 953–962. **196**

Lamborn, S. D., Dornbusch, S. M., and Steinberg, L. 1996. Ethnicity and community context as moderators of the relations between family decision making and adolescent readjustment. *Child Development, 67,* 283–301. **290, 340**

Lane, P., et al. 2002. *Mapping the healing journey: The final report of a First Nation research project on healing in Canadian Aboriginal communities.* Ottawa: Solicitor General of Canada, Aboriginal Corrections Policy Unit. **51, 388**

Laner, M. R., and Ventrone, N. A. 1998. Egalitarian daters/traditionalist dates. *Journal of Family Issues, 19*, 468–477. **185**

Langille, D. B., et al. 2003. Association of socio-economic factors with health risk behaviours among high school students in rural Nova Scotia. *Canadian Journal of Public Health, 94*, 442–448. **219**

Lansford, J. E., et al. 2001. Does family structure matter? A comparison of adoptive, two-parent biological, single-mother, stepfather, and stepmother households. *Journal of Marriage and Family, 63*, 840–851. **240**

Lansford, J. E., et al. 2009. Trajectories of physical discipline: Early childhood antecedents and developmental outcomes. *Child Development, 80*, 1385–1402. **286, 291, 292, 293, 294**

Laplante, B. 2006. The rise of cohabitation in Quebec: Power of religion and power over religion. *Canadian Journal of Sociology, 31*, 1–24. **191**

Laplante, B., Miller, C., and Malherbe, P. 2006. The evolution of beliefs and opinions on matters related to marriage and sexual behaviour among French-speaking Catholic Quebecers and English-speaking Protestant Ontarians. *Canadian Studies in Population, 33*, 209–239. **52, 191**

Lareau, A. 2003. *Unequal childhoods: Class, race, and family life.* Berkeley: University of California Press. **19, 20, 75, 161, 290, 422, 437**

Larkin, M. 2009. Life after caring: The post-caring experiences of former carers. *British Journal of Social Work, 39*, 1026–1042. **368, 438**

Laroche, D. 2007. *La violence conjugale envers les hommes et les femmes, au Québec et au Canada, 1999.* Québec: Gouvernement du Québec, Institut de la Statistique. **357, 384, 385, 386, 387**

LaRochelle-Côté, S., and Dionne, C. 2009. Family work patterns. *Perspectives on Labour and Income.* Statistics Canada, August. **102**

LaRossa, R. 2005. Grounded theory methods and qualitative family research. *Journal of Marriage and Family, 67*, 837–857. **29**

Larson, R. W., and Richards, M. H. 1994. *Divergent realities: The emotional lives of mothers, fathers, and adolescents.* New York: Basic Books. **101, 261, 295, 296, 265**

Larzelere, R. E., et al. 1998. Punishment enhances reasoning's effectiveness as a disciplinary response to toddlers. *Journal of Marriage and Family, 60*, 388–403. **287, 291**

Laszloffy, T. A. 2002. Rethinking family development theory: Teaching with the systemic family development (SFD) model. *Family Relations, 51*, 206–214. **16**

Laub, J. H., Nagin, D. S., and Sampson, R. J. 1998. Trajectories of change in criminal offending: Good marriages and the desistance process. *American Sociological Review, 63*, 225–238. **199, 219**

Laumann, E. O. 1996. Early sexual experiences: How voluntary? How violent? In M. D. Smith et al. (Eds.), *Sexuality and American social policy.* Menlo Park, CA: Henry J. Kaiser Family Foundation. **406**

Laumann, E. O., et al. 1994. *The social organization of sexuality: Sexual practices in the United States.* Chicago: University of Chicago Press. **208, 210, 211, 212**

Laumann-Billings, L., and Emery, R. E. 2000. Distress among young adults from divorced families. *Journal of Family Psychology, 14*, 671–687. **364**

Laurent, A. 1997. À propos des familles ou les parents sont battus par leur enfant. *Archives de Pédiatrie, 4*, 468–472. **407**

Laurent, A., and Derry, A. 1999. Violence of French adolescents towards their parents: Characteristics and contexts. *Journal of Adolescent Health, 25*, 21–26. **407**

Lavee, Y., and Katz, R. 2002. Division of labor, perceived fairness, and marital quality: The effect of gender ideology. *Journal of Marriage and Family, 64*, 27–39. **27**

Lavoie, Y. 1981. *L'émigration des Québécois aux États-Unis de 1830 à 1940.* Québec: Conseil de la langue française, direction des études et recherches. **42**

Lawrence, B. 2004. *"Real" Indians and others: Mixed-blood urban Native Peoples and Indigenous nationhood.* Vancouver: University of British Columbia Press. **48**

Lawrence, C. R., Carlson, E. A., and Egeland, B. 2006. The impact of foster care on development. *Development and Psychopathology, 18*, 57–76. **247**

Lawrence, E., et al. 2008. Marital satisfaction across the transition to parenthood. *Journal of Family Psychology, 22*, 41–50. **276**

Lawrence, R. 2007. *School Crime and Juvenile Justice,* 2nd Ed. New York: Oxford University Press. **166**

Le Bourdais, C., and Juby, H. 2002. The impact of cohabitation on the family life course in contemporary North America: Insights from across the border. In A. Booth and A. C. Crouter (Eds.), *Just living together* (pp. 107–118). Mahwah, NJ: Erlbaum. **193**

Le Bourdais, C., Lapierre-Adamcyk, E., and Pacaut, P. 2004. Changes in conjugal life in Canada: Is cohabitation progressively replacing marriage? *Journal of Marriage and Family, 66*, 929–942. **351**

Le Bourdais, C., et al. 2000. The changing face of conjugal relationship. *Canadian Social Trends, 56*, 14–17. **191**

Leathers, S. J. 2003. Parental visiting, conflicting allegiances, and emotional and behavioral problems among foster children. *Family Relations, 52*, 53–63. **245, 247**

Lebner, A. 2000. Genetic "mysteries" and international adoption: The cultural impact of biomedical technologies on the adoptive family experience. *Family Relations, 49*, 371–377. **239**

LeClere, F. B., and Kowalewski, B. M. 1994. Disability in the family: The effects on children's well-being. *Journal of Marriage and Family, 56*, 457–468. **325**

Lee, G. R., Peek, C. W., and Coward, R. T. 1998. Race differences in filial responsibility expectations among older parents. *Journal of Marriage and Family, 60*, 404–412. **196**

Lee, S. M., and Boyd, M. 2008. Marrying out: Comparing the marital and social integration of Asians in the US and Canada. *Social Science Research, 37*, 311–329. **187**

Lee, Y. 2009. Early motherhood and harsh parenting: The role of human, social, and cultural capital. *Child Abuse & Neglect, 33*, 625–637. **229**

Lefebvre, S. 2003. Housing: An income issue. *Canadian Social Trends, 68*, 15–18. **141**

Lemelin, J.-P., et al. 2007. The genetic-environmental etiology of cognitive school readiness and later academic achievement in early childhood. *Child Development, 78*, 1 855–1869. **23, 333, 337, 339**

Lenton, R. L. 1990. Techniques of child discipline and abuse by parents. *Canadian Review of Sociology and Anthropology, 27*, 157–185. **292**

Leon, I. G. 2002. Adoption losses: Naturally occurring or socially constructed? *Child Development, 73*, 652–663. **241, 242**

Leon, K. 2003. Risk and protective factors in young children's adjustment to parental divorce: A review of the research. *Family Relations,* 52, 258–270. **159**

Lerman, R. I. 2002. *Married and unmarried parenthood and economic well-being: A dynamic analysis of recent cohorts.* New York: The Urban Institute. **199**

Letourneau, N., et al. 2007. Longitudinal study of social-environmental predictors of behavior: Children of adolescent and older mothers compared. *Canadian Studies in Population, 34,* 1–27. **228**

Levan, M. B. 2001. *Creating a framework for the wisdom of the community: Victim services in Nunavut: Needs and recommendations.* Ottawa: Departement of Justice, Research and Statistics Division, Policy Centre for Victim Issues., RR03vic-3. **388**

Leve, L. D., et al. 2010a. Infant pathways to externalizing behavior: Evidence of genotype x environment interaction. *Child Development, 81,* 340–356. **285, 336**

Leve, L. D., et al. 2010b. The Early Growth and Development Study: Using the prospective adoption design to examine genotype-environment interplay, *Behaviour Genetics, 40,* 306–314. **289, 291, 336**

Levey, G. 2009. Lament for the iGeneration. *Toronto Life,* October, 33–38. **89**

Levin, I., and Trost, J. 1999. Living apart together. *Community, Work, and Family, 2,* 279–294. **78**

Levine, J. A., Pollack, H., and Comfort, M. E. 2001. Academic and behavioral outcomes among the children of young mothers. *Journal of Marriage and Family, 63,* 355–369. **18**

LeVine, R. A. 1990. Infant environments in psychoanalysis: A cross-cultural view. In J. W. Stigler, R. A. Shweder, and G. Herd (Eds.), *Cultural psychology: Essays on comparative human development* (pp. 454–476). New York: Cambridge University Press. **20**

Lewis, M. 1997. *Altering fate:Why the past does not predict the future.*New York: Guilford Press. **285**

Li, J.-C. A., and Wu, L. L. 2008. No trend in the intergenerational transmission of divorce. *Demography, 45,* 875–883. **355**

Lichter, D. T., and Carmalt, J. H. 2009. Religion and marital quality among low-income couples. *Social Science Research, 38,* 168–187. **176**

Lichter, D. T., and Qian, Z. 2008. Serial cohabitation and the marital life course. *Journal of Marriage and Family, 70,* 861–878. **196, 355, 356**

Liefbroer, A. C., and Dourlejn, E. 2006. Unmarried cohabitation and union stability: Testing the role of diffusion using data from 16 European countries. *Demography, 43,* 203–221. **355**

Lin, I.-F. 2008a. Consequences of parental divorce for adult children's support of their frail parents. *Journal of Marriage and Family, 70,* 113–128. **303**

Lin., I.-F. 2008b. Mother and daughter reports about upward transfers. *Journal of Marriage and Family, 70,* 815–827. **30**

Lincoln, C. E., and Mamiya, L. H. 1990. *The black church in the African American experience.* Durham, NC: Duke University Press. **174**

Lindsay, C. 2006. Women in Canada. Statistics Canada, *The Daily,* March 7. **96**

Lindsey, D., and Martin, S. K. 2003. Deepening child poverty: The not so good news about welfare reform. *Children and Youth Services Review, 25,* 165–173. **429**

Lindsey, E. W. 1998. The impact of homelessness and shelter-life on family relationships. *Family Relations, 47,* 243–252. **135**

Link, B. G., et al. 1987. The social rejection of former mental patients: Understanding why labels matter. *American Journal of Sociology, 92,* 1461–1500. **198**

Lipps, G., and Frank, J. 1997. The social context of school for young children. *Canadian Social Trends, 47,* 22–26. **163, 164**

Little, D. 2006. Consumer demand for entertainment services outside the home. Statistics Canada, *Services Industries Newsletter, 2,* June. **105**

Liu, H., and Umberson, D. J. 2008. The times they are 'a-changin': Marital status and health differentials from 1972 to 2003. *Journal of Health and Social Behavior, 49,* 239–253. **199**

Liu, M., et al. 2005. Autonomy- vs. connectedness-oriented parenting behaviours in Chinese and Canadian mothers. *International Journal of Behavioral Development, 29,* 489–495. **58**

Livingstone, S., and Bovill, M. 2001. *Children and their changing media environment: A European comparative study.* Mahwah, NJ: Erlbaum. **79**

Lockhead, C. 2000. The trend toward delayed first childbirth: Health and social implications. *ISUMA: Canadian Journal of Policy Research,* Autumn, 41–44. **230**

Logan, J. R., Alba, R., and Zhang, W. 2002. Immigrant enclaves and ethnic communities in New York and Los Angeles. *American Sociological Review, 67,* 299–322. **133**

Logan, J., and Smith, C. 2005. Face-to-face contact post adoption: Views from the triangles. *British Journal of Social Work, 35,* 3–35. **245**

Longmore, M. A., Manning, W. D., and Giordano, P. G. 2001. Preadolescent parenting strategies and teens' dating and sexual initiation: A longitudinal analysis. *Journal of Marriage and Family, 63,* 322–335. **184**

Longmore, M. A., et al. 2009. Parenting and adolescents' sexual initiation. *Journal of Marriage and Family, 71,* 969–982. **206**

Love, J., et al. 2005. The effectiveness of early Head Start for 3 year-old children and their parents: Lessons for policy and programs. *Developmental Psychology, 41,* 885–901. **157**

Lowe Vandell, P., et al. 2010. Do effects of early child care extend to age 15 years? Results from the NICHD study of early child care and youth development. *Child Development, 81,* 737–756. **155, 157**

Lowenstein, A., Katz, R., and Gur-Yaish, N. 2007. Reciprocity in parent-child exchange and life satisfaction among the elderly: A cross-national perspective. *Journal of Social Issues, 63,* 865–883. **305**

Lowry, D. T., and Towles, D. W. 1989. Soap opera portrayals of sex, contraception, and sexually transmitted diseases. *Journal of Communication, 39,* 76–83. **87**

Ludwig, J., Duncan, G., and Hirshfeld, P. 2001. Urban poverty and juvenile crime: Evidence from a randomized housing mobility experiment. *Quarterly Journal of Economics, 116,* 655–680. **130**

Luffman, J. 1998. When parents replace teachers: The home schooling option. *Canadian Social Trends, 50,* 8–10. **170**

Lukasiewicz, K. 2002. Ethnicity, politics and religion: Polish societies in Edmonton in the inter-war years. *Alberta History, 50,* 2–12. **47**

Lundquist, J. H., and Smith, H. L. 2005. Family formation among women in the U.S. military: Evidence from the NLSY. *Journal of Marriage and Family, 67,* 1–13. **78**

Luong, M. 2008. Study: Life after teenage motherhood. Statistics Canada, *The Daily,* May 23. **226, 227, 354**

Luong, M. 2010. Study: The financial impact of student loans. Statistics Canada, *Perspectives on Labour and Income 11,* January. **96, 301**

Luster, T., and Oh, S. M. 2001. Correlates of male adolescents carrying handguns among their peers. *Journal of Marriage and Family, 63,* 714–726. **127**

Luster, T., et al. 2000. Factors related to successful outcomes among preschool children born to low-income adolescent mothers. *Journal of Marriage and Family, 62,* 133–146. **339**

Luthar, S. S. 2003. The culture of affluence: Psychological costs of material wealth. *Child Development, 74,* 1581–1593. **125, 126**

Luthar, S. S., and Becker, B. E. 2002. Privileged but pressured: A study of affluent youth. *Child Development, 73,* 1593–1610. **125**

Lutz, W., O'Neill, B., and Scherbov, S. 2003. Europe's population at a turning point. *Science, 299,* 1991–1992. **420**

Luxton, M. 1997. Feminism and families: The challenge of neo-conservatism. In M. Luxton (Ed.), *Feminism and families* (pp. 10–26). Halifax: Fernwood. **24, 68**

Luxton, M. 2009. Conceptualizing families: Theoretical frameworks. In M. Baker (Ed.), *Families: Changing trends in Canada,* 6th Ed. (pp. 26–48). Toronto: McGraw-Hill Ryerson. **11, 23**

Luxton, M., and Corman, J. 2001. *Getting by in hard times: Gendered labour at home and on the job.* Toronto: University of Toronto Press. **21**

Lynch, S. K., et al. 2006. A genetically informed study of the association between harsh punishment and offspring behavioral problems. *Journal of Family Psychology, 20,* 190–198. **291, 292**

Lynn, M. M. 2003. Single-parent families. In M. Lynn (Ed.), *Voices: Essays on Canadian families,* 2nd Ed. (pp. 32–54). Toronto: Thomson Nelson. **64, 224**

Ma, L., Lerner, J., and Lerner, R. M. 2009. Academic competence for adolescents who bully and who are bullied. *Journal of Early Adolescence, 29,* 862–897. **405**

Ma, X., and Zhang, Y. 2002. *A national assessment of effects of school experiences on health outcomes and behaviours of children.* Technical Report. Ottawa: Health Canada. **159, 160**

Mac Con, K. 2006. The impact of family context on adolescent emotional health during the transition to high school. In K. McQuillan and Z. R. Ravanera (Eds), *Canada changing families. Implications for individuals and society* (pp. 160–178). Toronto: University of Toronto Press. **374, 416**

Maccoby, E. E., and Jacklin, C. N. 1983. The "person" characteristics of children and the family as environment. In D. D. Magnusson and V. L. Allen (Eds.), *Human development: An interactional perspective* (pp. 75–92). New York: Academic Press. **15**

Maccoby, E. E., and Lewis, C. C. 2003. Less day care or different daycare? *Child Development, 74,* 1069–1075. **155, 426**

Maccoby, E. E., and Martin, J. 1983. Socialization in the context of the family: Parent-child interaction. In E. M. Hetherington (Ed.), *Handbook of child psychology: vol. 4. Socialization, personality, and social development* (pp. 1–101). New York: Wiley. **288**

MacDermid, S. M., et al. 2004. *Child care use and satisfaction among military families with preschool children.* U.S. Military Family Research Institute, Purdue University. **78**

MacDonald, M. A. 1990. *Rebels and royalists: The lives and material culture of New Brunswick's early English-speaking settlers, 1758–1783.* Fredericton, NB: New Ireland Press. **41**

MacDonald, M., Phipps, S., and Lethbridge, L. 2005. Taking its toll: The influence of paid and unpaid work on women's well-being. *Feminist Economics, 11,* 63–94. **102**

Mackay, R., and Miles, L. 1995. A major challenge for the educational system: Aboriginal retention and dropout. In M. L. Battiste and J. Barman (Eds.), *First Nations education in Canada: The circle unfolds* (pp. 157–178). Vancouver: University of British Columbia Press. **168**

Mackenzie, C. S., et al. 2009. Associations between psychological distress, learning, and memory in spouse caregivers of older adults. *The Journals of Gerontology:* Series B, 64B, 742–750. **274**

MacKinnon, C. 2005. *Women's lives, men's laws.* Cambridge, MA: Harvard University Press. **25**

MacKinnon, C. 2006. *Are women human? And other international dialogues.* Cambridge, MA: Harvard University Press. **25**

MacMillan, H. L., et al. 1997. Prevalence of child physical and sexual abuse in the community: Results from the Ontario Health Supplement. *Journal of the American Medical Association Abstracts,* 9 July 9. **391**

MacMillan, H. L., et al. 2001. Childhood abuse and lifetime psychopathology in a community sample. *American Journal of Psychiatry, 158,* 1878–1883. **393**

Macmillan, R., and Copher, R. 2005. Families in the life course: Interdependency or roles, role configurations, and pathways. *Journal of Marriage and Family, 67,* 858–879. **16**

MacQueen, K. 2009. What Canadians really believe. *Maclean's,* November 30, 46–50. **7, 212**

MacTavish, K. 2007. The wrong side of the tracks: Social inequality and mobile home park residence. *Community Development, 38,* 74–91. **142**

Madden-Derdich, D. A., and Leonard, S. A. 2000. Parental role identity and fathers' involvement in coparental interaction after divorce: Fathers' perspectives. *Family Relations, 49,* 311–318. **22**

Madhavan, S. 2002. Best of friends and worst of enemies: Competition and collaboration in polygamy. *Ethnology, 41,* 69–84. **10**

Magdol, L., et al. 1998. Hitting without a license: Testing explanations for differences in partner abuse between young adults daters and cohabitors. *Journal of Marriage and Family, 60,* 41–55. **387**

Magee, K. 2008. "They are the life of the nation": Women and war in traditional Nadouek society. *The Canadian Journal of Native Studies, 28,* 185–199. **37**

Magnusson, D. 1995. Individual development: A holistic, integrated model. In P. Moen, G. H. Elder, Jr., and K. Lüscher (Eds.), *Examining lives in context* (pp. 19–60). Washington, DC: American Psychological Association. **15**

Mahoney, J. L., Lord, H., and Carryl, E. 2005. An ecological analysis of after-school program participation and the development of academic performance and motivational attributes for disadvantaged children. *Child Development, 76,* 811–825. **433**

Mallett, S., Rosenthal, D., and Keys, D. 2005. Young people, drug use, and family conflict: Pathways into homelessness. *Journal of Adolescence, 28,* 185–199. **134**

Mallon, G. P. 2005. *Gay men choosing parenthood.* New York: Columbia University Press. **248**

Malszecki, G., and Cavar, T. 2004. Men, masculinities, war & sport. In N. Mandell (Ed.), *Feminist issues: Race, class, and gender,* 4th Ed. (pp. 160–187). Toronto: Prentice Hall. **83, 86**

Man, G. 2001. From Hong Kong to Canada: Immigration and the changing family lives of middle-class women from Hong Kong. In B. Fox (Ed.), *Family patterns, gender relations,* 2nd Ed. (pp. 420–438). Toronto: Oxford University Press. **57, 58**

Mandelbaum, D. J. 1979. *The Plains Cree: An ethnographical, historical and comparative study.* Regina: Canadian Plains Research Centre. **36**

Mandell, N., and Sweet, R. 2004. Homework as home work: Mothers' unpaid educational labour. *Atlantis, 28.2,* 7–18. **69, 160, 163**

Manganello, J. A., and Taylor, C. A. 2009. Television exposure as a risk factor for aggressive behavior among 3-year-old children. *Archives of Pediatrics & Adolescent Medicine, 11,* 1037–1045. **85**

Manlove, J., et al. 2002. *Preventing teenage pregnancy, childbearing, and sexually transmitted diseases: What the research shows.* Washington, DC: Child Trends Research Brief. May. **159, 206**

Manlove, J., et al. 2008a. Factors associated with multiple-partner fertility among fathers. *Journal of Marriage and Family, 70,* 536–548. **110, 227**

Manlove, J., et al. 2008b. Pathways from family religiosity to adolescent sexual activity and contraceptive use. *Perspectives on Reproductive Health, 40,* 105–117. **175**

Mannheim, K. 1936. *Ideology and Utopia.* London: Routledge & Kegan Paul. **18**

Manning, M., and Baruth, L. 2000. *Multicultural education of children and adolescents.* Toronto: Allyn & Bacon. **165**

Manning, W. D. 2002. The implications of cohabitation for children's well-being. In A. Booth and A. C. Crouter (Eds.), *Just living together* (pp. 121–152). Mahwah, NJ: Erlbaum. **220**

Manning, W. D., and Lamb, K. A. 2003. Adolescent well-being in cohabiting, married, and single-parent families. *Journal of Marriage and Family, 65,* 876–893. **220, 221**

Manning, W. D., and Smock, P. J. 2000. "Swapping" families: Serial parenting and economic support for children. *Journal of Marriage and Family, 62,* 111–122. **352**

Manning, W. D., Stewart, S. D., and Smock, P. J. 2004. The complexity of father's parenting responsibilities and involvement with nonresidential children. *Journal of Family Issues, 24,* 645–667. **352**

March, K. 1995a. Perception of adoption as social stigma: Motivation for search and reunion. *Journal of Marriage and Family, 57,* 653–660. **241, 245**

March, K. 1995b. *The stranger who bore me.* Toronto: University of Toronto Press. **245**

Marcil-Gratton, N. 1998. *Growing up with mom and dad? The intricate life course of Canadian children.* Ottawa: Statistics Canada, Catalogue no. 89–566. **220**

Marcil-Gratton, N. 1999. Growing up with mom and dad? Canadian children experience shifting family structures. *Transition, 29,* September, 4–7. **352**

Marcil-Gratton, N., et al. 2003. Du passé conjugal des parents au devenir familial des enfants: Un example de la nécessité d'une approche longitudinale. *Sociologie et sociétés, 35,* 143–164. **354, 355, 372, 374**

Marcussen, K. 2005. Explaining difference in mental health between married and cohabiting individuals. *Social Psychological Quarterly, 68,* 239–257. **193**

Margolin, G. 1998. Effects of domestic violence on children. In P. K. Trickett and C. J. Schellenback (Eds.), *Violence against children in the family and the community* (pp. 57–101). Washington, DC: American Psychological Association. **393**

Marin, B. V. O., et al. 2006. Boyfriends, girlfriends and teenagers' risk of sexual involvement. *Perspectives on Sexual and Reproductive Health, 38,* 76–83. **207**

Markman, H. J., et al. 2010. The premarital communication roots of marital distress and divorce: The first five years of marriage. *Journal of Family Psychology, 24,* 289–298. **359**

Marks, G. N. 2006. Family size, family type and student achievement: Cross-national differences and the role of socioeconomic and school factors. *Journal of Comparative Family Studies, 37,* 18–24. **155, 318, 375**

Marks, L. 2004. Feminism and stay-at-home motherhood: Some critical reflections and implications for mothers on social assistance. *Atlantis, 28.2,* 73–83. **25, 99**

Marks, S. R. 2000. Teasing out the lessons of the 1960s: Family diversity and family privilege. *Journal of Marriage and Family, 62,* 609–622. **124**

Marquis, R. A., et al. 2008. The relationship of child neglect and physical maltreatment to placement outcomes and behavioral adjustment in children in foster care: A Canadian perspective. *Child Welfare, 87,* 5–26. **247, 396**

Marshall, K. 2006. General Social Survey: Paid and unpaid work. Statistics Canada, *Perspectives on Labour and Income, 7,* July. **100, 425**

Marshall, K. 2007. The busy lives of teens. Statistics Canada, *Perspectives on Labour and Income,* 8.

Marsiglio, W. 2004. When stepfathers claim stepchildren: A conceptual analysis. *Journal of Marriage and Family, 66,* 22–39. **243**

Martel, L., and Bélanger, A. 2000. Dependence-free life expectancy in Canada. *Canadian Social Trends, 58,* 26–29. **310**

Martikainen, P., et al. 2005. Differences in mortality by marital status in Finland from 1976 to 2000. *Population Studies, 59,* 99–115. **199**

Martin, A., Brooks-Gunn, J., and Ryan, R. M. 2010. When fathers' supportiveness matters most: Maternal and paternal parenting and children's school readiness. *Journal of Family Psychology, 24,* 145–155. **160**

Martin, G. 1974. British officials and their attitudes to the Negro community in Canada, 1833–1861. *Ontario History, 66,* 79–88. **44**

Martin, G. J., Jr. 1997. An agenda for family policy in the United States. In T. Arendell (Ed.), *Contemporary parenting: Challenges and issues* (pp. 298–324). Thousand Oaks, CA: Sage. **73**

Martin, S. P. 2000. Diverging fertility among U.S. women who delay childbearing past age 30. *Demography, 37,* 523–533. **230**

Martin, T. C. 2002. Consensual unions in Latin America: Persistence of a dual nuptiality system. *Journal of Comparative Family Studies, 33,* 35–55. **191**

Martin, V., Mills, M., and Le Bourdais, C. 2005. The consequences of parental divorce on the life course outcomes of Canadian children. *Canadian Studies in Population, 32,* 29–51. **362**

Martinez-Torteya, C., et al. 2009. Resilience among children exposed to domestic violence: The role of risk and protective factors. *Child Development, 80,* 562–577. **389**

Martin-Matthews, A. 1991. *Widowhood in later life.* Toronto: Butterworths/Harcourt. **368**

Martin-Matthews, A. 2000. Change and diversity in aging families and intergenerational relations. In N. Mandell and A. Duffy (Eds.), *Canadian families: Diversity, conflict, and change* (pp. 323–360). Toronto: Harcourt Canada. **17, 302**

Martin-Matthews, A. 2001. *The ties that bind aging families.* Ottawa: The Vanier Institute of the Family. **305, 306**

Martin-Matthews, A. 2007. Situating "home" at the nexus of the public and private spheres. *Current Sociology, 55,* 229–249. **25**

Mashburn, A. J., et al. 2008. Measures of classroom quality in prekindergarten and children's development of academic, language, and social skills. *Child Development, 79,* 732–749. **154**

Mason, M. A. 1998. The modern American stepfamily: Problems and possibilities. In M. A. Mason, A. Skolnick, and S. D. Sugarman (Eds.), *All our families: New policies for a new century* (pp. 95–116). New York: Oxford University Press. **243**

Masten, C. L., Juvonen, J., and Spatzier, A. 2009. Relative importance of peers. Differences in academic and social behaviors at three grade levels spanning late childhood and early adolescence. *Journal of Early Adolescence, 29,* 773–799. **298**

Mather, M., and Rivers, K. L. 2006. *The concentration of negative child outcomes in low-income U.S. neighbourhoods.* Population Reference Bureau. <www.prb.org>. **130**

Maxim, P. S., White, J. P., and Gyimah, S. O. 2003. Earnings implications of person years lost life expectancy among Canada's Aboriginal peoples. *Canadian Studies in Population, 30,* 271–295. **126**

Mayberry, M., et al. 1995. *Home-schooling: Parents as educators.* Thousand Oaks, CA: Corwin. **170**

Mayer, L. 2008. Aboriginal women and education: Overcoming a legacy of abuse. *The Canadian Journal of Native Studies, 27,* 35–48. **35**

Mayfield, M. 2001. *Early childhood education and care in Canada.* Toronto: Prentice Hall. **156**

McCabe, K. M., et al. 2005. The relation between violence exposure and conduct problems among adolescents: A prospective study. *American Journal of Orthopsychiatry, 75,* 575–584. **126**

McCarthy, E. D. 1996. *Knowledge as culture: The new sociology of knowledge.* London: Routledge. **18**

McCartney, K. 2003. On the meaning of models: A signal amidst the noise. In A. C. Crouter and A. Booth (Eds.), *Children's influence on family dynamics* (pp. 27–30). Mahwah, NJ: Erlbaum. **334**

McCartney, K., et al. 1997. Social development in the context of typical center-based child care. *Merrill-Palmer Quarterly, 43,* 426–450. **154**

McCartney, K., et al. 2010. Testing a series of causal propositions relating time in child care to children's externalizing behavior. *Developmental Psychology, 46,*1–17. **154, 155**

McCauley, J., et al. 1997. Clinical characteristics of women with a history of childhood abuse. *Journal of the American Medical Association, 277,* 162–1368. **394**

McClare, D. (Ed.) 1997. *The 1815 diary of a Nova Scotia farm girl, Louisa Collins of Colin Grove, Dartmouth.* Dartmouth, NS: Brook House Press. **41**

McClintock, E. A. 2010. When does race matter? Race, sex, and dating at an elite university. *Journal of Marriage and Family, 72,* 45–72. **187**

McCloskey, L. A., Figueredo, A. J., and Koss, M. P. 1995. The effects of systemic family violence on children's mental health. *Child Development, 66,* 1239–1261. **399**

McCurdy, K., and Daro, D. 1994. Child maltreatment: A national survey of reports and fatalities. *Journal of Interpersonal Violence, 9,* 75–94. **396**

McDaniel, S. A. 2002. Women's changing relations to the state and citizenship: Caring and intergenerational relations in globalizing Western democracies. *Canadian Review of Sociology and Anthropology, 39,* 1–26. **16**

McDaniel, S. A. 2003. Family/work challenges among mid-life and older Canadians. In M. Lynn (Ed.), *Voices: Essays on Canadian families,* 2nd. Ed. (pp. 152–176). Toronto: Thomson Nelson. **17**

McDaniel, S. A. 2009. The family lives of the middle-aged and elderly in Canada. In M. Baker (Ed.), *Families: Changing trends in Canada,* 6th Ed. (pp. 225–242). Toronto: McGraw-Hill Ryerson. **25, 265, 273, 305, 306**

McDonald, K. B., and Armstrong, E. M. 2001. De-romanticizing Black intergenerational support: The questionable expectations of welfare reform. *Journal of Marriage and Family, 63,* 213–223. **111, 130**

McDonald, R., et al. 2009. Children's adjustment problems in families characterized by men's severe violence toward women: Does other family violence matter? *Child Abuse & Neglect, 33,* 94–101. **389, 393**

McDonough, S., and Hoodfar, H. 2005. Muslims in Canada: From ethnic groups to religious community. In P. Bramadat and D. Seljak (Eds.), *Religion and ethnicity in Canada* (pp. 133–153). Toronto: Pearson. **173**

McGillivray, A., and Comaskey, B. 1999. *Black eyes all the time: Intimate violence, aboriginal women, and the justice system.* Toronto: University of Toronto Press. **389**

McHale, S. M., and Crouter, A. C. 1996. The family contexts of children's sibling relationships. In G. H. Brody (Ed.), *Sibling relationships: Their causes and consequences* (pp. 173–196). Norwood, NJ: Ablex. **322**

McHale, S., et al. 1995. Congruence between mothers' and fathers' differential treatment of siblings: Links with family relations and children's well-being. *Child Development, 66,* 116–128. **329**

McIlvane, J. M., Ajrouch, K. J., and Antonucci, T. C. 2007. Generational structure and social resources in mid-life: Influences on health and well-being. *Journal of Social Issues, 63,* 759–773. **303**

McIntosh, C. N., et al. 2009. Income disparities in health-adjusted life expectancy for Canadian adults, 1991 to 2001. Statistics Canada, *Health Reports, 20,* November. **113**

McIntosh, R. 2003. The boys in Nova Scotian coal mines: 1873–1923. In N. Janovicek and J. Parr (Eds.), *Histories of Canadian children and youth* (pp. 77–87). Toronto: Oxford University Press. **45**

McIntyre, L., et al. 2002. Food insecurity of low-income lone mothers and their children in Atlantic Canada. *Canadian Journal of Public Health, 93,* 411–416. **117**

McKay, A. 2005. Sexuality and substance use: The impact of tobacco, alcohol, and selected recreational drugs on sexual function. *The Canadian Journal of Human Sexuality, 14,* 47–57. **206**

McKay, A., and Barrett, M. 2010. Trends in teen pregnancy rates from 1996–2006: A comparison of Canada, Sweden, U. S. A., and England/Wales. *The Canadian Journal of Human Sexuality, 19,* 43–52. **225, 234, 421**

McLeod, N. 2000. Plains Cree identity: Borderlands, ambiguous genealogies and narrative irony. *Canadian Journal of Native Studies, 20,* 437–454. **36**

McLoyd, V. C. 1995. Poverty, parenting, and policy: Meeting the support needs of poor parents. In H. E. Fitzgerald, B. M. Lester, and B. Zuckerman (Eds.), *Children of poverty* (pp. 269–298). New York: Garland. **392, 393**

McLoyd, V. C. 1998. Socioeconomic disadvantage and child development. *American Psychologist, 53,* 185–204. **117, 219**

McLoyd, V. C., and Smith, J. 2002. Physical discipline and behavior problems in African American, European American, and Hispanic children: Emotional support as a moderator. *Journal of Marriage and Family, 64,* 40–53. **291**

McManus, P. A., and DiPrete, T. A. 2001. Losers and winners: The financial consequences of separation and divorce for men. *American Sociological Review, 66,* 246–268. **421**

McManus, S. 1999. Their own country: Race, gender, landscape, and colonization around the 49th parallel, 1862–1900. *Agricultural History, 73,* 168–182. **47**

McNeal, C., and Amato, P. R. 1998. Parents' marital violence: Long-term consequences for children. *Journal of Family Issues, 19,* 123–139. **389**

McNeil, J. 1975. Feminism, femininity and the television shows: A content analysis. *Journal of Broadcasting, 19,* 259–269. **82**

McNulty, J. K. 2008. Forgiveness and marriage: Putting the benefits into context. *Journal of Family Psychology, 22,* 171–175. **270**

McNulty, J. K., Neff, L. A., and Karney, B. R. 2008. Beyond initial attraction: Physical attractiveness in newlywed marriage. *Journal of Family Psychology, 22,* 135–143. **189**

McPherson, B. D. 1998. *Aging as a social process,* 3rd Ed. Toronto: Harcourt Brace. **50, 307**

McPherson, C. J., Wilson, K. G., and Murray, M. A. 2007. Feeling like a burden: Exploring the perspectives of patients at the end of life. *Social Science and Medicine, 64,* 417–427. **305**

McQuillan, J., et al. 2003. Frustrated fertility: Infertility and psychological distress among women. *Journal of Marriage and Family, 65,* 1007–1018. **233**

McQuillan, K. 2006. Conclusion: Family change and the challenge for social policy. In K. McQuillan and Z. R. Ravanera (Eds.), *Canada's changing families. Implications for individuals and society* (pp. 293–306). Toronto: University of Toronto Press. **420**

McRoy, G. R., Grotevant, H. D., and White, K. L. 1998. *Openness in adoption: New practices, new issues.* New York: Praeger. **245**

McWey, L. M., and Mullis, A. K. 2004. Improving the lives of children in foster care: The impact of supervised visitation. *Family Relations, 53,* 293–300. **247**

McWhinnie, A. 2001. Should offspring from donated gametes continue to be denied knowledge of their origins and antecedents? *Human Reproduction, 16,* 807–817. **235, 236**

Mead, G. H. 1934. *Mind, self and society.* Chicago: University of Chicago Press. **14, 15**

Mead, M. 1928. *Coming of age in Samoa.* New York: William Morrow. **295**

Meaney, M. J. 2010. Epigenetics and the biological definition of gene x environment interactions. *Child Development, 81,* 41–79. **23**

Meier, A. M. 2007. Adolescent first sex and subsequent mental health. *American Journal of Sociology, 112,* 1811–1847. **206**

Meier, A., Hull, K. E., and Ortyl, T. A. 2009. Young adult relationship values and the intersection of gender and sexuality. *Journal of Marriage and Family, 71,* 510–525. **189, 209**

Meijer, A. M., and van den Wittenboer, G. L. H. 2007. Contribution of infants' sleep and crying to marital relationship of first-time parent couples in the 1st year after childbirth. *Journal of Family Psychology, 21,* 49–57. **276**

Meilleur, N., and Lapierre-Adamcyk, E. 2006. Single parenthood and labour force participation: The effect of social policies. In K.

McQuillan and Z. R. Ravanera (Eds.), *Canada's changing families. Implications for individuals and society* (pp. 210–236). Toronto: University of Toronto Press. **425, 429**

Mejer, L., and Robert-Bobée, I. 2003. *Mortalité des femmes et environnement familial.* Paris: INSEE, April. **140**

Melzer, S. A. 2002. Gender, work, and intimate violence: Men's occupational violence spillover and compensatory violence. *Journal of Marriage and Family, 64,* 820–832. **385**

Menaghan, E. G., and Parcel, T. L. 1995. Social sources of change in children's home environments: The effects of parental occupational experiences and family conditions. *Journal of Marriage and Family, 57,* 69–84. **111**

Mendle, J., et al. 2009. Associations between father absence and age of first sexual intercourse. *Child Development, 80,* 1463–1480. **206, 229**

Menon, M., et al. 2007. The developmental costs of high self-esteem for antisocial children. *Child Development, 78,* 1627–1639. **19**

Merton, R. K. 1968. *Social theory and social structure.* New York: Free Press. **10**

Messner, M. 1997. *The politics of masculinity: Men in movements.* Thousand Oaks, CA: Sage. **24**

Metz, M. E., Rosser, B. R. S., and Strapko, N. 1994. Differences in conflict-resolution styles among heterosexual, gay, and lesbian couples. *Journal of Sex Research, 31,* 293–308. **269**

Metzger, J. 2008. Resiliency in children and youth in kinship care and family foster care. *Child Welfare, 87,* 115–121. **247**

Miall, C. E., and March, K. 2005. Open adoption as a family form: Community assessment and social support. *Journal of Family Issues, 26,* 380–410. **239**

Michelson, W., and Tepperman, L. 2003. Focus on home: What time-use data can tell you about caregiving to adults. *Journal of Social Issues, 59,* 591–610. **306**

Middelburg, M. J., et al. 2008. Neuromotor, cognitive, language, and behavioural outcome in children born following IVF or ICSI—a systematic review. *Human Reproduction Update, 14,* 219–231. **237**

Migliaccio, T. A. 2002. Abused husbands: A narrative analysis. *Journal of Family Issues, 23,* 26–52. **386**

Milan, A. 2000. One hundred years of families. *Canadian Social Trends, 56,* 2–12. **193, 211, 231, 232**

Milan, A. 2003. Would you live common-law? *Canadian Social Trends, 70,* 2–6. **191, 192**

Milan, A., and Hamm, B. 2003. Across the generations: Grandparents and grandchildren. *Canadian Social Trends, 71,* 2–7. **6, 18, 309**

Milan, A., and Hamm, B. 2004. Mixed unions. *Canadian Social Trends, 73,* 2–6. **133**

Milan, A., and Peters, A. 2003. Couples living apart. *Canadian Social Trends, 69,* 2–6. **78, 192**

Milan, A., and Tran, K. 2004. Blacks in Canada: A long history. *Canadian Social Trends, 72,* 2–7. **224**

Milan, A., Maheux, H., and Chui, T. 2010. A portrait of couples in mixed unions. *Canadian Social Trends,* 80. **187, 189**

Milan, A., Vézina, M., and Wells, C. 2009. *2006 Census: Family portrait: Continuity and change in Canadian families and households in 2006.* Statistics Canada, Demography Division, November 30. **308**

Milburn, N. G., et al. 2005. Predictors of close family relationships over one year among homeless young people. *Journal of Adolescence, 28,* 263–275. **134**

Miles-Doan, R. 1998. Violence between spouses and intimates: Does neighborhood context matter? *Social Forces, 77,* 623–645. **387**

Miller, B. C., et al. 2000. Comparisons of adopted and nonadopted adolescents in a large nationally representative sample. *Child Development, 71,* 1458–1473. **240, 241, 242**

Miller, B. D. 2005. *Cultural anthropology,* 3rd Ed. Boston: Pearson. **7, 19, 239**

Miller, F., Jenkins, J., and Keating, D. 2002. Parenting and children's behaviour problems. In J. D. Willms (Ed.), *Vulnerable children* (pp. 167–182). Edmonton: University of Alberta Press. **393**

Miller, K. S., Forehand, R., and Kotchick, B. A. 1999. Adolescent sexual behavior in two ethnic minority samples: The role of family variables. *Journal of Marriage and Family, 61,* 85–98. **204, 287**

Miller, L. C. 2005. International adoption, behavior, and mental health. *Journal of the American Medical Association, 293,* 2533–2536. **240**

Miller, P. J. E., Caughlin, J. P., and Huston, T. L. 2003. Trait expressiveness and marital satisfaction: The role idealization processes. *Journal of Marriage and Family, 65,* 978–995. **268**

Miner, S., and Uhlenberg, P. 1997. Intragenerational proximity and the social role of sibling neighbors after midlife. *Family Relations, 46,* 145–153. **330**

Minze, L. C., et al. 2010. Making sense of family conflict: Intimate partner violence and preschoolers' externalizing problems. *Journal of Family Psychology, 24,* 5–11. **388**

Mirrlees-Black, C., Mayhew, P., and Percy, A. 1996. *The 1996 British Crime Survey: England and Wales.* London: Home Office Statistical Bulletin, no. 19–96. **408**

Mitchell, B. A. 2000. The refilled "nest": Debunking the myth of families in crisis. In E. M. Gee and G. M. Guttman (Eds.), *The overselling of population aging* (pp. 80–99). Toronto: Oxford University Press. **300**

Mitchell, B. A. 2003. Would I share a home with an elderly parent? Exploring ethnocultural diversity and intergenerational support relations during young adulthood. *Canadian Journal on Aging, 22,* 69–82. **6**

Mitchell, B. A. 2004. Home, but not alone: Socio-cultural and economic aspects of Canadian young adults sharing parental households. *Atlantis, 28,* 2, 115–125. **70, 301, 302**

Mitchell, B. A., and Gee, E. M. 1996. Young adults returning home. Implications for social policy. In B. Galaway and J. Hudson (Eds.), *Youth in transition: Perspectives on research and policy* (pp. 61–71). Toronto: Thompson. **301**

Mitchell, K. 2003. Parental leave: More time off for baby. *Canadian Social Trends, 71,* 13–18. **427**

Mitchell, K. J., Finkelhor D., and Wolak, J. 2001. Risk factors for and impact of online sexual solicitation on youth. *Journal of the American Medical Association, 285,* June 20, 3011–3014. **87**

Mitnick, D. M., Heyman, R. E., and Smith Slep, A. M. 2009. Changes in relationship satisfaction across the transition to parenthood: A meta-analysis. *Journal of Family Psychology, 23,* 848–852. **268, 276**

Modell, J., and Goodman, M. 1990. Historical perspectives. In S. S. Feldman and G. R. Elliott (Eds.), *At the threshold: The developing adolescent* (pp. 93–122). Cambridge, MA: Harvard University Press. **295**

Mody, P. 2002. Love and the law: Love-marriage in Delhi. *Modern Asian Studies, 36,* 223–256. **59**

Moen, P., and Roehling, P. 2005. *The career mystique.* New York: Rowman & Littlefield. **95, 98, 100, 102**

Moffitt, T. E., et al. 2002. Males on the life-course-persistent and adolescence-limited antisocial pathways: Follow-up at age 26. *Development and Psychopathology, 14,* 179–206. **227**

Moghissi, H., Rahnema, S., and Goodman, M. J. 2009. *Diaspora by design.* Toronto: University of Toronto Press. **61, 64**

Mohammed, P. 2002. (Ed.). *Gendered realities. Essays in Caribbean feminist thought.* Barbados: University of the West Indies Press. **24**

Möhler, E., et al. 2009. Mothers with a history of abuse tend to show more impulsiveness. *Child Abuse & Neglect, 33,*123–126. **394**

Mollanen, K. L., et al. 2009. Growth and predictors of parental knowledge of youth behavior during early adolescence. *Journal of Early Adolescence, 29,* 800–825. **294, 299, 328**

Mollborn, S., and Morningstar, E. 2009. Investigating the relationship between teenage childbearing and psychological distress using longitudinal evidence. *Journal of Health and Social Behavior, 50,* 310–326. **227**

Monsebraaten, L. 2009. Native children flooding into aid societies. *Toronto Star.* November 22, A1, A14. **49**

Monserud, M. A. 2008. Intergenerational relationships and affectual solidarity between grandparents and young adults. *Journal of Marriage and Family, 70,* 182–195. **307**

Moore, K. A., Nord, C. W., and Peterson, J. L. 1989. Nonvoluntary sexual activity among adolescents. *Family Planning Perspectives, 21,* 110–114. **406**

Moore, M. R., and Chase-Lansdale, P. L. 2001. Sexual intercourse and pregnancy among African American girls in high-poverty neighborhoods: The role of family and perceived community environment. *Journal of Marriage and Family, 63,* 1146–1157. **131**

Moreno, M. A., et al. 2009. Display of health risk behaviors on MySpace by adolescents. *Archives of Pediatrics & Adolescent Medicine, 163,* 27–34. **89**

Morgan, S. P., Zhigand, G., and Hayford, S. R. 2009. China's below-replacement fertility: Recent trends and future prospects. *Population and Development Review, 35,* 605–629. **57**

Morris, J. F., Balsam, K. F., and Rothblum, E. D. 2001. Lesbian and bisexual mothers and nonmothers: Demographics and the coming-out process. *Journal of Family Psychology, 16,* 144–156. **208, 223**

Morris, M. 2004. What research reveals about gender, home care, and caregiving: Overview and the case for gender analysis. In K. R. Grant et al. (Eds.), *Caring for/caring about* (pp. 91–114). Aurora, On: Garamond Press. **136**

Morissette, R. 2002. On the edge: Financially vulnerable families. *Canadian Social Trends, 67,* 13–17. **106, 112**

Morissette, R., and Hou, F. 2008. Does the labour supply of wives respond to husbands' wages? Canadian evidence from micro data and grouped data. *Canadian Journal of Economics, 41,* 1185–1210. **98**

Morissette, R., and Zhang, X. 2001. Experiencing low income for several years. *Perspectives on Labour and Income, 2,* March, 5–15. **110, 112**

Morisette, R., and Zhang, X. 2006. Revisiting wealth inequality. *Perspectives on Labour and Income, 7,* December. **96**

Morissey, T. W. 2009. Multiple child-care arrangements and young children's behavioral outcomes. *Child Development, 80,* 59–76. **154**

Morrison, D. R., and Cherlin, A. J. 1995. The divorce process and young children's well-being: A prospective analysis. *Journal of Marriage and Family, 57,* 800–812. **367**

Morrison, D. R., and Ritualo, A. 2000. Routes to children's economic recovery after divorce: Are cohabitation and remarriage equivalent? *American Sociological Review, 65,* 560–580. **220**

Morrison, N. C., and Clavenna-Valleroy, J. 1998. Perceptions of maternal support as related to self-concept and self-report of depression in sexually abused female adolescents. *Journal of Child Sexual Abuse, 7,* 23–40. **399, 400**

Moscovitch, A. 2007. *Good servant, bad master? Electronic media and the family.* Ottawa: The Vanier Institute of the Family. **69, 79, 86**

Moss, K. 2004. Kids witnessing family violence. *Canadian Social Trends, 73,* 12–16. **118, 388**

Moss, M. H. 1998. *Manliness and militarism: Educating young men for war in the province of Ontario.* Ed. D. dissertation, University of Toronto. **45**

Mounts, N. S. 2001. Young adolescents' perceptions of parental management of peer relations. *Journal of Early Adolescence, 21,* 92–122. **287**

Moyers, S., Farmer, E., and Lipscombe, J. 2006. Contact with family members and its impact on adolescents and their foster placements. *British Journal of Social Work, 36,* 541–559. **247**

Moylan, C. A., et al. 2010. The effect of child abuse and exposure to domestic violence on adolescent internalizing and externalizing behavior problems. *Journal of Family Violence, 25,* 53–63. **393**

Mueller, M. M., and Elder, G. H., Jr. 2003. Family contingencies across the generations: Grandparent-grandchild relationships in holistic perspective. *Journal of Marriage and Family, 65,* 404–417. **307**

Mulvaney, M. K., and Mebert, C. J. 2007. Parental corporal punishment predicts problems in early childhood. *Journal of Family Psychology, 21,* 389–397. **292**

Murdie, R. A., and Teixeira, C. 2003. Towards a comfortable neighbourhood and appropriate housing: Immigrant experiences in Toronto. In P. Anisef and M. Lanphier (Eds.), *The world in a city* (pp. 132–191). Toronto: University of Toronto Press. **132**

Myers, D. G. 2000. *The American paradox: Spiritual hunger in an age of plenty.* New Haven, CT: Yale University Press. **125**

Myers, S. C. 1997. Marital uncertainty and childbearing. *Social Forces, 75,* 1271–1289. **316**

Myers, S. M. 1996. An interactive model of religiosity inheritance: The importance of family context. *American Sociological Review, 61,* 858–866. **174**

Myers, S. M. 2006. Religious homogamy and marital quality: Historical and generational patterns, 1980–1997. *Journal of Marriage and Family, 68,* 292–304. **188**

Myles, J., and Hou, F. 2004. Changing colours: Spatial assimilation and new racial minority immigrants. *Canadian Journal of Sociology, 29,* 29–55. **132, 133**

Myles, J., and Picot, G. 2006. Employment and earnings among lone mothers. Statistics Canada, *The Daily,* June 7. **111**

Nadesan, M. H. 2002. Engineering the entrepreneurial infant: Brain science, infant development toys, and governmentality. *Cultural Studies, 16*(3), 401–432. **286**

Nathers, M., and Rivers, K. L. 2006. *The concentration of negative child outcomes in low-income U.S. neighborhoods.* Population Reference Bureau. <www.prb.org>. **128**

National Council of Welfare. 2009a. *Poverty trends by family type, 1976–2007.* Ottawa, November. **428, 430**

National Council of Welfare. 2009b. *A snapshot of children living in poverty.* Ottawa, November. **429**

National Television Violence Study. 1998. *National televised violence study,* vol. 3. Santa Barbara: University of California, Center for Communication and Social Policy. **84**

Natsuaki, M. N., et al. 2009. Aggressive behavior between siblings and the development of externalizing problems: Evidence from a genetically-sensitive study. *Developmental Psychopathology, 45,* 1009–1018. **403**

Natsuaki, M. N., et al. 2010. Genetic liability, environment, and the development of fussiness in toddlers: The roles of maternal depression and parental responsiveness. *Developmental Psychology,* forthcoming. **285, 336**

Naumann, D. 2008. Aboriginal women in Canada: On the choice to renounce or reclaim Aboriginal identity. *The Canadian Journal of Native Studies, 28,* 343–362. **48**

Nayar, K. E. 2004. *The Sikh Diaspora in Vancouver: Three generations amid tradition, modernity, and multiculturalism.* Toronto: University of Toronto Press. **60**

NCHS (National Center for Health Statistics). 2010. *Marriage and cohabitation in the United States: A statistical portrait based on Cycle 6 (2002) of the National Survey of Family Growth.* Washington, DC: U.S. Department of Health and Human Services. **354, 355, 356, 420, 423**

Neff, C. 1996. Pauper apprenticeship in early nineteenth century Ontario. *Journal of Family History, 21,* 144–171. **46**

Neil, E. 2009. Post-adoption contact and openness in adoptive parents' minds: Consequences for child development. *British Journal of Social Work, 39,* 5–23. **245**

Nelson, A., and Robinson, B. W. 2002. *Gender in Canada,* 2nd Ed. Toronto: Pearson. **21, 33, 188**

Nelson, F. 1996. *Lesbian motherhood.* Toronto: University of Toronto Press. **274, 371**

Nelson, H. L. 1997. Introduction. In H. L. Nelson (Ed.), *Feminism and families* (pp. 1–9). New York: Routledge. **24**

Nelson, L. J., et al. 2007. "If you want me to treat you like an adult, start acting like one!" Comparing the criteria that emerging adults and their parents have for adulthood. *Journal of Family Psychology, 21,* 665–674. **300**

Nemr, R. 2009. *Family violence in Canada. Section 3. Fact sheet— police-reported family violence against children and youth.* Statistics Canada. Publication no. 85-224-X. **392**

Nett, E. M. 1993. *Canadian families: Past and present,* 2nd Ed. Toronto: Butterworths. **40**

Ney, P. G., Fung, T., and Wickett, A. R. 1994. The worst combinations of child abuse and neglect. *Child Abuse & Neglect, 18,* 705–714. **397**

NICHD (National Institute of Child Health and Human Development). Early Child Care Research Network). 2003. Does amount of time spent in child care predict socioemotional adjustment during the transition to kindergarten? *Child Development, 74,* 976–1005. **155**

NICHD (National Institute of Child Health and Human Development). Early Child Care Research Network. 2004. Are child developmental outcomes related to before- and after-school care arrangements? Results from the NICHD Study of Early Child Care. *Child Development, 75,* 280–285. **154**

NICHD (National Institute of Child Health and Human Development). Early Child Care Research Network. 2005. Duration and development timing of poverty and children's cognitive and social development from birth through third grade. *Child Development, 76,* 795–810. **116**

Nicholas, A. B. 2001. Canada's colonial mission: The great white bird. In K. P. Binda and S. Calliou (Eds.), *Aboriginal education in Canada* (pp. 933–947). Mississauga: Canadian Educators' Press. **168**

Nicholson, B. J. 1994. Legal borrowing and the origins of slave law in the British colonies. *American Journal of Legal History, 38,* 38–54. **44**

Nielsen, F. 2004. The ecological-evolutionary typology of human societies and the evolution of social inequality. *Sociological Theory, 22,* 292–314. **10**

Nielsen, F. 2006. Achievement and ascription in educational attainment: Genetic and environmental influences on adolescent schooling. *Social Forces, 85,* 193–216. **340**

Niranjan, S., Nair, S., and Roy, T. K. 2005. A socio-demographic analysis of the size and structure of the family in India. *Journal of Comparative Family Studies, 36,* 623–650. **59**

Noble, D. F. 1995. *Progress without people.* Toronto: Between the Lines. **418**

Nock, M. K., and Kazdin, A. E. 2002. Parent-directed physical aggression by clinic-referred youths. *Journal of Clinical Child & Adolescent Psychology, 31,* 193–205. **407**

Nock, S. L. 1998a. The consequences of premarital fatherhood. *American Sociological Review, 63,* 250–263. **194, 199, 422**

Nock, S. L. 1998b. Too much privacy? *Journal of Family Issues, 19,* 101–118. **143**

Nock, S. L. 1998c. *Marriage in men's lives.* New York: Oxford University Press. **178**

Noël, J. 2001. New France: Les femmes favorisées. In A. Prentice and S. Mann Trofimenkoff (Eds.), *The neglected majority,* vol. 2 (pp. 18–40). Toronto: McClelland & Stewart. **39**

Nokali, N. E. E., et al. 2010. Parent involvement and children's academic and social development in elementary school. *Child Development, 81,* 988–1005. **160**

Noller, P. 1996. What is this thing called love? Defining the love that supports marriage and family. *Personal Relationships, 3,* 97–115. **189**

Nomaguchi, K. M. 2008. Gender, family structure, and adolescents' primary confidants. *Journal of Marriage and Family, 70,* 1213–1227. **296**

Nooner, K. B., et al. 2010. Youth self-report of physical and sexual abuse: A latent class analysis. *Child Abuse & Neglect, 34,* 146–154. **30**

Northcott, H. C., and Wilson, D. M. 2008. *Dying and death in Canada.* Peterborough, ON: Broadview Press. **38, 306**

Notter, M. L., MacTavish, K. A., and Shamah, D. 2008. Pathways toward resilience among women in rural trailer parks. *Family Relations, 57,* 613–624. **142, 143**

Nyberg, G., et al. 2010. *Report of the Ontario Social Assistance Review Advisory Council.* Toronto: Ontario Ministry of Community and Social Services. **430**

O'Brien, C.-A., and Goldberg, A. 2000. Lesbians and gay men inside and outside families. In N. Mandell and A. Duffy (Eds.), *Canadian families: Diversity, conflict, and change,* 2nd Ed. (pp. 115–145). Toronto: Harcourt Brace. **5**

O'Brien, M. J. 1991. Taking sibling incest seriously. In M. Q. Patton (Ed.), *Family sexual abuse* (pp. 75–92). Newbury Park, CA: Sage. **404**

Odgers, C. L., et al. 2009. The protective effects of neighborhood collective efficacy on British children growing up in deprivation: A developmental analysis. *Developmental Psychopathology, 45,* 942–957. **130**

Ogbomo, O. 1997. *When men and women mattered: A history of gender relations among the Owan of Nigeria.* Rochester, NY: University of Rochester Press. **316**

Ogilvie, M. 2010. Homeless and pregnant. *Toronto Star.* March 13, I1, 4–5. **133**

Ogrodnik, L. 2009. *Family violence in Canada.* Section 5: Fact sheet—family homicides. Statistics Canada, Catalogue no. 85-224-X. **196, 385, 392**

O'Keefe, M. 1998. Factors mediating the link between witnessing interparental violence and dating violence. *Journal of Family Violence, 13,* 39–57. **389**

Oldehinkel, A. J., et al. 2008. Parental divorce and offspring depressive symptoms: Dutch developmental trends during early adolescence. *Journal of Marriage and Family, 70,* 284–293. **362**

Oldman, D. 1994. Adult-child relations as class relations. In J. Qvortrup et al. (Eds.), *Childhood matters: Social theory, practice and politics* (pp. 43–58). Aldershot, UK: Avebury. **74**

Ombelet, W., et al. 2006. Perinatal outcome of 12,021 singleton and 3,108 twin births after non-IVF-assisted reproduction: A cohort study. *Human Reproduction, 21,* 1025–1032. **237**

Ontario Heritage Foundation. 1997. *Home Children.* <www.heritagefdn.on.ca>. Accessed January 12, 2010. **46**

Onyskiw, J. E., and Hayduk, L. A. 2001. Processes underlying children's adjustment in families characterized by physical aggression. *Family Relations, 50,* 376–385. **184, 318, 390, 407**

Oreopoulos, P. 2006. The compelling effects of compulsory schooling: Evidence from Canada. *Canadian Journal of Economics, 39,* 22–52. **96**

Orpana, H. M., Lemyre, L., and Gravel, R. 2009. Income and psychological distress: The role of the social environment. Statistics Canada, *The Daily,* January 21. **20, 113, 124**

Orsini, F. 2007. *Love in South Asia: A cultural history.* New Delhi: Cambridge University Press. **61**

Orthner, D. K., and Rose, R. 2009. Work separation demands and spouse psychological well-being. *Family Relations, 58,* 392–403. **77**

Osborne, C., and McLanahan, S. 2007. Partnership instability and child well-being. *Journal of Marriage and Family, 69,* 1065–1083. **365**

Osborne, C., Manning, W. D., and Smock, P. J. 2007. Married and cohabiting parents' relationship stability: A focus on race and ethnicity. *Journal of Marriage and Family, 69,* 1345–1366. **220, 351**

Oster, E. 2009. Proximate sources of population sex imbalance in India. *Demography, 46,* 325–339. **60**

Oswald, R. F., et al. 2008. Structural and moral commitment among same-sex couples: Relationship duration, religiosity, and parental status. *Journal of Family Psychology, 22,* 411–419. **176**

Ouellette, F.-R., and Belleau, H. 2001. *Family and social integration of children adopted internationally: A review of the literature.* Montréal: Institut national de la recherche scientifique. Université du Québec. **244**

Owasu, T. 1999. Residential patterns and housing choices of Ghanaian immigrants in Toronto, Canada. *Housing Studies, 14,* 77–97. **132**

Oxford, M. L., et al. 2005. Life course heterogeneity in the transition from adolescence to adulthood among adolescent mothers. *Journal of Research on Adolescence, 15,* 479–504. **227**

Oyen, N., et al. 1997. Combined effects of sleeping position and pre-natal risk factors in Sudden Infant Death Syndrome: The Nordic Epidemiological SIDS study. *Pediatrics, 100,* 613–620. **219**

Ozawa, M. N., and Lee, Y. 2006. The net worth of female-headed households: A comparison to other types of households. *Family Relations, 55,* 132–145. **97**

Ozer, E. J. 2005. The impact of violence on urban adolescents: Longitudinal effects of perceived school connection and family support. *Journal of Adolescent Research, 20,* 167–192. **132**

Pagani, L., Boulerice, B., and Tremblay, R. E. 1997. The influence of poverty on children's classroom placement and behavior problems. In G. J. Duncan and J. Brooks-Gunn (Eds.), *Consequences of growing up poor* (pp. 311–339). New York: Russell Sage. **116, 373**

Page, C., et al. 2009. The effect of care setting on elder abuse: Results from a Michigan survey. *Journal of Elder Abuse & Neglect, 21,* 239–252. **409**

Paglia-Boak, A., et al. 2010. *The mental health and well-being of Ontario students 1991-2009.* Toronto: CAMH (Centre for Addiction and Mental Health. **89, 166, 350, 405**

Pagnini, D. L., and Rindfuss, R. R. 1993. The divorce of marriage and childbearing: Changing attitudes and behavior in the United States. *Population and Development Review, 19,* 331–347. **436**

Palameta, B. 2003. Who pays for domestic help? *Perspectives on Labour and Income, 4,* August, 2–15. **100**

Paletta, A. 2008. *Understanding family violence and sexual assault in the Territories, First Nations, Inuit and Métis Peoples.* Ottawa: Department of Justice. **384**

Pallas, A. M. 2002. Educational participation across the life course: Do the rich get richer? *Advances in Life Course Research, 7,* 327–354. **164**

Papp, L. M., Cummings, E. M., and Goeke-Morey, M. C. 2009. For richer, for poorer: Money as a topic of marital conflict in the home. *Family Relations, 58,* 91–103. **270**

Papp, L. M., Cummings, E. M., and Schermerhorn, A. C. 2004. Pathways among marital distress, parental symptomatology, and child adjustment. *Journal of Marriage and Family, 66,* 368–384. **279**

Pappano, L. 2001. *The connection gap—Why Americans feel so alone.* New Brunswick, NJ: Rutgers University Press. **141**

Parcel, T. L., and Dufur, M. J. 2001. Capital at home and at school: Effects on child social adjustment. *Journal of Marriage and Family, 63,* 32–42. **159**

Park, R. E., and Burgess, E. W. 1925. *The city.* Chicago: University of Chicago Press. **123**

Parr, J. 1980. *Labouring children.* London: Croom Helm. **98**

Parr, J. 1994. *Labouring children: British immigrant apprentices to Canada 1869–1924.* Toronto: University of Toronto Press. **46**

Parr, J. 2000. Rethinking work and kinship in a Canadian hosiery town, 1910–1950. In B. Bradbury (Ed.), *Canadian family history* (pp. 220–240). Toronto: Irwin Publishing. **97**

Parr, J. 2003. Introduction. In N. Janovicek and J. Parr (Eds.), *Histories of Canadian children and youth* (pp. 1–7). Toronto: Oxford University Press. **18, 45**

Parsons, S. 2005. *Rational choice and politics.* London: Continuum. **13**

Parsons, T. 1951. *The social system.* New York: Free Press. **11**

Parsons, T., et al. 1955. *Family, socialization and interaction process.* Glencoe, IL: Free Press. **11**

Pascal, C. E. 2009. *With our best future in mind. Implementing early learning in Ontario.* Toronto: Report to the Premier by the Special Advisor on Early Learning. **432, 433**

Pasley, K., Futris, T. G., and Skinner, M. L. 2002. Effects of commitment and psychological centrality on fathering. *Journal of Marriage and Family, 64,* 130–138. **22**

Passmore, N. C., and Chipuer, H. M. 2009. Female adoptees' perceptions of contact with their birth fathers: Satisfactions and dissatisfactions with the process. *American Journal of Orthopsychiatry, 79,* 93–102. **245**

Passmore, N. C., and Feeney, J. A. 2009. Reunions of adoptees who have met both birth parents: Post-reunion relationships and factors that facilitate and hinder the reunion process. *Adoption Quarterly, 12,* 100–119. **245**

Patterson, C. J. 2000. Family relationships of lesbians and gay men. *Journal of Marriage and Family, 62,* 1052–1069. **202, 211, 223**

Patterson, J. 2003. Spousal violence. In H. Johnson and K. Au Coin (Eds.) *Family violence in Canada: A statistical profile 2003* (pp. 4–20). Ottawa: Ministry of Industry. **388**

Paul, P. 2004. The porn factor. *Time,* February 9, 75–76. **73, 88**

Pauli-Pott, V., and Beckman, D. 2007. On the association of interparental conflict with developing behavioral inhibition and behavior problems in early childhood. *Journal of Family Psychology, 21,* 529–532. **279**

Paulson, M. J., Coombs, R. H., and Landsverk, J. 1990. Youths who physically assault their parents. *Journal of Family Violence, 5,* 121–133. **407**

Paupanekis, K., and Westfall, D. 2001. Teaching Native language programs: Survival strategies. In K. P. Binda and S. Calliou (Eds.), *Aboriginal education in Canada* (pp. 89–104). Mississauga, ON: Canadian Educators' Press. **168**

Payne, B. K., and Gainey, R. R. 2006. *Family violence and criminal justice: A life-course approach,* 2nd Ed. Cincinnati: Anderson. **409**

Pearce, L. D., and Axinn, W. G. 1998. The impact of family religious life on the quality of mother-child relations. *American Sociological Review, 63,* 810–828. **176, 177**

Pearce, L. D., and Thornton, A. 2007. Religious identity and family ideologies in the transition to adulthood. *Journal of Marriage and Family, 69,* 1227–1243. **174**

Pearce, M. J., et al. 2003. The protective effects of religiousness and parent involvement on the development of conduct problems among youth exposed to violence. *Child Development, 74,* 1682–1696. **175**

Pears, K. C., and Capaldi, D. M. 2001. Intergenerational transmission of abuse: A two-generational prospective study of an at-risk sample. *Child Abuse & Neglect, 25,* 1439–1461. **394**

Pearson, J. L., et al. 1997. Grandmother involvement in child caregiving in an urban community. *The Gerontologist, 37,* 650–657. **308**

Pedro-Carroll, J. 2001. The promotion of wellness in children and families: Challenges and opportunities. *American Psychologist, 56,* 993–1004. **364**

Pelkonen, S., et al. 2010. Perinatal outcome of children born after frozen and fresh embryo transfer: The Finnish cohort study 1995–2006. *Human Reproduction, 25,* 914–923. **237**

Pelton, L. 1991. Poverty and child protection. *Protecting Children, 7,* 3–5. **397**

Pelton, L. H. 1997. Child welfare policy and practice: The myth of family preservation. *American Journal of Orthopsychiatry, 67,* 545–553. **434**

Pena, D. 2000. Parent involvement: Influencing factors and implication. *Journal of Educational Research, 12*, 68–89. **160**

Pepler, D., et al. 2008. Developmental trajectories of bullying and associated factors. *Child Development, 79,* 325–338. **405**

Peralta, R. L., Tuttle, L. A., and Steele, J. L. 2010. At the intersection of interpersonal violence, masculinity, and alcohol use: The experiences of heterosexual male perpetrators of intimate partner violence. *Violence Against Women, 16,* 387–409. **386**

Peritz, I. 2010. Abortion. *The Globe and Mail,* June 19, A1, A15. **234**

Perkins, D. F., et al. 1998. An ecological, risk-factor examination of adolescents' sexual activity in three ethnic groups. *Journal of Marriage and Family, 60,* 660–673. **203**

Perozynski, L., and Kramer, L. 1999. Parental beliefs about managing sibling conflict. *Developmental Psychology, 35,* 489–499. **402**

Perry, Y. V., and Doherty, W. J. 2005. Viewing time through the eyes of overscheduled children and their underconnected families. In V. L. Bengtson et al., (Eds.), *Sourcebook of family theory & research* (pp. 255–258). Thousand Oaks, CA: Sage. **74**

Perry-Jenkins, M., and Crouter, A. 1990. Men's provider role attitudes: Implications for household work and marital satisfaction. *Journal of Family Issues, 11,* 136–156. **263**

Peters, A. 2002. Is your community child-friendly? *Canadian Social Trends, 67,* 2–5. **124, 129**

Petersilia, J. R. 2001. Crime victims with developmental disabilities: A review essay. *Criminal Justice and Behavior, 28,* 655–694. **394**

Petta, G. A., and Steed, L. G. 2005. The experience of adoptive parents in adoption reunion relationships: A qualitative study. *American Journal of Orthopsychiatry, 75,* 230–241. **246**

Pettit, G. S., et al. 1996. Stability and change in peer-rejected status: The role of child behavior, parenting, and family ecology. *Merrill-Palmer Quarterly, 42,* 267–294. **118, 131**

Pettit, G. S., et al. 1999. The impact of after-school peer contact on early adolescent externalizing problems is moderated by parental monitoring, perceived neighborhood safety, and prior adjustment. *Child Development, 70,* 768–778. **287**

Pettit, G. S., et al. 2007. Predicting the developmental course of mother-reported monitoring across childhood and adolescence from early proactive parenting, child temperament, and parents' worries. *Journal of Family Psychology, 21,* 206–217. **293**

Phillips, P., and Phillips, E. 2000. *Women & work.* Toronto: James Lorimer. **96, 441**

Pillemer, K., and Suitor, J. J. 1991. "Will I ever escape my children's problems?" Effects of adult children's problems on elderly parents. *Journal of Marriage and Family, 53,* 585–594. **303**

Pitt, K. 2002. Being a new capitalist mother. *Discourse & Society, 13,* 251–267. **152, 162**

Ploeg, J., et al. 2003. Helping to build and rebuild secure lives and futures: Financial transfers from parents to adult children and grandchildren. *Canadian Journal on Aging, 23S,* S113–125. **303**

Plomin, R., et al. 2008. *Behavior genetics.* New York: Worth. **22, 440**

Plotnick, R. D. 2009. Childlessness and the economic well-being of older Americans. *The Journals of Gerontology: Series B, 64B,* 767–773. **306**

Pogarsky, G., Thornberry, T. P., and Lizotte, A. J. 2006. Developmental outcomes for children of young mothers. *Journal of Marriage and Family, 68,* 332–344. **228**

Polgar, M. F., and North, C. S. 2009. Parenting adults who become homeless: Variations in stress and social support. *American Journal of Orthopsychiatry, 79,* 357–365. **134**

Pong, S. I. 1998. The school compositional effect of single parenthood on 10th-grade achievement. *Sociology of Education, 71,* 24–43. **159, 164**

Pong, S.-L., et al. 2003. Family policies and children's school achievement in single- versus two-parent families. *Journal of Marriage and Family, 65,* 681–699. **429**

Pontzer, D. 2010. A theoretical test of bullying behaviour: Parenting, personality, and the bully/victim relationship. *Journal of Family Violence, 25,* 259–273. **405**

Poonwassie, D. H. 2001. Parental involvement as adult education: A microstrategy for change. In K. P. Binda and S. Calliou (Eds.), *Aboriginal education in Canada* (pp. 155 165). Mississauga, ON: Canadian Educators' Press. **163, 168**

Poortman, A.-R., and Voorpostel, M. 2009. Parental divorce and sibling relationships. *Journal of Family Issues, 30,* 74–91. **325**

Porter, C. 2003. A wedding story. *Toronto Star* (a series of articles ending September 14, A1 and A8, following a Canadian-Pakistani male through the steps leading to his arranged marriage in Pakistan). **61**

Portes, A. 1998. Social capital: Its origins and applications in modern sociology. *Annual Review of Sociology, 24,* 1–24. **13**

Potter, J. 1996. *Representing reality: Discourse, rhetoric, and social construction.* London: Sage. **18**

Potter-MacKinnon, J. 1993. *While the women only wept: Loyalist refugee women.* Montreal, Kingston: McGill-Queen's University Press. **41**

Powell, B., and Steelman, L. C. 1993. The educational benefits of being spaced out: Sibling diversity and educational progress. *American Sociological Review, 58,* 367–381. **318**

Power, A. 2007. *City survivors: Bringing up children in disadvantaged neighbourhoods.* Bristol: The Policy Press. **128**

Powers, D. A., and Hsueh, J. C.-T. 1997. Sibling models of socioeconomic effects on the timing of first premarital birth. *Demography, 34,* 493–511. **322**

Presser, H. 1995. Are the interests of women inherently at odds with the interests of children and the family? A viewpoint. In K. Mason and A.-M. Jensen (Ed.), *Gender and family change in industrialized countries* (pp. 297–319). Oxford: Clarendon. **25**

Presser, S., and Stinson, L. 1998. Data collection mode and social desirability bias in self-reported religious attendance. *American Sociological Review, 63,* 137–145. **174**

Prigerson, H. G., Maciejewski, P. K., and Rosenbeck, R. A. 2000. Preliminary explorations of the harmful interactive effects of widowhood and marital harmony on health, health service use, and health care costs. *The Gerontologist, 40,* 349–357. **368, 369**

Prochner, L. 2000. A history of early education and child care in Canada, 1820–1966. In L. Prochner and N. Howe (Eds.), *Early childhood care and education in Canada* (pp. 252–272). Vancouver: University of British Columbia Press. **152**

Provencher, C., Le Bourdais, C., and Marcil-Gratton, N. 2006. Intergenerational transfer: The impact of parental separation on young adults' conjugal behaviour. In K. McQuillan and Z. R. Ravanera (Eds.), *Canada's changing families. Implications for individuals and society* (pp. 179–209). Toronto: University of Toronto Press. **176, 193, 354, 362, 369, 424**

Pruchno, R., Patrick, J. H., and Burant, C. J. 1996. Aging women and their children with chronic disabilities: Perceptions of sibling involvement and effects on well-being. *Family Relations, 45,* 318–326. **324**

Pruchno, R., Patrick, J. H., and Burant, C. J. 1997. African American and White mothers of adults with chronic disabilities: Caregiving burden and satisfaction. *Family Relations, 46,* 335–346. **305**

Prus, S. G. 2002. Changes in income within a cohort over the later life course: Evidence from income status convergence. *Canadian Journal on Aging, 21,* 475–504. **428**

Pryor, J., and Rodgers, B. 2001. *Children in changing families: Life after parental separation.* Oxford: Blackwell. **354**

Pyke, K. 2000. "The normal American family" as an interpretive structure of family life among grown children of Korean and Vietnamese immigrants. *Journal of Marriage and Family, 62,* 240–255. **286**

Pyper, W. 2002. Falling behind. *Perspectives on Labour and Income, 3,* July, 17–23. **224**

Quane, J. M., and Rankin, B. H. 1998. Neighborhood poverty, family characteristics, and commitment to mainstream goals: The case of African American adolescents in the inner city. *Journal of Family Issues, 19,* 769–794. **130**

Quart, A. 2003. *Branded: The buying and selling of teenagers.* New York: Perseus. **87**

Qvortrup, J. 1995. From useful to useful: The historical continuity of children's constructive participation. *Sociological Studies of Children, 7,* 49–76. **74**

Racine, Y., and Boyle, M. H. 2002. Family functioning and children's behaviour problems. In J. D. Willms (Ed.), *Vulnerable children: Findings from Canada's National Longitudinal Survey of Children and Youth* (pp. 149–165). Edmonton: University of Alberta Press.

Raikes, H., et al. 2006. Mother-child book reading in low-income families: Correlates and outcomes during the first three years of life. *Child Development, 77,* 924–953. **157**

Rajkhowa, M., Mcconnell, A., and Thomas, G. E. 2006. Reasons for discontinuation of IVF treatment: A questionnaire study. *Human Reproduction, 21,* 358–363. **236**

Rajulton, F., and Ravanera, Z. R. 2006a. Social status polarization in the timing and trajectories to motherhood. *Canadian Studies in Population, 33,* 179–207. **229**

Rajulton, F., and Ravanera, Z. R. 2006b. Family solidarity in Canada: An exploration with the General Social Survey on Family and Community Support. In K. McQuillan and Z. R. Ravanera (Eds.), *Canada's changing families. Implications for individuals in society* (pp. 239–263). Toronto: University of Toronto Press. **12, 304, 439**

Raley, R. K., and Wildsmith, E. 2004. Cohabitation and children's family instability. *Journal of Marriage and Family, 66,* 210–219. **220**

Raley, R. K., Crissey, S., and Muller, C. 2007. Of sex and romance: Late adolescent relationships and young adult union formation. *Journal of Marriage and Family, 69,* 1210–1226. **207**

Raneri, L. G., and Wiemann, C. M. 2007. Social ecological predictors of repeat adolescent pregnancy. *Perspectives on Sexual Reproductive Health, 39,* 39–47. **226**

Rapoport, B., and Le Bourdais, C. 2006. Parental time, work schedules, and changing gender roles. In K. McQuillan and Z. R. Ravanera (Eds.), *Canada's changing families. Implications for individuals and society* (pp. 76–104). Toronto: University of Toronto Press. **351**

Raschick, M., and Ingersoll-Dayton, B. 2004. The costs and rewards of caregiving among aging spouses and adult children. *Family Relations, 53,* 317–325. **306**

Ratcliffe, C., and Vinopal, K. 2009. *Are families prepared for financial emergencies?* U.S. The Urban Institute. <www.urban.org>. **106**

Ravanera, Z. R., and McQuillan, K. 2006. Introduction. In K. M. McQuillan and Z. R. Ravanera (Eds.), *Canada's changing families. Implications for individuals and society.* (pp. 3-11). Toronto: University of Toronto Press. **71**

Ravanera, Z., Beaujot, R., and Liu, J. 2009. Models of earning and caring: Determinants of the division of work. *Canadian Review of Sociology, 46,* 319–337. **260, 262**

Ravanera, Z. R., Rajulton, F., and Burch, T. K. 2003. Early life transitions of Canadian youth: Effects of family transformation and community characteristics. *Canadian Studies in Population, 30,* 327–353. **301**

Ravanera, Z. R., Rajulton, F., and Burch, T. K. 2004. Patterns of age variability in life course transitions. *Canadian Journal of Sociology, 29,* 527–542. **16**

Raver, C. C. 2003. Does work pay psychologically as well as economically? The role of employment in predicting depressive symptoms and parenting among low-income families. *Child Development, 74,* 1720–1736. **101**

Raver, C. C., and Zigler, E. F. 1997. New perspectives on Head Start. *Early Childhood Research Quarterly, 12,* 363–385. **157**

Ray, B. D. 2001. Homeschooling in Canada. *Education Canada, 41,* 28–31. **170**

Ray, B. D., and Wartes, J. 1991. The academic achievement and affective development of home-schooled children. In J. A. Van Galen and M. A. Pitman (Eds.), *Home schooling: Political, historical, and pedagogical perspectives* (pp. 43–62). Norwood, NJ: Ablex.**170**

Raymo, J. M. 2003. Premarital living arrangements and the transition to first marriage in Japan. *Journal of Marriage and Family, 65,* 302–315. **191**

RCAP (Report of the Royal Commission on Aboriginal Peoples). 1996. *Gathering Strength,* vol. 3. Ottawa: Canada Communication Group. **156**

Reboucas, L. 2002. Brazil confronts adolescent sexual health issues. *Population Reference Bureau.* **88**

Recht, M. 1997. The role of fishing in the Iroquois economy, 1600–1792. *New York History, 78,* 429–454. **37**

Rehman, U. S., and Holtzworth-Munroe, A. 2007. A cross-cultural examination of the relation of marital communication behaviour to marital satisfaction. *Journal of Family Psychology, 21,* 758–763. **269**

Reichman, N. E., Corman, H., and Noonan, K. 2004. Effects of child health on parents' relationship status. *Demography, 41,* 569–584. **276**

Reid, C. R. 2008. Quality of care and mortality among long-term care residents with dementia. *Canadian Studies in Population, 35,* 1–3. **438**

Reid, J. G. 1990. *Sir William Alexander and North American colonization: A reappraisal.* Edinburgh: University of Edinburgh, Centre of Canadian Studies. **40**

Reiss, D. 2003. Child effects on family systems: Behavioral genetic strategies. In A. C. Crouter and A. Booth (Eds.), *Children's influence on family dynamics* (pp. 3–25). Mahwah, NJ: Erlbaum. **336, 339**

Reiss, D., et al. 1995. Genetic questions for environmental studies: Differential parenting and psychopathology in adolescence. *Archives of General Psychiatry, 52,* 925–936. **328**

Renner, L. M, and Whitney, S. D. 2010. Examining symmetry and intimate partner violence among young adults using socio-demographic characteristics. *Journal of Family Violence, 25,* 91–106. **381**

Renzetti, C. M. 1997. Violence and abuse among same-sex couples. In A. P. Cardarelli (Ed.), *Violence between intimate partners* (pp. 70–89). Boston: Allyn & Bacon. **383, 384, 390**

Reynolds, A. J., and Robertson, D. L. 2003. School-based early intervention and later child maltreatment in the Chicago Longitudinal Study. *Child Development, 74*, 3–26. **157**

Reynolds, A. J., and Temple, J. A. 1998. Extended early childhood intervention and school achievement: Age thirteen findings from the Chicago Longitudinal Study. *Child Development, 69*, 231–246. **157, 433**

Reynolds, C. 2004. The educational system. In N. Mandell (Ed.), *Feminist issues: Race, class, and gender*, 4th Ed. (pp. 247–265). Toronto: Prentice Hall. **152**

Rezai-Rashti, G. 2004. Unessential women: A discussion of race, class, and gender and their implications in education. In N. Mandell (Ed.), *Feminist issues: Race, class, and gender*, 4th Ed. (pp. 83–99). Toronto: Prentice Hall. **24**

Richmond, M. K., Stocker, C. M., and Rienks, S. L. 2005. Longitudinal associations between sibling relationship quality, parental differential treatment, and children's adjustment. *Journal of Family Psychology, 19*, 550–559. **320, 321, 325, 328**

Rideout, V. J., Foehr, U. G., and Roberts, D. F. 2010. *Generation M^2. Media in the lives of 8- to 18-year-olds.* The Kaiser Family Foundation. <www.kff.org>. **79, 80**

Rifkin, J. 1995. *The end of work.* New York: Putnam's Sons. **419**

Riley, D., and Steinberg, J. 2004. Four popular stereotypes about children in self-care: Implications for family life educators. *Family Relations, 53*, 95–101. **104**

Ringstad. R. 2009. CPS: Client violence and client victims. *Child Welfare, 88*, 127–147. **247**

Rizk, C. 2003. *Le cadre des ménages les plus pauvres.* Paris: INSEE. **143**

Robinson, J. D., and Skill, T. 2001. Five decades of families on television: From the 1950s through the 1990s. In J. Bryant and J. A. Bryant (Eds.), *Television and the American family* (pp. 139–162). Mahwah, NJ: Erlbaum. **83**

Robinson, L. C., and Blanton, P. W. 1993. Marital strengths in enduring marriages. *Family Relations, 42*, 38–45. **273**

Robison, J., et al. 2009. A broader view of family caregiving: Effects of caregiving and caregiver conditions on depressive symptoms, health, work, and social isolation. *The Journals of Gerontology: Series B, 64B*, 788–798. **306**

Robitaille, N., Guimond, E., and Boucher, A. 2010. Intergenerational ethnic mobility among Canadian Aboriginal populations in 2001. *Canadian Studies in Population, 37*, 151–174. **48**

Robson, K. 2005. Canada's most notorious bad mothers: The newspaper coverage of the Jordan Heikamp inquest. *Canadian Review of Sociology and Anthropology, 42*, 217–232. **21, 415**

Roger, K. S., and Ursel, J. 2009. Public opinion on mandatory reporting of abuse and/or neglect of older adults in Manitoba, Canada. *Journal of Elder Abuse & Neglect, 21*, 115–140. **408**

Rogers, S. J., and White, L. K. 1998. Satisfaction with parenting: The role of marital happiness, family structure, and parents' gender. *Journal of Marriage and Family, 60*, 293–308. **275**

Rogoff, B., et al. 1991. Cultural variation in the role relations of toddlers and their families. In M. H. Bornstein (Ed.), *Cultural approaches to parenting* (pp. 175–184). Hillsdale, NJ: Erlbaum. **20**

Roosa, M. W., et al. 1997. The relationship of childhood sexual abuse to teenage pregnancy. *Journal of Marriage and Family, 59*, 119–130. **400**

Roper, S. O., and Yorgason, J. B. 2009. Older adults with diabetes and osteoarthritis and their spouses: Effects of activity limitations, marital happiness, and social contacts on partner's daily mood. *Family Relations, 58*, 460–474. **274**

Rosenberg, J. 2001. Boyhood abuse increases men's risk of involvement in a teenager's pregnancy. *Family Planning Perspectives, 33*, 184–185. **399**

Rosenthal, C J. 2000. Aging families: Have current changes been "oversold"? In E. M. Gee and G. M. Gutman (Eds.), *The overselling of population aging* (pp. 45–63). Toronto: Oxford University Press. **302, 305**

Rosenthal, C. J., and Gladstone, J. 2000. *Grandparenthood in Canada.* Ottawa: The Vanier Institute of the Family. **307**

Rosin, H. 2008. American murder mystery. *The Atlantic,* July/August, 40–54. **432**

Ross, C. E., and Mirowsky, J. 1999. Disorder and decay: The concept and measurement of perceived neighborhood disorder. *Urban Affairs Review, 34*, 412–432. **127**

Ross, C. E., Mirowsky, J., and Pribesh, S. 2001. Powerlessness and the amplification of threat: Neighborhood disadvantage, disorder, and mistrust. *American Sociological Review, 66*, 568–591. **126, 129**

Ross, C. J. 2006. Foster children awaiting adoption under the *Adoption and Safe Families Act of 1997. Adoption Quarterly, 9*, 121–131. **246**

Ross, E., et al. 2000. Adoption research review. Adoption Council of Canada, *Canada's Children, 2*, 31–34. **246**

Ross, L. E., et al. 2009. Policy, practice, and personal narratives: Experiences of LGBTQ people with adoption in Ontario, Canada. *Adoption Quarterly, 12*, 272–293. **222**

Rossi, A. S., and Rossi, P. H. 1990. *Of human bonding: Parent-child relations across the life course.* New York: Aldine de Gruyter. **297, 302, 302, 310, 313**

Rotermann, M. 2005. Sex, condoms and STDs among young people. Statistics Canada, *Health Reports, 16*, May. **206**

Rotermann, M. 2007a. Marital breakdown and subsequent depression. Statistics Canada, *Health Reports, 18*, 33–44. **109, 359, 360**

Rotermann, M. 2007b. Second or subsequent births to teenagers. Statistics Canada, *Health Reports, 18*, February. **226**

Rotermann, M. 2008. Trends in teen sexual behaviour and condom use. *Canadian Social Trends,* August 20. **203, 204**

Rothblum, E. D. 2002. "Boston marriage" among lesbians. In M. Yalom and L. L. Carstensen (Eds.), *Inside the American couple* (pp. 74–86). Berkeley, CA: University of California Press. **202, 208**

Rothermel, P. 2000. The third way in education: Thinking the unthinkable. *Education, 28*, 3–13. **171**

Rothman, B. K. 1989. *Recreating motherhood: Ideology and technology in a patriarchal society.* New York: W. W. Norton. **239**

Rothman, B. K. 1999. Comment on Harrison: The commodification of motherhood. In S. Coontz (Ed.), *American families: A multicultural reader* (pp. 435–438). New York: Routledge. **235, 238**

Rowe, D. C., Jacobson, K. C., and Van den Oord, E. J. C. G. 1999. Genetic and environmental influences on vocabulary IQ: Parental education level as moderator. *Child Development, 70*, 1151–1162. **336**

Roy, F. 2006. Changing patterns of women in the Canadian labour force. Statistics Canada, *The Daily*, June 15. **98**

Rubin, R. M., and White-Means, S. I. 2009. Informal caregiving: Dilemmas of sandwhiched caregivers. *Journal of Family and Economic Issues, 30*, 252–267. **440**

Rueter, M. A., and Koerner, A. F. 2008. The effect of family communication patterns on adopted adolescent adjustment. *Journal of Marriage and Family, 70*, 715–727. **286**

Rueter, M. A., et al. 2009. Family interactions in adoptive compared to nonadoptive families. *Journal of Family Psychology, 23*, 58–66. **240**

Ruggles, S. 2009. Reconsidering the Northwest European family system: Living arrangements of the aged in comparative historical perspective. *Population and Development Review, 35*, 249–273.

Ruggles, S., and Heggeness, M. 2008. International coresidence in developing countries. *Population and Development Review, 34*, 253–281. **38, 301**

Rushowy, K. 2004. Pre-school crucial time. *Toronto Star*. March 27, pp. A1, A4. **155, 158, 433**

Ruspini, E. 2000. Lone mothers' poverty in Europe: The cases of Belgium, Germany, Great Britain, Italy, and Sweden. In A. Pfenning and T. Bahle (Eds.), *Families and family policies in Europe* (pp. 221–244). Frankfurt am Main: Peter Lang. **248**

Russell, D., Springer, K. W., and Greenfield, E. A. 2010. Witnessing domestic abuse in childhood as an independent risk factor for depressive symptoms in young adulthood. *Child Abuse & Neglect, 34*, 448–453. **389**

Rutter, M. 2002. Nature, nurture, and development: From Evangelism through science toward policy and practice. *Child Development, 73*, 1–21. **22, 279, 285, 339, 368**

Rutter, M. L. 1997. Nature-nurture integration: The example of antisocial behavior. *American Psychologist, 52*, 390–398. **340**

Ryan, S., et al. 2008. Older sexual partners during adolescence: Links to reproductive health outcomes in young adulthood. *Perspectives on Sexual and Reproductive Health, 40*, 17–26. **207**

Ryan, S., et al. 2009. Family structure history: Links to relationship formation behaviors in young adulthood. *Journal of Marriage and Family, 71*, 935–953. **221**

Sabatelli, R. M., and Bartle-Haring, S. 2003. Family-of-origin experiences and adjustment in married couples. *Journal of Marriage and Family, 65*, 159–169. **271**

Sabatelli, R. M., and Shehan, C. L. 1993. Exchange and resources theories. In P. G. Boss et al. (Eds.), *Sourcebook of family theories and methods: A contextual approach* (pp. 385–417). New York: Plenum Press. **12**

Sacher, J. A., and Fine, M. A. 1996. Predicting relationship status and satisfaction after six months among dating couples. *Journal of Marriage and Family, 58*, 21–32. **184**

Saewyc, E., et al. 2008a. Trends in sexual health and risk behaviours among adolescent students in British Columbia. *The Canadian Journal of Human Sexuality, 17*, 1–13. **209**

Saewyc, E., et al. 2008b. Stigma management? The links between enacted stigma and teen pregnancy trends among gay, lesbian, and bisexual students in British Columbia. *The Canadian Journal of Human Sexuality, 17*, 123–140. **209**

Salzinger, S., et al. 1993. The effects of physical abuse on children's social relationships. *Child Development, 64*,169–187. **393**

Sameroff, A. 2010. A unified theory of development: A dialectic integration of nature and nurture. *Child Development, 81*, 6–22. **15**

Sampson, R. J. 1997. Collective regulation of adolescent misbehavior: Validation results from eighty Chicago neighborhoods. *Journal of Adolescent Research, 12*, 227–244. **130, 145, 418**

Sampson, R. J., Morenoff, J. D., and Earls, F. 1999. Beyond social capital: Spatial dynamics of collective efficacy for children. *American Sociological Review, 64*, 633–660. **13**

Sampson, R. J., Morenoff, J. D., and Gannon-Rowley, T. 2002. Assessing "neighbourhood effects": Social processes and new direction in research. *Annual Review of Sociology, 28*, 443–478. **127**

Sands, R. G., and Goldberg-Glen, R. S. 2000. Factors associated with stress among grandparents raising their grandchildren. *Family Relations, 49*, 97–105. **309**

Sanford, K. 2010. Assessing conflict communication in couples: Comparing the validity of self-report, partner-report, and observer ratings. *Journal of Family Psychology, 24*, 165–174. **254**

Sapolsky, B. S., and Tabarlet, J. L. 1991. Sex in prime time television: 1979 versus 1989. *Journal of Broadcasting and Electronic Media, 15*, 505–516. **88**

Sassler, S. 2004. The process of entering into cohabiting unions. *Journal of Marriage and Family, 66*, 491–505. **193, 194**

Sassler, S. 2010. Partnering across the life course: Sex, relationships, and mate selection. *Journal of Marriage and Family, 72*, 557–575. **12, 186, 196, 356, 370**

Sauvé, R. 2002. *Tracking links between jobs and families*. Ottawa: The Vanier Institute of the Family. <www.vifamily.ca>.**97. 199**

Sauvé, R. 2008. *The current state of Canadian family finances—2007 Report*. Ottawa: The Vanier Institute of the Family. <www.vifamily.ca>. **107**

Sauvé, R. 2009a. *The current state of Canadian family finances—2008 Report*. Ottawa: The Vanier Institute of the Family. <www.vifamily.ca>. **97, 110**

Sauvé, R. 2009b. The all-Canadian wealth test. *Canadian Business Online*, October 15. <www.canadianbusiness.com>.**96**

Savoie, J. 2007. Youth self-reported delinquency, Toronto, 2006. *Juristat, 27*, 6, Statistics Canada Catalogue no. 85-002-XIE. Ottawa. **372**

Savoie, J. 2008. Neighbourhood characteristics and the distribution of crime: Edmonton, Halifax, and Thunder Bay. *Crime and Justice Research Paper Series*. Statistics Canada, Catalogue no. 85-561-M1E no. 10. Ottawa. **126**

Savoie, J., Bédard, F., and Colins, K. 2006. Neighbourhood characteristics and the distribution of crime on the Island of Montreal. *Crime and Justice Research Paper Series*. Statistics Canada Catalogue no. 85-561-MIE. no. 7. Ottawa. **127, 166**

Sayer, L. 2005. Trends in women's and men's paid work, unpaid work, and free time. *Social Forces, 84*, 285–303. **261**

Scaramella, L. V., et al. 2002. Evaluation of a social contextual model of delinquency: A cross-study replication. *Child Development, 73*, 175–195. **294**

Scaramella, L. V., et al. 2008. Consequences of socioeconomic disadvantage across three generations: Parenting behavior and child externalizing problems. *Journal of Family Psychology, 22*, 725–733. **119**

Scarr, S. 1998. American child care today. *American Psychologist, 53*, 95–108. **20, 154**

Schermerhorn, A. C., et al. 2007. Children's influence in the marital relationship. *Journal of Family Psychology, 21*, 259–269. **276**

Schindler, H. S. 2010. The importance of parenting and financial contributions in promoting fathers' psychological health. *Journal of Marriage and Family, 72,* 318–332. **115**

Schlegel, A. 2003. Modernisation and changes in adolescent social life. In T. S. Saraswathi (Ed.), *Cross-cultural perspectives in human development* (pp. 236–257). New Delhi, India: Sage. **75, 298**

Schlegel, A., and Barry, H., III. 1991. *Adolescence: An anthropological inquiry.* New York: Free Press. **294**

Schmeeckle, M., et al. 2006. What makes someone family? Adult children's perceptions of current and former stepparents. *Journal of Marriage and Family, 68,* 595–610. **374**

Schneewind, K. A., and Gerhard, A.-K. 2002. Relationship personality, conflict resolution, and marital satisfaction in the first 5 years of marriage. *Family Relations, 51,* 63–71. **270**

Schneider, B., Waite, L., and Dempsey, N. P. 2000. Teenagers in dual-career families. *Family Focus,* December, F11, F13. **104**

Schnittker, J. 2008. Happiness and success: Genes, families, and the psychological effects of socioeconomic position and social support. *American Journal of Sociology, 114,* S233–259. **22, 116**

Schoen, R., and Canudas-Romo, V. 2006. Timing effects on divorce: 20th Century experience in the United States. *Journal of Marriage and Family, 68,* 749–758. **346**

Schoen, R., and Cheng, Y.-H. A. 2006. Partner choice and the differential retreat from marriage. *Journal of Marriage and Family, 68,* 1–10. **198**

Schoppe-Sullivan, S. J., et al. 2007. Marital conflict and children's adjustment: Evaluation of the parenting process model. *Journal of Marriage and Family, 69,* 1118–1134. **277**

Schor, J. B. 2001. Time crunch among American parents. In S. A. Hewlett, N. Rankin, and C. West (Eds.), *Taking parenting public* (pp. 83–102). New York: Rowan & Littlefield. **104**

Schteingart, J. S., et al. 1995. Homelessness and child functioning in the context of risks and protective factors moderating child outcomes. *Journal of Clinical Child Development, 24,* 320–331. **135**

Schultz, D., et al. 2009. The relationship between protective factors and outcomes for children investigated for maltreatment. *Child Abuse & Neglect, 33,* 684–698. **394**

Schulz, R., Boerner, K., and Hebert, R. S. 2008. Caregiving and bereavement. In M. S. Stroebe et al. (Eds), *Handbook of bereavement research and practice: Advances in theory and intervention* (pp. 265–285). Washington, DC: American Psychological Association. **368**

Schwartz, C. R. 2010. Earnings inequality and the changing association between spouses' earnings. *American Journal of Sociology, 115,* 1524–1557. **97**

Schwartz, P., and Rutter, V. 1998. *The gender of sexuality.* Thousand Oaks, CA: Pine Forge. **236**

Schwartz, S. J., and Finley, G. E. 2006. Father involvement, nurturant fathering, and young adult psychosocial functioning. *Journal of Family Issues, 27,* 712–731. **243**

Schwebel, D. C., and Plumert, J. M. 1999. Longitudinal and concurrent relations among temperament, ability estimation, and injury proneness. *Child Development, 70,* 700–712. **392**

SCIO (State Council Information Office of the People's Republic of China). 2000. *White paper—Fifty years of progress in China's human rights.* **56**

Scott, K. 2005. *The world we have: Towards a new social architecture.* Ottawa: Canadian Council on Social Development. **428**

Sedgh, G., et al. 2007. Legal abortion worldwide: Incidence and recent trends. *Perspectives on Sexual and Reproductive Health, 39,* 216–225. **234**

Seiter, E. 1993. *Sold separately: Children and parents in consumer culture.* New Brunswick, NJ: Rutgers University Press. **87**

Seljak, D. 2005. Education, multiculturalism, and religion. In P. Bramadat and D. Seljak (Eds.), *Religion and ethnicity in Canada* (pp. 178–200). Toronto: Pearson. **168**

Seltzer, J. A. 1998. Fathers by law: Effects of joint legal custody on nonresident fathers' involvement with children. *Demography, 35,* 135–146. **21**

Seltzer, J. A. 2000. Families formed outside of marriage. *Journal of Marriage and Family, 62,* 1247–1268. **194, 220**

Seltzer, M. M., et al. 1997. Siblings of adults with mental retardation or mental illness: Effects on lifestyle and psychological well-being. *Family Relations, 46,* 395–405. **324**

Selwyn, J., Frazer, L., and Quinton, D. 2006. Paved with good intentions: The pathway to adoption and the costs of delay. *British Journal of Social Work, 36,* 561–576. **241**

Serbin, L. A., et al. 1998. Intergenerational transmission of psychosocial risk in women with childhood histories of aggression, withdrawal, or aggression and withdrawal. *Developmental Psychology, 34,* 1246–1262. **227, 228**

Serbin, L. A., Peters, P. L., and Schwartzman, A. E. 1996. Longitudinal study of early childhood injuries and acute illness in the offspring of adolescent mothers who were aggressive, withdrawn, or aggressive-withdrawn in childhood. *Journal of Abnormal Psychology, 105,* 500–507. **228**

Sercombe, H. 2009. The gift and the trap: Working the "teen brain" into our concept of youth. *Journal of Adolescent Research, 25,* 31–47. **23, 295**

Sered, S. S. 1999. "Woman" as symbol and women as agents: Gendered religious discourses. In M. M. Ferree, J. Lorber, and B. B. Hess (Eds.), *Revisioning gender* (pp. 193–221). Thousand Oaks, CA: Sage. **178**

Sev'er, A. 2002. *Fleeing the house of horrors: Women who have left abusive partners.* Toronto: University of Toronto Press. **196, 360, 381, 382, 385, 386, 387, 388, 413**

Sev'er, A. 2009. More than wife abuse that has gone old: A conceptual model for violence against the aged in Canada and the US. *Journal of Comparative Family Studies, 40,* 279–296. **408**

Sev'er, A., and Yurdakul, G. 2001. Culture of honor, culture of change: A feminist analysis of honor killings in rural Turkey. *Violence Against Women, 7,* 964–998. **385**

Shaffer, A., et al. 2009. Intergenerational continuity in parenting quality: The mediating role of social competence. *Developmental Psychology, 45,* 1227–1240. **285, 408**

Shanahan, L., et al. 2008. Linkages between parents' differential treatment, youth depressive symptoms, and sibling relationships. *Journal of Marriage and Family, 70,* 480–494. **23, 329**

Shanahan, M. J., et al. 2008. Environmental contingencies and genetic propensities: Social capital, educational continuation, and dopamine receptor gene DRD2. *American Journal of Sociology, 114,* S260–286. **335, 339**

Shane, P. G. 1996. *What about America's homeless children?* Thousand Oaks, CA: Sage. **133**

Sharma, A. R., McGue, M. K., and Benson, P. L. 1998. The psychological adjustment of United States adopted adolescents and their nonadopted siblings. *Child Development, 69,* 791–802. **240**

Sharon, R. A. 1995. *Slaves no more: A study of the Buxton settlement, Upper Canada, 1849–1861.* PhD dissertation. Buffalo, NY: State University of New York. **44**

Shauman, K. A. 2010. Gender asymmetry in family migration: Occupational inequality or interspousal comparative advantage? *Journal of Marriage and Family, 72,* 375–392. **146**

Shephard, R. B. 1997. *Deemed unsuitable: Blacks from Oklahoma move to the Canadian Prairies in search of equality in the early twentieth century only to find racism in their new home.* Toronto: Umbrella Press. **45**

Shields, M. 2003. The health of Canada's shift workers. *Canadian Social Trends, 69,* 21–25. **99**

Shields, M., and Tremblay, S. 2005. Community belonging and self-perceived health. Statistics Canada, *The Daily,* December 21. **124**

Shook, S. E., et al. 2010. The mother-coparent relationship and youth adjustment : A study of African Amercian single-mother families. *Journal of Family Psychology, 24,* 243–251. **228**

Short, S., and Fengying, Z. 1998. Looking locally at China's one-child policy. *Studies in Family Planning, 29,* 373–387. **56**

Shuey, K., and Hardy, M. A. 2003. Assistance to aging parents and parents-in-law: Does lineage affect family allocation decisions? *Journal of Marriage and Family, 65,* 418–431. **306**

Shumway, D. R. 2003. *Modern love: Romance, intimacy and the marriage crisis.* New York: New York University Press. **189**

Shweder, R. A., et al. 2006. The cultural psychology of development: One mind, many mentalities. In W. A. Damon (Ed.), *Handbook of child development,* 5th Ed, vol. 1 (pp. 716–792). Chicago: University of Chicago Press. **71**

Sieving, R. E., et al. 2006. Friends' influence on adolescents' first sexual intercourse. *Perspectives on Sexual and Reproductive Health, 38,* 13–19. **207**

Silver, C. 2000. Being there: The time dual-earner couples spend with their children. *Canadian Social Trends, 57,* 20–29. **262, 263**

Silver, C. 2001. From sun-up to sundown: Work patterns of farming couples. *Canadian Social Trends, 61,* 12–15. **138**

Silverman, A. R. 1993. Outcomes of transracial adoption. *The Future of Children, 3,* 104–118. **243**

Silverstein, M., and Long, J. D. 1998. Trajectories of grandparents' perceived solidarity with adult grandchildren: A growth curve analysis over 23 years. *Journal of Marriage and Family, 60,* 912–923. **310**

Silverstein, M., Parrott, T. M., and Bengtson, V. L. 1995. Factors that predispose middle-aged sons and daughters to provide support to older parents. *Journal of Marriage and Family, 57,* 465–475. **306**

Silverstein, M., et al. 2010. Older parent-child relationships in six developed nations : Comparisons at the intersection of affection and conflict. *Journal of Marriage and Family, 72,* 1006–1021. **305**

Simms, G. P. 1993. Diasporic experience of Blacks in Canada: A discourse. *Dalhousie Review, 73,* 308–322. **44**

Simons, L. G., Simons, R. L., and Conger, R. D. 2004. Identifying the mechanisms whereby family religiosity influences the probability of adolescent antisocial behavior. *Journal of Comparative Family Studies, 35,* 547–563. **175**

Simons, R. L., et al. (Eds.). 1996. *Understanding differences between divorced and intact families.* Thousand Oaks, CA: Sage. **369**

Simons, R. L., et al. 1994a. Harsh corporal punishment versus quality of parental involvement as an explanation of adolescent maladjustment. *Journal of Marriage and the Family, 56,* 591–607. **291**

Simons, R. L., et al. 1994b. Economic pressure and harsh parenting. In R. D. Conger, G. H. Elder, Jr., and Associates (Eds.), *Families in troubled times: Adapting to change in rural America* (pp. 207–222). New York: Aldine de Gruyter. **139**

Simons, R. L., et al. 1994c. The impact of mothers' parenting, involvement by nonresidential fathers, and parental conflict on the adjustment of adolescent children. *Journal of Marriage and Family, 56,* 356–374. **293**

Simons, R. L., et al. 1995. A test of various perspectives on the intergenerational transmission of domestic violence. *Criminology, 33,* 141–172. **395**

Simons, R. L., et al. 1998. A test of latent trait versus life-course perspectives on the stability of adolescent antisocial behavior. *Criminology, 36,* 217–244. **382**

Simons, R. L., et al. 2002. Community differences in the association between parenting practices and child conduct problems. *Journal of Marriage and Family, 64,* 331–345. **129, 292, 293**

Singer, J. D., et al. 1998. Early child-care selection: Variation by geographic location, maternal characteristics, and family structure. *Developmental Psychology, 34,* 1129–1144. **154**

Singh, S., Darroch, J. E., and Frost, J. J. 2001. Socioeconomic disadvantage and adolescent women's sexual and reproductive behavior: The case of five developed countries. *Family Planning Perspectives, 33,* 258–268. **110**

Singh, S., et al. 2009. *Abortion worldwide: A decade of uneven progress.*Guttmacher Institute. **234**

Sinkewicz, M., and Garfinkel, I. 2009. Unwed fathers' ability to pay child support: New estimates accounting for multipartner fertility. *Demography, 46,* 247–263. **227, 352**

Skolnick, A. 1998. Solomon's children: The new biologism, psychological parenthood, attachment theory, and the best interests standard. In M. A. Mason, A. Skolnick, and S. D. Sugarman (Eds.), *All our families: New policies for a new century.* New York: Oxford University Press. **239**

Slomkowski, C., et al. 2001. Sisters, brothers, and delinquency: Evaluating social influence during early and middle adolescence. *Child Development, 72,* 271–283. **332**

Small, S. A., and Kerns, D. 1993. Unwanted sexual activity among peers during early and middle adolescence: Incidence and risk factors. *Journal of Marriage and Family, 55,* 941–952. **406**

Smith, D. E. 1993. The Standard North American family: SNAF as an ideological code. *Journal of Family Issues, 14,* 50–65. **19**

Smith, D. E. 1999. *Writing the social. Critique, theory, and investigations.* Toronto: University of Toronto Press. **24**

Smith, D. S. 1993. *Parent-generated home study in Canada: The national outlook, 1993.* Westfield, NB: Francombe Place.**19, 170**

Smith, G. C., and Hancock, R. 2010. Custodial grandmother-grandfather dyads: Pathways among marital distress, grandparent dysphoria, parenting practice, and grandchild adjustment. *Family Relations, 59,* 45–49. **309**

Smith, H. E. H., and Sullivan, L. M. 1995. Now that I know how to manage: Work and identity in the journals of Anne Langton. *Ontario History, 87,* 253–269. **41**

Smith, S. L., et al. 2006. A post-ASFA examination of adoption disruption. *Adoption Quarterly, 9,* 19–44. **241**

Smith, T. W. 1998. A review of church attendance measures. *American Sociological Review, 63,* 131–136. **172**

Smits, A., van Gaalen, R. I., and Mulder, C. H. 2010. Parent-child coresidence: Who moves in with whom and for whose needs? *Journal of Marriage and Family, 72*, 1022–1033. **304**

Smock, P. J., and Gupta, S. 2002. Cohabitation in contemporary North America. In A. Booth and A. C. Crouter (Eds.), *Just living together* (pp. 53–84). Mahwah, NJ: Erlbaum. **194, 356**

Smock, P. J., and Greenland, F. R. 2010. Diversity in pathways to parenthood: Patterns, implications, and emerging research directions. *Journal of Marriage and Family, 72*, 576–593. **220, 233, 352**

Smock, P. J., and Manning, W. D. 1997. Cohabiting partners' economic circumstances and marriage. *Demography, 34*, 331–341. **191**

Smyer, M. A., et al. 1998. Childhood adoption: Long-term effects in adulthood. *Psychiatry: Interpersonal and Biological Processes, 61*, 191–205. **241**

Smylie, L., Medaglia, S., and Maticka-Tyndale, E. 2006. The effect of social capital and sociodemographics on adolescent risk and sexual health behaviours. *The Canadian Journal of Human Sexuality, 15*, 95–113. **207**

Snyder, J., et al. 2008. Peer deviancy training and peer coercion: Dual processes associated with early-onset conduct problems. *Child Development, 79*, 252–268. **166**

Sobolewski, J. M., and King, V. 2005. The importance of the coparental relationship for non-resident fathers' ties to children. *Journal of Marriage and Family, 67*, 1196–1212. **365**

Solomon, J. C., and Marx, J. 1995. "To grandmother's house we go": Health and school adjustment of children raised solely by grandparents. *The Gerontologist, 35*, 386–394. **309**

South, S. D. 1996. Mate availability and the transition to unwed motherhood: A paradox of population structure. *Journal of Marriage and Family, 58*, 265–280. **110**

South, S. J., and Haynie, D. L. 2004. Friendship networks of mobile adolescents. *Social Forces, 83*, 315–350. **145**

South, S. J., Haynie, D. L., and Bose, S. 2005. Residential mobility and the onset of adolescent sexual activity. *Journal of Marriage and Family, 67*, 499–514. **145**

South, S. J., Trent, K., and Shen, Y. 2001. Changing partners: Toward a macrostructural-opportunity theory of marital dissolution. *Journal of Marriage and Family, 63*, 743–754. **354**

Spanier, G. B. 1976. Measuring dyadic adjustment: New scales for assessing the quality of marriage and similar dyads. *Journal of Marriage and Family, 42*, 15–27. **267**

Spencer, M. B., et al. 1996. Parental monitoring and adolescents' sense of responsibility for their own learning: An examination of sex differences. *Journal of Negro Education, 65*, 30–43. **288**

Spitze, G., and Trent, K. 2006. Gender differences in adult sibling relations in two-child families. *Journal of Marriage and Family, 68*, 977–992. **331**

Sprechner, S. 2001. Equity and social exchange in dating couples: Associations with satisfaction, commitment, and stability. *Journal of Marriage and Family, 63*, 599–613. **12**

Sprey, J. 2009. Institutionalization of the family and marriage: Questioning their cognitive and relational realities. *Journal of Family Theory & Review, 1*, 4–19. **5**

Stacey, J., and Biblarz, T. J. 2001. (How) does the sexual orientation of parents matter? *American Sociological Review, 66*, 159–183. **224**

Stack, S., and Eshleman, J. R. 1998. Marital status and happiness: A 17-nation study. *Journal of Marriage and Family, 60*, 527–536. **198**

Stambrook, F., and Hryniuk, S. 2000. Who were they really? Reflections on East European immigrants to Manitoba before 1914. *Prairie Forum, 25*, 215–232. **47**

Stanley, S. M., and Rhoades, G. 2009. "Sliding vs. deciding": Understanding a mystery. *Family Focus,* National Council on Family Relations, Summer. **193**

Stanley, S. M., Whitton, S. W., and Markman, H. J. 2004. Maybe I do: Interpersonal commitment and premarital or nonmarital cohabitation. *Journal of Family Issues, 25*, 496–519. **176, 195**

Stanley, S. M., et al. 2010. The timing of cohabitation and engagement : Impact on first and second marriages. *Journal of Marriage and Family, 72*, 906–918. **355**

Stanley, T. J. 2003. White supremacy, Chinese schooling, and school segregation in Victoria: The case of the Chinese students' strike, 1922–1923. In N. Janovicek and J. Parr (Eds.), *Histories of Canadian children and youth* (pp. 126–143). Toronto: Oxford University Press. **48**

Starrels, M. A., et al. 1997. The stress of caring for a parent: Effects of the elder's impairment on an employed adult child. *Journal of Marriage and Family, 59*, 860–872. **305, 306**

Statistics Canada. 2002a. *2001 Census of Canada: Profile of Canadian families and households: Diversification continues.* **3, 221, 368**

Statistics Canada. 2002b. 2001 Census: Marital status, common-law status, families, dwellings and households. *The Daily*, October 22. **141, 190, 191, 347**

Statistics Canada. 2003a. *Labour force historical review 2003.* Ottawa: Catalogue no. 71F0004XCB. **98**

Statistics Canada. 2003b. Family violence. *The Daily*, June 23. **380**

Statistics Canada. 2003c. Sexual offences. *The Daily*, July 25. **398**

Statistics Canada. 2003d. Household spending on domestic help. *The Daily*, August 26. **100**

Statistics Canada. 2003e. Witnessing violence: Aggression and anxiety in young children. *The Daily*, December 1. **387, 389**

Statistics Canada. 2003f. Grandparents and grandchildren. *The Daily*, Dec. 9. **307**

Statistics Canada. 2004a. Study: How long do people live in low income neighbourhoods? *The Daily*, January 21. **126**

Statistics Canada. 2004b. *Population 15 years and over by hours spent providing unpaid care or assistance to seniors, provinces and territories.* Accessed January 22, 2004. **304**

Statistics Canada. 2004c. *Owner households and tenant households by major payments and gross rent as a percentage of 2000 household income, provinces, and territories.* Accessed January 22, 2004. **140**

Statistics Canada. 2004d. *Families, households, and housing. Household activities.* Accessed February 21, 2004. **262**

Statistics Canada. 2004e. Study: Student reading performance in minority-language schools. *The Daily*, March 22. **167**

Statistics Canada. 2004f. Induced abortions. *The Daily*, March 31. **234**

Statistics Canada. 2004h. Low income in census metropolitan areas. *The Daily*, April 7. **54**

Statistics Canada. 2004i. Births. *The Daily*, April 19. **229, 232**

Statistics Canada. 2004j. Divorces. *The Daily*, May 4. **351**

Statistics Canada. 2004k. Aboriginal Peoples Survey: Children who live in non-reserve areas. *The Daily*, July 9. **156, 161**

Statistics Canada. 2004l. General Social Survey: Social engagement. *The Daily*, July 6. **13, 113, 172**

Statistics Canada. 2004m. Study: Economic consequences of widowhood. *The Daily*, June 22. **368**

Statistics Canada. 2005a. National Longitudinal Survey of Children and Youth: Home environment, income and child behaviour. *The Daily*, February 21. **111, 292**

Statistics Canada. 2005b. Adult correctional services. *The Daily*, December 16. **108**

Statistics Canada. 2005c. Social relationships in rural and urban Canada. *The Daily*, June 21. **136**

Statistics Canada. 2005d. Migration. *The Daily*, September 28. **144**

Statistics Canada. 2006a. Relationship between reading literacy and education outcomes. *The Daily*, June 7. **158**

Statistics Canada. 2006b. Readiness to learn at school among five-year-old children. *The Daily*, November 27. **158**

Statistics Canada. 2006c. Interreligious unions. *The Daily*, October 3. **188**

Statistics Canada. 2006d. *Report on the demographic situation in Canada: 2003 and 2004*. Catalogue no. 91-209-XIE. **354, 357, 371**

Statistics Canada. 2006e. Aboriginal people as victims and offenders. *The Daily*, June 6. **386, 388**

Statistics Canada. 2007a. Study: Canada's immigrant labour market. *The Daily*, September 10. **112**

Statistics Canada. 2007b. Study: Why are youth from lower-income families less likely to attend university? *The Daily*, February 8. **118**

Statistics Canada. 2007c. Study: Time with the family. *The Daily*, February 13. **104**

Statistics Canada. 2007d. *Mobility status 5 years ago, 2006 Census*. **144, 145**

Statistics Canada. 2007e. Marriages. *The Daily*, January 17. **197, 201, 202**

Statistics Canada. 2007f. *Population by marital status and sex*. Table 051–0010. **346, 368**

Statistics Canada. 2007g. *Census families in private households by family structure and presence of children, by province and territory (2006 Census)*. September 19. **218**

Statistics Canada. 2007h. 2006 Census: Families, marital status, households and dwelling characteristics. *The Daily*, September 12. **201, 209, 300, 439**

Statistics Canada. 2007i. Study: Self-reported delinquency among young people in Toronto. *The Daily*, September 25. **287, 372**

Statistics Canada. 2008a. 2006 Census: Ethnic origin, visible minorities, place of work and mode of transportation. *The Daily*, April 2. **48, 54, 57**

Statistics Canada. 2008b. Fathers' use of paid parental leave. *The Daily*, June 23. **53**

Statistics Canada. 2008c. *Farm operators by highest level of educational attainment, by sex and primary occupation, by province, 2001 and 2006*. **136**

Statistics Canada. 2008d. *Farm population and total population by rural and urban population, by province, 2001 and 2006*. **136**

Statistics Canada. 2008e. Agriculture-population linkage data for the 2006 Census. *The Daily*, December 2. **136**

Statistics Canada. 2008f. Divorces in Canada, 2005. *The Daily*, November 18. **346, 347, 348, 349**

Statistics Canada. 2008g. Children and youth. October 18. **100, 308**

Statistics Canada. 2008h. Study: Health and development of children of older first-time mothers. *The Daily*, September 24. **218, 229, 230**

Statistics Canada. 2009a. *Aboriginal peoples*. Ottawa: Statistics Canada, July 27. **48**

Statistics Canada. 2009b. *Immigration in Canada: A portrait of the foreign-born population, 2006 Census: Immigration: Driver of population growth*. Ottawa: Statistics Canada, May 05. **48**

Statistics Canada. 2009c. *Canada's ethnocultural mosaic, 2006 Census: National Picture*. Ottawa: Statistics Canada, September 03. **53**

Statistics Canada. 2009d. *Population by selected ethnic origins, by province, and territory (2006 Census)*. Ottawa: Statistics Canada, July 28. **57, 58**

Statistics Canada. 2009e. *Ethnic origin, single and multiple ethnic origin responses and sex for the population of Canada, 2006 Census*. Ottawa: Statistics Canada. July 26. **51**

Statistics Canada. 2009f. Study: Hours and earnings of dual-earner couples. *The Daily*, April 24. **97**

Statistics Canada. 2009g. Study: Earnings of women with and without children. *The Daily*, March 24. **97, 99**

Statistics Canada. 2009h. *Average earning by sex and work pattern*. Table 2002–0102. **96, 99**

Statistics Canada. 2009i. *Average total income by economic family types (2003–2007)*. Table 202–0403. **429**

Statistics Canada. 2009j. *Persons in low income before tax, by prevalence in percent (2003 to 2007)*. Table 202–0802. **106, 112, 428**

Statistics Canada. 2009k. Study: Immigrants' use of non-official languages in the workplace. *The Daily*, January 20. **112**

Statistics Canada. 2009m. Off-farm work by farmers. *The Daily*, March 9. **138**

Statistics Canada. 2009n. Canadian nine-year-olds at school, 2006–2007. *The Daily*, September 25. **158**

Statistics Canada. 2009p. *Canada's ethnocultural mosaic, 2006 Census: National picture. Mixed unions*. September 03. **187**

Statistics Canada. 2009q. Births. *The Daily*, September 22. **49, 231, 232**

Statistics Canada. 2009r. *Therapeutic Abortion Survey*. Table 106–9005, October 16. **234**

Statistics Canada. 2009s. *Crude birth rate, females 15 to 19 years, provinces and territories, for 2007*. Tables 102–4505. **225**

Statistics Canada. 2009t. Canada's population estimates: Age and sex. *The Daily*, November 27. **420**

Statistics Canada. 2010a. Chart 1. Religious attendance rates by sex, 1985 to 2008. *Canadian Social Trends*, Social Fact Sheet, 89, March 8. **173**

Statistics Canada. 2010b. Study: Police-reported dating violence. *The Daily*, June 29. **381**

Statistics Canada. 2010c. Study: The health of First Nations living off-reserve, Inuit and Métis adults. *The Daily*, June 23. **50**

Steele, F., et al. 2009. Consequences of family disruption on children's educational outcomes in Norway. *Demography*, 46, 553–574. **369**

Steinberg, L. 2001. We know some things: Parent/adolescent relationships in retrospect and prospect. *Journal of Research on Adolescence*, 11, 1–19. **438**

Steinberg, L., and Darling, N. 1994. The broader context of social influence in adolescence. In R. K. Silbereisen and E. Todt (Eds.), *Adolescence in context* (pp. 25–45). New York: Springer-Verlag. **287**

Steinberg, L., Brown, B. B., and Dornbusch, S. M. 1996. *Beyond the classroom: Why school reform has failed and what parents need to do*. New York: Simon and Schuster. **160, 288**

Steinberg, L., Dornbusch, S., and Brown, B. 1992. Ethnic differences in adolescent achievement in ecological perspective. *American Psychologist, 47*, 723–729. **290**

Steinberg, L., et al. 1995. Authoritative parenting and adolescent adjustment: An ecological journey. In P. Moen, G. H. Elder, Jr., and K. Lüscher (Eds.), *Examining lives in context* (pp. 423–466). Washington, DC: American Psychological Association. **130, 299**

Steinberg, L., et al. 2006. Patterns of competence and adjustment among adolescents from authoritative, authoritarian, indulgent, and neglectful homes: A replication in a sample of serious juvenile offenders. *Journal of Research on Adolescence, 16*, 47–58. **288**

Stenberg, S.-A. 2000. Inheritance of welfare recipiency: An intergenerational study of social assistance recipiency in postwar Sweden. *Journal of Marriage and Family, 62*, 228–239. **479**

Stephan, W. G., and Stephan, C. W. 1991. Intermarriage effects on personality, adjustment, and intergroup relations in two samples of students. *Journal of Marriage and Family, 53*, 241–250. **243**

Sternberg, K. J., et al. 1993. Effects of domestic violence on children's behavior problems and depression. *Developmental Psychology, 29*, 44–52. **393**

Stevenson, K. 1999. Family characteristics of problem kids. *Canadian Social Trends, 55*, 2–6. **288, 318**

Stevens-Simon, C., Nelligan, D., and Kelly, L. 2001. Adolescents at risk of mistreating their children: Part 1: Prenatal identification. *Child Abuse & Neglect, 6*, 737–751. **228**

Stewart, S. D. 1999a. Disneyland dads, Disneyland moms? How nonresident parents spend time with their absent children. *Journal of Family Issues, 20*, 539–556. **352**

Stewart, S. D. 1999b. Nonresident mothers' and fathers' social contact with children. *Journal of Marriage and Family, 61*, 894–907. **352**

Stewart, W., Huntly, A., and Blaney, F. 2001. *The implications of restorative justice for Aboriginal women and children survivors of violence: A comparison overview of five communities in British Columbia.* Vancouver, BC: Aboriginal Women's Action Network. **388**

Stimpson, J. P., Peek, M. K., and Markides, K. S. 2006. Depression and mental health among older Mexican American spouses. *Aging and Mental Health, 10*, 386–393. **266**

Stobert, S., and Kemeny, A. 2003. Childfree by choice. *Canadian Social Trends, 69*, 7–10. **231**

Stolzenberg, R. M., Blair-Loy, M., and Waite, L. J. 1995. Religious participation in early adulthood: Age and family life cycle effects on church membership. *American Sociological Review, 60*, 84–103. **178**

Stoneman, Z., et al. 1999. Effects of residential instability on Head Start children and their relationships with older siblings: Influences of child emotionality and conflict between family caregivers. *Child Development, 70*, 1246–1262. **146**

Story, L. B., and Repetti, R. 2006. Daily occupational stressors and marital behavior. *Journal of Family Psychology, 20*, 690–700. **266**

Stouffer, A. P. 1992. *The light of nature and the law of God: Antislavery in Ontario, 1833–1877.* Baton Rouge, LA: Louisiana State University Press. **44**

Stouthamer-Loeber, M., et al. 2001. Maltreatment of boys and the development of disruptive and delinquent behavior. *Development and Psychopathology, 13*, 941–955. **393**

Straus, M. A. 1979. Measuring intrafamily conflict and violence: The Conflict Tactics (CT) Scales. *Journal of Marriage and Family, 41*, 75–88. **384**

Straus, M. A. 2008. Ending spanking can make a major contribution to preventing physical abuse. *Family Focus.* National Council on Family Relations. December. **291, 292**

Straus, M. A., and Kaufman-Kantor, G. 2005. Definition and measurement of neglectful behavior: Some principles and guidelines. *Child Abuse & Neglect, 29*, 19–29. **396**

Straus, M. A., and Ulma, A. 2003. Violence of children against mothers in relation to violence between parents and corporal punishment by parents. *Journal of Comparative Family Studies, 34*, 41–60. **407**

Straus, M. A., Gelles, R. J., and Steinmetz, S. K. 1980. *Behind closed doors: Violence in the American family.* Garden City, NY: Anchor. **402**

Strawbridge, W. J., et al. 1997. New burdens or more of the same? Comparing grandparents, spouse, and adult-child caregivers. *The Gerontologist, 37*, 505–510. **309**

Strazdins, L., et al. 2006. Unsociable work? Nonstandard work schedules, family relationships, and children's well-being. *Journal of Marriage and Family, 68*, 394–410. **99**

Strohschein, L. 2005. Parental divorce and child mental health trajectories. *Journal of Marriage and Family, 67*, 191–206. **116, 367**

Strohschein, L. 2010. Generating heat or light? The challenge of social variables. *Journal of Marriage and Family, 72*, 23–28. **223, 248**

Strohschein, L., Noralou, R., and Bronwell, M. 2009. Family structure histories and high school completion: Evidence from a population-based registry. *Canadian Journal of Sociology, 34*, 83–104. **350, 364**

Stromberg, B., et al. 2002. Neurological sequelae in children born after in-vitro fertilization: A population-based study. *Lancet, 359*, 461–465. **237**

Sturge-Apple, M., Davies, P. T., and Cummings., E. M. 2006. Hostility and withdrawal in marital conflict: Effects on parental emotional unavailability and inconsistent discipline. *Journal of Family Psychology, 20*, 227–238. **277**

Su, T. F., and Costigan, C. L. 2009. The development of children's ethnic identity in immigrant Chinese families in Canada. *Journal of Early Adolescence, 29*, 638–663. **58**

Sui-Chu, E. H., and Willms, J. D. 1996. Effects of parental involvement on eighth-grade achievement. *Sociology of Education, 69*, 126–141. **163**

Suitor, J. J., and Pillemer, K. 2000. Did mom really love you best? Exploring the role of within-family differences on parental favoritism. *Motivation and Emotion, 24*, 104–119. **326**

Suitor, J. J., and Pillemer, K. 2007. Mothers' favoritism in later life: The role of children's birth order. *Research on Aging, 29*, 32–55. **303, 327**

Suitor, J. J., Pillemer, K., and Sechrist, J. 2006. Within-family differences in mothers' support to adult children. *Journals of Gerontology, 61B*, S10–17. **303**

Suitor, J. J., et al. 2009. The role of perceived maternal favoritism in sibling relations in midlife. *Journal of Marriage and Family, 71*, 1026–1038. **329**

Sullivan, A. 1995. *Virtually normal: An argument about homosexuality.* New York: Alfred A. Knopf. **201**

Sun, Y., and Li, Y. 2008. Stable postdivorce family structures during late adolescence and socioeconomic consequences in adulthood. *Journal of Marriage and Family, 70*, 129–143. **362, 374**

Sussman, D. 2006. Wives as primary breadwinners. *Perspectives on Labour and Income, 7.* **97**

Suzuki, D., and Taylor, R. D. 2009. *The big picture: Reflections on science, humanity, and a quickly changing planet.* Vancouver: Greystone. 72

Sweeney, M. M. 2010. Remarriage and stepfamilies: Strategic sites for family scholarship in the 21st century. *Journal of Marriage and Family, 72,* 667–684. 370

Sweet, R., and Anisef, P. (Eds.). 2005. *Preparing for post-secondary education: New roles for governments and families.* Montreal: McGill-Queen's University Press. 152

Swinford, S. P., et al. 2000. Harsh physical discipline in childhood and violence in later romantic involvements: The mediating role of problem behaviors. *Journal of Marriage and Family, 62,* 508–519. 381, 393

Swisher, R. R., et al. 1998. The long arm of the farm: How an occupation structures exposure and vulnerability to stressors across role domains. *Journal of Health and Social Behavior, 39,* 72–89. 138

Swiss, L., and Le Bourdais, C. 2009. Father-child contact after separation: The influence of living arrangements. *Journal of Family Issues, 30,* 623–652. 352

Szinovacz, M. E. 2000. Changes in housework after retirement: A panel analysis. *Journal of Marriage and Family, 62,* 78–92. 264

Szinovacz, M. E., and Davey, A. 2005. Retirement and marital decision-making: Effects on retirement satisfaction. *Journal of Marriage and Family, 67,* 387–398. 273

Tach, L., and Halpern-Meekin, S. 2009. How does premarital cohabitation affect trajectories of marital quality? *Journal of Marriage and Family, 71,* 298–317. 356

Tach, L., Mincy, R., and Edin, K. 2010. Parenting as a "package deal": Relationships, fertility, and nonresident father involvement among unmarried parents. *Demography, 47,* 181–204. 352

Talbani, A., and Hasanali, P. 2000. Adolescent females between tradition and modernity: Gender role socialization in south Asian immigrant culture. *Journal of Adolescence, 23*(5), 615–627. 61

Talbott, S. L. 1995. *The future does not compute: Transcending the machines in our midst.* Sebastopol, CA: O'Reilly & Associates. 419

Tan, T. X. 2009. School-age adopted Chinese girls' behavioral adjustment, academic performance, and social skills: Longitudinal results. *American Journal of Orthopsychiatry, 79,* 244–251. 244

Tang, P. N., and Dion, K. 1999. Gender and acculturation in relation to traditionalism: Perceptions of self and parents among Chinese students. *Sex Roles, 41,* 17–29. 58

Tanimura, M., et al. 2007. Television viewing, reduced parental utterance, and delayed speech development in infants and young children. *Archives of Pediatrics & Adolescent Medicine, 161,* 618–619. 89

Tarver-Behring, S., and Barkley, R. A. 1985. The mother-child interactions of hyperactive boys and their normal siblings. *American Journal of Orthopsychiatry, 55,* 202–209. 293

Tasker, F., and Golombok, S. 1995. Adults raised as children in lesbian families. American Journal of Orthopsychiatry, 65, 203–215. 222, 224

Tasker, F. L., and Golombok, S. 1997. *Growing up in a lesbian family: Effects on child development.* New York: Guilford Press. 222

Tatara, T. 1993. Understanding the nature and scope of domestic elder abuse with the use of state aggregate data: Summaries of the key findings of a national survey of state APS and aging agencies. *Journal of Elder Abuse and Neglect, 5,* 35–57. 409

Taylor, A. 2002. Keeping up with the kids in a wired world. *Transition,* Autumn, 3–6. 84, 88, 89

Taylor, D. M., et al. 2004. "Street kids": Towards an understanding of their motivational context. *Canadian Journal of Behavioural Science, 36,* 1–16. 133

Taylor, J. E., and Norris, J. A. 2000. Sibling relationships, fairness, and conflict over transfer of the farm. *Family Relations, 49,* 277–283. 138

Taylor, J. L., et al. 2008. Siblings of adults with mild intellectual deficits or mental illness. Differential life course outcomes. *Journal of Family Psychology, 22,* 905–914. 324

Taylor, R. J., Chatters, L. M., and Levin, J. 2004. *Religion in the lives of African Americans.* Thousand Oaks, CA: Sage. 53, 172

Taylor-Butts, A. 2009. *Family violence in Canada. Section 2: Fact sheet—police-reported spousal violence in Canada.* Ottawa: Statistics Canada. Publication no. 85-224-X. 385

Teachman, J. 2003. Childhood living arrangements and the formation of coresidential unions. *Journal of Marriage and Family, 65,* 507–524. 221

Teachman, J. D. 2004. The childhood living arrangements of children and the characteristics of their marriages. *Journal of Family Issues, 25,* 86–111. 369

Teachman, J. D. 2008. Complex life course patterns and the risk of divorce in second marriages. *Journal of Marriage and Family, 70,* 294–305. 350, 355, 370

Teachman, J. D., and Tedrow, L. 2008. Divorce, race, and military service: More than equal pay and equal opportunity. *Journal of Marriage and Family, 70,* 1030–1044. 77

Teti, D. M., et al. 1996. And baby makes four: Predictors of attachment security among preschool-age firstborns during the transition to siblinghood. *Child Development, 67,* 579–596. 316

Theurer, K., and Wister, A. 2010. Altruistic behaviour and social capital as predictors of well-being among older Canadians. *Ageing and Society, 30,* 157–181. 13

Thibaut, J. W., and Kelly, H. H. 1959. *The social psychology of groups.* New York: Wiley. 12

Thomas, A., and Sawhill, I. 2005. For love and money? The impact of family structure on family income. *Future of Children, 15,* 57–74. 110

Thomas, D. 2010. Foreign nationals working temporarily in Canada. *Canadian Social Trends, 90,* June 8. 113

Thompson, L. 2010. *Are you the descendant of a Home Child?* Ontario Historical Society, April 2010 Bulletin. <www.ontariohistoricalsociety.ca>. 46

Thorne, B. 1992. Feminism and the family: Two decades of thought. In B. Thorne and M. Yalom (Eds.), *Rethinking the family: Some feminist questions* (rev. Ed., pp. 3–30). Boston: Northeastern University Press. 24

Thornton, A. 2005. *Reading history sideways.* Chicago: The University of Chicago Press. 6, 38, 67

Thornton, A., and Lin, H.-S. 1994. *Social change and the family in Taiwan.* Chicago: University of Chicago Press. 335

Thornton, A., and Young-DeMarco, L. 2001. Four decades of trends in attitudes toward family issues in the United States: The 1960s through the 1990s. *Journal of Marriage and Family, 63,* 1009–1037. 212

Tieman, W., et al. 2008. Young adult international adoptees' search for birth parents. *Journal of Family Psychology, 22,* 678–687. 245

Tillman, K. H. 2008. "Non-traditional" siblings and the academic outcomes of adolescents. *Social Science Research, 37,* 88–108. 372

Tilly, L. A., and Scott, J. W. 2001. The family economy in modern England and France. In B. J. Fox (Ed.), *Family patterns, gender relations*, 2nd Ed. (pp. 78–107). Toronto: Oxford University Press. **41**

Torr, B. M., and Short, S. E. 2004. Second births and the second shift: A research note on gender equity and fertility. *Population and Development Review, 30,* 109–130. **419**

Torres, J. 2009. *Children & cities: Planning to grow together.* Ottawa: The Vanier Institute of the Family. **124**

Townsend, A. L., and Franks, M. M. 1997. Quality of the relationship between elderly spouses: Influence on spouse caregivers' subjective effectiveness. *Family Relations, 46,* 33–39. **273**

Townsend-Batten, B. 2002. Staying in touch: Contact between adults and their parents. *Canadian Social Trends, 64,* 9–12. **302, 303**

Treas, J., and Giesen, D. 2000. Sexual infidelity among married and cohabiting Americans. *Journal of Marriage and the Family, 62,* 48–60. **176, 195, 212**

Tremblay, J., et al. 2002. Valeur prévisionnelle de la différenciation de soi et des stratégies religieuses d'adaptation dans l'étude de la satisfaction conjugale. *Revue Canadienne des Sciences du Comportement, 34,* 19–27. **176, 355**

Trentacosta, C. J., and Shaw, D. C. 2008. Maternal predictors of rejecting parenting and early adolescent antisocial behavior. *Journal of Abnormal Child Psychology, 36,* 247–259. **279**

Trocmé, N., et al. 2003. Nature and severity of physical harm caused by child abuse and neglect: Results from the Canadian Incidence Survey. *Canadian Medical Association Journal, 169,* 911–919. **392**

Trocmé, N., et al. 2005. What is driving increasing child welfare caseloads in Ontario? Analysis of the 1993 and the 1998 Ontario Incidence Studies. *Child Welfare, 84,* 341–362. **395**

Trudel, M. 1973. *The beginnings of New France 1524–1663.* Toronto: McClelland and Stewart. **37, 44**

Trusty, J. 1998. Family influences on educational expectations of late adolescents. *The Journal of Educational Research, 5,* 260–270. **160**

Tu, W., et al. 2009. Time from first intercourse to first sexually transmitted infection diagnosis among adolescent women. *Archives of Pediatrics & Adolescent Medicine, 163,* 1106–1111. **87**

Tucker, C. J., Marx, J., and Long, L. 1998. "Moving on": Residential mobility and children's school lives. *Sociology of Education, 71,* 111–129. **145**

Tucker, C. J., McHale, S. M., and Crouter, A. C. 2003. Dimensions of mothers' and fathers' differential treatment of siblings: Links with adolescents' sex-typed personal quality. *Family Relations, 52,* 241–248. **326**

Tudge, J. 2008. *The everyday lives of young children: Culture, class, and child rearing in diverse societies.* New York: Cambridge University Press. **10, 74**

Turcotte, M. 2006. General Social Survey: Commuting times. *The Daily,* June 12. **104**

Turcotte, M., and Schellenberg, G. 2007. *A portrait of seniors in Canada.* Ottawa: Statistics Canada, Publication no 89-519-XWE, February 27. **305, 409, 419, 439**

Turcotte, M., and Vézina, M. 2010. Migration from central to surrounding municipalities in Toronto, Montréal and Vancouver. *Canadian Social Trends, 90,* June 8. **144**

Turcotte, P. 2002. Changing conjugal life in Canada. *The Daily,* July 11. **193, 370, 420**

Turcotte, P., and Bélanger, A. 1997. *The dynamics of formation and dissolution of first common-law unions in Canada.* Ottawa: Statistics Canada. **193**

Turner, H. A., Finkelhor, D., and Ormrod, R. 2007. Family structure variations in patterns and predictors of child victimization. *American Journal of Orthopsychiatry, 77,* 289–295.

Turner, R. J., Sorenson, A. M., and Turner, J. B. 2000. Social contingencies in mental health: A seven-year follow-up study of teenage mothers. *Journal of Marriage and Family, 62,* 777–791. **226**

Twenge, J. M., Campbell, W. K., and Foster, C. A. 2003. Parenthood and marital satisfaction: A meta-analytic review. *Journal of Marriage and Family, 65,* 574–583. **233**

Tyler, K. A., and Bersani, B. E. 2008. A longitudinal study of early adolescent precursors to running away. *Journal of Early Adolescence, 28,* 230–251. **133**

Tyler, T. 2004. Ottawa backs gay divorce. *Toronto Star.* July 22, A1, A19. **346**

Tyyskä, V. 2001. *Long and winding road: Adolescence and youth in Canada today.* Toronto: Canadian Scholars' Press. **295**

UAPS (Urban Aboriginal Peoples Study). 2010. (Led by M. Adams.) Environics, April. **50**

Udry, J. R. 2003. How to string straw into gold. In A. C. Crouter and A. Booth (Eds.), *Children's influence on family dynamics* (pp. 49–54). Mahwah, NJ: Erlbaum. **340**

Uecker, J. E. 2008. Religion, pledging, and the premarital sexual behavior of married young adults. *Journal of Marriage and Family, 70,* 728–744. **207**

Uecker, J. E., and Stokes, C. E. 2008. Early marriage in the United States. *Journal of Marriage and Family, 70,* 835–846. **78**

Uhlenberg, P. 2009. Children in an aging society. *The Journals of Gerontology: Series B, 64B,* 489–497. **75**

Uhlenberg, P., and Hammill, B. G. 1998. Frequency of grandparent contact with grandchild sets: Six factors that make a difference. *The Gerontologist, 38,* 276–285. **375**

Umberson, D. 2003. *Death of a parent: Transition to a new adult identity.* Cambridge, UK: Cambridge University Press. **310**

Umberson, D., et al. 2005. As good as it gets? A life course perspective on marital quality. *Social Forces, 84,* 493–512. **258, 276**

Umberson, D., et al. 2006. You make me sick: Marital quality and health over the life course. *Journal of Health and Social Behavior, 47,* 1–16. **271**

United Nations. 2008. *Demographic yearbook.* New York: United Nations. **347**

United Way of Toronto. 2001. *A decade of decline: Poverty and income inequality in the City of Toronto in the 1990s.* **106, 126**

Updegraff, K. A., and Obeidallah, C. L. 1999. Young adolescents' patterns of involvement with siblings and friends. *Social Development, 8,* 52–69. **321**

U.S. Commission on Civil Rights. 1977. *Window dressing on the set: Women and minorities in television.* Washington, DC: A report of the U.S. Commission on Civil Rights.

U.S. Department of Health and Human Services. 2002. *Trends in sexual risk behaviors among high school students—United States, 1991–2001.* Center for Chronic Disease, September 27. **88**

Uzzell, O., and Peebles-Wilkins, W. 1989. Black spouse abuse: A focus on relational factors and intervention strategies. *Western Journal of Black Studies, 13,* 10–16. **387**

Vaaler, M. L., Ellison, C. G., and Powers, D. A. 2009. Religious influences on the risk of marital dissolution. *Journal of Marriage and Family, 71,* 917–934. **176, 177**

Vaillancourt, R. 2009. *Family violence in Canada. Section 4: Police-reported family violence against older adults.* Ottawa: Statistics Canada, Catalogue no. 85-224-X. **408, 409**

van den Akker, O. 2007. Psychosocial aspects of surrogate motherhood. *Human Reproduction Update, 31,* 53–62. **238**

van den Akker, O. B. A. 1994. Something old, something new, something borrowed, and something taboo. *Journal of Reproductive and Infant Psychology, 12,* 179–188. **236**

Vanderschelden, M. 2006. *Les ruptures d'unions: plus fréquentes, mais pas plus précoces.* Paris: INSEE, 1107, Novembre. **350**

Vanfraussen, K., et al. 2003. Family functioning of lesbian families created by donor insemination. *American Journal of Orthopsychiatry, 73,* 78–90. **223**

van Ijzendoorn, M. H., et al. 2005. Adoption and cognitive development: A meta-analytic comparison of adopted and non-adopted children's IQ and school performance. *Psychological Bulletin, 131,* 301–316. **240, 247**

Vanier Institute of the Family. 2002. *Sources of diversity: geography, ethnicity, gender, kinship ties and technology.* Ottawa: Vanier Institute of the Family. <www.vifamily.ca>. Accessed December 8. **239**

Vanier Institute of the Family. 2004. *Profiling Canada's families. III.* Ottawa: Vanier Institute of the Family. **246**

Van Kirk, S. 1992. The custom of the country: An examination of fur trade marriage practices. In B. Bradbury (Ed.), *Canadian family history.* Toronto: Copp Clark Pitman. **43**

van Roode, T., et al. 2009. Child sexual abuse and persistence of risky sexual behaviors and negative social outcomes over adulthood: Findings from a birth cohort. *Child Abuse & Neglect, 33,* 161–172. **401**

Varga, D. 1997. *Constructing the child: A history of Canadian day care.* Toronto: James Lorimer. **152**

Veblen, T. 1899. *The theory of the leisure class.* New York: Modern Library. **105**

Vézina, M., and Turcotte, M. 2009. *Forty-year-old mothers of preschool children: A profile.* Ottawa, Statistics Canada. **229, 230**

Vézina, M., and Turcotte, M. 2010. Caring for a parent who lives far away: The consequences. Statistics Canada, *The Daily,* January 26. **440**

Viding, E., et al. 2005. Evidence for substantial genetic risk for psychopathy in 7-year-olds. *Journal of Child Psychology and Psychiatry, 46,* 592–597. **337**

Villeneuve-Gokalp, C. 1997. Vivre en couple chacun chez soi. *Population, 5,* 1050–1982. **78**

Viner, R. M., and Tayler, B. 2005. Adult health and social outcomes of children who have been in public care: Population-based study. *Pediatrics, 115,* 894–899. **247**

Voisey, P. 1987. *Vulcan: The making of a Prairie community.* Toronto: University of Toronto Press. **47**

Volling, B. L. 1997. The family correlates of maternal and paternal perceptions of differential treatment in early childhood. *Family Relations, 46,* 227–236. **327, 329**

Voorpostel, M., and Blieszner, R. 2008. Intergenerational solidarity and support between adult siblings. *Journal of Marriage and Family, 70,* 157–167. **331**

Vosko, L. F. 2002. Mandatory "marriage" or obligatory waged work. In S. Bashevkin (Ed.), *Women's work is never done* (pp. 165–199). New York: Routledge. **109, 248**

Votruba-Drzal, E., Coley, R. L., and Chase-Lansdale, P. L. 2004. Child care and low income children's development: Direct and moderated effects. *Child Development, 75,* 296–312. **155**

Vroegh, K. S. 1997. Transracial adoptees: Developmental status after 17 years. *American Journal of Orthopsychiatry, 67,* 568–575. **243**

Wagmiller, R. L., Jr., et al. 2006. The dynamics of economic disadvantage and children's life chances. *American Sociological Review, 71,* 847–866. **116**

Waite, L. J., and Gallagher, M. 2000. *The case for marriage.* Cambridge, MA: Harvard University Press. **198, 357**

Waite, L. J., et al. 2002. *Does divorce make people happy?* Institute for American Values. **359**

Waite, L. J., Luo, Y., and Levin, A. C. 2009. Marital happiness and marital stability: Consequences for psychological well-being. *Social Science Research, 3,* 201–212. **360**

Walby, S. 1997. *Gender transformation.* London: Routledge. **248**

Waldfogel, J., Han, W.-J., and Brooks-Gunn, J. 2002. The effects of early maternal employment on child cognitive development. *Demography, 39,* 369–392. **101**

Walker, A. J., and McGraw, L. A. 2000. Who is responsible for responsible fathering? *Journal of Marriage and Family, 62,* 563–569. **351**

Walker, J. 1976. *The Black Loyalists: The search for a promised land in Nova Scotia and Sierra Leone, 1783–1807.* London: Longman. **45**

Walker, J. M. 1980. *A history of Blacks in Canada.* Ottawa: Minister of State for Multiculturalism and Supply and Services Canada. **44**

Wall, C. S., and Madak, P. R. 1991. Indian students' academic self-concept and their perceptions of teacher and parent aspirations for them in a band-controlled school and a provincial school. *Canadian Journal of Native Education, 18,* 43–51. **167**

Wall, G. 2001. Moral construction of motherhood in breastfeeding discourse. *Gender and Society, 15,* 592–610. **20**

Wall, G. 2004. Is your child's brain potential maximized?: Mothering in an age of new brain research. *Atlantis, 28.* 2, 41–50. **19, 72, 162, 163, 286**

Wall, G. 2009. Childhood and child-rearing. In M. Baker (Ed.), *Families: changing trends in Canada,* 6th Ed. (pp. 68–90). Toronto: McGraw-Hill Ryerson. **285**

Wallace, H. 1999. *Family violence: Legal, medical, and social perspectives,* 2nd Ed. Boston: Allyn & Bacon. **402**

Wallace, M., Wisener, M., and Collins, K. 2006. *Neighbourhood characteristics and the distribution of crime in Regina. Crime and Justice Research Paper Series.* Ottawa, Statistics Canada Catalogue no. 85-561-MIE. no. 8. **127**

Wallerstein, J. S. 1998. Children of divorce: A society in search of policy. In M. A. Mason, A. Skolnick, and S. D. Sugarman (Eds.), *All our families: New policies for a new century* (pp. 66–94). New York: Oxford University Press. **365**

Walsh, C., MacMillan, H., and Jamieson, E. 2002. The relationship between parental psychiatric disorder and child physical and sexual abuse: Findings from the Ontario health supplement. *Child Abuse & Neglect, 26,* 11–22. **393**

Wang, Y., and Marcotte, D. E. 2007. Golden years? The labor market effects of caring for grandchildren. *Journal of Marriage and Family, 69,* 1283–1296. **309**

Ward, C. 1998. Community resources and school performance: The Northern Cheyenne case. *Sociological Inquiry, 68*, 83–113. **168**

Ward, R. A., Spitze, G., and Deane, G. 2009. The more the merrier? Multiple parent-adult child relations. *Journal of Marriage and Family, 71*, 161–173. **371**

Warman, C. 2007. Ethnic enclaves and immigrant earnings growth. *Canadian Journal of Economics, 40*, 401–422. **112**

Warner, T. D. 2010. Violent acts and injurious consequences: An examination of competing hypotheses about intimate partner violence using agency-based data. *Journal of Family Violence, 25*, 183–193. **381**

Wartella, E., Caplowitz, A. G., and Lee, J. H. 2004. From Baby Einstein to Leapfrog, from Doom to the Sims, from instant messaging to Internet chat rooms: Public interest in the role of interactive media in children's lives. *Social Policy Report, 18*, 3, 19. **86**

Watamura, S. E., et al. 2003. Morning-to-afternoon increases in cortisol concentrations for infants and toddlers at child care: Age differences and behavioral correlates. *Child Development, 74*, 1006–1020. **155**

Waters, J. L. 2002. Flexible families? Astronaut households and the experiences of mothers in Vancouver, British Columbia. *Social & Cultural Geography, 3*, 117–134. **76**

Weaver, S. E., Coleman, M., and Ganong, L. H. 2004. The sibling relationship in young adulthood: Sibling functions and relationship perceptions as influenced by sibling pair composition. *Journal of Family Issues, 24*, 245–263. **331**

Wegar, K. 1997. *Adoption, identity, and kinship: The debate over sealed birth records.* New Haven, CT: Yale University Press. **239**

Wekerle, C., et al. 2009. The contribution of childhood emotional abuse to teen dating violence among child protective services-involved youth. *Child Abuse & Neglect, 33*, 45–58. **382, 394**

Welsh, M. 2006. "The game." *Toronto Star.* April 29, A1, A26–27. **128**

Wentzel, K. R. 2002. Are effective teachers like good parents? Teaching styles and student adjustment in early adolescence. *Child Development, 73*, 287–301. **159**

Westhead, R., and Aulakh, R. 2009. Lost brides. *Toronto Star.* Nov. 15. A1, A6. **60**

Westoff, C. F., and Frejka, T. 2007. Religiousness and fertility among European Muslims. *Population and Development Review, 33*, 785–809. **172**

Whalen, C. K., Henker, B., and Dotemoto, S. 1980. Methylphenidate and hyperactivity: Effects on teacher behavior. *Science, 208*, 1280–1282. **293**

Whisman, M. A., and Snyder, D. K. 2007. Sexual infidelity in a national survey of American women: Differences in prevalence and correlates as a function of method of assessment. *Journal of Family Psychology, 21*, 147–154. **30, 212**

Whisman, M. A., Gordon, K. C., and Chatav, Y. 2007. Predicting sexual infidelity in a population-based sample of married individuals. *Journal of Family Psychology, 21*, 320–324. **212**

White, D., and Mill, D. 2000. The child care provider. In L. Prochner and N. Howe (Eds.), *Early childhood education and care in Canada* (pp. 236–251). Vancouver: University of British Columbia Press. **154**

White, J. M. 1999. Work-family stage and satisfaction with work-family balance. *Journal of Comparative Family Studies, 30*, 163–175. **263**

White, J. M. 2005. *Advancing family theories.* Thousand Oaks, CA: Sage. **10, 13**

White, J. M., and Klein, D. M. 2002. *Family theories*, 2nd Ed. Thousand Oaks, CA: Sage. **3, 12, 14, 15, 16**

White, L. 2001. Sibling relations over the life course: A panel analysis. *Journal of Marriage and Family, 63*, 555–568. **331**

Whiteman, S. D., and Christiansen, A. 2008. Processes of sibling influence in adolescence: Individual and family correlates. *Family Relations, 57*, 24–34. **321**

Whiteman, S. D., McHale, S. M., and Crouter, A. C. 2003. What parents learn from experience: The first child as a first draft? *Journal of Marriage and Family, 65*, 608–621. **327**

Whiteman, S. D., McHale, S. M., and Crouter, A. C. 2007. Longitudinal changes in marital relationships: The role of offspring's pubertal development. *Journal of Marriage and Family, 69*, 1005–1020. **275**

Whiting, B. B., and Edwards, C. P. 1988. *Children of different worlds.* Cambridge, MA: Harvard University Press. **20**

Whiting, J. B., and Lee, R. E. 2003. Voices from the system: A qualitative study of foster children's stories. *Family Relations, 52*, 288–295. **247**

Whitton, S. W., et al. 2008. Effects of parental divorce on marital commitment and confidence. *Journal of Family Psychology, 22*, 789–793. **355**

Wickrama, K. A. S., and Bryant, C. M. 2003. Community context of social resources and adolescent mental health. *Journal of Marriage and Family, 65*, 850–866. **130**

Widmer, E. D. 1997. Influence of older siblings on initiation of sexual intercourse. *Journal of Marriage and Family, 59*, 928–938. **322**

Widmer, E. D., Treas, J., and Newcomb, R. 1998. Attitudes toward nonmarital sex in 24 countries. *Journal of Sex Research, 35*, 349–358. **212**

Widom, C. S., and Morris, S. 1997. Accuracy of adult recollections of childhood victimization: Part 2: Childhood sexual abuse. *Psychological Assessment, 9*, 34–36. **401**

Wieke, V. R. 1997. *Sibling abuse: Hidden physical, emotional and sexual trauma*, 2nd Ed. Thousand Oaks, CA: Sage. **402**

Wienke Totura, C. M., et al. 2009. Bullying and victimization among boys and girls in middle school. *Journal of Early Adolescence, 29*, 571–609. **406**

Wiik, K. A., et al. 2009. A study of commitment and relationship quality in Sweden and Norway. *Journal of Marriage and Family, 71*, 465–477. **355, 356**

Wilcox, K. L., Wolchik, S. A., and Braver, S. L. 1998. Predictors of maternal preference for joint or sole legal custody. *Family Relations, 47*, 93–101. **351**

Wilcox, W. B. 2002. Religion, convention, and parental involvement. *Journal of Marriage and Family, 64*, 780–792. **178**

Wilcox, W. B., and Nock, S. L. 2006. What's love got to do with it? Equality, equity, commitment and women's marital quality. *Social Forces, 84*, 1321–1346. **254, 264, 266, 268**

Wildeman, C. 2009. Parental imprisonment, the prison boom, and the concentration of childhood disadvantage. *Demography, 46*, 265–280. **425**

Wiley, A. R., Warren, H. B., and Montanelli, D. S. 2002. Shelter in a time of storm: Parenting in poor rural African American communities. *Family Relations, 51*, 265–273. **177**

Wilkie, J. R., Ferree, M. M., and Ratcliff, K. S. 1998. Gender and fairness: Marital satisfaction in two-earner couples. *Journal of Marriage and Family, 60*, 577–594. **261, 264**

Wilkins, R., Bertholet, J.-M., and Ng, E. 2002. *Trends in mortality by neighbourhood income in urban Canada from 1971 to 1996.* Supplement for Health Reports, vol. 13, Catalogue no. 82–003. **126**

Williams, C. 2001a. Connected to the internet, still connected to life? *Canadian Social Trends, 63,* 13–15. **84**

Williams, C. 2001b. The evolution of communication. *Canadian Social Trends, 60,* 15–18. **84**

Williams, C. 2001c. Family disruptions and childhood happiness. *Canadian Social Trends, 62,* 2–5. **362, 363**

Williams, C. 2002. Time or money? How high and low income Canadians spend their time. *Canadian Social Trends, 65,* 7–11. **104**

Williams, C. 2003. Finances in the golden years. *Perspectives on Labour and Income, 4,* November, 5–13. **426**

Williams, C. 2008. Work-life balance of shift workers. *Perspectives on Labour and Income, 9.* **99**

Williams, K., and Dunne-Bryant, A. 2006. Divorce and adult psychological well-being: Clarifying the role of gender and child age. *Journal of Marriage and Family, 68,* 1178–1196. **359**

Williams, L. M., and Banyard, V. L. 1997. Gender and recall of child sexual abuse: A prospective study. In J. D. Read and D. S. Lindsay (Eds.), *Recollections of trauma: Scientific evidence and clinical perspective* (pp. 371–377). New York: Plenum Press. **401**

Williams, S. T., Conger, K. J., and Blozis, S. A. 2007. The development of interpersonal aggression during adolescence: The importance of parents, siblings, and family economics. *Child Development, 78,* 1526–1542. **322**

Willms, J. D. 2002a. A study of vulnerable children. In J. D. Willms (Ed.), *Vulnerable children* (pp. 3–22). Edmonton: University of Alberta Press. **30**

Willms, J. D. 2002b. Socioeconomic gradients for childhood vulnerability. In J. D. Willms (Ed.), *Vulnerable children* (pp. 71–103). Edmonton: University of Alberta Press. **30, 118, 163, 228**

Wills, J. B., and Risman, B. J. 2006. The visibility of feminist thought in family studies. *Journal of Marriage and Family, 68,* 690–700. **24**

Willson, A. E., Shuey, K. M., and Elder, G. H., Jr. 2003. Ambivalence in the relationship of adult children to aging parents and in-laws. *Journal of Marriage and Family, 65,* 1055–1072. **307**

Wilmoth, J., and Koso, G. 2002. Does marital history matter? Marital status and wealth outcomes among preretirement adults. *Journal of Marriage and Family, 64,* 254–268. **200, 370**

Wilson, S. 2009. Partnering, cohabitation, and marriage. In M. Baker (Ed.), *Families: changing trends in Canada,* 6th Ed. (pp. 68–90). Toronto: McGraw-Hill Ryerson. **186**

Wilson, W. J. 1987. *The truly disadvantaged.* Chicago: University of Chicago Press. **110, 148**

Wilson, W. J. 1996. *When work disappears: The world of the new urban poor.* New York: Knopf. **129**

Winks, R. W. 2000. *The Blacks in Canada: A history,* 2nd Ed. Montreal, Kingston: McGill-Queen's University Press. **44**

Wolak, J., et al. 2008. Online "predators" and their victims: Myths, realities, and implications for prevention and treatment. *American Psychologist, 63,* 111–128. **88**

Wolfe, S. M., Toro, P. A., and McCaskill, P. A. 1999. A comparison of homeless and matched housed adolescents on family environment variables. *Journal of Research on Adolescence, 9,* 53–66. **134**

Wolff, E. N. 2001. The economic status of parents in postwar America. In S. A. Hewlett, N. Rankin, and C. West (Eds.), *Taking parenting public* (pp. 59–82). New York: Rowan & Littlefield. **104**

Woodward, L. J., Fergusson, D. M., and Horwood, L. J. 2006. Gender differences in the transition to early parenthood. *Development and Psychopathology, 18,* 275–294. **227**

Woodward, L., Fergusson, D. M., and Horwood, L. J. 2001. Risk factors and life processes associated with teenage pregnancy: Results of a prospective study from birth to 20 years. *Journal of Marriage and Family, 63,* 1170–1184. **227**

Wu, Z., and Hart, R. 2002. The effects of marital and nonmarital union transition on health. *Journal of Marriage and Family, 64,* 420–432. **359**

Wu, L. L. 1996. Effects of family instability, income, and income instability on the risk of a premarital birth. *American Sociological Review, 61,* 386–406. **365**

Wu, Z. 1995. Remarriage after widowhood: A marital history study of older Canadians. *Canadian Journal on Aging, 14,* 719–736. **368**

Wu, Z. 2000. *Cohabitation: An alternative form of family living.* Toronto: Oxford University Press. **193, 194, 196**

Wu, Z., and MacNeill, L. 2002. Education, work, and childbearing after age 30. *Journal of Comparative Family Studies, 33,* 191–213. **233**

Wu, Z., and Schimmele, C. M. 2003. Childhood family experience and completed fertility. *Canadian Studies in Population, 30,* 221–240. **224, 369**

Wu, Z., and Schimmele, C. M. 2005. Repartnering after a first union disruption. *Journal of Marriage and Family, 67,* 27–36. **369**

Wu, Z., and Schimmele, C. M. 2009. Divorce and repartnering. In M. Baker (Ed.), *Families: Changing trends in Canada,* 6th Ed., (pp. 154–178). Toronto: McGraw-Hill Ryerson. **346**

Wu, Z., et al. 2000. Age-heterogamy and Canadian unions. *Social Biology, 47,* 277–293. **188**

Wu, Z., et al. 2004. "In sickness and in health": Does cohabitation count? *Journal of Family Issues, 24,* 811–838. **196, 198**

Wulczyn, F. 2004. Family reunification. *The Future of Children, 14,* Winter, 95–113. **247**

Wulczyn, F. 2009. Epidemiological perspectives on maltreatment prevention. *The Future of Children, 19,* 39–65. **396**

Xu, L., Gauthier, A. H., and Strohschein, L. 2009. Why are some children left out? Factors barring Canadian children from participating in extracurricular activities. *Canadian Studies in Population, 36,* 325–345. **126**

Xu, X., Hudspeth, C. D., and Bartkowski, J. P. 2006. The role of cohabitation in remarriage. *Journal of Marriage and Family, 68,* 261–274. **355, 370**

Yabiku, S. T., and Gager, C. T. 2009. Sexual frequency and the stability of marital and cohabiting unions. *Journal of Marriage and Family, 71,* 983–1000. **194, 210, 211**

Yaman, A., et al. 2010. Parenting and toddler aggression in second-generation immigrant families: The moderating role of child temperament. *Journal of Family Psychology, 24,* 208–211. **285**

Yanca, C., and Low, B. S. 2003. Female allies and female power: A cross-cultural analysis. *Evolution and Human Behavior, 25,* 9–23. **9**

Yancey, G. 2002. Who interracially dates?: An examination of the characteristics of those who have interacially dated. *Journal of Comparative Family Studies, 33,* 179–190. **187**

Ybarra, M. L., et al. 2009. Associations between blocking, monitoring, and filtering software on home computer and youth-reported unwanted exposure to sexual material online. *Child Abuse & Neglect, 33,* 857–869. **70**

Yee, S. 1994. Gender ideology and Black women as community-builders in Ontario, 1850–70. *Canadian Historical Review, 75,* 53–73. **45**

Young, V. H. 1974. A Black American socialization pattern. *American Ethnologist, 1,* 415–431. **288**

Yount, K. M., and Li, L. 2009. Women's "justification" of domestic violence in Egypt. *Journal of Marriage and Family, 71,* 1125–1140. **387**

Yu, T., et al. 2010. The interactive effects of marital conflict and divorce on parents—Adult children's relationships. *Journal of Marriage and Family, 72,* 282–292. **277, 366**

Zaidi, A. U., and Shuraydi, M. 2002. Perceptions of arranged marriages by young Pakistani Muslim women living in a Western society. *Journal of Comparative Family Studies, 33,* 495–514. **60, 61, 204**

Zajonc, R. B. 2001. The family dynamics of intellectual development. *American Psychologist, 56,* 490–496. **316**

Zajonc, R. B., and Mullally, P. R. 1997. Birth order: Reconciling conflicting effects. *American Psychologist, 52,* 685–690. **318, 319**

Zelizer, V. A. R. 1985. *Pricing the priceless child: The changing social value of children.* New York: Basic Books. **232**

Zeman, K., and Bressan, A. 2008. *Factors associated with youth delinquency and victimization in Toronto, 2006.* Ottawa: Statistics Canada. **228, 372**

Zerk, D. M., Mertin, P. G., and Proeve, M. 2009. Domestic violence and maternal reports of young children's functioning. *Journal of Family Violence, 24,* 423–432. **389**

Zhu, W. X., Lu, L., and Hesketh, T. 2009. China's excess males, sex selective abortion and one child policy: Analysis of data from 2005 national intercensus survey. *British Medical Journal, 338,* 1211–1217. **57**

Zielinski, D. S. 2009. Child maltreatment and adult socioeconomic well-being. *Child Abuse & Neglect, 33,* 666–678. **394**

Zimmerman, J. 2003. *Made from scratch: Reclaiming the pleasures of the American hearth.* New York: Free Press. **101**

Zlotnick, C. 2009. What research tells us about the intersecting streams of homelessness and foster care. *American Journal of Orthopsychiatry, 79,* 319–325. **246**

Zuckerman, M. 2005. *Psychobiology and personality,* 2nd Ed. Cambridge, UK: Cambridge University Press. **2791**

Zysk, K. G. 2002. *Conjugal love in India.* Boston: Brill. **61**

Subject Index

Photo Credits